Morningside Heights

The Columbia History of Urban Life, Kenneth T. Jackson, General Editor

Morningside

COLUMBIA UNIVERSITY PRESS   NEW YORK

Heights

Andrew S. Dolkart

Columbia University Press

Publishers Since 1893
New York   Chichester, West Sussex

Copyright © 1998 Columbia University Press
All rights reserved
Library of Congress Cataloging-in-Publication Data

Dolkart, Andrew S.
    Morningside Heights : a history of its architecture and
development / Andrew S. Dolkart.
        p.   cm. — (The Columbia history of urban life)
    Includes bibliographical references and index.
    ISBN 0-231-07850-1 (cloth)—ISBN 0-231-07851-x (paper)
        1. Architecture—New York (State)—New York.   2. Architecture,
Modern—19th century—New York (State)—New York.   3. Architecture,
Modern—20th century—New York (State)—New York.   4. New York
(N.Y.)—Buildings, structures, etc.   5. Morningside Heights (New
York, N.Y.)—Buildings, structures, etc.   6. New York (N.Y.)—History.
7. Morningside Heights (New York, N.Y.)—History.
I. Title.   II. Series.
NA735.N5D65   1998
720'.9747'1—dc21   97–44482

Publication of this book was made possible in part by a grant from
Futhermore, the publication program of the J. Kaplan Fund, and the
Schoff Trust Fund of Columbia University's University Seminars.
The Press gratefully acknowledges their assistance.

c 10 9 8 7 6 5 4 3
p 10 9 8 7 6 5 4 3 2 1

To my parents, Ellen and Irwin Dolkart

THE COLUMBIA HISTORY OF URBAN LIFE

Kenneth T. Jackson, General Editor

NEW YORK IS A CITY OF NEIGHBORHOODS. A NEW YORKER GENERALLY
identifies his or her home as being located in one of those neighborhoods, such
as the Upper West Side, the Lower East Side, Forest Hills, Harlem, or Flatbush.
Each neighborhood has its own history, character, and story. Together these local stories create the rich and complex history of New York City. Among the
city's diverse neighborhoods, Morningside Heights stands apart, unique both in
the history of its development and in the concentration of distinguished architecture. Although it is a relatively small geographical section on the west side of
Manhattan Island, Morningside Heights boasts the city's largest ensemble of institutional complexes as well as an extensive concentration of early-twentieth-
century middle-class apartment buildings. The extraordinary development of
Morningside Heights took place within a relatively brief period from 1887 to
about 1910. It is this period of development that is the major focus of this book,
with additional attention devoted to the further expansion of the area's institutions into the early 1930s.

Morningside Heights: A History of Its Architecture and Development is a study
primarily of the physical fabric of Morningside Heights. Although the focus
of the book is on issues of architecture and urban development, these themes
do not exist in a vacuum. Thus, this study seeks to place these developments
within a broader social framework. The introduction discusses general issues
that affected the development of Morningside Heights, such as its unusual geology, the identification of the area's boundaries and name, and the forces that
made the area ripe for institutional and residential development. Chapter 1
traces the history of the area prior to its urbanization, including histories of
the insane asylum and orphanage that occupied much of the plateau, a discussion of efforts by real estate interests to force the removal of the insane asylum,
and an examination of the creation of the parks that border the area on the east
and west.

This background chapter is followed by more detailed explorations of the
histories of the institutions that moved onto Morningside Heights, beginning
with the announcement in 1887 that a monumental Episcopal cathedral would

be erected in the area. Chapter 2 discusses the area's major religious institutions, the Cathedral of St. John the Divine and Riverside Church. Following are chapters focusing on St. Luke's Hospital and other health-related facilities (chapter 3), the early history of Columbia's presence on Morningside Heights (chapter 4), the expansion of Columbia's campus through the 1934 completion of Butler Library (chapter 5), the construction of campuses for Barnard College and Teachers College (chapter 6), the second wave of institutional development on Morningside Heights including the construction of Union Theological Seminary, the Institute of Musical Art/Juilliard School, and Jewish Theological Seminary (chapter 7), and, finally, a detailed examination of the residential development of the area, focusing on the creation of a singular middle-class apartment-house community in the early years of the twentieth century (chapter 8). Although the post-World War II history of Morningside Heights could easily be the subject of a separate work, a brief Afterword concludes this study by examining a number of issues in the development of the neighborhood in the second half of the twentieth century that relate to issues developed in earlier chapters.

The institutional and residential development of Morningside Heights in the last years of the nineteenth century and first decades of the twentieth century is extremely complex, with significant events occurring simultaneously throughout the community. Since a simple chronological approach would have required jumping back and forth among many different institutions and residential developments within each period, I have decided, as described above, to treat each institution separately. However, a chronology has been provided which will make it easier for the reader to understand the overlapping histories of the area's institutional and residential development. An appendix provides a building list, which includes the name, address, architect, owner, and date of construction of each important building on Morningside Heights. Finally, because the endnotes are extremely detailed, only a brief bibliography, listing major sources, is included.

The completion of this book would not have been possible without the aid and support of many people. Since it was crucial to illustrate this book extensively, I am extremely grateful for two financial grants that helped to pay for the photographs and for the high quality production of the book, one from Furthermore, the publication program of the J. M. Kaplan Fund and the other from the Schoff Trust Fund of Columbia University's University Seminars. I was helped enormously by my official and unofficial readers whose comments and encouragement were not only greatly appreciated, but also contributed to the completeness and clarity of the final text, notably Mary Beth Betts, Debra Gardner, Dorothy Miner, and Marjorie Pearson, who read the entire manuscript, Bette Weneck, who commented on the Teachers College section, and, most importantly, Paris R. Baldacci, who scrupulously read and edited the text several times.

I was especially lucky to have chosen a topic where so much archival material survives. In fact, so much material was available that the project took far longer to research than was initially planned. I would like to acknowledge the extraordinary assistance given to me by the archivists and librarians who maintain these various collections, especially Adele Lerner, archivist of New York Hospital/Cornell Medical Center, which maintains the records of the Bloomingdale Insane Asylum; the manuscript librarians at the New-York Historical Society, which is the repository for the records of the Leake and Watts Orphan Asylum; Wayne Kempton, archivist for the Episcopal Diocese of New York, which owns extensive material on the Cathedral of St. John the Divine; Jonathan Dorn, archivist at Riverside Church and Valerie Comar and Katharine Keim at the Rockefeller Archives Center, which retains extensive information on the Rockefeller Family's interests on Morningside Heights, including Riverside Church, Claremont Park, Teachers College, Barnard College, and International House, as well as the papers of Edward Harkness, who funded the construction of Columbia's Butler Library; Joan Carvajal, archivist at the St. Luke's Hospital Archives, which maintains the records of this hospital as well as of Woman's Hospital; Jane Lowenthal at the Barnard College Archives and David Ment and Bette Weneck at the Teachers College Archives, who took special interest in the project. Cynthia Frame, at the Union Theological Seminary Archives; Stephen E. Novak, at the Juilliard School of Music Archives; Julie Miller, at the Joseph and Miriam Ratner Center for the Study of Conservative Judaism at the Jewish Theological Seminary; and Sharon Lieberman-Mintz and Elka Dietsch at the Jewish Theological Seminary Library provided invaluable assistance in researching material on the second wave of institutional development on Morningside Heights.

Of the many who assisted me at Columbia University, I would especially like to thank, Rhea E. Pliakus and Linea M. Anderson of the university's new archives; Sara Vos, keeper of the university's correspondence files; Hollee Haswell, curator of the Columbiana Collection; Janet Parks and Dan Kany of the Avery Archives; Bill O'Malley, Avery Library's rare books librarian; and the librarians at Columbia's Rare Books and Manuscripts Library, which contains the voluminous papers of university presidents Seth Low and Nicholas Murray Butler. Additional records relating to Columbia University were warmly made available to me at the McKim, Mead & White Collection at the New-York Historical Society, overseen by architectural curator Mary Beth Betts. In addition, librarians and staff members at Columbia's Avery Library and Butler Library, the New York Public Library's United States History, Local History and Genealogy Division, the New-York Historical Society Library, the Library of Congress, the Berkshire Athenaeum, and the New York State Library also provided valuable assistance.

The book could not have been completed without the assistance of many friends and colleagues who contributed ideas and information and helped with research, including Paul Bentel, Barry Bergdoll, George Chauncey, Ken Cobb, Stephen Facey, Wendy Feuer, Carl Forster, Sheila H. Gillams, Christopher Girr, Hugh Goodman, Christopher Gray, Laura Hansen, Gale Harris, Marilyn Ibach, Sarah Bradford Landau, Roger Lang, Irwin Lefkowitz, Emily Lloyd, Robert A. McCaughey, Lynden Miller, Dorothy Miner, Susan Montgomery, Dale Neighbors, Chris Neville, Tony Pisani, Elise Quasebarth, Robin Rhodes, Bob Roistacher, Lisa Rosenthal, Bill Scott, Peter Shaver, Jay Shockley, Richard Southwick, Anne Steinert, Michael Stoller, Janet Adams Strong, Susan Swiatosz, Chris Townsend, and Carol Willis.

Kate Wittenberg, Leslie Bialler, and Linda Secondari at Columbia University Press and indexer Alan M. Greenberg were a pleasure to work with and made the task of completing the book extremely smooth. Bill Higgins and Anne Covell's home in Lenox, Massachusetts, proved to be the perfect place for extended periods of writing and I thank them for providing this comfortable space for three successive summers. Most importantly, my life-partner Paris Baldacci was not only my great support during the years of research and writing, but was also the greatest supporter of the project, editing the text, discussing ideas, and insisting that it was worth all of the time and effort . . . which it was.

Andrew Scott Dolkart

October 1997

1754   King's College established.

1760   King's College erects building on Park Place and Church Street.

1771   New York Hospital organized.

1776   Battle of Harlem Heights.

1784   King's College renamed Columbia College.

1808   New York Hospital opens facility for mental patients.

1811   Commissioners Plan establishes New York City's street grid.

1816   New York Hospital begins buying land on Morningside Heights.

1821   New York Hospital's Bloomingdale Insane Asylum opens on Morningside Heights.

1828   Bishop John Henry Hobart proposes that New York build an Episcopal cathedral on Washington Square.

1832   Leake and Watts Orphan Asylum established.

1839   Union Theological Seminary incorporated.

1842   Croton Aqueduct completed.

1843   Leake and Watts Orphan Asylum opens on Morningside Heights.

1853   St. Luke's Hospital receives first patients.

1856   Columbia relocates to Madison Avenue and East 49th Street.

       Woman's Hospital established.

1858   St. Luke's Hospital's building on Fifth Avenue and West 54th Street completed.

1868   New York Hospital purchases property in White Plains for Bloomingdale Asylum.

1870   113th Street gatehouse of Croton Aqueduct constructed.

       First use of term "Morning Side."

1872	Bishop Horatio Potter revives interest in an Episcopal cathedral.
1873	Frederick Law Olmsted and Calvert Vaux commissioned to design Morningside Park.
	Frederick Law Olmsted commissioned to design Riverside Park and Drive.
	Cathedral of St. John the Divine officially incorporated.
1879	Ninth Avenue elevated begins service.
1885	Macy Villa erected at Bloomingdale Asylum.
1886	Campaign to drive Bloomingdale Asylum off Morningside Heights begins.
1887	Leake and Watts Orphan Asylum sold as site for Episcopal Cathedral.
1888	New York Hospital announces that Bloomingdale Asylum will relocate to White Plains.
1889	Competition for design of Cathedral of St. John the Divine.
	New York Hospital auctions a portion of its Morningside Heights property.
	Seth Low becomes president of Columbia.
	Barnard College holds first classes.
	Teachers College chartered.
1891	Leake and Watts Orphan Asylum relocates to Yonkers.
	Heins & La Farge win design competition for Cathedral of St. John the Divine.
	Seth Low announces Columbia's intention to move to Morningside Heights.
1892	Cornerstone laid for St. John the Divine.
	Columbia purchases portion of New York Hospital's Bloomingdale Asylum on Morningside Heights.
	St. Luke's Hospital purchases land on Morningside Heights; Ernest Flagg wins design competition.
	Teachers College purchases land on Morningside Heights; William Potter appointed architect.
1893	McKim, Mead & White appointed architect for Columbia's campus.
1894	Bloomingdale Asylum relocates to White Plains.
	Charles McKim submits plan for Columbia's campus.

Main Hall and Macy Hall completed at Teachers College and classes commence.

Construction begins on the first group of speculative rowhouses on Morningside Heights.

1895   William C. Schermerhorn donates $300,000 for Schermerhorn Hall at Columbia.

Seth Low donates $1 million to Columbia for Low Memorial Library.

Barnard College purchases property on Morningside Heights from New York Hospital; Charles Rich appointed architect.

1896   St. Luke's Hospital opens on Morningside Heights.

1897   Low Library, Schermerhorn, Fayerweather, Havemeyer, and Engineering (now Mathematics) halls, South Court, and gymnasium and power plant completed and classes commence at Columbia College.

Milbank and Brinckerhoff halls completed and classes commence at Barnard College.

Home for Old Men and Aged Couples constructed on Amsterdam Avenue.

Grant's Tomb completed.

Milbank Hall completed at Teachers College.

1898   St. Luke's Home for Indigent Christian Females constructed on Broadway and West 114th Street.

Fiske Hall completed at Barnard.

1899   Crypt at St. John the Divine dedicated.

1901   Seth Low resigns as Columbia's president; Nicholas Murray Butler appointed his successor.

Horace Mann School and Whittier Hall dormitory completed at Teachers College.

1902   Woman's Hospital purchases land on Cathedral Parkway; Allen & Collens appointed architect.

Earl Hall opens at Columbia.

Jewish Theological Seminary of America chartered.

1903   Daniel Chester French's *Alma Mater* unveiled at Columbia.

Columbia purchases South Field from New York Hospital; McKim, Mead & White prepares plan.

Funds provided for St. Paul's Chapel at Columbia; Howells & Stokes appointed architect.

Elizabeth Milbank Anderson purchases property between 116th and 119th streets for expansion of Barnard.

Classes commence at Jewish Theological Seminary on West 123rd Street.

1904   IRT subway begins service beneath Broadway.

Institute of Musical Art established.

1905   School of Mines Building (now Lewisohn Hall) and Columbia's first two dormitories, Hartley and Livingston halls, open.

Thompson Hall, Teachers College's gymnasium, opens.

Union Theological Seminary purchases land on Morningside Heights.

Thirty-seven new apartment buildings begun on Morningside Heights.

1906   Woman's Hospital completed.

Margaret J. Plant Pavilion completed at St. Luke's Hospital.

Allen & Collens wins competition for design of Union Theological Seminary.

1907   St. Paul's Chapel and Hamilton Hall completed at Columbia.

Brooks Hall, Barnard's first planned dormitory, opens.

1908   Charles McKim dies; McKim, Mead & White partner William Kendall becomes architect in charge of Columbia designs.

1909   Household Arts Building (now Grace Dodge Hall) opens at Teachers College.

Institute of Musical Art purchases property on Morningside Heights; Donn Barber appointed architect.

Construction begins on Eglise de Notre Dame on Morningside Drive.

Thirty-five new apartment houses begun on Morningside Heights, including many impressive buildings on Riverside Drive and Claremont Avenue.

1910   St. Faith's House erected on cathedral grounds.

Columbia purchases East Campus block between 116th and 117th streets.

Union Theological Seminary commences classes on Morningside Heights.

Institute of Musical Art commences classes on Morningside Heights.

1911   Initial construction phase completed at St. John the Divine.

Heins & La Farge removed as architect of cathedral; Ralph Adams Cram appointed.

Kent Hall and Philosophy Hall completed at Columbia.

1912   Avery Hall and President's House completed at Columbia.

Broadway Presbyterian Church completed on Broadway and 114th Street.

1913   Synod House and Choir School completed on cathedral grounds.

Furnald Hall and Journalism Hall completed at Columbia.

1914   Bishop's House and Deanery completed on cathedral grounds.

1916   Travers Pavilion completed at St. Luke's Hospital.

1917   Students' Hall (now Barnard Hall) opens at Barnard.

1919   Columbia and Teachers College purchase first apartment buildings on Morningside Heights.

1923   Faculty Club completed at Columbia.

1924   Business School (now Dodge Hall) completed at Columbia.

Russell Hall and Grace Dodge Hall Extension completed at Teachers College.

International House opens.

1925   Major fund raising drive for completion of cathedral begins.

Harry Emerson Fosdick agrees to become minister of Riverside Church.

John D. Rockefeller, Jr., purchases Morningside Heights site for Riverside Church.

Johnson Hall (now Wien Hall), first women's dormitory at Columbia, and Hewitt Hall, Barnard dormitory, open.

1926   Institute of Musical Art merges with Juilliard School of Music.

Allen & Collens and Henry C. Pelton appointed architects for Riverside Church.

1927   Pupin Hall, John Jay Hall, and Casa Italiana completed at Columbia.

John D. Rockefeller, Jr., commissions redesign of Claremont Park (now Sakura Park).

1928   Chandler Chemistry Laboratory completed at Columbia.

Scrymser Pavilion completed at St. Luke's Hospital.

Refectory, social hall, and Brown Memorial Tower completed at Union Theological Seminary.

1929   Schermerhorn Extension completed at Columbia.

1930   Riverside Church opens for services.

Jewish Theological Seminary relocates into new building on Broadway at 122nd Street.

1931   Edward Harkness agrees to fund construction of Butler Library at Columbia.

Juilliard School of Music buildings completed.

1932   McGiffert Hall completed at Union Theological Seminary.

1934   Butler Library completed at Columbia.

1935   Corpus Christi R.C. Church erected on West 121st Street.

1941   Nave and west front of St. John the Divine dedicated.

World War II begins; construction of cathedral stops.

1945   Nicholas Murray Butler resigns as Columbia's president.

1947   Fourteen Morningside Heights institutions organize Morningside Heights, Inc..

1951   Auburn Hall completed at Union Theological Seminary.

1954   Florence Stokes Clark Building completed at St. Luke's Hospital.

1957   Morningside Gardens apartment complex completed.

Stuyvesant Building, replacing the Norrie Pavilion, completed at St. Luke's Hospital.

1958   Interchurch Center opens.

1959   Carman Hall dormitory and Ferris Booth Hall completed at Columbia.

Dickinson Hall completed at Union Theological Seminary.

Adele Lehman and Helen Reis halls completed at Barnard.

1960   Riverside Church Parish House completed.

1961   Law School (now Greene Hall) and Seeley Wintersmith Mudd Hall completed at Columbia.

1962   Woman's Hospital's building sold.

1964   Uris Hall, Columbia School of Business, completed.

1966   Seeley Wintersmith Mudd Extension completed at Columbia.

1967   St. Hilda and St. Hugh's School opens on West 114th Street.

Plimpton Hall completed by Barnard College.

1968   Columbia begins construction of gymnasium in Morningside Park; Columbia campus occupied by student protesters; gymnasium project abandoned.

Woman's Hospital Annex completed at St. Luke's Hospital.

1968   I. M. Pei commissioned to prepare master plan for Columbia.

1969   Millicent McIntosh and Helen Goodhardt Altschul halls completed at Barnard.

Juilliard School moves to Lincoln Center; Manhattan School of Music moves into its former home.

1970   School of International Affairs building completed at Columbia.

Mitzi Newhouse Pavilion completed at Manhattan School of Music.

Bank Street College opens on West 112th Street.

1973   Thorndike Hall completed at Teachers College.

1974   Marcellus Hartley Dodge Physical Fitness Center completed at Columbia.

1977   Avery Hall Extension completed at Columbia.

1978   Revival of construction on cathedral announced.

1981   East Campus Housing completed at Columbia.

1983   Computer Science building completed at Columbia.

1984   Uris Hall addition completed at Columbia.

1985   Jewish Theological Seminary Extension and Library completed.

1988   Havemeyer Hall Extension and Morris A. Shapiro Hall completed at Columbia.

1989   Iphigene Ochs Sulzberger Hall completed at Barnard.

1991   Dorothy Doubleday Babcock Building completed at St. Luke's Hospital.

1996   Ferris Booth Hall at Columbia demolished; construction begins on Alfred Lerner Student Center; Greene Hall Extension and William C. Warren Hall completed.

1997   Exterior of cathedral dome restored.

Designs prepared for Columbia dormitory on Broadway and West 113th Street.

Map of Morningside
Heights

WEST 125TH STREET

WEST 122ND STREET

WEST 120TH STREET

WEST 116TH STREET

WEST 112TH STREET

WEST 110TH STREET (CATHEDRAL PARKWAY)

RIVERSIDE DRIVE

CLAREMONT AVENUE

BROADWAY

AMSTERDAM AVENUE

MORNINGSIDE DRIVE

1. Site of Woman's Hospital
2. Cathedral of St. John the Divine
3. Site of Home for Old Men and Aged Couples
4. St. Luke's Hospital
5. St. Luke's Home
6. Columbia University Original Campus
7. Columbia University South Field
8. Columbia University East Campus
9. Barnard College
10. Teachers College
11. Interchurch Center
12. Riverside Church
13. Union Theological Seminary
14. Institute of Musical Art / Juilliard School / Manhattan School of Music
15. Jewish Theological Seminary
16. Claremont Park / Sakura Park
17. International House
18. Grant's Tomb
19. Riverside Park
20. Morningside Park

Morningside Heights

Introduction

No more beautiful sight is found in New York on a bright winter's day than the spectacle of the late afternoon sun shining upon the domes, spires and windows of the new modern buildings which have been built, and which are still in the process of construction, on Morningside Heights, which has been rightly termed the Acropolis of the new world.[1]

"The Acropolis of the new world"—quite a grandiose designation for a neighborhood that in 1896 had more vacant land than new modern buildings and in which domes and spires were often more the vision of architects and institutional administrators than a reality for the viewer on the street. Yet this was not an unusual description of Morningside Heights in the last years of the nineteenth century, when the high rocky plateau west of Harlem was dubbed "New York's Acropolis," "America's Acropolis," or, as in the case of the hyperbolic article from Dayton, "the Acropolis of the new world."[2]

Morningside Heights apparently was first compared to the Acropolis of Athens in 1887, soon after the announcement that an Episcopal cathedral would rise on the edge of the escarpment north of 110th Street. In that year, the *Uptown Visitor* observed that "a cathedral on this commanding elevation will be as nobly housed as the Parthenon was on the Acropolis."[3] Indeed, just as the Parthenon had been the center of Athenian religious life, the cathedral's benefactors envisioned their church as a center for the religious life of their city and their nation. When Columbia College, St. Luke's Hospital, and other institutions also purchased property on the Morningside Plateau, the use of the term "acropolis" came to have a broader metaphorical significance, likening New York's developing religious, academic, and institutional center to the great symbol of the flowering of culture in Periclean Athens.[4]

Of course, "Acropolis of the new world" simply referred to a New York City neighborhood. Nevertheless, the use of the term was not inappropriate since this neighborhood is set apart from the rest of New York City, both physically and in terms of its developmental history. Indeed, I was attracted to study Morningside Heights not only because the area is filled with enough extraordinary buildings to draw the admiration of any architectural historian and by my attachment to Columbia University and its great architectural library, but most especially because of the neighborhood's unique developmental history. It is the only neighborhood that was skipped by the general pattern of urbanization on Manhattan Island that began at the Battery at the southern tip of the island and flowed north up to Marble Hill. This divergence from the general development pattern had three causes: the topographic isolation of the area on a plateau rising above the Harlem Lowlands; the presence, for much of the nineteenth century, of an insane asylum in the center of the plateau, which depressed land values and inhibited real estate investment; and the lack of public transit facilities on the plateau long after elevated rail lines had been extended into areas to the south and east.

Geology was the key: Morningside Heights is set on a rocky plateau that begins its rise at 110th Street and then rapidly descends into the Manhattan or Manhattanville Valley beginning at 122nd Street. This narrow plateau, extending only about 2,000 feet between cliffs now incorporated into Morningside and Riverside parks, is formed of mica or Manhattan schist, a hard metamorphic rock, and is a section of the Manhattan Ridge, part of an ancient, now worn-down mountain range. To the east, the Harlem Plain or Harlem Lowlands is formed from a softer Inwood marble that has eroded, creating the Morningside cliff that forms a barrier between these two geologic regions.[5] The *Evening Post* described the topography of Morningside Heights in 1896:

> Nature has dealt bountifully with this little eminence on her face. . . . Its boundaries are the Hudson River [on the west] . . . ; Manhattan valley on the north . . . ; Harlem plains on the northeast and east, with the Harlem [River] and Long Island Sound in distant view . . . ; Central Park and the great teeming city to the southeast and south. In the midst of these surroundings the plateau rises, at first abruptly, and then by easy slopes from elevations of 80 to over 140 feet above the level of the sea. No view could be more varied or interesting. Its natural drainage is unexcelled, and no place could be more salubrious.[6]

Despite the beauty of the plateau and its natural amenities, its physical separation would isolate it from the development that occurred in surrounding areas in the late nineteenth century.

The presence of the Bloomingdale Insane Asylum (to be discussed in chapter 1) also inhibited development. By 1821 it occupied a building in the very center of the Morningside Plateau, with extensive grounds laid out as a therapeutic garden and farm for the "inmates." The insane asylum was joined on the plateau in 1843 by the Leake and Watts Orphan Asylum, which opened a handsome new building on land purchased from New York Hospital (see chapter 1). Property surrounding these institutions remained in private hands, but little development occurred to change the region's semi-rural character. Real estate interests believed that there could be no profitable residential development so long as the insane asylum occupied such a large and key site on Morningside Heights. Not only were this institution and its patients seen as a blight on the neighborhood, but the presence of the asylum in the center of the plateau also meant that streets between 114th and 120th could not be cut through to connect privately held property near Morningside and Riverside parks.[7] Private real estate interests forced the insane asylum to announce in 1888 that it would leave the area (see chapter 1), raising the value of nearby properties. Even so, major residential development did not immediately occur since there still was no mass transit connecting the heights with the rest of the city.

When elevated railroads were erected through northern Manhattan in the late 1870s, the companies involved avoided this physically isolated region of asylums, preferring instead to run their trains through the broad flat expanses of Harlem. Since speculative residential investment generally followed the routes of transit lines, there was little residential development during the late nineteenth century. Instead, a number of New York City institutions seeking large tracts of land on which to relocate and expand their enterprises were drawn to this relatively undeveloped area. As the *New York Times* observed in 1894, "Population already has surrounded these heights with a great band of life, but the heights themselves are still largely undeveloped. By their configuration they offer precisely the conditions which such institutions need—accessibility to a large population, together with a certain retirement from the noise and disturbance of surrounding life."[8] These institutions would begin construction of distinguished new complexes in the early 1890s, creating a concentration of distinctive institutional buildings unlike anything found elsewhere in the city (see chapters 2–7). Major residential development would await the opening of the subway beneath Broadway in 1904, resulting in Morningside Heights becoming the city's first middle-class apartment-house neighborhood (see chapter 8).

Determining the Area's Boundaries and Name

Since Morningside Heights is defined as a distinct neighborhood primarily by its topography, it should be easy to determine the area's boundaries. Indeed, to the west and east, the geology clearly demarcates the neighborhood. To the west is the Riverside cliff and the Hudson River, while the Morningside cliff to the east separates the area from Harlem. To the south, 110th Street is generally considered the neighborhood's boundary since this is where the plateau begins. This demarcation was made more pronounced in the late nineteenth century when 110th Street was widened and officially renamed Cathedral Parkway, providing a landscaped boulevard connecting the northern end of Central Park with Morningside Park and Riverside Park and Drive. In this study, the south side of Cathedral Parkway is used as the southern boundary of Morningside Heights.

Determining the northern boundary of Morningside Heights is more problematic. Today, West 125th Street is generally considered the northern edge of the area.[9] This street, however, does not correspond to the edge of the plateau, which begins its steep descent at 122nd Street. This descent is evident where the Broadway subway emerges from its tunnel at 122nd Street and spans the Manhattanville Valley on a viaduct. In the late nineteenth century and the first years of the twentieth century, as Morningside Heights was undergoing rapid transformation, 122nd Street was generally cited as the northern end of the new neighborhood.[10] With the exception of Riverside Drive and Claremont Avenue, where the plateau extends farther north, development north of 122nd Street, beginning in the 1890s, generally took the form of working-class tenements, a type of building unrelated to the development patterns that eventually characterized construction on the higher land of the plateau. In fact, the blocks north of 122nd Street and east of Claremont Avenue were not viewed as being part of the Morningside Heights area until the 1950s, when the deterioration of the tenements was viewed as threatening the image and economy of Morningside Heights and it was decided that they should be replaced by an urban renewal project (see Afterword). However, because this expansion of Morningside Heights' northern boundary to 125th Street is relatively recent, in this study the north side of 122nd Street will generally be considered the northern boundary of Morningside Heights.

With the neighborhood's boundaries established, it is also necessary to determine how the area was named. The poetic appellation "Morningside Heights" is not a historic name dating back to New York's early history, as are such old neighborhood names as Harlem, Chelsea, and Greenwich Village; nor does it refer to a famous resident, as does Murray Hill, Hamilton Heights, or Washington Heights; nor is it geographically descriptive, as is Upper West Side or Lower East Side. Indeed, the choice of the name Morningside Heights was not inevitable. In the late eighteenth century, the area was sometimes referred to as Vandewater Heights (referring to the Vandewater family which owned much of the land) or Harlem Heights.[11] By the late 1880s and early 1890s, when the Cathedral of St. John the Divine, St. Luke's Hospital, Columbia College, and Teachers College were announcing the purchase of property on this rocky plateau north of 110th Street, no single neighborhood name was generally accepted to designate the location. Articles sometimes merely described the boundaries of the proposed sites or referred to a location "at Bloomingdale."[12] During the 1890s other names appeared in newspapers and magazines, all incorporating the term "heights," including Bloomingdale Heights, Riverside Heights, Columbia Heights, and University Heights.[13] However, only two names developed widespread currency—Morningside Heights and Cathedral Heights.

"Morningside" was the name that had been given to the adjacent park where the steep cliff catches the rays of the rising sun. The earliest reference to the park as "Morningside" is contained in a recommendation of the Commissioners of Public Parks, dated September 13, 1870, that a topographic survey be undertaken "of a place known as Morning Side [sic] Park."[14] Terms such as "Morningside Plateau" and "Morningside Hill" were also in general use as early as 1892.[15] Only the Morningside Park Association seems to have employed the name "Morningside Heights" at this early date.[16] Ironically, considering the argument that would develop between advocates of the two names, Columbia's President Seth Low reported in February 1895 that he had sat beside the Cathedral's chief advocate, Bishop Henry Potter, at a dinner party and had "spoke[n] with him about the name of the Heights where our new site is. He proposed that we call it Morningside Heights."[17] The following month, the Columbia trustees reported that all of the local institutions had decided on the Morningside Heights designation. However, this announcement proved premature, since the trustees of the cathedral objected to the choice of the secular "Morningside Heights" over "Cathedral Heights," their preferred name for the area.[18]

Although the neighborhood's institutions were anxious for uniformity in the choice of a name, they could not settle on which name was more appropriate, with the leaders of the Cathedral and St. Luke's Hospital not surprisingly preferring Cathedral Heights, and Columbia and Teachers College campaigning for Morningside Heights. The cathedral's trustees argued that since it was the first institution to purchase land on the heights, its choice of Cathedral Heights should be binding.[19] "In a spirit of courtesy," Low agreed to support the use of Cathedral Heights, just as Potter had earlier acquiesced to Morningside Heights.[20] However, just as Potter had been thwarted by his trustees, the trustees of Columbia insisted upon Morningside Heights.[21] Teachers College, located at some distance from the cathedral, was especially adamant about maintaining the use of the term Morningside Heights, arguing that all of its printed documents used this name.[22] In 1897 New York City's Common Council officially designated "Cathedral Heights" as the name for the portion of the plateau between Cathedral Parkway and 114th Street and Morningside Drive and Amsterdam Avenue, but this designation was widely ignored.[23] Indeed, the following year a *Tribune* editorial wondered why if Cathedral Heights was an acceptable name for the entire heights, then why not Hospital Heights, or Asylum Heights, or Columbia Heights, or Teachers College Heights; but concluded emphatically that "'Morningside Heights' it was and is and shall be."[24] And so it was! No official action ever established Morningside Heights as the sole designation for the area. However, despite continued use of "Cathedral Heights" at St. John the Divine (the address on Bishop William Manning's stationery in the 1920s was "Cathedral Heights, New York"), "Morningside Heights" increasingly appeared in the press and in common usage, and soon became firmly established as the neighborhood's name.

A Neighborhood of Institutions

Morningside Heights is generally thought of as a neighborhood of institutions. Indeed, these institutions create the neighborhood's special character. The institutional character of Morningside Heights began to take shape between 1887 and 1892, when several prominent organizations decided to purchase large land parcels for the construction of new institutional complexes. In 1887 Episcopal Bishop Henry Codman Potter announced that the planned Cathedral of St. John the Divine would rise on the site of the Leake and Watts Orphan Asylum (see chapter 2). In 1892 three other institutions announced their move to Morningside Heights: the Episcopal-affiliated St. Luke's Hospital, which exchanged its site on the corner of Fifth Avenue and West 54th Street for a new home on West 113th Street across from the Cathedral grounds (see chapter 3); venerable Columbia College, which abandoned its overcrowded and noisy home on Madison Avenue and East 49th Street to build a new campus on a segment of New York Hospital's Bloomingdale Asylum property (see chapter 4); and the nascent Teachers College, which would erect a new home across 120th Street from Columbia's chosen site (see chapter 6). These pioneering institutional settlers sowed the seeds of a community which continues to nurture "the threefold nature of man," attending to the needs of the mind, the body, and the spirit.[25]

Other institutions would soon consider relocating to the area. For example, pressure mounted on the newly established New York Public Library to join with Columbia in creating a "center for the polite arts" on Morningside Heights and there was talk of the New-York Historical Society building on the plateau.[26] Neither of these proposals materialized, but in the next few decades other educational, medical, and religious organizations would settle on Morningside Heights—notably Riverside Church (see chapter 2), Woman's Hospital (see chapter 3), Barnard College (see chapter 6), Union Theological Seminary (see chapter 7), Jewish Theological Seminary (see chapter 7), and the Institute of Musical Art (later the Juilliard School of Music; see chapter 7). Most of these institutions thrived on Morningside Heights and became well-established in New York's institutional universe. They found in Morningside Heights a neighborhood that provided the perfect blend of quiet seclusion and urban excitement.

Today, these institutions are so much a part of the city that it is easy to forget the difficulties they experienced as they struggled to build on Morningside Heights and to thrive in a commercial city where academics, religion, music, and art have not always been high priorities. In fact, one institution, the National Academy of Design, utterly failed in its effort to move to Morningside Heights, even after an impressive Beaux-Arts design by Carrère & Hastings won a competition for a building on the organization's new site at Cathedral Parkway and Amsterdam Avenue.[27] As other institutions sought to establish their presence in the city by building on Morningside Heights, the ideals of their founders or those who had initiated their move to Morningside Heights were often compromised, and the visions of their architects were frequently not fully realized. Nonetheless, Morningside Heights contains many of the most spectacular institutional complexes in New York City. The stories of the struggles of these institutions to find homes, raise money, and erect great architectural monuments that would signify their importance in New York City's life are central to this study.

The institutions that settled on Morningside Heights interacted with each other and some were very closely allied: the Cathedral of St. John the Divine and St. Luke's Hospital were both affiliated with the Episcopal Church and had major supporters in common; Barnard College and Teachers College purposely chose Morningside Heights sites in order to be in close proximity to Columbia's campus and became officially affiliated with the larger university; the theological seminaries also chose Morningside Heights because of the academic environment fostered by Columbia; the major early supporters of Jewish Theological Seminary and the Institute of Musical Art, Felix Warburg and James Loeb, were relatives; and names such as Vanderbilt, Dodge, Schiff, James, Milbank, Harkness, and Rockefeller appear on the donor lists of several of these organizations. However, there is no evidence of a deliberate, coordinated effort among the leaders of these various organizations to create a unified institutional center. As the argument over an appropriate neighborhood name attests, there were often tensions and conflicting interests among the institutions, sometimes exacerbated by the fact that they were seeking funds from the same small pool of wealthy philanthropic New Yorkers.

When the intentions of the first group of institutions to relocate onto Morningside Heights became known, some commentators envisioned a great future for the area with a harmonious architectural ensemble providing "an architectural crown such as no other American city is ever likely to wear."[28] In 1892, as Columbia was seeking a design for its new site, an editorial in the *New York Times* urged upon Columbia, St. Luke's Hospital, and the cathedral the need for a unified "cloistral neighborhood" with appropriate architecture and landscaping that would not "vulgarize the quarter." The editorial writer confidently assured readers that "The Trustees of the hospital, we may be reasonably sure, will not sanction any building that is manifestly and defiantly at variance in its expression with the architectural character that should belong to a building that will form a member of the architectural group of which the cathedral is the centre. We may be equally assured respecting the action of Columbia."[29] However, in December 1893, just a little more than a year after this editorial, St. Luke's accepted Ernest Flagg's impressive French Renaissance hospital design, a design that could not have been more "manifestly and defiantly at variance" with the character of the proposed Romanesque/Gothic/Byzantine cathedral directly across the street. In addition, that same month Columbia rejected proposals for a Gothic campus that might have harmonized the

Episcopal-affiliated college with the Episcopal cathedral, opting instead for Charles McKim's "pure classic" proposal.[30]

This question of design uniformity, as proposed in the *New York Times* editorial and other publications, versus institutional individuality was hotly debated. The popular critic Royal Cortissoz, writing for *Scribner's Magazine* in 1895, approved of the choice of different architectural styles by each institution. Impressed with the monumentality of the individual designs, he found each proposed project "Interesting by itself," creating an appropriate "tone religiously meditative near the church, imbued with the equability of learning near the college, silent with the silence of a place of healing [at St. Luke's Hospital], between the two."[31] *Harper's Weekly,* on the other hand, found the lack of uniformity especially disturbing. "Visionary persons," mused an editorial writer early in 1897, "began to dream of a segregated and cloistered quarter devoted to the humanities. . . . There was indeed an opportunity offered that is very rare . . . to make a quarter of which all the parts should be in keeping. . . . It cannot be said that these expectations have been realized." The writer observed that "The buildings of Columbia are designed without reference to the cathedral" and that the design of the hospital building exhibits a certain "disrespect" of the nearby church.[32] This line of criticism culminated in 1910 with architectural critic Montgomery Schuyler's scathing indictment of Columbia's "pompous" architecture and the "alien" design of St. Luke's, both of which eschewed the architectural character initially established by St. John the Divine and thus ran afoul of Schuyler's own desire for a unified "secluded and cloistral" neighborhood.[33]

Few of the institutions that settled on Morningside Heights were well-established, thriving organizations. They either were recently founded and intent upon establishing themselves as important players in New York and in their respective fields, or, like Columbia, were seeking to redefine themselves in a rapidly changing, highly competitive urban context. Thus, each institution sought a distinctive architectural design that would aid in establishing its unique identity, ignoring the admonitions of some critics and editorial writers that they collaborate on a unified design scheme. Although each institution was profoundly concerned about design issues and committed to architectural and design excellence, each made design decisions only in terms of its own project. Architects were individually chosen by the various institutional boards, by wealthy donors, or as a result of a design competition. Indeed, some of America's most talented architects were commissioned to design institutional buildings on Morningside Heights, including McKim, Mead & White, Carrère & Hastings, Ernest Flagg, William Potter, Allen & Collens, and Howells & Stokes. However, the notion that the design of a particular complex should be bound by that of a nearby building already under construction was inimical to the leaders of these institutions and to their architects.

Accordingly, the trustees of the Cathedral of St. John the Divine planned a church of towering grandeur as a representation of the primacy of Episcopalians in the city's religious and social life and of New York's supremacy among North American cities. St. Luke's Hospital, wishing to erect a home that would associate it with modern medicine's rapid advances, planned a complex employing popular French forms and clean, light-colored materials.[34] Columbia's president, Seth Low, and his allies on the college's board of trustees specifically rejected a Gothic design, consciously seeking a monumental style that would reflect the transformation of a relatively hidebound institution into one of America's great educational centers and a powerful force in New York City.[35] Some years later, when Union Theological Seminary planned its buildings on Morningside Heights, it recognized that the seminary was part of a larger educational community, but the program for its design competition called for a complex of "such individuality of treatment as to make evident . . . [the seminary's] organic distinctness and peculiar character."[36] Thus, there is no harmony in the architectural style of institutional buildings erected on Morningside Heights. Instead, the neighborhood has many distinguished complexes, each characterized by the individuality of its design.

A Neighborhood of Apartment Houses

Not every building on Morningside Heights was erected to exalt the mind, the body, or the spirit. Much of the neighborhood consists of residential buildings erected by speculative builders, who exalted the promise of financial profit. While it is easy to assume that the development of the residential community was intimately tied to the arrival of Columbia and its neighboring institutions, this is not the case. Residential development actually proceeded independently of the presence of these institutions.

Although several dozen rowhouses, largely unsuccessful, were built on Morningside Heights in the 1890s, major residential development in the area did not occur until after the opening of the subway beneath Broadway in 1904, which finally made Morningside Heights convenient to downtown and, therefore, attracted investment from speculative developers who erected apartment buildings for the middle-class families now interested in moving to the neighborhood. The land that had not been purchased by the institutions was rapidly transformed, with apartment buildings rising within a few years on almost every available site. As a result, Morningside Heights became New York City's first middle-class apartment house neighborhood, with upper middle-class households settling in impressive twelve-story apartment buildings on Broadway, Riverside Drive, Claremont Avenue, and Cathedral Parkway, and less prosperous households moving into more modest six- to eight-story buildings on the side streets and on Morningside Drive. As such, Morningside Heights provides an excellent opportunity to study the early development of the middle-class apartment house which, while it is a common residential type in New York City, has largely been neglected by those studying apartment buildings (see chapter 8).

Not only was the development of apartment buildings on Morningside Heights unrelated to the nearby presence of institutions, but also few of the early apartment renters were affiliated with the institutions. Rents were generally too high for institutional employees, especially in the better apartment buildings with their spacious units and, in many cases, expansive views. The academic institutions became increasingly concerned about high rents in the area since, without a concentration of resident faculty and staff, Morningside Heights would lack the "college life" seen as vital to establishing an intellectual community. Since little land remained on which to erect faculty housing and since the academic institutions lacked the money for such ventures even if vacant sites had been available, Columbia University and Teachers College purchased several apartment buildings in 1919 and 1920. A few additional apartment buildings were purchased by the area's institutions during the 1930s, 1940s, and 1950s. However, widespread property acquisition did not occur until the 1960s, when Columbia purchased more than 100 buildings (and other institutions purchased a few) seeking both to stabilize what the university's administrators perceived as a deteriorating neighborhood and to acquire apartments that could be rented to university affiliates. Thus, only in the later half of the twentieth century did these two separate strands of neighborhood develop-

FIGURE

INTRODUCTION 1

Aerial view of Morningside Heights looking northwest, c. 1935.

ment—that of the institutions and of the residential buildings—merge, so that today most of the apartment buildings and rowhouses are owned by the institutions and these buildings, along with many of those in private ownership, house people affiliated with Columbia University and the area's other prestigious institutions.

Almost every building standing today on Morningside Heights is the original structure erected on that site (frontispiece). The early farmhouses and mansions are gone, as are a few of the institutional buildings, primarily medical facilities that became obsolete due to advances in health care. Some rowhouses and a few apartment buildings were demolished, generally for institutional expansion. By and large, however, the area's architecture illustrates the phenomenal expansion of some of New York City's major institutions in the years between about 1890 and the early 1930s, as well as reflecting the impact of the subway system on the creation of this residential neighborhood in the years after 1904. Morningside Heights contains a densely packed collection of speculative residential construction that typifies neighborhood development and residential design in the early twentieth century, as well as being home to some of New York's leading institutions and several of the city's greatest works of architecture. Both the ordinary and extraordinary are the subject of this book.

FIGURE 1.1
Claremont House, early
nineteenth century.

CHAPTER ONE

At Bloomingdale

The Pre-History of Morningside Heights

IN THE SEVENTEENTH AND EIGHTEENTH CENTURIES AND FIRST years of the nineteenth century, Morningside Heights was a quiet rural region far from the city at the southern tip of Manhattan Island. The area was even isolated from the small rural villages that dotted the west side of the island, including Bloomingdale to the south and Manhattanville to the north.[1] With the exception of the Revolutionary War Battle of Harlem Heights on September 16, 1776, little occurred to disturb the area's rural tranquility.[2] The only buildings on Morningside Heights during this early period were rural cottages and farmhouses, and a few riverside mansions, such as Michael Hogan's "Claremont" (figure 1.1), erected c. 1804 at the northwestern edge of the Morningside Plateau, and merchant and banker Andrew Carrigan's impressive Greek Revival home, erected c. 1836 on what would become the northeast corner of Riverside Drive and 114th Street.[3] The area was accessible only by the Bloomingdale Road, the northern extension of Broadway, which, on Morningside Heights, generally followed the route traversed today by Riverside Drive and Claremont Avenue, including an S-curve at 116th Street that accounts for the odd shape of the apartment buildings currently standing on that corner. The first significant intrusions into the rural farmland on the Morningside Plateau occurred in 1816 when the Society of the New York Hospital began purchasing large parcels of land for an insane asylum. The asylum opened in 1821 and was joined some years later by the Leake and Watts Orphan Asylum, thus establishing the Morningside Plateau as an area of large asylums.

Asylums on the Morningside Plateau

The Society of the New York Hospital purchased large tracts of land on the Morningside Plateau between 1816 and 1820 with the intention of moving its asylum for the mentally ill from its overcrowded building on Broadway and Leonard Street to this spacious rural locale.[4] New York Hospital had begun admitting patients with mental disorders shortly after its founding in 1771 as New York City's first hospital.[5] It erected a hospital on Broadway between Duane and Worth streets, which was then the northern fringe of the city. During the early years of the hospital's existence, its mental patients were housed in filthy, ill-lit basement cells, typifying the prison-like conditions to which mental patients were subjected at the time. However, in 1806 the hospital's governors and staff, who were among the first medical professionals in America to seek the "humane" treatment of mentally ill patients, erected a separate building for these patients adjacent to the hospital. A contemporary account recorded that "The eye is not offended in this institution with the sight of padlocks and bolts, nor the ear by the rattling of fetters and chains. And it is believed that the discipline can be established among the maniacs without the use of the whip."[6] Since it was the only institution in the state at that time caring for people with mental disorders, New York Hospital's caseload was continually growing. The hospital appealed to the New York State Legislature for funding and in 1806 it was assured of an annual grant of $12,500 to last until 1857.[7]

In 1815 New York Hospital board member Thomas Eddy undertook a campaign to further improve the care of mental patients provided by the hospital. Eddy had been impressed by advances in mental health care in England and France, especially at the Quakers' "retreat" near York, where experiments in the humane treatment of mentally ill patients in a rural environment had shown success.[8] Accordingly, Eddy proposed that treatment at New York Hospital be reorganized and "that a lot, not less than ten acres, should be purchased by the Governors, conveniently situated, within a few miles of the city, and to erect a substantial building, on a plan calculated for the accommodation of fifty lunatic patients; the ground to be improved in such a manner as to serve for agreeable walks, gardens, etc., for the exercise and amusement of the patients."[9] As a result of Eddy's appeal, the Board of Governors appointed a committee to consider the purchase of land outside of the city since "there are many reasons for believing, that the recovery from a State of insanity would be greatly promoted, by having a considerable space of ground adjoining the Asylum . . . , in which many of the patients might have the privilege of walking or taking other kinds of exercise."[10]

The committee recommended the purchase of 38 acres "at Bloomingdale," approximately seven miles north of Wall Street. The proposed site extended from 107th Street north to 113th Street, generally bounded by Morningside Drive and Columbus Avenue on the east and Amsterdam Avenue on the west.[11] The governors thought that this was appropriate for the planned asylum since "The prospect is very commanding and beautiful. . . . [It] is as Salubrious, as any other that could be selected in the neighborhood of the City. . . . The extent of the grounds, their capacity to afford Gardens, and rural walks, the beauty of the scenery, and the retirement of the situation . . . recommend it strongly."[12] The governors took title to the Bloomingdale property in August 1816. Designs for five separate buildings were accepted in early 1817, but, since funds were limited, it was decided to erect only a single structure that would house both male and female patients.[13] As planning for construction proceeded, however, the governors decided that there was no suitable site for the proposed building on the newly purchased property. Thus, a separate site north of 113th Street and west of Amsterdam Avenue was assembled between 1818 and 1820.[14]

Thomas C. Taylor, a builder and a member of the Board of Governors, took charge of construction, although it is unclear who actually designed the hospital building. Board minutes note that Taylor "prepared all the plans," but in 1820 James O'Donnell submitted a claim for payment, asserting that he was the architect. This claim was initially rejected by the governors, but was paid in full in 1821.[15] Initial plans called for construction of a building with a front elevation clad in marble. When this proved too expensive, Taylor suggested using a less expensive brownstone from Newark, New Jersey, but on the entire structure, not only on the facade, since, he noted "all the building is equally exposed to view, and ought to be built of the same materials."[16] Taylor successfully argued that "this may appear extravagant to some of the Governors, but they should remember this building ought to have the appearance of a Palace, rather than a Gaol, and by that means it will command the most wealthy patients in the United States."[17] The cornerstone was laid on May 7, 1818, and the 211-foot-long, elegantly detailed Federal style brownstone building, constructed at the center of the site, facing south toward the developing city, was occupied in June 1821 (figure 1.2). During the first decades after the asylum opened on Morningside

building 1818
finished 1821

FIGURE 1.2

Bloomingdale Insane Asylum, 1834.

Heights, a visitor from New York City would reach the institution via the Bloomingdale Road. At about what is now Riverside Drive and 111th Street, the visitor would turn onto an old lane (sometimes referred to as Asylum Lane) that led to the asylum's grounds (figure 1.3). To a close observer, this lane is still evident, its route having been preserved in the odd shape of several buildings: the oblique walls of 2867, 2869, and 2871 Broadway and the canted rear facades of the apartment buildings at 521 West 112th Street and 530 West 113th Street (figure 8.18).

By 1826 the asylum had already outgrown its original building and plans were considered both for its extension and the construction of free-standing pavilions for "noisy" patients. Architect and board member Ezra Weeks was asked to site the buildings and prepare plans and cost estimates. Weeks proposed an additional wing on the east side of the existing hospital and two new buildings at the rear, each designed to house twenty-five patients.[18] A brick building for "noisy" male patients (the Men's Lodge) was erected in 1829 behind the east side of the hospital. This building may have been constructed to Weeks's designs, but more likely was the work of John McComb, Jr., one of the architects of City Hall, who was also a board member and was consulted about the plans and specifications for the lodge early in 1829.[19] A similar pavilion to care for "noisy" women patients (the Women's Lodge) was erected in 1835–37 to the designs of James H. Dakin on a site behind the west side of the asylum.[20]

FIGURE 1.3

Map of Morningside Heights with original route of the Bloomingdale Road (left) and Asylum Lane; scattered frame buildings, 1885.

additions 1829, 1835

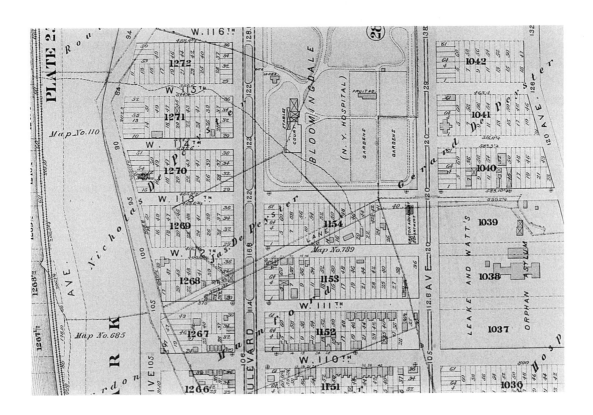

These two buildings were only the first of many additions and alterations constructed over the next five decades to accommodate additional patients, to improve care, or to add modern conveniences such as plumbing and heat (figure 1.4). Later construction included a bowling alley (c.1845), superintendent's house (c.1852; figure 1.10), two-story additions to the lodges (1854), laundry (1854), wings connecting the original building and lodges (west wing, 1860–62, additional story 1867; east wing, 1886), chapel (c.1865), conservatory (1875), heating plant and kitchen (1877), and the John C. Green Memorial Building (Ralph Townsend, 1879–80), a pavilion attached to the west wing to accommodate educated and "refined" women whose problems were deemed curable.[21] In 1879 a porter's lodge was erected on Broadway at 115th Street, at what had become the asylum's main entrance when the Bloomingdale Road was discontinued and realigned as present-day Broadway in the late 1860s (figure 5.9).[22] The last building erected at the asylum was Macy Villa, designed by Ralph Townsend in 1885 (figure 4.30). This homey brick pavilion with deep wooden porches was donated by William H. Macy, a member of the Board of Governors, for wealthy male patients who would live in a residential rather than institutional environment. Construction of Macy Villa occurred at the same time that the hospital's governors were fending off attacks from real estate interests that eventually forced the asylum to vacate its Morningside Heights property. Macy Villa is the only asylum building that survives.[23]

The grounds of the asylum were laid out with walks and gardens in which the patients could engage in what were considered therapeutic outdoor agricultural and horticultural pursuits (figure 1.5). The landscaping included pas-

further additions

FIGURE 1.4
Bloomingdale Insane Asylum, c. 1890; from left, John C. Green Memorial Building, west wing, original building, and east wing.

ture land below 113th Street, vegetable gardens and barns between 114th and 115th streets, lawns extending north to the main buildings at 117th Street, and additional pasture land and groves of trees to the north between 119th and 120th streets. The grounds were considered quite beautiful, as Edward Ruggles recounts in his 1846 guidebook to New York City:

> The approach to the asylum from the southern entrance, by the stranger who associates the most sombre scenes with a lunatic hospital, is highly pleasing. The sudden opening of the view, the extent of the grounds, the various avenues gracefully winding through so large a lawn; the cedar hedges, the fir, and other ornamental trees, tastefully distributed or grouped, the variety of shrubbery and flowers, is fine, the assemblage of so many objects to please the eye, and relieve the melancholy mind from its sad musings, strike him as one of the most successful and useful instances of landscape gardening.[24]

FIGURE 1.5

Map of the Bloomingdale Insane Asylum with buildings and path system, c. 1890.

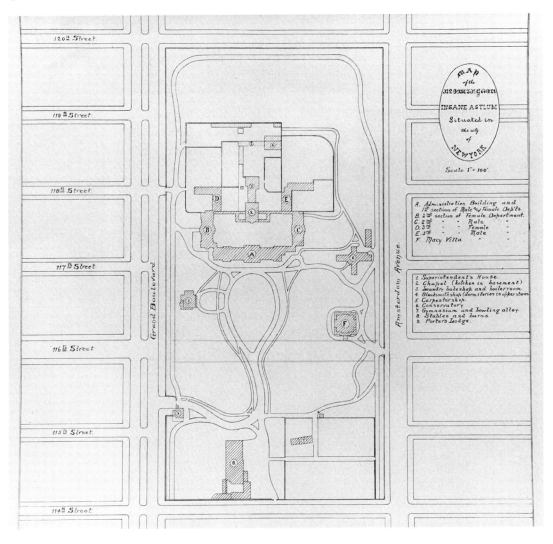

In its early years, the asylum was quite successful, caring for a mix of curable and incurable patients, including those who paid for their care and those who were charity cases subsidized by the state and placed at the Bloomingdale Asylum because it received an annual government stipend. Soon, however, the asylum became a dumping ground for poor "chronic" patients and the quality of care deteriorated.[25] In the 1840s, poor patients were removed to the city's new asylum on Blackwell's Island (now Roosevelt Island) or to the state's first asylum in Utica, thus ending Bloomingdale's extensive service to the poor, a point that would become an issue in the 1880s when the hospital would be embroiled in a fight to save its tax exemption.[26]

As early as November 1821 the Board of Governors considered selling the property south of 113th Street and east of Amsterdam Avenue, which was physically separate from the site on which the asylum had been built, to raise capital for the operations of the new asylum.[27] However, the governors were unable to divest themselves of a significant portion of this land until 1834, when much of the property was sold to the Leake and Watts Orphan Asylum. The orphan asylum had only recently been founded as the unanticipated result of a bizarre condition in the will of John G. Leake. At his death in 1827 John Leake left most of his fortune to Robert Watts 2nd, the son of his close friend John Watts, but only under the condition that Robert change his surname to Leake. If Robert refused this condition or died underage or without an heir, the bequest was to go to the Protestant Episcopal, Presbyterian, and Dutch churches to "erect and endow a building in the Suburbs of the City for the reception[,] maintenance and education from time to time forever thereafter of as many helpless Orphan children (paying no regard to the country or religious persuasion of their deceased parents) until they shall severally arrive at an age to be put out apprentices to trades."[28] Leake's will further specified that none of his money was to be expended on the construction of orphan asylum buildings, but only for operational costs. Rather, construction costs were to be paid from the rents on several downtown properties that were also part of the bequest.

When Robert Watts accepted the proviso of Leake's will, his father was "struck with grief," not only because his friend had stipulated that Robert Watts change his name to Leake, but also that Robert had actually agreed to this requirement.[29] Robert's unexpected death only two years later, in 1829, further complicated the issue, since his father then inherited his estate, which included Leake's bequest. Watts did not want Leake's money, since he had so vehemently objected to the will's provisions. Instead he used the funds to establish the orphan asylum and named it both for its original benefactor and himself.

A board of directors was established in 1832 for the fledgling institution. One of its first duties was to find a site in the "Suburbs of the City," as originally requested by Leake. A site committee examined many potential properties, including Alexander Hamilton's Grange south of 145th Street and several sites on Morningside Heights adjoining the Bloomingdale Asylum. The committee was "particularly pleased" with the unused asylum property. New York Hospital was anxious to sell the entire 38 acres, but the Leake and Watts board agreed to purchase only the 24.755 acres lying between 109th and 113th streets, leaving the hospital with land south of 109th Street.[30] Having acquired land for an asylum, the board was then faced with the problem of funding construction of an appropriate building. Leake's proviso that only income from rents on downtown properties could be spent for construction provided an inadequate amount of money for this purpose. Thus, in 1834, board members petitioned the New York State Legislature for an appropriation, noting that the asylum would relieve the public of the need to care for the swelling numbers of orphans resulting from recent cholera epidemics, and, according to asylum board members, from increasing immigration. Playing to the emotions of the state's lawmakers, the board exhorted, "Private aid has not been invested, it is trusted, in vain! But that unassisted by public efforts is incompetent to afford the support requisite to render these destitute, friendless beings fit members of a community whose individual intelligence, morality & religion constitute the true basis of its public character."[31] However, this plea fell on deaf ears and no government funding was approved.

In June 1835 Ithiel Town, one of the most prestigious architects in New York, submitted plans to the board for the new asylum.[32] The board had hoped to erect an orphanage of granite, marble, or other durable stone, but these options were too expensive. As a result, Town redesigned the building several times to scale back costs. Nevertheless, the board was finally compelled to postpone construction until sufficient capital could be raised. In 1837, after selling the portion of their property south of 110th Street and taking out a mortgage on other land owned by the corporation, the board again began planning for construction. They asked architect Joseph Trench to draw plans based on those submitted by builder Phineas Burgess.[33] However, in October of 1837, the board credited Town's work as the basis for the orphanage design, resolving "that Ithiel Town be paid Seventy five dollars for the plans of the Orphan House heretofore submitted to this board and the specifications accompanying the same—which plans, altho' not wholly approved, were the basis for the present plan."[34] Finally, in late 1837 construction began on a plot in the center of the asylum's property at about 112th Street between Morningside Drive and Amsterdam Avenue, with Samuel Thomson selected to superintend construction.[35] The new orphanage was occupied in 1843 (figure 1.6). The building, constructed of brick and designed in Ithiel Town's favored Greek Revival style, had austere Ionic temple fronts facing north and south (the columns were brick covered in stucco with wooden capitals) flanked by simple two-story wings and projecting end pavilions.[36] Although deteriorated, a portion of the building survives on the site of the proposed south transept of the Cathedral of St. John the Divine. It is the oldest extant structure on Morningside Heights.

Public Works: The Croton Aqueduct, Parks, and a Firehouse

The Bloomingdale Insane Asylum and Leake and Watts Orphan Asylum, which together occupied more than half of Morningside Heights, established a rural institutional character on the Morningside Plateau that would last for several decades. With the exception of the buildings erected to house these two institutions and a few houses constructed on private property nearby, major construction on Morningside Heights prior to the 1890s was limited to public works projects—the Croton Aqueduct, Morningside Park, Riverside Park and Drive, and a small firehouse on West 113th Street.

The Croton Aqueduct was the first system to transport fresh water to New York City. In the early decades of the nineteenth century, the prosperity of New York City was hampered by lack of an inexpensive, continuous supply of fresh water. Local wells and the water system of the Manhattan Company provided foul water and even then only in limited quantity. Potable water was difficult and expensive to acquire, streets could not be cleaned, and it was almost impossible to fight fires efficiently. In 1835, after much debate about how to assure an adequate supply of fresh water to the city, the Croton watershed in Westchester County was chosen as a source and construction commenced on a dam and gravity-driven aqueduct. Fresh water was finally available to New Yorkers on July 4, 1842.[37] In Manhattan, the Croton Aqueduct ran down Amsterdam Avenue on a raised structure that bisected Morningside Heights.

Croton Aqueduct

1842

FIGURE 1.6
Leake and Watts Orphan Asylum, c. 1860s.

In the 1840s, the areas of Manhattan through which the aqueduct ran were sparsely populated. Thus, an aqueduct built above ground was not considered a problem. As the city grew, however, the aqueduct structure became an impediment to development and to the flow of traffic on and across Amsterdam Avenue. In 1865 the New York State Legislature mandated the removal of the masonry conduit between West 85th and 92nd streets. This decision was followed by two further acts directing New York City's Department of Public Works to remove the aqueduct between West 92nd and 113th streets and then from 113th Street north. Instead of the raised aqueduct, a masonry conduit with iron pipes was to be constructed below the street. As a result, six mains were placed beneath the center of Amsterdam Avenue.

The most visible feature of the reconstructed water system was a series of gatehouses with machinery that controlled the flow of water into and out of the pipes. These structures were designed as seemingly impenetrable fortresses, symbolically protecting the lifeline of the city. Gatehouses at West 92nd Street (demolished) and West 113th Street were begun in 1870. For the 113th Street gatehouse, the city purchased the southwest corner of Amsterdam Avenue and 113th Street from the Leake and Watts Asylum, which owned a small piece of property on the west side of the avenue. A small but monumental structure constructed of massive blocks of granite was built on this corner site (figure 8.8).[38] Another gatehouse was erected several years later on the southeast corner of Amsterdam Avenue and West 119th Street.[39] Although no longer used as part of the water system, both buildings remain standing, their odd juxtaposition of diminutive scale and massive stonework creating two of the neighborhood's most unusual structures.[40]

Even before residential development was contemplated on Morningside Heights, the city invested in the planning and eventual construction of Morningside Park and Riverside Park and Drive at either edge of the plateau. Both parks incorporated steep escarpments that were not conducive to residential development and both were conceived, at least in part, as amenities that would raise land values and spur residential construction. Morningside Park serves as the eastern boundary of Morningside Heights, hugging the edge of the cliff from 110th to 123rd Street, originally including a small western panhandle at 122nd Street (now the site of P.S. 36, completed in 1967). Morningside Park had first been proposed by the Central Park Commissioners in 1867, but was delayed when the Commission was abolished in 1870.[41] In 1873 the city commissioned Frederick Law Olmsted and Calvert Vaux to transform the wasteland along the high cliffs into a small park.[42] Although Olmsted and Vaux's report on the design of the park makes clear their opposition to the conversion of land unsuitable for residential development, such as the Morningside cliff, into parks without any regard for the city's actual needs, he and Vaux proposed a design for the park.[43] However, the economic depression following the Panic of 1873 prevented the implementation of the plan since there was no necessity for expending scarce resources on the creation of a park in an area where few people lived and few would visit.

In 1887, after the elevated railroad had opened and Harlem was rapidly being developed as a middle-class community, Olmsted and Vaux were asked to alter their initial concept to accommodate new conditions.[44] In both the original and later designs they incorporated the natural features of the site, proposing meadows at the base in the flat area where the park borders Harlem, paths and dense plantings in the rugged terrain along the cliffs (figure 1.7), and a promenade with observation platforms on top of the cliffs on Morningside Heights where viewers could scan "far out across a wide range of beautiful country, and over the waters and islands of the river and sound, the eastern sea-gate of the metropolis."[45] In the 1887 design, Olmsted and Vaux acknowledged the presence of the elevated railroad station at 116th Street and Eighth Avenue by adding a passage across the park at 116th Street and a long staircase along the cliff. Construction began almost immediately on the revised plan and a steep and precarious link was created between Morningside Heights and the elevated station.[46]

Riverside Park and the adjacent Riverside Drive were also planned to take advantage of panoramic views.[47] A park and separate drive along the western edge of Manhattan Island from 72nd Street to about 129th Street were first proposed by the Parks Department in 1865 as a means of spurring development on the West Side. Although this area was beautifully sited, with gentle slopes and dramatic cliffs leading to the river and spectacular views across the Hudson to the New Jersey Palisades, it was not without problems. The proposed parkland

Morningside Park

Riverside Park

FIGURE 1.7
Morningside Park, view looking north, with stairs leading to 116th Street, c. 1900.

would not reach to the water since the tracks of the Hudson River Railroad (later the New York Central Railroad) ran near the edge of the island and the waterfront itself was planned for commercial uses. Nevertheless, in 1867 the New York State Legislature enacted a law that permitted the city to acquire land for the proposed park.[48] In the initial design for the project, Riverside Avenue (as Riverside Drive was known until 1908) was to be a straight road that did not follow the undulating contour of the cliffside. Criticism of this unimaginative and impractical scheme prompted the hiring of Olmsted in 1873. His task was to design a narrow linear park that would shield visitors from the unsightly commercial aspects of the riverfront as well as highlight the natural drama of the site. Olmsted discarded the original plan and proposed a seemingly simple, yet for its time, remarkable design concept, which combined into a single unified design a picturesque park taking advantage of the natural attributes of a dramatic site and an urban parkway providing a landscaped environment for a residential community. As presented early in 1875, the project consisted of a series of narrow sections aligned along the edge of the island: a park with paths set into the cliffs and slopes leading toward the water; a tree-lined promenade atop the cliff, from which strollers could admire the impressive views across the Hudson River; and a landscaped drive that followed the gentle curves of the is-land's edge.[49]

Riverside Drive was to serve as a scenic carriageway for those out on a plea-sure drive and would also be an access route to the villas that wealthy people were expected to build along the landscaped boulevard. In several locations, where the park is especially wide, the drive is divided by landscaped islands sep-arating the main carriageway from narrower access routes, increasing the feel-ing of a residential community set in a park. On Morningside Heights, the park is especially beautiful. The parkland here is particularly wide, serving to hide the railroad tracks, and from 110th Street to 114th Street wide landscaped islands hug a steep slope, creating a naturalistic setting for residential buildings that ap-pear to be perched on top of a hill. North of 114th Street, the route of the drive is almost straight, providing an esplanade that culminates in the view of the Hudson River and Palisades from the northern edge of the Morningside Plateau (figure 1.8).

Olmsted envisioned the possibility of a "suitable terminal feature" at the north end of the park that would enhance the magnificent views, but he was concerned that the 1885 proposal to erect Grant's Tomb at this site might block "the great northern view" and that "it will be extremely unfortunate if . . . the remains of the dead are brought into close association with the gayety [sic] of the Promenade at the culminating point."[50] Olmsted, who no longer lived in New York City, suggested that Calvert Vaux be called upon to advise on the de-sign and placement of the monument, but this idea was ignored. An incon-clusive competition for the Grant memorial was held in 1888–89, requiring a second competition in 1890. John Duncan's Classical Revival monument, modeled after the Mausoleum of Halicarnassus, was selected and its construction completed in 1897 (figure 1.9).[51] Although it is an impressive structure, its presence at the north end of the park, as Olmsted had feared, hides the vista to the north.

In the years prior to the area's major development, the city financed one other project on Morningside Heights—Engine Company 47's firehouse of 1889–91, located on West 113th Street just west of Amsterdam Avenue, adjacent to the 113th Street gatehouse.[52] This firehouse was one of a large group erected by the city in the late nineteenth century as the New York City Fire Department became an increasingly professional municipal service. Beginning in 1879, the city undertook a campaign of erecting technologically up-to-date firehouses, generally on narrow, inexpensive side street plots. As the city expanded northward, firehouses were built in the newly populated districts, but in some cases firehouse construction preceded the influx of new residents. Such was the case on Morningside Heights. For the 113th Street firehouse Napoleon LeBrun & Son, the architectural firm responsible for all of the city's new firehouses between 1879 and 1894 (more than sixty were built), designed an elegant Romanesque Revival structure faced in yellow brick, brownstone, and red terra-cotta, with a cast-iron vehicular entry symbolically ornamented with fish scales and water.[53]

Early Residential Buildings on Morningside Heights

Although for many decades the insane and orphan asylums were the major land owners on the Morningside Plateau, they never owned all of the land in the area. The Bloomingdale Asylum owned property in the center of the plateau, while Leake and Watts held title to the southeast. The asylums never acquired any of the riverside property, and most of the northern, western, southwestern, and northeastern sections of the neighborhood also remained in the hands of private individuals. Many parcels were held by real estate investors, including the Astor and Goelet families, two of New York's largest landowners. Much of this property was retained as long-term investments by owners who awaited the day when development would

raise land values. By the 1880s, only a few residential buildings were scattered through the area, ranging from wooden shanties, to old farmhouses, to substantial mansions (figures 1.10 and 1.11). In 1886 the earliest multiple dwellings were erected on Morningside Heights, an anomalous pair of modest four-story tenements at 2848 and 2850 Broadway between 110th and 111th streets.

More typical of the area were the wooden houses scattered across the Morningside Plateau. Some of these were permanent dwellings and others were makeshift shanties (figure 1.12). The largest group of wooden houses was located in "Dixonville," at the southern edge of the neighborhood along 110th

FIGURE 1.10
View from the Bloomingdale Insane Asylum looking southwest, c. 1890; Superintendent's House is at right.

FIGURE 1.11
View from the Bloomingdale Insane Asylum looking northwest toward Manhattanville, c. 1890.

Street. These modest wooden dwellings were built by William Dixon and rented to "men of the laboring class," many of whom were Irish or German immigrants (figure 1.13).[54] Following the opening of the subway in 1904, Dixonville was briefly transformed into "Little Coney Island," a street of beer gardens, snack stands, and concert halls, that the *Real Estate Record* referred to as "inferior amusement resorts" (figure 1.14).[55] West 110th Street was an ideal site for such entertainment facilities. The area was not yet heavily developed, yet a subway station at the corner of Broadway and 110th Street provided convenient access. In addition, 110th Street was well-traveled, since it connected the northern end of Central Park with Morningside Park and Riverside Park and Drive. Thus, those on an outing between the parks could stop for refreshment and entertainment on 110th Street.

Between 1884 and 1887 three substantial mansions were built along the Morningside Heights portion of Riverside Drive. The new houses were not part of the general residential development of Morningside Heights which would not begin for another decade (see chapter 8); rather, they were part of a separate development of large residences along Riverside Drive. Olmsted had planned Riverside Drive under the assumption that large freestanding houses would rise along the landscaped boulevard. Although a number of such houses were scattered along the Drive, "for some reason or another," a writer noted in 1898, "the Drive failed to attract many such [residences]."[56] Riverside Drive's inability to live up to development expectations may be explained by the lack of adequate mass transit on the far west side and the drive's distance from other areas with concentrations of wealthy residents. In addition, although Riverside Drive was extremely attractive, with its park frontage and river views, it was also exceptionally narrow in most places and was marred by the presence below of the busy and noisy freight tracks of the New York Central Railroad.

The three mansions erected on Morningside Heights took advantage of the river views available from the bluffs along the east bank of the

Hudson River. In addition they were located in a section where the park and drive are relatively wide, thus partially shielding residents from the noise and unsightly appearance of the railroad tracks and the commercial riverfront below. These houses were erected for the households of wealthy businessmen: George Noakes, a restauranteur who ran the eponymous establishment on Greenwich Street in Lower Manhattan founded by his father, built on a site between 113th and 114th streets in 1884 (figure 1.15); Joseph J. Kittel, until his retirement in 1888 one of America's largest dealers in china and glassware, known in the trade as "the Napoleon of China," and John J. Gibbons, a partner in the famous glass and china emporium of Gilman, Collamore & Co., built houses just south of 122nd Street on the present site of Riverside Church in 1885 and 1887 respectively (figure 2.29).[57] These mansions joined the earlier Claremont and the Carrigan House along the river frontage. The three houses were all designed by Arthur Bates Jennings, who lived in Manhattanville just north of Morningside Heights. In the 1880s, early in his career as an archi-

tect, Jennings designed a number of homes, including these three Riverside Drive dwellings, in a picturesque version of the Romanesque Revival style.[58] The Noakes House was faced with rough-textured blocks of stone and massed in an especially eccentric manner, with recessed portico and loggia, open terrace, projecting oriels and corner bartizan, and steeply sloping roof profiles.[59] The somewhat smaller nearby houses erected for the china merchants are equally picturesque, with gables, towers, and chimneys creating dynamic silhouettes.

Development Pressures and the Elevated Railroad

Although the Bloomingdale Insane Asylum had been established on Morningside Heights so that patients could be cared for in a rural environment far from the bustle of the city, it could not avoid urban development forever. As early as 1865 "frequent and annoying trespassing on the asylum grounds" was reported.[60] The following year, the Board of Governors of the Society of the New York Hospital seriously considered removing the Bloomingdale Asylum from the city. The board realized that the surrounding area might soon be developed and that streets would be opened in the area including some that might actually be pushed through the asylum grounds (noting in particular the city's desire to turn Eleventh Avenue into a boulevard that would become the northern extension of Broadway and would divide the asylum property).[61] Thus, New York Hospital's Board of Governors acknowledged "the expediency of the selection of a substitute location."[62] This resulted in the acquisition of slightly over 292 acres in White Plains in 1868. Although Richard Morris Hunt was hired

FIGURE 1.14
Broadway and West 110th Street, c. 1905. Saloons occupy the corner buildings; a roof garden theater, at right, is ornamented with mock medieval and Renaissance structures; temporary buildings line 110th Street; six new apartment houses stand on 111th Street; the dome of St. Luke's Hospital rises in the background; the arch of the Cathedral of St. John the Divine looms at right.

FIGURE 1.15
George Noakes House, c. 1891.

as architect in 1871, no construction occurred.[63] The economic depression of the 1870s halted all additional planning. Instead, beginning in 1875, the asylum expanded on Morningside Heights, erecting several new buildings. However, the Bloomingdale Asylum's continuing presence on Morningside Heights now faced mounting pressures from real estate interests and their political and journalistic allies who believed that the presence of the asylum was depressing land values and retarding residential development on the heights. People who owned land on Morningside Heights hoped that if they could force the removal of the asylum from the center of the Morningside Plateau, they would profit from land sales and residential development.

While it was true that few builders were willing to invest in high-class residential development in the area immediately surrounding the Bloomingdale Insane Asylum, the asylum's presence was not the major reason why development on Morningside Heights lagged behind that in surrounding neighborhoods. Development in areas of Manhattan located long distances from the downtown business, manufacturing, entertainment, and shopping districts could not occur until modes of mass transportation were established that permitted people to live uptown and easily commute south. The key event in the history of residential development in the uptown neighborhoods on the west side was the completion of construction on the Ninth Avenue elevated railroad in 1879. Service from South Ferry ran up Ninth Avenue (now Columbus Avenue) through the Upper West Side to 110th Street, where the tracks turned eastward on an S-curve, popularly dubbed "Suicide Curve" (figure 2.11), continuing north into Harlem on Eighth Avenue to a terminus at 155th Street.[64] The inception of service on this elevated line directly influenced the development of the areas through which it traversed. For the first time middle- and working-class people could live in uptown neighborhoods and commute at a reasonable cost and in a relatively rapid and comfortable manner to the city's business and commercial neighborhoods, to jobs, shops, and places of entertainment. To meet the demand for housing in newly accessible areas, thousands of small- and large-scale speculators and builders invested in the transformation of the open land near the els into residential communities. In the 1880s and 1890s, the neighborhoods that bordered Morningside Heights developed as middle-class residential sections to varying degrees. The Upper West Side, south of 110th Street, was almost entirely built up with single-family rowhouses, a few apartment houses (such as the Dakota) for affluent families, and some tenements for working-class households. In Harlem, to the east and northeast of Morningside Heights, handsome rowhouses were erected in clusters near parks or on streets convenient to the elevated stations. To the north, on Hamilton Heights, breaks in the cliff that forms the barrier between the Heights and the Harlem Lowlands at 141st and 145th streets permitted easy access to el stations, providing a suitable environment for rowhouse developers.[65]

Morningside Heights was bypassed by the Ninth Avenue el and the physical barrier created by the steep cliff separating the plateau from Harlem made the area virtually inaccessible from the elevated station at 116th Street and Eighth Avenue. Even the construction of steps in Morningside Park as part of Olmsted and Vaux's 1887 park design did not solve this problem, since the steep steps provided only a precarious route to and from the elevated station. At 110th Street, where there would have been easy access to the lowlands to the east, there was no station; in fact, there was no stop between 104th and 116th streets. Only in 1903 was a 110th Street station added to the line. However, by that time the presence of this station was irrelevant since construction was well underway on the subway beneath Broadway, which would open in 1904. It was the subway that would be the key force in creating a residential neighborhood on Morningside Heights.

Subway makes residential area [handwritten marginalia]

The Social Elite vs the Real Estate "Pooh-Bahs"

The lack of mass transit was clearly the major factor retarding residential development on the heights in the late nineteenth century, but local real estate interests continued to focus on the presence of the Bloomingdale Insane Asylum as the cause for depressed land values and limited development opportunities. Real estate owners, many of whom had purchased property as investments, hoping to profit from eventual development, believed that if the asylum could be removed, land values might rise and residential development might begin as it had to the south, east, and north. Ultimately, it was pressure from owners of real estate in the vicinity of the Bloomingdale Asylum that forced the Society of the New York Hospital to announce in May 1888 that the asylum would relocate to White Plains. This was not accomplished, however, without a fierce battle between the hospital's governors and the real estate community. The real estate owners were led by former State Senator Francis Bixby and lawyer Dwight H. Olmstead, both of whom owned land on Morningside Heights to the east of the asylum property. They were supported by local politicians, who were anxious to increase their constituency with the residential development of the Morningside Plateau, and they were abetted by several local newspapers, particularly the *New York Herald* and Joseph Pulitzer's *New York World,* each of which published an extensive series of articles condemning the hospital.[66]

1888 asylum leaves [handwritten marginalia]

The political battle to remove the asylum began in earnest in 1886, when State Assemblyman John McManus introduced a bill to repeal the asylum's tax exemption. Since its organization, the Bloomingdale Asylum had benefitted from several laws passed by the New York State Legislature exempting the property from taxation as a charitable institution and prohibiting the opening of streets through the Bloomingdale property between West 114th and 120th streets.[67] McManus argued that the asylum was no longer a true charitable institution deserving of an exemption from taxes since it did not care for poor patients as it had in its early years. Both the proponents and opponents published broadsides, entitled "A Good Bill" and "A Bad Bill," that compared their adversary's behavior to the corrupt machinations of Boss Tweed.[68] Those in favor of the bill argued that the asylum received a public grant equivalent to $100,000 per year by its tax exemption, but that the public received no benefit at all from this. Strong support for this position came from members of the real estate community. Most vocal was Dwight H. Olmstead who, claiming to "have no personal interest in the matter" (even though he owned property near the asylum), unequivocally stated that the asylum "interferes with the growth of the city's improvements . . . deteriorating the value of adjoining property."[69] In response, the hospital defended its care of patients from all social strata and also noted that it was not the city that was interested in the passage of this bill, but only "a number of REAL ESTATE SPECULATORS . . . who within the last fifteen years have bought up at low prices a large number of vacant lots between the Asylum and Morningside Park." These realtors hoped, the hospital governors argued, that cutting streets through the asylum's property or burdening the hospital with onerous taxation would force it to sell its land and that "they fondly trust to create a market for their own lots."[70] Although the 1886 efforts to remove the asylum failed, the realtors continued their fight, culminating in another legislative battle two years later.

The 1888 effort to force the removal of the Bloomingdale Asylum was instigated by the Morningside Park Association, a new organization founded by a small number of local real estate owners, led once again by Bixby and Olmstead. The association submitted a "memorial" or petition to the legislature requesting an investigation of the asylum. The memorial listed eight complaints against the institution, requesting that the legislature investigate whether the asylum was a charity, whether streets should be opened through the property, and whether or not the asylum "is detrimental to property in the neighborhood or unsafe for persons residing or who might reside there, and whether the said asylum should be permitted to continue in that location."[71] A committee of the New York State Senate held five hearings that examined the accusations of the Morningside Park Association.[72] At these hearings, Bixby and Olmstead presented witnesses who commended the beauty of the asylum site and argued that the asylum lowered real estate values and inhibited development. The testimony of Leopold Friedman, one of several speakers who owned land in the area, was typical. Although Friedman described the asylum property as "the most elevated and handsomest" in New York "and the most desirable," he also protested that the presence of the insane asylum "paralyzes the development of all that region."[73] In defense of the asylum, counsel John Cadwalader called members of the Board of Governors, the superintendent of the asylum, and the superintendents of other asylums, as well as realtors, who argued that the asylum did not lower values since there was no demand for building on Morningside Heights because of the inaccessibility of the locale due to a lack of adequate transit.

The Morningside Park Association had strong allies in the New York City press. The *New York World* and *New York Herald* were particularly vocal in their support of the removal of the asylum. They reported in detail the comments of the association's supporters, barely mentioning the testimony of those in favor of the hospital. Inflammatory headlines and subheadings made the newspapers' positions clear, referring to the hospital as "an incubus," "a blight on the west side," or "a so-called charitable asylum." [74] The argument was framed as one involving the "people" or the "citizens" against a hospital run by and for members of New York's elite. An insane asylum run by and primarily for the city's social elite was a natural target for newspapers competing for readers among the city's growing working- and middle-class communities. It was true that New York Hospital's board was composed of members from some of the oldest and wealthiest families in New York and that most patients did pay for at least a portion of their care. However, the hospital's opponents who had petitioned the legislature were clearly not representative of "the people," but were a small group of developers who sought personal pecuniary advantage through the removal of the asylum. As Cadwalader noted in his summation at the hearings, "This is not the public against the Bloomingdale Asylum, but it is Bixby & Olmstead against the public." [75] Hospital governor Elbridge T. Gerry less diplomatically referred to Bixby and Olmstead as "two respectable 'pooh-bahs.'" [76]

Although the Senate Committee's report of May 1888 sided with New York Hospital, it was clear to the governors that their days on Morningside Heights were numbered. They had spent a great deal of money fighting the real estate interests, who, it was certain, would continue their campaign. In fact, the hospital had little time to savor its victory in the State Senate, for on the same day that one senate committee supported the hospital, another issued a report recommending street openings. [77] As a result, late in May of 1888, the Board of Governors officially announced that the Bloomingdale Asylum would be transferred to White Plains, but only if this Westchester County land was exempted from taxation. [78] The White Plains site had all of the advantages of a quiet rural setting not too far from settled parts of New York City that Morningside Heights had offered seventy years earlier. In 1890 architect James Brown Lord designed the new hospital and in the following year F.L. Olmsted & Co. was hired to landscape the property. The asylum finally relocated to White Plains in 1894.

Even after the announcement of its imminent departure from New York City, the asylum continued to fight encroachments on the property, but lost this battle in 1889 when a law was passed mandating the opening of 116th Street through the asylum property. [79] The governors had not decided how to dispose of their vast tract on Morningside Heights and wished to forestall any changes that might lower the value of their property. New York Hospital had no interest in divesting itself of its land at a financial loss, nor were the governors, for obvious reasons, especially interested in selling most of their property to the local realtors. In any event, in 1889, perhaps in order to placate the real estate interests and to buy time to design and build a new hospital in White Plains, the governors announced that a small portion of their holdings would be auctioned off (see chapter 8). In 1891 the governors came to an agreement with Columbia College for the sale of a large part of the hospital's remaining property (see chapter 4). This arrangement must have given great satisfaction to the asylum's board members, since they had been able to sell a portion of their property to an elite institution at a substantial price, thus assuring a healthy income to the hospital, while at the same time keeping the property out of the hands of Bixby, Olmstead, and their cohorts.

While the Bloomingdale Asylum was embroiled in its fight to remain on Morningside Heights, the neighboring Leake and Watts Orphan Asylum quietly continued its work, although its building had become overcrowded and was aging. Its tax-exempt three-block site, through which no streets had been cut, was ignored by the Morningside Park Association. The realtors were apparently not particularly concerned about the orphanage since its property was at the southeast corner of Morningside Heights and did not inhibit development or block the flow of traffic across the plateau. In addition, while "lunatics" might be considered poor neighbors, Christian orphans apparently did not depress real estate values. It is thus ironic that Leake and Watts announced plans to relocate outside of New York City before the Bloomingdale Asylum. At a meeting of the Board of Directors of the orphanage on May 17, 1887, a motion was passed appointing a committee "to consider the expedience of selling the property."[80] The Board acted in response to interest from members of the Episcopal church in purchasing the property as the site for a proposed cathedral (see chapter 2). Nevertheless, after the property was appraised at between $803,000 and $970,000, the Board rejected a proposal from the Cathedral Committee to sell for only $800,000. Although it recommended a sale price of $875,000, the Board of the orphanage finally accepted an offer of $850,000 in 1887 on condition that the orphanage be permitted to remain on the site rent free until a new home was constructed.[81] The following year, Leake and Watts purchased land in Yonkers and hired architect Charles C. Haight and the landscape architectural firm of F.L. Olmsted & Co. to complete the new asylum. Leake and Watts finally left Morningside Heights in 1891.

By the last years of the 1880s, with the Bloomingdale Insane Asylum and the Leake and Watts Orphan Asylum committed to leaving Morningside Heights, the neighborhood was poised for change. The proposed construction of a grand Episcopal cathedral was sure to focus attention on Morningside Heights with its vast tracts of undeveloped land. Nevertheless, after fighting so insistently for the removal of the Bloomingdale Asylum, realtors and builders did not rush to erect homes on Morningside Heights. Indeed, John Cadwalader and New York Hospital's witnesses before the Senate Committee in 1888 had been correct. There was really no immediate demand for residential construction in the area, not because of the presence of the asylum, but because the lack of transit facilities made the Morningside Plateau relatively inaccessible. Some landowners profited from the sale of their properties to a new group of institutions and it was these new owners who began the transformation of the undeveloped plateau into modern Morningside Heights.

FIGURE 2.1
Column capital with the
prophet Jeremiah in nave
of Riverside Church.

CHAPTER TWO

Building for the Spirit

The Cathedral of St. John the Divine and Riverside Church

THE ERA OF MAJOR INSTITUTIONAL DEVELOPMENT ON MORNINGSIDE
Heights begins and ends with the construction of a monumental religious structure. The announcement in 1889 that the Cathedral of St. John the Divine would be built at the southeast corner of the rugged plateau first drew New Yorkers' attention to the potential for institutional development on Morningside Heights; the completion of Riverside Church in 1930, at the northwest corner of the area, marked the completion of major institutional development in the area. Although these two churches, begun almost thirty years apart, might seem to have little in common, their histories are closely intertwined since Riverside Church was erected as a response to the cathedral's reluctance to become an ecumenical center and force for Protestant unity.

1889 - St.John
1930 - Riverside

A[n Episcopal] Cathedral For New York

When Bishop Henry Codman Potter, leader of New York City's Episcopalian community, proclaimed on June 1, 1887, that a great Protestant cathedral would rise in the city, he set in motion a series of events that would, within the decade, transform the Morningside Plateau from a rural area into the center of the city's spiritual and intellectual life.[1] Although never a significant percentage of the city's population, Episcopalians were a powerful social and political force in New York City.[2] Many of New York's wealthiest families and many of those who wielded the greatest economic and political power were Episcopalian communicants. They held such sway in the social realm that many people converted to the Episcopal faith as their wealth increased in order to secure their place at the highest echelons of New York society. Among the wealthy New Yorkers active in Episcopal church affairs who became generous donors to the cathedral were the Astors, descendants of Calvinist immigrant John Jacob Astor; the Vanderbilts, whose Moravian ancestors had settled on Staten Island in the seventeenth century; and August Belmont, a German-Jewish immigrant.

Episcopalians - $ + power

Bishop Potter's announcement was the fulfillment of what had long been a dream of New York's Episcopal community. The construction of a great cathedral had been considered twice before. The project was first proposed in 1828, when Bishop John Henry Hobart suggested a cathedral on Washington Square, then a relatively undeveloped area at the northern edge of the city.[3] However, anti-British feelings lingering from the War of 1812 made the construction of a cathedral by the American wing of the Anglican church untenable. The movement for the establishment of an Episcopal cathedral waned with Bishop Hobart's death in 1830. By 1872, a time of dramatic growth in New York's wealth and population, an Episcopal cathedral was a more viable project than it had been nearly a half century before. The Episcopalian community had grown in numbers and in wealth, and could more readily afford an impressive new building. An additional impetus for a cathedral was undoubtedly the construction of a monumentally scaled cathedral for the city's Roman Catholics on a Fifth Avenue site in the heart of New York's newest premier residential district. To the city's powerful Episcopalian community, the fact that the largest church and only cathedral in the city was being built by Roman Catholics (the religion of many of their Irish servants), under the leadership of Irish-immigrant Archbishop John Hughes, must have been especially galling. As a result, they desired to erect an even grander cathedral of their own. Thus, under the leadership of Bishop Horatio Potter, the Cathedral of St. John the Divine was officially incorporated on April 16, 1873, and shortly thereafter a site committee was organized. The site committee chose a prime location—two vacant blocks just south of Central Park between 57th and 59th streets and Sixth and Seventh avenues. However, the Panic of 1873 and the ensuing economic depression killed this project, since the resulting precarious finances of most of the cathedral's subscribers and potential donors made fundraising impossible.

Although the cathedral project was shelved once again, it was not forgotten. Bishop Horatio Potter's nephew and successor, Bishop Henry Codman Potter, revived the search for an appropriate and affordable site. Henry Codman Potter served as bishop of the Episcopal diocese of New York for more than twenty years, from 1887 until his death in 1908. Born into a well-connected Episcopalian family—his father, Alonzo Potter, was bishop of Pennsylvania, his uncle was the previous bishop of New York, and his grandfather was president of Union College—Potter was at home both with church governance and with the socially elite patrons of the church. He was, however, committed to expanding Episcopal-church activities from its narrow base among this small segment of the population. Thus, Potter actively supported ministries to the poor, reform efforts, and the settlement-house movement.[4] His commitment to the construction of a cathedral in New York City was part of these efforts to broaden the church community and to attract large numbers of people from varied social backgrounds.

Bishop Potter's desire to erect one of the great churches of the world in New

York City was also part of New York's rise as the preeminent economic, cultural, and intellectual center of North America, and the efforts of many prestigious New Yorkers to create a metropolis rivaling the great cities of Europe. During the 1880s, this movement was manifested in the increasing interest among wealthy New Yorkers in adapting features of notable European architectural landmarks for their palatial new homes and in modeling the design of major public buildings on European monuments. The final decades of the nineteenth century saw the formation or expansion of cultural and civic organizations that sought to emulate the established institutions of European cities, resulting in the inauguration of major institutional building campaigns: the erection of the Metropolitan Opera House (1881–84) and Carnegie Hall (1889–91), the city's grandest concert halls; the dramatic expansion of New York's two major museums, the American Museum of Natural History (beginning in 1888) and the Metropolitan Museum of Art's monumental new complex on Fifth Avenue (beginnning in 1894); the founding of the New York Public Library in 1895 and the ensuing construction on its magnificent French-inspired building (1898–1911); the organization and first phase of construction on large complexes in the Bronx by The New York Botanical Garden (1891) and New York Zoological Society (1892); and the development of three major university campuses—Columbia (beginning in 1892) and City College (beginning in 1897) in Manhattan, and New York University (beginning in 1892) in the Bronx. All of these projects were deemed by the city's social elite to be necessary for a city that vied for international status.[5]

On June 1, 1887, only a few months after becoming Bishop of New York, Potter appealed "To the Citizens of New York," seeking their support for the construction of a Protestant cathedral.[6] In his appeal, Potter spoke to the sense of pride that affluent and well-educated New Yorkers had in their city. He quoted the apostle Paul's claim of being "a citizen of no mean city" and compared this declaration to the civic affections of "those whose lot is cast in the metropolitan city of America."[7] Potter challenged New Yorkers to aid in the construction of a building where "great moral and spiritual ideas" would be embodied. His general entreaty to all the citizens of New York courted civic pride in an ecumenical manner, calling for the erection of a cathedral "worthy of a great city."

The response to the bishop's appeal was overwhelmingly supportive with newspaper editorials lauding the bishop and the civic promise of the new cathedral. The bishop's ecumenical call attracted support from non-Episcopalians. One of the first donors was prominent Presbyterian layman D. Willis James, who contributed $100,000 and informed Potter that although he recognized that this was an Episcopalian project, he was confident that it would be "a permanent power for good to the nation through its entire history."[8] However, many others interpreted the bishop's appeal as being not only ecumenical, but also a call for a cathedral that would operate in a nondenominational manner. They were soon disappointed, finding that while their financial support was welcome, this was to be an Episcopal, not a nondenominational Protestant cathedral.[9] As might be expected, Roman Catholics were less enthusiastic than Protestants about the proposal. They already had a cathedral, the presence of which had been ignored by Bishop Potter and by those whose praise of the Episcopalian project implied that it would be the first cathedral in New York City. "What business is it of anyone else if the Protestants of the United States want to erect a large building in New York and desire to call it a Cathedral?," asked the *American Catholic News,* which then concluded, "Let the children have their toy." [10] A few months later, after Morningside Heights was chosen as the cathedral's site, the *Catholic American and Semi-Weekly Catholic Review* would quip that since an Episcopal Cathedral was "not intended for the people, its location is in a sufficiently out of the way place to keep it for the select and wealthy who will 'patronize' it." [11]

With the generally supportive response to the proposed cathedral project from New York's Protestant community, the Cathedral Committee once again sought a location. The committee members searched for a site that would be large enough for the construction of a monumental building, while assuring its visibility. Locations such as Park Avenue and 92nd Street (next to an open railroad cut) and the Polo Grounds at Eighth Avenue and West 155th Street were rejected since, as the *Real Estate Record* reported, "no one would dream for one moment of placing the *chef d'oeuvre* of ecclesiastical architecture in the United States alongside of a railroad with its shrieking engines, or in a second or third rate neighborhood." [12] By the autumn of 1887 the search focused on Morningside Heights. The favored site was on Morningside Drive between 116th and 119th streets, but as soon as the cathedral's interest became known, the price rose to a prohibitive level. This property was held by several owners, including Dwight Olmstead, who had been a leading force in the drive to displace New York Hospital's Bloomingdale Asylum (see chapter 1). According to the cathedral's representative, Olmstead, "that dreadful lawyer," persuaded those with larger land holdings to double their prices "in order to get off his own land at the same rates." [13] Although the higher elevation north of 116th Street was the favored location, the cathedral's site committee turned to the Leake and Watts Orphan Asylum's property on Amsterdam Avenue between 110th and 113th streets after it became apparent that no agreement would be reached with Olmstead and the other private owners. Legend has it that board member George Macculloch Miller noticed the site while on a stroll up Fifth Avenue.[14] At 111th Street he is said to have turned his gaze westward, spotting the asylum perched on the Morningside Plateau. In negotiating the sale, cost was a significant concern to both parties. The cathedral had little money in hand and would have to raise funds both for the purchase and for building construction. The asylum needed funds so that it could buy a new site and erect buildings without jeopardizing its ability to care for its charges. The two groups finally agreed on a price of $850,000, the Leake and Watts board reasoning that, while they might have received more money from another buyer, the asylum's founders would have supported the property's new use.[15]

Although less elevated than the 116th Street site, the 110th Street site was, nevertheless, an ideal location for the new cathedral: it was a large plot consisting of three square blocks with no bisecting cross streets, since these had already been legally closed; the property hugged the southern and eastern edges of the plateau, permitting the construction of a highly visible building; the site was close to the northern end of Central Park; it was near rapidly developing residential neighborhoods; and it was in an area that seemed likely to evolve into a center of New York's civic life within a few decades as the city's core moved farther and farther north. Most of the newspaper commentary on the choice of the site was positive. The *New York Times* called the location "commanding and appropriate," while the *Uptown Visitor* boasted that no "cathedral in the world has a site at all comparable." [16] The vision of the cathedral's benefactors in erecting a highly visible symbol of New York's preeminence was captured, in somewhat exaggerated fashion, by a writer for the *Real Estate Record*:

> The new Cathedral will be seen rising above the city as prominently as St. Paul's is over London. Like a beacon it will be visible from the Palisades and from miles up the Hudson; in another direction it will be seen beyond the Harlem; to the foreigner in New Jersey flats and meadows its spires will serve to mark the seat of civilization; it will be one of the first things seen by the incoming immigrant in the lower bay, and the Staten Islander can turn his face towards it in the morning as the Egyptian does towards the Mosque at Cairo, and see its pinnacles brightening in the light of the rising sun.[17]

The excitement that followed Bishop Potter's challenge to New Yorkers and the positive response to the choice of a site on Morningside Heights bode well for the future of the enterprise. Unfortunately, these were the only unalloyed successes in the history of the design and construction. A poorly managed architectural competition that alienated much of the press and public, selection of a compromise design that did not have the full support of the bishop or many of the trustees, arguments over the siting of the building, design changes, setbacks in fund raising, serious unforeseen construction problems, waning enthusiasm among New Yorkers for spending money on a cathedral, friction between the architects and Bishop Potter and his trustees, and, finally, the removal of the original architects and their replacement with a new architect who completely redesigned the building took their toll on the project, resulting in a building that has never been completed.

DESIGNING THE CATHEDRAL   Almost immediately after the Cathedral Committee agreed to purchase the Morningside Heights site, a Committee on Architecture was established to organize a design competition.[18] Columbia architecture professor William R. Ware was consulted on how best to do so. Four-teen architects were invited to submit designs, each to be paid $500.[19] Other ar-chitects were invited to submit designs, but they would not be paid. Sixty-eight completed submissions were presented to the trustees by January 1889.[20] The public was not permitted to view the designs (some of the architects objected to a public display), leading to increasingly vocal complaints provoked by an irate press. In addition, many architects were disturbed because the board members who were choosing the design had little or no knowledge of architecture. As the criticism mounted, the cathedral board invited Ware, architectural professor Charles Babcock, and engineer John Bogart to evaluate the plans. Even with this professional committee in place, little news was made public and complaints continued. The prominent Episcopal magazine the *Churchman,* which rarely criticized the Episcopal establishment, admitted "restlessness and impatience under the action of the Cathedral Competition Committee."[21]

Finally, in May 1889, George Miller announced that four designs had been selected for a second and final competition, but neither the designs nor the names of the architects were released to the public. City newspapers, which zealously sought information about the competitors, eventually leaked the iden-tities of three of the four finalists.[22] It was not, however, until May 17, 1889, that the trustees publicly identified the finalists. The designs of William Potter and R. H. Robertson, Huss & Buck, and William Halsey Wood had already been widely discussed in the press, but the choice of the design of Heins & La Farge was a surprise.[23] The *New York Times* noted that "All guesses were wide of the mark with regard to the authorship of this last design, which was generally at-tributed to Richard M. Hunt or J. Cleveland Cady."[24] The response to the choice of finalists was not positive. Critics decried the secretive nature of the delibera-tions and the absence of any of America's leading architects from among the finalists. The *Times* summed up the general displeasure when it editorialized that "There is no denying that the result of the competition for the design of the cathedral thus far has not been such as to encourage the belief of the better-informed part of the public in the final success of the project."[25] This type of complaint could not have pleased the Cathedral Board, as it was relying on this "better-informed part of the public" for financial support.

As the board began judging the four final designs, again in secret, criticism intensified. Henry Y. Satterlee, the rector of Calvary Episcopal Church, finally sent an open letter to the Board of Trustees that was widely published in the daily newspapers, reminding the judges that "Public sentiment is not aroused in behalf of any project that is conducted in the spirit of a close corporation."[26] Additional controversy arose over the fact that one of the finalists, William Pot-ter, was Bishop Potter's half brother. Fearing charges of nepotism, the bishop hoped to disqualify Potter & Robertson, but the trustees permitted the archi-tects to remain in the competition, claiming that the design had been fairly chosen in a blind competition.[27]

Although the four finalists had been instructed to complete revised submissions for the final round of competition by February 1890, the deadline was extended when the Morningside Plateau was proposed as the site for the World's Columbian Exposition.[28] Powerful business interests in New York, supported by publications such as *Scientific American,* argued for a New York site for the exposition, but this proposal gained only lukewarm support from the boards of the cathedral and New York Hospital, the two largest landowners on Morningside Heights.[29] At any rate, the campaign for a New York City venue failed when the United States Senate selected Chicago as the site for the fair.

Finally, in April 1891, the finalists' designs for the cathedral were completed and placed on public exhibition.[30] While the trustees debated which of the finalists would be chosen as the architect, the public's enthusiasm for the cathedral project waned. An editorial in *American Architect and Building News* summarized the perception of the competition as a fiasco, lamenting the fact that "the entire undertaking, from first to last, has been attended by so many unpleasant features . . . [that] instead of being one of the pleasantest professional events that have occurred in this generation, the great competition has been one of the most disagreeable."[31] In addition, critical opinion on the individual designs was generally negative. A back-handed compliment in a *New York Times* editorial was typical: "Should any one of these plans be chosen, that of HEINS and LA FARGE [sic] presents the only one the faults of which are not radical."[32]

The cathedral trustees, again meeting in secret, finally chose Heins & La Farge's eclectic Byzantine/Romanesque/Gothic design for the cathedral in July 1891 (figure 2.2).[33] This selection, however, was not an unconditional endorsement of the firm or its proposal. It was a compromise. The unimaginative English Gothic scheme of Huss & Buck had been favored by some of the trust-

FIGURE 2.2
Cathedral competition entry of Heins & La Farge, 1891.

ees (figure 2.3), while others had been drawn to William Halsey Wood's romantic, but impractical proposal (figure 2.4). William Potter and R. H. Robertson's Romanesque/Gothic design (figure 2.5) had probably been viewed favorably by many, but it had to be rejected in light of Bishop Potter's fear that the choice of his half-brother would jeopardize the cathedral project. As the trustees took vote after vote, no design emerged as a clear favorite. Indeed, Heins & La Farge's submission had consistently been the trustees' second choice. According to William Partridge, an assistant to William Ware during the period of Ware's involvement with the cathedral competition, "to break the complete deadlock, it was decided to give Hines [sic] and La Farge the commission, there being no other competitor upon which the Trustees could agree." [34]

FIGURE 2.3
Cathedral competition
entry of Huss & Buck,
1891.

Bishop Potter was especially unhappy with this compromise choice. In letters to Heins, John Codman Ropes, a Boston lawyer and vestryman at Trinity Church, Boston, who had an intimate knowledge of cathedral affairs, commented on the bishop's "animus" toward the Heins and La Farge proposal, referring to a letter in which Bishop Potter "goes out of his way to throw discredit on your plans . . . [and] makes it very plain that the action of the committee in selecting you & Grant [La Farge] as the architects of the Cathedral was ex-

FIGURE 2.4
Cathedral competition entry of William Halsey Wood, 1891.

FIGURE 2.5
Cathedral competition entry of Potter & Robertson, 1891.

ceedingly disappointing to him, and that you have got to count on his hostility throughout."[35] Indeed, Potter's discontent was evident at the ceremonies for the laying of the cornerstone, when he failed even to mention the architects' names.[36]

Heins & La Farge was a relatively new firm in 1891, having little experience designing large-scale buildings. That both architects were only in their thirties was not necessarily viewed as an impediment, for, as the *New York Tribune* commented, several of the finalists "are young, a fact which is of interest, because years of supervision will be necessary when the construction of the Cathedral is once begun, and this could be given only by a man under middle-age to-day."[37] Both Heins and La Farge came from privileged backgrounds and, ironically, both were Roman Catholics.[38] George Lewis Heins studied at the University of Pennsylvania and MIT, and Christopher Grant La Farge, son of the painter and stained-glass master John La Farge, also studied at MIT before entering the architectural office of Henry Hobson Richardson. Both architects worked together briefly in Cass Gilbert's St. Paul, Minnesota office and then became architectural assistants to John La Farge before establishing a formal partnership in 1886. Their only major building prior to the competition for New York's cathedral was the Roman Catholic Cathedral of the Blessed Sacrament in Providence, Rhode Island.[39]

The competition entry of Heins & La Farge was a building combining round-arch Romanesque and Byzantine elements with Gothic detail on the exterior. The centrally massed plan (figure 2.6), with its apsidal end, apsidal chapels, and rounded transepts was also based on Romanesque and Byzantine precedents, while the richly ornamented interior surfaces were derived from Byzantine design (figure 2.7). The key element of the interior was the large unobstructed space for congregational worship in the crossing, close to the sanctuary, not unlike that provided by Henry Hobson Richardson at his influential Trinity Church, Boston (1872–77). Such an arrangement would guarantee that the largest number of people could both see and hear the service, elements not always possible in a traditional church with pews in a long nave, side aisles, and transepts. The nave planned by Heins & La Farge would create a dignified approach to the sanctuary and would accommodate additional worshippers, but would not be the main seating area.[40] Heins & La Farge objected to em-

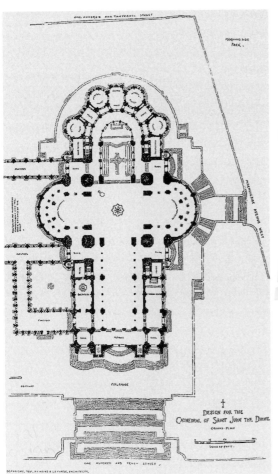

FIGURE 2.6

Plan of Heins & La Farge's competition entry, 1891.

ploying Gothic arches in the new cathedral since they felt that such construction would be unnecessarily expensive. Instead, they proposed barrel vaults and domes of tile-arch construction. The crossing would be created by four enormous round arches supporting a dome crowned by a massive tower. Glittering mosaics in a Byzantine style would adorn the tile surfaces. Heins & La Farge's inspiration for the central plan, domes, and mosaics was Santa Sophia in Istanbul, considered by the architects to be the "first great Expression of a Typically Christian Form of Religious Architecture," and the form from which, they argued, English vaulted design had developed.[41]

FIGURE 2.7
Interior of crossing in Heins & La Farge's competition entry, 1891.

Heins & La Farge's design was not accepted without reservation. The trustees, unenthusiastic to begin with, expected extensive revisions which would give the cathedral "a more Gothic appearance, and in consequence conforming more nearly to what is understood by the governing body of the intended cathedral as the Early English style of architecture." [42] Since a Gothic cathedral was not what Heins & La Farge envisioned, there was significant discord between architects and trustees from the start. Heins & La Farge eventually altered their design in response to the trustees' demands, increasing the building's length, redesigning the towers in a traditional Gothic manner, lengthening windows, and adding Gothic decorative detail and Gothic porches, creating what a *New York Times* editorial referred to as "a compromise cathedral"(figure 2.8).[43]

compromise design

The most serious change to the planned cathedral, however, was not the gothicizing of the design, but the total realignment of the building from north-south to east-west. The competition had called for a cathedral with its front elevation facing south onto 110th Street. With that positioning, the building would rise above the city from the high elevation at the edge of the Morningside Plateau and the tall spires would welcome visitors arriving from the populous regions to the south and east. Unfortunately, this north-south alignment was not in accord with traditional Episcopal doctrine, which mandated that the chancel end of a church face east toward the rising sun, symbolic of the resurrection. The cathedral trustees bowed to this tradition and reoriented the planned cathedral so that the front facade would align with West 112th Street and the apse would rise at the eastern end of the site. Subsidiary buildings would be erected to the south, creating a close.

The realignment of the cathedral had the disastrous effect of removing the building from a site where its facade and soaring towers would be a prominent feature of the city's skyline. Instead, the facade would now be buried within the urban grid, with the accessory buildings blocking the view of the cathedral from the city to the south. Only from Harlem to the east would the cathedral be seen dramatically perched at the edge of the Morningside escarpment (figure 2.9). Heins & La Farge opposed this realignment, realizing that it would diminish the presence of the building. As a compromise, the architects suggested that "to secure additional architectural effect when viewed from the east or the south" the building be shifted so that the entry axis was on West 111th Street.[44] This repositioning, they unsuccessfully argued, would heighten the visibility of the south facade and allow the south transept to soar above 110th Street. In addition, placing the cathedral farther south on the site would open land at the north end of the property where the subsidiary buildings could form a less obtrusive close that might also include the Episcopal Church's St. Luke's Hospital (see chapter 3).[45]

final design 1892

THE SLOW PROCESS OF BUILDING THE CATHEDRAL Heins & La Farge's revised design was accepted by the trustees in 1892, with construction to begin with the choir at the east end of the site. Coinciding with this work, the

FIGURE 2.8
Heins & La Farge's
revised design, late 1891.

FIGURE 2.9
Heins & La Farge's
revised design viewed
from southeast with
Morningside Park,
late 1891.

trustees also hoped to erect seven chapels radiating from the apsidal east elevation. The "Chapels of Tongues" were, as a trustee's report stated, to connect "in some way with the various racial elements that have entered into the structure of our national and, more especially, our municipal population."[46] The *New York Times* described the chapels as a "strictly American and democratic institution" that would "represent the various foreign races which have fused with the Anglo-Saxons in making the modern American."[47] The choice of the races to be represented in the chapels was quite limited, however, primarily representing European groups deemed acceptable by the Episcopal elite. As planned, the three chapels to the south were to represent the "Latin races" and those to the north the "Germanic and Celtic races." The trustees sought an individual donor for each chapel, with the donor having the privilege of choosing an architect. Heins & La Farge would be the designer of only two of the seven chapels.[48]

The cathedral cornerstone was laid on St. John's Day, December 27, 1892, in a formal ceremony attended by more than a thousand guests, marking what the *Evening Post* described as "the first step in the development of the Morningside Plateau in a permanent way."[49] Construction did not begin until the following spring, but was stopped only a few months later when workers digging the foundation discovered a deep pocket of soft stone instead of the solid bedrock that had been anticipated.[50] The trustees considered the idea of moving the building from 112th Street to the 111th Street site previously advocated by Heins & La Farge. Engineer William Sooy Smith felt that the building could be erected at either site, but he argued that "the Southern site is manifestly preferable."[51] However, further consideration of this proposal was foreclosed because of the superstition that moving the cornerstone would be an omen "considered unpropitious for the fortunes of the new cathedral."[52] Instead, several years were wasted with test borings and extensive excavations at the original site. Smith excavated individual pits to bedrock level, rather than constructing a continuous foundation as had been planned. Concrete was then poured into these pits to support the great piers and the apsidal east end.[53] Heins likened the process to filling a dental cavity.[54] After a three-year delay and extensive cost overruns, the foundations were finally completed in 1895. Unfortunately, this construction delay further diminished confidence in the success of the entire project. Only J. P. Morgan's donation

FIGURE 2.10
Cathedral crypt, 1904.

of $500,000, "to get us [the cathedral] out of a hole," prevented the entire enterprise from failing.[55]

Work at the site continued, but by 1900 more than two million dollars had been spent with little visible progress. The crossing arch at the east end stood as a stark masonry mass, evoking curious gazes from commuters on the elevated line at 110th Street (figure 2.11). Only the crypt, consecrated in January 1899, had opened for services. The richly ornamented crypt was a Byzantine-inspired installation with scintillating glass mosaics originally designed by Louis Comfort Tiffany for the World's Columbian Exposition and subsequently donated to the cathedral and transported to New York (figure 2.10).[56] Finally, early in the new century, the cream-colored Lake Mohegan, New York, granite superstructure of the cathedral began to rise. However, construction once again slowed as structural problems awaited solutions and designs were altered.

Many of the problems that occurred during the initial phase of construction resulted from the overreaching nature of the entire cathedral project. Among the most daunting challenges was the erecting of eight monumental columns at the east end of the apse. Each of these 54-foot-high columns, with a diameter of 6 feet and weighing 130 tons, was to be a monolith cut from a single piece of polished gray granite. They would be the largest columns ever quarried in America and the second largest stone columns in the world, after those at the Cathedral of St. Isaac in St. Petersburg. The columns were so large that they had to be in place before work could begin on the outer walls of the choir. Although

[handwritten margin note: $ probs delays]

[handwritten margin note: ↑ large columns]

FIGURE 2.11

Crossing arch of cathedral, with elevated railroad on 110th Street in foreground, and St. Luke's Hospital, Low Library, and various apartment buildings and rowhouses in background, 1902.

monolithic columns would be a spectacular visual statement, their cost would also be high since special equipment would have to be devised for cutting and setting. To meet this cost, the columns were used as a fundraising opportunity, like the radiating chapels, with each column standing as a memorial paid for by an individual donation of $20,000.[57]

The granite for the columns was quarried in Vinal Haven, Maine by the Bodwell Granite Company.[58] The company constructed a special lathe (the largest in America) to turn the columns, but ultimately was unable to cut monoliths of such extraordinary weight.[59] Three columns cracked while still on the lathe, one fracturing within only a few hours of its completion.[60] As a result, the trustees were forced to settle for columns divided into two sections, one 37 feet, 6 inches tall, weighing 90 tons, and the other 17 feet, 5 inches, weighing between 40 and 45 tons.[61] Even these smaller shafts were difficult to transport to the site. The columns were shipped from Maine by water and unloaded at a dock at West 135th Street and then, during the summer of 1903, slowly transported individually to the cathedral site on a truck specially constructed in Maine. The truck rested on massive oak wheels, each about 20 inches thick, with iron tires. Thirty horses were to haul the truck, but when it became clear that this was an impossible task, a plan was devised to pull the truck forward by a horizontal hoist (figure 2.12). A huge engine was anchored to the street, either by creating a "deadman," by placing large blocks around the wheels, or by removing granite paving blocks and sinking the wheels into the ground. A steam winch connected to the engine then hoisted or dragged the loaded truck 270 feet. The engine and winch were then moved forward, reanchored, and the drum hoisted forward again. For each drum, this process was repeated twenty-six times. It took nineteen days to move the first column, but other columns took only six days to transport.[62] Once the drums had arrived on the cathedral grounds, their placement presented additional problems. Wood derricks tall enough and strong enough to support the columns were not available in New York, so the cathedral trust-

FIGURE 2.12

A cathedral column moving along Amsterdam Avenue, 1903.

ees were forced to order special tree trunks from the Pacific Northwest (figure 2.13).[63] As a result of these time delays and cost overruns, each column apparently cost about $25,000—$5,000 more per column than the individual donations (figure 2.14).[64]

The progress of construction was also hampered by difficulties in fundraising resulting from diminishing enthusiasm for the project among much of the populace. *Scientific American* reported that the cathedral "is progressing slowly, largely owing to a lack of funds."[65] An elite segment of the Episcopal community continued its support, often presenting substantial financial gifts for discrete elements of the building, such as the apsidal chapels or the choir columns. The largest of these gifts was $600,000 pledged by former vice-president and former New York State governor Levi P. Morton for the completion and furnishing of the choir.[66] However, the outpouring of support from the general public did not meet Bishop Potter's expectations, perhaps because the public had quickly come to realize that the cathedral project was not as ecumenical as had initially been implied or because of the public's disillusionment with the secretive process of choosing a design.[67] In addition, many New Yorkers, including many Episcopalians, began to feel that a cathedral was not necessary for their personal spiritual well being. As early as November 1887, the *Real Estate Record* had published a letter that noted that "many people doubt the pressing necessity for the Cathedral from a religious point of view"; by 1892 the *New York Times* was suggesting that "it is not absolutely certain that the present needs of worshippers demand a cathedral."[68]

In his initial announcement of the cathedral project and in later statements, Bishop Potter had claimed that the cathedral would stand as proof of the spiritual elevation of the American people by demonstrating that their largess was not limited to the construction of lavish business buildings.[69] The bishop's statement notwithstanding, New York's Episcopalians (and members of other denominations as well) had not limited themselves to supporting commercial architecture, but also had generously donated funds for the construction of impressive, architecturally distinguished neighborhood churches. This was especially evident on

FIGURE 2.13

A cathedral column hoisted into place, 1903.

FIGURE 2.14

Chapel of St. Saviour, apsidal columns, and crossing arch, looking south, August 26, 1905.

the Upper West Side and in Harlem, neighborhoods that were developing as prosperous communities during the period when initial fundraising for the cathedral was undertaken and in which a significant number of architecturally distinguished contemporary Episcopal churches were erected.[70] As the *Real Estate Record* commented, "It is true that America cannot boast of very many cathedrals; but no one can accuse the American people of any stinginess in building and endowing churches. A nation builds what it needs. Cathedrals are not needed; small churches are."[71] Many agreed with this sentiment and, accordingly, the cathedral project suffered.

In 1903, as the contractors were pursuing the daunting task of setting the apsidal columns, the cathedral's trustees decided to begin work on the vast crossing in order to assure adequate room for worshippers as the initial construction phase was completed.[72] Meanwhile, relations between the trustees and their architect further deteriorated. In 1906 some trustees even questioned the structural stability of Heins & La Farge's massive masonry crossing arches and pressured the firm to substitute reinforced concrete which, they argued, would be stronger and less expensive. Heins & La Farge rejected this demand, arguing that concrete-arch construction had not proven itself and that masonry construction was more appropriate for a cathedral.[73] This tension between the trustees and the architect was further exacerbated by the slow progress of construction, cost overruns, the architect's miscalculation regarding how many people could be seated in the choir (Heins & La Farge had estimated 5,000, but the actual number was less than half that), and accusations (not unjustified) that Heins & La Farge was involved in too many other projects and was not giving full attention to the cathedral project. Board member John P. Peters, the rector of St. Michael's Episcopal Church, was especially concerned that Heins & La Farge "have taken on themselves apparently much more than they are able to carry."[74] Peters complained in 1905 that Heins & La Farge's staff was far too small and that the architects, who were consulting for New York State, designing subway stations, and spending time in Seattle, where they were building a Roman Catholic Cathedral, were not giving the Episcopal cathedral project the attention that it required. Peters felt that the architects should be dismissed and new designers hired, and when this did not happen, he resigned from the board's building committee in protest.[75]

The *New York Times* made light of the slow pace of construction, commenting that "In a hustling country like this a work which has taken sixteen years and is still extremely far from being completed may, and in fact does, occasion wonder. As compared with the great cathedrals of the Old World, however, the progress on St. John's has been rapid."[76] Nonetheless, many of the cathedral's supporters were frustrated that work was not proceeding more rapidly and that, after more than a decade and a half, there was so little to show for the huge amount of money expended.

In September 1907, as work was slowly moving ahead and as arguments between the architects and trustees were intensifying, George Heins died. With Heins's death, the trustees had the contractual right to change architects. Several board members, supported by Cathedral Canon Robert Ellis Jones, campaigned for La Farge's removal. However, after much argument, he was kept on to complete work on the choir and crossing.[77] By late 1908 the choir (figure 2.15) was roofed, leaving only the glazing, completion of the floor, and addition of furnishings in this section of the building. The arches of the crossing were also nearly complete. Temporary walls and roofing were about to be constructed, with these features designed so they could be removed when the nave, transepts, and crossing tower were begun.

The roof constructed over the crossing, intended only as a temporary expedient while funds were raised for the crossing tower, remains one of the most significant features of the structure.[78] For this temporary roof, the trustees chose a saucer dome constructed of Guastavino tiles. Rafael Guastavino, a Spanish immigrant, had been influenced by the ancient Catalan technique of timbrel vaulting. After coming to America in 1881, Guastavino patented a system of structural tile vaulting and established the Guastavino Fireproof Construction Company. His distinctive vaulting was used on more than 1,500 buildings throughout the United States. On Morningside Heights, Guastavino vaulting appears not only at the cathedral, but also throughout Columbia University's St. Paul's Chapel, on the dome of Columbia's Earl Hall, at Union Theological Seminary, and at Riverside Church. Guastavino's structural system was exactly the type of tile vaulting that Heins & La Farge had proposed in its original design submission. The architectural firm had become proficient in the use of these tiles, having previously employed them at the Elephant House at the Bronx Zoo and the City Hall station on the IRT, and in the choir, chancel, and other sections of the cathedral (figure 2.16). Following Guastavino's death in 1908, his son, Rafael Guastavino, Jr., took control of the company and it was he who was responsible for the execution of the masterful crossing dome of the cathedral.[79]

The dome was not only a spectacular engineering feat, but it also saved money, since no false work or structural supports were needed during construction. Its construction was described at the

FIGURE 2.15

Crossing arches and east end of the cathedral, viewed from Amsterdam Avenue, December 14, 1908.

FIGURE 2.16

Choir and choir dome with Guastavino tiles, c. 1912.

time as "a bold undertaking" that was "nothing short of audacious," "mark[ing] a new epoch in the construction of masonry domes."[80] Beginning on May 1, 1909, Guastavino first constructed tiles in the four pendentives (the triangular-shaped areas that rise from the crossing piers and support the dome). The tile pendentives were a permanent installation upon which the crossing tower would eventually rest. Each pendentive is 12 inches thick, composed of nine layers of tile. The thickness of each tile is only one inch, with the cement mortar accounting for the remaining depth. By overlapping the tiles so that the joints do not align, Guastavino greatly enhanced their strength. The dome, which rests on the pendentives, was completely self-supporting throughout construction. Tiles were laid from the outer edge and, with the completion of each row, a nonstructural scaffold was erected on top of the work, permitting the construction of the next band of tile. The finished dome is 98 feet in diameter, with its thickness varying from about 7.5 inches at the base to only about 4 inches at the crown. Metal rods, running radially, were built into the shell of the dome for additional structural strength. Amazingly, the entire dome was completed in a mere fifteen weeks.

With the crossing covered, La Farge could now turn his attention to interior finishes and furnishings. Heins & La Farge designed many of the interior details, notably the choir stalls, with figures of musicians, which were modeled after those at the San Domenica Cathedral in Taormina, Sicily.[81] One of the finest interior features is the choir floor, paved with an extensive array of tile selected by Heins & La Farge from the Grueby Faience Company of Boston, a leading manufacturer of hand-made art tiles and pottery.[82] Heins & La Farge chose geometric and representational tiles that recall the tiles employed on the floors of many medieval cathedrals.

The completed apse, choir, crossing, and first two apsidal chapels were finally consecrated on April 19, 1911 (figure 2.17). The extent of local newspaper coverage of this historic event varied greatly. The *New York Herald* reserved extensive space for the consecration beginning on the front page, but other newspapers did not feel that it was a front page story.[83] Perhaps this decision reflected a waning of interest on the part of the public in the cathedral project after so many years of construction or the view that the Episcopal cathedral was no longer an essential civic project. All of the reports, however, no matter their length or placement in the paper, praised the building. In addition, editorials lauded the beauty and nobility of the design and also frequently commented on Bishop Potter's notion of constructing a great religious monument that would counterbalance the city's prominent commercial structures.[84] In its extensive discussion of the completed east end of the cathedral, *American Architect* spoke for much of the professional architectural world when it noted that "the new cathedral is about the most interesting object in New York to a student of church architecture, and the most worthy of his careful consideration."[85] Yet, less than a month later, the cathedral trustees removed Christopher Grant La Farge as cathedral architect and, in a controversial move, hired Ralph Adams Cram in his place.

HEINS & LA FARGE VS RALPH ADAMS CRAM   Boston-based Gothicist Ralph Adams Cram, a specialist in ecclesiastical architecture, was contacted by the cathedral trustees shortly after the initial section of St. John the Divine was consecrated.[86] On May 24, 1911 only thirty-five days after the consecration ceremony, the cathedral's trustees entered into an agreement with Cram, appointing him as their new architect. Cram had a long standing interest in the design of St. John the Divine. The firm of Cram & Wentworth had submitted a proposal to the initial cathedral competition, which, ironically, had combined Romanesque and Gothic features, as had the revised Heins & La Farge design.[87] In the years after the Heins & La Farge design had been accepted, Cram had criticized it as not suitable for an Episcopal cathedral since it did not follow English precedents.[88] There is even evidence that Cram actively sought the removal of Heins & La Farge as cathedral architect prior to the completion of construction on the east end. A 1907 letter to La Farge, marked "private and confidential," warned the architect that Cram's firm was "energetically scheming to get the Cathedral work in a very discreet and astute manner."[89]

1911 Cram – new architect

FIGURE 2.17

East end of the cathedral overlooking Morningside Park, with Leake and Watts Orphan Asylum to left and St. Luke's Hospital to right, 1910.

The hiring of Cram caused an uproar and created a public relations disaster for the cathedral. The fact that Cram had been hired before La Farge had been notified of his removal as cathedral architect created a situation that even Cram had to admit was "fraught with complications, embarrassments, and the considerations of personal and professional relationships." [90] Indeed, the first inkling that La Farge apparently had of his replacement came in a letter from Cram sent to La Farge's New York office, even though it was known that La Farge was in Europe.[91] The news had to be cabled to La Farge by his new partner, Benjamin Wistar Morris.

Seeking to remove any suspicion of his having gone behind La Farge's back, Cram claimed in an interview with a *New York Times* reporter that he had accepted the commission only after assurances from the trustees that they had no contract with La Farge and had no intention of working with him in the future and that they wished to dramatically revise the plans.[92] Cram also sought to quiet his critics by publicly suggesting the appointment of an architectural commission consisting of himself, Henry Vaughan (another Boston-based Gothicist), and La Farge, knowing full well that the trustees who wished to rid themselves of La Farge would never agree to this.[93] After this suggestion was rejected, Cram proposed an idea that had even less hope of being accepted—appointing La Farge as architect and himself as a consultant. One board member responded that he was "astonished," since he was sure that Cram "has been informed that Mr. La Farge was not desired as architect of the Cathedral." [94]

Cram sought support from other architects and from the American Institute of Architects, all of whom assured him that in accepting the job he was within the bounds of professional ethics.[95] Although the AIA exonerated Cram, New York newspapers were often less charitable. The daily papers, especially the *New York Times,* gave extensive space to the story, generally to the detriment of the cathedral's interests. The *Times* went so far as to print a front page article consisting almost entirely of a letter from Benjamin Wistar Morris supporting La Farge and condemning the behavior of the cathedral trustees and Cram.[96] In an editorial, the *Times* accepted the trustees' right to change architects and defended Cram's talents, but noted that "nevertheless they [the trustees] are open to just criticism for their inconsiderate treatment of Mr. La Farge." [97] The professional journal *Architectural Record* also questioned the behavior of the trustees in dropping La Farge and their inability to explain their action adequately: "The more they [architects] have read the newspapers on the subject, the deeper has probably been their puzzlement over the reasons for the change." The *Record* commented on the general acclaim accorded the completed sections of the cathedral, noting that the only criticism had been that it was not English Gothic. The replacement of La Farge, "who has given twenty years of his life" to the project, with an architect "whose own work shows an entire lack of sympathy with what has thus far been done on Morningside Heights" was seen as analogous to the "business men who had changed their minds about the kind of building they wanted, holding that the rights of an artist in his work of art were strictly limited to the letter of his contract." [98] It is ironic that the trustees were seen to be acting like businessmen in light of Bishop Potter's expressed desire to erect a great cathedral that would stand as a monument to spiritual values in contrast to business's deification of petty commercial interests.

La Farge returned from Europe on June 27, 1911, but refused to comment on the cathedral issue. [99] In fact, La Farge never commented in public about what must have been his greatest professional humiliation. The only glimpse of his feelings in this matter is in a short personal letter written to Cram ten years later. In response to a letter of apology from Cram concerning an article published in the *Churchman* under Cram's name, but not entirely written by him, that had criticized the Heins & La Farge work, La Farge referred to the entire episode as a "greasy performance" and, quoting Cervantes, remarked that "the more you stir it the worse it stinks." [100]

The decision by the cathedral's board of trustees to replace La Farge with Cram was the culmination of the professional and personal disagreements between Heins & La Farge and the trustees that dated back to the firm's initial appointment as cathedral architect. [101] More significant, however, was that by 1911 Heins & La Farge's Byzantine-inspired plan with its central congregational space was hopelessly out of date. Following the brief interlude of stylistic diversity ushered in by H. H. Richardson's Trinity Church, Boston, Episcopal-church architecture had returned to English Gothic precedents. By the first years of the twentieth century, most Episcopal churches were being designed in the more historically correct manner that was popularized by Cram and his Boston competitor Henry Vaughan. The trustees of St. John the Divine would have been familiar with this new Gothicism, especially its use for monumental cathedral projects. English architect William Bodley and Henry Vaughan's straightforward English-inspired design had been accepted for Washington Cathedral in 1906, Giles Gilbert Scott's Neo-Gothic Liverpool Cathedral was under construction, and English Gothic-inspired Episcopal cathedrals were in the design stage for Denver and Boston. [102]

REBUILDING THE CATHEDRAL   By 1911, when Cram received the commission for St. John the Divine, the trustees had exhausted all the construction funds, leaving no money for major new work on the cathedral. Without pressure to begin construction immediately, Cram carefully developed a plan for transforming the cathedral into a towering Gothic edifice that would, as he stated, represent "in principle and form the best possible expression of Christianity by the Anglo-Saxon people." [103] Transforming Heins & La Farge's scheme into a Gothic cathedral would not be an easy task since Cram intended not only to design new portions of the cathedral in a Gothic style, but also "to Gothicize what already existed." [104] Cram worked on the design for two years, publicly presenting a preliminary proposal in late 1913. He initially intended to employ an

English Gothic form at St. John the Divine, but the height of the existing crossing and the vast plan of the proposed cathedral proved to be inconsistent with the lower-scale, horizontal massing of English Gothic cathedrals. Thus, Cram was forced to turn to French Gothic prototypes. He designed an enormous, five-aisled structure adapting features of Bourges (the great example of a five-aisle cathedral), Notre Dame, Amiens, and Rheims in France, and Wells in England (figure 2.18). His intention, as he noted, was to meld "the great verticals of Bourges and Wells" with their five-part fronts "with the powerful horizontals" of the other French cathedrals.[105] In fact, the portals designed by Cram for the three major entrances to St. John the Divine are closely modeled after the three great entrance portals to Bourges Cathedral. The most unusual aspects of the plan were the placing of the triforium and clerestory in full-height central aisles rather than in the nave, and the inclusion of small chapels in each bay of the side aisles (figure 2.19).[106]

Cram's greatest challenge was designing an appropriate scheme for the crossing tower. He redesigned this central feature several times, proposing a low square tower and pair of tall spires, an octagonal tower, and a single tall square tower, before finally opting, in 1942, for a soaring fleche inspired by those at Amiens Cathedral and Sainte Chapelle in Paris (figure 2.20).[107] Cram's redesign of the cathedral displayed a rigorously academic re-creation of medieval architecture, illustrating the architect's mastery of Gothic detail and proportion, but without much individual creativity. In this respect, Cram's design is in marked contrast to Liverpool Cathedral, the most famous Gothic cathedral of the era, where architect G. G. Scott did not merely imitate medieval cathedrals, but sought instead to create a modernized Gothic form appropriate for the twentieth century.

Although there was no construction on the cathedral itself immediately after Cram's appointment as architect, Cram did oversee construction on the close south of the cathedral. The four buildings of the cathedral close are set around a large lawn with a central open air pulpit designed by Howells & Stokes in 1913.[108] Although these small-scale

FIGURE 2.19
Ralph Adams Cram's
proposed design for nave
and aisles.

FIGURE 2.20
Ralph Adams Cram's
final proposal for a
crossing tower, 1942.

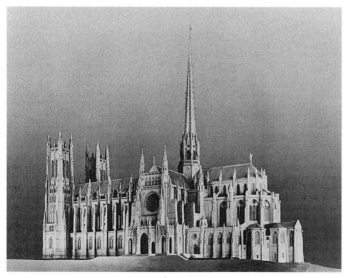

structures were not meant to be impressive architectural statements, they are, in fact, among the finest architectural features of the cathedral complex. As with the apsidal chapels and monumental columns in the cathedral itself, construction of each of these buildings was possible only through individual donations. The first auxiliary building to be constructed was St. Faith's House, designed by La Farge in 1909, before Cram's arrival at the cathedral. St. Faith's House was erected for the Training School and Home for Deaconesses on a site along Cathedral Parkway, in the middle of the block between Morningside Drive and Amsterdam Avenue. The Training School had been established in 1890 by Rev. William Reed Huntington, minister of Grace Church and a cathedral trustee. It occupied a site on the cathedral grounds by special permission of the trustees. The building is a Collegiate Gothic structure constructed of brick with limestone and terra-cotta trim (figure 2.21).[109]

Cram's first completed project on the cathedral grounds was the Synod House of 1911–13, located on the corner of Amsterdam Avenue and Cathedral Parkway (figure 2.21). Synod House, perhaps the finest building of the entire cathedral complex, was constructed in response to the announcement in 1910 that the General Convention of the Episcopal Church would convene in New York in 1913. J. P. Morgan and W. Bayard Cutting, deputies representing the Diocese of New York at the Synod, offered to split the cost of an impressive meeting hall for the convention. Cram confided that he "wanted to make this Hall the most beautiful thing in New York . . . [with] a colour combination that would be unique, (so far as America is concerned), and at the same time strikingly beautiful."[110]

Synod
House
1911-1913

FIGURE 2.21

Synod House photographed during the General Convention of the Episcopal Church, 1913; St. Faith's House at far right and cathedral at left.

He succeeded in creating a lively and original adaptation of French Gothic architecture (the design was inspired, in part, from the Knight's Hall at Mont St. Michel and the Papal Palace at Avignon) for this small-scale work that contrasts with his colder cathedral design.[111] A pink Kingwood stone, apparently never before used in New York City, was employed on the exterior. The building hugs the lot line on 110th Street, where an austere wall appears to be a part of the natural rock formation of the Morningside Plateau. The main entrance is a deep portal just east of Amsterdam Avenue (figure 2.22) with carved figures of six Christian rulers (Constantine, Charlemagne, Emperor Alexis of Byzantium, King Gustavus Adolphus of Sweden, St. Louis of France, and Alfred the Great, King of Wessex) flanking the massive oak double doors. In place of the tradi-

FIGURE 2.22

Entrance portal to Synod House with central figure of George Washington.

tional figure of Christ or a saint between the entrance doors, the most prominent figure on the Synod House entry is George Washington. Above the entrance portal, there is a tympanum consisting of three ranges filled with thirty-
six small figures. Some figures represent saints, but others portray the labors
and works of men and women involved in the arts, science, craft, and industry,
including figures of a painter, sculptor, cobbler, musician, chemist, miner, engineer, and, of course, an architect, represented by Ralph Adams Cram holding
a model of the cathedral.[112] The spacious hall (figure 2.23), planned to seat up
to 1,200 people on the main level and in a gallery, was highly decorated, with a
painted roof and trusswork, gray-brown woodwork, white plaster walls, and
grisaille glass.[113]

St. Faith's House and the Synod House were followed in 1912–13 by a choir
school set on Morningside Drive adjacent to the south elevation of the cathedral's apse (figure 2.24). Architects Walter Cook and Winthrop A. Welch chose
an English-inspired Collegiate Gothic style since this was seen as appropriate
for a choir school and because they were seeking a design that would harmonize
with the new cathedral design, which they had incorrectly, but quite reasonably,
assumed would be English Gothic.[114]

Finally, in 1912, Cram began work on the fourth and final building in the
close—the Episcopal Residence, also known as the Cathedral House, consisting of the Bishop's House and Deanery (figure 2.24). This attached, double residence, completed in 1914, is a large gray granite structure modeled on the form
of a medieval French chateau. These two substantially sized residential units
were to share a private chapel, but this chapel was never built.[115] The Episcopal
Residence was sited toward the center of the close, adjacent to the location of
the proposed south transept. The main elevation of the Bishop's House, facing
west onto the close, was sited for maximum visibility, reflecting the significance
of the bishop's office. The Deanery was placed in a more secluded location to
the rear and faces south toward Cathedral Parkway. This hierarchy is also evident on the exterior detail. The grander Bishop's House is ornamented with
symbols of the office, including miters and small figures of bishops holding
their staffs, while the ornamental detail on the Deanery is more domestic, including flowers and a cat.

The location of the Bishop's House and Deanery caused some controversy.
In 1912, George Miller, the only surviving member of the original board of trustees, wrote Bishop David Greer of his concern that the building would obstruct
views from the south.[116] Miller reminded Bishop Greer that the original plans
had left this space unoccupied so that there would be an unobstructed view of
the cathedral from the south. Miller's criticism of the siting was ignored, but his
concern was justified, for the Episcopal Residence does block the view of the
cathedral from the south, and, along with the other buildings of the close, creates a walled effect, just as Heins & La Farge had feared in 1892. Also problematic

FIGURE 2.23
Synod House interior.

FIGURE 2.24
Episcopal Residence, the bishop's house (left) and deanery (center), with choir school (right) and cathedral (rear), 1917.

was the magnitude of the houses. The Bishop's House was designed with twenty-eight rooms and seven baths, and the Deanery with twenty rooms and five baths. Several of the rooms in the Bishop's House were palatial in scale and contained beamed ceilings and enormous fireplaces. Dean William M. Grosvenor was concerned that these homes were "too large and imposing . . . [and] too expensive to live in" and that the cost of maintenance would limit the election of bishops and deans who were rich and could afford the upkeep on the expansive homes.[117] Cram argued that the size was not unreasonable, noting that the house erected by the Bishop of Philadelphia was larger. In response to Dean Grosvenor's concerns that the cost of maintaining such a large house would preclude the selection of a bishop who was not rich, Cram suggested that a maintenance fund be established for the residences.[118]

After a hiatus of several years, construction resumed in May 1916 on the cathedral itself with work on the nave foundations (figure 2.25). However, by November of that year funds had once again been depleted and construction again was halted.[119] World War I and uncertain economic conditions following the war postponed further work until 1924, when construction started on the baptistry, located to the north of the choir. The baptistry was the gift of Augustus Van Horn Stuyvesant and his sisters Anne and Catherine in memory of their parents.[120] Following the example of the great baptistries at Florence and Pisa, the cathedral's baptistry is octagonal, with the French marble font placed in the center. The space has a complex iconographic scheme, including polychromatic arms of the twelve apostles, decorative details and coats-of-arms relating to the

FIGURE 2.25
Cathedral of St. John the Divine, c. 1920, after foundations had been laid for nave, looking east from Amsterdam Avenue; Leake and Watts building and Bishop's House at right.

Stuyvesant family and their Dutch heritage, and statues of figures of importance in the history of the Netherlands, New Amsterdam, and New York, including Dutch Governor Peter Stuyvesant and Hendrick Hudson.[121]

The oft-postponed project to complete Cram's cathedral design was finally inaugurated with a major fund-raising campaign that began in early January 1925, under the leadership of Franklin D. Roosevelt, with an enormous rally at Madison Square Garden.[122] A contract for the construction of the nave was signed and major building work began anew.[123] Also in 1925 construction of the west front was added to the project with money raised by the Business Men's Division of the Committee for the Completion of the Cathedral.[124] As the baptistry, nave, and west facade were being built (figure 2.26), plans were progressing for other portions of the cathedral. In December 1927 construction started on the north transept, dubbed the Women's Transept, to be funded entirely by donations from women.[125]

The search for funds to complete the cathedral during the 1920s reignited the confusion over whether St. John the Divine was an Episcopal or nondenominational church. At the Madison Square Garden fundraising event in 1925, Bishop William T. Manning emphasized that the cathedral would be "a shrine of prayer and worship for all people" and a "common centre for the religious

FIGURE 2.26

West front and north buttresses under construction, November 1926.

life of our whole city."[126] Yet the conservative Manning, like Bishop Potter decades earlier, was not willing to open cathedral governance fully to members of other Christian denominations. This denominational tension culminated in February 1925 when John D. Rockefeller, Jr., a Baptist, donated $500,000 to the cathedral and requested an appointment to the board of trustees, noting that "The purpose of the cathedral is so lofty, so broad and so nobly stated, and it is being carried out so liberally" that laymen of other churches should be considered for the board.[127] Although Rockefeller's gift was accepted, his application for board membership was refused. Bishop Manning declared that the time had not yet arrived when members of other denominations could join the board.[128] Bishop Manning's rejection of Rockefeller's bid for board membership prompted Rockefeller to support the construction on Morningside Heights of what became known as Riverside Church. Despite Manning's rejection of Rockefeller as a board member, and of ecumenicism in general, he continued to press the ecumenical theme geared to successful fund raising, referring to the cathedral, in his public pronouncements, as an "illustration of universal Christianity."[129]

Even though the Great Depression of the 1930s halted most other building projects, work continued on the cathedral. In the face of possible criticism about expending such vast sums for a building during such difficult economic times, Bishop Manning likened the cathedral to a public works project, asserting that employment on the project was "of inestimable help to the craftsmen and workmen engaged and to their families."[130] Construction continued without interruption until completion of the nave and west facade (figure 2.27) and the partial redesign of Heins & La Farge's choir and sanctuary in a Gothic manner. The expanded cathedral was dedicated on November 30, 1941.[131] Although the cathedral had been successful at raising money and great progress had been made in constructing large sections of the building, Cram's conservative design was not highly regarded by many critics, let alone hailed as a masterpiece. For example, architect Philip N. Youtz, writing for *Creative Art,* found the nave more "a memorial to bygone days than . . . a beacon of future progress," noting that the

FIGURE 2.27

West front nearing completion, c. 1941.

cathedral "is archeology, not architecture. Archeology deals with death, architecture with life."[132]

The November 30, 1941 dedication ceremony occurred only seven days before the bombing of Pearl Harbor and the United States' entry into World War II. With the advent of war, construction and fundraising was more difficult and work ceased with the Women's Transept only one-third complete, and with no work begun on the south transept, west towers, central tower, and other aspects of the design.[133] On the interior, the result of the cessation of construction produced a curious juxtaposition of Heins & La Farge's monumental apsidal columns, Cram's highly finished nave, and the raw stonework of the incomplete crossing with its "temporary" dome, a juxtaposition that many find is one of the most dramatic features of the building today.

In June 1945, as the war was ending, Bishop Manning issued a new plea for $10 million to complete the cathedral, but only five months later he suspended this plan in favor of a national campaign to raise $5 million to fund the reconstruction of Episcopal missions destroyed during the war.[134] At the age of 79, and only one year away from retirement, Manning must have been sorely disappointed that he could not continue the cathedral project after so much progress had been made under his leadership. Manning's successor, the Rt. Rev. Charles Gilbert, brought to the cathedral a burning concern for the social problems of the surrounding area. Gilbert and other cathedral officials felt that continuing to spend large sums of money on the construction of a grand building while poverty increased in surrounding areas was inconsistent with Christian charity and faith. As a result, construction was halted for three decades.

In 1978 Dean James Parks Morton announced that work would once again resume on the cathedral, with local young people employed as apprentices and taught the art of stone cutting. As architectural critic Paul Goldberger noted in a review of the cathedral's resumed construction, the project "represents a return to the making of cathedrals as they were in the Middle Ages . . . in the way that it is a product of an entire community joining to build itself a symbolic center."[135] The initial phase of Dean Morton's project would be to complete the tall towers of the west front and the carving of sculptural elements on this facade. A stoneyard was established on vacant land to the north of the nave in 1980 and, two years later, the first stone was set in the southwest tower.[136] Although Dean Morton continued Cram's design for the towers, he wanted a modern design for the south transept. Following the precedent set by the original cathedral trustees, Morton organized a competition for a contemporary south transept that would take the form of a bioshelter. The winner of the competition was a greenhouse-like structure designed by Spanish-born French architect Santiago Calatrava. Architect Philip Johnson, one of the competition judges, noted that Calatrava was the "only entrant who successfully incorporated Modern forms into a Gothic structure."[137] Ultimately, the efforts to continue construction on the cathedral, begun with great optimism, failed as insufficient funds were donated to the project. With no money to pay its workers, the stoneyard was closed and work was again halted, with only a small portion of the southwest tower having been built. Only the carving of figures on the central portal was continued.

The tension between the cathedral as a celebration of the Episcopal community and the cathedral as an ecumenical symbol of New York City's greatness was finally resolved in the 1970s when the cathedral became the vital ecumenical center that many had long hoped for and the cathedral's constitution was amended to permit the service of non-Episcopalians on the board. In addition, the cathedral began to draw diverse crowds with its innovative religious, social, and cultural programming. In the 1980s, when the major fundraising campaign for the new construction project was organized, the cathedral again sought donations from all segments of the population. This time a committee was established with "business and civic leaders of all faiths" who would solicit funds for continuing construction of a cathedral that was "a world model of ecumenism." [138]

Emphasis on the cathedral's ecumenical role continued into the late 1990s with the appointment in September 1996 of the Rev. Dr. Harry H. Pritchett, Jr., to succeed Dean Morton, who had retired. Rev. Pritchett was especially impressed with the cathedral's "strong sense of being a house of prayer for all people so it has an interfaith, interdenominational and international tone to its ministry." [139] The cathedral's new leadership committed itself to the restoration and repair of the buildings already constructed, rather than any new construction, hiring the architectural firm of Polshek and Partners to undertake this work. [140] Today, the partially completed church stands both as a monument to the faith of many New Yorkers, but also as a monument to the overreaching of those who planned such an enormous and inevitably impractical building project.

Riverside Church: John D. Rockefeller, Jr. Builds a Church for All People

[handwritten: 1925 Rockefeller gift]

John D. Rockefeller, Jr.'s, $500,000 donation in February 1925 to the building fund for the Cathedral of St. John the Divine was a substantial gift, even for so wealthy and philanthropic a man. His generosity was particularly remarkable given the fact that Rockefeller was not an Episcopalian, but a devoted Baptist and loyal member of the Park Avenue Baptist Church. [141] His gift was even more surprising given that only eight years earlier Rockefeller had rejected a solicitation from Bishop David Greer for similar support, informing Greer that since he only contributed toward the construction of individual Baptist churches he attended, "I can hardly conceive of any reason why we should contribute to the erection of a church of another denomination." [142] Rockefeller was attracted to a broad, inclusive view of Christianity that was not limited by the doctrines of a particular denomination. As a result, he was closely involved in an ecumenical movement that sought to bring all Christians together in the service of a better and more peaceful world. It was undoubtedly because of this goal that Rockefeller eventually changed his attitude and donated to the Episcopal cathedral. Bishop William T. Manning had spoken enthusiastically about turning the Episcopal cathedral into an ecumenical force for Protestant unity, assuring Rockefeller that the cathedral would be "a great democratic Church for all who will use it, a House of Prayer for all people. We need it as a common centre and rallying point for the forces of Protestant Christianity, a powerful influence and instrument for closer fellowship and unity."[143]

Rockefeller hoped that his gift would inspire the bishop and the cathedral trustees not only zealously to pursue an ecumenical mission, but also to open the cathedral's governance to laymen of other denominations to further reflect its stated purpose of ministering to all Protestant adherents. Thus, his gift came with a statement expressing his "hope that, if not now, in the near future it may be deemed right and fitting to invite representatives of Protestant communions other than the Protestant Episcopal Church to a share in the control and direction of the erection, maintenance and management of the Cathedral of St. John the Divine."[144] This bold move on Rockefeller's part was supported by other non-Episcopalians, including some who were not even Christian. Reform Rabbi Stephen S. Wise wrote Rockefeller that "I wish you to know how glad I am that you have raised the question of Cathedral management with the Bishop of New York. It has seemed to a number of us very clear that, if the Episcopal Church of New York desires the help of all folk in New York in the building of a Cathedral, they should give some part to non-Episcopalians in the direction of the Cathedral as an institution of the city's life,—not, of course, with reference to strictly denominational services but touching other things."[145]

The doctrinally conservative Manning was happy to profess the ideals of ecumenism, but he had no intention of permitting anyone who was not an Episcopalian onto the cathedral's board. He thanked Rockefeller for his gift, but rejected as premature his proposal for expanding the board.[146] Manning publicly announced "Mr. Rockefeller's noble gift" on February 5, 1925, but failed to include any mention of Rockefeller's qualifying remarks.[147] Rockefeller was infuriated by the bishop's disingenuousness, informing Manning some weeks later that "I could not disabuse myself of the feeling that the fullest publicity had been given to the endorsement involved in the amount of the gift and the name of the giver,—an endorsement which to the public appeared to be one hundred per cent,—while the fact that the endorsement carried with it a certain qualification was withheld."[148] Rockefeller also provided the newspapers with copies of his correspondence with the bishop so they would publish full accounts of the gift and its "qualification."[149]

Rockefeller's failure to move Bishop Manning toward a more open stance on cathedral governance convinced him that if he was to further the interests of Protestant unity he would have to look elsewhere since the Episcopal cathedral was determined to remain an insular, sectarian organization for the foreseeable future. Fortunately, an opportunity was near at hand—an alliance with the prominent liberal theologian Harry Emerson Fosdick. Fosdick was an ordained

Baptist minister who, like Rockefeller, whom he had known for many years, was a strong supporter of Protestant unity and liberal theology, refusing to adhere to any formal creed. At the time Rockefeller was corresponding with Bishop Manning about the cathedral's ecumenical potential, Fosdick was ending his controversial rectorship at New York's First Presbyterian Church where conservative fundamentalists had accused him of heresy because of his liberal views.[150] In addition, a group of prominent progressive Protestants had for several months been discussing the idea of building what would become known as Riverside Church as a center for Fosdick's liberal teachings. Rockefeller became aware of this proposal in late January 1925. However, only after his relationship with the cathedral soured because of Manning's rejection of his governance proposal did he fully commit his time and especially his money to the project.

The idea for a progressive Protestant church on Morningside Heights was apparently that of Harry E. Edmonds, founder of International House, a dormitory for students from all over the world. The large, vaguely Renaissance-inspired International House building on Riverside Drive and 124th Street (figure 2.36), designed by Louis Jallade of the firm of Jallade, Lindsey & Warren, with William Welles Bosworth as consulting architects, had been built in 1921–24 with funds provided by Rockefeller.[151] Building on his relationship with Rockefeller, Edmonds wrote his benefactor on January 20, 1925, about his idea for a church "to strengthen progressive Christian thought in the City and throughout our country and the world."[152] He suggested that Dr. Fosdick lead the project and that the church building rise on Riverside Drive and West 122nd Street to the south of International House.

Rockefeller was impressed with Edmonds's idea and had an agent examine the proposed site. He also discussed the plan with other leaders at the Park Avenue Baptist Church. That congregation, which had recently completed construction on a new Neo-Gothic church building on the corner of Park Avenue and East 64th Street (figure 2.28), designed by Henry Pelton and Allen & Collens, was seeking a new minister.[153] In fact, Fosdick had already been approached by the Park Avenue church, but he had rejected an offer to become its leader.[154] Fosdick is said to have informed Rockefeller that "I do not want to be known as the pastor of the richest man in the

FIGURE 2.28
Park Avenue Baptist
Church, c. 1922.

country"; to which Rockefeller is supposed to have replied, "do you think that more people will criticize you on account of my wealth than will criticize me on account of your theology?"[155] In any event, Fosdick soon reconsidered and in May 1925 accepted the offer of the Park Avenue Baptist Church on the condition that they erect a church building near Columbia, as had been suggested by Edmonds. He also insisted that the new church be given a name with no specific denominational connotations, similar to such names as Plymouth Church and the Broadway Tabernacle (both of which were Congregational churches). Most importantly, Fosdick desired "an inclusive church," with an interdenominational congregation open to all Christians and with doctrinal issues such as baptism left to the conscience of individuals rather than to strict ecclesiastical regulation.[156] The independent congregational structure of the Baptist Church, with no control from a higher central ecclesiastical authority, permitted the new congregation to embrace Fosdick's vision of an ecumenical church. Thus, although all of the founders of the new enterprise were Baptists and the new church retained its affiliation with the Southern New York Baptist Association, the independent congregational structure permitted experimentation in doctrine and church organization, resulting in the transformation of the Park Avenue Baptist Church into the ecumenical Riverside Church.[157]

Once Fosdick joined the endeavor to create a great ecumenical Protestant church, Rockefeller committed himself fully to its realization. The construction of the church became a largely private enterprise, with Rockefeller donating more than $8,000,000 for land and construction. Rockefeller was sensitive to concerns that the new church might appear to be his church, rather than a project of the Park Avenue Baptist Church as a whole. Accordingly, he tried to omit his name from discussions and reporting about the building. "I think it highly important," he wrote architect Charles Collens, "that there should be no more connecting of our name with this whole enterprise than is absolutely necessary."[158] This effort was, of course, ineffectual since Rockefeller's name was inevitably linked with the Riverside Church project. Indeed, the *New Yorker*'s architectural critic "T-Square" quipped that the church was "known to most secular minds as the Rockefeller Cathedral."[159] Although Rockefeller was committed to building the church on Morningside Heights, he was not wedded to a site on Riverside Drive. He seriously considered two sites on Morningside Drive, since at those locations the new church would stand not only as a theological challenge but also, with its proposed tall carillon tower, loom as a visible challenge to the still incomplete Episcopal cathedral.[160]

Some Episcopalians also supported Rockefeller's challenge to the conservative hierarchy of the cathedral. The *Churchman,* taking the view of liberal Episcopalians, noted that Rockefeller's plan "has made practical a vision cherished by many Episcopalians for the Cathedral of St. John the Divine." The article quoted from a recent sermon given by the Rev. Russell Bowie at Grace Church, which declared that "Something ought to be done and done quickly by the board of trustees [of the cathedral] to recognize, not only the passive right of

FIGURE 2.29
Aerial view of the River-
side Church site (right),
c. 1926, occupied by the
Kittel and Gibbons
houses, and three apart-
ment buildings; Grant's
Tomb (center), with
International House and
Claremont Park behind;
along Claremont Avenue
(middle), from left, are
apartment buildings, the
Institute of Musical Art,
Union Theological
Seminary, and Barnard
College; Teachers College
and Columbia University
campus at upper center

worshipping there [by non-Episcopalians], but the active right of planning and working for its larger ministry." [161]

Rockefeller soon abandoned the idea of building on Morningside Drive, realizing that the proposed site on Riverside Drive was more advantageous. With a Riverside Drive location, the "skyscraper church" would be clearly visible from the Hudson River. It would also be seen by the crowds of people strolling, bicycling, or driving up Riverside Drive toward Grant's Tomb, one of New York's leading attractions, which was immediately across the street from the proposed site. Rockefeller purchased the site proposed by Edmonds on the south side of West 122nd Street between Riverside Drive and Claremont Avenue, including the entire 200-foot frontage on West 122nd Street and 225-foot frontages on Riverside Drive and Claremont Avenue. When Rockefeller acquired the site in the spring of 1926, it was not a vacant plot, but contained three apartment buildings, one on Riverside Drive and two on Claremont Avenue, as well as the Riverside mansions of Joseph J. Kittel and John J. Gibbons, erected in the 1880s, and a stable to the rear of the Gibbons house (see chapter 1 and figure 2.29).[162] Rockefeller hoped to retain, at least temporarily, some of the apartment houses to generate income for the support of the church.

Rockefeller had no preconceived idea regarding the type of building he

wished to erect for Riverside Church. His one requirement was that the building include a tower for a carillon since he intended to move the carillon that he had recently donated to the Park Avenue Baptist Church. Rockefeller instituted a careful search for an architect whose ideas would be appropriate to the new venture. Some people suggested that the new church be a Colonial-inspired structure resembling a New England meeting house, accenting the Americanism of the progressive movement toward Christian unity, while others suggested an English Gothic style that would contrast with the French Gothic employed at St. John the Divine.[163] Like Rockefeller, Fosdick had no stylistic preference, but he sought first a building of great beauty and harmony and, secondly, a building that was also warm and intimate. Fosdick wrote to Rockefeller that "The second can be had always cheaply by sacrificing the first; the first can be gotten by any good architect, but often with frigidity, oppressive stateliness that would freeze any congregation and take the heart out of any sermon."[164]

Rockefeller sought to avoid the publicity attendant upon a public design competition. Instead, he decided to solicit ideas from individual architects and discuss these findings with Fosdick and the building committee of the Park Avenue Church. Since, as Rockefeller wrote to Fosdick, it was considered professionally unethical to commission designs from several architects at the same time, he privately commissioned plans from individual architects one at a time, paying each in full before beginning discussions with the next candidate.[165] He first consulted Burt Leslie Fenner, a partner at McKim, Mead & White, because "I thought their firm about the most likely to give us satisfaction."[166] The McKim office was asked to design a large church that incorporated an income-producing apartment building. The firm designed several schemes, at least two of which were in a northern Italian Romanesque style (figure 2.30). The result was a plan that Rockefeller and the other members of the building committee found satisfactory, but elevations with which they were not pleased, possibly because the church structure was lost in the massive apartment complex. Rockefeller realized that creating a church of great monumentality in a building that combined the church with an apartment building was impossible and he proposed the removal of the income-producing element and provided a donation to cover any additional costs.[167] He asked McKim, Mead & White to prepare another proposal, but the firm declined. Rockefeller then turned to Charles Collens, a part-

and right; the vacant site at upper left would later house Jewish Theological Seminary.

FIGURE 2.30
McKim, Mead & White's proposal for Riverside Church, rendered by Hugh Ferris, 1925.

ner in the Boston firm of Allen & Collens, and New York architect Henry C. Pelton, who had successfully associated on the completion of the Park Avenue Baptist Church's new home in 1922. He also solicited design ideas from Ralph Adams Cram and York & Sawyer.

Each of these proposals placed the church on 122nd Street, preserving the Riverside Drive apartment building and one apartment house on Claremont Avenue. In the fall of 1925 Collens and Pelton, who were no longer under contract with Rockefeller, suggested another possibility: aligning the new church along Riverside Drive with the tall carillon tower located to the south where it would abut a proposed apartment building for missionaries planned by Union Theological Seminary (whose architect, not coincidentally, was Allen & Collens). They also proposed that the church and the college residence hall both be designed in a Gothic style (the style of Union's earlier buildings; see chapter 7), although each would be "distinct enough, so that their [individual] identities would not be destroyed." This proposal, the architects felt, would also provide scale to the lofty carillon tower which would now rise from the center of a Gothic complex.[168] Even though they were no longer employed by Rockefeller, who was now officially dealing with Ralph Adams Cram, Rockefeller found Allen & Collens' proposal tantalizing.[169] Sensing Rockefeller's interest, Collens and Pelton decided to avail themselves of an earlier offer made by Rockefeller to fund a trip to France and Spain for the study of Gothic churches. Collens and Pelton returned from their travels with numerous ideas, which they translated into design proposals for Rockefeller. They gambled that their past relationship with Rockefeller in successfully completing the Park Avenue Baptist Church and Collens's relationship with neighboring Union Theological Seminary would place them in an excellent position to receive this prestigious commission. Thus, they spent considerable time preparing designs at no cost to Rockefeller. Their efforts were successful.

In February 1926 the trustees of the Park Avenue Baptist Church announced that they would erect a new church for Dr. Harry Emerson Fosdick on Riverside Drive and West 122nd Street and that its architect would be Allen & Collens in association with Henry C. Pelton.[170] Rockefeller sent a selection of newspaper clippings about the announcement to Fosdick, commenting on the references to the "Fosdick church" and the "Rockefeller church." Fosdick remarked in reply that "This competition in the newspapers as to whether we are a 'Rockefeller' or a 'Fosdick' church is likely to wax fast and furious. I wonder which will win! I judge that at present writing we are, as you say, breaking about even, and that you are tarred with my stick about as much as I am with yours."[171]

Rockefeller had two reservations with the Collens and Pelton proposal to build on Riverside Drive—there was no room for a chapel and there would be no entrance to the church from the east on Claremont Avenue. In order to address these concerns, Rockefeller sought additional land to the south owned by Union Theological Seminary. He offered Union a trade: he would give the seminary the apartment building at 99 Claremont Avenue, which could immediately be used to house students and missionaries, and they would give the church 40 feet of their 130-foot frontage on Riverside Drive and 20 feet on Claremont Avenue.[172] This deal was consummated in May 1926 and the architects added a chapel at the south end of the church and a cloister providing entry from Claremont Avenue. The design was made public late in December 1926 and the response was overwhelmingly positive (figure 2.31).[173]

According to Eugene C. Carder, a member of the building committee, Collens "was the guiding genius and recognized specialist in all decisions concerning the Gothic tradition," while Pelton "figured significantly in the ground plan of Riverside Church and in practically every decision that was made in the day-by-day and week-by-week sessions over a period of about five years."[174] Collens and Pelton designed a church with Gothic detail that combines a sanctuary seating 2,500, a smaller chapel, and a tower rising 392 feet that incorporated twenty-two floors of offices, classrooms, and meeting rooms, capped by a belfry housing a seventy-two-bell carillon. The tower and its carillon, the largest in the world, were dedicated as memorials to Rockefeller's mother, Laura Spelman

FIGURE 2.31

Allen & Collens and Henry C. Pelton's design for Riverside Church, 1926.

Rockefeller. The sanctuary is sited on the northern portion of the plot with the apsidal end facing 122nd Street. The tower, incorporating the chapel and main entrance in its base, rises to the south. The architects acknowledged that Chartres Cathedral was a major inspiration for the design.[175] They did not copy Chartres, however, but echoed the simplicity of Chartres's Gothic facade articulated by large windows and ornamented at entrances and other key areas with elaborate carving, as well as adapting the massing of Chartres's apse and the design of its main entrance.

Chartres was not the only source for Collens and Pelton's design. In fact, the architects actually employed various other French and Spanish Gothic forms, many of which they had seen on their trip to Europe. For example, the placement of the main entrance on the side of a church was inspired by the entry at Bordeaux Cathedral, although the design of the entrance portal itself resembles that of the Royal Portal at Chartres. The auditorium (figure 2.32) is massed with

FIGURE 2.32
Interior of Riverside
Church, c. 1930.

a low wide vault (60 feet wide and 102 feet high), unlike the high vaults employed on English and northern French churches which were widely emulated by American Gothicists. Collens and Pelton first studied such low wide vaults in Barcelona and Gerona, and then viewed them again in Perpignan, Carcassonne, and Albi. They then adapted this form to meet Fosdick's desire for a large but intimate space and for a building with no obstructions restricting the congregants' ability to see and hear the service. The chapel (figure 2.33) was inspired by the nave of the pointed Romanesque cathedral at Carcassone.[176] By choosing an architectural form earlier than Gothic for the chapel, the architects played with the conceit of a small chapel appearing to be the earliest portion of a larger church, with the main sanctuary having been erected some centuries later.[177] The building is faced entirely in Indiana limestone, with the interior of limestone and acoustical blocks cast in a matching color by the Guastavino company, which had also provided the structural vaulting tiles at St. John the Divine.

The Gothic "style" of Riverside Church is limited to ornament and massing and is not incorporated into its structure. Riverside Church lacks the crucial load-bearing wall construction of medieval Gothic design. Structurally, the church is totally modern, with a steel frame and curtain walls (figure 2.34).[178] The use of such a steel frame for a building with Gothic details was controversial and was criticized, notably by Walter A. Taylor, an architect and lecturer in architectural history at Columbia, in an essay in *American Architect*.[179] Taylor felt that the church was a "theatrical pseudo-Gothic" structure that was "a violation and betrayal of both Gothic tradition and steel construction."[180] He was especially disappointed that a congregation with one of the most progressive preachers in America, had opted for "reactionary" architecture rather than a modern design idiom that reflected its "forward-looking gospel."[181] In response to Taylor's commentary, Charles Crane, an architect in Henry Pelton's office, defended the design, commenting that the significance of Gothic design to the twentieth century was its "fundamentally Christian" nature which made it an appropriate choice for the church and that, in the Riverside Church project, the Gothic architecture of medieval Europe was adapted to "the necessities of today's conditions."[182]

Crane's defense notwithstanding, criticism of the architecture of Riverside Church continued. A year after Taylor's article was published, Philip N. Youtz wrote a scathing review of the church, referring to it as a "lithic ghost," and contrasting the vi-

FIGURE 2.33
Allen & Collens and
Henry C. Pelton's design
for Riverside Church
chapel, 1926.

tality of the modern religious thought practiced in the church with the choice
of Gothic forms which, Youtz believed, "can only be interpreted as an outward
confession that religion is dead, and powerless to inspire an architecture of contemporary significance."[183] From Rockefeller's point of view, the use of Gothic
design and a steel structure was not incongruous. Not only was Rockefeller conservative in his architectural taste, but also the choice of a Gothic style building
erected with modern construction techniques ensured the rapid completion of
Riverside Church and thus provided a dramatic contrast with the incomplete
Cathedral of St. John the Divine, which was being built slowly in the medieval
manner with load-bearing walls and structural vaults.

While the ornament was traditional Gothic in style, it was not always traditional in subject matter. For example, the arches of the main entrance portal
display distinguished scientists, philosophers, and religious leaders, including
several humanist leaders more indicative of Rockefeller and Fosdick's beliefs
than those of more traditional Christian leaders. The press found the choice of
figures especially noteworthy, pointing out the presence of Ralph Waldo Emerson among the philosophers and Charles Darwin and Albert Einstein (who was
still living and was Jewish) among the scientists.[184]

Construction began on Riverside Church in 1927. Work was set back by a fire
in January 1929 which destroyed much of the interior, but this delay did not hold
up construction for long.[185] On October 5, 1930, the first service was held at
Riverside Church (figure 2.35).[186] John D. Rockefeller, Jr., was not in attendance
(he had left the country several days earlier), undoubtedly because he did not
wish to have the church too closely identified with his patronage. Thousands of
people were turned away from the opening ceremonies even after the basement
and virtually every inch of standing room had been filled. Rockefeller's deter-

FIGURE 2.34
Steel skeleton frame of
Riverside Church,
May 18, 1928.

mination that Riverside Church be completed, in stark contrast with the cathedral, was dramatically vindicated when on the same day that Riverside Church opened and Reverend Fosdick gave his first sermon to the assembled throngs, Bishop Manning, speaking from the pulpit of the still incomplete Cathedral of St. John the Divine, yet once again announced that additional millions of dollars would be needed to complete construction on the cathedral.[187]

Although work on Rockefeller's great church was now complete, Rockefeller was not completely satisfied, since he found the physical setting of the church unworthy of his new monument. To the north, between Riverside Church and International House, was unkempt Claremont Park which, in 1927, Rockefeller offered to redesign at his own expense in order to create a better environment for the church and the international residence hall, both of which he had funded, as well as for Grant's Tomb which was immediately to the west. Frederick Law Olmsted, Jr., partner in the Olmsted Brothers firm, which had earlier proposed a landscape design for Columbia University's Morningside Heights campus (see chapter 5), was asked by Rockefeller to examine conditions in the park. Olmsted reported that it "is certainly a rather characterless as well as a shabby

FIGURE 2.35
Riverside Church with miniature golf course in foreground, 1930.

affair, and very poorly related to its surroundings." [188] The most serious problem with the small park was the fact that the land sloped toward Claremont Avenue and 122nd Street, with ragged rocky edges. In order to counteract this problem, Olmsted Brothers proposed leveling the site and building a tall retaining wall along Claremont Avenue. The wall proved to be the most difficult element to design successfully. Olmsted Brothers consulted frequently with Collens and Rockefeller regarding this element of the design, finally settling on a wall of Manhattan schist (to correspond with the facades of nearby Union Theological Seminary), with limestone trim (echoing the material on the Institute of Musical Art, located immediately to the east, and on International House and Riverside Church). [189] Olmsted Brothers also laid out paths and planted hedges, lawns, and formal rows of European lindens, providing the city with a magnificently transformed park in June 1934 (figure 2.36). [190] The project cost John D. Rockefeller, Jr. $306,987.24. [191]

More problematic was how to improve conditions on the land to the immediate south and east of the church. A vacant lot to the south was still owned by Union Theological Seminary, while on the corner of 120th Street and Riverside Drive, the setting was marred by a seasonal miniature golf course/ice skating rink with unsightly signage (figure 2.35)! This latter property and the entire block south of 120th Street were part of an estate whose elderly owner, a Mrs. Fitzgerald, had refused offers to sell. At her death in 1927 she left the property to St. Luke's Hospital, providing in her will that the hospital could not sell the property. To the east of the church stood two Claremont Avenue apartment houses, one still owned by Rockefeller and the other given to Union by Rockefeller as part of the 1926 land swap. Neither of these rather ordinary apartment houses provided a suitable architectural context for the impressive church building.

In 1930, when Union was planning a new dormitory on the site of the Alderson Apartments at 99 Claremont Avenue, Rockefeller offered to trade his apartment building on the corner of Claremont and 122nd Street for Union's land to the south of the church on Riverside Drive. This trade would permit the seminary to erect a dormitory on an expanded Claremont Avenue site. Rockefeller also offered to provide $652,000 toward construction of the dormitory if the seminary could raise all additional funds. [192] The seminary was not enthusiastic about this proposal, but it was difficult to say no to so wealthy a philanthropist as John D. Rockefeller, Jr. As a result, in 1931 the property was traded and the seminary's new dormitory begun (see

FIGURE 2.36
Redesigned Claremont Park looking north toward International House, August 1935.

chapter 7). The dormitory, designed by Allen & Collens in the Neo-Gothic style employed on other seminary buildings, provides a suitable setting for Riverside Church. In 1935 Rockefeller was also finally able to acquire the final piece of the Riverside Drive blockfront from St. Luke's Hospital. The hospital had successfully petitioned the court in 1933 for permission to sell the Fitzgerald property and in 1935 the land at the northeast corner of Riverside Drive and West 120th Street was purchased by Rockefeller for $200,000.[193]

Rockefeller hoped to complete the Riverside Drive blockfront with an addition to the church for the expansion of office and classroom facilities and asked Collens to prepare proposals. The massing of Collens's schemes, closely related to the massing of the church nave, providing a balanced setting for the tower. It was not, however, until 1955 that plans for a parish house addition were seriously considered. The new building was to provide space for expanding programs and to meet the needs of new programs.[194] Rockefeller offered to build, furnish, and fully equip the parish house as a gift in celebration of the twenty-fifth anniversary of Riverside's dedication. The design was a simplified version of Allen & Collens's earlier scheme, creating what was seen as a modern Gothic design. The firm of Collens, Willis & Beckonert, successors to Allen & Collens, designed the addition, with Harold Willis architect in charge.[195] Completed in 1959, the seven-story parish house contained classrooms, an assembly hall, a radio station, recreation rooms for use by the increasingly large Spanish-speaking community on Morningside Heights, and a two-story underground parking garage.[196] The building was paid for entirely by Rockefeller.

Riverside Church is not one of the most creative or stirring works of religious architecture in New York City, yet it was an institutional success, creating an ecumenical Protestant religious center that attracted people from all over the city and became a center for progressive religious, social, and cultural programs. Dr. Fosdick remained at Riverside Church until his retirement in 1946. He was succeeded by preachers who continued his theological liberalism. Riverside is one of the most visible church structures in New York City and a prominent landmark on the city's Hudson River skyline. With its tall tower soaring into the sky, Riverside stands in marked contrast to the truncated west front of the still incomplete Cathedral of St. John the Divine, bereft of towers and with its transepts and crossing tower unbuilt.

The two monumental churches that flank Morningside Heights mark the beginning of the transformation of the area into a vibrant neighborhood and the end of the era of major institutional migration to Morningside Heights. Although differing in the intentions of their founders and providing a radical contrast in their present architectural form, these two churches have succeeded in becoming vital religious, social, and cultural centers for the entire city, drawing thousands of local residents and visitors, and adding a religious dimension to the diverse Morningside Heights community.

FIGURE 3.1
Ernest Flagg's revised
design for St. Luke's
Hospital, 1893.

CHAPTER THREE

Building for the Body

St. Luke's Hospital and Other Health-Related Facilities on Morningside Heights

FOR SEVERAL YEARS AFTER THE DECISION IN LATE 1887 TO BUILD the Cathedral of St. John the Divine on Morningside Heights, the cathedral remained the only institution committed to locating in the area. However, in 1892 the institutional character of the neighborhood was firmly established when St. Luke's Hospital, Columbia College, and Teachers College each purchased land on Morningside Heights. The hospital's choice to relocate to West 113th Street was influenced primarily by the availability of a large urban site with plentiful light and fresh air, but the presence of the cathedral and the close relationship between members of the hospital's Board of Managers and the cathedral's supporters were also important elements in that decision. St. Luke's relocation established the first medical presence on Morningside Heights. However, it was soon followed by another major medical institution, Woman's Hospital, as well as two homes for the aged. Each of these organizations hired a prominent architectural firm and, within limited means, each erected a building of distinction to house its facilities.

St. Luke's Hospital

St. Luke's Hospital was incorporated in 1850 as the fourth general hospital in New York City—only New York Hospital (established in 1771), Bellevue (1826), and St. Vincent's (1849) are older. In 1846 William Augustus Muhlenberg, the dynamic minister of the Church of the Holy Communion on Sixth Avenue and 20th Street, had proposed an Episcopal hospital that would serve the city's poor without regard for religious affiliation.[1] In 1853 the hospital's first patients were housed at the church complex while a site for a separate hospital building was sought. The following year, the institution acquired a large plot at Fifth Avenue, West 54th Street, and West 55th Street, only a few blocks from both the land that had just been acquired for St. Patrick's Roman Catholic Cathedral and the site to which Columbia College would soon relocate. At that site the hospital erected an Early Romanesque Revival style red brick structure amidst landscaped grounds; it opened in 1858 (figure 3.2).[2] The hospital was a narrow rectangle with a wing at either end and a projecting central pavilion flanked by towers. Within this prominent central pavilion was the chapel, "the distinctive feature of the Hospital," reflecting the hospital's religious character.[3] At the time St. Luke's purchased the Fifth Avenue property, 54th Street was on the northern outskirts of the city. However, within only a few years of its opening, the surrounding neighborhood began its transformation into a wealthy residential community of palatial mansions and prestigious churches.[4] By 1885 the hospital building had become medically obsolete, while the presence of this austere brick hospital caring for the poor seemed incongruous. Accordingly, the hospital's Board of Managers appointed a committee to seek a new location farther uptown. However, no site was selected and the hospital would remain in its increasingly outdated quarters until 1896.[5]

The rapidly changing character of the hospital's Midtown neighborhood and its urgent need for a larger modern facility that would incorporate advances in medical research and sanitary care soon made a move imperative. A February 1891 editorial in the *Tribune*, observing that the hospital's land was exceedingly valuable, suggested an uptown move, "perhaps, in the neighborhood of the spot chosen for the new Episcopal Cathedral."[6] A month after the *Tribune's* editorial, a new site committee was established. George Macculloch Miller, president of the Board of Managers and prime instigator of the cathedral's purchase of Morningside property, was instrumental in persuading the board that the hospital should join the cathedral on Morningside Heights. He had been interested in a union between the cathedral and hospital since 1886 when he had proposed that St. Luke's occupy part of the cathedral's grounds. He again broached this subject with Bishop Henry Codman Potter in April 1891.[7] While building a hospital on the cathedral's property was not very practical, since it would have limited the size and future expansion of the institution, the hospital agreed in February 1892 to purchase the block immediately north of the cathedral for $500,000.[8] This property seemed perfect to Miller and the other Episcopalian board members who were either actively involved or sympathetic to the cathedral project. Its location would bring two prominent Episcopal institutions together in the same neighborhood, while assuring a distinctive and appropriate setting for the hospital. With the planned cathedral to the south and the steep Morningside escarpment

FIGURE 3.2

St. Luke's Hospital, West 54th Street and Fifth Avenue, c. 1866.

to the east, uninterrupted light and air, the first essential of good hospital planning in the late nineteenth century, was guaranteed. For the cathedral's planners, the hospital's choice provided a complementary use for a crucial neighboring plot and the presence of what they presumed would be an architecturally significant complex that would enhance the setting. Perhaps some of the board members also saw in the placement of cathedral and hospital a historic allusion to the proximity of Notre Dame Cathedral to the adjoining Hôtel Dieu in Paris. Unfortunately for the hospital, purchase of the Morningside block was difficult and costly, entailing negotiations with eight separate owners and the employment of a middleman to buy the property "in order to prevent the separate owners suspecting the purchase by the Hospital" and, thus, raising their prices.[9] With this choice site purchased, the Board of Managers set about selling its Fifth Avenue property so that the proceeds could be dedicated to the erection of a new hospital.[10]

St. Luke's Hospital's Board of Managers now faced a complex task in building their new hospital. The project required both sophisticated planning and quality design to meet the practical demands of a modern medical facility and the institutional need for a prominent structure that would establish a favorable image for the institution and reflect positively on the hospital and its trustees. A design competition was proposed as the method most likely to obtain the best possible building. Under George Macculloch Miller's leadership, five well-known architects were invited to submit competition entries, with each to be paid $400: Heins & La Farge, James Brown Lord, George E. Harney, James Renwick, Jr. (firm of Renwick, Aspinwall & Renwick), and Charles W. Clinton. Renwick and Clinton chose not to accept the offer. Other architects were free to enter the competition, but would receive no remuneration.[11] Miller asked Heins & La Farge to draft competition rules and a general outline of the hospital's needs.[12] Ultimately, ten schemes were submitted—three from invited architects and seven from others, mostly young architects or obscure firms with little or no experience in hospital design or in the design of large projects.[13] Although the competition for St. Luke's was not as controversial as the cathedral competition, it was not without problems, which perhaps accounted for the lack of interest among well-known firms and the submissions from those ill-suited to the project. The *Real Estate Record* noted some of the objections to the competition: plans "were not to be submitted under a *nom de plume*," thereby opening the judges to accusations of favoritism since they would be able to identify favored competitors; there would be no outside judges to assure a disinterested selection; and there was no assurance that a winning proposal would actually be adopted.[14]

Most of the designs that were submitted attempted to be in harmony with the proposed cathedral.[15] As might be expected, Heins & La Farge designed a building combining Romanesque and Gothic features that closely resembled the firm's cathedral design. Other architects worked in a more traditional

Gothic mode, even though the cathedral was not pure Gothic. Only one design, the French Renaissance proposal of Ernest Flagg, was a "radical departure from the cathedral idea."[16] The Building Committee selected four designs for further study—those of the three invited architects and Flagg.[17] On November 28, 1892, Flagg was awarded the commission.[18]

Flagg was an inexperienced architect, only recently returned from study at the Ecole des Beaux-Arts in Paris; he had yet to build anything. Especially considering this inexperience, his St. Luke's design was impressive, reflecting his sophisticated knowledge of French architecture and his skill in drafting expertly detailed drawings. However, his precocious talent alone would not have guaranteed him this prestigious assignment. Rather, Flagg's relationship with Cornelius Vanderbilt II, chair of the hospital's executive committee, assured the commission for him. Flagg was related by marriage to Vanderbilt and, as Marges Bacon notes in her study of Flagg, the architect had become Vanderbilt's "surrogate son."[19] Vanderbilt had financed the architect's European studies and he undoubtedly influenced the St. Luke's building committee to chose the dramatic design of the untested architect.

Despite Vanderbilt's support, the Building Committee entertained misgivings about Flagg's abilities. In November, Miller requested that Flagg provide information regarding his qualifications. Flagg replied that he had extensive experience in creating building plans, including work on Madison Square Garden and on apartment houses designed by Charles W. Clinton. He also noted his study in Paris, his involvement in the competition for the Corcoran Gallery (a commission that he would soon receive), and his designs for the proposed Tilden Trust Library (later the New York Public Library, a commission he would not receive). Flagg concluded that he "had ten years experience in architecture and am competent to carry out any work which may be entrusted to me."[20] Despite his self-confidence, Flagg suggested that if the committee remained unsatisfied, he would arrange to have Clinton or some other architect act as a consultant. This reply was apparently satisfactory and Flagg was finally appointed architect for the new St. Luke's, with Clinton serving as his associate at Flagg's expense.

Although it is apparent that Flagg ultimately received the St. Luke's commission through his connection to Vanderbilt, his hospital design had exceptionally beautiful elevations (figure 3.3) and a skillfully thought out plan. The proposed building was modeled on the Renaissance-inspired garden facade of the Luxembourg Palace in Paris.[21] *Harper's Weekly,* commenting on the quality of Flagg's design, observed that the proposal had "that appearance of symmetrical perfectness so royal to the French Renaissance, and a harmonious beauty in the rendering of detail, which two essentials all the other plans submitted in competition lacked."[22] Others, however, criticized Flagg's choice of style as being incongruous with the design of the cathedral. The issue of a lack of harmony between the cathedral and the hospital, later heightened by the disparate designs of other institutions, notably Columbia, was of great concern to many critics who had hoped that a unified institutional ensemble would be created on Morningside Heights (see Introduction). A *Real Estate Record* editorial bemoaned this loss of an architecturally harmonious neighborhood, commenting that "The dream has already been dispelled, and the promise been rudely broken. The design of St. Luke's hospital is a quite wanton affront to the Cathedral, which it is almost to adjoin, and an offense to every disinterested lover of architecture."[23] The competition instructions, however, had not specified that the proposals conform with the cathedral's design. The hospital's board undoubtedly wished to establish a visual identity independent from that of the cathedral and a French Renaissance project of such great beauty and individuality as that proposed by Flagg would do just that. Architect Walter B. Chambers, in praising his friend's design, cited historical precedent in favor of such architectural diversity, noting that the Hôtel Dieu and Notre Dame stand side by side in Paris, but "there is no attempt at harmony, and both buildings gain by contrast."[24]

Flagg's proposed hospital complex consisted of nine major pavilions with the focus on a central administration pavilion (a requirement of the competition) crowned by a dome not unlike that on the entrance screen of the Luxembourg Palace. This central pavilion was to be set back from 113th Street with a small court in front. The entry would be guarded by a pair of gatehouses connected by impressive iron gates. Eight 4.5-story pavilions were to be symmetrically arranged to either side of the main building, four on West 113th Street facing south, and four to the north on West 114th Street. Each pavilion was to be faced with brick and stone, ornamented with paired pilasters, and crowned by a mansard roof.[25] The arrangement of pavilions was a successful solution to the

FIGURE 3.3
Ernest Flagg's St. Luke's Hospital competition design, 1892.

problem of contemporary hospital planning. Pavilions housing patient wards would line West 113th Street with the wards facing south to maximize the flow of light and air into each room. A home for nurses and a private patient pavilion were planned for West 114th Street. Flagg also provided rooms for the increasingly specialized needs of a modern hospital resulting from advances in patient care. From the perspective of a hospital strapped for funds, the pavilion plan had the added advantage of permitting the construction of only a portion of the plan, with the remainder awaiting future financing.

St. Luke's choice of a pavilion plan for its new building also placed the hospital in the forefront of the evolution of the design of large American hospitals. The pavilion hospital, a development of the second half of the nineteenth century, would dominate hospital design in Europe and America until the 1920s.[26] In the United States, the precedent for the pavilion plan was Johns Hopkins Hospital in Baltimore, begun in 1877.[27] This large institution had a central administration building capped by a prominent dome with two parallel rows of ward pavilions. *Harper's Weekly* commented on the similarities in the plans of the Baltimore and New York hospitals, but immodestly concluded that St. Luke's "will be a notable improvement over the Baltimore institution, and will be, when completed, the finest hospital, without exception, in the world."[28]

Although the board of managers chose Flagg's entry, it also made clear that the choice "does not carry with it the adoption of his plans as presented, which are to be modified or changed as directed by the Building Committee."[29] In fact, Flagg made important alterations to his proposal in 1893, keeping the French Renaissance style and basic plan, but improving circulation and lowering costs (figure 3.1). The gatehouses were removed and the administration building pulled forward toward 113th Street to dominate the design. In front of this central pavilion Flagg placed an open court, which was to be flanked by gently curved colonnades leading from the street to the main entrance; these colonnades were never constructed. The removal of the gatehouses also accentuated the effect of the tower-like administration building with its ornate fifth-story clock, increasing the visibility of its three-story porticoed frontispiece which was closely modeled on that of the garden front of the Luxembourg Palace. Flagg's revised design also improved the visual presence of the dome and lantern which now dominated the design and were visible throughout the Morningside neighborhood and also towered over Harlem.[30] Although the dome came to serve as a symbol of the presence of the hospital and its great new building in the city, it actually had the purely utilitarian purpose of hiding the water tower. The drum below the dome, marked by arched windows, paired Corinthian columns, and corner temples crowned by sculpted figures of the four apostles, housed the surgical theater (figure 3.4). By placing the operating theater at the highest elevation within the building's most prominent architectural element, Flagg emphasized the growing importance of surgery in the hierarchy of medical disciplines.[31] Flagg also simplified the street elevations of his competition design by removing the paired pilasters that would have been expensive to carve. Instead, he enlivened the white brick facades, with their white Georgia marble base and trim, with inexpensive, but vibrant, yellow brick diaperwork. He also made several changes to the interior (figure 3.5), the most significant of which was moving the stairs to locations outside of the ward pavilions so that individual wards could be efficiently quarantined without affecting vertical circulation. As part of the redesign project, Flagg submitted his proposals to Charles Clinton, who found the plans "strong and at the same time simple and economical."[32]

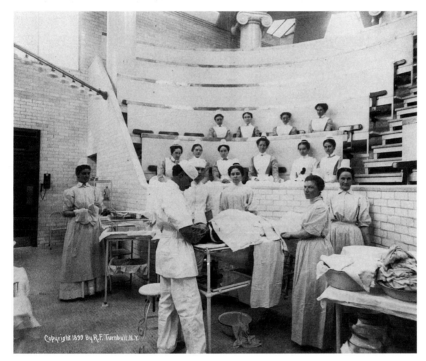

FIGURE 3.4
St. Luke's Hospital's
surgical theater, 1899.

FIGURE 3.5
Revised plan for
St. Luke's Hospital, 1893.

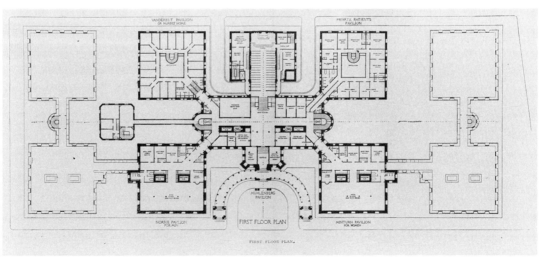

The realignment of the administration building not only made it a more visible element of the overall design of the hospital complex, but also created space for a separate chapel wing to the rear. As at the original hospital building on Fifth Avenue, the chapel held primary importance in this church-affiliated facility (figure 3.6). Modeled on seventeenth-century precedents such as Philibert de l'Orme's Chapelle de la Sainte-Trinité at the château of Fontainebleau, the chapel is placed on axis with the main entrance to the hospital. Architecturally it is the most beautiful interior feature of the building and remains one of the great late nineteenth-century religious spaces in New York.[33]

The cornerstone of the new hospital was laid on May 6, 1893. Work began on the administration building (designated the Muhlenberg Pavilion, in honor of the hospital's founder), the chapel wing, a pavilion for women on West 113th Street to the east of the administration building (Minturn Pavilion, named for the hospital's first president, Robert B. Minturn), a similar pavilion for men to the west (Norrie Pavilion, in memory of Gordon Norrie, treasurer for twenty-nine years), a single wing on West 114th Street to the west of the chapel for nurses' housing that contained a spectacular open stairway with wrought-iron railings (Vanderbilt Pavilion, in honor of William H. Vanderbilt whose legacy of $100,000 had paid for the Vanderbilt Annex at the original hospital and whose family was still actively engaged with the institution; figure 3.7), and two small one-story structures: an ambulance stable and apartments for the ambulance drivers and stablemen located in the center of the block to the east of the hospital, and a pathology building set to the west.[34] Unfortunately, construction did not proceed smoothly. While the untried Flagg was a designer of enormous talent, his inexperience in supervising a major construction project and his arrogant personality soon took their toll.[35]

Major problems first arose with the marble supplied by the Piedmont Marble Company of Georgia. Blocks of suitable size were slow in arriving at the hospital site and Flagg rejected much of what was finally delivered as unsuitable. The Building Committee blamed Flagg for the delay. Although Flagg was probably correct in rejecting the marble, his adversarial response to the committee's protestations, which had been communicated to Flagg by Vanderbilt,

FIGURE 3.6
St. Luke's Hospital Chapel with stained glass by Henry Holiday, early twentieth century.

blaming them for insisting on Piedmont's marble, did not foster an amicable relationship between the architect and most committee members.[36] Problems also arose over the speed of construction, with Flagg placing the entire blame on the contracting firm of Robinson & Wallace. The incensed contractors responded to Flagg's allegations, complaining to the trustees that the architect's "statement that we are incompetent, that we are trifling with the Committee and that we show no executive ability clearly shows his animus. He should be more careful in casting such reflections upon men of our experience and reputation."[37] Having antagonized the building committee and the contractor, Flagg went on to battle with the J.B. & J.M. Cornell Ironworks, one of the city's most prominent suppliers of cast iron, over the provision of dormers that Flagg had failed to include in the initial specifications and regarding door frames that Flagg complained were not being installed in a timely manner, but which Cornell insisted could not be installed because of inadequate preparatory work.[38]

The most heated dispute occurred in 1893–94 between Flagg and the prominent English stained-glass artist Henry Holiday, who was commissioned to provide the large window lighting the chapel. Gordon Norrie had offered to provide a great window for the chapel in early 1893 as a memorial to his parents.[39] Although there were talented American stained-glass makers active in the 1890s, including Louis Comfort Tiffany and John La Farge, the St. Luke's window was to be designed in England. Initially, Clayton & Bell, a major commercial stained-glass firm, was considered, but eventually Holiday, a more artistic stained-glass maker, received the commission. The design for a window on the theme of Christ the Consoler, crowned by roundels representing the Seven Acts of Mercy (figure 3.6), was approved by a committee consisting of Bishop Potter, the donor, and representatives of the hospital. However, delays arose when Flagg failed to provide Holiday with adequate information about the design of the chapel. As work progressed, Flagg redesigned portions of the chapel, forcing Holiday to alter his window design.[40] Holiday was driven to writing Superin-

FIGURE 3.7
Open stair in Vanderbilt Pavilion, 1900.

tendent George S. Baker that "it is impossible for me to stultify a design which has been a work of great care, in order to meet an architectural afterthought."[41] In addition, Flagg's failure to describe the architectural context within which the window would be placed and his failure to identify architectural elements that might intrude upon the window, such as a projecting reredos below the window, forced Holiday to undertake additional changes.[42] After Flagg wrote an insulting letter to Holiday, calling his design "effeminate" and "medieval," the irate glass artist replied to Flagg's "impertinence" by informing Baker that "Mr. Flagg's letter to me was of a character that rendered it undesirable to communicate with him directly. He must I suppose be a young man who knows as little about figure-drawing as about manners."[43]

These multiple construction delays caused the trustees grave concern since they had agreed to leave the old hospital by the end of 1894. They considered a temporary move to the Cancer Hospital on Central Park West and 106th Street, but rejected this idea, eventually arranging with the new owners of the Fifth Avenue property to vacate only part of the old building, while retaining use of the remainder until July 1, 1895.[44] Even this reprieve failed to provide enough time to complete the new building. Patients were not finally transferred to the new hospital until January 1896, although construction continued for several more months.[45]

Despite the delays in construction, problems with materials, Flagg's personality, and the architect's inadequacies in superintending such a large-scale construction project, St. Luke's was ultimately provided with a hospital building that was not only one of the most beautiful institutional structures in New York (figures 3.8 and 3.9), but was also as efficiently planned as any hospital in America.[46] *Scientific American* went so far as to refer to St. Luke's as "the most magnificent hospital building in the world, with the exception of one instance."[47] Unfortunately, this "exception" is not identified. With the demand for hospital services increasing rapidly in New York City, St. Luke's soon outgrew the complex and sought funds to erect the additional planned pavilions. Especially pressing was the need for a private patient pavilion, since the hospital's ability to care for the indigent depended on income generated by these paying patients. When the hospital opened, private patients were temporarily housed on two floors of the Vanderbilt Pavilion, which had been erected to house nurses. This arrangement not only crowded the nurses, but also provided poor service to wealthy paying patients. As a result, St. Luke's lost crucial income as potential patients chose New York Hospital and Presbyterian Hospital. The trustees feared that other potential patients would choose Mt. Sinai and Woman's hospitals when construction was completed on those institutions' new buildings.[48]

Unfortunately, St. Luke's was "seriously retarded in its development by lack of sufficient income."[49] Although the hospital accepted patients of all creeds, and, in fact, Episcopalian patients were always a minority, it was officially an

Episcopal institution. This affiliation limited likely donors to a small, albeit wealthy group. Even among the city's Episcopalian social elite, St. Luke's was not the most prestigious medical institution. Wealthy Episcopalians were far more likely to donate to New York Hospital, the city's oldest medical facility, than to St. Luke's. In addition, in the 1890s many worthy organizations were vying for the philanthropic donations of the wealthy. St. Luke's had to compete with other Episcopal institutions seeking to erect new buildings or expand their campuses, including the Cathedral of St. John the Divine and Columbia University, as well as with new or expanding secular institutions (libraries, museums, botanical gardens, etc.) that reflected the civic aspirations of affluent New Yorkers.

It was not until late 1903, when Margaret J. Plant offered to fund a private patients pavilion, that work on this crucial wing began.[50] The pavilion, located on the corner of Morningside Drive and West 113th Street, was designed by Flagg, but there is no indication that the architect had any responsibility for super-

FIGURE 3.8
St. Luke's Hospital, main facade on West 113th Street, 1904; from left, Norrie Pavilion, administration building, Minturn Pavilion, and ambulance stable.

FIGURE 3.9
St. Luke's Hospital, rear elevation on West 114th Street, c. 1899; from left, ambulance stable, Minturn Pavilion, chapel wing, Vanderbilt Pavilion, and pathology building.

intending its construction. The Margaret J. Plant Pavilion contained sixty-five private rooms, an operating room and other medical facilities, staff housing, and an apartment for the hospital's superintendent.[51] On the exterior, the pavilion is similar to those erected earlier, except that the east facade, overlooking Morningside Park, incorporates French-inspired iron balconies where patients could sit in the morning sun, breath fresh air, and admire the view over Harlem and the Bronx toward the Long Island Sound. Two additional pavilions were later erected to Flagg's designs, the Travers Pavilion (1908–16) on West 114th Street east of the chapel and Scrymser Pavilion (1925–28) at the corner of Morningside Drive and West 114th Street.[52]

By the post-World War II period, radical changes occurring in medical treatment and in the design of hospitals made Flagg's building obsolete. In the 1950s, St. Luke's began a slow process of modernization that resulted in the demolition of the Norrie and Vanderbilt pavilions and the construction of several banal additions.[53] Not only are these structures of mediocre design, but their scale conflicted with Flagg's pavilions. In addition, the majestic dome that Flagg designed as the crowning element of the Administration Building was demolished in 1966 and the four marble statues that once encircled the surgical theater below the dome had deteriorated so badly that they too had to be removed.[54] A series of alterations also occurred to other wings, all partially a result of serious deterioration to the marble that had given Flagg so much trouble during the initial construction. The hospital also erected buildings on adjacent blocks and expanded its presence in the community by purchasing apartment houses either for demolition or for staff housing.[55] Today, Ernest Flagg's St. Luke's complex is a pale reflection of its original grandeur, with two pavilions demolished and others unsympathetically altered. As the obsolete pavilions that remain are vacated, the future of these still significant buildings becomes increasingly problematic.

Woman's Hospital and Other Health Facilities

St. Luke's Hospital was not the only institution ministering to the welfare of the body that relocated to Morningside Heights near the proposed Episcopal cathedral. Opposite the planned western entrance to the cathedral, on the northwest corner of Amsterdam Avenue and West 112th Street, the Home for Old Men and Aged Couples began construction of a Gothic-inspired building in 1897; while to the south, Woman's Hospital, the oldest hospital in America dedicated to women's health issues, purchased a large site on Cathedral Parkway in 1902. Several blocks away, on the southeast corner of Broadway and West 114th Street, the St. Luke's Home for Indigent Christian Females acquired land in 1896 and moved from the Upper East Side to Morningside Heights.

Both the Home for Old Men and Aged Couples, established in 1872 for "those who, having been accustomed to the comforts, and in many cases the elegancies of life, through loss of property or other causes, find themselves in their old age without means for their support," and the St. Luke's Home for Indigent Christian Females, organized in 1852 to assist poor Episcopalian women over the age of fifty, were Episcopal-church affiliated institutions with Bishop Potter as an ex-officio member of each of their boards of trustees.[56] Both institutions had initially occupied rowhouses on Hudson Street in Greenwich Village, adjoining St. Luke's Chapel. The St. Luke's Home had moved to Madison Avenue and East 89th Street in 1870, but by the end of the century, both institutions were seeking larger and more modern facilities. Since neither home required an enormous site, affordable land could easily have been purchased on the Upper West Side, in Harlem, or in other developing neighborhoods, yet the trustees of each institution chose to buy on Morningside Heights. Undoubtedly, proximity to the cathedral prompted the relocations to this neighborhood. The cathedral would serve as a convenient place for the Episcopalian residents of each home to attend services and, in turn, the construction of new buildings by these institutions would aid in creating a fitting architectural setting for the cathedral. The Home for Old Men and Aged Couples hired the firm of Cady, Berg & See and erected a distinguished neo-Gothic building, with a fine pointed-arch portico and picturesque roofline of gables and dormers (figure 3.10).[57] A writer for *Harper's Weekly,* who bemoaned the general lack of architectural unity among the Morningside Heights institutions, found the home to be one of "the only buildings in the neighborhood which seem to have been designed with any other than a disrespectful reference to the minster."[58] Sadly, this structure was demolished in the 1970s and replaced by Amsterdam House, a thirteen-story retirement home that is one of several undistinguished newer buildings that have marred the cathedral's setting.[59] The St. Luke's Home chose the socially well-connected firm of Trowbridge & Livingston for its new building, erecting a simple, but spacious six-story Renaissance-inspired structure (figure 3.11). The building served as a retirement home until the 1970s when it was sold to Columbia University, which commissioned the architectural firm of R. M. Kliment & Frances Halsband to convert the former home into a dormitory and administrative offices, renamed Hogan Hall.[60]

A far more significant presence on Morningside Heights than either of these two old-age homes was Woman's Hospital. Founded in 1856, Woman's Hospital was a nondenominational organization with a Board

FIGURE 3.10
Home For Old Men and
Aged Couples, c. 1897.

of Governors and a women's Board of Managers composed of members of many of the city's prominent Protestant families, including those who were involved with other Morningside Heights institutions.[61] The hospital, established by pioneering surgeon J. Marion Sims, was the first in America to minister specifically to the needs of women, giving special emphasis to gynecology and obstetrics. The hospital had initially occupied a rowhouse on Madison Avenue and East 29th Street. In 1857 New York City gave the hospital the block bounded by Park and Lexington avenues and East 49th and 50th streets (presently the site of the Waldorf-Astoria Hotel). In 1866 construction began on a hospital build-

ing (figure 3.12); the hospital was enlarged with the construction of a second building on the same plot in 1873–77. In 1857 the Park Avenue site was in a relatively undeveloped area where light, air, and quiet were abundant. However, as the nineteenth century progressed, Park Avenue became an increasingly unpleasant thoroughfare with noisy trains belching smoke into the hospital as they traveled to and from Grand Central Terminal. By the 1890s, the increasing traffic on the rail lines and extensive development on blocks surrounding the hospital, including the presence of the F. & M. Schaefer Brewery on the block to the north and the National Ice Company to the south, made relocation of the hospital imperative. In 1892 land was purchased on Central Park West between West 92nd and 93rd streets, but with the onset of an economic depression the following year, fundraising for construction on the new site became impossible.

Conditions at the aging and ill-sited hospital buildings continued to deteriorate and in 1897 the Board of Governors finally determined to settle the issue of either moving or building a new hospital on the Park Avenue site. Attempts to sell the Park Avenue property failed and, with money tight, the board of Woman's Hospital decided to sell the Central Park West site and use the proceeds to rebuild on Park Avenue.[62] Designs were solicited from four architectural firms, with the French Renaissance proposal of the Boston firm of Allen & Vance ultimately selected (figure 3.13).[63] The selection of Allen & Vance was undoubtedly influenced by Mary Thompson, an active supporter of Woman's Hospital, as well as an important donor to Teachers College (see chapter 6). Thompson was a native of the Finger Lakes, New York town of Canandaigua, where she and her husband, Frederick Ferris Thompson, worshipped during the summer at the local Congregational Church. The church's minister was the brother of architect Frederick R. Allen and the Thompsons became close friends. Allen designed additions to Sonnenberg, the Thompsons' Canandaigua estate, as well as most of the buildings that the Thompsons donated to various institutions, including the Thompson Memorial Chapel at Williams College, the Frederick Ferris Thompson Memorial Library at Vassar College, and the Thompson Memorial Hospital (now the Ontario County Building) and the Woodlawn Cemetery Chapel, both in Canandaigua.[64]

Plans for the construction of the new Woman's Hospital building were proceeding when a broker suddenly proposed selling the Park Avenue site. The possibility of a sale encouraged the trustees to once again search for a new location for the hospital. Negotiations for the sale of the Park Avenue property advanced slowly and in January 1902 the hospital decided that a sale would have to be finalized within two weeks or construction would begin on Allen & Vance's scheme for the Park Avenue site.[65] Finally, in February 1902, the land was sold for $450,000 to the New York Central Railroad, which needed the site for the enlargement of its facilities as part of the construction of a new Grand Central Terminal.[66]

This unexpected sale occurred before Woman's Hospital was able to erect

FIGURE 3.11
St. Luke's Home For Indigent Christian Females, c. 1897.

FIGURE 3.12
Woman's Hospital, Fourth Avenue (Park Avenue) and East 50th Street, 1866, view from west side of Fourth Avenue looking northeast.

FIGURE 3.13
Allen & Vance's proposal for Woman's Hospital, 1899.

a new building and the institution was forced to close for several years until a new hospital could be constructed. A building site was rapidly assembled on Cathedral Parkway (West 110th Street) extending to West 109th Street between Columbus and Amsterdam avenues, opposite the grounds of the Cathedral of St. John the Divine and just east of the land recently purchased by the National Academy of Design (see Introduction).[67] The hospital chose this site because it was large enough for the erection of a substantial new building, was within walking distance of an elevated station, and would be even more conveniently located when the subway was completed in 1904; and it was affordable. Unlike those involved with St. Luke's Hospital and the two old-age homes, most of the board members of Woman's Hospital were not Episcopalians and they did not have a close relationship with the cathedral and its supporters. Thus, the proximity of the cathedral was not a determining factor in the hospital's choice of a Morningside Heights location. However, the presence of the Cathedral of St. John the Divine across the street must have increased the appeal of the Cathedral Parkway property since this meant that the surroundings would be quiet (a dramatic change from the old site) and views from the hospital would be toward a beautiful church and its landscaped grounds.

FIGURE 3.14
Woman's Hospital,
c. 1909.

Frederick R. Allen, by 1902 a partner in the firm of Allen & Collens, remained the hospital's architect and his Park Avenue design was adapted for the new site (figure 3.14). The building was designed with the main facade set on a

stone terrace along sloping Cathedral Parkway. At this location it would overlook a wide boulevard and the grounds of the cathedral to the north and would impressively anchor the main entry to Morningside Heights from Central Park and the East Side. The U-shaped building had a court on 109th Street where southern light would shine onto a garden and into the patient wards. Entry was through an imposing *porte-cochère* on the western elevation.[68] As at St. Luke's Hospital, the most impressive interior space at Woman's Hospital was a chapel—here designed with simple Gothic features. The hospital opened late in 1906.[69]

Woman's Hospital prospered at this new location and two large extensions were added to the building. In 1913 Mary Thompson gave the hospital four lots immediately to the east of the original building for construction of a nurses' residence. The building, which was completed in December 1914, was largely funded by a gift of $125,000 from Maria Jesup, wife of the prominent banker and philanthropist Morris K. Jesup (a significant supporter of Union Theological Seminary; see chapter 7). Thompson also paid for the Thompson Pathological Building, which was erected to the west of the original hospital in 1913–15, replacing the *porte-cochère*. Both of these additions were designed by Allen & Collens in a style that matched the original design, but they lacked the picturesque roofline of the original and significantly altered the proportions of the building.

The organization of local hospitals changed considerably after World War II as large general hospitals, such as St. Luke's, sought to provide comprehensive care. Smaller specialized hospitals, such as Woman's, could not compete with these larger and better funded institutions. Many of these smaller hospitals merged or closed their doors completely. When St. Luke's decided to add an obstetrics department, Woman's future as an independent institution was called into question. In 1952 the board decided to merge Woman's Hospital with St. Luke's, creating the Woman's Hospital Division of St. Luke's Hospital. This division remained in its original hospital building until 1968, when a new building was completed on Amsterdam Avenue between 114th and 115th streets. The 110th Street site was sold in 1962 and the entire hospital complex demolished in the mid-1970s for the construction of Davis, Brody & Associates' Cathedral Parkway Houses.

The Cathedral of St. John the Divine and nearby institutions, especially St. Luke's Hospital and Woman's Hospital, provided an institutional anchor at the southeastern portion of Morningside Heights. Although the cathedral and the hospitals were major construction projects, they did not have a significant impact on the development of other projects in the Morningside area, since their constituencies had no special interest in the surrounding neighborhood. In contrast, Columbia College's decision to relocate to Morningside Heights and erect a monumental new campus for its expanding academic programs and its rapidly increasing student body would have the most profound influence on the character of the evolving Morningside Heights neighborhood.

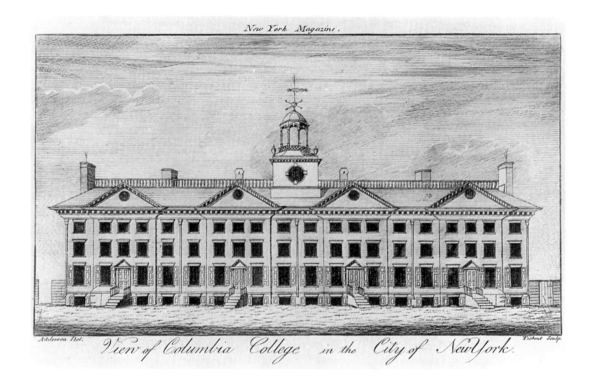

FIGURE 4.1

"View of Columbia
College in the City of
New York," 1790.

CHAPTER FOUR

Building for the Mind I

Columbia University and the Transformation of Morningside Heights

BISHOP HENRY CODMAN POTTER'S PROCLAMATION IN 1887 THAT AN Episcopal Cathedral would rise on the site of the Leake and Watts Orphan Asylum suddenly placed Morningside Heights in the public eye. Although the Cathedral of St. John the Divine is significant in the architectural and cultural history of New York City (see chapter 2), its construction on Morningside Heights did not have a tremendous influence on the future character of the area. Rather, it was Columbia College's purchase of a portion of New York Hospital's Bloomingdale Asylum property in 1892 that began the transformation of the Morningside Plateau into a center for prestigious educational institutions. Columbia's monumental complex of academic buildings, the creation of college president Seth Low and his architect Charles Follen McKim, not only physically transformed the Morningside Heights neighborhood, but also stood as a visible symbol of change at the institution as it became a major force in the intellectual life of the expanding city. As Columbia grew physically and in academic prestige over the next century, the university would have an increasingly significant impact on its neighborhood, attracting other educational institutions to the area and, as the school's enrollment increased, expanding its presence into the surrounding residential community.

King's College/Columbia College:
Columbia University's Early History

King's College was established in 1754 as the first institution of higher learning in what was then the Province of New York.[1] Classes for the first eight students were held at Trinity Church on Broadway and Wall Street. The royal charter, issued on October 31, 1754, mandated that an Anglican hold the position of president, but neither the board of trustees nor the student body was ever exclusively Episcopalian. Indeed, the charter specifically provided that admission be open to men of all religions, although attendance at Episcopal chapel services was mandatory.[2] Thus, from its inception, Columbia had a close affiliation with the Episcopal Church, but was not an official church institution. In 1760 the fledgling college moved into a building erected on land donated by Trinity Church at Park Place and Church Street (figure 4.1). After closing during the Revolutionary War, King's College, rechartered as Columbia College, resumed classes in 1784.

During the first half of the nineteenth century the trustees continued to come primarily from a small group of established Episcopalian families, including many clergymen. The small student body was drawn primarily from elite local families. The curriculum remained a conservative scholarly one, stressing the classics as opposed to law, mechanics, or other professional fields necessary in a burgeoning commercial city.[3] The school soon outgrew its colonial-era building. In 1813 engineer James Renwick, the father of the prominent architect James Renwick, Jr., proposed a new Gothic Revival complex for the downtown site, but it was never erected.[4]

By the 1850s the trustees could no longer ignore the need of the expanding city for citizens educated in the professions, but disagreed over the extent to which Columbia should accommodate its curriculum to this exigency. The aged building on Park Place was impractical for a modern college; the curriculum was uninspired; and the school's place at the center of higher education in New York City was being challenged by the elite New York University (then known as the University of the City of New York), founded primarily by wealthy Presbyterians, and the more egalitarian, publicly sponsored Free Academy (later renamed City College).[5] In 1853 a committee of the board of trustees proposed that the college institute two significant changes to meet these challenges—a move to a new site and the addition of "University Education" (i.e., professional programs) to the undergraduate offerings.[6] However, neither of these suggestions was acted upon immediately. Although the proposal to relocate met with wide favor, resources were insufficient for its realization. The addition of professional training to the scholarly curriculum was a far more controversial proposal and the trustees chose not to alter the character of the school in such a radical way.

Relocating the college to a new site should not have been difficult since Columbia owned a large plot of land on the west side of Fifth Avenue between 47th and 51st streets, known as the "Upper Estate" (now the location of Rockefeller Center), that was suitable for a new campus. The Upper Estate was originally the Hosack Botanic Garden, a tract of land given to Columbia by New York State in 1814 after the school had pleaded with the State Legislature for financial assistance.[7] In 1855, two years after the trustees' committee proposed a move north, serious consideration was given to relocating to this property. Not all trustees were in favor of such a move; George Templeton Strong felt that construction on the site would be too expensive and that it was a "suburban waste" that resembled a "pig-sty premises."[8] Nonetheless, the board commissioned Richard Upjohn, one of America's preeminent architects, to design a new college on the Upper Estate property. Upjohn planned a building in a Venetian Gothic style that was to be built of polychromatic brick.[9] However, rather than immediately building this impressive permanent complex, Strong recommended "the removal of the college to temporary accommodations."[10] After the trustees rejected a proposal to move the college to rural Westchester County to the north of Manhattan, Strong's suggestion was accepted.[11] In 1856 the trustees voted to relocate the college temporarily in the former Deaf and Dumb Asylum complex on the block between Madison and Fourth (now Park) avenues and East 49th and 50th streets, just east of the Upper Estate, while a new campus was being erected on the college's Fifth Avenue property.[12] This "temporary" relocation, however, would last forty years, since no effort was ever made to erect college buildings on the Upper Estate. Instead, Columbia's trustees warehoused the property, gambling that the area on and adjacent to Fifth Avenue would develop into a prestigious residential neighborhood. The trustees' wager paid off. Mansions and townhouses soon rose on Fifth Avenue lots leased by Columbia and speculative builders erected rowhouses on the side street properties. Payments on the land leases generated a substantial income for the college.[13]

On May 7, 1857, the cornerstone of the original college building on Park Place was "disinterred" (it had been buried six feet below ground) and transferred to the former Deaf and Dumb Asylum site.[14] Four days later, classes assembled on this new uptown campus and demolition began on the original college building.[15] The new campus was in a part of the city that was still largely undeveloped, as is clear from an 1857 description published in the *Evening Post*:

> The new location of the College is a delightful one, and undesirable only on account of the distance up town—an objection which, by the tendency of population, will be in a few years obviated. The old asylum buildings have been altered somewhat, repaired, and greatly improved. The two wings have been separated from the main building. . . . A beautiful lawn slopes from the college southward down to 49th street, and is ornamented by some fine old trees. . . . The site is on a commanding eminence, affording an extensive and pleasant view. That part of the city is still quite new, and the hand of improvement is visible in all directions. 'Potters Field' is within a stone's throw, and we are sorry to say the ends of rows of coffins, filled with the bones of the unknown dead, are still to be seen protruding from the bank of earth left by the cutting through of the 4th Avenue.[16]

While the residential population of the area was still small, a number of other institutions were making significant investments in the neighborhood: St. Patrick's Cathedral was under construction on a block catercorner from the college's new property; St. Luke's Hospital was completing construction nearby (see chapter 3); and, in the same year that Columbia relocated to the area, New York City presented Woman's Hospital with land across Fourth Avenue from Columbia's property (see chapter 3).

Coincident with Columbia's move, the trustees broadened the educational curriculum, permitting senior students to study science or history and law, as well as the classics. This movement toward an expanded curriculum responsive to the professional needs of a growing commercial city was embraced by Frederick A. P. Barnard, president of Columbia from 1864 until his death in 1889.[17] Under Barnard's aegis Columbia undertook a few small steps toward accommodating new fields of study; the School of Mines and the School of Political Science were established and an architecture program was instituted.[18] However, many of Barnard's proposals were rejected by the conservative trustees, including his efforts to admit women to Columbia and his proposal for the establishment of professional training in education.[19] These expanded programs required increased space, even though Columbia's student body remained small in comparison to that of Harvard, Yale, and other colleges. Barnard suggested moving to a new site since the college needed new buildings, and "the continual noise of the locomotives and cars" along Fourth Avenue, following the opening of Grand Central Depot in 1871, disrupted the academic environment.[20] In 1872 Columbia purchased about eight acres near West 161st Street and the Hudson River waterfront in Washington Heights for a new campus, but for unknown reasons the trustees decided not to build so far uptown.[21]

Rather than relocating the college, Columbia's trustees chose to erect a series of striking new buildings on its cramped Midtown site: Hamilton Hall (figure 4.2), extending along the entire Madison Avenue frontage, in 1878–79; the

FIGURE 4.2

Hamilton Hall, Madison Avenue between East 49th Street and East 50th Street, c. 1885; Villard Houses visible at far left.

School of Mines, on the Fourth Avenue frontage, in 1880–84; and a magnificent library with brick interior walls and a vaulted roof supported by exposed cast-iron trusses permitting an uninterrupted space measuring 113 by 75 feet, completed in 1883 (figure 4.3).[22] These new buildings, all of which were constructed of brick with Potsdam sandstone trim, were designed in an English-inspired Collegiate Gothic style by architect Charles Coolidge Haight. The Columbia commissions were among Haight's earliest important designs. That the trustees chose Haight as their architect is not surprising, since he had a close relationship with both Columbia itself and the city's Episcopal hierarchy. He was a graduate of Columbia and his father, Benjamin Haight, had been a minister at Trinity Parish as well as a Columbia trustee, serving from 1843 until his death in 1879. Much of Haight's work was for Episcopal institutions, including several churches, the Sheltering Arms Home, St. Stephen's College in Annandale, New York, the College of the South in Sewanee, Tennessee, and, most significantly, a series of structures for Trinity Parish and a magnificent complex for General Theological Seminary in Chelsea.[23]

Soon after moving to 49th Street, Columbia found itself in the midst of a prestigious residential neighborhood as fine mansions and rowhouses were erected on Fifth Avenue, Madison Avenue, and adjacent side streets, including McKim, Mead & White's sumptuous Villard Houses of 1882–85 on the Madison Avenue blockfront immediately north of Hamilton Hall. Thus, while Columbia's space needs were increasing, expansion beyond the Madison Avenue block was becoming difficult. With its cramped and inadequate facilities, a location not conducive to learning, and few opportunities for advanced study at a time when graduate and professional education were becoming more and more important at American schools, most elite families in New York City, including the families of most of the trustees, did not enroll their sons at Columbia, but instead sent them off to Harvard, Yale, Princeton, or other prestigious northeastern colleges. Columbia, in fact, was becoming increasingly irrelevant as a center of higher education.

If Columbia were to survive and thrive in a competitive educational environment, the institution would have to undergo substantial changes in its curriculum, its relationship with the city, and, just as significantly, in its physical fabric. The death of President Barnard in 1889 and the need to choose a successor presented the trustees with just such an opportunity to chart a new future for Columbia. They reluctantly opted for progress by choosing Seth Low as college president in October 1889.

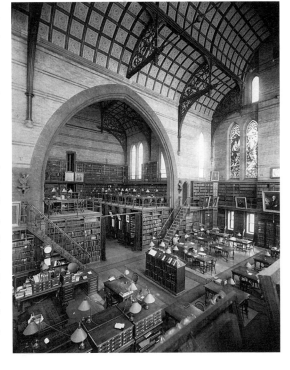

FIGURE 4.3
Interior of Charles Haight's Columbia College Library, c. 1885.

Seth Low and the New Columbia

Seth Low was a native of Brooklyn, born in 1850 into one of that city's wealthiest mercantile families.[24] His grandfather, also named Seth Low, had established a business in Salem, Massachusetts, importing pharmaceutical drugs from India. He had relocated to New York in 1829, joining a major migration of New Englanders to the New York area as the importance of Salem and other New England commercial centers dwindled. Like many other New Englanders, Low settled in Brooklyn, which was beginning its development as a prosperous, largely residential city. He was a founder of Brooklyn's First Unitarian Church (the Church of the Saviour). This Unitarian heritage may partly account for the younger Seth Low's commitment to progressive reform and belief in equal opportunity for all people. Seth Low's father, Abiel Abbot Low, owned one of the largest fleets of clipper ships in the country and dominated American trade with China. Abiel Abbot Low entered this trade in the 1830s, the beginning of a lucrative period for Americans in China as British dominance was being challenged. After spending several years in China, he returned to New York and established the firm of A. A. Low & Brothers in 1840. From his base on Burling Slip (now John Street) in Manhattan, Abiel Low organized a thriving trade in silk, tea, and other goods (including opium, which was shipped from Turkey and India, and exchanged for Chinese goods).[25]

Seth Low grew up in an enormous brownstone-fronted mansion at 3 Pierrepont Place in Brooklyn Heights.[26] The house overlooked New York Harbor, where Seth could view his father's clipper ships as they entered and left the port. He was educated at Brooklyn Polytechnic Institute before matriculating at Columbia College. Upon graduating in 1870, Low briefly entered his father's firm. However, as heir to a great commercial fortune, Low did not have to worry about finances and was able to forsake business and enter the world of reform politics. In 1881 Low was elected mayor of Brooklyn, serving two consecutive two-year terms. During his tenure, Low sought to make the entire civic governance system more efficient and to remove what he and other progressives saw as the corrupting influence of the Tammany Hall Democratic machine. Among his most important achievements as mayor were the institution of civil service reform, revision of the tax and franchise systems, expansion of municipal services into new areas of a rapidly growing city, and the improvement of the public school system, including the construction of new schools, free distribution of textbooks, and the opening of all schools to black students.[27] Shortly after his election as mayor, Low built one of Brooklyn's most beautiful Queen Anne style houses on the corner of Pierrepont Street and Columbia Heights, just across the street from his childhood home.[28]

On November 7, 1881, one day before his election as Brooklyn's mayor, Low was also elected a trustee of Columbia. Although his commitment to the college would inevitably be limited by his new political obligations, Low accepted the appointment. It was not until he stepped down as mayor in 1885 that Low was able to participate fully in college affairs.[29] After serving only a few years as an active trustee, Low was elected president of the college. Although he was a graduate of Columbia and a trustee, Low was not the unanimous choice of the trustees since his views on modernizing the school were well known and they conflicted with those of the more conservative board members. Low was elected president by a bare majority of only seven to six.[30] Despite this lukewarm endorsement, Low was offered the position since there was no other candidate on whom the divided board could agree. He was installed as Columbia's president at a ceremony at the Metropolitan Opera House on February 3, 1890.

Low was the perfect choice for those trustees and alumni interested in transforming Columbia into a modern university. He was an Episcopalian (still a requirement for the college presidency; he had left the Unitarian Church in 1872), an alumnus of the college, a board member, and the president of the alumni association.[31] While Low was not an academician, he was a leader among the progressive activists within the city's elite community. He also had a proven record for successful reform and was recognized by his peers as someone who understood the nature of the contemporary city and could translate this understanding into a vision for creating a great academic institution within an urban setting. *Century Magazine,* a publication intended for educated and affluent readers who would be concerned about higher education in America, editorialized that Low was the perfect choice for creating "the great metropolitan university," adding, "The American Republic never needed more than it does now, at the dawn of its second century, an insistence in all its educational enterprises— from the kindergarten to the university—upon *training in citizenship.*"[32] Low was eminently qualified to lead Columbia in providing this training.

Low's tenure would be characterized by an aggressive response to the challenges of transforming Columbia into a center of modern education by expanding the curriculum, increasing the size and improving the quality of the faculty, and opening the college to men from varied ethnic, religious, and class backgrounds.[33] Low was especially proud of his relationship with the Jewish community and, as part of his ecumenical emphasis for the college, he did away with compulsory chapel attendance. His development of professional and graduate programs led to Columbia's becoming a university in 1896.[34] In addition, to accommodate the physical and educational needs of the growing institution, Low oversaw Columbia's move from the relatively new buildings on the overcrowded, Midtown campus to a monumental home on Morningside Heights.

Up to Morningside Heights

After spending his first years as president improving Columbia's academic offerings, Low turned his attention to the college's inadequate facilities. In 1891 Low established a committee to investigate potential new locations for Columbia.[35] The committee considered three options for the school's future: a move to the country, the fragmentation of the college among a variety of locations within the city, and the purchase of a new site on Manhattan Island. The first two were quickly rejected. Although some trustees and a segment of the New York community supported the country option, it was strongly opposed by Low and several other trustees who recognized the educational advantages to training men "under city conditions and under metropolitan conditions. The great city itself gives a view of life which is no slight part of the student's education." [36] Low also realized that a city location could be the school's greatest asset in attracting students and would also set it apart from rival institutions. Fragmenting the college remained a possibility, but only if no other option was available since such a policy would prove costly and would preclude interaction among departments.[37] Thus, a new site had to be found that would permit the entire college to relocate as a single unit. Finding an affordable site of such a scale on Manhattan Island would not be easy since the school had little money, land costs were extremely high, and much of the island was already developed.

New York Hospital's Bloomingdale Asylum tract on Morningside Heights was first suggested as an appropriate site for Columbia by John B. Pine, the clerk of the Board of Trustees.[38] Pine had graduated from Columbia College in 1877 and from the law school two years later. Although he was involved with many civic and philanthropic efforts, Columbia occupied most of his time. Pine became a member of the board of trustees in 1890 and, on his death in 1922, Columbia President Nicholas Murray Butler wrote, "It may be doubted whether in all the long history of Columbia any of her sons has loved her more ardently or has served her with more tireless devotion." [39] As clerk, he was closely involved in the planning for the new campus. Shortly after his appointment, Low wrote his friend and fellow trustee George Rives that "the college cannot always secure as clerk a man who is both as competent as Pine and as willing to give to the college so much time and attention for nothing." [40] This comment not withstanding, Low's relationship with Pine was not always amicable and the two were often at odds over building and design issues.

Pine's suggestion that Columbia consider the Bloomingdale property was contained in a report he prepared in the summer of 1891. After enumerating all of the advantages of the site, Pine summarized his findings: "It is well within the city limits, and in a portion of the city likely to be well built up, and . . . it retains all of the advantage of a city university which our present site possesses, while infinitely superior in all other respects." [41] Columbia entered into secret negotiations with New York Hospital for the northern portion of the hospital's holdings—the four blocks between West 116th and 120th streets and Amsterdam Avenue and Broadway, which the hospital offered to sell for $2 million.[42] Columbia eventually accepted this offer.

It has been suggested that the elite boards of New York Hospital and Columbia College contrived to protect Morningside Heights from immigrant speculators who might otherwise have transformed the plateau into a tenement district and that these prestigious institutions sought to affirm "the long-term hegemony of the elite" over the area.[43] There is, however, little evidence for such a conspiratorial theory. While the board members of the hospital and college were undoubtedly familiar with one another through business, social, and religious connections, and while the hospital wished to sell a section of its property in a manner that would not detract from the value of its remaining holdings in the area, it was not interested in selling at anything less than the highest possible price. In fact, the hospital made few financial concessions to the college, despite the elite Protestant backgrounds of members of each board.[44] The $2 million price that the hospital demanded of Columbia reflected the maximum value of this land, not a conspiratorial sweetheart deal. In fact, the sale price was equivalent to $6,525 per lot, higher than the going price for land in the area. It is clear that maximizing revenue from land sales in order to construct a state-of-the-art asylum in White Plains was more important to the hospital than guaranteeing the future character of a neighborhood that it was being forced to abandon or even than assisting Columbia College in its purchase of a new campus site. However, since Columbia was interested in a large tract, undivided by cross streets, and since the property contained substantial buildings that could be put to temporary use by the college, Columbia's trustees did not deem $2 million to be "an unreasonable price."[45]

The high cost of the property was a potential stumbling block for Low and his allies on the Columbia board since the college did not have funds for such a major purchase and the school had never been successful at raising money from its graduates or from the general citizenry of New York. Dean John W. Burgess described how in the recent past "Columbia had received from individual donors hardly enough as a permanent endowment to pay the salary of a single professor . . . while individual residents of New York had given millions to Harvard, Yale and other institutions."[46] Those on the Columbia board who favored the move to Morningside Heights realized that in order to gain support and financial backing they had to carefully publicize the proposal in a way that would excite the alumni and other New Yorkers about the potential for a great university in their city. Low and Pine planned the public announcement to be "so framed as to carry the most weight and to excite confidence in and enthusiasm" for the project. They also sought to control the release of information regarding the project so that newspapers would not have "a chance to publish any misleading and prejudicial statements[, for] we cannot afford to have the project 'leak out' in a garbled and perverted form."[47]

It was decided that Low would announce the decision to take an option on the Morningside Heights property at an alumni dinner on December 15, 1891. Low's speech was carefully constructed. It was imperative that he ask the alumni to join with the board in considering the land purchase and that graduates not think that the decision to purchase the property had been finalized without their involvement. At Pine's suggestion, Low emphasized that the proposal was only tentative and was being announced "for consideration and discussion and for the purpose of ascertaining whether public sentiment will support us."[48] In addition, Pine urged Low not to mention that the Episcopal college would be moving to a site on Morningside Heights near that of the proposed Episcopal cathedral. Pine observed that this would be obvious to Episcopalians, but that such a direct connection might work against the interests of the college by discouraging support from adherents of other denominations.[49] Low followed Pine's advice in his speech, playing upon the pride of the alumni, seeking both their advice on the suitability of the proposed move and their support in raising money. Although the cathedral was mentioned, along with Grant's Tomb, as sites that would attract visitors to the area, no mention was made of any religious connection between the cathedral and college.[50] Pine and Low's care in preparing the announcement succeeded and the alumni greeted the proposal with great enthusiasm. The speech was followed in January 1892 by a report from a committee of the trustees discussing the proposed move in detail and by a meeting of the alumni the following month who, after an impassioned speech by Low, strongly supported the trustees' plan.[51]

In the months following Low's initial speech, the city's newspapers began publishing editorial comments. At first editorial sentiment was mixed, but eventually most newspapers enthusiastically supported Columbia's plan. All editorials agreed that Columbia needed to move if it was to become a leader among the nation's institutions of learning and some papers were excited about the specifics of Low's proposal. The *New York Recorder* summed up the views of those who saw the move as assuring a great future for the college:

> The proposal of the Faculty of the Columbia College . . . [is] wise and timely. . . . While Columbia has for years been an old-fashioned rather conservative school, it has not been accorded the place which should belong to a leading college of the metropolis and one so richly endowed. Harvard and Yale have outstripped it in educational fame. Princeton, Cornell and the University of Virginia are better known. There is no reason why, with a liberal, progressive government, Columbia should not hold the primacy to which it is entitled. A long step towards this would be the building of a college worthy of Columbia.[52]

Other editorials were essentially supportive, but also sought more information about the decision to remain in an urban setting rather than relocating to a more traditional rural environment. At a subsequent alumni meeting, in February 1892, Low forcefully supported the choice of an urban site and editorial sentiment soon became almost universal in favor of Columbia's decision to move to Morningside Heights.[53] Only a few papers remained hostile to the plan, questioning the selection of a site on densely populated Manhattan Island. The *New York Mercury* was most vociferous in its opposition, asserting that the $2 million purchase was "a foolish piece of extravagance" since the school would soon be subject to the same problems of urbanization that it suffered on 50th Street and would then have to move again.[54] The *Real Estate Record and Builders Guide* also opposed the purchase, perhaps reflecting disappointment that its constituency of speculative builders would not profit from developing New York Hospital's property.[55] The *Evening Post* was more pointed in its concern for real estate interests, commenting that while the owners of surrounding property might be delighted with Columbia's plans, "This sale in bulk will be a great disappointment to many real-estate operators, who expected to profit by the gradual increase in values that would have followed a large auction of lots."[56]

Low's announcement of Columbia's move to Morningside Heights was made only a few months after New York University had announced that it had purchased a site for a new campus on Fordham Heights in the Bronx.[57] The decision by the city's two private colleges to relocate precipitated a proposal by a wealthy banker, Jacob Schiff, a leader of New York's German-Jewish community and one of the city's most generous benefactors, that the two schools affiliate in some way.[58] There was some logic to Schiff's proposal since the institutions had similar goals and were about to inaugurate major fundraising campaigns targeting similar segments of the city's wealthy elites. Although wealthy Episcopalians were more likely to donate to Columbia than to NYU, which had a strong affiliation with the Presbyterian community, Low hoped to broaden support for Columbia and attract substantial gifts from philanthropists of other faiths. Low was not disposed to accept an alliance with NYU, but he could not reject the plan out of hand since Schiff apparently had promised a substantial gift to a consolidated university and, no matter what the outcome of the proposal, Low undoubtedly hoped for generous donations from Schiff and other members of the German-Jewish establishment.[59]

Low made it clear in his letters to Schiff and NYU's chancellor Henry MacCracken that Columbia, as the older of the two institutions, would only accept a full consolidation of NYU and Columbia, and that Columbia would not consider changing its name. This demand, Low knew, would be unacceptable to MacCracken, who favored a federation in which NYU would retain its identity and much of its independence. Rives and Pine agreed with Low's approach. Rives suggested that Low not reject MacCracken's federation proposal out of hand, but that he simply state that it was Columbia's belief that only a merger would be appropriate.[60] Pine was much more direct, telling Low that Columbia should be on record as "open to any reasonable proposition for the consolidation of [New York] University, and to place the University on record as refusing to make any such proposition. We may well feel certain that Presbyterian prejudice will prevent the University from making any such proposition at present, and a refusal to do so will greatly prejudice the University in the minds of Mr. Schiff and others holding his views in that it will betray the narrowness and bigotry which characterizes the University."[61] Neither Low nor MacCracken was enthusiastic about Schiff's merger proposal, but neither was willing to antagonize this powerful figure. For more than a year they exchanged guarded communications, but ultimately nothing came of Schiff's proposal.[62]

Once Low had gained significant support for Columbia's proposed move from most of the trustees, alumni, and press, he must have imagined that he would have no problem raising the funds needed for the purchase of the Morningside property. Unfortunately, this was not the case. The alumni's sorry tradition of limited financial support continued. In addition, the collapse of the financial market in June 1893 would make fundraising even more difficult. In fact, the campaign to raise funds for the land purchase netted only $427,150, with the alumni donating a mere $136,150, of which $100,000 was a gift of a single alumnus, William C. Schermerhorn.[63] In an effort to generate larger gifts, Low wrote personal letters to some of the city's wealthiest residents, including William Waldorf Astor, Andrew Carnegie, and Theodore Havemeyer.[64] J. P. Morgan and Cornelius Vanderbilt each gave Columbia $100,000, D. Willis James, who had already donated $100,000 to the cathedral's fundraising campaign and who would be Union Theological Seminary's major benefactor, donated $50,000, and a few other wealthy individuals contributed, but the school was still forced to rely on the sale of the old Madison Avenue campus and a $1 million mortgage to complete the purchase.

Fundraising came to a virtual halt in March 1892 when Low and the entire Columbia community were forced into a brief, but time-consuming battle to keep the New York State Legislature from splitting the Morningside Heights property in two by opening West 119th Street between Amsterdam Avenue and Broadway. Early in March, state senator George Washington Plunkett, a prominent Tammany politician, introduced a bill requiring the opening of 119th Street. Plunkett's support of this bill may have reflected animosity toward Low's anti-Tammany politics, but more likely it was simply a continuation of Plunkett's previous support for street openings as a way of augmenting his power in the Morningside Heights district through residential development and increased population. In an editorial, the *Evening Post* accused the corrupt Plunkett of self-interest in his efforts to thwart Columbia, commenting that "What Mr. Plunkett's purpose is in introducing this bill is not difficult to imagine. Nobody has asked him to present it, and nobody except himself will be found to say a word in its favor. He is in politics for business purposes only, and has presented this measure in the ordinary course of business under the belief that it will prove offensive enough to 'have something in it for Plunkett.'"[65] Even Dwight Olmstead and Charles Bixby, the local landowners who had actively sought the removal of the Bloomingdale Asylum by forcing the opening of cross streets through the asylum's property, supported Columbia, realizing that the college would provide opportunities for profitable land sales and development.[66]

Whatever Plunkett's motives, his bill was a threat that could not be ignored since Columbia could not possibly proceed with its option to purchase if the property were threatened with subdivision. As soon as Plunkett's intentions became known, Pine had Low write to the senator seeking his support for keeping the tract intact. Low carefully framed his argument to appeal to Plunkett's concern for increasing real estate values in his district, writing that the removal of Columbia to Morningside Heights "would bring to it as a place of residence a large number of professors and students . . . permanently increasing the value of all property in the neighborhood."[67] As word of Plunkett's plan reached the public, the alumni began circulating a petition to Mayor Hugh Grant, eventually signed by more than 5,000 people, seeking his support for the protection of the Bloomingdale property. Articles and editorials in local newspapers, even those that previously had led the fight against the presence of the Bloomingdale Asylum on Morningside Heights, supported Columbia.[68] Columbia's trustees were optimistic that they would prevail in their efforts to maintain the Bloomingdale property and on March 7, 1892, the trustees officially voted to purchase the site so long as a bill permanently closing 117th, 118th, and 119th streets was passed by the State Legislature.[69]

In order to ensure that the new campus site was preserved, Low and trustee Cornelius Vanderbilt met privately in early March with Mayor Grant, a Tammany Democrat (and a graduate of Columbia Law School), whose support was necessary if Plunkett was to be persuaded to amend his bill. At that meeting, the representatives of Columbia proposed a compromise. In exchange for preserving the integrity of the property, Columbia offered to cede a strip of land on the south side of West 120th Street, permitting the city to lay out a boulevard one hundred feet wide.[70] With the support of Mayor Grant, local real estate interests, Columbia alumni, and many other powerful and influential citizens, Plunkett acceded to Columbia's compromise. On March 18, 1892, he amended his bill, providing that so long as the property was owned by Columbia, West 117th, 118th, and 119th streets between Amsterdam Avenue and Broadway would remain closed and that, in exchange, Columbia would give a 40-foot-wide strip on 120th Street to the city.[71] The bill immediately passed the state senate by a unanimous vote and soon after also passed the assembly; it was signed into law on April 7, thus ending a battle that could have permanently derailed Columbia's move to Morningside Heights and its renaissance as a leading urban university.[72] Low and his supporters could now focus their energies on the more important task of planning a major new campus.

Designing the New Columbia

With the integrity of the Morningside Heights site secure, Low turned to the issue that would define the character of the institution—the complex problem of designing a suitable campus. Low, although without any preconceived idea regarding the form the campus should take, was well aware that a wide spectrum of people had high expectations for the new Columbia campus, anticipating that the school would present New York City with a great ensemble of architecturally distinguished buildings. *Harper's Magazine,* a publication popular in affluent middle-class households, saw the new campus as "the magnificent and adequate representative of the just aspirations of the city for an institution which is symbolical of the higher interests of every great and prosperous community"; the religious publication *Christian Union* reasoned that "the city ought to see to it that the magnitude of its [Columbia's] life and the range of its interests are symbolized by a nobler group of buildings, sacred to science and scholarship, on the height which nature has made the crown of the island"; while the *Real Estate Record* editorialized, "It will rest with the authorities of Columbia . . . more than those of any other institution to treat their plot so as to add a real architectural monument to New York."[73]

Low hoped that the new campus would provide an identity for Columbia and symbolize its prominence within the life of the city. He was also sensitive to issues of architectural quality, having grown up in one of Brooklyn's finest mansions and having commissioned a stylish home for himself. However, Low had no experience or training in creating or designing an institutional complex of the scale necessary to meet his expectations and those of the wider public for Columbia. In order to choose a campus design that would fit Columbia's educational needs and provide a fitting architectural symbol of the school's importance, and that could be built within the institution's limited financial resources, Low sought the advice of others. He relied especially on his friend and fellow trustee George Lockhart Rives. Like Low, Rives came from a wealthy family and, throughout much of his adult life, was involved in public and philanthropic affairs. He had graduated from Columbia College and Columbia Law School, had been appointed a trustee in 1882, and would become chairman of the board in 1903.[74]

Rives proposed the framework within which Low and the trustees would consider design ideas and choose an architect. Rives realized that with limited funds for construction and with no assurance of substantial donations from the alumni and general public, the school could initially erect only essential buildings, leaving additional construction for the future. While Rives did not want to hamper Columbia's educational functions by building too little or squander funds by building too much, he believed that problems arising from either of these excesses could be eventually rectified. He understood, however, that it was essential to select a design that would assure a "dignified, harmonious and artistic whole," since an artistic mistake and the construction of a mediocre group of buildings "will be irreparable." Rives appreciated the significance of quality design in enhancing Columbia's position in New York City life and furthering its objective of becoming an institution of influence in the city. He commented that "the unequalled opportunities of our new site . . . will only be fulfilled by the erection of buildings that will be an ornament to the locality and an honor to the College."[75]

At Rives's suggestion, Low initiated a survey of departmental needs. The responses were to be only advisory, but they would assist in ensuring that the new campus buildings would provide sufficient and appropriate space for modern educational demands.[76] With data from the survey, Low and the trustees were able to determine what the school needed to build immediately, what could await future funding, and what activities could be placed temporarily within existing asylum structures. With these questions addressed, Low and the trustees faced the crucial issues of campus planning and building design. These were perplexing problems, not only because Low and the trustees were aware that many people were expecting an impressive project, but also because of the physical limitations of the new site. While the Bloomingdale property was considerably larger than the Midtown campus, it was still much smaller than those of other universities. Accordingly, the arrangement of buildings would have to be more compact than the expansive layouts of most American colleges. In addition, the peculiar topography of the property, a rocky plateau running north from West 116th Street with a steep drop of about fifteen feet at approximately West 119th Street, would present difficult challenges in designing the campus as a unified whole.

In order to provide a number of alternative solutions to these problems for the consideration of the trustees, Rives suggested that the college seek the advice of three eminent designers rather than immediately hiring a single architect to design the campus. Rives hoped that the trustees would keep "an open mind which shall not permit us to become the victims of preconceived notions based on only an incomplete study of our complex problems."[77] In publicly explaining why a decision had been made to proceed in this manner, Low indicated, "We want to avoid mistakes in the beginning . . . [since] it may be many years before the whole plot is covered with buildings. . . . Perhaps the final buildings in our plan may not be erected for a hundred years."[78]

In May 1892, the trustees agreed to appoint what they referred to as an architectural "commission," consisting of Charles Coolidge Haight, Richard Morris Hunt, and Charles Follen McKim.[79] Charles Haight could be considered Columbia's "house architect," since he had designed the buildings for the Midtown campus only a decade or so earlier. He also had experience designing other academic institutions, including a master plan for New York's General Theological Seminary which was nearing completion. Richard Morris Hunt was the dean of the American architectural profession.[80] The first American to study at the Ecole des Beaux-Arts in Paris, he had, over several decades, received some of the most prestigious architectural commissions in the country, among which were buildings for Columbia trustee Cornelius Vanderbilt and his relatives, such as the Breakers, Vanderbilt's palatial Newport, Rhode Island estate. Hunt was also known to several of the older trustees, notably F. Augustus Schermerhorn, since he had been Schermerhorn's choice to direct Columbia's architecture program when it had been established in 1881 (an offer Hunt had turned down).[81]

In 1892, when Hunt was approached by Columbia to serve on the architectural commission, he was at work on the Administration Building at the World's Columbian Exposition in Chicago, a world's fair which was to open one year later. Beaux-Arts-trained Charles McKim was one of the leading architects in America and a partner in what was rapidly becoming the country's most prestigious firm, McKim, Mead & White. This firm had skyrocketed to the top of the architectural profession since its establishment in 1879. It had designed or completed many of New York's most significant landmarks, including the Century Association, Metropolitan Club, Villard Houses (across from the 50th Street campus), Madison Square Garden, and Washington Square Arch.[82] McKim was also the architect of the Agriculture and New York State buildings, then under construction at the World's Columbian Exposition. In addition, in 1892, McKim, Mead & White was at work on a small stable for George Rives's Newport estate.[83] Most of the trustees would also have known McKim since he traveled in the highest social circles and was a member of the Century Association and other clubs frequented by Columbia's leaders.

The trustees hoped for a joint proposal from their architectural commission, but this was not likely from three such independent architects. Instead, the architects formulated general ideas that would govern each design and then each prepared one or more campus plans independently. Undoubtedly, each architect hoped that his plans would impress the trustees and win him the prestigious appointment as architect for the college. However, the trustees had not envisioned the architectural commission as a design competition, seeing it rather as a means of generating ideas and discussion. In order to guide their evaluation of the plans submitted by Haight, Hunt, and McKim, the trustees requested the assistance of William R. Ware, chair of Columbia's architecture program, and William Trowbridge, head of the engineering faculty (Trowbridge died in the summer of 1892, before the designs were completed). Landscape architect Frederick Law Olmsted was later invited to join Ware in evaluating the proposals since it was clear that the campus plan would involve landscaping as well as building issues. Olmsted had extensive experience with university design, having given, as Olmsted reminded Ware, "similar advice . . . to Harvard, Yale, Cornell, Amherst, Johns Hopkins, Stanford, Chicago, and other Universities."[84]

Although the trustees wished to get the broadest range of options from their architects, and in some cases purposely kept their own ideas from the architects so as not to influence their work in any way, they did require that each architect include certain features in his plans.[85] The trustees required that each proposal contain a chapel, a refectory, an observatory, a gymnasium, administrative offices, a single academic hall, a boiler room, and a home for the president. Dormitories could be included, although the trustees had yet to decide if they wished to provide such residences on the campus.[86]

The architects worked on their proposals through 1892 and into early 1893. Finally, in April 1893, the commission submitted its recommendations to the

trustees. The joint proposals covered general issues involving use of the site, relationships between proposed buildings and open space, and selection of materials. The architects suggested that the natural levels of the site be preserved,
thus avoiding unnecessary and expensive grading; that courts, enclosed on three
sides, be a feature of the plan, with each court wider than the maximum five-
story height proposed by them for the buildings; that connections between
buildings be provided by covered walkways; that buildings be fireproof structures of stone, preferably Indiana limestone, or, should this prove too expensive, red brick with stone trim; and that the plan and design of the entire group
be finalized before any construction was undertaken.[87] Although not all of these
suggestions were ultimately included in the final design, they did provide a basis upon which further planning proceeded.

Within these parameters, each architect prepared at least one plan representing his proposal for the layout of the campus.[88] The plans were accompanied by
explanatory texts discussing practical aspects of the proposals and the reasons
for the choice of style and materials.[89] As would be expected from his earlier
work at Columbia's Madison Avenue campus and his design for General Theological Seminary, Haight proposed a complex of buildings designed in a Collegiate Gothic style reminiscent of Oxford and Cambridge. Haight felt that this

FIGURE 4.4
Charles Haight's plan for
Columbia, 1893.

style was "admirably adapted for use
on the irregular levels of the new
site."[90] The main entry to the campus would be from Amsterdam Avenue, which Haight believed would
continue to be the main point of
access for the site. His plan (figure
4.4) was extremely dense, with large
and small enclosed or semi-enclosed
courts. The chapel was in the center,
flanked by the library and administration building facing Amsterdam
Avenue and a refectory and theater
near Broadway; a gymnasium in the
center of the plot completed the central core. Classroom buildings were
located at the north end of the site,
with a spine running along 120th
Street and wings extending south, an
arrangement successfully employed
by Haight at General Theological
Seminary. To the south, closer to
116th Street, Haight provided a
house for the president and a series

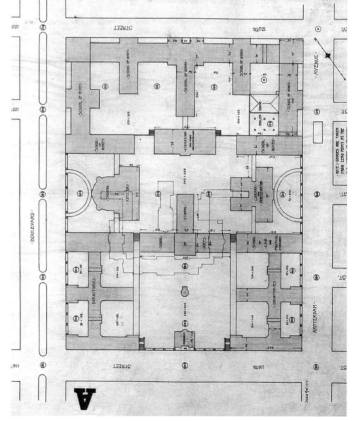

of dormitory units. Haight's plan was thus an attempt to create an enclosed complex on the model of English colleges. However, his proposal was not especially spacious or elegant. The courts and other open areas were awkwardly shaped and, while there was ample classroom space, major buildings, such as the library and gymnasium, were exceptionally small. In addition, his plan did not exploit the multileveled topography of the site and also failed to provide a grand entrance to the campus or impressively scaled buildings that would serve as fitting symbols for the reinvigorated university.

Hunt prepared several plans, each with a large central courtyard surrounded by Italian Renaissance-inspired pavilions that created smaller courts, many of which opened onto the flanking streets (figure 4.5). Although some of the pavilions were connected, major structures such as the administration building and chapel were freestanding. The pavilion plan was not based on precedents of university design, but on French hospital planning, bearing a decided resemblance to the plans of Martin-Pierre Gauthier's Hôpital Lariboisière (1839–54) in Paris.[91] Like Haight, Hunt placed the campus entrances on the east and west, although he sited the main entry on Broadway at 118th Street, which he felt would provide the "grandest approach to the property."[92] Although his report spoke of using the varied levels of the site, the actual design, like Haight's, failed

FIGURE 4.5

One of several plans by Richard Morris Hunt for Columbia, 1893.

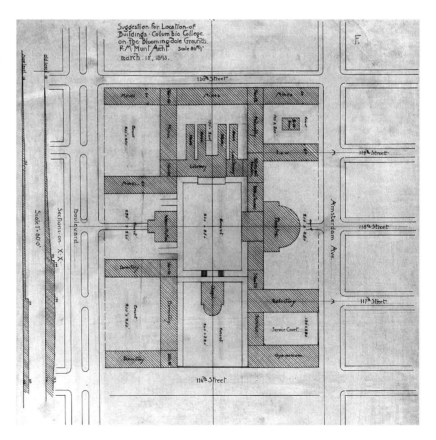

to successfully exploit the topography. Given Hunt's successful design of monumental projects, such as the World's Columbian Exposition, his proposals for Columbia were surprisingly uninspired, with no clear focus to the plan and no attempt at a monumental architectural statement.

Although McKim's three original plans have been lost, his design ideas are clearly described in the report that accompanied his submission. McKim sought to maximize the use of the property, accenting the fact that this was a "city property" and that the design must be "wholly municipal [in] character."[93] He noted that the creation of a university in a densely built up city was not unique to Columbia, but was identical to that faced only a few years earlier by the authorities at the Sorbonne in Paris.[94] Responding to the multilevel topography of the site, McKim divided the campus into two separate zones. All of the major buildings were to be placed on the higher southern platform, south of West 119th Street. The plans were formal and symmetrical, inspired by the French Beaux-Arts ideas with which McKim was intimately familiar. Each of McKim's three proposals centered around variously configured entrance courts (a rectangular court running north/south, a rectangular court running east/west, and a square court). Entry would be from the south, up a single steep flight of stairs, and would focus on a monumental building "of pure Classic forms" that incorporated all of the most important college functions.[95] Placed around this central core were subordinate classroom structures. McKim's dynamic proposals used the limited size of the plot to great advantage, creating a dramatic approach and an impressive arrangement of buildings.

The plans submitted by Haight, Hunt, and McKim varied in so many particulars that they did not provide the trustees with a clear direction in which to proceed. The trustees adopted McKim's idea of entry from the south and the division of the campus into two sections, with the northern portion left for future development. Other decisions, including the arrangement of buildings, style, and materials, remained unresolved. Since the trustees were not willing to choose any one of the schemes submitted by the three architects, they asked Ware and Olmsted to propose a new plan that "combines many of the best points of all the others."[96] The trustees particularly praised Haight's provision of space for lecture halls, Hunt's external courts, and McKim's symmetrical and monumental architectural grouping.[97] Besides adopting McKim's proposal to divide the site into two zones and his idea of entrance from 116th Street, Ware and Olmsted also incorporated McKim's central entrance court and axial massing, but adopted an arrangement of pavilions modeled after Hunt's proposals.

The plan that Ware and Olmsted submitted to the trustees (figure 4.6) centered on a large, fully enclosed, south-facing court.[98] On 116th Street, a flight of steps (divided horizontally into three sections) led to an extremely shallow court. From this court, a monumental gateway of five arches "forming a sort of *Propylaea* to the Acropolis" led onto the main court.[99] Buildings of two to three stories were to flank this grand classical entry. At the north end of the court was a single prominent building combining a centrally placed academic theater, chapel to the left, library to the right, and the refectory below. Open and enclosed courts surrounded by classroom structures completed the plan. Ware and Olmsted's completely enclosed campus effectively separated Columbia from the city, with the main court becoming a private space instead of a civic square easily accessible to the public.

After approving the Ware and Olmsted scheme, the Committee on Buildings and Grounds, following a somewhat convoluted process, once again returned to Haight, Hunt, and McKim requesting that each prepare sketches by September 30, 1893, suggesting how the Ware and Olmsted plan could be realized. McKim's distaste for that plan is evident in a letter to Hunt in which he refers to it as "a pudding—and a very indigestible one indeed!" [100] Just before the deadline for the submission of proposals, the three architects prepared a memo condemning the proposal.[101] They judged the design to be "radically defective," adding that it "cannot be successfully developed from an artistic and an architectural point of view." [102] The three architects strongly recommended the selection of a single architect to plan the entire complex.[103] The trustees agreed that this approach was now appropriate. However, they did not immediately announce who the architect would be.

Following almost a year of discussion and the presentation of the plans devised by Haight, Hunt, McKim, and Ware and Olmsted, the Committee on Buildings had agreed on a number of key issues regarding the design and construction of the new campus. These decisions would guide their choice of the architect most appropriate for the job. In addition to the design elements previously agreed upon, many of which had been adopted from McKim's proposal, the Committee on Buildings had also accepted McKim's idea that the princi-

FIGURE 4.6
Ware and Olmsted proposal for Columbia, drawn over a plan of the Bloomingdale Asylum buildings, 1893.

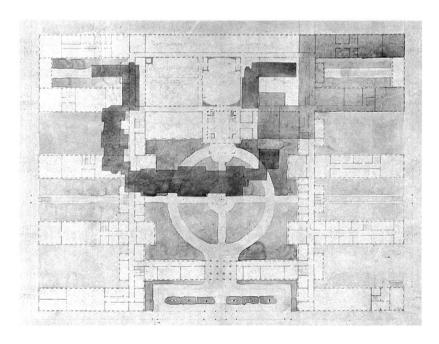

pal structures—the library, chapel, theater, office of administration, refectory, and possibly a gymnasium—should be situated in the center of the grounds. Around these major buildings would be classroom structures of not more that four stories, each with large windows admitting a maximum of natural light. The classroom buildings would also have flexible floor plans, with the floors supported independently of the partitions "as in modern office buildings." The trustees also chose to take advantage of the uneven topography by placing the boiler room and other service facilities out of view in the northern section of the property at the base of the incline, with a private delivery road running through the property at about West 119th Street.[104]

The trustees were also concerned about securing "the best architectural effect" and determining the appropriate architectural style for the campus structures.[105] This goal was crucial for a building complex that was to establish Columbia as the centerpiece of New York City's intellectual life. The trustees wanted a style that was practical and flexible enough to permit varied building forms, while at the same time securing a "general harmony of effect." It was also important to them that many architects have expertise in the chosen style so that, if necessary, more than one architect could design campus buildings. Finally, and most importantly, the trustees wanted the style to be one "which will appeal most strongly to the taste and judgment of the educated public" and would be "appropriate to the municipal character of the situation." [106] The construction of a complex of "municipal character" was something that Low had sought from the very start of planning for the new Columbia campus.

Renaissance

In late-nineteenth-century America two architectural styles were generally considered appropriate for a college campus—Collegiate Gothic and variations on classical design, such as Ancient Roman, Italian Renaissance, or Colonial. By the 1890s, the Collegiate Gothic, with its association with such historic educational institutions as the colleges at Oxford and Cambridge, had been adopted by the architects of several prestigious American colleges, including Henry Ives Cobb in 1893 for the new University of Chicago (figure 4.7), an urban university funded by John D. Rockefeller and a potential rival of the revitalized Columbia.[107] Charles Haight, who had designed Columbia's Madison Avenue campus in the Collegiate Gothic style, was clearly a proponent of this mode of design and proposed that Collegiate Gothic also be employed for the buildings on Columbia's new campus. The Columbia trustees considered Collegiate Gothic a style that was flexible and adaptable, and could, therefore, be employed on buildings of different sizes and uses. In addition, it was believed to be an appropriate style for urban buildings that could provide the college with buildings of great beauty.

While acknowledging the positive aspects of the Collegiate Gothic, the trustees had many reservations regarding the adoption of this style. They were concerned that the style would not allow for sufficient light since it did not generally incorporate large windows. Also, in the early 1890s, there were few architects in New York City, besides Haight, who were proficient in its use. In addition, by choosing Collegiate Gothic, the trustees would have given the appearance of imitating traditional English college architecture rather than choosing a style more appropriate to the school's goal of creating a new American synthesis of higher education and urban life. Further, Low and the other trustees on the Building Committee may have wished to avoid a design that could be compared with the Gothic design of the University of Chicago. Perhaps most significant to the trustees' decision to reject the Gothic was that the choice of Haight and a Collegiate Gothic design would have linked the new campus and its buildings with the old complex that was being abandoned. Such a backward looking reference was inconsistent with the plans of Low and his allies among the trustees who were seeking to remake Columbia into a dynamic modern university.

Like the Collegiate Gothic, "a classic style such as the Renaissance" was seen as being flexible and adaptable, but the trustees viewed it as more practical for lighting and ventilation since classical design could easily accommodate large windows.[108] A classic style was also deemed especially appropriate to a site on a ridge where monumental college buildings could rise above surrounding structures much as the Parthenon and other classical monuments rose above their surroundings. While the choice of such a classical architectural vocabulary would be a departure from more traditional collegiate architecture, this, the trustees felt, "offers certain strong recommendations" since it would set Columbia apart from its rivals.[109] In addition, as the World's Columbian Exposition had made clear, many architects were adept at using classical forms and "in the opinion of the Committee it is the style which will appeal most strongly to educated popular taste."[110] Low had visited the exposition and had written ecstatically about its "surpassing beauty." He was especially impressed with the man-

FIGURE 4.7
Henry Ives Cobb's
Collegiate Gothic design
for the University of
Chicago, 1893.

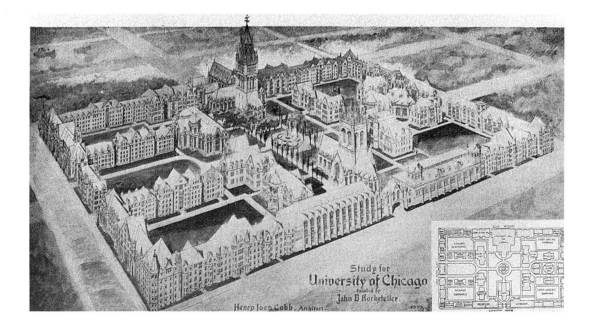

Study for
University of Chicago
Erected for
John D Rockefeller.

Henry Ives Cobb, Architect.

ner in which "the most modern knowledge and experience have entered into the adaptation" of classical architecture.[111] Many educated Americans judged the fair and its classical design to be a high point in the development of taste in their nation. Thus, it was the academic classicism popularized at the 1893 exposition that was the logical choice for Columbia's great metropolitan campus.

Given all of these considerations, it was clear that McKim was the appropriate architect for Columbia. Haight's work was not consistent with the school's new forward-looking vision. Not only was his choice of the Collegiate Gothic a return to Columbia's past, but also his design proposal was uninspired. Although Hunt was a leading proponent of classical and Renaissance design and was responsible for the most prominent building at the World's Columbian Exposition, he had not provided the trustees with especially creative design ideas and, as an older architect, he was not among the leaders of the new generation who could provide a progressive university with new ideas. In addition, in 1893 Hunt was in ill health, as the Committee on Buildings and Grounds noted (he would die only two years later), and could not be counted on to guide Columbia through years of construction.[112] Thus, Charles McKim and his firm were the logical choice. Not only was McKim, Mead & White a leading proponent of monumental classicism as an expression of America's growing power and prestige, but also McKim was a well-liked individual who could easily work with Low and the other trustees. McKim's creative ideas also assured that, should adequate funds be raised, Columbia would be housed in a complex of buildings that would be appropriate for what was envisioned as the great university of the leading metropolis of North America. The completion of an impressive campus, representative of the college's paramount importance in New York City, was especially important because in early 1892, Columbia's rival, New York University, announced that McKim's partner Stanford White would design its new Bronx campus.[113] It is indeed one of the great ironies of late-nineteenth-century American architecture that the same firm, albeit different senior partners, was commissioned to design the campuses of these rival institutions that had recently rejected a merger proposal. In November 1893 Columbia officially engaged McKim to plan an urban campus that would efficiently exploit the limited space available on Morningside Heights, rival in grandeur the complex planned for NYU, and visually establish Columbia as a major institutional presence in the city.[114]

McKim Designs Columbia

McKim and Low worked closely together, planning a campus that would efficiently utilize the limited space on Morningside Heights and create a complex of great architectural distinction. The two men developed a close rapport which enabled them to resolve problematic design issues without rancor. Low protected McKim from criticism leveled at his designs by Ware and especially by Pine, particularly in 1894, when Low requested that Pine refrain from mounting an individual campaign for design changes. Low told Pine that he and other trustees must "make me the medium of communication with the architect." [115] On May 7, 1894, McKim, Mead & White submitted a proposal for the arrangement of buildings to the Board of Trustees (figure 4.8). [116]

The basic feature of the plan was the placement of buildings around four courts or quadrangles, all of which were set on a platform on the lower two-thirds of the plot: a large southern entrance court focusing on a massive rectilinear library building; a secondary court to the north, bounded on the south by the rear elevation of the library and on the north by a unified dining hall, gymnasium, and academic theater structure (soon to be named University Hall) arranged longitudinally; and two long narrow side courts, each bounded by six classroom structures and one formal building (the chapel to the east and an assembly hall to the west). Secondary entrances led from Amsterdam Avenue and Broadway into these quadrangles. The south court was not fully opened to 116th Street. Instead, an administration building and a house for the university president were placed along the street. Three relatively narrow staircases flanked these buildings and led from the public street onto the court.

Certain aspects of McKim's initial plan were not fully successful and clearly needed additional consideration. For example, Columbia required a striking central building to create a strong image for the college, but the rather stolid library proposal did not adequately serve this purpose. The ill-proportioned stair leading from the court to the library and the awkward scale of the side quadrangles also marred the harmony of the design. Further, the close lateral relationship of the assembly hall, library, and chapel near the center of the platform, with only modest passageways between, created a wall dividing the campus into two distinct sections, interrupting the spatial flow.

McKim and his assistants, William Kendall, Austin Lord, and Egerton Swartwout, worked on addressing the problems with the initial campus plan, as well as designing the facades of the library, University Hall, and two prototypical classroom buildings. Low was especially concerned about these subsidiary classroom structures, admonishing

FIGURE 4.8
McKim, Mead & White's
first proposal for the
arrangement of buildings
on the Columbia
campus, May 1894;
dotted lines indicate
asylum buildings.

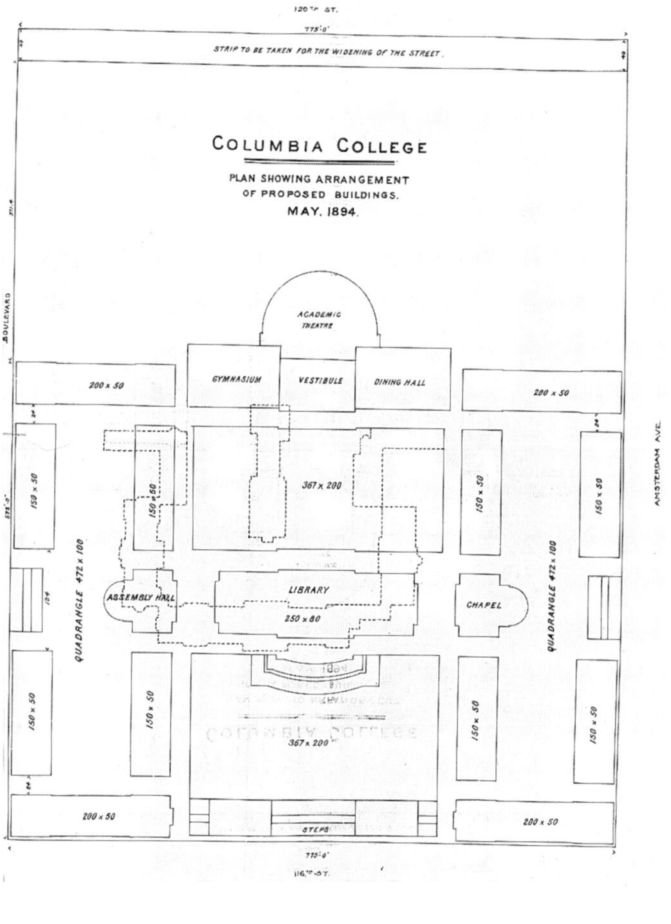

McKim "not [to] overlook the two typical buildings of which we spoke. More depends on those facades, or elevations, than perhaps we realize."[117] McKim was also dissatisfied with the design of the library and spent much time rethinking its form. He wrote to his partner William Rutherford Mead in July that "The Library has undergone many changes and at one time . . . I felt sick of it . . . but last week we struck it and are now awaiting official notice to commence working drawings."[118] In late September 1894 a final plan was submitted to the Building Committee and, on October 1, it was approved by the Board of Trustees (figure 4.9).[119]

McKim's final plan proposed that Columbia build an impressive formal ensemble focusing on a monumental classical library. It is not surprising that McKim chose the library as the central feature, since both he and Low considered the library to be the most important building of a great academic institution. Thus, even though Columbia was still linked with the Episcopal Church, the library, not the chapel, would physically and symbolically dominate the campus. The design for the library was finalized in July and was, in McKim's words, "Roman in scale and, generally speaking, in type."[120] Its plan was that of a Greek-cross with angled corners, crowned by a shallow dome set on a drum articulated with large half-round windows. The facade (figure 4.10), facing south toward the entrance to the campus and the city beyond, would be embellished with a portico of ten Greek Ionic columns. Unlike the rectilinear library in the earlier plan, which had been squeezed into a dense arrangement of buildings, this library is clearly the dominant structure on the campus. In addition, its compact centralized form opens up the spatial relationships of the ensemble of buildings, permitting views to subsidiary buildings and creating an open flow of space.

McKim's library adapts features from two of the most important ancient Roman buildings, the Pantheon and the Baths of Caracalla, both of which represent aspects of ancient culture that were also to be embodied in the library. The basic form of a centralized structure with a shallow dome is derived from the Pantheon, perhaps the greatest surviving monument from ancient

FIGURE 4.9
McKim, Mead & White's final plan for the Columbia campus, September 1894.

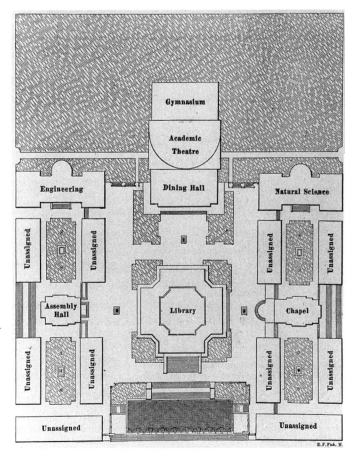

Rome. The Pantheon had long been valued as a symbol of the greatness of classical civilization serving, for example, as the model for Thomas Jefferson's Rotunda at the University of Virginia.[121] McKim explicitly drew a parallel between
the Columbia library and Roman baths, such as the Baths of Caracalla, the
grandest of the ancient thermae. The design of the great half-round windows
on the drum of the library dome is clearly modelled on those of the baths. The
architect reminded the trustees that besides being places of physical culture, the
baths were public libraries and academies where public lectures were delivered
and philosophers held court. He also observed that they were "provided with
every possible comfort and accommodation to insure the health of the body
and the education of the mind." He specifically requested that the trustees "note
as a precedent in the use of architectural forms drawn from these sources, their
appropriateness in view of the similarity in aim."[122]

McKim's adoption of a centrally planned library also placed this building
within a long history of library design. For example, architect Egerton Swartwout, a draftsman in the McKim, Mead & White office, reported that James
Gibbs's Radcliffe Camera (1737– 49) at Oxford was studied.[123] Prominent recent
libraries with central reading rooms and separate book stacks also probably
influenced McKim and his assistants, notably the British Museum Library, dating from 1854–56, and the Library of Congress, which was nearing completion
at the time McKim, Mead & White was working on the Columbia proposal.[124]
In addition, at the time that McKim and his team were perfecting their Columbia library proposal, Stanford White had already designed a centralized domed
library on a Greek-cross plan for rival New York University.[125]

FIGURE 4.10
Design for Low Library
and South Court with
proposed gates on
116th Street.

The imposing design of the Columbia library demanded an equally impressive approach. Accordingly, McKim radically reconfigured the original plan for the entry court, removing the administration building and president's house from the 116th Street frontage and incorporating an enormous piazza and series of stairways culminating at the portico of the library. With this new entry configuration, McKim created one of the most dramatic and awe-inspiring progressions of architectural spaces in America. The architect also significantly changed the placement of the campus's three secondary structures—the assembly hall, chapel, and University Hall—in order to enhance the setting of the library and improve the spatial arrangement of the campus. The chapel and assembly hall, originally squeezed close to the library, were pulled back, creating small square courts in front of each structure and providing each of these important buildings with an appropriately imposing setting. This reconfiguration also divided the two awkwardly scaled side quadrangles of the original plan into four more intimate courts or quadrangles. Each of these was to be enclosed by three Renaissance-inspired classroom buildings and the side of the assembly hall or chapel (figure 5.21). The landscaped courts would provide places of quiet seclusion for the students and faculty, in contrast to the grander, more public entry court. Finally, University Hall, to the rear of the library, was reconfigured so that rather than a wide front elevation facing the library, a narrower facade faced south, thus opening views on either side of the building toward the landscaped northern portion of the site generally referred to as the "green" or the "grove," which was reserved for future construction (figure 4.11).

The fifteen buildings that were to enframe the library were carefully de-

FIGURE 4.11
The Green, c. 1910–15
with Teachers College at
right.

FIGURE 4.12
Columbia University
campus from Broadway,
1907; from left,
Havemeyer, Engineering
(now Mathematics), Earl,
and the School of Mines
(now Lewisohn). The
landscaped garden and
vacant lot are part of
Barnard's campus.

FIGURE 4.13
Broadway and West 116th
Street entrance to the
Columbia campus, with
the School of Business
(now Dodge Hall) left
and Kent Hall right, late
1920s.

signed to provide a unified ensemble. The twelve classroom structures were to harmonize in size, massing, materials, and detail, but each was also to have an individualized design. The actual form of the facade of each building depended on its location within the ensemble. McKim developed an architectural hierarchy among these subsidiary structures. The most important of the secondary buildings were the specialized structures located immediately east, west, and north of the library—the chapel (figure 5.12), assembly hall (now Earl Hall; figure 5.1), and University Hall (figure 4.29). Each would have an individualized design that would complement the design of the library. Like the library itself, each was planned with a colonnade extending across its front facade. The chapel and assembly hall were to be flanked by the four inner classroom buildings (only Avery Hall was built; figure 5.20), each of which was to be entered through a monumental columned portico. Thus, a virtually continuous colonnade would form a noble setting for the library.

In the hierarchy of classroom buildings, the most significant were the two at the south end of the campus, anchoring the approaches along 116th Street from Amsterdam Avenue and Broadway (now Dodge Hall and Kent Hall). These buildings were the most visible components of the complex when viewed from the major north-south public thoroughfares that flank the campus and from 116th Street, which was at that time a public street, on which these structures fronted. When viewed from the south, the buildings would appear to flank the library (figure 5.9). Thus, each was designed with a two-story colonnade on the 116th Street elevation (figure 4.13), on the second and third stories, which appear to extend the library's colonnade virtually the full width of the campus. These buildings also have monumental entrance porticos facing north onto the campus (figure 5.18). The two classroom buildings that demarcate the north end of the complex (now Schermerhorn Hall and Havemeyer Hall) lack such grand entry porticos, but they are the most boldly massed of the twelve classroom structures (figures 4.17 and 4.19). Each has projecting end pavilions, a central pavilion crowned by a pediment, heavy sculptural detail, and a semicircular rear projection housing a large lecture hall that extends onto the lower classroom level.[126] The inner classroom buildings (now Fayerweather Hall, Mathematics Hall, Lewisohn Hall, and Philosophy Hall) were to be more modest structures, with campus facades that are flatter and less heavily detailed (figures 4.19, 5.17, and 5.19). This design choice was appropriate since, once the entire campus was completed, their facades would face onto courtyards and would be barely visible from the main campus walkways. However, since these buildings are set at the edges of the campus, fronting onto Broadway or Amsterdam Avenue, these elevations were designed with high granite bases contributing to the effect of a walled enclosure that can only be penetrated at specific entry points, each clearly marked by a gate (figure 4.12).

In order to appreciate fully the success of McKim's plan, it must be remembered that in 1894, when he laid out the campus, West 116th Street was a public thoroughfare and the land to the south was not owned by the college and its future use was unknown.[127] A visitor arriving at Broadway and 116th Street would have approached the center of the campus by walking eastward alongside the high granite wall of a classroom building (what is now Dodge Hall; figure 4.13).[128] The only other campus building that would be visible is the corresponding building at the corner of Amsterdam Avenue (now Kent Hall). The presence of a similarly designed building at each of these corners immediately establishes the overall symmetry of the campus plan. However, the placement and length of the 116th Street buildings also mask the breadth of the interior campus. Indeed, the visitor's eye might easily ignore the interior campus altogether and be pulled along 116th Street toward the horizon if not for one especially subtle feature.

McKim draws attention to the enclosed campus by placing a huge stone urn high up on a pedestal near the corner of the side elevation of the classroom building on 116th Street at the opposite side of the campus (from Broadway one would see the urn adjacent to the side elevation of Kent Hall; figure 4.13). This urn, the only significant architectural feature visible from 116th Street and Broadway, provides the first clue to the presence of an interior space and serves to draw the visitor forward toward it. By the time the visitor has reached the center of Dodge Hall, McKim has still provided very little additional information about the campus. Another urn, located several yards north of the first urn, can now be seen, pulling one's eyes further in toward the enclosed campus. Granite walls and a staircase leading up to the main platform then indicate to the visitor that the campus is arrayed on several levels, but neither the full width nor the depth of the court is yet revealed. As the visitor walks further along, the extent of the single

low staircase leading from 116th Street to the main plaza gradually becomes visible, indicating the width of the interior court. However, most of the interior space still remains hidden. More of the court comes slowly into view only as the visitor approaches the end of the classroom building. Yet it is only at the last moment that the full scale of the design suddenly explodes into view, sweeping one's gaze over the lower court and up the long flights of stairs to the portico and dome of the library (figure 4.14).

The visitor is then invited up onto the court by a low flight of stairs that runs along 116th Street (figure 4.14). This court, which resembles such great European urban spaces as the Piazza Navona in Rome, provides a public space in which the academic community and the general public can mingle, share marble benches, or linger by the fountains that punctuate the space. The Roman-inspired herringbone-patterned brick paving of this impressive space further accentuates the classical nature of the design.[129] McKim had proposed an enormous iron fence in front of the piazza (figure 4.10 above), but Low objected to this feature, probably because it seemed to create a private enclave and not a great public forecourt for the college.[130]

While the open court (known as South Court) welcomes the public, the upper terrace containing the college buildings does not. This academic precinct is a more cloistered environment, separated from the public court by a high, more

FIGURE 4.14
Low Library and
South Court, c. 1900;
Engineering Hall and the
Bloomingdale Asylum's
West Hall are visible
at left.

daunting, and less inviting, staircase. Students and faculty, climbing the stairs toward the terrace, pass *Alma Mater* (figure 4.15), Daniel Chester French's sculptural embodiment of the institution cast in bronze that was originally "heavily plated with pure gold leaf and toned to a dull, uniform finish."[131] McKim had planned a statue that was symbolic of the university for a site at the center of the stair, but the actual design was not chosen until 1900, when Harriette Goelet and her children offered to pay for the statue as a memorial to their husband and father Robert Goelet.[132] McKim was concerned about the quality of this statue since it would be sited in such a prominent location. He reported that he went to see French's proposal "in some fear and trembling, feeling that upon Mr. French depended the final making or marring of the whole composition of the Court and Library upon which we had worked so long."[133] McKim was "delighted" with French's "creation [of] a figure dignified, classic and stately . . . exhibiting as much perception of the spirit and freedom of the Greek as any modern can."[134] The completed sculpture was unveiled during commencement exercises in 1903.

Alma Mater is a woman robed in an academic gown, regally sitting upon a throne. In one arm she holds a scepter surmounted by a crown, representing King's College, while the other arm is outstretched, welcoming members of the academic community. An open book of learning sits on her lap and flaming torches of truth, set on the arms of her throne, light the way to knowledge. Knowledge, however, does not come easily. The student must search the folds of Alma Mater's dress to find the hidden owl of wisdom, just as one must search for knowledge in one's studies.[135] After passing *Alma Mater* and reaching the campus level, the seeker after academic knowledge must climb an even longer stairway, symbolically a "stairway to knowledge," to reach the entrance to the library. From the top of the stairs, members of the select Columbia community could turn and look out over New York, secure in the belief that they were contributing to the

FIGURE 4.15
Alma Mater, c. 1903.

rapid transformation of their city into a world center of intellectual and professional endeavor.

The Columbia campus was the first monumental urban ensemble designed in America following the World's Columbian Exposition. Through McKim's design, the Beaux-Arts ideal of urban spaces arranged along axial vistas lined with impressive classical buildings that had defined the temporary city in Chicago was translated into a permanent university campus. Richard Morris Hunt's great domed Administration Building, the focus of the major vista at the exposition, was translated by McKim into a library rising above a vast court.[136] Just as the exposition had been an attempt by America's arbiters of taste to re-create the glories of European culture in the New World, so too McKim's design for Columbia, with its grand European piazza and classical library, explicitly placed the expanding college in the tradition of European culture and sought to recast Columbia as a rival to the universities of the Old World.

McKim's final plan was initially received with great praise. Even Pine was impressed, expressing to Low his "admiration of the wonderful piece of work which you have accomplished."[137] The plans received extensive coverage in newspapers and in national magazines, with reports, often accompanied by drawings, describing the campus in detail.[138] However, many design issues remained to be resolved and Pine's admiration turned out to be short lived. He soon became a vocal critic of aspects of the proposal. Other trustees also raised a number of reservations. Although Low publicly defended McKim, he could not ignore the specific critical comments of the trustees and he dutifully asked McKim to justify each of the contested aspects of the design. McKim patiently replied to each concern, presenting architectural history lessons to the trustees that justified his choice of form or detail by placing it in its historical context. His charm and persuasiveness eventually prevailed regarding almost every disputed issue.

The concerns of the trustees centered around two major aspects of the proposal—the low dome on the library and the expansiveness of South Court, with its wide stairway at 116th Street. The criticism of the shallow dome was not surprising since, according to Columbia architecture professor A. D. F. Hamlin, the shallow dome had become popular only after its introduction at the World's Columbian Exposition, where such domes were employed on McKim's Agriculture Building and Charles Atwood's Art Palace.[139] Thus, many of the trustees were not as familiar with this form as they were with the more typical high dome. McKim directed his critics' attention to the low Roman dome, which he described as "the classic dome par excellence . . . [and] of a higher order of composition and much more monumental in its character than the later forms." He specifically referred the trustees to the low domes on the Pantheon and the baths of Agrippa and Caracalla, and particularly to the low dome of St. Sophia, "the last note of the classic dome, [which] is usually regarded as the most perfect dome in the world."[140]

Criticisms of the South Court were primarily generated by three aspects of its design: the width of the low flight of stairs, the uneven rise of the stairs due to a grade change along 116th Street, and what Pine noted was "its expanse of pavement [which] would make the court a desert of stone."[141] In response to the criticism of the stairs, McKim again called upon historic precedents, suggesting comparisons with Versailles, St. Mark's in Venice, and St. Peter's and Santa Maria Maggiore in Rome with their wide, low stairs; and with St. Peter's, the Grand Trianon at Versailles, the New Market and Loggia of S. Paolo in Florence, and, closer to home, with McKim's own Boston Public Library, all of which had stairs of uneven height.[142]

As for the scale of the court, McKim was most emphatic in his defense of the plan, praising the formality of his design and describing it as "the vestibule so to speak of the whole University" creating "the most natural arrangement for showing off to the best advantage all the buildings."[143] He again cited historical sources in urban architecture for this plan, including the Louvre, Sorbonne, St. Mark's, and St. Peter's, which "no one ever thinks of calling 'deserts of stone.'"[144] Nevertheless, Pine suggested to Low that he ask Frederick Law Olmsted to review the court design. While Low initially balked at this idea, he eventually wrote to Olmsted, Olmsted & Eliot requesting a review of the plans for the court and adjoining stairs.[145] The landscape architects generally supported McKim, referring to the stairs as "simple, dignified and convenient" and asserting that the criticism of the expansive plaza "holds as to almost all noble and dignified streets and public spaces in cities." They further assured Low that "the advantages will in the long run far outweigh [the disadvantages]."[146]

The Olmsted firm had only one suggestion, the addition of fountains, an idea that McKim immediately incorporated into his plan with the addition of a pair of round granite basins with simple Renaissance-inspired fountains that once forcefully spouted water (figure 4.16).[147] The response of the Olmsted firm

FIGURE 4.16
South Court fountain with School of Mines (now Lewisohn Hall) at rear, c. 1910.

apparently assuaged the concerns of most of the trustees and they moved ahead with plans for the actual construction of the new Columbia.

Building Columbia

In the early autumn of 1894, as McKim, Mead & White was completing the final designs for Columbia, a potential crisis almost derailed the project even before construction could begin—the possibility that Low might resign as president in order to run as a reform candidate for mayor of New York. In the spring of 1894 a group of prominent New Yorkers privately offered Low the mayoral nomination, arguing, according to Low, "that in their judgement I was perhaps the only person in the city upon whom all the anti-Tammany elements could be united in the coming campaign."[148] Low was a dynamic, well-respected public figure who had received a great deal of positive press attention since his ascension to the presidency of Columbia. From his tenure as mayor of Brooklyn, he was perceived as a successful anti-Tammany reformer with progressive ideas and experience governing a large municipality. Thus, he was judged to be an ideal candidate to defeat the entrenched Tammany Hall machine. Low's resignation would have been a terrible blow to the dream of a new Columbia campus. It was his vision and energy and his personal involvement in almost every detail of the proposed move and choice of an appropriate design that had energized the institution. It was not clear that there was anyone else with such dedication and drive who could carry the project to fruition.

Low undoubtedly experienced a tremendous sense of conflict between his commitment to Columbia and the potential for accomplishing great things as the leader of the city. Nevertheless, he assured Columbia trustee Joseph W. Harper in May 1894 that he would not forsake Columbia at this crucial period in its history.[149] However, efforts to induce Low to run for the mayoralty continued. In August, the executive committee of the Citizens' Alliance, a prominent reform organization, unanimously adopted a resolution endorsing Low's nomination for mayor.[150] He again rejected the offer, but shrewdly left the door open to the possibility of accepting the nomination should public pressure make it difficult to refuse. Low informed Dean Burgess, "if a situation arises in which it becomes clear that a union against Tammany can be made around me and not around anybody else, . . . I should feel obliged at every sacrifice to answer the call."[151] Low discussed this possibility with the trustees who, according to Nicholas Murray Butler, were not happy with the possibility of losing Low at such a crucial juncture in Columbia's rejuvenation.[152] Fortunately for Columbia, the reformers were able to rally behind William L. Strong, permitting Low to focus his efforts on translating McKim's plan from paper to bricks and mortar.[153]

From the start of planning, the trustees had realized that completion of the campus plan would take many years. In order to facilitate the construction of discrete elements of the campus, McKim designed twelve individual classroom pavilions and four separate structures for general campus activities. The trustees decided to begin construction with the library, University Hall (which would incorporate the campus power plant and gymnasium in its basement), and four classroom buildings. Most of the new classroom buildings were planned specifically for departments that required custom-built laboratories, since it was decided that until money was available to erect additional classrooms, liberal arts departments could be temporarily housed in the remaining Bloomingdale Asylum buildings.[154] The first classroom pavilions would be erected at the north end of the platform, with later construction proceeding toward the south.

In the initial phase of construction, Columbia would build the university's infrastructure, including the main platform on which the campus would sit amd the boiler facility using its own funds. This created the framework for the construction of the buildings. Unfortunately, the college did not yet have funds for the library or University Hall and had only enough money to erect two of the four proposed classroom structures.[155] The money for one of the classroom buildings came from the 1891 bequest of Daniel B. Fayerweather which the trustees decided to put toward the construction of a home for the physics department (now Fayerweather Hall).[156] Before actual building construction could begin, the trustees had to raise the funds for the other buildings, especially the library, without which, they felt, the project should not proceed. Since Columbia had not been successful in attracting large numbers of donors to support the purchase of the Morningside site, which had been made possible only by the donations of a few wealthy supporters and a $1 million mortgage, the trustees feared that there would be similar difficulties in attracting financial support in 1894 to finance construction of the campus. However, McKim's plans were so compelling that Pine, even with his reservations about some aspects of the design, had no doubt "that they will commend themselves to our prospective benefactors to such an extent as will ensure the means for their construction."[157]

Seth Low staked his reputation on the successful development of the Morningside Heights campus. He had rejected the entreaties of prominent local reformers that he leave Columbia and run for mayor in order to complete the transformation of his alma mater. Yet, in early 1895, without the money to complete the first phase of construction, the success of his vision for Columbia was at risk. When the final plans had been announced to the public in October 1894, Low stated that "It is my earnest hope that the buildings to be erected . . . will come to the college, without exception, by gift."[158] Despite a depressed economy in 1895, Low continued to be optimistic, "still entertain[ing] the hope that, to a considerable extent at all events, the buildings which are immediately necessary will be given to the College."[159] However, no gifts were immediately forthcoming and Low's reputation as an effective leader was in question. Finally, on April 20, 1895, board chairman William C. Schermerhorn, the one alumnus who had generously donated money for the purchase of the Morningside property, broke this stalemate, offering $300,000 for a natural science building.[160] This gift was a positive development, but it was still not clear where money would come from for the library, the most important academic structure at any university and the centerpiece of McKim's design. Low's solution to this problem was dramatic and, apparently, a surprise to most of the trustees. On May 6, 1895, Low announced that he would personally give up to $1 million for the construction of the library as a memorial to his father, "a merchant who taught his son to value the things for which Columbia College stands."[161]

With Low's generous gift, Columbia could begin construction on the new campus buildings. Such generosity to Columbia was typical of Low's civic-minded character. He had withdrawn from his family's business enterprises to dedicate himself to political and social reform and then to the creation of a great urban university. After inheriting his father's fortune in 1893, Low was able to actually effect his plans for Columbia and to save the project on which he had staked his reputation. There is no evidence that Low donated the library as a means of furthering his political career, as has been suggested.[162] He had, after all, recently declined the entreaties of leading reformers and rejected a run for political office. Thus, there was no basis in 1895 to believe that Low was calculating a future political career or would again consider running for mayor. Rather, the gift was the culmination of Low's efforts to establish Columbia as the preeminent academic institution in the preeminent city of North America.

The outpouring of praise for Low's generosity was overwhelming. Newspapers and magazines hailed this "great public benefaction" that "is so magnificent as to make the reader catch his breath."[163] Low received appreciative letters from all over the country, none perhaps as poignant as that of *Century Magazine* publisher Richard Watson Gilder, who asserted that Low's gift "makes us able to hold up our heads as Americans and as citizens of New York."[164] McKim, too, was moved, informing Low "that if, when the Library building shall be completed, your confidence in our firm prove not to have been misplaced, I shall regard it one of the greatest happinesses of my life."[165] To some apologists for America's mercantile wealth, Low's lavish gift of money from his father's trading fortune, "legitimately acquired through hard work and shrewd business deals rather than through the exploitation of labor," was a vindication of American commerce.[166] "There is no blood upon this gift of a million. It is pure gold," affirmed the *Commercial Advertiser,* the voice of New York City's business community.[167] The *Boston Evening Transcript* was even more direct, noting the repugnance with which some people held Standard Oil founder John D. Rockefeller because of the exploitative methods that he had employed in acquiring the wealth that had been used to establish the University of Chicago. In contrast, commented the author of the *Transcript* article, "The severest critic among us . . . can in nowise reproach Mr. Low with the source of his wealth."[168]

Although construction was now underway on the platform and power house and funding was assured for the library and for the first two classroom buildings, the trustees could not be complacent. Speaking on behalf of the trustees, John Pine used the recent Low and Schermerhorn gifts as an opportunity to remind New Yorkers that Columbia required additional contributions to complete the first phase of construction "in a way worthy of the great city to which it is a historic part." Pine estimated that $1.5 million was needed and appealed "to the generous people of New-York who are proud of their city" for gifts.[169]

Before construction on any of the buildings could begin, many specific decisions about the designs still needed to be resolved. No decision was more important than that regarding the choice of facade materials. Almost as soon as McKim, Mead & White had submitted the final design proposal in October 1894, Low expressed concern about the choice of materials, requesting from McKim studies on how to combine brick and marble or brick and stone on the subsidiary buildings if a single material was chosen for the library, or how he would use brick and stone on the library if a less expensive alternative was necessary.[170] Low was apprehensive about the use of marble, because of its expense. Instead, he observed that "My own preference is for as large a use of brick in all the buildings as is consistent with a fine effect" and even offered to visit Independence Hall in Philadelphia or other buildings that McKim might suggest in order to adequately study the use of this material.[171] McKim agreed with Low on the importance of choosing the correct materials, asserting that "No question has arisen since the selection of the site itself and the distribution of the buildings so fundamental and important to the successful issue of the undertaking as this one of materials."[172] He felt that the municipal character of the planned complex, its symmetrical massing, and its commanding site demanded "the use of one material having a monumental character; or if this is not possible, then a combination with brick."[173]

By the end of 1894 the trustees had resolved that the library would be erected of limestone (with granite for the base), since limestone was strong, durable, beautiful, and workable, but that brick with limestone trim would satisfy for all of the other buildings in order to control costs.[174] The trustees then began examining buildings faced with brick as possible models for the facades of Columbia's buildings. Pine praised McKim's recently completed Harvard Club for its warm combination of brick and limestone, while Low suggested as a model the Berwind House on Fifth Avenue and East 64th Street with its dark red brick and black mortar.[175] Only when construction was about to begin on the first classroom buildings in early 1896 did the trustees finally choose Harvard brick, a hand-pressed, burned, dark red brick that resembles the brick used on the colonial buildings of Harvard Yard.[176]

This decision to use brick on the classroom buildings was somewhat problematic, since they were to be Renaissance in character. Few of the great monuments of the Italian Renaissance were faced with brick. Most were either entirely faced with stone or with stucco imitation of stone. McKim resolved this problem by designing the facades of the classroom buildings in an innovative hybrid design that combines Italian Renaissance massing and ornamental detail with Colonial-inspired brickwork (figure 4.17). The rectilinear massing of each of these buildings is strongly influenced by Renaissance design, as is the symmetry of each facade, the rhythm of window and door openings, and the preponderance of such classical ornamental details as sculptural window enframements, quoins, pediments, and rusticated stone blocks. Most of the contemporary descriptions of the classroom buildings note this affinity with Renaissance architecture.[177] However, William Ware correctly noted that the buildings have an "almost Colonial character."[178] This "colonial character" resulted from the use of Harvard brick. With the decision to use brick and not stone as the predominant material of the buildings set around the library, McKim looked to American collegiate architecture for inspiration. McKim had briefly been a student at Harvard and, by 1895, had designed several Colonial-inspired gates around the eighteenth-century Harvard Yard, employing the same variegated colors and textures of the handmade early American brick used on the original Harvard Yard buildings and also traditional Colonial-era Flemish bond (i.e., long bricks alternating with short bricks).[179] McKim adopted similar brickwork for Columbia's buildings, combining this Colonial-inspired use of brick with the classical and Renaissance details appropriate to buildings that would surround his great classical library, thus lending the buildings what Columbia architecture professor A. D. F. Hamlin referred to as their "half-Georgian" character.[180] This combination of variegated dark red colonial-inspired brick laid in Flemish bond with heavy white limestone Renaissance detail established a new mode of design that influenced other architects in New York, notably McKim's friends George Fletcher Babb and Walter Cook, who employed this style at their Fifth Avenue mansion for Andrew Carnegie (1899–1903), and Ernest Flagg, who incorporated brick and bold limestone detail at his Alfred Corning Clark House (1898–1900) on Riverside Drive.[181]

While McKim and the Columbia trustees were deciding what materials to use, other aspects of the project had been going forward. By the fall of 1895 work had progressed on the campus infrastructure: construction of the platform had begun, excavations for the library's foundation were underway, sewer and water lines were being laid, the retaining wall at 119th Street had been completed, and work on the fence along the east, west, and north perimeters of the site

FIGURE 4.17
Schermerhorn Hall,
c. 1902.

had started.[182] Low had hoped to hold a ceremony in late 1895 to celebrate the laying of the library's cornerstone, but this plan was abandoned when NYU announced a "great opening" in October, with the mayor and governor in attendance. Low told McKim that he was "most unwilling to interfere with the eclat of such an occasion by preparing for one so similar," but he must also have been concerned that Columbia's ceremony might easily have been overshadowed by NYU's earlier event.[183] Thus, the cornerstone of the library was laid in a small private ceremony in December. A grand public event dedicating the campus site and celebrating the laying of the cornerstones of Schermerhorn and Fayerweather halls was not held until May 2, 1896.[184]

By May 1896, when the dedication ceremony was held, the university had much to be thankful for. Not only had Low's gift of the library and Schermerhorn's for a classroom building made construction possible, but planning was also underway for a gymnasium in the semicircular north end of the basement of the proposed University Hall. The gymnasium was to include a play space with a gallery incorporating an indoor running track that was supported by Doric columns (figure 4.18) and, set one level below, a semicircular swimming pool also adorned with marble Doric columns, underlining the rela-

FIGURE 4.18
Gymnasium, c. 1900.

FIGURE 4.19
Engineering Hall (now Mathematics Hall) and Havemeyer Hall, c. 1910–15.

tionship between Columbia's classical buildings and the Roman thermae.[185] In addition, two classroom structures were now planned for the northwest corner of the platform (figure 4.19). Engineering Hall (now Mathematics Hall) was to be paid for from the college's own funds.[186] The second building, planned for the chemistry department, was to be financed from a memorial gift from the four sons, two daughters, and nephew of Frederick Christian Havemeyer, class of 1825.[187] Design for these two buildings began in February 1896 as McKim was setting off for a cruise up the Nile. Stanford White took temporary charge of the chemistry building's design and William Rutherford Mead that of the engineering building.[188] Each partner adhered to McKim's design precedents. Havemeyer Hall, and its companion on the opposite side of the campus, Schermerhorn Hall, were built at the edge of the terrace, overlooking the

Green. Each has a semicircular extension that incorporated a large lecture hall with a shallow arched ceiling (figure 4.20).[189]

Early in 1897, just a few months after Havemeyer and Engineering were begun, another major step toward the completion of the campus was taken when the trustees announced that the college would pay for the construction of South Court in order to create a suitable approach to Low Library. McKim carefully

FIGURE 4.20
Lecture hall in
Havemeyer, unknown
date.

FIGURE 4.21
South Court with
original paving of red
Catskill brick and white
Joliet stone, 1904;
construction is
proceeding on the School
of Mines (now Lewisohn
Hall), visible at right.

planned a paving pattern consisting of brick laid on edge in a herringbone pattern set around panels of buff-colored Joliet [Illinois] limestone, forming "a great carpet of red and white panels" (figure 4.21).[190] The brick chosen was dark red Catskill [New York] brick with smooth surfaces and rounded corners. The same brick, with Joliet stone edges and curbs, was used for the campus's walks and secondary courts.[191] This use of brick and a light-colored stone created the same color effect as McKim had achieved on the classroom buildings by combining Harvard brick and limestone, thus linking the court's design to that of the rest of the campus.[192]

Once construction had finally started in late 1895 and early 1896, Low turned his attention to planning virtually every detail of the library, thus assuring that the building would be a fitting memorial to his father. McKim's plan for the interior of the library (figure 4.22) included a series of impressive public spaces

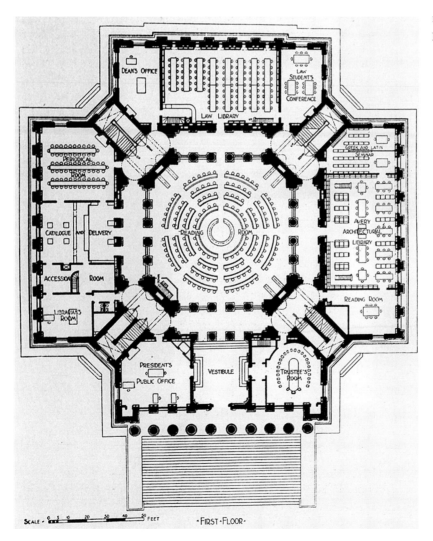

FIGURE 4.22
Plan of Low Library.

leading from the low entrance doors, through a highly ornate vestibule, then past a screen of columns into an ambulatory, then through another column screen into the central octagonal rotunda. Just as McKim had hidden the expansiveness of South Court from the pedestrian entering the campus (see above), the full breadth of the rotunda is not revealed until the last moment.

McKim had proposed entry into the library through a pair of great bronze doors, but Low, rejecting this as "out of harmony with our ideals and with the ideals of my father," chose, instead, more modest oak doors.[193] Once past the doors, the tall vestibule with its enormous hanging lamp provides an imposing entry to the building. The central feature of this room is a fluted column shaft supporting a bust of Minerva, goddess of wisdom, set in the center of a ring of brass zodiac signs by sculptor George William Maynard (class of 1859) that had been installed in McKim's New York State Building at the World's Columbian exposition and were donated to Columbia by their fabricator, John Williams.[194] The vestibule is flanked by imposing doors leading to two major administrative spaces, the president's public office to the left and the trustees' room to the right (figure 4.23). The latter is an intimate, artfully designed space evoking Columbia's eighteenth-century heritage. Paneled in beautifully carved oak provided by the decorating firm of Herter Brothers, the room's central feature is a Georgian mantel with broken pediment on which sits an iron crown

FIGURE 4.23
Trustees' Room, 1898.

preserved from King's College. The cornerstone of the original college building is set into the mantel, as is a portrait of Samuel Johnson, the institution's first president.[195]

The library's rotunda itself originally served as the main reading room (figure 4.24), with a round bookcase in the center surrounded by four concentric ranks of desks accommodating up to seventy-five students, an arrangement modeled after that of the reading room at the Library of Congress. The space is supported by four enormous stone piers between each of which are four massive Ionic columns. Oak bookcases were set between the columns and piers,

FIGURE 4.24
Low Library rotunda photographed after the addition of the central clock in 1900.

creating a sense of enclosure in the vast space. Sixteen classical statues of Istrian marble were to be installed on the parapets of the open galleries above each of these groups of columns, but only four statues were executed, including one donated by McKim as a gift to the university.[196] Two specialized libraries were placed in the arms of the Greek cross—the Law Library to the north and the Avery Architectural Library, with its ceiling beams inscribed with the names of architects, to the east (figure 4.25). Color was also an important aspect of the interior design of the library, not only in the choice of stone, but also regarding decoration of the walls. McKim hired mural painter Elmer E. Garnsey to execute a complex color scheme that was to harmonize the entire interior. Garnsey incorporated dull Pompeiian red, yellow, black, and various shades of white, all rubbed, glazed, and waxed "until the surface has the texture of an old billiard-ball."[197]

As construction on the library proceeded during 1896, several questions of crucial importance to the character of the final design required Low's input. Several times in this process, Low and McKim were forced to compromise in order to complete the building on schedule. First, as work on the walls and piers of the library proceeded, a decision on the engineering of the dome was re-

FIGURE 4.25
Avery Architectural
Library in east arm of
Low Library, c. 1900.

quired. McKim had originally proposed a concrete dome supported by iron trusses and clad in limestone. Ware, who almost never missed a chance to criticize McKim, disapproved of this proposal, finding it "disturbing and distasteful" since by using iron supports it did not follow traditional techniques of dome construction, and it was, therefore "not a real dome, . . . [but] only an ingenious contrivance to produce the effect of one."[198] In May 1896 McKim suggested a Guastavino tile dome, an alternative Ware approved of. However, the contractor, Norcross Brothers, perhaps America's most prestigious firm of contractors and builders, questioned this construction method, possibly because the firm was advocating an unreinforced concrete dome of its own devising.[199] After much discussion, McKim and Low approved the Norcross Brothers' design and amended the application they had submitted to the New York City Department of Buildings. In typical fashion, the Department of Buildings had trouble with such a novel design and the permit was delayed for several months. It was finally issued in November, but by then fear of frost, which would weaken the concrete, would have delayed construction until the spring. Instead, Norcross Brothers designed a more traditional outer dome of brick set in Portland cement, which was then covered with limestone facing (figure 4.26). Below the brick outer dome, a steel frame was constructed to support a false inner dome of plaster, which hangs 105.5 feet above the rotunda floor and was painted blue to resemble the night sky.[200]

Low's biggest disappointment came in the compromise involved in the selection of marble for the eighteen interior columns. Low had hoped that all of the columns would be made of green Connemara marble from Ireland, thought by many to be the world's most beautiful stone. Unfortunately, in June 1896 Columbia was informed that only two columns could be provided from this rare material (figure 4.27), probably because of the difficulty in quarrying pieces of the diameter required for the project.[201] Only a few weeks after Columbia had received the frustrating news about the Irish stone, NYU was able to get Connemara marble for the sixteen more slender columns of the rotunda of its new library. That the rival institution was able to acquire this beautiful marble must have been galling for Low. Stanford White particularly noted the competition between these two institutions when he gloated in a letter to NYU's Chancellor MacCracken, "I find that columns in [the] Library dome can be made of Connemara Irish Green Marble. . . . This is the marble they endeavored to use in Columbia, but which had to be abandoned because it was impossible to get the marble in so large diameter. It is the most beautiful green marble in the world, and it would be a great thing to use it after having had to give it up in Columbia."[202] Columbia's two extraordinary Connemara marble columns were placed in the most prominent position within Low Library, forming a screen that is visible as soon as one enters the building. Critic Charles H. Caffin enthused that "No description can give an adequate idea of their stateliness, the exquisite mystery of graded greens and grays and black, their tempestuous streakings and tender veining, and the perfect texture of their polished surface. The most heedless visitor cannot pass them unadmired, the connoisseur will be enthusiastic."[203]

With Connemara marble out of the question for the sixteen rotunda columns, Low settled on a green granite from Ascutney Mountain in Vermont. Fortunately, the subtle green Vermont granite chosen to harmonize with the Irish stone more closely resembles marble than more traditional granites. It proved an extraordinarily beautiful material. These magnificent columns, each capped by an Ionic capital of bronze plated in tawny gold, form an especially impressive frame for the reading room. As work on the library progressed, Low expressed his delight with the project. Upon returning from vacation in mid-September 1896 Low was inspired to write McKim that:

> I reached the city Wednesday evening, and yesterday morning went to the New Site. On account of the rain I saw everything under the worst pos-

FIGURE 4.26
Setting the last stone on the Low Library dome, June 14, 1897.

sible conditions, and yet I must tell you that the buildings surpass even my hopes. I was partially prepared for the progress of the Library by the photograph you brought to me in Boston, but no photograph can do justice to the building itself. I was much moved as I stood in the future reading room by the promise of its majestic proportions. I congratulate you very heartily.[204]

Columbia's trustees were very much concerned with providing adequate light for the reading room, an issue to which McKim devoted a great deal of attention. During the day, artificial light provided by individual desk lamps was augmented by natural illumination flowing through four huge half round windows below the dome. After dark, however, McKim "wanted to have a soft, general illumination for this space, independent of the special lighting for the reading tables, etc., and declared that there was no more beautiful light than moonlight, so he wanted moonlight."[205] To create this effect, McKim designed a wooden "moon" about seven feet in diameter, painted a grayish white, that was suspended from the dome on an invisible ¼-inch steel rope, creating the appearance that the "giant pearl, seen against the dark blue of the interior of the dome," was floating in the air. Eight arc lights, positioned in the balconies, beamed indirect light off of the globe providing "moonbeams" to illuminate the space (figure 4.28).[206]

FIGURE 4.27
Installation of the Connemara marble columns in the vestibule of Low Library, October 1, 1896.

One exterior design issue that continued to dog McKim and Low was their desire to place an extensive series of inscriptions on the entablatures and along the frieze of the library. Both Low and McKim were committed to this proposal, but they received little support from the trustees, who were divided regarding whether inscriptions would "cheapen the effect of a building otherwise dignified and impressive" and whether the proposed inscriptions should be in English or Latin.[207] McKim was adamant that the inscriptions were an important part of his design and that, as an artist, he was "entitled to have the building completed as he had designed it."[208] When the trustees rejected all inscriptions except that above the portico, Low suggested that McKim "enter upon a campaign of education."[209] Although the architect had earlier succeeded in guiding the trustees to accept his proposals for South Court and the library dome, he was unsuccessful regarding the library inscriptions.

Low Memorial Library was to be a symbol of Columbia's academic achievement and preeminence (or attempts at preeminence) as an institution and a monumental memorial to Abiel Abbot Low, but also was to be a functional building at the heart of the academic experience on the new campus. To this end, McKim provided a reading room for undergraduates set beneath the great dome, specialized law and architectural libraries occupying individual rooms in the arms of the cross, and seminar and study rooms placed on the upper floors. Extensive book stacks were located in the basement, on balconies, and in study rooms. Other spaces were temporarily given over to the faculties of political science and philosophy while they awaited the construction of their own buildings. Initially the library could accommodate about 450,000 books, with space for another 600,000 volumes to become available when the liberal arts departments vacated their temporary quarters. This capacity made Low Library second in size in the United States only to the Library of Congress.[210] For an institution that had only about 215,000 books in its collection in 1896 and was acquiring approximately 12,000 new volumes a year, the library was a facility that would, apparently, meet the university's needs for decades.[211] Indeed, early critical pronouncements applauded the library's extraordinary design. One commentator described it as "a utilitarian scheme artistically carried out."[212]

Low Library was designed to meet space demands based on late-nineteenth-century acquisition practices and the modest size of student enrollment at that time. Unfortunately, the library was not able to keep up with the demands caused by an explosion in book publishing and acquisitions that soon overwhelmed its capacity. In addition, since the expected move of the liberal arts departments did not occur because of a delay in construction of classroom buildings, the anticipated room for stack expansion was also delayed. Even more significantly, the university's rapidly increasing enrollment burdened the library with more students than could reasonably be accommodated. In 1898 the undergraduate school had only 326 students, but by 1915 1,118 students matriculated and enrollment in all programs at the Morningside Heights campus rose from 1,353 to 4,225.[213] As early as 1902 Low's successor as president, Nicholas Murray Butler, expressed concern for the crowded conditions in the library.[214] As these space problems with the building became apparent, its design began to be criticized. In 1902, for example, *American Architect* praised the monumental character of the design and the general arrangement of the reading rooms and study rooms, but also commented that "architecturally this building is very fine, and to obtain this fine effect it is evident that one or two utilitarian points have been rather sacrificed."[215] The harshest criticism came from architectural critic Montgomery Schuyler, who disliked the entire Columbia complex because Columbia had rejected his favored Collegiate Gothic style. In 1910 Schuyler sarcastically referred to a "French friend's" comment "that the library of Columbia is a 'library de luxe and not de books.'"[216] By the 1920s the cramped

FIGURE 4.28
Design of Low Library
rotunda with suspended
"moon."

conditions in the library had become critical, virtually paralyzing the facility. Finally, in 1931, design began on South Hall (now Butler Library; see chapter 5) to replace Low Library. Upon South Hall's completion in 1934, Low Memorial Library was transformed into a ceremonial and administrative center, and most of its desks, stacks, and other library furnishings were removed.

The only structure planned as part of the initial construction phase that was not built was University Hall, a failure that was the result of the inability of the alumni to raise the necessary funds. University Hall had been planned as a multipurpose building that would rise to the north of the library and anchor the north end of a large court (figure 4.29). It was to consist of a long limestone portico of twelve Corinthian columns, behind which would rise a central basilican pavilion flanked by heavy brick wings. This complex structure was to be built at the edge of the terrace so that the power plant and gymnasium could be placed on lower levels, separated by a service drive. The upper section, visible from the campus, would contain a monumental vaulted memorial hall that would serve as the university dining room and an academic theater seating 2,500 people, which could be used by the entire academic community for graduation and other special events. The idea for a building combining a theater, dining room, and memorial was adopted from Harvard's successful Memorial Hall, completed in 1874.[217] A dining room was especially important at Columbia since it was a school of "day scholars" located in an area that did not yet have any commercial development. Thus, it was necessary to provide the university community with a place to eat in a central location on the campus that would also en-

FIGURE 4.29
McKim, Mead & White's design for University Hall, c. 1897.

courage the development of college social life. The power plant and gymnasium, set below the main campus platform, were part of the first wave of construction.[218] Unfortunately, no alumni donations were forthcoming to complete the building. Construction plans were revived in 1899 and efforts to raise funds from the alumni resulted in contributions of only $1,000! Sufficient funds were available, however, to begin construction on the first story which included a modest refectory.[219] Completed in 1900, this fragment of McKim's larger project burned in 1914 and had to be rebuilt.[220] Although interest in completing University Hall continued, other pressing needs channeled funds elsewhere. In the 1920s President Butler again proposed completing University Hall, suggesting that it become an extension of the library. Finally, in the early 1960s, this "eyesore of the Columbia University campus" was demolished to be replaced by an even greater "eyesore," the Business School's Uris Hall, designed by Moore & Hutchins.[221]

On October 4, 1897, classes met for the first time on Morningside Heights, thus marking the completion of the first phase of campus construction and fulfilling Low's dream of moving Columbia to a monumental new urban campus (figure 4.30).[222] No grand public ceremony inaugurated the campus. Instead, "a simple service was held in the great reading-room of the new library," and Low gave a brief address to the assembled students, faculty, and trustees, welcoming them to Columbia's new home.[223]

FIGURE 4.30

Columbia College and its surroundings, looking northwest from Amsterdam Avenue and 115th Street, c. 1900. From left, Bloomingdale Asylum's Superintendent's House, Engineering, the asylum's West Hall, Low Library, the asylum's Macy Villa, Teachers College (at rear), chimney of Columbia's power house, Schermerhorn, and Fayerweather.

At a cost of $6,879,011.90, Low had discharged his commitment to the trustees to see Columbia successfully relocate to Morningside Heights when he had rejected the offer of a mayoral nomination.[224] With this goal accomplished, Low tendered his resignation on the day the campus was inaugurated in order to run as a reform candidate to be the first mayor of Greater New York.[225] The trustees chose to postpone consideration of Low's resignation until after the election, which, as it turned out, he lost, coming in second in a field of three candidates. The resignation was withdrawn and Low remained president until finally resigning four years later to run again for mayor—this time successfully.[226]

Although the college year opened with little fanfare, October 4, 1897 was one of the most significant days in Columbia's history. The school had at last found a home where it could take its place in the top rank of American universities and play a major role in the civic life of New York City. Columbia College joined Teachers College which had already occupied its new buildings on West 120th and 121st streets for several years (see chapter 6), and Barnard College which also moved to Morningside Heights in October 1897 (see chapter 6). Students arriving at the new colleges discovered a largely undeveloped neighborhood of vacant lots and farm plots, with the grand new institutional structures

FIGURE 4.31
Columbia College on October 1, 1897, three days before classes began, looking north from 114th Street.

contrasting dramatically with this semi-rural landscape (figure 4.31). The initial phase of Columbia's construction, successfully completed under Low's direction, set the stage for the expansion of the university over the next few decades as buildings that were part of McKim's initial plan were constructed and his plan was expanded onto surrounding blocks, extending Columbia's presence on Morningside Heights.

1931 - Butler

FIGURE 5.1
Earl Hall, c. 1910–15.

CHAPTER FIVE

Building for the Mind II

The Growth and Expansion of Columbia

WITH THE INAUGURATION OF CLASSES IN THE NEW MORNINGSIDE
Heights buildings in October 1897, Columbia was transformed from a modest
institution with antiquated facilities into a modern educational enterprise. Columbia had acquired a library of great magnificence, and classroom and laboratory buildings that were among the most advanced in the country. In addition, Barnard College and Teachers College had joined Columbia on Morningside Heights (see chapter 6), thus providing the seeds for the creation of an
academic neighborhood. However, many issues concerning the Columbia campus and its place in the Morningside Heights neighborhood remained unresolved. No provisions had been made for housing Columbia's students, many
of whom continued to reside with their parents or in shabby boarding houses
located at some distance from the campus. The trustees had to determine
whether Columbia should follow the example of other American colleges and
erect dormitories, or, in the spirit of continental European schools, have students live in the urban community and split their time between the academic
and civic realms. As described in chapter 4, the initial construction phase of the
campus had included only a small portion of the planned structures. The university was uncertain who would fund the remaining buildings of the original
plan which were needed for Columbia's continued growth. The chapel, symbol
of the college's historic roots in New York's Episcopal community, had yet to be
funded, nor were there funds for the student assembly hall or for classroom
buildings to house the undergraduate college and the university's liberal arts departments. With construction beginning on the subway along Broadway and
the resultant rise of property values in the neighborhood, Columbia was also
faced with resolving the long-delayed issue of land acquisition for expansion
before cost would make this prohibitive. It would fall to Columbia's new president, Nicholas Murray Butler, to resolve these issues and to find the capital to
fund the growth and expansion of the university.

Earl Hall: The First Addition on Morningside Heights

While Seth Low still guided Columbia through its first years on Morningside Heights, continuing his efforts at creating a great urban university that would play a key role in New York City affairs, only one additional building—the assembly or students hall, donated in 1900 by William Earl Dodge—was erected on the new campus before Low resigned in 1901 to run what would be a successful campaign for mayor.[1] The construction of what came to be known as Earl Hall on a key site to the west of the library completed an important piece of McKim's plan and provided a place for student activities (figure 5.1). The building was planned especially for activities of a religious nature and it embodied Low's goal of creating a university open to all qualified students regardless of their religious background.

William Earl Dodge, Jr., was the scion of one of the wealthiest mercantile and industrial families of America and an officer in the family's metallurgy firm of Phelps, Dodge & Co.[2] Dodge was a Presbyterian, active in the development and expansion of the Young Men's Christian Association in New York City. His daughter Grace had been the guiding force behind the establishment of Teachers College in the late 1880s (see chapter 6). Although Dodge was not a graduate of Columbia nor involved with its board of trustees, he was deeply committed to the advancement of religious causes and shared Low's liberal Christianity, respecting the spiritual beliefs of all and seeking to accommodate all beliefs within the framework of an institution of higher learning. Thus, despite his personal religious affiliation with the Presbyterian church, he offered Columbia $100,000 for the construction of a building for the spiritual development of the entire student body of Columbia and its affiliated colleges (Barnard College and Teachers College). He believed that this spiritual center would complement the intellectual and physical training provided in other campus buildings. Even though activities in the new students hall were to be directed by the YMCA, Dodge required as a term of his gift that Roman Catholic and Jewish students be permitted to hold meetings as freely as Protestant students. Dodge also hoped that women students at Barnard and Teachers would be as welcome in the hall as Columbia's men.[3] The building would contain reading and meeting rooms, but it would center on a hall where students could attend or participate in lectures, concerts, and debates. The trustees gratefully accepted Dodge's offer and hoped to dedicate the building with his surname, continuing a policy begun with Schermerhorn and Havemeyer halls of naming new buildings for their donors. Dodge demurred at such a public recognition, but finally agreed to the use of his middle name.[4]

Earl Hall was placed to the west of the library on a site occupied at that time by West Hall, the former John C. Green Memorial Building of the Bloomingdale Asylum, which had been adapted for classrooms. In order to preserve these classrooms as long as possible, Earl was constructed in two sections—first the central and rear portions that had no impact on West and then, after the demolition of the portion of West that stood in the way of construction, the portico, stairs, and front facade (figure 5.2).[5] McKim and his assistant William Kendall designed Earl as a miniature version of the library, with a long flight of entrance stairs, a limestone portico, and a shallow dome.[6] In its basic form, the building resembles a small centralized Italian Renaissance church, such as the Pazzi Chapel in Florence. Since Earl Hall was a subsidiary structure placed to the side of the library, it was constructed of the same dark red brick employed on the classroom buildings. The design is not totally successful, perhaps because McKim and Kendall were unable to resolve Dodge's desire for a "homelike" structure with the project's location on a key secondary site that was planned for a small, yet monumental building. Thus, an imposing portico and elegant dome, which usually indicate a grand interior space, are jarringly combined with facades regularly punctuated by rather pedestrian rectangular windows indicating that the interior is actually divided into two floors and a number of individual rooms, the most significant of which is the domed theater and lecture hall on the second floor.[7]

Ironically, the opening of Earl Hall on March 8, 1902, was the first building dedication presided over by Columbia's new president, Nicholas Murray Butler, a man who did not share Low's vision of a municipal university equally accessible to students of all religious faiths. Only a few months after dedicating Earl Hall as a place for the spiritual development of students of all denominations, John Pine wrote Butler a letter about how to deal with the "Hebrew question" and "the often repeated assertion that Columbia is a 'Jew' college." It is clear that Butler shared Pine's prejudices, since, as Pine noted, Butler did not "need to be convinced, for I am very sure you will agree with all I write."[8] In fact, a few years later, Butler would be responsible for restricting the admission of Jews to Columbia College, a policy completely antithetical to Low's vision of inclusion. Although Low remained on the board of trustees, his voice was muted and he eventually resigned over Butler's repellant anti-Semitic policies.[9]

Butler also changed the nature of Columbia's relationship with New York City. Unlike his predecessor, Butler did not see the necessity of the university's playing an active role in the life of New York. Rather, he strove to create a separate environment where Columbia's elite students could be trained as future leaders.[10] To this end, he strongly promoted the expansion of the university. During the early years of his presidency, Butler was an aggressive fundraiser. The university received many gifts from wealthy capitalists

FIGURE 5.2
Earl Hall under
construction, c. 1901 after
the demolition of a
portion of West Hall.

and was able to construct a number of impressive new buildings, including a series of classroom halls and a magnificent chapel. In addition, Butler resolved the "dormitory question" and secured new land for university expansion. It was also under Butler's leadership that Columbia finally entered the first ranks of modern American academic institutions, but it no longer sought to become a powerful force for progressive social change in New York City.

University Life and the Dormitory Question

As soon as Columbia College announced that it would move to the Morningside Plateau, alumni and students pressured the trustees to build dormitories, which, they argued, would aid in creating the university community life that was so lacking downtown. Indeed, the alumni association had "hope[d] that a dormitory would be the first new building to be erected" on the new campus.[11] The dormitory issue was a contentious one, pitting Low and his vision of a European-inspired urban university integrated into the life of the city against Pine and the Alumni Association, who favored the more traditional American ideal of a boarding college where a student's first loyalty was to the institution.[12] Dormitories were not universal at institutions of higher learning. German, Italian, and French universities, and those in London, Edinburgh, and other British cities did not provide housing for their students. Instead, students returned to their residences in the city after the completion of their daily studies. This was the model that Low hoped to establish at Columbia—a university of day scholars who would divide their time and talents between Columbia and the neighborhoods of New York City, commuting to school through the streets of the city, perhaps even following Low's own example of traveling by bicycle.[13]

In contrast to this European model, almost all American colleges of the nineteenth century provided dormitories where students lived and where their behavior was carefully prescribed. Since most American schools were established at some distance from population centers, providing housing was necessary. Even at schools such as Harvard that were near large cities, dormitories, modeled after those at Oxford and Cambridge, were considered essential. Proponents of dormitories argued that a true college spirit was instilled "only by the intimate association of college-room life."[14] To that end, dormitories were envisioned as a means of fostering student social interaction and student activities, thus creating a group of loyal college alumni. In addition, dormitories were seen as a way of attracting additional students from outside the New York City area, since such students would no longer be forced to rent a private apartment, find accommodations in one of the many dreary, low-cost student boarding houses in Harlem, the Upper West Side, and other nearby neighborhoods, or seek admittance into a selective fraternity.[15] Some of Columbia's fraternities purchased the neighborhood's new rowhouses; Alpha Delta Phi, for example, bought the house at 614 West 113th Street in 1898, as soon as it was completed.

Only three of the Greek letter societies erected clubhouses in the vicinity of the campus. The earliest of these custom-built fraternities was the Alpha Club, home of Delta Psi, which commissioned a building from Wood, Palmer & Hornbostel in 1898. The firm designed a sculptural Beaux-Arts structure that remains a distinguished presence on Riverside Drive just south of 116th Street.[16] The Alpha Club was soon followed by the Lambda Association's Colonial Revival building (housing the Psi Upsilon fraternity), designed in 1900 by Little & O'Connor for a site on West 115th Street between Broadway and Riverside Drive (figure 5.3), and Delta Phi's French Neoclassical clubhouse on West 116th Street, just east of Riverside Drive, designed by Thomas Nash in 1906.[17]

Pine led the dormitory advocates among the trustees, exacerbating his already strained relationship with Low. Low, understanding that there was strong sentiment for the establishment of a dormitory system, was politically astute enough not to oppose dorms publicly. He realized that Columbia had little to gain if he antagonized dormitory supporters who were also potential donors for other aspects of the project. Instead, he simply avoided commenting on the issue. When reporters asked for comments regarding an 1894 alumni resolution urging the trustees to provide dormitories, Low simply replied, "I must decline to discuss that now."[18]

The issue of dormitories, however, did not go away. As the move to Morningside Heights became imminent, pressure on Low to build dormitories escalated. Although Low's opposition to residence halls on campus continued, he was willing to support the construction of privately funded dormitories on sites near the campus; in November 1896 the trustees passed a resolution authorizing the university treasurer "to receive gifts to be applied to the purchase of land or the erection of a building or buildings" for dormitories.[19] Low's strategy was a shrewd response to demands for dormitories since it placed the onus for raising money on the historically parsimonious alumni. In addition, any off-campus dormitories actually erected under this system would be officially independent of the university and would not transform Columbia into a residential college. In fact, at the time the trustees' resolution was passed, planning was already underway for what was called "the largest and handsomest college dormitory in this country," a ten-story building for 920 students on the east side of Amsterdam Avenue between 121st and 122nd streets to be erected by a corporation of

FIGURE 5.3
Lambda Association's Psi Upsilon Fraternity House, c. 1902.

stockholders friendly to the college.[20] Named Hamilton Court, after Alexander Hamilton, one of Columbia's most illustrious early graduates, this dormitory was to be a Dutch-inspired structure with scrolled gables (figure 5.4) designed by Heins & La Farge, architect of the nearby Cathedral of St. John the Divine. The *Evening Post* found the design "in complete harmony . . . with the classical and Renaissance style of the buildings of the university grounds, but nevertheless possessing a strong individuality"; while the *Mail and Express,* emphasizing the contrast between the dormitory's design and that of McKim's college buildings, noted that this artistic diversity "will increase the interest growing out of the variety of architectural styles that will adorn the city's Acropolis."[21]

Just as each of the institutions that moved to Morningside Heights sought a distinguishing design for its buildings, the sponsors of this dormitory wished to build a structure that would stand out as an individual entity and would not be seen as part of the larger Columbia College campus, even though the building was specifically planned for use by Columbia's students. Although the scheme to build Hamilton Court was received with great enthusiasm by local newspapers, the capital needed to purchase the site and erect the building could not be raised. As a result, this proposal became the first of several off-campus dormitory projects that failed due to the inability of the alumni to fund their construction.[22]

Pressure for university-sponsored dormitories continued, with Pine reminding the trustees, "We can continue to ignore, but we cannot alter the fact that the absence of dormitories tends to repel many students, as well those living in the city as at a distance, and that without them the University cannot attain its

FIGURE 5.4
Heins & La Farge's design for the proposed Hamilton Court dormitory, 1896.

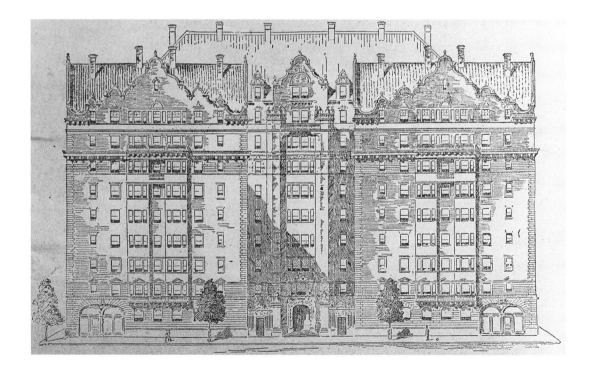

legitimate and normal growth." [23] He also reminded Low that Columbia needed to stay competitive with Harvard, Yale, and Princeton, even listing Columbia trustees whose sons had chosen to attend these other schools rather than Columbia "on account of the college life that they would get there." [24] In June 1898 Low finally agreed that if dormitories were to be erected on campus, the Green was the only appropriate spot.[25] At Low's behest, McKim, Mead & White prepared a plan for four five-story dorms designed in a style compatible with the classroom buildings (figure 5.5). They were sited along the edges of the Green, so that the center would remain a landscaped court. As might be expected, Low made little effort to find major donors to fund the dormitories. Surprisingly, the alumni also failed to launch a campaign to raise money for this project, which they had so vocally supported, and the dormitories on the Green were never constructed.

Although the university's lack of dormitories obviously limited the development of a social life similar to that at other prestigious colleges, Columbia's move to Morningside Heights did begin to instill a "college spirit" in the undergraduates. The location of the campus at some distance from the city's established commercial and residential neighborhoods encouraged a strong collegiate environment on the relatively isolated campus. In addition, the open space, especially the library stairs, provided popular venues for student interaction and activities. "Meet me on the library steps" became the slogan of undergraduates who would then "stand upon the steps or lean against the Ionic columns of the [library] portico. There is a ledge on the side of the balustrade, where they perch

FIGURE 5.5

McKim, Mead & White's design for dormitories on the Green, 1899.

like birds of good omen, with their hands in their pockets and breathing the incense of tobacco from bulldog pipes." [26] Or, if not puffing on their pipes, they might be heard singing:

> Here at the pleasant twilight hour
> When daily tasks are o'er,
> We gather on the library steps
> To sing our songs once more.[27]

Nevertheless, as the size of Columbia's physical plant and student body expanded, and as the surrounding neighborhood began to be built up with apartment houses that were too expensive for most students (see chapter 8), the construction of dormitories became an increasingly pressing issue. However, it was not until 1905, four years after Low's resignation as president, that the first two dormitories, Hartley Hall and Livingston Hall, were actually completed. By that time, Columbia had purchased South Field, between 114th and 116th streets, which provided extensive property on which a dormitory system could be developed.

South Field and the Expansion of the University

Columbia College had been forced to abandon its Madison Avenue site in part due to the density of surrounding development which precluded expansion. The four square blocks comprising the Morningside Heights property was considerably larger, but the possibility that Columbia would again be hemmed in by surrounding development had caused some critics to oppose the school's relocation to this urban site (see chapter 4). Concern also arose over the character of construction that might surround the Morningside Heights campus. The land to the south and west was owned by New York Hospital, which was holding the property for profitable future sale. As early as 1892 Pine had advocated the purchase of the hospital's holdings south of 116th Street, as well as its land west of Broadway, even suggesting that the block between 119th and 120th streets between Broadway and Claremont Avenue might be leased to Barnard College (see chapter 6).[28] The following year, Frederick Law Olmsted and William Ware had warned the trustees of the "danger that buildings will be erected, on ground adjoining the College, of the extremely lofty class now becoming common for hotels and apartment houses," and suggested that the college seek to restrict construction on the south side of 116th Street to private dwellings. Concern for the character of this adjoining property continued, as is evident in a 1900 editorial in the *Columbia University Quarterly,* which argued that "The permanent security of this embellishment [the Columbia campus] and its final value will depend in large measure upon the final disposition of the now vacant property on the south side of 116th Street. The erection upon it of commonplace or ugly buildings or of lofty structures would tend greatly to diminish the beauty and effectiveness of the present approach to the University." [29] Indeed, beginning in

1896, Columbia had actively supported an unsuccessful attempt by the Morn-ingside Protective Association to establish restrictive covenants over the entire Morningside Plateau (see chapter 8), thus assuring that tall buildings would not mar the campus's setting.

While it may have been advisable for Columbia to control property in the vicinity of the new campus, especially the land south of 116th Street across from South Court and the library, the institution had no money for land purchases. It was unlikely that the alumni, who had failed to contribute significant sums for the original land purchase and for construction of new buildings, would fund the purchase of additional property. In the early twentieth century, be-cause of the imminent completion of the subway beneath Broadway, the na-ture of the development on adjoining property became a pressing concern. The subway would finally provide a convenient transit link between Morningside Heights and downtown and attract major residential development (see chapter 8). If Columbia did not own the property south of 116th Street, it could not con-trol what would be constructed in its "front yard."

Columbia was especially interested in acquiring the two square blocks stretching from West 114th to West 116th Street between Amsterdam Avenue and Broadway, known as South Field. Since 1897 New York Hospital had per-mitted Columbia free use of the property for athletics and had promised to of-fer the college the option of purchasing the land when it was put up for sale. Co-lumbia had attempted to buy the site in 1899 for $2 million, but New York Hos-pital's asking price of $2.6 million was simply too high for the university.[30] Early in 1902 President Butler was informed that the property was on the market for $2.25 million. This price was considerably more than the $1.7 million Colum-bia's trustees felt the property was worth and far more than they could afford. However, President Butler was determined to acquire the land. By May he had arranged for a group of wealthy Columbia supporters, led by James Stillman, James Speyer, and Stuyvesant Fish, to purchase South Field from New York Hospital as a temporary expedient for $1.9 million ($400,000 in cash and the remainder in a mortgage), almost the same price that Columbia had paid for double the acreage less than a decade earlier. As part of this arrangement, Co-lumbia would have until July 1903 to raise funds to buy the land from Stillman, Speyer, and Fish at cost plus expenses.[31] The trustees were anxious to meet this challenge, since, as Finance Committee chair Francis S. Bangs noted, "we re-gard this land as essential to the future development of the University."[32]

As usual, no major donations were forthcoming. With the threat that the mortgage holder would immediately begin building on the site if Columbia did not pick up its option to purchase, Butler announced in June that the trustees had agreed to find the necessary funds to secure the purchase.[33] When the trustees took title to the property in October 1903, John Pine indicated to the *New York Times* that "As regards the amount of money the university has raised toward its purchase we have nothing to say."[34] This was an apt comment since, in fact, the university had raised almost no money for South Field. Rather, Columbia was forced to sell the block between Fifth and Sixth avenues and 47th and 48th streets on its Upper Estate to fund the purchase.[35]

With ownership of this large parcel of land assured, a master plan for South Field was requested from McKim, Mead & White. During the summer of 1903 Mead devoted his attention to this project and McKim added his ideas upon his return from vacationing in Europe.[36] With the new buildings on the original campus primarily planned for the expanding graduate programs, South Field was to be largely devoted to the undergraduate college. The architects sought to organize South Field as a continuation of the original campus, integrating the undergraduate college within the larger university structure. Many schemes for the arrangement of buildings on South Field were devised by McKim, Mead & White, including one with quadrangles of four- and five-story buildings and another culminating at 114th Street with tall buildings capped by enormous domes.[37] Another proposal called for two long, narrow quadrangles, each surrounded by four rectangular buildings, including enormous structures running parallel to Broadway and Amsterdam Avenue.[38]

In the South Field proposal that was ultimately submitted to the university trustees (figure 5.6), McKim, Mead & White planned a terrace along 116th Street with stairs leading onto the lower field, paved in red brick and stone and ornamented with two fountains that parallel the fountains on South Court. A pair of classroom buildings would face onto 116th Street, mirroring the placement of as yet unbuilt classroom structures to the north. These classroom buildings would echo the cornice line of those on the original campus, but would be a story taller to compensate for the lower elevation on South Field. Extending south from the classroom buildings, McKim, Mead & White planned east and west quadrangles, each comprised of five 9.5-story dormitories and a classroom structure. Although this plan would have provided Columbia with substantial dormitory space, the buildings would have been placed so close to one another that the resulting claustrophobic quadrangles would have received only minimal light. In fact, Columbia never actively considered erecting the inner rows of dorms and, as early as 1914, they were omitted from proposals for campus additions.[39]

The future disposition of the center of the tract facing Low Library remained unresolved. At some point, possibly in 1907, McKim, Mead & White proposed that the center of South Field be laid out with formal lawns outlined by pleached trees and hedges, and ornamented with vases, statues, and an obelisk.[40] This proposal would have totally displaced the students' athletic field, and since there was, as yet, no alternative field for undergraduate sports, Columbia chose temporarily to leave the field open. The southern end of the plot, bordering on West 114th Street, was especially problematic. Several designs by McKim, Mead & White placed a building on this site, closing off the view from the library terrace south toward the city.[41] For example, a design illustrated in a magnificently delineated watercolor drawing by Jules Crow shows a U-shaped building crowned with a cupola (figure 5.7) that has a sizable footprint extending into South

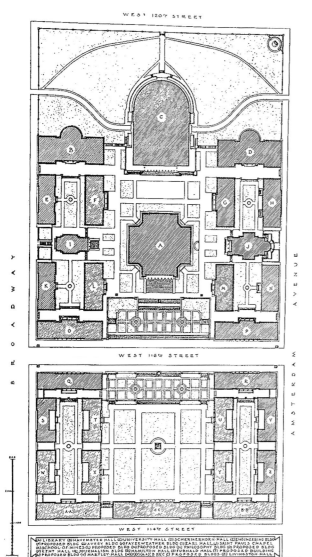

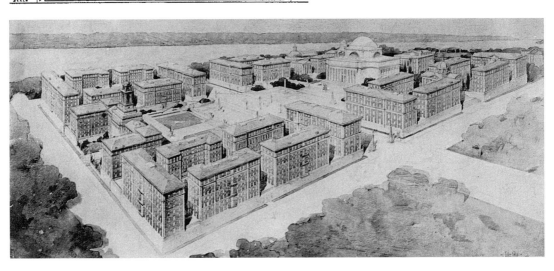

Field.[42] The McKim, Mead & White South Field landscape proposal included a shallow building along 114th Street, but contained a note stating, "this building omitted in estimate," apparently because the trustees did not need a cost estimate for a building that was not seriously under consideration.[43] Indeed, no serious plan to develop this portion of South Field was considered until 1922.

The university decided to use one of the new classroom buildings planned for South Field to house the lecture rooms and offices of the undergraduate college. A building for the undergraduate college was a pressing need, since most of the buildings erected on the campus had been planned for the professional schools, with college classes squeezed into the library and former asylum structures. McKim, Mead & White had designed a four-story College Hall in 1900 for the classroom site on the northeast corner of Broadway and 116th Street (now the site of Dodge Hall; figure 5.8), but there was no money to build this structure. When trustee John Stewart Kennedy suggested to Butler late in 1904 that he might fund construction of a new building, the president informed Kennedy that the buildings "for which we are in desperate straits" were halls for the undergraduate college and the law school. Kennedy, an enormously wealthy banker and railroad entrepreneur, met this need for an undergraduate academic center by quietly offering $500,000 in 1905 to build such a structure, which would be called Hamilton Hall.[44]

With money now available, McKim, Mead & White simply transferred its earlier design for College Hall to the new site on the southwest corner of Amsterdam Avenue and 116th Street, adding a rusticated limestone first story below the earlier four-story proposal (figure 5.9).[45] As with the south elevations of the buildings planned for the north side of 116th Street, the south elevations of this

FIGURE 5.8
McKim, Mead & White's original design for College Hall, 1900.

new classroom building, erected in 1905–7, and its companion to the west (now Journalism Hall, erected in 1912–13) were also to be articulated by tall limestone columns, providing a subtle visual continuation of Low Library's colonnade; there were also to be columns on the north elevations of these buildings, echoing those on the planned classroom buildings across 116th Street.

President Butler's announcement in 1903 regarding Columbia's commitment to purchasing South Field had coincided with a gift of $300,000 from Helen Hartley Jenkins and her nephew Marcellus Hartley Dodge, president of the class of 1903, for the construction of a dormitory in honor of her father and his maternal grandfather, munitions dealer Marcellus Hartley. Marcellus Hartley had died in 1902 leaving much of his wealth to his grandson whose classmates promptly voted him "luckiest" member of the class.[46] This gift, the first donation received for a new building under Butler's presidency, resulted from Butler's aggressive solicitation of funds for the expansion of the university. On March 13, 1902, just two months after the death of Marcellus Hartley, Butler wrote Helen Jenkins that, in recognition of Hartley's importance in New York, she and her relatives might wish to fund a memorial to him at Columbia, "the great University which represents so fully the city."[47] Marcellus Hartley Dodge's decision to fund a dormitory was an appropriate gift since it came, as the student newspaper noted, "from one who has himself been made conscious . . . of the need which he now comes forward to supply."[48] Along with this gift, the university committed itself to the construction of a companion dormitory (Livingston Hall, now Wallach Hall), thus guaranteeing the erection of two substantial residential halls on South Field and the recasting of Columbia as a residence college.[49]

FIGURE 5.9
South Field and the original Columbia campus, looking northeast from Broadway and 114th Street, c. 1915. Clockwise from lower right, St. Luke's Home, the Bloomingdale Asylum's gatehouse, Furnald, Journalism, School of Mines, Engineering, Havemeyer, dome of Earl, Teachers College's Household Arts Building, Low Library, Avery, Fayerweather, St. Paul's Chapel, the asylum's Macy Villa (relocated from its original site), Kent, Hamilton, Hartley, and Livingston.

Hartley and Livingston halls are large-scale versions of the Renaissance/ Colonial design form adopted by McKim, Mead & White for all of the subsidiary campus buildings and are faced, as are the earlier buildings, with dark red brick with limestone trim (figures 5.9 and 5.33). On the interior, the dormitories originally contained bedrooms and impressive ground-floor lounges and other public spaces with high, beamed ceilings, massive fireplace mantels, and stained-glass windows.[50] The room arrangements were planned, according to Butler, "in the interest of true democracy," for, although rent depended on size and location, expensive and inexpensive rooms were interspersed, permitting "the poorer student to live in the same building and in the same entry with him who is better off, and so avoids the chasm between rich and poor living in separate buildings, of which there is so much complaint at Harvard."[51]

These two dormitories opened in 1905 as an experiment in urban dormitory living at Columbia. Until their success was assured, Butler opposed the construction of additional dormitories, requesting, as noted above, that trustee John S. Kennedy fund a classroom hall rather than another dormitory.[52] The dormitories quickly filled with students, but they did not immediately become the center of undergraduate college life that had been predicted. Instead, they attracted both undergraduates and a significant number of male students in the professional and graduate programs (no dormitories were available to women enrolled in graduate programs).[53] In fact, most undergraduates continued to live at home and commute to school, or resided in apartments, boarding houses, or fraternities. Some building owners in the general vicinity of Columbia continued to cater specifically to students, advertising economical apartments "for you and your chums."[54] Off-campus accommodations were often less costly than the dormitories and offered the freedom precluded by the closely controlled dormitory environment. The dorms eventually gained in popularity and in 1911 200 students had to be turned away because of insufficient space.[55]

The university was promised an additional dormitory in 1907, when businessman Francis Furnald left funds in his will for a residence hall as a memorial to his son Royal Blacker Furnald of the class of 1901. The money, however, would not be transferred to Columbia until the death of Furnald's wife, Sarah E. Furnald, since she was to receive the income from the investment willed to Columbia. In 1911 Columbia hoped to erect the proposed Furnald Hall on South Field in conjunction with the construction of Journalism Hall on the southeast corner of Broadway and 116th Street, thus saving money by building neighboring structures concurrently. In order to build Furnald at that time, the university offered Mrs. Furnald annual payments for life in an amount equal to the annual interest on the investment if she would advance the money for construction of the dormitory that would bear her deceased son's name. This offer was accepted and Columbia was able to erect its third dormitory in 1912–13 (figure 5.10). The university made annual interest payments to Mrs. Furnald until her death in 1920.[56]

In 1906 Columbia's trustees thought that they had found a solution to the problem of athletic facilities, one that would permanently free South Field from use as an undergraduate sports center. In March 1906, plans were announced for the construction of a large stadium on landfill in the Hudson River adjacent to Riverside Park and the New York Central Railroad's tracks from 116th Street north to 120th Street (figure 5.11).[57] The scheme, which the *New York World*

FIGURE 5.10
Furnald Hall and
Journalism Hall, c. 1914.

FIGURE 5.11
Palmer & Hornbostel's
design for proposed
stadium in the Hudson
River adjoining Riverside
Park, 1907.

thought was "daring and original," called for fields, grandstands, a running track, a recreation pier that would be open to the public, and boat houses.[58] In addition, there would be an impressive "water gate," a ceremonial entrance onto Manhattan Island where distinguished visitors could arrive by boat to visit the tomb of Ulysses S. Grant. According to the *Tribune,* this was necessary because "When warships of this or foreign nations have gone up the river to salute the tomb of General Grant there has been no easy way for the officers to reach the tomb."[59]

The architect for the project was Palmer & Hornbostel, a firm comprised of Columbia graduates who had previously designed the Alpha Club fraternity (see above). The idea of building the proposed facility in the river was approved by the mayor and the New York State Legislature. Although Columbia worked closely with New York City officials to finalize the proposal, it was never built. The *Evening Mail* was clearly not familiar with Columbia's parsimonious alumni when it editorialized that the construction of the water gate "involves the little matter of raising a million dollars by private subscription, but what is a million dollars when a matter of such interest to the whole city is broached? Could not the amount be raised in twenty-four hours?"[60] Plans for an even more ambitious water gate and playing field were announced in 1912, with the state to erect the water gate on a site between 114th and 116th streets as a memorial to Robert Fulton.[61] This proposal would have entailed a financial outlay of $10 million, which was never forthcoming, and the project was quietly shelved.

Notwithstanding the failure to build a new stadium, Columbia soon received a flurry of large gifts for other projects, permitting Butler to direct the rapid expansion of facilities on campus and the acquisition of additional property on Morningside Heights. As a result, Butler would oversee not only the construction of Hamilton Hall and the Hartley, Livingston, and Furnald dormitories, but also seven additional buildings erected on the campus before the outbreak of World War I. Almost all of these buildings were funded through large donations from wealthy New Yorkers, many of whom had no previous connection with Columbia. In addition, smaller donations, many from class fundraising campaigns, provided the campus with gates, lamps, sculpture, stained-glass windows, stone pylons (figure 4.13), a sundial in the form of a granite sphere (figure 5.33), and other ornamental embellishments.[62]

St. Paul's Chapel

The year 1903 was especially propitious for Columbia. Besides acquiring title to South Field and receiving funds for the school's first dormitory, the trustees also received an offer for the chapel which was to be named for St. Paul, the early Christian teacher. This gift was received with tremendous excitement at the university, but with deep disappointment by McKim, Mead & White, since the donors, Olivia Egleston Phelps Stokes and her sister Caroline Phelps Stokes, required that this important commission, given in honor of their parents, go to their nephew I. N. Phelps Stokes of the architectural firm of Howells & Stokes.[63] Butler confidentially informed McKim of the design stipulation as soon as the offer was received "because I want you to feel fully informed as to what is going on here and to know that the architects for the chapel are the personal choice of the donors."[64] McKim, Mead & White had always known of the possibility of other architects designing buildings at Columbia. Seth Low had made it clear that donor requests would be honored, even choosing a classical style for the campus, in part, because many architects had the ability to work in this design mode. However, this issue did not arise during the initial phase of construction. Now McKim, Mead & White had lost the commission for one of the key campus structures to a young architect with little experience in designing imposing public buildings.

The Columbia chapel was one of Stokes's earliest major buildings and his masterpiece (figure 5.12). It would be Howells & Stokes's second building on Morningside Heights, coming only two years after the completion of the Horace Mann School for Teachers College, which had been co-designed with Edgar A. Josselyn (see chapter 6). Isaac Newton Phelps Stokes studied architecture at Columbia in 1893–94 and at the Ecole des Beaux-Arts from 1894 until his return to New York in 1897, when he opened an office with John Mead Howells.[65] The Columbia chapel project was obviously a prestigious commission for Stokes, but it placed the architect in an awkward position since he was displacing Charles McKim, one of the leading architects in the country, which could easily foster an antipathy that could harm Stokes's professional advancement. Stokes wrote to both McKim and Butler offering to resign the commission since, as he informed Butler, "it would not be consistent with professional etiquette or with our own professional wishes to take upon ourselves the designing of a building forming part of a group which is so essentially the creation of another firm of architects."[66] Since the trustees were anxious to retain the Stokes sisters' chapel donation, they requested that Howells & Stokes proceed with the building, suggesting that McKim, Mead & White act as consulting architect.[67] Both Stokes and McKim acquiesced, and Howells & Stokes agreed to pay McKim, Mead & White one-fifth of their commission.[68]

Stokes was constrained in designing the chapel by the guidelines established in McKim's master plan and by the liturgical demands of the Episcopal service. The siting, general ground plan,

FIGURE 5.12

St. Paul's Chapel, 1909; Schermerhorn Hall at left.

FIGURE 5.13
I. N. Phelps Stokes's
proposal for a campanile
on the east elevation of
St. Paul's Chapel, c. 1904.

FIGURE 5.14
Final design for the east
end of St. Paul's Chapel,
1904.

cornice line, and exterior materials were to follow the requirements for all university buildings, while the plan of the building, with its chancel, choir, and nave, was to meet the specific liturgical needs of an Episcopal chapel. Within these parameters, Stokes created a spectacular building, adapting Northern Italian Renaissance church design to the particular requirements of the Columbia project. Stokes experimented with many designs, including one that included a tall campanile on the Amsterdam Avenue facade (figure 5.13), before finally settling on the impressive final design that, according the architectural critic Russell Sturgis, "fills a place . . . among pseudo-classic edifices . . . without introducing one discordant element" [69] (figure 5.14). The building is cruciform in plan (figure 5.15), which was not only appropriate for an Episcopal chapel,

but also harmonious with the arrangement of the surrounding buildings. Stokes knew that the chapel had to relate architecturally to the four classroom buildings that would eventually enclose the site (only three of which were built). He reported to John Pine that "Happily, the very form of plan which would most gracefully accept these four angles . . . was precisely a cruciform plan, with its re-entering angles corresponding to the projecting angles of the [proposed classroom] building[s]." [70]

The exterior of the chapel is faced with dark red brick and limestone, as are other campus buildings, but the facades are also enlivened with highlights of yellow marble, green ceramic roof tiles supplied by the Ludowici Roofing Tile Company of Ohio, and real scallop shells. The scallop shells, a symbol of welcome for pilgrims on the road to Santiago de Compostela, are set in groups of four within panels located on either side of the entrance portico. [71] Unlike other major buildings at Columbia, with their freestanding porticos, the chapel's portico is recessed, creating a narthex-like space that is actually on the exterior of the building. [72] The chapel is crowned by a raised dome, as is Earl Hall on the other side of Low Library, but here the low dome is more fully integrated into the design than on Earl. The drum of the dome is pierced by sixteen arched windows that flood the interior with light. Stokes also planned four bas relief lunettes over the side entrances of the chapel, representing scenes from

the life of Christ. Rough-stone blocks were put in place, but the only panel actually completed is the one adjacent to the southwest corner of the chapel, a 1912 gift from Stokes himself.[73]

It is on the interior of St. Paul's Chapel that Stokes was especially creative (figure 5.16). Stokes was intent upon erecting a chapel that was structurally honest, "with nothing false or deceptive, and everything—even the treatment of the interior decoration—structural and permanent."[74] He described his goal as seeking "to produce effect rather by an interesting combination of carefully selected materials than by richness of detail or profusion of applied decoration," in order

FIGURE 5.15
Plan of St. Paul's Chapel and its relationship to adjoining buildings, 1904.

"to make the Chapel an example of good, honest, logical and truthful construction."[75] This emphasis on structural honesty is an indication of Stokes's adherence to European architectural theories ignored by most of his compatriots who had also studied at the Ecole des Beaux-Arts, but who were more interested in designing buildings with superficial applied ornamentation.

Unfortunately, Stokes's design choices led to major cost overruns. Completion of the chapel as designed would cost over $260,000, but Stokes's aunts had committed only $200,000. Stokes explained the design in detail to his aunts in a letter (they preferred not to meet in person), informing them that "A very large savings could have been made by substituting for the stone, brick and tile vaulting used in the interior, rough brick and lath finished in plaster. This is the usual form of construction in this country, but it was our ambition, as well as that of the Trustees, to make this Chapel a lasting monument not only of good design but of the best construction."[76] Although they withheld their decision regarding additional funding for several weeks, Olivia and Caroline Stokes finally agreed to pay the extra cost. Indeed, having taken such a possessive interest in the chapel, they added even more money to their donation over the next few years for stained-glass chancel windows, woodwork, and other incidentals, rather than allowing any other donor to be identified with an aspect of the building.[77]

Because of the simplicity and structural honesty of the interior, the choice of each material and finish was crucial. Thus, Stokes selected each component of the interior with great care. Once Stokes had settled on brick as the appropriate material for the highly visible walls and piers, and for the inner surface of the drum of the dome, selection of an appropriate brick became his most critical decision. After rejecting many possibilities, Stokes chose a Roman brick that he had seen on the West End Presbyterian Church on Amsterdam Avenue and West 105th Street.[78] Stokes felt that this salmon-colored brick with "an undertone of yellow" produced "a very decided pink flush ... [that] would give a soft, warm, sympathetic and, with all, cheerful interior."[79] Subtle terra-cotta ornament was employed on the arches, at the cornice lines, and in other key locations. This terra cotta, supplied by the Atlantic Terra Cotta Company of Tottenville, Staten Island, complements the color of the brick. Iconographically, the terra-cotta detail refers to religious subjects, including the fig and its leaves, the vine, the poppy, the cross, and the pilgrim's shell; much of this ornament was modeled after designs by Renaissance artists Lucca della Robbia and Mino da Fiesole.[80] The most prominent terra-cotta elements are the insignia of the four evangelists in the keystones of the crossing arches, designed by Adolph Weinman, one of the leading sculptors of the era.[81] It was also important for the unity of the interior design that the brick and terra cotta harmonize with the pink hue of the tiles of the spandrels, central dome, chancel dome, apsidal half dome, transept vaults, stairways, and portico roof, which form one of the most significant installations of Rafael Guastavino's structural tiles.[82] This successful combination of brick, terra cotta, and tile prompted *Craftsman Magazine* to declare the building "an epic in clay."[83]

Since the interior of the church contained little applied decorative ornament other than the terra-cotta detail, Stokes realized that the stained glass, especially that in the three chancel windows, would play an especially significant role in the decorative scheme. Stokes understood that these windows needed to be dark, limiting the amount of sunlight entering through them, since the congregation would be facing the glass and excessive sunlight would obscure views toward the chancel.[84] It was also essential that the color of the glass and the masonry materials harmonize. Early in the project, Stokes sought advice regarding the design of these windows from John La Farge, one of the most talented American stained-glass artists of the period.[85] La Farge designed three figurative windows centering on a scene of St. Paul, "the intellectual and teaching representative of early Christianity," preaching to the Athenians on Mars Hill.[86] Appropriately, the Parthenon, the crowning temple on the Athenian Acropolis, stands in the background, reminding viewers that they are attending a service in a chapel atop New York's Acropolis. The remaining windows in the chapel were to be glazed with more transparent glass to allow more natural light into the building. The sixteen arched windows in the drum of the dome are among the few features of the chapel that the Stokes sisters allowed others to fund. These windows, designed by Maitland Armstrong, are gifts from individual families in honor of important Columbia graduates, with each displaying the donor-family's coat of arms.[87]

The only major decorative detail in the chapel that is not part of the structure is the exquisite, intricately inlaid carved walnut woodwork of the choir and apse. Florentine craftsmen Mariano and Figli Coppedé won a competition arranged by Stokes while he was in Italy early in 1905 to select a designer for the woodwork.[88] Stokes was anxious to use Italian craftsmen not only because their work was cheaper than that of American wood carvers, but more importantly, because he felt that it was of a higher quality than comparable work produced in America. Stokes's plan for decorating the chapel with these imported furnishings almost backfired when the U.S. Customs Service refused to permit free entry. It took Stokes almost a year to persuade the government that the Coppedés' pieces were works of art that should pass duty free and not taxable commercial furniture.[89]

The chapel received a tremendous amount of favorable publicity upon its completion in 1907, with articles or illustrations appearing in almost all of the architecture and design periodicals. Architecture professor A. D. F. Hamlin called it "an architectural masterpiece" with "the most noble and stately church interior in the United States."[90] The two leading architecture critics of the day agreed with Hamlin. In the opinion of Russell Sturgis, "nothing better has ever been done in New York."[91] Stokes must have been especially proud of Montgomery Schuyler's judgement that the interior is "one of those rare architectural successes which, being of no style, yet unmistakably have style."[92] These comments and others like them undoubtedly also delighted President Butler, for the building had a special significance to him and his ambitions for Columbia. Butler wished to reassert the Christian nature of Columbia, as opposed to the more ecumenical view of the college espoused by Low and symbolized by Earl Hall. Thus, St. Paul, the central teacher among the early Christians, was an appropriate choice for the dedication of the university chapel. To Butler, "the Chapel declares to the whole University in terms of the God of Christianity the ultimate force in the whole universe which the scientists and men of letters are seeking in their respective laboratories and seminar rooms."[93] Butler insisted that "Columbia University is a Christian institution," and, indeed, it was his desire to Christianize the university that would lead to restrictive admissions, which would significantly reduce non-Christian enrollment at Columbia.[94]

Design and Construction, 1904–1914

In 1904, the year after McKim, Mead & White lost the chapel commission, the firm was informed that it had also lost the contract for the first classroom building to be constructed under Butler's leadership. Adolph Lewisohn had offered to erect a building for the School of Mines (now Lewisohn Hall) so long as Arnold Brunner was appointed architect. As with the chapel, McKim agreed to consult on the project, thus assuring the trustees that Brunner's building would be in keeping with McKim's overall campus design.[95] In compensation for the loss of these commissions, Butler informed McKim, Mead & White of the trustees' intent to appoint the firm as Columbia's official consulting architect, thus publicly formalizing a relationship that had been informally in effect for over a decade.[96]

Adolph Lewisohn's interest in the School of Mines resulted from his business in mining, smelting, and refining copper and other metals.[97] He was a prominent member of New York's German-Jewish community and a generous philanthropist.[98] Arnold Brunner, Lewisohn's choice of architect, was New York City's leading German-Jewish designer and was responsible for many of the public buildings commissioned by that community, including Barnard Hall, donated to Barnard College by Jacob Schiff in 1916, Lewisohn Stadium at City College (demolished), and buildings at Mt. Sinai Hospital on Fifth Avenue and Montefiore Hospital in the Bronx.[99] As required by McKim's master plan, Brunner's School of Mines Building uses the same dark red brick and white limestone found on other classroom structures, but its detailing is more sculptural, reflecting its architect's taste for French Beaux-Arts design (figure 5.17).[100]

The construction of the School of Mines in 1904, on Broadway, south of Earl Hall, was quickly followed by the funding and construction of five additional classroom buildings—Hamilton (1905–7), Kent (1909–11), Philosophy (1910–11), Avery (1911–12), and Journalism (1912–13), all designed by McKim, Mead & White. In addition, in 1908 McKim, Mead & White prepared designs for all four of the inner classroom buildings flanking the library (only Avery was erected).[101]

The undergraduate college's Hamilton Hall was the first of these new classroom buildings to be erected (see above). Butler had told John S. Kennedy in 1904 that the university's two priorities were the college hall, which he funded, and a law school building. Construction on the law school had to wait until additional benefactors came forward. Sufficient funds were finally raised by 1909 through a series of bequests and Kent Hall, named for James Kent, the school's first law professor, was erected on the northwest corner of Amsterdam Avenue and 116th Street (figure 5.18).[102] As noted in chapter 4, McKim planned that the buildings placed to the north and south of 116th Street would be designed to continue the line of the Low Library colonnade. Thus, Kent has four monumental columns on its south elevation and an impressive entry portico on its north face. The entrance level of Kent originally housed the Law Library (now the Starr East Asian Library), one of McKim, Mead & White's most splendid Columbia interiors. This long, narrow room with vaulted ceiling, book alcoves, galleries, and tall end windows recalls such great historic libraries as the Bodleian at Oxford and Christopher Wren's Trinity College Library, Cambridge.[103]

Shortly after construction began on Kent Hall in 1909, work started on Philosophy Hall, located on Amsterdam Avenue between Kent and St. Paul's Chapel (figure 5.19). Construction was made possible by a second gift from Helen Hartley Jenkins. In 1910 Jenkins offered $350,000 for a building in which research in electrical and mechanical sciences would be conducted. Such a research facility was not a pressing need at Columbia, since the School of Engineering already had a new building, but an agreement was reached with Jenkins whereby her gift could be used to build a hall for liberal arts study that would include, in its basement, the Marcellus Hartley Research Laboratory specializing in electromechanics.[104] As with the other buildings forming the east and west edges of the original campus complex, whose inner facades would be hid-

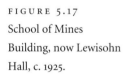

FIGURE 5.17
School of Mines
Building, now Lewisohn
Hall, c. 1925.

den by the construction of the proposed inner range of classroom buildings, the facade of <u>Philosophy Hall</u> had a modest design—one without the impressive columns included on the more centrally placed classroom buildings. The arched entry, however, contains beautiful crafted wrought-iron screens, decorative iron and glass outer doors, and neoclassical urns carved into the

FIGURE 5.18
Kent Hall, 1915.

FIGURE 5.19
Philosophy Hall, c. 1915.

limestone enframement. This detail is typical of the ornamentation at the entries to the classroom buildings erected during the 1910s.

With the completion of Kent in 1911, the law school and its library vacated Low Library, permitting a reallocation of space in that overcrowded building. Butler recognized that this rearrangement also provided an opportunity to remove another specialized collection from Low Library, the Avery Architectural Library, which had outgrown its limited space in the east arm of Low. Samuel Putnam Avery and his wife had established the Avery Architectural Library in 1890 as a memorial to their son, architect Henry Ogden Avery. In 1910 Butler reminded Avery that he had previously offered funding for a separate building to house the architecture library.[105] A year later, Avery committed up to $330,000 toward a building that "shall be primarily devoted to the Avery Library and exclusively so devoted whenever the growth of the Library demands."[106] He agreed that the upper floors could temporarily house the School of Architecture, but he envisioned a time when the studios and offices of the school would be displaced by the expanding library. McKim, Mead & White spent a great deal of time designing this building (figure 5.20), since, as Butler informed Avery, the firm "attached great importance to the proposed building and have felt a sort of professional pride in designing it as attractively and as carefully as possible."[107] The entrance to Avery is through a monumental portico, following McKim's proposal that the inner classroom buildings flanking Low Library have impressive colonnaded entrances echoing and extending the library's columns and piers. The lower two stories of Avery are devoted to the architecture library, which was planned in the alcove format previously employed at the law library. The ceiling is coffered and ornamented with three large squares embellished with portrait medallions of twelve Italian Renaissance architects and patrons. Since Avery was the only one of the proposed inner classroom buildings ever erected, its completion in 1912 created the only one of McKim's small quadrangles ever realized. This was an intimate landscaped space formed by Avery, Fayerweather, Schermerhorn, and St. Paul's Chapel (figure 5.21).[108]

In 1903 Joseph Pulitzer offered a $1 million endowment for a school of journalism, including funds for the construction of a building that would rise after his death, thus becoming the first person since Seth Low to donate such a substantial sum to Columbia. In a letter sent to Butler, Pulitzer wrote that "my idea is to recognize that journalism is, or ought to be, one of the great and intellectual professions; to encourage, elevate and educate in a practical way the present and still more, future members of that profession, exactly

FIGURE 5.20

Avery Hall, c. 1912.

as if it were the professions of law and medicine."[109] This novel idea was not universally acclaimed. An editorial writer in the *Real Estate Record* recognized that Columbia would be the first university in America with a school of journalism, but hoped that it would also be the last, opining that this "is a superfluous piece of educational machinery." This journalist did not believe that journalism was a learned profession, but rather felt that all a good reporter really needed was a sound general education and some on-the-job training.[110] Nonetheless, Columbia was proud to accept Pulitzer's substantial gift. The journalism building was erected in 1912, a year after Pulitzer's death (figure 5.10). After several possible locations were considered, the building was eventually sited on the southeast corner of Broadway and 116th Street, and was designed with colonnades similar to those already employed at Hamilton Hall across South Field on the corner of 116th Street and Amsterdam Avenue.[111]

In the early twentieth century, Charles McKim began to spend less and less time designing the specifics of the Columbia projects. With the overall plan for the campus in place and the basic design intent of the new buildings established, McKim's input was not always essential. In addition, McKim never developed as close a rapport with Butler as he had had with Low. McKim was extraordinarily busy during this period, working on such major projects as Pennsylvania Station, the Army War College in Washington, D.C., and the expansion of the Metropolitan Museum of Art. He also was serving as president of the American Institute of Architects and director of the American Academy in Rome. At the same time, McKim's health was beginning to fail, forcing him to spend less and less time working on the firm's projects. Finally, on January 1, 1908, McKim quietly retired; the following year he died.[112]

William Mitchell Kendall took McKim's place as the lead architect for Columbia's projects. Kendall, who had joined the McKim, Mead & White office in 1882 and became a partner in 1906, had assisted McKim since the inception of planning for the Columbia campus. Responsible for much of the detailing on Low Library and Earl Hall, he was the actual designer of many of the new buildings erected during Butler's tenure.[113] Kendall continued to design buildings in the same style and using the

FIGURE 5.21
Small quadrangle created by St. Paul's Chapel, Fayerweather (left), Avery (right), and Schermerhorn.

materials established by McKim, but his designs generally incorporated the use of raised brick patterning not generally seen on McKim's work. This is evident, for example, in the panels of raised brick at Kent Hall and the window surrounds and rectangular panels on the elevations of the President's House.[114]

In addition to presiding over the erection of a significant number of new buildings in the early years of the twentieth century, Butler also oversaw the expansion of the university's land holdings on Morningside Heights, purchasing not only South Field, but also East Campus, the block east of Amsterdam Avenue between 116th and 117th streets. By early in 1910, it had become apparent to the trustees that this block would be sold for speculative development if it was not acquired by Columbia.[115] Gifts from several generous friends of the university allowed Columbia to buy the 116th Street frontage for $1 million, with the intention that this site would become the new home of the medical school.[116] The trustees hoped to acquire the remainder of the block and planned an interconnected group of five buildings designed in a manner consistent with the character of the buildings on the main campus.[117] The 117th Street half of the block was purchased for $475,000 in 1914.[118] In 1911, even before the entire block had been assembled, the trustees decided to erect a president's house on East Campus at the corner of Morningside Drive and 116th Street (figure 5.22).[119] Kendall designed an impressive residence of brick laid in English bond (alternating courses of headers and stretchers) with a deeply channeled rusticated base.[120] In this residence, Butler could live in elegant style and lavishly entertain university guests and those who had the potential for donating to Columbia's rapidly expanding facilities.

Since the university was using most of its money for improving the academic position of various departments and erecting impressive buildings, it had little left for landscaping. In fact, no landscape plan had been proposed in conjunc-

FIGURE 5.22
President's House, c. 1912; rowhouses on 117th Street visible at right.

tion with McKim's initial plan and planting on the campus had been undertaken in a somewhat ad hoc manner. Early in his tenure, Butler, along with
McKim, became concerned about the setting of the campus buildings and the
fact that the landscaping did not match the grandeur of the built structures.
By the early twentieth century, McKim's disquiet over the poor quality of
the plantings around his buildings led him to ask Frederick Law Olmsted, Jr.
(the son of the more famous landscape architect, who had contributed ideas
to Low and McKim in the 1890s) to visit the campus and evaluate the landscaping. Olmsted was unimpressed with what he viewed as "restless and trivial,
not to say fussy" plantings.[121] McKim sent Olmsted's critical letter to Butler,
with a recommendation that the university avail itself of the landscape architect's services.[122] As a result, in 1905 Olmsted Brothers was commissioned to
study the extant plantings on the portion of the campus north of 116th Street
and to recommend improvements. The firm submitted a detailed report and
plan on September 10, 1906 (figure 5.23), that recommended formal plantings

FIGURE 5.23
Olmsted Brothers'
proposed landscape
design for the campus
north of 116th Street,
1906, showing all of the
proposed classroom
buildings and the four
proposed quadrangles.

of the type "often found in squares and formal gardens of European countries, where the conditions and surroundings are somewhat similar to those at Columbia."[123]

The most important idea suggested by Olmsted Brothers was the removal of the poplars that had initially been planted in each of the beds at the corners of the library and their replacement with European lindens, with up to twenty trees in each bed. The trees were to "be planted so close together that their branches in a few years will intermingle with each other, thereby making a solid canopy of branches and foliage."[124] The trees were to be pleached (i.e., trimmed into rectilinear box-like forms) in the European manner to form solid, architectonic masses that would complement the buildings. In 1907, the Buildings and Grounds Committee of the trustees authorized the superintendent of the grounds "to proceed with as much work as could be covered by money to be obtained by gift."[125] Unfortunately, there were few gifts forthcoming for this project and Columbia's landscaping has retained, to the present day, a poorly planned, ad hoc quality. In fact, only one of Olmsted Brothers' suggestions was implemented—the addition of eight grass panels to South Court, four at each fountain (figure 5.24). McKim was enthusiastic about this idea when it was suggested by Olmsted Brothers at a meeting in April 1906 and it was implemented even before Olmsted Brothers had submitted their final report.[126]

FIGURE 5.24

South Court with grass panels, c. 1912.

Design and Construction in the 1920s

After the start of work on Furnald and Journalism in 1912, no new construction was begun for a decade. The rapid increase in classroom and dormitory space between 1904 and 1912 had diminished the immediate need for new buildings. In addition, World War I interrupted almost all nonmilitary construction in America, including Butler's plan to build a home for the recently established School of Business on the northeast corner of Broadway and 116th Street. Butler had aggressively sought a donor for this project. On October 18, 1916, he wrote to public utilities magnate Emerson McMillin, appealing to him "as a man of affairs keenly interested in business and in having business carried on by well-trained men in accordance with the highest standards" to provide funds for a building to house the School of Business in facilties at least equal to those of Columbia's other professional schools.[127] McMillin was a Congregationalist with no previous connection with Columbia, but he was known to be a man with a keen interest in business education. His advocacy of professional training for businessmen attracted Butler's attention. Butler was persuasive, writing McMillin about the need for the building and discussing the proposal over private luncheons. On November 13, 1916, McMillin made a "formal offer of ducats"—approximately $600,000 to be paid in stock.[128] However, construction was delayed by the war and the volatility of labor conditions and construction costs immediately following the armistice. By 1919, McMillin had provided Columbia with the necessary funds, including an inadvertent transfer of additional stock worth $100,000 more than he had promised. When this mistake was brought to his attention, he allowed the university to keep the windfall, leading Butler to dub McMillin "the most princely benefactor that any institution of learning ever had."[129]

A segment of Columbia's faculty was opposed to the construction of the Business School Building on the planned site since this would entail the demolition of the Bloomingdale Asylum's superintendent's house which had been converted into the Men's Faculty Club.[130] In order to calm the faculty, Butler promised them a new Faculty Club. Money left to Columbia in the will of trustee F. Augustus Schermerhorn paid for its construction in 1922–23 on a site adjacent to the president's house on East Campus.[131] It is McKim, Mead & White's most uninspired building on the Columbia campus (figure 5.25). The old

FIGURE 5.25
Faculty House, c. 1923.

Men's Faculty Club Building was demolished and the Business School (now Dodge Hall) finally constructed on this key site at the entrance to the campus in 1923–24 (figure 4.13).[132] McKim, Mead & White designed most of the classroom buildings with ornamental detailing that made each structure distinctive. Even with McMillin's additional gift, Kendall was forced to remove much of the ornament from the Business School's facade, leading someone, perhaps Kendall himself, to scrawl on one of the firm's drawings of the proposed south elevation that it had been "cheapened by omission of ornament."[133] Still, the completed building had an imposing colonnade facing 116th Street and included a large public lecture hall and theater named for the donor.[134]

In his *Annual Report of the President* for 1919, Butler impressed upon the trustees the need for immediate expansion of university facilities due to the rapid rise in student enrollment after the war. "It is plain," Butler wrote, "that unless the work of the University is to be thrown into confusion, immediate steps must be taken to provide new buildings both for academic work and for residence."[135] Butler proposed building several of the classroom buildings initially proposed in the McKim, Mead & White plan of 1894—a building to the southeast of the library for the departments of philosophy, political science, and pure science on the present-day site of Buell Hall, creating a quadrangle with St. Paul's Chapel, Kent, and Philosophy, and another building for the departments of botany and zoology on a site to the northwest of the library, creating a quadrangle with Havemeyer, Engineering (now Mathematics), and Earl.[136] In 1927 McKim, Mead & White designed this latter building, which was to be called Pierce Hall, but neither of these classroom structures was erected.[137] During the 1920s, President Butler became increasingly involved in projects outside of Columbia, including Republican politics (he sought the presidential nomination in 1920) and the Carnegie Endowment for International Peace. As a result, he had less time to raise money for new construction at Columbia.[138] Thus, many projects proposed during this decade were never built.

In 1926 Butler laid out another ambitious set of building priorities that was not completely realized.[139] This proposal included the perennial dream of completing University Hall, as well as new construction on the Green at the north end of the campus, on South Field, and on East Campus. The Green was a promising site for large new buildings since this land, incorporating approximately one square block, was still undeveloped in the early 1920s. Accordingly, substantial plans were formulated for new construction, with most of the proposed buildings earmarked for improved science facilities. Extensions to Havemeyer and Schermerhorn halls were projected along the Broadway and Amsterdam Avenue borders of the Green for chemistry and natural science laboratories and classrooms. Chandler Chemistry Laboratories (figure 5.26), the extension to Havemeyer Hall, was begun in 1925, and construction began on the Schermerhorn Extension in 1928.[140] In addition, a row of buildings was planned along 120th Street. An impressive 1926 scheme by McKim, Mead & White called for five buildings at this location at the northern edge of the campus—slender skyscraper towers of more than twenty stories on the Broadway and Amsterdam Avenue corners (the former for chemical engineering laboratories), a seventeen-story structure with a pyramidal tower in the center, and a pair of bulky twelve-story structures in between (figure 5.27). The twelve-story building located to the west had actually already been designed and was under construction, opening in 1927 as the Pupin Physics Laboratory.[141] In a proposal from 1928, the building in the center of the block was redesigned as a four-story art center with grand arched windows.[142] Pupin was the only part of the scheme that was completed and the remainder of the Green would remain undeveloped for several more decades.

FIGURE 5.26
Chandler Laboratories, c. 1928, with, from left, corner of Pupin, Low, rear of Havemeyer with semicircular lecture hall extension, Broadway facades of Havemeyer, Engineering (now Mathematics), Mines (now Lewisohn), Business (now Dodge), and Journalism.

FIGURE 5.27
McKim, Mead & White's proposal for West 120th Street between Amsterdam Avenue and Broadway, 1926.

In the 1919 *Annual Report,* Butler had also first broached the idea of building on the central plot at the southern end of South Field, along 114th Street, suggesting that this site, adjacent to the undergraduate dormitories and classroom building, would be an appropriate location for a university commons.[143] By 1922 this proposal had been expanded into a Students Hall that was to include an assembly hall, dining room, modern gymnasium, and rooms for various student clubs and organizations that would "make adequate material provision for the care and satisfaction of undergraduate students."[144] With the completion in 1922 of Baker Field, a sports stadium on Broadway and 218th Street at the northern tip of Manhattan Island and the removal of most organized outdoor sports activities from South Field, Butler and the trustees felt that this land could be used for other purposes.[145] McKim, Mead & White considered a large number of ideas, finally settling on a pompous, overscaled classical design (figure 5.28). The massive building was to be only slightly lower in height than the crown of the dome on Low Library. The final scheme and almost all of the alternative versions of the design included a two-story limestone colonnade on the north facade that was set at a height parallel with the colonnade in front of Low Library.[146] The cost estimate for the building was $3 million, far more than Columbia could afford and the plans were shelved, the trustees deciding "that it will be necessary to re-study the problem in all its aspects."[147]

Another building project initiated in the mid-1920s had not been foreseen by Butler in 1919 when he had proposed the expansion of the university's facilities. Casa Italiana, an Italian cultural center, was donated in 1925 by real estate developers Joseph and Michael Paterno and Anthony Campagna (see chapter 8) and erected in 1926–27 on the northeast corner of Amsterdam Avenue and West 117th Street, replacing an earlier residential building (figure 5.29). As might be expected, this building closely resembles an Italian Renaissance palazzo. It is the only building designed by McKim, Mead & White at Columbia, besides Low Library, that is clad in limestone.[148] The building contained offices, classrooms, and, on the second floor, a magnificent Renaissance-inspired auditorium that remains one of the most beautiful interior spaces on Morningside Heights (figure 5.30).[149]

FIGURE 5.28
McKim, Mead & White's design for north elevation of Students Hall, 1922.

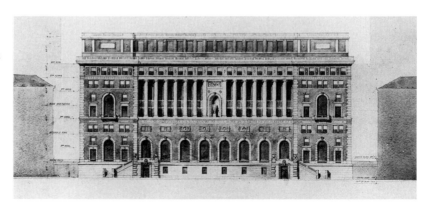

FIGURE 5.29
Casa Italiana, c. 1927.

FIGURE 5.30
Auditorium of Casa
Italiana, c. 1927.

As enrollment expanded following World War I, the university faced not only a growing demand for classrooms, but also for additional dormitories. Students were experiencing increasing difficulty finding affordable lodging in the Morningside Heights area or in any other convenient New York City location as postwar rents skyrocketed.[150] Women who attended programs in the graduate schools faced particular housing difficulties since Columbia provided no dormitory space for their use.[151] In 1924 and 1925 Columbia began construction of its two largest residence halls, one for women and one for men. Planning for the women's residence hall began in 1922, with a decision to place what would be named Johnson Hall (now Wien Hall; figure 5.31) on East Campus where it would be far removed from the men's dormitories on South Field.[152] The building was to include 370 bedrooms, a dining room and lounge, and the Women's Faculty Club. The club would occupy two floors in the north wing of the dormitory and be connected to the recently completed Men's Faculty Club by a small passageway.[153] Funding problems delayed the start of construction until 1924 and the dormitory was completed the following year.[154] Of all McKim, Mead & White's buildings on the Columbia campus, the women's residence was designed with the most overt references to American colonial architecture, employing such motifs as an enormous segmental-arch pediment at the main entrance, large fanlights with webbed sash, splayed window lintels, and blind brick arches. Colonial-inspired design, which was closely associated with domestic life in the early decades of the twentieth century, was undoubtedly chosen for this women's dormitory in order to lend the residence hall an especially "homey" quality thought to be appropriate for women students.[155] This "homey" character is especially evident in the lounge, with its Colonial Revival furniture and Persian rugs (figure 5.32). Butler hoped that Johnson would become a part of a larger complex of East Campus buildings. McKim, Mead & White sketched a pair of additional buildings, one on Amsterdam Avenue that was similar in scale to Johnson and another on 117th Street with paired towers, but neither was built.[156]

For men, Columbia decided to erect a dormitory on a site at the southeast corner of South Field adjacent to Livingston Hall that would incorporate features planned for the aborted Students Hall project. The enormous new Students Hall, named John Jay Hall in 1925, is a twelve-story structure that is several stories taller than the building McKim, Mead & White had planned for this site in the 1903 plan for South Field (figure 5.33).

FIGURE 5.31
Johnson Hall (now Wien Hall), c. 1925.

FIGURE 5.32
Johnson Hall (now Wien Hall) lounge, unknown date.

FIGURE 5.33
South Field looking east. From left, Hamilton, Hartley, Livingston (now Wallach), and John Jay; granite sundial at left, c. 1927.

John Jay Hall was erected with 484 rooms, as well as the refectory and club rooms that had been planned for the larger Students Hall several years earlier.[157] McKim, Mead & White created several impressive public rooms in the building, including a two-story entrance lobby with mezzanine balcony, large wood-paneled lounge, dining room with finely detailed wood paneling, coffered ceiling, and leaded-glass windows (figure 5.34), and a smaller grill room in the basement with beamed ceiling and enormous fireplace.[158] The wood beams, dark paneling, and other detail were considered to have a far more "masculine" feel than the Colonial-inspired motifs employed at Johnson Hall.

The construction of John Jay was the culmination of Butler's efforts to increase the enrollment of students from outside the New York area who might attend Columbia if assured a suitable place of residence. Butler's efforts to increase the geographic diversity of students has been interpreted by some as his way of limiting the large number of Jewish students at the university, most of whom were from New York City. By this scheme, the university did not need to resort to express quotas, but could limit the admission of qualified local applicants, many of whom were Jewish, in favor of Protestant students from outside of the city. In addition, the dormitory would segregate the largely Christian residential students from the more religiously and ethnically diverse population of local commuting students.[159]

Columbia's students were not the only ones affected by the rapid rise in rents on Morningside Heights after World War I. Faculty at Columbia and affiliated

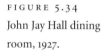

FIGURE 5.34
John Jay Hall dining
room, 1927.

institutions also found it difficult to afford the rents on local apartments, which "in some cases," noted Columbia's trustees, "[were] as large as the generous increases in salary recently granted." [160] As faculty members who had settled on Morningside Heights moved out of the neighborhood in order to find affordable housing, people unaffiliated with the institutions took their place. The Barnard Dean, Virginia Gildersleeve, reported:

> The extreme increase in the rents in this neighborhood has been driving a number of our officers away from the vicinity of the College to residence in the lower part of the city or in the suburbs. This must inevitably have a bad effect upon our college life. Indeed, the congestion in living conditions in New York and the influx of non-university people into this neighborhood, presents the whole of the University a problem with which it must grapple very seriously in the immediate future. [161]

None of the Columbia-affiliated institutions had funds for the construction of housing for faculty. Instead, in 1919 Columbia instituted a policy that was to have a significant impact on Morningside Heights real estate. The university purchased four apartment buildings on Claremont Avenue in 1919 and 1920, and, after securing possession of apartments from tenants as their leases expired, let these units to university affiliates at affordable rents. [162] These real estate purchases were the beginning of the transformation of the residential housing stock on Morningside Heights from privately held apartment buildings to buildings largely owned by the area's institutions (see Afterword).

Butler Library

By the end of the 1920s, the university still had one especially pressing need—a large new library to replace Low Library, which had long ago proved inadequate for the expanding university's needs. In 1921 Butler had informed the trustees that "pressure upon the Library of the University has become such as well nigh to paralyze it." [163] In his *Annual Report* of 1921–22, Butler first suggested that the oft-delayed University Hall might be completed for library use. [164] Serious consideration of the idea of extending Low Library into University Hall apparently followed a letter from Charles Williamson, the director of Columbia's library, to Butler in August 1927 that detailed the needs of the library and how they could be met by erecting an enormous University Hall addition. [165] By the late 1920s, Butler was actively seeking a substantial donation for this project from Edward S. Harkness. [166] Harkness was one of the wealthiest men in America (in 1926 he paid the sixth largest income tax in the country), having inherited the fortune of his father, a founder of the Standard Oil Company. [167] Harkness spent most of his adult life giving away money, largely to educational and medical organizations. He was an especially generous donor to Yale (his alma mater), to Harvard, and to Presbyterian institutions, such as Presbyterian Hospital. Butler and Harkness became acquainted in 1925 when Columbia's Medical School affiliated with Presbyterian Hospital and construction began on the vast Columbia University-Presbyterian Medical Center at 168th Street and Broadway. Harkness funded a portion of the new Presbyterian Hospital and, in 1929, also offered two million dollars for a dormitory for Columbia's medical students (Bard Hall).

In order to increase the likelihood of another major gift from Harkness, Butler hired Harkness's favorite architect, James Gamble Rogers, to adapt McKim, Mead & White's University Hall as a library.[168] Rogers had designed most of Harkness's projects, including the Columbia medical center buildings, after having established a close relationship with the philanthropist during the design of Harkness's house on Fifth Avenue and 75th Street in 1907–9. Butler never considered McKim, Mead & White for this project and there is no indication that he even informed the firm that he was seeking designs from another architect, as he had decades earlier regarding the design of St. Paul's Chapel and the School of Mines Building. It was Rogers who finally wrote to William Kendall early in 1931, after he had been involved with the library project for several years, informing Kendall that "I did not apply for this work but was asked by Columbia to take it up."[169] Relations between McKim, Mead & White and Columbia had, in fact, deteriorated to such a level that McKim, Mead & White would never again design a building for Columbia.[170]

In 1930 Rogers planned an enormous project, connecting Low Library and University Hall, both underground and by a bridge.[171] However, the idea of using University Hall as a library proved impractical since the project would have been extremely costly and the weight of books would have required a major reconstruction of the portion of the building that had already been completed. In addition, engineering concerns relating to the presence of the power plant and gymnasium in the basement would have precluded efficient library services.[172] Thus, in December 1930, Butler altered his request to Harkness, seeking support for constructing a separate library building on 114th Street, at the south end of South Field.[173]

The future of this site had been left undetermined by the trustees in the 1903 master plan for South Field. Although McKim, Mead & White's 1922–23 designs for a Students Hall at this location would have closed off the view from Low Library's portico toward the city to the south, it was the decision to erect the library at the south end of the campus that effected this change. This architectural barrier between the university campus and the city can be seen as symbolic of Butler's efforts to create a university separated from the city. However, in reality, the vista from Low Library toward the city had been destroyed years before. With the construction of six- and eight-story apartment buildings on the blocks between Amsterdam Avenue and Broadway in the earlier years of the twentieth century (see chapter 8), rather than the three- and four-story row-houses that Low and McKim had assumed would rise on the midblock sites, the view from the Low Library portico to the city to the south had already been largely blocked (figure 5.35). Indeed, the view south was neither grand nor elegant, focusing on rowhouses and speculative apartment buildings with rooftop water towers. The decision to erect South Hall in 114th Street, now fully enclosing the entire campus precinct, created an educational "acropolis" that historian Thomas Bender has noted was now "in the city, but not of it."[174]

James Gamble Rogers's initial design for the proposed library would have cost an estimated $5.5 million.[175] This was more than Harkness contemplated spending for a library at Columbia and Butler was forced to ask Rogers to redesign the building.[176] The revised design, completed in April 1931, was estimated to cost $4 million. In order to save money, Rogers had simplified the facade, removed an impressive entry lobby and stairway, and compromised on many utilitarian elements of the building, including the number of books that could be held in the stacks.[177] Even with these changes, Harkness would not commit to fund the library and Butler had to plead with him. Since Harkness often funded laboratory and research facilities, Butler impressed upon him that the library he wished to erect was "a laboratory building to furnish what are in effect laboratory facilities for all those departments of the University which lie

FIGURE 5.35
View looking south from Low Library during construction of John Jay Hall, c. 1926.

outside the field of experimental sciences, of law, and of medicine."[178] Finally, on May 8, 1931, Harkness agreed to fund the $4 million library scheme.[179]

While supporting the need for a new library, some students and faculty (especially from the Department of Physical Education) were not happy with the decision to erect the library on a portion of the undergraduates' athletic field.[180] Students were especially irate that their opposition had been muted by the timing of the trustees' announcement in May 1931, just as they were occupied studying for finals and after their newspaper, the *Columbia Spectator,* had ceased publication for the year. This timing was actually a coincidence, since Harkness had only agreed to fund the project in May. In defense of the plan, the *Alumni News* noted that Columbia opted for "the pursuit of mental exercises rather than . . . the pursuit of physical exercises."[181] Once students had dispersed for their summer vacations, groundbreaking proceeded smoothly.

Rogers's final design for Columbia's new library (figure 5.36) was constrained not only by cost, but also by the necessity of providing a building within the design context established by McKim, Mead & White. He used limestone and brick as the facade materials and a style of architecture that was similar to that of Low Library. He also attempted to be deferential to McKim's masterpiece, informing Butler that "the fact that this new working library is at a much lower level makes me feel quite sure that this new building will in no

FIGURE 5.36
Butler Library, 1934, with
John Jay Hall at left.

way detract from the dominance of the beautiful Low Library." [182] Rogers was adept at producing monumental Collegiate Gothic university complexes, such as those at Yale and Northwestern University, but, for all his effort, he provided Columbia with a Classical Revival structure more notable for its size than the grace of its exterior design and the utility of the interior. [183] The building has a long limestone central pavilion with twelve Ionic columns echoing those of Low Library. This feature copies the colonnade proposed by McKim, Mead & White several years earlier for their Students Hall design for the same site. To either side are small, poorly proportioned brick wings with limestone trim, designed to connect the building visually to the brick and limestone structures of the surrounding campus. Butler was interested in every detail of the new library's design, even so far as choosing the names of the men of letters inscribed on the frieze that runs around the east, north, and west elevations, and the twelve American statesmen and twelve American literary figures whose names are carved in pairs above the reading room windows. [184] As Aaron Betsky discusses in his study of Rogers, the completed building was widely criticized by the Columbia community, which found it to be a dry and uninspired work. [185]

Choosing a name for the new library proved to be somewhat complicated. In November 1931 Butler proposed to Harkness that the library be named Alexander Hamilton Hall, since, Butler argued, "Hamilton remains, after all the years that have passed, the most distinguished alumnus of Columbia in any of the stages of its history." [186] However, Columbia's trustees had other ideas. They wished to name the library for Butler, but since he was still president, this was not possible. Instead, the trustees decided to use the name "South Hall" as a temporary expedient. [187] South Hall was renamed Butler Library in 1946, a year after the president's retirement.

The completion of South Hall in 1934 brought to a close a major phase in Columbia's development under Butler's leadership. Butler continued to propose grand plans for Columbia's expansion, announcing, for example, a major initiative in February 1938 that included a new School of Engineering Building, a new Law School, the completion of University Hall, a Fine Arts Building, a theater, two dormitories, a classroom building for the Faculty of Political Science, and other structures. [188] These proposals were never seriously acted upon and campus expansion and new construction ceased because of the Depression and World War II. In 1945, at the age of 83, after serving as president for more than four decades, Butler resigned.

With the completion of South Hall in the 1930s and the resignation of Butler in the 1940s, Low's and McKim's architectural vision of a unified, monumental campus, was forgotten. Buildings erected in the 1950s and 1960s, such as Ferris Booth Hall (a student center; demolished), Carman Hall (a dormitory), Seeley Mudd Hall (a new engineering school building), and Uris Hall (for the business school) are not only stylistically out of place on the campus, but also excruciatingly banal individually.[189] Beginning in the 1970s, following criticism from the architectural and popular press and from students and faculty, Columbia attempted to commission designs from more prominent architects and build more distinguished buildings. In 1972 James Stewart Polshek, dean of the School of Architecture, was asked to assist in the selection of architects and the planning for new construction and building renovations, resulting in campus additions of a higher quality than those of previous decades, notably Mitchell/Giurgola Associates' Sherman Fairchild Center for the Life Sciences (1974–77), R. M. Kliment and Frances Halsband's Computer Science Building (1981–83; figure 5.37), and Davis, Brody & Associates' Havemeyer Extension (1984–89).[190] Plans during this period also included the construction of a science laboratory at the northeast corner of the campus that was to have been designed by British architect James Sterling, but, unfortunately this building was never erected.[191] New projects were undertaken in the late 1990s, notably the Lerner Student Center (1996–99; figure afterword.4), designed by James Polshek's successor as dean of the School of Architecture, Bernard Tschumi. The massing of this controversial stone, brick, and glass building is a bold attempt at a contemporary

FIGURE 5.37
Computer Science
Building, 1983; at left,
Schermerhorn Extension,
at right, Sherman
Fairchild Hall.

adaptation of McKim, Mead & White's South Field proposal.[192] Although the McKim, Mead & White buildings and campus plan have not always been treated with the greatest respect by Columbia, the work of McKim and his office survives as one of the great institutional ensembles in America and as the physical representation of Seth Low's vision of a great university in the greatest metropolis of North America.

FIGURE 6.1

Terra-cotta cartouche on facade of Milbank Hall.

CHAPTER SIX

Building for the Mind III

Barnard College and Teachers College—
Women's Education on Morningside Heights

COLUMBIA COLLEGE'S DECISION IN 1892 TO TRANSFER ITS OPERA-
tions to Morningside Heights attracted other academic institutions to the neighborhood. The earliest to follow Columbia's lead were Barnard College, founded
in 1888 as a women's college affiliated with Columbia, and Teachers College,
founded in 1889, which wished to arrange a similar affiliation with Columbia.
These two colleges introduced a major women's educational presence on Morningside Heights. They also consciously sought to erect impressive academic
buildings in order to establish their institutional identities in the growing
metropolis.

Barnard College: A Women's College for New York

Barnard College has become such an important presence on Morningside
Heights and such a significant part of New York City's academic community
that it is easy to forget how controversial the very idea of higher education for
women once was.[1] As we saw in chapter 4, Columbia was not in the forefront of
educational reform for much of the nineteenth century. Therefore it is not surprising that the trustees, who hesitated to undertake educational reforms for the
men who enrolled, would balk at the even more radical notion of admitting
women. The fight for women's higher education in New York City occurred long
after the admission of women at Oberlin College, a religious institution founded
in Oberlin, Ohio in 1833 as America's first coeducational college.[2] Despite the
example of Oberlin, higher education did not become a viable option for most
women until the mid-nineteenth century, when schools began to respond to
the demands for secondary education for women equivalent to that available to
men. Some coeducational religious colleges were established during this period, including Antioch College, Bates College, and Boston University. In addition, newly incorporated state universities, especially those in the Midwest,
slowly began admitting women, although not without serious hesitation.[3]

In the northeast, with its well-established men's colleges, educational options for women were far fewer since these entrenched institutions were unwilling to permit women to study alongside men. As a result, independent women's colleges were established, beginning with Vassar in 1865 and Wellesley and Smith in 1875.[4] The creation of these women's colleges was controversial, not only because some doubted whether women should receive a college education at all, but also because even among those who supported education for women there was a concern that separate colleges would be seen as second-best when compared to men's colleges. Thus, many reformers continued to advocate the opening of older all-male schools to women. Lobbying for such reforms centered in urban areas such as Boston and New York with their large populations of educated women who sought entry into prestigious local colleges. Harvard resisted pressure to admit women and, instead, established a women's "annex" in 1879, where young women would study with Harvard professors and take Harvard's exams, but would not be granted Harvard degrees. Instead, as *Harper's Weekly* reported, even the most brilliant woman student was compelled "to accept the certificate of the Society for the Collegiate Instruction of Women in lieu of the diploma which she had fairly earned."[5] The refusal of Harvard's trustees to grant degrees to women resulted in the establishment in 1894 of Radcliffe College, an independent institution located near Harvard's campus that sought to give women the equivalent of a Harvard education.[6] This development decreased pressure on Harvard to admit women, but did little to dispel the view that separate women's colleges, especially those established as parallels to men's colleges, were inferior.

By the 1880s, at least some form of higher education was available to women in such cities as Baltimore, Boston, Chicago, and New Orleans. However, New York City still offered women no opportunities for advanced study. New York's women first sought admission to Columbia in 1876 when Sorosis, a women's club established in 1868 for "the promotion of agreeable and useful relations among women of literary, artistic and scientific tastes" unsuccessfully petitioned for the admission of women to Columbia's classes.[7] Three years later, the trustees also refused women the privilege of auditing the school's science lectures.[8] Despite these setbacks, there was great optimism in the early 1880s that Columbia would soon grant women the right to an education equal to that of men. Those who believed that coeducation at Columbia was inevitable based their optimism on the increasing number of independent women's colleges as well as coeducational institutions; Oxford and Cambridge, as well as Harvard, had opened women's annexes. More important, Columbia's president Frederick Barnard, who had attempted to introduce many new ideas to the college, was a vocal proponent of education for women and, beginning in 1879, his annual reports to the trustees spoke eloquently of Columbia's responsibility to women's higher education.[9] However, his efforts were vigorously opposed by Dean John Burgess and consistently thwarted by the trustees.

A major campaign for the admission of women to Columbia was initiated in April 1882, when the Association for the Promotion of the Higher Education of Women held a meeting at the conservative Union League Club to discuss the issue. That evening many prominent New Yorkers demanded equal educational opportunities for women at coeducational institutions, none perhaps more forcefully than lawyer Joseph Choate, who declared, "If you ask why we insist on Columbia's actually opening her doors to women, we answer because there is no reason why they should submit to gather in an annex the crumbs which fall from their master's table, when they might have a right to an equal seat at the board."[10] As a result of this meeting, a petition to Columbia's trustees was drafted demanding that "in view of the present state of public opinion, both here and in other countries, touching the justice and expediency of admitting women to the same educational advantages as men," Columbia's policy regarding the admission of women should be liberalized.[11] The petition was signed by more than 1,400 people, including former United States presidents (Arthur and Grant), governors and mayors, judges, ministers, lawyers, and a wide range of other New Yorkers.[12] The Columbia trustees were unmoved. Some years later, *Harper's Weekly*, a supporter of women's education, sarcastically condemned this rejection by Columbia's trustees:

> But in the still seclusion of the college this kindly voice of an orderly multitude, eager to advance the cause of law and order, intelligence and morality, was exaggerated [by the trustees] into the frenzied shriek of a ribald mob, bent on trampling down the safeguards of society. Certain of the trustees, not all of them, declared that they would oppose such an innovation to the bitter end, and the association for the promotion of the higher education of women received, in effect, the classic reply—*nullum tui negotium.*[13]

Although the trustees were unwilling to admit women to Columbia's classes, they evidently realized that the pressure to offer women opportunities for higher education would continue. Finally, in 1883, Columbia announced the establishment of a Collegiate Course for Women that would allow women to pursue an educational program parallel to that offered to men, so long as no women attended Columbia's classes. Women students would meet with professors at the beginning of each term in order to receive reading assignments, but they could not attend lectures. They were free to study at home or at another school and then were to reappear at Columbia for final exams. Should all work be completed satisfactorily, Columbia would grant a degree. This approach differed from that followed at Harvard. Harvard offered women an education similar to that given to men, but refused to grant degrees; Columbia offered a degree, but refused to extend an equivalent educational experience to women. Needless to say, few women enrolled in this sham program and even fewer completed their studies. The absurdity of the Collegiate Course for Women was summarized by one of its original students, Annie Nathan, who described her desolation when seated for her first examination:

> I had read the pages assigned to me, their content I was sure I knew; yet I could make nothing at all of the questions before me! As I grew calmer, I realized where the trouble lay. The Professor had, it is true, told me to read certain pages and I had done so; but he had calmly proceeded to base his questions, not on the textbooks assigned, but entirely upon the lectures which he had given to his classes—lectures which I, of course, had not been permitted to attend. . . . Was I, then, to flunk what hosts of boys would pass? Perish the thought! Getting a grip on myself, I answered fully such questions as I understood, and then coolly wrote in the examination paper that certain questions evidently referred to the Professor's lectures, which I had not had the privilege of hearing. The Professor had a sense of justice—or possibly, a sense of humor—for he passed me.[14]

Annie Nathan remained in the collegiate course for only one year, abandoning her studies to marry Dr. Alfred Meyer, but not abandoning her commitment to women's education. Annie Nathan Meyer went on to lead the campaign that culminated in the establishment of Barnard College in 1889, an independent institution affiliated with Columbia that offered women an education equivalent to that at Columbia, capped by the awarding of a Columbia College degree. Although Annie Nathan was a member of one of New York City's oldest Jewish families (ironically, one of her ancestors, Gershom Seixas, had been an original trustee of Columbia), her success in this enterprise is somewhat surprising since she came from a middle-class household and had few connections among the wealthy New Yorkers whose support would be necessary to ensure the success of a women's college. In addition, she had no experience with grassroots organizing. However, her commitment to the establishment of a women's college made her unstoppable as she—perhaps somewhat immodestly—details in her memoir, *Barnard Beginnings*.[15]

Meyer credits Columbia's librarian Melvil Dewey as the inspiration for her campaign to create a separate women's college in New York. After she had explained to Dewey how ridiculous she considered the Collegiate Course, Dewey exploded with enthusiasm. As Meyer recounts:

> He agreed with me that the present scheme was utterly absurd. Obviously, if women could get from a few examinations all that men got from daily intercourse with Faculty and with students, and from hundreds of lectures, and work in the laboratories, then either women were miraculously gifted or else—and this was an alternative pretty serious to contemplate—all the millions and millions at the moment locked up in college endowments, in laboratories and lecture halls, were just so much sheer waste![16]

Dewey then urged Meyer to start a college herself. Meyer launched her crusade to create a separate women's college with an article published in the *Nation* on January 21, 1888.[17] In that article, she noted that Bryn Mawr, Smith, Vassar, Wellesley, and Cornell matriculated fifty-seven women from New York (the actual number was sixty-seven, but, as Meyer later admitted, her math had been faulty), observing that if these "girls can leave their homes and encounter the discomforts of an independent life for the sake of pursing a collegiate education, how many would attend college gladly, enthusiastically, were it not necessary to face the obstacle of leaving home?"[18] She then set out her idea for an independently funded college, located near Columbia, where women would be instructed by Columbia's professors and receive Columbia degrees.

Meyer met with anyone in New York who could assist her in her efforts, including meeting and seeking the support of each of Columbia's trustees. Another petition urging Columbia to offer a course to women was drafted, but instead of seeking general support as with the first petition, the proponents focused their campaign on collecting signatures from fifty carefully selected New Yorkers representing a wide variety of interests, including politics, religion, business, law, education, and philanthropy.[19] The petition was presented to the Columbia trustees at their March 5, 1888 meeting, resulting in the establishment of a special committee to examine the proposal.[20] Meyer and her allies waited expectantly for the committee's response and word from the full board, but heard nothing. In fact, the trustees had discussed the issue at their March meeting and in May had voted to recognize a women's college.[21] Unfortunately, the board's secretary was on leave of absence and there was no public announcement of this decision. It was not until November, when Meyer herself asked one of the trustees, that she learned of the favorable recommendation.[22] Columbia's trustees approved the idea of a separate women's college, but also insisted that only Columbia professors teach at the new school and that the annex meet all of its own expenses. Only seniors who were enrolled in graduate courses would be permitted to take classes on the Columbia grounds with Columbia men. The new women's school was to open on a trial basis, with Columbia reviewing its commitment to the project after four years.[23]

After having rejected coeducation for so long, why did the trustees of Columbia so readily acquiesce to the plan for a women's annex? Although the trustees remained unalterably opposed to undergradute coeducation, they apparently had no strong objections to the general notion of educating women. The trustees realized that pressure for advanced education for women, including the idea of coeducation, would escalate if the proposed annex were rejected. In contrast to accepting women into Columbia College itself, the establishment of an "annex" for women would have only a minimal effect on the school. Thus, since the creation of an annex was a relatively conservative step, entailing no financial commitment on Columbia's part and continuing the ban on women in undergraduate college classrooms, the trustees' decision was a strategic way to defuse this highly charged issue.

If the trustees' decision approving a women's college had been announced in May rather than November, the proponents of the college might have attempted to open the still unnamed college in the fall of 1888. The delay, however, provided time in which to establish a board of trustees, locate and furnish a site near Columbia's campus for classes, advertise for students, and, most importantly, attempt to raise the money needed to pay for the venture. A board of twenty-one men and women, among them some of New York's wealthiest and most prestigious citizens, was formed with Arthur Brooks, minister of the socially-prominent Episcopal Church of the Incarnation, as chair. On April 28, 1889, prior to the school's opening, President Barnard of Columbia died. The trustees of the new college voted to name the school in his honor, even though Barnard had opposed the creation of a separate college for women, preferring, instead, the admission of women to Columbia. Barnard's widow declared that she "was going to fight the establishment of an 'Annex.'" However, she agreed to support the school since "you have done my husband the honor of naming the College for him, you have taken the wind from my sails. I cannot very well fight a College which bears his name."[24]

Finding a site for the school that was near Columbia's Madison Avenue campus and was also affordable proved difficult. The college finally rented a four-story and basement brownstone rowhouse at 343 Madison Avenue between East 44th and 45th streets only four blocks from Columbia's campus (figure 6.2).[25] Even with a roster of prestigious board members and vocal support from large segments of New York's elite, the new venture was in danger of collapsing since this support was not followed by significant financial assistance. Jacob Schiff even suggested that the school postpone its opening since "the response of the people had not been generous enough to warrant it."[26] This suggestion was ignored and, on October 7, 1889, the new women's college opened its doors to fourteen degree candidates and twenty-two special students.[27]

During its four-year trial period, Barnard succeeded in enrolling an increasing number of qualified women seeking a college degree. However, financially, the college was bordering on insolvency, with an endowment of only $6,000 as the trial period was nearing its end in 1892. Jacob Schiff, who was serving as the college treasurer, announced that he would resign "unless ways and means can be found to better arouse public spirit on behalf of Barnard College."[28] To make matters worse, in late 1891 Columbia's president Seth Low had announced that the college hoped to move to a new campus on Morningside Heights. Barnard was not included in Columbia's planned move. If the women's college wished to retain its affiliation with Columbia, it would have to consider a move as well. Unfortunately, such a venture would also mean that this new college would be competing with the larger established institution for funds to purchase land and erect a new building.

Luckily for Barnard, a benefactor came forward at this critical juncture. In 1892, Mary E. Brinckerhoff offered the college $100,000 to construct a building, under the condition that within four years the school purchase a site located no more than 1,000 feet from Columbia's new Morningside Heights campus.[29] Since Brinckerhoff had no association with the campaign for a women's college, her gift came as a complete surprise, apparently resulting from a suggestion by her lawyer, Barnard trustee Frederick Wait.[30] However, before Brinckerhoff's money would be made available to Barnard, the college had to locate an appropriate site and raise the funds to purchase it. The *Evening Post,* a consistent supporter of Barnard, did not envision a problem, affirming "that a mere statement such as this of the needed sum would be sufficient to bring in fresh dona-

Binckerhoff

FIGURE 6.2
Barnard College's original home at 343 Madison Avenue between East 44th and East 45th streets.

tions."[31] The *Evening Post*'s optimism was far removed from the reality of the situation.

Barnard's supporters immediately started investigating potential sites. Only a few days after the Brinckerhoff gift was announced, John Pine, the clerk of the Columbia board of trustees, suggested to Columbia President Seth Low that Columbia acquire New York Hospital's property west of Broadway between 116th and 120th streets, and lease the block between 119th and 120th streets to Barnard "as a means of concentrating educational institutions about us."[32] Unfortunately, Columbia's serious financial constraints prevented the purchase of the hospital's land. Various real estate agents, including Dwight Olmstead, the landowner who had led the fight to evict the Bloomingdale Asylum (see chapter 1), sought to interest Barnard in purchasing other land near Columbia.[33] Despite initial efforts to locate a site, it was not until 1895 that Barnard actually purchased land on Morningside Heights. There is no documentation as to why it took so long to purchase property, especially since so many sites were available, but the school's financial plight is undoubtedly the explanation. Barnard, like Columbia, found itself caught in the intersection of the long history of New Yorkers' lack of interest in lending financial support to local educational institutions and the economic depression that began in June 1893, which inhibited donations from those who otherwise might have been persuaded to view local colleges as worthy objects of their philanthropy.

In February 1895 Barnard's trustees finally announced that an option had been taken on the New York Hospital plot between 119th and 120th streets that Pine had suggested several years earlier. The price was $160,000. To secure this site, the trustees took out a mortgage, but, pursuant to the terms of Brinckerhoff's gift, the mortgage had to be retired before her money could be spent on construction. Since Barnard had managed to raise only $16,000 in the three years since Brinckerhoff's offer, "a $144,000 vacuum still exist[ed] between this worthy institution of learning and the realization of its desires for needed accommodations."[34] Shortly after settling on a site, Barnard announced a second $100,000 gift for the erection of another building, from "a lady who desires that her identity should not be made known."[35] Thus, the college had pledges for $200,000 to erect two buildings, but still lacked most of the funds needed to buy the land on which to actually build. Barnard's supporters organized a series of afternoon parlor meetings for socially prominent women at which Barnard's dean, Emily Smith, various trustees, and prominent guests—including Episcopal Bishop Henry Potter, Joseph Choate, Abram Hewitt, and Seth Low—solicited gifts.[36] Editorial writers urged support, asserting that Barnard's failure would reflect poorly on New York, comparing the backward state of women's education in this city with the progress elsewhere in America.[37] Finally, in May 1896, within 24 hours of Brinckerhoff's four-year deadline for purchasing a Morningside Heights site, a gift for the final $23,000 averted the failure of the

entire project. *Harper's Weekly* editorialized on the slow and piecemeal response of New Yorkers to Barnard's appeal for funds:

> It is not for New York men and women to be very proud of such an
> episode, for it means that the money essential to the continued life of
> Barnard had to be wrung from them by the hardest kind of work. And
> this should not have happened.[38]

Building Barnard

The anonymous donor of Barnard's second $100,000 gift (later increased to
$170,000) was Elizabeth Milbank Anderson. Elizabeth Milbank was born in
New York City in 1850, the daughter of wealthy financier Jeremiah Milbank
whose $10,000,000 fortune came primarily from the organization of the Bor-
den Condensed Milk Company.[39] Elizabeth and her brother Joseph, a supporter
of Teachers College, inherited this money in 1884. In 1887, Elizabeth Milbank
married the fashionable academic painter Abram A. Anderson. Elizabeth Milbank Anderson had not been involved in the establishment of Barnard, nor was
the women's college her first choice of philanthropy. She had offered a medical
building to Roosevelt Hospital, sending her architect, Charles Rich, to Europe
to study modern hospital design, but Roosevelt eventually refused the gift because of restrictions Anderson placed on it.[40] She turned her attention to
Barnard after attending one of the fundraising parlor meetings at which her
minister and Barnard's board chairman Arthur Brooks spoke. Elizabeth Milbank Anderson soon became Barnard's most generous patron, as well as a
member of its board of trustees.[41] Her loyalty to the school assured its survival
and expansion at a time when few other New Yorkers were extending substantial assistance to the new women's college.

As Elizabeth Milbank Anderson became increasingly involved in philanthropic ventures, including donating buildings to several institutions, she insisted that Charles Rich design the projects.[42] In the autumn of 1895, for example, Anderson telegraphed Barnard's dean, succinctly informing her that
"My gift is a building[;] as condition I of course choose architect."[43] Since Mary
Brinckerhoff had not requested a specific architect for the building that she
funded, Rich became the architect for the entire original campus.[44] Charles
Rich had studied engineering at Dartmouth and received architectural training
in the United States and Europe before settling in New York and forming the
partnership of Lamb & Rich in 1882.[45] Lamb & Rich was an extremely prolific
firm, designing numerous speculative rowhouses (especially on Manhattan's
Upper West Side) and apartment buildings, and a significant number of institutional structures. Between 1899 and 1903 Rich worked independently before
establishing a new firm, Rich, Mathesius & Koyl. Rich designed many collegiate
buildings, including sixteen at Darmouth, erected between 1896 and 1914, and

two at Wesleyan.[46] Rich never reached the top rank of New York architects. Although he designed in a wide range of fashionable styles, his work was rarely as sophisticated as that of his better trained contemporaries such as McKim, Mead & White, William Potter, and Howells & Stokes, all of whom also designed institutional buildings on Morningside Heights.

Rich prepared an imposing plan for Barnard's new site, which was located across from the undeveloped north end of the Columbia campus, just southwest of the recently completed buildings of Teachers College (see below). The site was relatively small, measuring only 200 feet wide on 119th and 120th streets, and just under that length on Broadway and Claremont Avenue. Although New York Hospital owned all of the land between Broadway and Claremont Avenue as far south as 116th Street, John Pine had suggested this more northern location for Barnard and there is no evidence that the women's college sought to purchase the more prominent site facing onto 116th Street, across from the entrance to Columbia's campus, then under construction. Barnard, as an adjunct to Columbia and with significantly limited funds, was simply not able to compete with its larger, older, and more prestigious associate. Thus, as a result of the size and location of its site, Barnard would not have as significant a physical presence in the neighborhood as Columbia.

Although funding was in hand for only two buildings, Rich devised a unified design for three interconnected four-story structures (figure 6.3). Writing in *Harper's Bazaar,* Annie Nathan Meyer credited Rich's rejection of an individual design for each building to the influence of the World's Columbian Exposition, remarking that the fair "has made such errors forever impossible to us," and es-

FIGURE 6.3
Charles Rich's design for
Barnard College, 1896.

pecially praising the fact that Rich had designed a third building to complete the ensemble even though its construction was not immediately contemplated.[47] The campus was planned as a symmetrical U-shaped complex with a central courtyard oriented to the south (figure 6.4). Milbank Hall (named in honor of Anderson's parents) was to be the central building, with the wing along Broadway erected with the Brinckerhoff gift. Entry to Barnard's buildings would be through an impressive doorway in Milbank Hall, set beneath a columned cloister. Rich's plan echoes, on a significantly reduced scale, that of Columbia, with a group of buildings oriented to the south, focusing on an open court. Rich planned to enclose this court with a colonnade in much the same way that McKim had initially planned to enclose the Columbia court with an iron fence, neither of which was ever completed. As at Columbia, which did not yet own the land south of 116th Street, Barnard also faced the prospect of unrelated and perhaps inappropriate development immediately to the south of its campus across 119th Street should New York Hospital sell its remaining property.

As was appropriate for a school affiliated with Columbia, Rich adapted the design and materials chosen by McKim for the Columbia classroom structures

FIGURE 6.4

Charles Rich's plan for Barnard College, 1896.

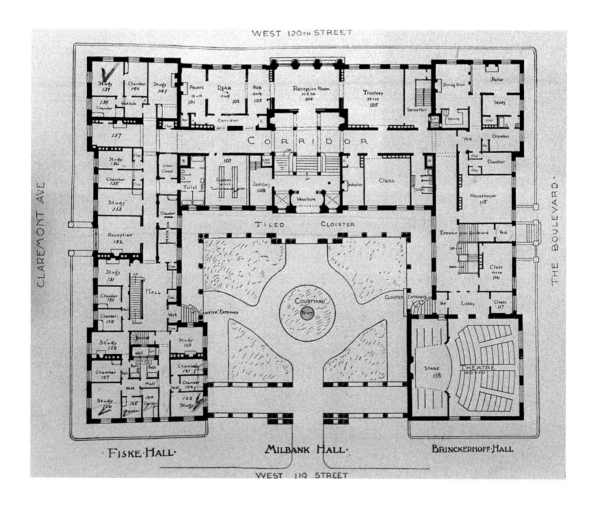

then under construction. Accordingly, the Barnard buildings are faced with dark red brick with contrasting white trim, similar to that employed at Columbia. The details on the first story and the major ornamental flourishes of the upper floors are limestone, with the remainder of the ornament, including corner quoins, huge cartouches (figure 6.1), and ornamental roundels executed in a less costly white terra-cotta that imitated the look of limestone.[48] The buildings were often described at the time as designed in the style of Henri II, referring to sixteenth-century early French Renaissance architecture.[49] The U-shaped plan of the complex certainly echoes the layout of sixteenth-century French chateaux and the heavy ornament, especially the quoins and keyed window enframements, also resembles French motifs, but the design more closely follows the combination of Italian Renaissance and American colonial forms employed at Columbia, as was acknowledged in several contemporary newspaper articles about the Barnard buildings.[50]

Milbank Hall originally contained several notable interior spaces. Just as the lobby of Low Library was designed as a grand space with ornate marblework and a monumental chandelier, Rich planned an impressive entrance into Milbank Hall (figure 6.5). By manipulating the floor levels in the entrance vestibule and employing fine ornamental details, Rich sought to turn the small entry into a complex and dramatic space. The visitor enters Milbank Hall through a vestibule articulated by columns of Mycenian marble that form screens, breaking up the space and disguising its small dimension. The overscaled quality of a number of features in the vestibule, such as a shallow central dome that originally appeared to be supported by four massive cartouches and a huge spheri-

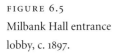

FIGURE 6.5
Milbank Hall entrance
lobby, c. 1897.

cal chandelier (all destroyed), provided the formal space with a sense of expansive breadth. A handsome cast-iron stair with ornate railings leads to the upper floors. In 1897 Anderson commissioned the Tiffany Glass and Decorating Company to design a window for the stairway landing between the first and second stories and to decorate the college library on the second story, which was an alumnae memorial to Ella Weed, the college's first dean. For the library, the Tiffany company provided oak furnishings, green-tinted walls and ceiling, and a mantel in scintillating glass mosaic.[51]

Milbank and Brinckerhoff halls were completed in time for Barnard to join Columbia in inaugurating classes on Morningside Heights in October 1897. In May 1897, several months before the original buildings were completed, Martha T. Fiske (always referred to as Mrs. Josiah Fiske) presented the college with $140,000 in memory of her husband to fund the third building of Rich's campus plan.[52] This building, erected along Claremont Avenue, was initially planned as a science laboratory, with its exterior design mirroring that of Brinckerhoff. However, in 1898 the trustees decided that Barnard was in greater need of a dormitory in order to attract additional students from outside New York City. Thus, Rich had to add additional windows to this wing in order to light the dormitory rooms, creating the crowded fenestration on Fiske Hall that compromises the symmetry of the original design (figure 6.6).[53]

Unfortunately, the Brinckerhoff, Anderson, and Fiske gifts did not meet all of the construction expenses and the college was burdened with a debt of $127,911.50, a substantial sum for an institution with no endowment and few financial resources. The board of trustees feared that unless this debt was paid off, the college's limited funds would be spent on interest payments rather than on education. In January 1898, board chairman Abram S. Hewitt donated $1,000 to a fund that he established to retire the debt. Almost immediately an

FIGURE 6.6
Barnard College, c. 1900; from left, Fiske Hall, Milbank Hall, and Brinckerhoff Hall.

anonymous friend of the college, who turned out to be Elizabeth Milbank Anderson, promised $25,000 under the condition that funds to pay off the entire debt be raised by the time the second year of classes began on October 3, 1898. Although John D. Rockefeller (whose wife sat on the board) and J. P. Morgan each donated $10,000, raising this relatively small sum of money proved difficult. On the morning of October 3, subscriptions were still $9,000 short. Fortunately, by the end of the day another anonymous "friend" (undoubtedly Elizabeth Anderson) had bailed out the college and the entire debt was paid off.[54]

By the start of classes in October 1898, Barnard was finally poised to become a major academic force in the city. The affiliation with Columbia was a success, permitting Barnard's students to receive a quality education, a Columbia degree, and admission to many of the university's graduate programs;[55] the school had a new complex of buildings that provided modern classrooms and social facilities; enrollment was increasing as the school gained in prestige; and the college was free from debt. Unfortunately, Barnard still had no endowment by which to assure its future prosperity and advancement, and fundraising continued to be a problem. These financial difficulties again became evident when, in June 1901, John D. Rockefeller promised Barnard $200,000 for a desperately needed endowment if a like amount could be raised by January 1, 1902. When that date arrived, the college had managed to raise only $120,000. Even with an extension to April 1, $3,500 was still lacking on the last morning. Although many wealthy people were interested in supporting Barnard (77 people had donated to the endowment fund), few were committed enough to give the college more than modest gifts of $1,000.[56] As with the campaign to pay off the original debt, only last-minute donations rescued the challenge gift.

Barnard Expands

In 1902 New York Hospital decided to divest itself of all of its remaining land on Morningside Heights. That May, Columbia optioned the property south of 116th Street between Amsterdam Avenue and Broadway, thus protecting its southern flank from unwanted development (see chapter 5). The land south of Barnard, however, was in danger of falling into the hands of the speculative developers who envisioned large profits from constructing apartment houses on vacant Morningside Heights property that would soon be conveniently linked to Lower Manhattan by a new subway line (see chapter 8).[57] Barnard desperately needed additional space for a student center and for the construction of a dormitory to replace Fiske Hall, which was about to be reconfigured for its originally intended purpose as a hall of science. Thus, the college was anxious to buy land on Morningside Heights before prices increased, but did not have the resources to undertake a costly land transaction.[58]

New York Hospital's vacant property south of Barnard between 116th and 119th streets was an obvious site for the college's expansion (figure 6.7). However, it was unclear how Barnard would acquire the funds needed to purchase this land. After all, Columbia, a far larger and more established school, was itself struggling to find the $1.9 million required for the purchase of South Field and Barnard had only recently experienced difficulty in raising a mere $200,000. It was unlikely that the funds needed to buy New York Hospital's land could easily be found. Nevertheless, in February 1903 Barnard's treasurer, George A. Plimpton, began negotiating with New York Hospital for the property. Plimpton was authorized by the trustees to offer up to $1 million, and after a lower price was rejected by the hospital he pleaded with H. H. Cammann, chairman of New York Hospital's Real Estate Committee, to accept the $1 million offer: "I sincerely hope that the Hospital will accept this offer. If it does not the college will lose the chance, now for the first time presented to add a million dollars to its assets and its development and public usefulness will be seriously impaired."[59] New York Hospital accepted Barnard's proposal. Barnard was able to offer $1 million because an anonymous donor—once again Elizabeth Milbank Anderson—offered to buy the property and transfer ownership to the college.[60] In recognition of Anderson's "most opportune and splendidly munificent gift," the trustees designated the new property "Milbank Quadrangle."[61]

Barnard now owned an additional narrow strip of land incorporating three small blocks (116th to 119th streets), measuring only 200 feet on the north and south, and 725 feet along Broadway and Claremont Avenue. As was also the case with Columbia's recent land acquisition, Barnard's newly acquired property was undivided by streets, but in both cases the sites lay across existing streets from the original campuses (116th Street at Columbia and 119th Street at Barnard).[62] A Buildings and Grounds Committee was established with Anderson as chair to consider how the new property should be developed. Anderson

FIGURE 6.7
Vacant site south of Barnard's campus, January 13, 1906; view looking north from 116th Street with Grant's Tomb at left and the Horace Mann School at right.

submitted an outline plan drawn by Rich, but the committee, following Columbia's example of seeking suggestions from three architects before actually
choosing a designer, decided to solicit ideas from Charles McKim and another
architect who would be chosen later, with Columbia architecture professor Talbot Hamlin acting as an adviser.[63]

Charles McKim expressed some interest in the project, but only Rich is
known to have provided Barnard with a master plan for the development of the
new property. In 1903–4 Rich prepared a bombastic, crudely detailed Beaux-
Arts-inspired design (figure 6.8), consisting of four enormous six-and-one-
half-story buildings raised on a terrace, focusing on a domed auditorium building set in front of a formal plaza or quadrangle. "Woven into the Quadrangle,"
recounts *Architecture,* "will be secluded nooks of shrubbery, filled with antique
bits of statuary, picturesquely interspersed with gardens, flowers and vases."[64]
Adapting a feature from his original complex (which itself was to be increased
in height to match the new buildings), Rich proposed a series of columned
cloisters to connect the individual buildings. Not only was this scheme far beyond Barnard's financial means, but also the awkwardly detailed massive buildings were completely out of scale with the narrow site. In addition, Rich presumed that the privately owned block between 116th and 120th streets and
Claremont Avenue and Riverside Drive would be converted into a park. Thus,
he oriented the new campus to the west toward a formally landscaped park,
with Riverside Drive, Riverside Park, and the Hudson River beyond.

FIGURE 6.8
Charles Rich's proposal
for the enlargement of
Barnard College, 1904,
view looking east with
Columbia in background.

There was, in fact, a movement initiated by the Morningside Heights institutions to persuade New York City to acquire the land from 116th Street to
122nd Street between Claremont Avenue and Riverside Drive for the enlargement of Riverside Park (figure 6.9). This proposal was obviously an expedient
way for institutions that were unable to raise funds to purchase the property

BARNARD COLLEGE

themselves to acquire the amenity of an additional park. This effort culminated in 1906 when the city's Board of Estimate and Apportionment was asked to spend approximately $3 million for the property, ostensibly to protect the view toward Grant's Tomb and preserve the site of the Battle of Harlem Heights. One member of the Board of Estimate perceptively noted that "the plan is purely one for the boosting of real estate values . . . and to preserve the present outlook from Columbia University."[65] Although the Morningside Heights institutions actively supported the proposal and *Architecture* congratulated New York City on this impending park expansion, the proposal received little public support.[66] The *New York Times* opined that "it would be difficult to select a site where that advantage [a park] is less needed."[67] Ultimately, the Board of Estimate rejected the proposal and the property was soon developed with some of Morningside Heights' finest apartment houses (see chapter 8).

Despite its problematic character, Rich's master plan was approved, but for-tunately only one structure, Brooks Hall (1906–8; figure 6.10), the dormitory needed to replace Fiske Hall, was ever built. Funds for Brooks were largely con-tributed by Elizabeth Milbank Anderson, who chose to name the building after her minister and the first president of Barnard's Board of Trustees, the Rev. Arthur Brooks. As would be expected, the building was to be designed by Rich. Brooks Hall, located at the southern end of the new property along 116th Street,

FIGURE 6.9
The block bounded by Claremont Avenue, Riverside Drive, West 119th Street, and West 116th Street, January 13, 1906; view looking southwest toward the Hudson River.

where the master plan indicated dormitories should rise, was planned as the first wing of a larger complex. Although the eight-story dormitory was taller than the classroom buildings, Rich used the same materials and design vocabulary, including a one-story cloister-like portico, continuing his efforts at creating a unified campus. In addition to ninety-seven apartments of varying sizes renting at different rates, the building also included a large dining room and comfortably furnished parlors. Interior decorator Elsie de Wolfe was hired to design and furnish all of the interiors. She chose antique and reproduction antique furniture, chintz and silk fabrics, oak and mahogany woodwork, and subtly tinted paints in an effort to create traditional interiors where the women from elite families, who could afford the cost of room and board, would presumably feel at home (figure 6.11).[68] Brooks Hall was not immediately successful since Barnard's enrollment was still composed largely of commuters from the New York City area. However, as more affluent out-of-town students were admitted, the dormitory was soon filled.

Barnard's enrollment increased and the college quickly outgrew its classroom facilities. The *New York Times* observed in 1913 that "At present the equipment and the resources of Barnard are totally inadequate for its greatly increased number of students. . . . The lecture halls and laboratories are filled to overflowing."[69] As a result, Rich prepared plans for the construction of two additional stories on the original buildings, as he had proposed in his 1904 master plan, and he also designed an open-air rooftop gymnasium—none of which were constructed. In 1915 the trustees authorized the construction of a Students' Building that, with its gymnasium, swimming pool, library, lecture hall, cafeteria, offices for student organizations, and study rooms, was to become a center of student life. Although Rich prepared designs for this building, it did not fit within his master plan. With the view toward the Hudson River now blocked by the twelve-story apartment houses that lined Claremont Avenue and Riverside Drive, there was no longer any reason to align the campus to the west. Instead, the Barnard campus was reoriented to the east toward Columbia, with the front entrance of the new building facing east on an axis with Columbia's Earl Hall. The new building was also set back from Broadway behind a new entrance gate leading from Broadway onto the campus.[70] Unfortunately, the visual link with Columbia was extremely weak since the

FIGURE 6.10

Brooks Hall, c. 1911, with apartment buildings on West 116th Street at rear.

Barnard entry gate and Students' Hall were aligned with a secondary entrance to Columbia and focus on the rather undistinguished rear facade of Earl Hall.

In 1916 Jacob Schiff offered Barnard $500,000 toward the cost of constructing the Students' Building.[71] The gift was in celebration of the fiftieth anniversary of his arrival in America from Frankfurt.[72] Rich's design was set aside when Schiff insisted that he choose the architect.[73] Schiff chose Arnold Brunner, as he had earlier commissioned Brunner to design the original home of the Jewish Theological Seminary (see chapter 7), and just as Adolph Lewisohn, another member of the city's German-Jewish establishment, had done twelve years earlier when he donated the School of Mines Building to Columbia (see chapter 5). Brunner worked on the Barnard project in association with the firm of Buchman & Fox. Brunner's design for the Students' Building is a simplified version of the Columbia classroom structures, employing dark red brick laid in Flemish bond with a monumental limestone Corinthian entrance portico placed on axis with the new Barnard entrance and the secondary entrance to Columbia across Broadway (figure 6.12). A marble tablet set into the floor of the lobby commemorates Jacob Schiff's gift.[74] For many years, the tablet was the central meeting place for Barnard students who arranged to "meet on Jake."[75] This tablet is the only recognition of Schiff's gift. In 1926, a few years after Schiff's death, Students' Hall was renamed Barnard Hall, rather than Schiff Hall. The Barnard trustees argued that they had chosen the name "Barnard Hall" for the building closest to the campus entrance gate because strangers had trouble locating Barnard. Annie Nathan Meyer found this argument "palpably disingenuous."[76] According to Meyer, the Schiff family was humiliated by this rejection of their father and their family name. In 1934 Meyer spearheaded a campaign to

FIGURE 6.11
Brooks Hall Parlor decorated by Elsie de Wolfe, c. 1908.

redress "the impression which the Schiff family has unfortunately received, that the College is unwilling to place upon one of its buildings the name of a Jew."[77] Not surprisingly, considering the anti-Semitic views held both by Columbia's president, Nicholas Murray Butler (see chapter 5), and by Barnard's dean, Virginia Gildersleeve, the effort to rename the building in honor of Schiff was rejected and the redundancy of Barnard Hall at Barnard College remains to this day.[78]

Following World War I, Barnard was again in desperate need of additional dormitory facilities. A housing crisis following the war made it increasingly difficult for students to locate off-campus apartments. This development not only increased demand for dormitory rooms but also made it more difficult to attract students from outside of the New York area. Thus, in 1924 the college commissioned McKim, Mead & White to design the western wing of the dormitory complex on the south end of the campus. Several historians have noted that the construction of this dormitory was part of a concerted effort on the part of Dean Gildersleeve and certain trustees to increase the "geographic diversity" of students, a euphemism for the admission of elite Protestant students from outside of New York City in place of local students of Eastern European Jewish background.[79] The new dorm, known as Hewitt Hall, connected with Brooks and extended along Claremont Avenue. Hewitt Hall is a refined, Renaissance-inspired building erected of the same brick, limestone, and terra cotta found elsewhere on the Barnard campus. It originally contained 240 dor-

FIGURE 6.12

Students' Hall (now Barnard Hall), late 1920s, with original Barnard buildings at right.

mitory rooms, plus dining rooms and lounges treated in an "early American" manner.[80] As with Brooks Hall, a woman, in this case Emma B. Hopkins of the J. R. Bremner Co., was hired as interior designer to create "settings as intimate as those of private homes."[81] The private homes that served as models for these interiors were the suburban dwellings with Colonial-inspired interiors with which elite students might have been familiar. Such settings were seen as appropriate for a woman's college that was seeking to become an urban version of such prestigious rural colleges as Wellesley, Smith, and Mount Holyoke.[82]

With the construction of Hewitt Hall, building on the Barnard campus ceased for more than thirty years. This hiatus did not result from any lack of need for new facilities. Barnard's classrooms and laboratories were over-crowded, dormitories were so full that students were housed in nearby Columbia-owned apartment houses, and, even with an expansion into a former lecture room, the library in Barnard Hall did not have nearly enough space. Rather, the Depression and World War II, coupled with Barnard's perennial inability to raise funds, combined to prevent any new building construction. In 1935 Barnard acquired the block between 119th and 120th streets to the west of the original campus, bordering on Riverside Drive, and planned a new academic building.[83] The college was unable to raise funds for this project and, in 1954, was pressured into selling the property to John D. Rockefeller, Jr., where he erected the Interchurch Center (see Afterword). When construction on the campus resumed in the late 1950s, Barnard commissioned a dormitory, library, student center, and classroom tower. Unfortunately, Barnard's continuing relationship to Columbia is all too obvious in these new buildings, which rival contemporaneous buildings at Columbia in their mediocrity.[84] The only bright spot in Barnard's post–World War II building came in 1989 with the completion of James Stewart Polshek & Partners Iphigene Ochs Sulzberger Hall (originally known as Centennial Hall; figure 6.13), a seventeen-story dormitory that both blends with the campus's older buildings and, with its massing in the form of a bell tower, creates an identifiable focus for the college.[85]

Although Barnard's original campus structures are not the most distinguished buildings on Morningside Heights, they identified the college as an important institution. The placement of the buildings on their own block and the creation of a unified complex of three buildings established an independent identity for Barnard. Nevertheless, the style and materials chosen by Charles Rich and the board of trustees are also clearly linked to those

FIGURE 6.13
Iphigene Ochs Sulzberger Hall, 1989.

employed by Charles McKim at Columbia, accenting the close relationship between these two centers of learning. As Barnard expanded, efforts were made to continue a unified design scheme, but this ultimately failed when the narrow site was filled with the densely packed collection of disparate structures that characterize the campus 100 years after its move to Morningside Heights.

Teachers College and the Professional Education of Teachers: The Early Years

Teachers College, like Barnard, was established to offer educational opportunities not provided by more established colleges. A small group of dedicated benefactors interested in establishing professional training for teachers on a par with the training offered to doctors, lawyers, and other professionals organized Teachers College in 1889.[86] However, the roots of Teachers College extend back even earlier, to the 1880 establishment by a group of affluent women of the Kitchen Garden Association. The main force behind the Kitchen Garden Association was Grace Hoadley Dodge, a wealthy evangelical Presbyterian who, like many of her peers, was inspired by the "Social Christianity" or "Social Gospel" movement popular in progressive Protestant circles and was the impetus for much liberal social action in the late nineteenth century.[87] Dodge grew up in a wealthy New York City family.[88] Her grandfather was a founder of the metals and mining firm of Phelps, Dodge & Co., and her father, William Earl Dodge, donor of Columbia University's Earl Hall, was a partner in that firm. She grew up in a deeply religious home where philanthropy was an important part of family life. Dodge rejected the typical late-nineteenth-century woman's role of wife and mother. She never married and spent much of her time and money on evangelical and philanthropic work, primarily assisting needy women. However, Dodge was not content with merely passive involvement with worthy causes, but often took an active interest in managing the organizations that received her support.[89] Dodge was also a substantial benefactor of the Young Women's Christian Association and supported other organizations that improved opportunities for girls and young women.[90] Her interests in education led to her appointment as one of the first two women on the New York City Board of Education. Perhaps more than any other project, Dodge focused her time, energy, and money on establishing Teachers College as a powerful force in American education. She was so involved with the founding and early operation of the school that James E. Russell, who became dean in 1898, observed that Teachers College was Dodge's "oldest child."[91]

The Kitchen Garden Association was established as a charitable organization founded "for the promotion of the domestic industrial arts among the laboring classes, by giving to the children of the same . . . gratuitous instruction in household arts."[92] The school trained young, primarily immigrant, girls in do-

mestic skills. The girls were taught such practical tasks as cleaning, dish wash-
ing, table setting, bed making, and laundering. By combining practical lessons
using toy appliances with songs and games, "the children of poverty acquire the
order, precision, and neatness, essential to household service."[93] These pursuits
not only taught useful household skills and trained potential domestic servants,
but also were thought to impart discipline to the children's lives and improve
their moral fiber. From the start, the organizers of the Kitchen Garden Association were interested not only in teaching children, but also in training teachers in the Kitchen Garden system, commenting that "the managers cannot lay
too much stress upon the importance of teachers being trained for the work."[94]

In 1884, four years after it was organized, Dodge and her supporters transformed the Kitchen Garden Association into the Industrial Education Association (IEA), a technical education center that was one of a number of schools established in the late nineteenth century with the mission of teaching poor and
working-class children trade skills.[95] The intention behind schools such as the
IEA, Cooper Union, Pratt Institute, the New-York Trade-School, and the Hebrew Technical Institute, was to ensure that young people had the skills to find
jobs so that they would not become economic burdens on society. These
schools also provided trained workers for the increasingly specialized tasks demanded by modern industrial establishments.[96] To social reformers such as
Dodge, manual training was believed to achieve more than merely utilitarian
goals. They maintained that such training also taught moral values, such as
economy and industriousness, thus instilling civic virtues which would be of
value to students no matter what they did in their future life.[97] Dodge also believed that such training would develop the mind, as well as the eye and the
hand, creating well-rounded, mature individuals.[98]

According to an 1887 directory of local charitable societies, the IEA taught
"classes in cooking, sewing, domestic economy, and industrial drawing and clay
modeling, the latter being open to boys as well as girls."[99] As the organization
expanded, it needed a larger building and in 1887 moved into the former home
of Union Theological Seminary on University Place.[100] The organization also
expanded its course offerings, placing increasing emphasis on training teachers
of the manual and domestic arts. According to the school's initial catalogue,
"The Trustees and Faculty view teaching as a profession for which careful
preparation is necessary. They believe manual training should be a part of the
curriculum, and the ability to give instruction in it and to understand it a part
of the Teacher's equipment."[101] Indeed, the IEA's program of teacher training
set it apart from other schools, which simply taught classes in technical fields
such as the manual and domestic arts. In order to experiment with progressive
teaching ideas and also fully train teachers in classroom techniques, the IEA established the coeducational Horace Mann School in 1887.

As the education of teachers who would carry the message of the practical
and civic value of manual and domestic training to the public schools became

the central focus of the IEA, Grace Dodge realized that she did not have the background or credentials to continue at the helm.[102] Thus, in 1887, she called upon Nicholas Murray Butler to become the IEA's president. Butler was then a young professor at Columbia, a recent Ph.D. graduate of that school, and confidant of Columbia's president Frederick Barnard. Barnard was a supporter of the IEA and was deeply committed to professional training for teachers. He had attempted to establish a Department of Science and Art of Education at Columbia in 1881, but, as with other progressive ideas, the proposal was rejected by Columbia's conservative trustees.[103] Years later, after Butler became president of Columbia University, he remarked that Barnard "might just as well have urged a Department of the Science and Art of Aviation, then unknown, because neither the faculty nor trustees would hear of it under any circumstances."[104] Since Barnard had been thwarted in his attempt to establish a school of education at Columbia, he turned his energies to assisting in the creation of an independent teacher's college that might later become affiliated with the college. As education historian Bette Weneck has observed, "Barnard saw Dodge's plan to expand the IEA as an opportunity to establish a department of pedagogy outside of Columbia and affiliate it with the University, later on."[105] What could be a more appropriate way of carrying out this plan than having his protege, Nicholas Murray Butler, assume the presidency of the organization?

After Butler became the president of the IEA, the school completely dropped from its curriculum the courses in technical education offered to the poor. Rather, the IEA school became an institution exclusively for professional teacher training. In January 1889, the school, renamed the New York College for the Training of Teachers, received a provisional charter from the New York State Board of Regents. It received its permanent charter in 1892 and was officially renamed Teachers College.[106] The significance of the transformation of the school was summarized in the inaugural issue of *Teachers College Bulletin,* which proclaimed that the school's "purpose, at first purely philanthropic, has become entirely educational. *To train teachers for the schools,* it holds to be the shortest and the surest way to social reform."[107] According to Butler, teachers would be "trained so as to view manual training in the light of the history and principles of all education, and not as a special—and more or less accidental and temporary—addition to the course of study."[108] From the start, the overwhelming majority of students at the new college were women since they comprised the bulk of teachers in American primary and secondary schools in the late nineteenth century.[109] As the school grew in the 1890s and early years of the twentieth century, its mission expanded and its curriculum came to include courses in general education, psychology, chemistry, botany, and other scientific subjects, although manual and domestic training remained important aspects of the educational philosophy of the college. Increasingly, Teachers College became a center for training school administrators and supervisors and not primarily a school for training the school-room teacher.

The Move to Morningside Heights and the Growth of Teachers College

In October 1890, the Board of Trustees of the Teachers College addressed the inadequacy of the school's accommodations and the impracticality of expanding on University Place, indicating "that if the College is to extend its work as it is clear that it is able to do and should do steps must be taken to secure a building of suitable size and arrangement."[110] No action was immediately taken on this proposal, but by the following autumn the college was actively seeking a new site and real estate interests were offering plots in various Manhattan locations.[111] The search for a site was led by the college's new board chairman, architect William Appleton Potter.[112] At the same time that the trustees were looking for a new location, they also opened a dialogue with Columbia College's new president Seth Low, hoping to establish an alliance between the two educational institutions.[113] Under Low's leadership, Columbia was rapidly expanding its curriculum into fields other than classical education. As the importance of graduate and professional programs and departments became more apparent, it was logical that a professional teachers-training school should become a part of the university. In addition, a teachers-training school would further advance Low's efforts at transforming Columbia into a university whose students, faculty, and graduates would actively contribute to the civic and economic life of the great metropolis of New York.

If Teachers College were to ally itself with Columbia, it was important that the school seek a site near the Columbia campus. By late 1891, it had become public knowledge that Columbia was searching for a new home and that negotiations were proceeding between Columbia and the Society of the New York Hospital for the purchase of a portion of the Bloomingdale Insane Asylum property on Morningside Heights (see chapter 4). Butler, who left Teachers College in 1891 to assume the position of dean of the Faculty of Philosophy at Columbia, claims that he kept his colleagues at Teachers College abreast of Columbia's plans to move. In his autobiography, Butler recalls "I took Mr. [George W.] Vanderbilt into our confidence and suggested his acquiring for Teachers College the property adjoining whatever land the College might decide to buy."[114]

Whether on his own initiative or at Butler's suggestion, Vanderbilt visited Morningside Heights and by February 1892, when it became clear that Columbia would indeed buy the asylum property, he purchased twenty lots on West 120th and 121st streets in the middle of the block between Amsterdam Avenue and Broadway and donated them to Teachers College.[115] Although Vanderbilt's purchase was announced several days before Columbia finalized its agreement with New York Hospital, given Teachers College's desire to locate near Columbia, the deal would not have been completed if Vanderbilt and other Teachers College trustees had not known of Columbia's impending move to Morningside Heights.[116] This securing of a Morningside Heights site by Teachers College not only assured that the college would own property large enough for the erection of an up-to-date building for its progressive educational mission, but also virtually guaranteed an alliance between Teachers College and Columbia.

The effort to ally Teachers College with Columbia moved significantly forward in early 1892, when the Teachers College board submitted a formal proposal to the Board of Trustees of Columbia College seeking a consolidation. Teachers College proposed that it would remain independent for five additional years and then merge with Columbia University, with Teachers College ceasing to exist as a separate entity on July 1, 1897.[117] Columbia found Teachers College's offer unacceptable, since it would have meant that Columbia, with its perennial fundraising problems, would have been burdened with the financial responsibility for a professional program in education. In addition, the plan would have thrown open Columbia's classes to the significant number of women who enrolled at Teachers College. This project was unthinkable coming only a few years after Columbia had rejected coeducation and established Barnard College as a separate annex.[118] In response, Low proposed that Teachers College retain its independent identity and financial status, but that it also become a constituent part of Columbia's university system, with Columbia awarding degrees to Teachers College's graduates.[119] On the basis of Low's proposal, the two institutions reached an affiliation agreement that took effect in 1893.

Shortly after acquiring a site on Morningside Heights for a new Teachers College building, the trustees established a Building Committee to secure plans.[120] William Potter resigned as president of the board of trustees so he could serve as architect for the new school buildings.[121] Teachers College was fortunate in acquiring the services of William Potter, for not only was he supportive of the progressive goals of the institution, but he was also one of the most talented architects active in New York City in the final decades of the nineteenth century. He was best known for his churches and had, in fact, been one of the four finalists in the competition for the design of the Cathedral of St. John the Divine (see chapter 2). However, he also had extensive experience designing academic buildings, including the Park Avenue campus of Union Theological Seminary (figure 7.1) and structures at Princeton University and Union College.[122] Potter's proposal consisted of two interconnected buildings, Main Hall on West 120th Street (figure 6.14), which

FIGURE 6.14
Main Hall, c. 1894.

would contain administrative offices, classrooms, library, gymnasium, and assembly hall, and space for the Horace Mann School, and, on West 121st Street, a building specifically for manual arts training (figure 6.15). Since the college did not have extensive funds for construction, the complex was prudently planned with relatively inexpensive facades of brick with brownstone trim. However, a significant amount of money was invested in providing the buildings with technologically advanced elevators, electric lighting, plumbing, heating, and ventilating.[123]

Potter designed the Teachers College buildings in what the *Real Estate Record* alternatively referred to as the "Collegiate Gothic" or "secular Gothic" style.[124] Potter articulated the exteriors in an extremely picturesque manner, with steeply sloping roofs enlivened with gables, dormers, and lantern towers. Brownstone banding, perhaps inspired by contemporary English architecture, and beautifully carved stone entranceways enliven the dark red, pressed-brick facades. Main Hall was planned with a central pavilion flanked by asymmetrical wings. Curiously, Potter did not place the entrance in the prominent central pavilion, but in the east wing. At the east end of the building he added a separate entrance porch that led directly into the assembly hall, permitting the public to attend lectures and other functions without disturbing the work of the school.[125] There is no record as to why Teachers College chose a Collegiate Gothic design nor is there evidence that the trustees ever even discussed the issue of architectural style. Since Potter was experienced in Gothic design, it was not surprising that he would use this style for the new college, linking it with the great college buildings of Oxford and Cambridge.[126]

FIGURE 6.15
William A. Potter's design for the West 121st Street facade of Teachers College, 1893.

In order to create a unified complex, Potter designed the individual buildings as if they formed a single freestanding complex on a large site. Surprisingly, the east and west facades were finished with the same materials employed on the street elevations and not with a cheaper brick, and they were also articulated with windows that open onto narrow courts. This use of costly materials seems extraordinarily shortsighted on the part of the trustees and their architect. In 1892, Teachers College did not own the land to either side of its site. The neighboring lots could easily have been developed with buildings that would have virtually abutted the college, not only hiding the brick and stone facades, but also blocking light and air in the classrooms and assembly hall. The result would have been the same even if the college itself acquired the adjacent properties and erected additional buildings.[127]

Work began in the fall of 1892 on the central and east wings of Main Hall. Teachers College was therefore the first institution on Morningside Heights to actually begin construction. As the first phase of construction proceeded, the trustees sought funding to complete the project. To their surprise, on February 15, 1893, "two gentlemen called representing a Lady who[,] . . . [r]ealizing the great need for a Mechanical Art Building . . . most generously states that she will be glad to immediately erect and equip the building (whose plans have been accepted by the Trustees) as a memorial to her husband."[128] The "lady's" only conditions were that the building cost no more than $200,000, that it be named for her husband, and that the name of the donor should not be revealed to anyone, including members of the board of trustees, until she gave her permission. The trustees readily accepted this offer, even persuading William Earl Dodge, who had previously donated $25,000 toward the cost of this building, to transfer his gift to the General Building Fund.[129]

The mysterious donor was Caroline Everit Macy, who gave the building in memory of her husband Josiah Macy, Jr. This gift was the first major donation toward building construction at Teachers College by a member of the Macy family, which would soon become the most active supporter of the college. The Macys were Quakers, who traced their ancestry to early settlers on Nantucket. Josiah Macy, Jr., had acquired an enormous fortune as one of John D. Rockefeller's early partners at the Standard Oil Company. At Josiah's death in 1876, most of his fortune, estimated at over $20 million, was inherited by his young son V. Everit Macy.[130] At an early age, V. Everit Macy became interested in manual or mechanical arts training and taught woodcarving to poor boys. He later studied architecture at Columbia, but never practiced. In 1892, he was appointed to the board of Teachers College (he became vice chairman in 1896 and chairman in 1905). Influenced by her son, Caroline Macy donated funds to Teachers College for what would be known as the Macy Manual Arts Building (now Macy Hall). Since the building had already been designed by Potter, work could begin immediately on what was referred to as "the finest building devoted to the purpose of art education and instruction in manual arts in the world."[131]

Main Hall was completed in time for the start of classes in the fall of 1894 and Macy Hall was ready to receive students a year later.[132] The students arriving at Teachers College in October 1894 were pioneers in a neighborhood that would one day become a great institutional center. However, in 1894, Morningside Heights was largely vacant parcels of land interspersed with a few construction sites. St. Luke's Hospital was under construction, but its architect was arguing with contractors over delays (see chapter 3); work had halted at the Cathedral of St. John the Divine because of problems with the foundations (see chapter 2); Charles McKim was completing his initial designs for Columbia's campus prior to beginning construction (see chapter 4); and Barnard College was still searching for a site in the area on which to relocate (see above). For several years after the completion of construction on its first buildings in 1894, Teachers College was isolated on Morningside Heights, not only because construction on neighboring institutions was incomplete (Columbia College and Barnard College began classes on Morningside Heights in October 1897), but also because access to the area was limited and often difficult. *Teachers College Bulletin* instructed students and visitors to take a street car up Amsterdam Avenue or Broadway (a very slow ride from downtown neighborhoods). Alternatively, the *Bulletin* advised a trip on the Ninth Avenue elevated to the 104th Street station and then a walk one block west to Amsterdam Avenue where a street car would complete the ride to 120th Street. One could also exit the elevated at 125th Street and then walk or take a street car west to Amsterdam Avenue, and then either continue walking south or transfer to another street car for the ride to 120th Street.[133]

The trustees of Teachers College were justifiably proud of their new buildings. However, they were soon aware of the need for additions, especially the planned west wing of Main Hall, and expressed the desirability of securing the lots adjacent to the college for the "purpose of giving light, air and play grounds for both students and pupils."[134] In March 1896, a "gentleman, not associated with the school," finally offered up to $250,000 for the west wing, including a chapel (figure 6.16).[135] In May 1897, after the school was released from its promise to keep the donor's name anony-mous, the newspapers announced that banker Joseph Milbank, the brother of Barnard benefactor Elizabeth Milbank Anderson, had presented the gift as a memorial to his parents, Jeremiah and Elizabeth Lake Milbank.[136]

Potter had planned that the west wing of Main Hall contain a gymnasium, kindergarten classrooms, reading rooms, and the domestic arts department, including rooms

for instruction in sewing and cooking.[137] However, the main feature of the building as it was finally erected is Milbank Memorial Chapel. Joseph Milbank, who "has always been a man of strong religious convictions" and was a member of the board of trustees of the Madison Avenue Baptist Church, specified that a chapel be included in the wing.[138] This requirement must have delighted Teachers College founder Grace Dodge who, as Bette Weneck has noted, "believed, in no uncertain terms, that God had guided her in establishing Teachers College."[139] Potter's chapel (figure 6.17), designed to seat 250 people, is a fanciful Gothic space with a wide pointed arch framing a shallow raised platform. The chapel's piers and walls are paneled with quartered-oak wainscot. Above the wainscot is colorfully patterned stencilled decoration, primarily green and gold, designed by the Tiffany Glass and Decorating Company. The decoration includes TC and M initials and a centrally placed winged angel. The ceiling is paneled in oak with ornate pseudo-Gothic coffers. The five stained-glass windows located at the rear of the chapel, representing science, literature, art, the New Testament, and the Old Testament, are not by Tiffany, but are the work of Clayton & Bell of London. This space, virtually unknown outside of the Teachers College community, remains largely intact and is one of New York City's finest surviving late-nineteenth-century interiors.[140]

With the opening of Milbank Memorial Hall in September 1897, Potter's original plan for Teachers College was fully realized. The trustees, however, were not content. Increasing enrollment and the expansion of the curriculum demanded more space than Potter's design provided. They expressed their concern that "The growth of the inner development of the College must stop if the School is not enlarged and made more satisfactory. Also the growth of certain departments must stop if room is not found for them."[141] Thus, they set about raising funds to erect a gymnasium, a dormitory where women could live near to the campus, and a building specifically dedicated to the needs of the Horace Mann School. In January 1899, the trustees announced that if a benefactor came forward to present the college with a minimum gift of $350,000 for construction of a new building, they would raise the necessary funds for the acquisition of land. Through the generosity of its board members, the college received sufficient funds by 1902 to build all three buildings considered crucial to its survival. This success in fundraising was in marked contrast to the problems with raising money experienced by Columbia and especially by Barnard. Teachers College was especially fortunate that its innovative educational ideas con-

FIGURE 6.17
Milbank Memorial
Chapel, c. 1897.

tinued to attract the support of a few exceptionally generous supporters, mostly liberal Protestant philanthropists, who loyally provided the college with needed facilities.[142]

The first new building funded was a separate home for the Horace Mann School. V. Everit Macy and his wife, Edith Carpenter Macy, offered Teachers College funding for construction of Horace Mann early in 1899 as a memorial to Caroline Macy, the donor of Macy Hall.[143] In the spring of 1899, Teachers College purchased the Broadway blockfront between 120th and 121st streets as the site for the school at a cost of only $100,000, a sum considered to be substantially below market value.[144] Difficulties arose in selecting an architect for the building (surprisingly, it does not appear that William Potter was considered). A building committee consulted with both architect Edgar A. Josselyn and the architectural firm of Howells & Stokes (I. N. Phelps Stokes was related to Grace Dodge). Neither architect submitted a proposal that was fully satisfactory: one provided a superior interior plan and the other a more impressive exterior. Unfortunately, there is no record regarding which design was judged exemplary for which aspect of the proposal.[145] As a result, the committee suggested that the competing architects collaborate on a joint proposal.[146] Howells & Stokes and Josselyn discussed the suggestion and agreed to present a joint design.[147] The architects' proposal for the Horace Mann School would have filled most of the space between Broadway and Milbank Memorial Hall, but the project was ultimately cut back to a freestanding structure extending only about 100 feet east from Broadway, with a large vacant plot to its rear. The structure has a longmeadow sandstone base with red brick enlivened with a diaper pattern of darker burned bricks above (figure 6.18). The symmetrical Broadway

FIGURE 6.18

Teachers College, c. 1905. View looking northeast along West 120th Street from Broadway, with, from left, Horace Mann School, Thompson Hall, Milbank Memorial Hall, Main Hall, Whittier Hall.

facade combines Northern European Gothic and Renaissance features, such as the diaper work, steeply sloping roof, flat-topped gables, arched entry flanked by paired columns, and carved shields. The design centers on the entrance pavilion in the center of the Broadway frontage, with its steep gabled roof capped by a cupola that was originally crowned with a weathervane in the form of a quill pen.

Construction of such an impressive new building for Horace Mann, substantially enlarging the school's facilities, reflected a major change in the character of the institution. Horace Mann was no longer simply a "working laboratory" for educational experimentation or a training ground for unskilled teachers. Instead, it became a "demonstration school" where Teachers College students would learn through the "observation and demonstration of superior class teaching and school management."[148] As a result, Horace Mann was transformed into an exclusive private school serving as an alternative to the public schools with their diverse student body. As part of this development, the school instituted a selective admissions policy that discriminated against the city's Jewish population. In 1899, the school became embroiled in a nasty incident in which three Jewish boys were expelled for being disciplinary problems and "unclean." Jacob Schiff was asked to investigate and, while ultimately satisfied that the expulsions had been justified, noted that it was clear that Jews were being excluded from the school.[149] Virgil Prettyman, Horace Mann's principal, wrote an amazingly revealing letter to Dean Russell in August 1899, confirming the accuracy of Schiff's judgment: "Jews are excluded, and an attempt is constantly made to keep the social tone of the Horace Mann School much above that of the public schools of New York City. In following this policy the Principal believes that he is carrying out the wish of the Trustees, President, and Dean of Teachers College."[150]

Since the experimentation with new teaching methods and ideas previously conducted at Horace Mann also had to continue as a part of Teachers College's educational program, the college established an experimental school on 126th Street just a few blocks north of Horace Mann, in the heart of the poor Manhattanville neighborhood. This school, named the Speyer School after trustee James Speyer who gave $100,000 for its construction, was to be run in conjunction with the University Settlement House with the aim of promoting "the study of educational problems, especially those concerned with the improvement of public school instruction and the development and coordination of the various educational forces in social life."[151] Poor youngsters were to be trained in traditional subjects, as well as "in the industrial and domestic arts, in the fine arts, and in those occupations and recreations which make for upright moral character and good citizenship."[152] To house the new school, Edgar Josselyn designed an elaborately decorated, German Renaissance-inspired building that provided up-to-date facilities for teaching poor immigrant children.[153]

No construction took place on the midblock site between Horace Mann and Milbank until 1902–4, when a gymnasium was erected there. In November 1901

Dean Russell had indicated that construction of a gym was a priority for the college.[154] William Potter had planned a gym in the west wing of Main Hall, but when a chapel was added to that building the gym was eliminated. Four months after Dean Russell's request for funding for a gym, Mary Thompson, a member of Teachers College's board, presented the school with $250,000 to erect the building as a memorial to her husband, a founder of First National Bank, who had died in 1899. The gift was later increased to $400,000.[155] Thompson was a generous philanthropist, who would later pay for substantial construction at Woman's Hospital (see chapter 3) and who would also donate $150,000 to Teachers College in 1913 to assist in the construction of a new boys' high school for Horace Mann in the Riverdale section of the Bronx.[156] Neither Howells & Stokes nor Josselyn was asked to design the gymnasium, nor was Thompson's favorite architect, Frederick Allen of Boston. Instead, the design was entrusted to Parish & Schroeder, undoubtedly because Grace Dodge's brother, Cleveland Dodge, was married to Wainwright Parish's sister.[157] The asymmetrical 120th Street facade of Parish & Schroeder's gymnasium is similar to the proposal made by Howells & Stokes and Josselyn in 1899 to connect the Horace Mann School with Milbank Hall. Indeed, with its freestanding entrance portico, diaper brickwork, gables, dormers, and crowning cupola, Thompson Hall is virtually indistinguishable from the facade of Horace Mann (figures 6.18 and 6.19).

The completed gymnasium, named Frederick Ferris Thompson Memorial Hall, provided advanced physical education facilities for women students. This amenity was a breakthrough on Morningside Heights since women were barred from entry into Columbia's gymnasium. Although it was equipped with a swimming pool, handball courts, bowling alleys, exercise rooms, locker and

FIGURE 6.19
Parish & Schroeder's presentation drawing of Thompson Hall.

shower rooms, and a sizable gymnasium, the building was more than a recreational center. It was also planned as an educational facility, with classrooms, laboratories, and an examination room for students planning careers in teaching physical education. As George Maylan, the director of physical education at both Columbia and Teachers College, explained shortly after the gymnasium opened, "It has been recognized that to become a teacher of physical training requires a university course in scientific study quite as important and intellectual as that taken for law or medicine. In this university [Teachers College] at present the teaching of gymnastics is upon precisely the same basis as instruction in Latin and Greek."[158]

The interior of Thompson Hall retains several remarkable features, include the original swimming pool; an open-cage elevator (no longer in working order); first-story halls clad in mustard-colored octagonal tiles capped with a leaf and berry border (figure 6.20), all manufactured by the Grueby Faience Company, the art pottery which also created tiles for Grace Dodge Hall and for the floor of the choir at the Cathedral of St. John the Divine (see chapter 2); and a marble bas-relief, memorializing Frederick Ferris Thompson (along with his dog, Uncle Fred), carved by prominent American sculptor Augustus St. Gaudens.[159]

The most serious issue facing Teachers College following the completion of its first buildings was the housing of the young women who were arriving in New York from all over the United States in order to enroll in classes. Whereas it was socially acceptable for Columbia's men to be left on their own to find housing in fraternities, boarding houses, and shared apartments, it was not considered proper for young women to live on their own unchaperoned. In addition, rents in "respectable" neighborhoods of New York were often too high for women on limited budgets. In 1899, Teachers College leased one of the first residential buildings erected on Morningside Heights, a four-story structure on the northeast corner of Amsterdam Avenue and 117th Street, referred to as Teachers College Hall (figure 8.3). Here students could rent small rooms and live under the supervision of a house-mother who assured that "life at the Hall is made home-like and pleasant."[160] Thirty-one students and three Teachers College staff members took advantage of these accommodations.[161] Unfortunately, the rents proved to be too high and the accommodations poor, and the lease agreement was not renewed.[162] The college then sought to house some students at Barnard's Fiske Hall, but this was clearly not a permanent solution to a pressing problem. Thus, in 1900, a committee of the trustees "urge[d] most strongly the prompt consideration by the Board of Trustees of some Dormitory plan, by

FIGURE 6.20
Grueby Faience
Company's drawing for
leaf and berry tile.

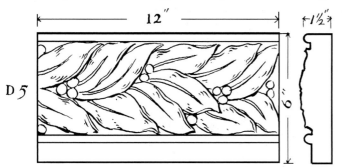

which women students can secure cheap rooms, proper board, under wise direction. The importance of this cannot be underestimated." [163]

Teachers College did not have the money to erect this desperately needed dormitory. However, several of the school's loyal supporters, led by Spencer Trask, and including V. Everit Macy, Joseph Milbank, and William Earl Dodge, solved the problem by acquiring the Amsterdam Avenue blockfront adjoining the college buildings. They incorporated as the Morningside Realty Company, a stock company, that issued 4,000 shares each valued at $1,000. [164] In June 1900 the Morningside Realty Company began construction of a dormitory and apartment building on the Amsterdam Avenue site (figures 6.21 and 6.22). The building was split into four wings—two central wings for dormitory rooms (called Longfellow and Whittier) and two end wings with commercial rental apartments (Lowell and Emerson). For the design of the building, the stockholders did not use any of the architects who had previously worked for Teach-

FIGURE 6.21
Bruce Price and J. M. Darragh's design for Teachers College's dormitory, now known as Whittier Hall, originally referred to as, from left, Lowell, Longfellow, Whittier, and Emerson halls.

FIGURE 6.22
Teachers College, 1909. View looking northwest from Amsterdam Avenue and 119th Street with Columbia University's Green in foreground; from right, Whittier Hall, Household Arts Building (now Grace Dodge Hall), Main Hall and Macy Hall, Milbank Memorial Hall, Thompson Hall, and Horace Mann School, with Grant's Tomb at rear left.

ers College. Instead, they turned to Bruce Price in association with J. M. A. Dar-ragh, a young designer in Price's office.[165] Price had been a leading member of New York City's architectural world for more than two decades when he re-ceived the dormitory commission. It was rare for an associate in any architec-tural office to be given credit for a design, yet Price and Darragh were given equal credit on their submitted drawings and in most written accounts. Some sources cite Darrach as the sole designer. The *World* noted that it was Darrach "who prepared the plans."[166] The building is a large-scale version of the Horace Mann School, located on the opposite end of the block. As at Horace Mann, the facade has a sandstone base above which are elevations clad in red brick laid in a diaper pattern and trimmed with stone, and the massing features prominent gables and a central cupola.

Whittier Hall, the name generally used to denote the entire complex, opened in December 1901. As the dormitory was not completed until after the school year had begun, not all the rooms were rented. In order to attract residents, rooms were made available to all "single women of approved character, regard-less of their occupation."[167] Even so, Dean Russell reported that the first year had been "a disaster."[168] The two apartment wings had presented special prob-lems. Construction had been shoddy, apartments were small and poorly laid out, rents were high, and there was little demand in 1901 for apartments in what was still a relatively inaccessible area (see chapter 8).[169] On January 1, 1909, the stockholders of the Morningside Realty Company officially transferred the property to Teachers College (along with a $600,000 mortgage), ending the le-gal charade of private ownership.[170] Once Teachers College assumed direct re-sponsibility for the building, it became a lucrative enterprise.[171] Whittier Hall eventually became so popular that the *Evening Post* proclaimed it "a bee-hive of single femininity."[172] The article went on to describe the ground-floor stores that catered to these women, notably the corner drugstore with its soda foun-tain where students could imbibe such concoctions as a "Horace Mannikin," a "Co-ed Frappé," or a "College Yell" ("a very yellow, long-drawn-out drink").[173]

In 1902 Teachers College's financial good fortune continued when John D. Rockefeller offered the college a gift of $500,000 for its endowment. This was the second largest gift that Rockefeller had made to an academic institution, ex-ceeded only by his support to the University of Chicago.[174] The gift was "a thanks offering to Almighty God" in recognition of the safe evacuation of the Rockefeller household from its Pocantico Hills house, which had been de-stroyed by fire on the night of September 17, 1902.[175] Rockefeller was undoubt-edly attracted to Teachers College by the school's efforts to further manual edu-cation (a subject that appealed to industrialists such as Rockefeller), by its roots in the liberal evangelical Protestant community in which he was also active, and by its concern for the education of women (another field in which Rocke-feller took a deep interest).[176] Rockefeller generally conditioned his gifts on an institution's raising additional funds. With the Teachers College donation, Rockefeller stipulated that the school raise $190,000 to pay off its debt and an additional $250,000 for the endowment. Unlike Barnard, which had struggled to meet the conditions of its $200,000 gift from Rockefeller, Teachers College was able to raise the matching funds within a few years, with most of the money coming from the college's small group of loyal supporters.[177] These donations were especially welcome at a college for teachers, since as noted by *Harper's Weekly,* "The college could hardly hope to profit to any material extent from the generous inclinations of its graduates, who have seldom large means of their own."[178]

By 1904 the Teachers College complex offered extensive classroom space, a well-furnished manual arts building, an up-to-date gymnasium, a large dormitory, and modern facilities for a model school. However, the college still lacked adequate accommodation for advanced training in the domestic arts. It is surprising that an extensive domestic arts building had not been one of the earliest projects at Teachers College, since the school's roots, going back to the Kitchen Garden Association, lay in the promotion of the domestic arts as a morally uplifting educational tool. This field was of special interest to Grace Dodge and it was she who finally donated funds for the construction of what was originally known as the Household Arts Building (now Grace Dodge Hall). Early in 1907 Dodge offered $400,000 for construction of a domestic arts building as a memorial to her mother. As with many of the donors of earlier buildings at Teachers College, Dodge requested anonymity. She had Parish & Schroeder design the building for a site on 121st Street just east of the Macy Manual Arts Building (figure 6.22). The firm provided a Collegiate Gothic structure of red brick with longmeadow sandstone trim, the same materials employed on other Teachers College buildings, but this building's design is somewhat more academic than the earlier sections of the college complex. The major feature is a clock tower containing the building's main entrance, said to have been modeled after a tower at Magdalen College, Oxford.[179] Instead of facing the main elevation onto 121st Street, Parish & Schroeder aligned the building to the south, facing the landscaped Columbia University Green. Since at the time of construction the land on 120th Street south of the Household Arts Building was a vacant lot, the new building was quite visible. However, it was expected that this front elevation would eventually face onto an inner court when additional buildings were erected on 120th Street.[180] With the construction of Russell Hall in 1922–24, the court was enclosed and the front elevation of Dodge rendered barely visible.

The front entrance to the Household Arts Building is now rarely used. Thus, few people ever enter the vestibule, which contains the building's most significant design feature. For this space, Parish & Schroeder commissioned six tile panels (figure 6.23), which were to be set high on the east and west walls, from Henry Mercer's Moravian Pottery and Tile Works, one of America's foremost art tile studios. The designs, on the theme of "home industries and home work of the Colonial housewife" (sewing, spinning, churning, candle dipping, weaving, and cooking at an open fire) were prepared by students in the Art Department of Teachers College.[181] Each scene was then interpreted in the mosaic tile process that Henry Mercer patented in 1902. The scenes are composed of solid-colored glazed pieces of clay in varied shapes and sizes, bonded by wide mortar joints, creating colorful panels that are similar in effect to a stained-glass window with its pieces of solid-colored glass connected by metal cames.[182] The mosaic panels are surrounded by additional bands of Moravian tile. The floor of the vestibule and the floor and walls of the stair hall located just beyond are clad in tiles made by the Grueby Faience Company of Boston.[183]

With the completion of the Household Arts Building, not only were facilities for domestic arts study significantly expanded, but also the entire program was professionalized by replacing the departments of Domestic Arts and of Domestic Science with the School of Household Arts.[184] This new school was proclaimed "a new creation which proposes a school of collegiate rank, devoted to the household arts and sciences and intended primarily to train teachers of these subjects for public, technical and collegiate education."[185] In addition, the school would train women to enter professional positions in large residential and institutional settings and in such fields as dietetics, interior design, and laundry management. The school, it was felt, would enlarge the possibilities for women's professional work, just as engineering colleges had opened up new fields for men.[186] To this end, novel facilities were provided, such as laundry laboratories for training women in the management of institutional laundries using "just the same kind of machinery that a large hotel or hospital might have . . . so that any graduate could run an entire laundry as a business or part of a business";[187] cooking laboratories for the study of institutional cooking; work rooms for the study of textiles and clothing; and a model apartment consisting of "six rooms, arranged like the typical city apartment, which will be utilized for instruction in interior decoration and house furnishing, in dining room instruction, housewifery, and home nursing, and many other subjects of the household arts which can best be taught by utilizing a set of living rooms."[188]

FIGURE 6.23

Moravian tile panels in vestibule of Household Arts Building (now Grace Dodge Hall); from left, weaving, cooking, and candle dipping, c. 1909.

On the second floor, the building contained a Table Service Laboratory, "a room providing space for exercises in table setting, and in the service of meals" (Fig. 6.24).[189] This room was designed in the Arts & Crafts style by Helen Kinne, the director of the household arts program, in association with Arthur Wesley Dow, a professor of art at Teachers College. It contained medieval-inspired oak paneling, a floor paved in hexagonal Grueby tiles, and "mission" style furniture.[190] The choice of Arts & Crafts decor at Teachers College's household arts center is not surprising since the progressive Arts & Crafts movement sought to reform household life through what was considered to be morally uplifting, simply designed, hand-crafted objects and decoration, just as the college hoped to uplift its students and the larger society by training women in the moral virtues of domestic education.[191]

Teachers College grew at an extraordinarily rapid pace. The number of graduates increased from 29 in the first graduating class to 686 in 1911, with thousands of students enrolled in the school's varied programs.[192] With so many students, the college soon was in desperate need of a larger library and additional classrooms. In 1911 Dean Russell suggested building these facilities on the vacant land on 120th Street between Main Hall and Whittier Hall.[193] During the next few years overcrowded conditions worsened and in 1916 a committee was finally established to look into the erection of a new library.[194] Undoubtedly through the influence of Mary Thompson, design sketches were requested from Allen & Collens, her favorite architectural firm (see chapter 3).[195] However, with America's entry into World War I in 1917, this project was postponed. Toward the end of the war, Allen & Collens requested permission to enlarge on its preliminary design. In November 1919 the firm's plans were approved and funds were sought for construction.[196]

The library project was temporarily derailed when Teachers College decided to buy apartment buildings in order to increase housing options for its students. In April 1919 Dean Russell informed the board of trustees that housing accommodations for students were inadequate and that conditions were rapidly getting worse due to the increasing number of students and the decreasing number of available apartments as New York City experienced a severe housing crisis.[197] It was clear that the school would either have to build new housing (a difficult proposition since there was little vacant land left on Morningside Heights) or buy extant apartment buildings. Fortuitously, the Bancroft apartment building

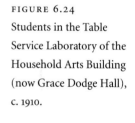

FIGURE 6.24
Students in the Table Service Laboratory of the Household Arts Building (now Grace Dodge Hall), c. 1910.

(figure 8.31) on the north side of West 121st Street between Amsterdam Avenue and Broadway, with 108 suites of two and three rooms each that could house 375 students, was for sale. A contract for the purchase of the building for approximately $575,000 was signed in May 1919.[198] Leases for Bancroft tenants expired on September 1, 1919, and Teachers College was able to acquire rights to all of its apartments. However, a few months later, an additional $590,000 was spent for the Janus Court at 106 Morningside Drive on the southwest corner of 121st Street (renamed Seth Low Hall), where many leases ran for up to two more years. Teachers College could not gain immediate control of most apartments. In addition, a housing law passed in April 1920 seeking to bar the eviction of tenants so landlords could substantially raise rents encouraged even tenants whose leases had expired to remain in their apartments in hopes of protecting themselves from dislocation.[199] As a result, by the fall of 1920, Teachers College had gained access to only 37 of the Seth Low's 80 apartments. The antieviction housing law was scheduled to expire in November 1922, but, as expected by the Teachers College trustees, it was renewed and the college was again prevented from dispossessing tenants and gaining access to the apartments. In fact, it was not until 1927 that Teachers College was able to acquire many of the Seth Low Hall apartments.[200] This struggle between nonaffiliated resident tenants and Teachers College marked the beginning of a conflict that would become a central issue within the Morningside Heights community in the 1960s and 1970s, especially as the Morningside Heights institutions increased their real estate portfolios and sought to obtain possession of apartments in order to improve housing opportunities for their faculty, students, and staff (see Afterword).

In 1922, Teachers College again turned its attention to the construction of the library and intensified its efforts to fund the project. Loyal supporters such as Mary Thompson, V. Everit Macy, and James Speyer once again made substantial contributions, as did members of a new group of supporters including board member Felix Warburg, who would soon be the main funder of a new building for Jewish Theological Seminary (see chapter 8), and Edward Harkness, who, almost a decade later, would fund a new library at Columbia (see chapter 5).[201] As money was solicited for a library, the school also decided that there was a pressing need for a dining hall and restaurant, and proposed a building on the vacant site on 121st Street between Grace Dodge Hall and Whittier Hall that would provide for these needs along with additional classrooms. It was envisioned that this building would also be designed by Allen & Collens and erected at the same time as that firm's new library. The library and the Grace Dodge Hall extension were erected in 1922–24.

Library construction entailed the demolition of the east entrance porch and entire east facade of Main Hall. During construction, it was decided to name the library Russell Hall, in honor of James Russell's quarter century of service to Teachers College.[202] While not as creative and exciting a design as Allen &

Collens' nearby Union Theological Seminary complex (see chapter 7), the rather staid Neo-Gothic Russell Hall (figure 6.25) typifies Allen & Collens' generally more academic work of the 1910s and 1920s. The building harmonizes with the earlier campus structures, virtually completing the picturesque West 120th Street frontage, and also provides the college with a central focus and prominent entry, both of which had been lacking. The key element of the Russell Hall design is its tall entrance tower, capped by a dramatically placed turret, that rises above the roofline of the other college buildings. The tower is clearly visible from both Broadway and Amsterdam Avenue, drawing attention to the college complex and to its main entrance in the middle of the block. The main mass of the building, set to the east of the tower, contains large windows which light the library reading rooms and a gabled roofline that continues the picturesque massing of the gables and dormers that project from other campus roofs.[203]

With the construction of Russell Hall and the Grace Dodge Extension, work on Teachers College's impressive central complex of medieval-inspired buildings was complete. The school, of course, continued to grow. In 1954, a house for the president was erected on the lot between Russell and Whittier.[204] The final building constructed on the block owned by Teachers College was Thorndike Hall, erected on West 121st Street between the Horace Mann School and Grace Dodge Hall as part of a master plan for the college prepared by Hugh Stubbins & Associates of Boston in 1973. Fortunately, this massive and jarring concrete structure was all that was built of the master plan, which also proposed the demolition of almost the entire residential block to the north and construction of a giant highrise dormitory and classroom complex.[205]

Teachers College remains an independent institution allied with Columbia University and America's leading center for the study of education.[206] Its location at the north end of the Morningside Plateau, far from a subway station and from the commercial bustle of Broadway south of 116th Street, has tended to keep this extraordinary architectural complex from being more generally known and appreciated.[207] Fortunately, all of Teachers College's extraordinary historic buildings survive, standing as monuments to a vision of professional teacher training and to the commitment of a few individuals willing to devote considerable time and money to the realization of this vision.[208]

FIGURE 6.25
Russell Hall, c. 1930;
Main Hall at left.

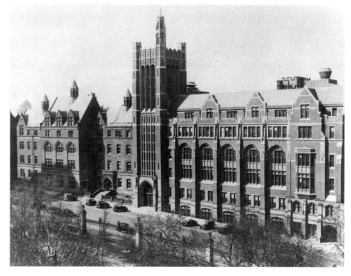

FIGURE 7.1

Union Theological
Seminary's complex on
Park Avenue between
East 69th Street and East
70th Street.

CHAPTER SEVEN

Building for the Mind and Spirit

Theological Seminaries and a Musical Institute on Morningside Heights

THE SECOND PHASE OF INSTITUTIONAL DEVELOPMENT ON MORN-
ingside Heights began in 1905 with Union Theological Seminary's decision to
move onto the northwest portion of the Morningside Plateau. The seminary's
acquisition of the long, narrow block between Broadway and Claremont Avenue and West 120th and 122nd streets marked the beginning of the transformation of this section of Morningside Heights into an institutional quarter, with
Union soon being joined by the Institute of Musical Art, Jewish Theological Seminary, and Riverside Church (see chapter 2). The northwest portion of
Morningside Heights was inviting to religious and academic institutions in the
early twentieth century since it was close to Columbia University, Barnard College, and Teachers College, yet still retained large sections of undeveloped land
that had not been subdivided into small building plots. The area north of 120th
Street had remained largely undeveloped (with the notable exception of Teachers College) since it was the most remote and inaccessible section on Morningside Heights, far from the elevated railroad on Eighth Avenue and some distance from the subway stations at Broadway and 116th Street and Broadway
and Manhattan Avenue (now 125th Street).[1] Thus, institutions were able to purchase sizable plots from single owners economically and efficiently, on which
they constructed a series of impressive new structures to house their institution
enterprises.

Union Theological Seminary: Liberal Protestant Education
Comes To Morningside Heights

In October 1835 a small group of Presbyterians met to consider the organization
of a sectarian theological seminary in New York City.[2] Although the city was
home to many prominent churches, it was not yet a center of theological education. The Episcopalians' General Theological Seminary, established in 1817,

was the only important seminary in the city. The city's wealthy Presbyterian merchants and industrialists were undoubtedly anxious to organize a rival school. Thus, in January 1836, New York Theological Seminary was founded, with courses commencing at the end of that year. In December 1838, the fledgling seminary moved into a new building on Jackson Avenue (now University Place) near East 8th Street. Three months later, in March 1839, the seminary was officially incorporated and its name changed to Union Theological Seminary in the City of New York.[3] As the number of seminarians increased and the curriculum expanded, stories were added to the original building and additions were constructed. However, by 1870 it became evident that the seminary could no longer expand in the densely built up area north of Washington Square and that this increasingly commercial neighborhood was not conducive to quiet study and meditation.

In 1870 Union Theological Seminary purchased sixty lots in the vicinity of St. Nicholas Avenue between West 130th and 134th streets, becoming one of the first urban institutions in New York City to acquire a site for a new home in the semi-rural northern regions of Manhattan, years before the decision to build the Cathedral of St. John the Divine on Morningside Heights was announced in 1887 (see chapter 2). The seminary's trustees hoped to raise $500,000 in order to erect classrooms, a library, a chapel, a dormitory for 250 students, and a house for each professor on this site.[4] Nothing came of this proposal, perhaps because West 130th Street was simply too far north and too inconvenient in 1870 before elevated rail lines had penetrated the northern areas of Manhattan or because the financial panic in 1873 made major fundraising for this project virtually impossible.[5] Nevertheless, the seminary's pressing need for new accommodations persisted and, in 1881, the trustees bought the blockfront on Park Avenue between East 69th and 70th streets.[6] This property was more accessible than the 130th Street site since the Second Avenue and Third Avenue elevated lines had recently opened. In addition, the area was rapidly developing into a pleasant residential community of middle-class rowhouses, and land on Park Avenue was affordable for institutions such as Union Theological Seminary and Presbyterian Hospital (located on the block immediately north of the seminary) because the presence of the New York and Harlem River Railroad, running in a semi-open cut along the avenue, depressed land values. William Potter (who would later design the first buildings for Teachers College; see chapter 6) and his partner James Brown Lord designed a picturesque Gothic-inspired complex for Union that focused on a central chapel with steep sloping roof and tall octagonal tower, completed in 1884 (figure 7.1).[7]

By the early years of the twentieth century, Union had outgrown its Park Avenue complex. The seminary could not easily expand on the Upper East Side, since this area was now filled with residential buildings and land values were rapidly rising as it became a fashionable location for the city's wealthiest households. In late 1903 or early 1904 the seminary's president Charles Cuthbert

Hall wrote to wealthy Presbyterian benefactor and seminary board member D. Willis James seeking a gift of two million dollars for the purchase of a new site and construction of an expanded seminary.[8] As recounted by the president of the board, John Crosby Brown, a partner in the Brown Brothers banking firm, he and James explored various possible building sites on the west side of Manhattan and, on January 18, 1904, James confidentially informed Brown that he would contribute $1 million toward the project.[9] James decided that the seminary should relocate to a site near Columbia University and in January 1905 he funded the $850,000 purchase of the block bounded by West 120th and 122nd streets, Broadway, and Claremont Avenue. Payment of the remaining $150,000 of the promised $1 million gift, plus an additional donation of $100,000 to compensate for the fact that the land had cost more than expected, completed James's gift.[10]

James's extraordinarily generous donation coincided with a major change in the theological sectarianism of the seminary. Union was established as a Presbyterian institution and, although it welcomed students from other evangelical Protestant denominations, it required that all directors and professors declare acceptance of the Presbyterian church's Westminster Confession of Faith. On November 15, 1904, the Board of Directors of the seminary unanimously voted to change the seminary from a sectarian Presbyterian institution into a nondenominational center for liberal Protestant theology, welcoming members of all evangelical Protestant denominations to the faculty and board of directors and dropping the requirement of acceptance of the Westminster Confession.[11] As a direct response to this announcement, the widow of William Earl Dodge (donor of Columbia University's nondenominational student center, Earl Hall; see chapter 4) and lawyer Morris K. Jesup (whose wife, Maria, was an important donor to Woman's Hospital; see chapter 3) each gave the seminary $120,000 to endow professorships.[12]

John Crosby Brown maintained that James's gift was also a direct result of this theological liberalization of the seminary: "The action," Brown stated, "had one important consequence not contemplated by the Board at the time. It made possible the removal of the Seminary to the new buildings on Morningside Heights, for, as subsequently appeared, it was one of the conditions which determined Mr. D. Willis James to make the munificent gift."[13] This connection would not be surprising, since James was a prominent promoter of ecumenical Protestantism. He had been, for example, one of the first major donors to the campaign to build the Cathedral of St. John the Divine (see chapter 2), even though the cathedral was an Episcopalian undertaking.[14] However, Brown's claim is not corroborated by the timing of James's action. Although James officially made his gift to Union in January 1905, a few weeks after the board's decision to transform the school into a nonsectarian institution, he had already committed himself a year earlier, in January 1904, to give a substantial gift toward Union's relocation and he had been searching for a new site with Brown for some months prior to the board's announcement. Although Brown asserted that only he and one other member of the board were aware of James's intended gift at the time that the trustees voted to liberalize the seminary, it is possible that James had lobbied for the liberalization. It is more probable, however, that the gift was unrelated to this development and that Brown, a supporter of the board's decision to open the seminary equally to all Protestants, used the announcement of James's gift as an argument justifying the controversial change. In any event, it was James's generous contributions that enabled Union to move to a new building complex on Morningside Heights. James continued to donate generously to the seminary until his death in 1907, giving an additional $400,000 during his life and leaving a bequest of $100,000 in his will. In addition, James's wife, Ellen Curtiss James, presented Union with $300,000 in 1908 for construction of a chapel in memory of her husband, and their son, Arthur Curtiss James, actively supported Union for several decades. The James family gifts toward construction of the new seminary complex were augmented by $125,000 donated by John Crosby Brown and his wife, and an additional $359,059.15 raised from the sale of the Park Avenue property.[15]

In order to secure an appropriate design for the new campus, Union's Board of Directors organized an architectural competition, as had other New York institutions that had settled on Morningside Heights. Four architectural firms— Cram, Goodhue & Ferguson, Cass Gilbert, Lord & Hewlett, and Palmer & Hornbostel—were specifically invited to enter the competition, but any other architect could apply for permission to submit designs. These designs were to be judged by architects Warren P. Laird of Philadelphia, Walter Cook of New York, and Robert Peabody of Boston.[16] Laird prepared a detailed program for competition entrants.[17] The program required a complex with classroom space, a library, a chapel, a refectory, a student dormitory, faculty housing, and a home for the president. The main entrance to the seminary was to be from the southeast, English Gothic was suggested, but not required, as the style for the new buildings, and there was also a suggestion that a tower might be appropriate.[18]

The competition program specifically emphasized the place of the seminary within the complex of institutions on Morningside Heights: "[T]he Seminary will maintain with neighboring institutions, an interchange of facilities for instruction, study and recreation and must therefore be regarded as an integral part of the educational community in which it will be located."[19] However, the directors of the seminary did not want a building that would be indistinguishable from those of neighboring institutions. Rather, they believed that this "institution of higher learning made distinctive by religious rather than purely academic motive . . . [requires a] suitable expression . . . which should, on the one hand, be so in consonance with neighboring groups as to promote an harmonious ensemble and, on the other, have such individuality of treatment as to make evident their organic distinctness and peculiar character."[20] This approach was typical of the history of institutional design in the area, where each organization sought an individual design that would define its character in the burgeoning metropolis (see Introduction).

Late in 1906 thirty-five architects submitted designs to the competition.[21] The three judges met twice to discuss the merits of the various designs, unanimously awarding the commission to the Collegiate Gothic proposal of the Boston architectural firm Allen & Collens.[22] Unlike the problematic competitions for the cathedral and St. Luke's Hospital, *Architecture* reported that "The program [for the Union Theological Seminary competition] was a model of careful preparation and detail and the whole competition was conducted with such rare good judgment and fairness as we are pleased to commend."[23] Frederick R. Allen and Charles Collens specialized in the design of Gothic-inspired buildings and were responsible for many Neo-Gothic churches in New England and New York, and for several significant Collegiate Gothic academic structures.[24] The seminary complex was the second building on Morningside Heights designed by Allen & Collens; the Union Theological Seminary competition was underway as the firm's Woman's Hospital opened on Cathedral Parkway in December 1906 (see chapter 3). The firm would eventually become the most active institutional architect in the neighborhood, receiving the commissions for Russell Hall and the Grace Dodge Hall extension at Teachers College (see chapter 6) and Riverside Church (see chapter 2). In order to assure that the design process and construction would proceed efficiently, Allen & Collens formed an association with local architect Louis E. Jallade.[25]

As had been suggested in the competition program, Allen & Collens's winning entry proposed an English Gothic style structure reminiscent of college designs at Oxford and Cambridge. The complex was to be divided into two quadrangles. To the south would be the administrative offices, classrooms, president's house, library, and chapel focusing on a tall tower at the corner of Broadway and West 120th Street. The library would be the main feature along Broadway and the chapel, marked by a squat square tower, would be sited on quieter and more secluded Claremont Avenue. The president's house was planned for the corner of Claremont Avenue and West 120th Street, between the administrative wing and the chapel. On Broadway, a single-story carriage entrance would separate the library from a dormitory, which was to extend across the plot to Claremont Avenue, dividing the courtyard into two quadrangles. The use of the northern portion of the plot, along West 122nd Street, was not yet determined.

Over the next year Allen & Collens worked with the seminary on finalizing the proposal.[26] The double quadrangle was changed to a single large quadrangle with a raised terrace at its south end. The entire seminary complex would now be arrayed around the perimeter of the site, with a covered cloister incorporated into the courtyard elevations. The student dormitory was to occupy the northern portion of the Broadway frontage and part of the area along 122nd Street.[27] Allen & Collens also increased the height of the chapel tower and added a third tower above the carriage entry at Broadway and 121st Street. These two towers, plus the proposed entrance tower on Broadway and 120th Street, were planned as the seminary's three most prominent visual features. In 1908 the Board of Directors suggested that money from the sale of the old seminary site on Park Avenue be used for construction of a faculty apartment building on the corner of Claremont Avenue and 122nd Street, and Allen & Collens incorporated this residence into its design, thus completing the quadrangle.[28] In addition, Allen & Collens successfully resolved the complex issue of creating a unified design for this grouping of so many diverse elements (classrooms, offices, dormitory rooms, faculty apartments, chapel, library reading room, book stacks, refectory, etc.), each requiring a different massing and fenestration pattern (figures 7.2 and 7.3). This result was achieved by the careful and consistent use of materials and English Gothic ornament, and the harmonious placement of towers, projecting oriels, rooftop gables, and terra-cotta chimney pots (carefully cast in imitation of limestone).

One of the most interesting aspects of the design, and, at first, its most controversial element, was Allen & Collens's decision to construct the seminary of rough-textured Manhattan schist quarried during foundation excavations. In contrast, a light-colored mortar would bond the dark-hued stones and ornamental details would be carved from smoothly finished white Indiana limestone. Union was not the first Collegiate Gothic complex built of schist quarried on site. Architect George B. Post was employing this stone, trimmed with bright white terra cotta, for the Collegiate Gothic buildings under construction on the City College campus in 1906 while Union Theological Seminary was

FIGURE 7.2
Union Theological Seminary, c. 1910; view looking northwest from Broadway and West 120th Street; from left, President's House, Administration Building, memorial entrance (now base of Brown Memorial Tower), library wing, James Tower, and dormitory.

holding its design competition. Nevertheless, the *Real Estate Record* reported that "there was some uncertainty as to what the appearance of the college [i.e. seminary] would be when completed" if the schist were used. As a result, the seminary decided on "the novel expedient" of erecting a sample wall on the center of the plot.[29] The wall satisfied the seminary's directors and the excavated stone was used for the building's exterior walls. This still somewhat novel use of schist continued to fascinate the editors of the *Real Estate Record,* who mused:

> The wonders of Manhattan increase. The tight little island . . . can still fall back upon some of its natural resources, at least when it comes to erecting attractive and costly structures. With the finest of face brick at its threshold, with unsurpassed granite within a few hours' haul, with the exquisite Italian marble at available prices, this patrimony of Father Knickerbocker . . . provides the raw material for the facade of what will be one of the best examples of collegiate architecture in the country. And more, still, it comes from the site of the building—the Union Theological Seminary. This anomaly in the history of New York, the transformation of excavated rock into the exterior facing of an educational plant that will involve the outlay of over $1,000,000 and the use of two city blocks, conjures up in the mind the old idea of attempting to lift oneself by one's bootstraps.[30]

The cornerstone for the initial construction phase of the Seminary, consisting of the office and classroom wing, library, and residential buildings, was laid

FIGURE 7.3
Union Theological Seminary, view looking northeast from Claremont Avenue and West 120th Street, 1910; from right, Administrative wing, President's House, James Chapel, and faculty residence.

on November 17, 1908, and work on the chapel was begun shortly thereafter.[31] This initial construction phase did not include the refectory, which would eventually connect the chapel and residential buildings along Claremont Avenue, or the corner tower, both of which awaited future gifts. Construction proceeded smoothly with blocks of excavated schist piled in the center of the lot before the stones were cut and applied to the facades (figure 7.4). The seminary was ready for occupancy in the fall of 1910.[32] The project included several notable public interiors. Perhaps the most beautiful is Memorial Hall, the original entrance hall (now no longer in use; figure 7.5). This round space, with a complex marble floor pattern, contains four limestone clustered columns from which spring complex vaults. Hallways lead to the administrative offices and to what was originally a museum, while a twisting corkscrew stair leads to classrooms and the library. The religious heart of the seminary is the impressive James Memorial Chapel (dedicated to the memory of D. Willis James), which originally had a hammer beam ceiling of red oak, quartered oak wainscot, and English stained glass.[33] The chapel was referred to by the *Evening Post* as "a perfect example of the Gothic style in ecclesiastical architecture."[34] Other notable features of the original seminary complex are the library, said to have been modeled after the refectory at Christ Church College, Oxford, with its beamed ceiling, the Moravian Tile fireplace in the dining room of the president's house, and the cloisters with Guastavino vaulting.[35] The dormitory provided quarters for all of Union's seminarians, thus creating the type of residential collegiate community that other Morningside Heights educational institutions eagerly sought, but had been unable to achieve. This sense of community was augmented by the adjoining faculty housing that provided professors and their families with spacious apartments of up to twelve rooms and facilitated their active involvement in seminary life.[36] Unfortunately, the three men who had initiated, planned, and funded the project all died without seeing the fruits of their work—seminary president Charles Cuthbert Hall, who had suggested relocating the institution, had died in 1908; benefactor D. Willis James, in 1907; and board president John Crosby Brown, in 1909.[37]

In contrast to most of the other institutions that had relocated to Morningside Heights, Union Theological Seminary's building project ran smoothly. The competition was a success, construction proceeded rapidly, the design of Allen & Collens was well received and was considered

FIGURE 7.4
Excavations on the site of Union Theological Seminary, looking north from West 120th Street, October 5, 1908; Manhattan schist quarried on site is piled in the center of the lot.

appropriate for a religious institution, and the completed complex was widely praised in popular newspapers and magazines and in the professional real estate and architectural press. The *Evening Post* judged that "the country will be the richer by one of the handsomest bits of architecture of Gothic type this side of the Atlantic" and boasted, perhaps somewhat hyperbolically, that the quadrangle at the New York institution could stand comparison with those of Ox-

FIGURE 7.5

First floor plan of main entrance lobby of Union Theological Seminary, 1908.

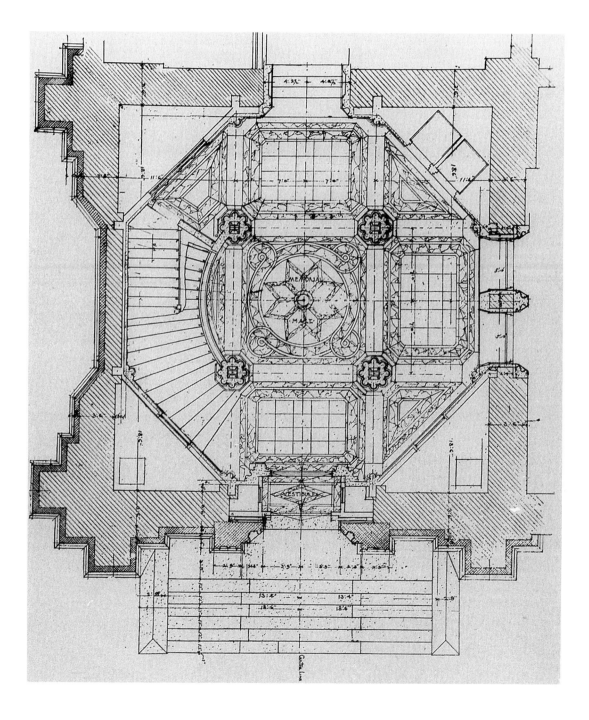

ford and Cambridge.[38] *Outlook* magazine's editorial writer maintained "That this school of theology is as superbly housed as any of the financial and commercial interests of the city [and] is eloquent testimony that even in this great business center spiritual values are as strongly accented as the material"—a sentiment that more than twenty years earlier, Bishop Potter had hoped would lead to an outpouring of financial support for his cathedral project (see chapter 2).[39] The *Real Estate Record* claimed that the building is "Considered by some authorities as the best example in America of English scholastic Gothic architecture" and later asserted that "many consider it the most . . . charactered range of institutional buildings that has yet been erected in New York and devoted to education."[40] *American Architect* found the seminary to be a "notable addition to the splendid educational and religious buildings on Cathedral Heights."[41] Finally, the prominent architectural critic Montgomery Schuyler observed, in his survey of New York City university design which also included a vociferous condemnation of Charles McKim's work for Columbia, that Union's new complex was "even better worth looking at [than the old buildings on Park Avenue], being equally artistic and much more extensive," concluding that "It is not only one of the best of our collegiate buildings, but one of the most notable architectural ornaments of New York."[42]

Union Theological Seminary commenced classes in the fall term of 1910, establishing a liberal, ecumenical Protestant presence on Morningside Heights. The seminary's role as a center of liberal theology was further accentuated by the presence of controversial liberal preacher Harry Emerson Fosdick as a part-time instructor (see chapter 2). In 1915 Fosdick became the Morris K. Jesup Professor of Practical Theology and moved into the faculty residence hall.[43] He remained a Union professor until 1934, when his duties as pastor at neighboring Riverside Church forced him to resign his position at Union.[44] Union thrived on Morningside Heights. Enrollment increased and the seminary became a center of nondenominational Protestant education, admitting men and a small number of women, and considered by many to be one of the most important Protestant seminaries in the country.[45]

Increasing enrollment and prestige also brought with it a demand for additional facilities. In 1912 Louis Jallade was hired to design a gymnasium, funded by Mrs. D. Willis James, on leased land at the northwest corner of West 120th Street and Claremont Avenue. Jallade, who had assisted Allen & Collens with the initial construction of the seminary, created a simple Neo-Gothic structure, known as the "stone gym," erected of the same schist used on the seminary's earlier buildings.[46] By 1921 the seminary was anxious to expand its programs and complete construction of the full initial plan for its core complex.[47] A fundraising campaign was initiated in the fall of 1924, with several million dollars donated by John D. Rockefeller, Jr., Edward Harkness, Arthur Curtiss James, and other supporters of the liberal Protestant cause.[48] This campaign resulted in the completion, in 1928, of the remainder of Allen & Collens's design. To the north of the James Memorial Chapel, a building housing the Charles

Cuthbert Hall Refectory and the Francis Brown Social Hall was built, while the Brown Memorial Tower was erected on the corner of Broadway and 120th Street above the main entrance to the complex. This tower was funded primarily through a $200,000 donation from friends and members of the Brown family (figure 7.6).[49]

Besides finishing its core complex, Union also hoped to erect housing for returning missionaries on property that it owned on the block to the west, across Claremont Avenue. Allen & Collens designed an English Gothic structure for this purpose.[50] However, instead of erecting this new building, in 1927 the seminary converted the Alderson Apartments at 99 Claremont Avenue, which had been acquired in a trade with John D. Rockefeller, Jr., in 1926 (see chapter 2), into a Missionary Apartment House.[51] This building was used to house missionaries and their families for only a few years. In 1931 John D. Rockefeller, Jr., persuaded Union to trade property it owned on the Riverside Church block so that the church could expand to the south toward 120th Street. As part of the deal, Union acquired a second apartment house on Claremont Avenue. The seminary then demolished both Claremont Avenue buildings and, in 1931–32, with the financial assistance of Rockefeller, erected McGiffert Hall (named for Arthur C. McGiffert, eighth president of the seminary) on the southwest corner of Claremont Avenue and 122nd Street as a residence for students, including married and women students, as well as for missionaries and young faculty.[52] Since Allen & Collens was the architect of both Riverside Church and Union Theological Seminary, the firm designed McGiffert Hall to complement both the neighboring church and the seminary across the street (figure 7.7) . The building is a Neo-Gothic style structure erected of the same Manhattan schist used on the seminary, but its design is more heavily influenced by the French Gothic architecture of the church than the English Gothic aesthetic of the seminary itself. Since the dormitory abuts Riverside Church on 122nd Street, that street elevation was carefully planned so that the church and dormitory would appear as a

FIGURE 7.6
Union Theological Seminary with newly constructed Brown Memorial Tower, c. 1928.

unified design. For the juncture of the two buildings, Allen & Collens designed a round, French-inspired turret. The turret is clad entirely in limestone and, although it is actually part of the dormitory, it appears to be a section of Riverside Church.

Union Theological Seminary has continued to occupy its original complex, sensitively adding to the physical fabric or undertaking generally sympathetic alterations to meet the changing needs of modern theological education. In 1939, for example, the Auburn Theological Seminary, a nondenominational seminary that continued to have strong links to the Presbyterian church, moved from Auburn, New York, to Union Theological Seminary's campus. Although Auburn remained an independent institution, it no longer matriculated its own students, but was responsible for the theological needs of Union's Presbyterian students.[53] To accommodate Auburn and also give Union additional space, Collens, Willis & Beckonert, the successor firm to Allen & Collens, was commissioned in 1949 to design the Neo-Gothic Auburn Hall for a site on the terrace at the north end of the quadrangle. This building was dedicated on October 22, 1951.[54] In 1957–59, Dickinson Hall, a small sensitively designed Neo-Gothic structure with classrooms and offices, was built as an infill project in the space between the chapel and president's house. This addition was funded, in part, by the Sealantic Fund, one of John D. Rockefeller, Jr.'s foundations.[55] Early in the 1980s, Union's library was in need of modernization and renovation, for which the firm of Mitchell/Giurgola (architect of Sherman Fairchild Hall at Columbia) designed modern additions for a new periodical room and stair tower that adapt the grids of the original Gothic windows to a modern glass and metal structure.[56] A few years later, James Stewart Polshek & Partners (architect of Barnard's Sulzberger Hall) redesigned Hastings Hall, the seminary's dormitory, restoring the exterior and virtually gutting the interior in order to transform its small dark rooms into spacious suites suitable for both single students and married students with families. In addition to work on the dorm, the Polshek firm also placed new gates at the carriage entrance on Broadway at West 121st Street, creating a handicapped-accessible main entry into the entire seminary complex.[57]

Union Theological Seminary's presence on Morningside Heights extended the institutional character of the neighborhood as far north as the south side of West 122nd Street, with the seminary adjoining Barnard

FIGURE 7.7
McGiffert Hall, c. 1950, with Riverside Church at right.

College immediately to the south, Columbia University catercorner to the southeast, and Teachers College to the east. Union's move to the northwest end of the Morningside Plateau also influenced further institutional development in this area, as the Institute of Musical Art and Jewish Theological Seminary erected their new homes on the north side of 122nd Street.

Music on Morningside Heights: The Institute of Musical Art and the Juilliard School of Music

In 1910, as construction work was proceeding on the new home of Union Theological Seminary, it was joined at the northern end of Morningside Heights by the Institute of Musical Art. Although the institute was only five years old when it purchased the site on the northeast corner of Claremont Avenue and West 120th Street, it was rapidly growing into a prestigious music conservatory. The organization of the institute and its early growth were the achievements of music educator Frank Damrosch and the school's chief benefactor during its early years, James Loeb. Frank Damrosch was born in Germany into a family of professional musicians (he was the godson of Franz Liszt). When Damrosch was a child, his family moved to New York. Damrosch became increasingly interested in music education, serving as supervisor of music education for the Denver public school system and, after returning to New York in 1885, founding the People's Singing Classes, the People's Choral Union, and the Symphony Concerts for Young People. He also served as chorus master at the Metropolitan Opera, conductor of the Oratorio Society of New York, and, from 1897 until 1905, supervisor of music for New York City's public schools.[58] James Loeb was a member of one of New York's wealthiest and most prominent German-Jewish families. His father was a founder of the banking firm of Kuhn, Loeb & Company. Although more interested in music and the arts than in business (he played the cello, piano, and organ), Loeb dutifully entered the family's banking firm, but remained only until his father's death in 1901. Having inherited a large fortune, Loeb was then able to pursue his artistic interests and also became a generous philanthropist.[59] This union of Loeb and Damrosch, a wealthy philanthropist and dedicated professional, in successfully spearheading the establishing of a major institution in Morningside Heights would be paralleled some years later in the development of neighboring Riverside Church, an organization established and largely supported through the financial generosity of John D. Rockefeller, Jr., working with the famous preacher Harry Emerson Fosdick (see chapter 2).

By the late nineteenth century, New York had become "the musical centre of the Union."[60] The Music Hall (later known as Carnegie Hall) had opened in 1891, providing New Yorkers with one of America's finest concert halls. The city was also home to several orchestras and choral societies and a number of music schools that provided professional training.[61] The organization of the Institute of Musical Art is a part of this larger development of music in New York City. In 1901 Frank Damrosch proposed that a music school of national prominence be established in New York that would not only provide the highest level of professional training and instruction, but also establish a "true musical culture" in America by offering classes to those who wished to pursue music for their personal enjoyment. His hope was that such a school would create a climate whereby music would become as much a part of the life of Americans as it was for Europeans.[62]

Damrosch had first suggested this idea for a music school to Andrew Carnegie in 1901. However, Carnegie was not interested in lending his support to the project.[63] In May 1903 Damrosch met his old acquaintance James Loeb on a boat heading toward Atlantic Highlands, New Jersey, and described his conservatory idea to him.[64] Loeb found Damrosch's proposal attractive, not only because of his interest in music, but also because he wanted to create a memorial to his recently deceased mother, who had been a great lover of music. Loeb soon agreed to raise $500,000 as an endowment for the music school, giving $50,000 of this sum himself. However, by the spring of 1904, Loeb had decided that he did not wish to spend time raising money and gave the entire $500,000, establishing the Betty Loeb Memorial Endowment Fund. This fund was to be used to establish a music school that would be open to both men and women, and would not discriminate on the basis of race, creed, or color.[65] According to the *New York Tribune,* Loeb also hoped to interest ten friends in contributing an additional $50,000 each, thus doubling the endowment.[66] These gifts did not materialize, perhaps because Loeb continued to avoid active fundraising and never made a concerted effort to find ten additional donors. In fact, during its early years, the Institute of Musical Art was virtually the private philanthropic enterprise of James Loeb and his immediate family.

The Institute of Musical Art of the City of New York was established in 1904, with a board of directors that consisted, among others, of Loeb, Damrosch, Loeb's brothers-in-law, Paul Warburg and Isaac Seligman, music publisher Rudolph Schirmer (who donated a music library), Union Theological Seminary benefactor Arthur Curtiss James, and Elkan Naumburg, who would later establish the famous concert band that bore his name.[67] Damrosch immediately set off to Europe to find prominent teachers who would be willing to relocate to New York and teach at the new school. If the school were to succeed, it would require a prestigious faculty capable of attracting large numbers of students. For this purpose recognized European professionals were crucial, since few Americans at that time had such standing in the musical world. Loeb impressed upon Damrosch that "The school needs a *big very big* foreign name to give it a proper send-off."[68]

Although Carnegie had previously shown little interest in Damrosch's project, the *Tribune* reported that he had offered Damrosch the use of Carnegie Hall for the school.[69] Carnegie had actually offered to give the school the Rembrandt apartments, located next to the concert hall, for its home. Negotiations over the use of the Rembrandt bogged down, apparently over funding for necessary alterations. Carnegie's patience wore thin and in February 1905 he wrote Damrosch, "Knowing what I do to-day, if I had to do it over again, I would not make you that promise [to use the Rembrandt free of rent]. It is made, however, and I will keep it, but please do not ask me to do anything more."[70] Nothing more was done and negotiations with Carnegie broke off.

On October 11, 1905, the Institute of Musical Art opened in a Gothic Revival mansion that had been built in the 1850s on Fifth Avenue and 12th Street by James Lenox and that was temporarily loaned rent free to the institute by Thomas Fortune Ryan.[71] James Loeb contributed $19,000 toward furnishing the house and supplying it with musical instruments, including an organ.[72] Damrosch had succeeded in attracting a faculty of European singers and musicians that the *New York Times* commented was an "instructing force that . . . is particularly strong."[73] The initial prospectus published by the new institute in 1905 set forth the objectives of the school which, "simply stated . . . are to advance the art of music by providing for students the highest class of musical instruction in all its branches—practical, theoretical, aesthetic; to encourage endeavor, reward excellence, and generally to promote knowledge and appreciation of the art in the community."[74] The Institute of Musical Art was enormously successful, with enrollment rising from 281 students at the opening to 467 in early 1906.[75]

In the spring of 1909, Ryan informed Damrosch that the institute would have to vacate the Fifth Avenue property within a year. A search began for a site on which a new school building could be erected. The board of trustees required that the property be in a location accessible to the subway and surface car lines, on a corner site with maximum light, in a quiet location where the work of the school would not be disturbed by noise, and which was to cost no more that $150,000.[76] Paul Warburg contacted realtors and examined possible sites, but supposedly discovered the property on the corner of Claremont Avenue and 122nd Street by chance while out for a pleasure drive along Riverside Drive. Although smaller than desired, the site was convenient to streetcar lines and not too far from the recently opened subway. It also faced Claremont Park, which permanently guaranteed light, and the academic nature of the surrounding community provided a suitable environment. In addition, the vacant land cost only $77,500.[77] Loeb, who had left New York in 1905 and resettled permanently in Germany, was delighted, writing to Damrosch, "You can imagine how happy I am to know that the Institute is to build just in the region which I had always regarded as the most ideal part of New York for us to be in."[78]

With the property secured, Damrosch and Warburg, who were in direct communication with Loeb in Germany, and the other members of the board of trustees turned their attention to commissioning a design for the new music school. They solicited proposals from three architects—Donn Barber, Philip

Sawyer, and an architect with the surname of "Leo." [79] The proposals were sent to Loeb in Germany and he chose Barber as architect for the project. [80] Donn Barber was a leading figure in the New York architecture world in the first decades of the twentieth century. He had studied at Columbia and at the Ecole des Beaux-Arts, and was responsible for a number of important residential, public, and institutional buildings. [81] He was also an active member of many design organizations and was the editor of *The New York Architect,* a magazine that published high-quality illustrations of major new buildings. For the Institute of Musical Art, Barber designed a relatively sober four-story Beaux-Arts structure capped with a mansard roof (figure 7.8). [82] The limestone building has a rusticated first story, projecting stone and iron balconies, a central entrance on Claremont Avenue capped by an ornate cartouche, and a handsome iron railing. Appropriately for a music school, the Claremont facade is enlivened with symbols of music: third-story window spandrels carved with French rococo-inspired emblems with musical instruments; a lyre carved into the entry cartouche; a pair of cameo-shaped panels, each with a classically garbed woman, one holding and the other playing a lyre; and still more lyres in the iron balconies. Damrosch praised the "noble exterior which will proclaim the purpose of the building and will be an ornament to this great metropolis." [83] On the interior, "which will contain everything necessary to the best work, comfort and safety of the students," the major space was a recital hall seating 400 and "decorated with a rich simplicity which approaches perfection." [84]

Cost estimates for erecting Barber's building were higher than the institute had hoped, and in order to fund the project, Loeb suggested "an earnest & assiduous effort to get some of the 'richards' of New York to loosen their pursestrings." [85] Damrosch detailed ways to control construction costs, such as substituting brick for stone and pipe rails for ornate wrought iron, but he was not enthusiastic about compromising the artistic quality of the building in any way:

> We all felt that inasmuch as the building is in such a prominent and beautiful location and will be seen by not only New York's inhabitants who frequent Riverside Drive but also by thousands of strangers who visit Grant's Tomb, it would be a pity not to take advantage of this opportunity to contribute something really beautiful and artistic to that part of the city, not to mention the fact that the more attractive our building appears to the eye, the better it will advertise the Institute. [86]

Thus, Damrosch and the institute's trustees increased their fundraising efforts, collecting a little over $100,000 from a small group of civic-minded New Yorkers, including $10,000 donations from Union Theological Seminary's chief benefactors D. Willis James and John Crosby Brown, and from Thomas Fortune Ryan, who had given the new institute use of his Fifth Avenue property for its first home. The institute also borrowed $150,000 from the Betty Loeb Memorial Fund. [87] With these additional funds, no compromises had to be made in the design and construction proceeded as originally planned. The cornerstone of the school was laid on March 26, 1910, and construction was completed in only twenty-one weeks. The building was opened for classes in the fall of 1910.[88] At the dedication ceremony on November 5, the Reverend Francis Brown, president of Union Theological Seminary, noted that he had felt disappointment when apartment buildings had risen to the west of the seminary on Claremont Avenue and 122nd Street (buildings that Union later acquired and demolished), but he proclaimed, "It is with quite a different feeling that we turned northward and saw this structure with its beautiful proportions and exquisite finish taking its place on this corner. It is the kind of neighbor that a respectable person or group of persons rejoices in, feels proud to have, and is grateful to be allowed to recognize."[89]

The new home of the Institute of Musical Art proved to be a great success. The institution thrived on Morningside Heights, with its student body rising so rapidly that by 1919 Damrosch asked the trustees to acquire property to the rear of the building for construction of an addition.[90] Several trustees donated $20,000 for land acquisition. Finally, in the fall of 1923, when enrollment had increased to 840 students, Damrosch "begged the Trustees to consider the plan of building an annex on the property belonging to the Institute in the rear of our building."[91] In 1924 Barber was asked to design a simple rear addition with administrative offices, studios, classrooms, and a large rehearsal room that would not alter the appearance of the original structure.[92] In order to fund the addition, Loeb hoped that "there are enough people in New York and in other towns so well persuaded of the excellent work we are doing, that they might open their purses and defray a good part of the cost of the building."[93] As it turned out, however, the entire $128,000 estimated cost of construction was donated by James Loeb, his siblings, and their immediate relations.[94]

The construction of the addition to the Institute of Musical Arts occurred at a critical time in the school's history, with its preeminence as a center of musical education being challenged by the Juilliard Foundation, which had been established as a result of a major bequest by Augustus D. Juilliard in 1919. Juilliard, who had been born at sea while his French Protestant parents were emigrating to America, made his fortune in the textile business and, later, as a director of banks and other financial institutions.[95] Although Juilliard's interest in music had been

FIGURE 7.8

Institute of Musical Art, 1910.

evident in his active support of the Metropolitan Opera (at the time of his death in 1919, he was president of the Metropolitan Opera & Real Estate Company, the holding corporation for the opera company), the provisions of his will came as a total surprise. The will stipulated that most of Juilliard's substantial fortune, approximately $13 million, be used to establish a foundation that would support musical education.[96] Juilliard particularly wished that the foundation aid students in receiving a musical education, sponsor concerts that would educate the public, and support the production of operas at the Metropolitan Opera, so long as that company did not make a profit.[97] The Juilliard Foundation was established in 1920, with its board composed primarily of businessmen, many with little knowledge of music or musical education. The director of the foundation was Eugene A. Noble, a retired minister. Although the foundation had a great deal of money, it was slow to make its mark on the local music scene.

Among the trustees of the Juilliard Foundation were Paul Warburg and Paul Cravath, both of whom were also on the board of the Institute of Musical Art. Warburg and Cravath suggested that the Juilliard Foundation aid the Institute rather than establish a rival school. However, according to John Erskine, who would later become the director of the Juilliard School, Damrosch rejected this suggestion because he was not willing to permit outside directors who knew little about music to interfere with his school.[98] With its overture to the Institute of Musical Art rejected, the Juilliard Foundation announced in May 1924 that it would organize a graduate school of music with classes to be held in a former apartment building at 49 East 52nd Street.[99] Although Damrosch hoped for amicable relations between the two institutions, he also feared that Juilliard's financial resources might lure teachers away from his school.[100] Nevertheless, in early June 1924, shortly after the Juilliard program was announced, Damrosch gloated (perhaps unadvisedly) in a letter to Loeb, "The Juilliard Foundation's 'Graduate School' has Twelve Million Dollars to back it, but money will not buy everything and I understand that Dr. Noble, who is to be the Director, is already finding it very difficult to secure good teachers of the type he would like to have."[101]

The initial slowness of the Juilliard Foundation's work led its committee of musical advisers to resign in late 1925. In January 1926 the surprising announcement was made that the Juilliard Graduate School and the Institute of Musical Art would merge after all, with the two schools sharing a common board of directors, but with each retaining its independent identity.[102] The Institute of Musical Art would become the undergraduate conservatory of the Juilliard Musical Foundation, with James Loeb's $500,000 endowment kept as a separate fund with its own administrators. This merger was greeted with enthusiasm by the local press. An editorial in the Evening Post hailed the merger as "one of the most important developments concerning music that have ever occurred in this country," boasting that "The resulting institution will give this city a music center comparable to the Paris Conservatoire."[103] The Sun felt that

"Only good will come from the union," while a *New York Times* editorial stated that "The trustees of the Juilliard Foundation . . . started last year what was intended to be a graduate school to obviate the need for American students studying abroad. They naturally have found that such a school is not created over night, and that even with enormous financial resources the right kind of functioning can be attained only through skill, wisdom, experience and musical knowledge. The partnership now to be made will unite many of the elements needed for the perfection of a great musical institution."[104]

Although there is no record of why the trustees of the Institute of Musical Arts decided to merge with the Juilliard Foundation, it is probable that they were finally forced to face the future viability of the institute at a time when the school's founders were aging and newer and wealthier conservatories were competing with the institute for top students and faculty. In 1926 James Loeb was in his sixties and, since 1905, had been living in Germany. Loeb had continued to be the institute's major supporter, but, given his age, the trustees were undoubtedly concerned about the future of the school after his death, especially since the Juilliard Foundation had a large endowment on which to continue its efforts and the institute had never been able to increase the size of the $500,000 endowment originally donated by Loeb. In addition, Damrosch was 66 and had recently suffered a heart attack. Thus, it was clear that he too would not be able to guide the institute for much longer.[105] Besides competition from the new school established by the Juilliard Foundation, the institute also had to compete for faculty and students with two other new music schools, each of which was handsomely endowed—the Eastman School of Music in Rochester, which had opened in 1921 with an initial endowment of $4.5 million, and the Curtis Institute of Music in Philadelphia, which had been established in 1924 with an endowment of $12.5 million.[106] In this newly competitive environment, a merger with the Juilliard Musical Foundation would guarantee funding to extend the institute's work into the future, but, of course, would also result in the loss of much of the institute's independence. In October 1926 the board of trustees of the Institute of Musical Art agreed to the merger and in the following month the New York State Board of Regents approved the plan for the establishment of the Juilliard School of Music.

As part of the merger, the Juilliard School's graduate program was to relocate to the institute's Morningside Heights building. Juilliard agreed to move uptown, away from the center of musical life in Midtown, because its home on East 52nd Street was seriously overcrowded and lacked an auditorium. However, the Institute of Musical Art's building, even with its new extension, did not have sufficient space for Juilliard's classes. Thus, beginning in 1927, the Juilliard Foundation began purchasing the buildings adjacent to the institute, with the intention of emptying the apartments and demolishing the buildings in order to expand facilities. Between 1927 and 1929 the foundation acquired five apartment buildings on Broadway and Claremont Avenue.[107] Preliminary sketches for a new building were prepared as early as 1928. These proposals greatly upset Damrosch because the plans entailed major alterations to the institute's build-

ing. He wrote to Juilliard's president John Erskine that "Any such alterations would not only destroy a nearly perfect building, but entail a large and needless expense. Moreover, the activities of the school would have to be suspended during reconstruction."[108] As more land became available, Erskine agreed to retain the institute's original building.

In the summer of 1929 the trustees of the Juilliard Foundation voted to commission an addition from architect Arthur Harmon.[109] Harmon's design was planned to harmonize with Barber's original building. The addition consists of a series of austere cubic forms—with restrained Renaissance and Art Deco detail— a seven-story structure north of the original building, stretching from Claremont Avenue to Broadway (figure 7.9), a smaller wing on 122nd Street and a four-story pavilion at the corner of Broadway and 122nd Street (figure 7.10). The modest facade details subtly echo motifs on Barber's original building, notably on the Claremont Avenue building, with its rusticated base, round-arch entrances, projecting balconies, and pair of roundels ornamented with musical instruments.[110] Recessed within the arched entrances on Claremont Avenue are magnificent Art Deco style metal and glass doors set within marble frames. Above each door are stylized carved baskets overflowing with flowers. Construction of the additions entailed the demoli-

tion of the institute's 1926 addition and the removal of Barber's mansard roof so that the old building would match the simplified form of the newer structures (figure 7.10). Damrosch kept Loeb abreast of the radical architectural changes occurring at the Institute of Musical Art, sending him blueprints of Harmon's design, praising the fact that the Claremont Avenue and West 122nd Street elevations "will present a pleasant aspect inasmuch as the general style of our building will be preserved in the additions." [111] The addition did not occupy the entire site. Vacant land was preserved at the north end of the lot, possibly for construction of a concert hall for an opera school. [112]

While the design process went smoothly, construction—which was to begin late in 1930—did not, since the foundation had difficulty in completely emptying the apartment buildings that were to be demolished. For example, one tenant at the Buckingham at 3089 Broadway refused to move and for six months was served by a superintendent, two elevator boys, full-time switchboard operators, and other staff. He was finally bought out for $1,000. [113] Even with all of the residential units of the Buckingham vacated, the foundation still faced the additional headache of a remaining commercial tenant, a bookstore located in the basement, whose owner refused to vacate the premises until her lease expired in May 1931. As the building was demolished around her, her shop was flooded twice, but she still refused to move. Finally, in August 1930, after a settlement of what was reputed to be $10,000, she vacated the store, demolition was completed, and construction proceeded. [114]

The new school and its elegant Moderne concert hall were dedicated in November 1931 with a concert by the student orchestra conducted by Leopold Stokowski. [115] The design of the concert hall (figure 7.11), according to a critic for the school's magazine *The Baton*, "climaxes the modern idea of the whole

FIGURE 7.9
Juilliard School, Claremont Avenue elevation, c. 1931.

FIGURE 7.10
The Juilliard School, view looking northwest from Broadway and West 122nd Street, c. 1931; at left, original Institute of Musical Art building with mansard roof removed.

FIGURE 7.11
Juilliard School concert hall, c. 1931.

building." [116] The lower walls of the auditorium were paneled in grayish hare-wood, trimmed with walnut and black wood highlights. Peach-colored walls, dull silver metal work and striped fabrics in "autumnal shades" highlighted the room. [117] The interior decorator for the new school was Elsie Sloan Farley, who provided almost every space with a rich color palette, employing various marbles in the foyer and painted walls elsewhere. The foyer ceiling was painted in three shades of blue that contrasted with the gray, rose, and black marbles on the walls; halls were painted green; and studios and offices were painted in a variety of pastel hues.

The new building served the needs of the Juilliard School and Institute of Musical Art until their complete merger in 1946 and then served as the home to the Juilliard School of Music until 1969, when its operations were transferred to a new home at Lincoln Center. [118] The building has continued to house a music conservatory of national reputation. Juilliard sold the complex to the Manhattan School of Music, which had been established as a settlement school in 1917 on the Upper East Side and ten years later had commissioned a new building on East 105th Street in East Harlem from Donn Barber. In 1969 the Manhattan School of Music relocated to Morningside Heights. [119] As part of this move, the school commissioned a handsome, modestly scaled, modern extension of concrete and glass, facing onto Broadway, that was designed by MacFayden & Knowles. The music school building remains much as it was when completed in 1931 and continues to be a vital component of institutional Morningside Heights and one of New York City's important musical centers.

The Jewish Theological Seminary of America: Building for Traditional Judaism with an American Character

The last major institutional complex begun on Morningside Heights before the Great Depression and World War II was the impressive new home of the Jewish Theological Seminary of America erected in 1929–30 on Broadway between West 122nd and West 123rd streets, across the street from the Juilliard School and the Institute of Musical Art. The seminary traces its history to the establishment in 1886 of the Jewish Theological Seminary Association, founded to train American Jews in rabbinical studies and traditional Jewish faith while recognizing the necessity of adapting these traditional practices to modern American life. [120] The Seminary Association was established by Orthodox rabbis and laymen during a period of great ferment in the American Jewish community as traditional Orthodox beliefs were being challenged both by the Reform movement, which was especially popular among assimilated German Jews and by a secular Judaism that found popularity among many Eastern European immigrants faced with the realities of adjusting to life in America. [121] The founders of the seminary hoped to revitalize Orthodoxy in a way that would meet the needs of the bulk of Jews in America who, while increasingly uncomfortable with European Orthodoxy, were unwilling to give up traditional Jewish beliefs. However, the nascent seminary failed to attract a large following or the financial assistance needed for the creation of an institution that would have a major impact on American Judaism.[122] With the death of many of its founders between 1894 and 1901, the seminary also lacked the vigorous leadership necessary to find the funds to lead it into the future.[123]

By 1899 several of New York's most prominent Jewish residents, led by Jacob Schiff and Leonard Lewisohn (the brother of Adolph Lewisohn, donor of the School of Mines Building to Columbia) became interested in reorganizing the seminary.[124] In 1901 they persuaded Cyrus Adler, one of the leading Jewish scholars in the United States, to divide his time between his home in Washington and New York City so that he could become president of the board of trustees of an independent, revitalized seminary.[125] Adler, who eventually relocated to New York City, was a vocal advocate for the adaptation of "traditional" or "historical" Judaism to modern life, writing in 1919 that the Jewish Theological Seminary is "a religious institution with a definite aim in view to preserve the Jewish tradition and make it livable in modern surroundings."[126] In addition, Schiff and his supporters lured prominent scholar Solomon Schechter from Cambridge University to New York, appointing him president of the new seminary.[127] Adler met with the leaders of the floundering Jewish Theological Seminary Association in March 1902, seeking a merger of the association with the new seminary. This union was finalized later in 1902.[128]

Financial backing for the new seminary came from Jacob Schiff, Leonard Lewisohn, and Daniel and Simon Guggenheim. Their gifts totalled $250,000, which was considerably less than Adler had hoped they would donate.[129] Ironically, these donors were all adherents of the Reform movement. Indeed, Schiff and other successful assimilated German Jews did not accept the theological doctrines of the seminary. However, they believed that the rituals and lifestyle of the old-world Orthodoxy of immigrant Eastern European Jews were incompatible with assimilation into American life. They also felt that the spread of these practices and lifestyles would result in increased anti-Semitism. Thus, as historian Gerald Sorin has noted, Schiff "saw that a revitalized seminary might succeed, where Reform Judaism had not, in building a bridge to help immigrants cross over to American Judaism and the American mainstream."[130] Schiff's discomfort with traditional Orthodoxy is evident in the letter that he sent to the conferees discussing the seminary merger:

> What will be taught to the students should be sufficiently conservative to satisfy the reasonable orthodox Jew, while at the same time it should, with tolerance to all views, enable those who graduate from the new seminary to choose for themselves what course to follow, and to become in any event dignified ministers and teachers, to whom Jews of every shade of belief can look up with respect.[131]

Further evidence that the seminary was to be an Americanizing institution was the fact that English was to be the language of the institution and not the Yiddish spoken by the Orthodox Jewish immigrants from Eastern Europe who would comprise most of the student body.[132]

The merged theological seminary received a new charter from New York State in 1902 under the name "Jewish Theological Seminary of America," enlarged its faculty, and planned the construction of a building that would give the institution a visual presence in the city. In January 1902 Jacob Schiff purchased land for a new building on the north side of West 123rd Street between Amsterdam Avenue and Broadway at the northern fringe of Morningside Heights. The *New York Times* noted that "The selection of a site on Morningside Heights, in close proximity to Columbia University, is not without significance," and the *New York Tribune* explained that the site was chosen because "The seminary has unofficial relations with Columbia University, in that the majority of its students receive their academic education at the latter institution, and it was for this reason that the present location was selected."[133] It is not clear why Schiff chose land on the slope descending from the Morningside Plateau to the Manhattan Valley when many more prominent sites were available on Morningside Heights, including some much closer to Columbia. Schiff also paid for the construction of the new seminary building and chose its architect.[134] Schiff's choice was Arnold Brunner, the German-Jewish architect who designed many of the public projects funded by Schiff and his peers, including the School of Mines Building at Columbia University (see chapter 5) and the Students' Hall at Barnard College (see chapter 6). For the seminary, Brunner designed a beautifully proportioned Classical Revival building with a limestone facade, two-story rusticated base, arched third-story windows lighting the library, and an imposing entry flanked by fluted Doric columns that stood out amidst the brick tenements rising on nearby lots. The seminary's first permanent home was dedicated on April 26, 1903.[135]

The new Jewish Theological Seminary of America succeeded in drawing an increasingly large number of students interested in the evolving synthesis of traditional Judaism with American culture that would later be known as "Conservative Judaism."[136] Besides teaching future rabbis, the seminary also organized a Teachers Institute in 1909 to train teachers for religious schools. Most of this institute's classes were held not at the Morningside Heights building, but on the Lower East Side in the heart of New York City's immigrant Jewish community at locations such as the Hebrew Technical Institute and at various small Torah schools.[137] By the late 1910s, as the number of students increased and as the role of the seminary in Jewish theological education grew, the school was rapidly outgrowing its quarters. In 1919 Adler informed the board of directors "that the Seminary building, adequate and commodious as it was considered seventeen years ago . . . has been entirely outgrown."[138] The size of the library's collection had grown enormously and in 1924 Felix Warburg and Mortimer Schiff (Jacob Schiff's son) proposed the construction of a separate library building as a memorial to Jacob Schiff, who had recently died.[139] Besides a new library, the seminary also needed permanent space for its Teachers Institute and President Schechter also hoped to construct a dormitory to improve student life.[140] Funding to build facilities for all of these needs was soon forthcoming. Warburg, taking responsibility for the library, had Arnold Brunner design a new building, but his plans were considered "inadequate."[141] In 1924 Warburg purchased the two tenements to the east of the seminary with the intention of replacing them with a new library, but this plan was not realized.[142] A year later, the seminary received a gift of $200,000 from Israel Unterberg, president of the Jewish Education Association, for construction of a Teachers Institute building on the Lower East Side.[143] Finally, in 1927, the seminary was informed that Louis S. Brush had unexpectedly left it $1,467,113 in his will, half of which was dedicated to the construction of a dormitory, an idea that had been suggested to Brush by President Schechter.[144] Thus, by 1927 the seminary had funds for a library that was to rise on West 123rd Street adjacent to the overcrowded seminary, a Teachers Institute that would be sited downtown, and a dormitory for which no site had yet been selected. Felix Warburg suggested the idea of combining all of these buildings into a single unified complex and by February 1927 this notion was under serious consideration by the seminary's board of directors.[145]

A large site would be needed for the combined seminary buildings and affordable plots were difficult to find, especially on Morningside Heights near the seminary's classroom building, which was to remain in use. Fortuitously, a large vacant property on Broadway between West 122nd and West 123rd streets, just south of the original seminary building, had suddenly become available for purchase when plans to erect the world's tallest building on this site had fallen through. With the exception of the Fitzgerald block on Riverside Drive and West 120th Street, which was embroiled in an estate problem (see chapter 2), this Broadway plot at the north edge of Morningside Heights was the largest available parcel in the neighborhood in the late 1920s.

On September 1, 1925, page one articles in the *New York Times* and *New York Herald Tribune* had proclaimed that this Broadway site was to house the world's tallest building.[146] Oscar E. Konkle, president of Realty Sureties, Inc., the owner of many apartment houses, including several on Morningside Heights, announced the construction of the Christian Missionary Building in thanksgiving for the recovery of his son Howard from a serious bout with lockjaw in 1913 when he was six. After unsuccessfully attempting to erect the Christian Missionary Building on the Bowery and on several Upper West Side parcels, Konkle settled on the Morningside Heights plot. The building was to be a combined nondenominational church, hospital, bank, and hotel with 4,500 rooms that was to rise approximately eight feet higher than the then-record-holding Woolworth Building. Drinking and smoking were to be banned in the building and Konkle also considered banning all Sunday newspapers. Ten percent of the building's profits were to go toward the founding and maintenance of a medical mission on the shores of Lake Victoria in Africa. The building was to be designed by Shreve & Lamb, who would later actually design what would for years be the world's tallest building, the Empire State Building.[147] Foundation excavations began for the Christian Missionary Building early in 1926, but work stopped on March 31 when a rock slide killed five workers.[148] Litigation against the contractor effectively ended the project and Konkle put the property up for sale.[149] The plot, immediately across the street from the seminary's home on West 123rd Street, was perfectly located, and the seminary acquired the property on the last day of 1927.[150]

With the land purchased and the Brush, Unterberg, and Warburg donations in hand, the seminary decided to begin immediate planning for the building. By early February 1928, Adler and the seminary directors were discussing design issues.[151] Since three distinct building sections had been funded, Adler decided that a quadrangle would be appropriate, with the fourth side left open for the later construction of a building to house the expanding rabbinical seminary.[152]

FIGURE 7.12

Jewish Theological
Seminary, c. 1950.

Arnold W. Brunner Associates, the firm formed after the seminary's original architect died in 1925, was commissioned to design the building. In 1928 this firm was renamed Gehron, Ross & Alley; David Levy served as associate architect. William Gehron, the architect in charge of the seminary project, designed a building with three interconnected wings in the Colonial Revival style (figure 7.12).[153] Colonial Revival was chosen as the style for the seminary because in his bequest Louis S. Brush had required that the building "be constructed in severe Colonial style."[154] According to Abrahams, members of the building committee "spent several weeks traveling around the country looking at colonial styles. We finally designed on the basis of William and Mary College in Virginia, using similar colonial arches." [155] Among the colonial-inspired features incorporated into the building are the use of red Harvard brick laid in Flemish bond, multipaned windows, pedimented lintels, and a quadrangle with an open arcade (figure 7.13). Abrahams's comment notwithstanding, this arcade is more closely modeled on those designed by Thomas Jefferson for the outer ranges of the University of Virginia than any design at William and Mary. [156]

Brush's insistence on a colonial style for the Jewish seminary might seem, at first blush, rather incongruous. However, as Jewish immigration increased during the first decades of the twentieth century, so too did anti-Semitism, with its belief that Jews were alien to American customs and would not be easily assimilated into American life. [157] During the 1920s Henry Ford was especially virulent in his attacks against Jews, accusing them of being "Internationalists" and not loyal Americans. [158] Among many assimilated Jews, Colonial Revival design was adopted as an explicit and visible affirmation of their acceptance of American values. [159] Thus, for Jewish Theological Seminary, which had been founded in an effort to create an American version of traditional Judaism, a colonial-inspired design was an appropriate symbol of the institution's American outlook.

The major exterior feature of the seminary's new building was a tall entrance tower that housed the library's book stacks and the trustees' room. The entrance tower anchors the corner of Broadway and West 122nd Street and is aligned toward the other institutions of Morningside Heights, giving Jewish Theological Seminary a visual presence within the area's academic community. The tower is embellished with a stylized representation of the burning bush, symbolizing the presence of God, carved by prominent sculptor Lee Lawrie. [160] In 1934 Frieda Warburg presented Jewish Theological Seminary with magnificent wrought-iron entrance gates as a memorial to her parents Jacob H. and Therese Loeb Schiff (the sister of James Loeb; figure 7.14). These gates, ornamented with such Jewish symbols as lions of Judah, a menorah modeled after that on the arch of Titus, a crown of the Law, and fruits of Palestine (pomegranate, palm, and citron) were the work of Samuel

FIGURE 7.13
Gehron, Ross & Alley's design for the arcaded courtyard of Jewish Theological Seminary, c. 1928.

Yellin, the leading American designer of ornamental ironwork in the early decades of the twentieth century.[161]

While the public face of the building was modeled after eighteenth-century American colonial design precedents, the more private interiors were planned with a freer mix of stylistic forms. For example, colonial wood paneling and furnishings in the plans for a dormitory lounge contrast with the stylized classicism of the Teachers Institute's basement auditorium and with the coffered ceiling (with alternating sunbursts and six-pointed stars) and stylized Ionic piers of the library's manuscript room.[162] As initially designed, the library's reading room was to have a richly polychromed beamed ceiling with the stylized middle-eastern decoration, referred to in the 1920s as "semitic," that was popular in contemporary synagogues (figure 7.15).[163] Construction on the seminary building was completed in the fall of 1930; the Schiff Library and Unterberg Building were dedicated on October 19; the Louis S. Brush Memorial Dormitory a week later.[164] Many interior alterations have been made in these buildings to adapt them to the needs of Jewish Theological Seminary as a major center for Conservative Jewish study in New York City.[165]

Union Theological Seminary, the Institute of Musical Art, and Jewish Theological Seminary geographically extended the academic presence on Morningside Heights to the neighborhood's northern boundary. Each of the institutions completed a distinguished architectural complex that provided expanded space for its educational needs and, in the case of the seminaries, dormitories for the residential needs of students and faculty. These complexes complement those erected previously by Columbia University, Barnard College, Teachers College, and the neighborhood's other institutions, but, like those other institutions, each of the complexes in the northern portion of the neighborhood was built in a style that gave it a distinct identity and presence on Morningside Heights. The line of institutional buildings, extending diagonally from the Cathedral of St. John the Divine and Woman's Hospital in the southeast corner of the Morningside Heights neighborhood to Riverside Church, the Institute of Musical Art, and International House at the northwest corner of the area created a spectacular concentration of late nineteenth- and early-twentieth-century academic, religious, and philanthropic buildings. However, the institutional complexes are also set within a larger neighborhood context, sharing the Morningside Plateau with a densely-built-up residential neighborhood that is of significant architectural and historical interest in its own right.

FIGURE 8.1

Grotesques supporting
the balcony of the
Britannia, 527 West 110th
Street, 1909

CHAPTER EIGHT

Building for Profit

The Development of a Residential Community on Morningside Heights

PRIOR TO 1890, THE SMALL RESIDENTIAL COMMUNITY ON MORNINGSIDE Heights was housed in a few wooden farmhouses and shanties, two small brick tenements, and several riverside mansions (see chapter 1), not in speculative rowhouses of the type that were rapidly becoming the predominant residential structures in the nearby neighborhoods of the Upper West Side and Harlem. Landowners and real estate speculators, realizing as early as the 1880s the potential for future residential development on Morningside Heights, had successfully fought to rid the area of the Bloomingdale Insane Asylum (see chapter 1). Yet, even with the 1889 announcement that the asylum would relocate to White Plains, residential development continued to be impeded by the geographical isolation of the area and the lack of mass transit, which caused speculative builders to remain wary of investing in residential construction on the heights. A few rowhouses were erected during the 1890s, but these were not especially successful real estate ventures. A reticence toward large-scale development persisted even after Columbia College, Teachers College, St. Luke's Hospital, and other institutions had committed themselves to erecting impressive complexes in the neighborhood. However, with the advent of subway service through Morningside Heights in 1904, the area suddenly became a convenient place in which to live and the entire Morningside Plateau was rapidly transformed into an early example of a middle-class apartment house neighborhood.

Early Speculative Development:
Rowhouses on Morningside Heights

Ironically, the first step toward the transformation of Morningside Heights into a residential neighborhood was taken by the Society of the New York Hospital, which had long fought the developers' attempts to force its Bloomingdale Asylum off of Morningside Heights. The governors of New York Hospital had finally agreed in 1887 to move the Bloomingdale Asylum from Morningside Heights to White Plains (see chapter 1). Perhaps as a means of forestalling additional pressure to immediately sell all of its Morningside property, the governors announced in March 1889 the impending auction of 98 lots, each approximately 25 feet wide by 100 feet deep, on an irregularly shaped site at the southern edge of the hospital's holdings, from 112th to 114th streets between Amsterdam Avenue (then known as Tenth Avenue) and Broadway (then known as the Boulevard or the Grand Boulevard), including the avenue frontages.[1] In order to assure that these lots would command high prices, the governors included restrictive covenants in the deeds, forbidding noxious uses and restricting the types of residences that could be erected on the lots for a period of twenty years. On the side street properties, development was limited to private houses of at least four stories. Quality materials were mandated: brick or stone for the walls and slate, tin, or other fireproof materials for the roofs. Tenements were completely prohibited on any of the lots, but dwellings "commonly known as 'apartment houses' and 'flats,' usually consisting of a suite of rooms upon single floors and adapted and intended each as the residence of a single family" were permitted on the avenue frontages, extending back onto the side streets for 100 feet.[2]

Although far from universal in New York's developing late-nineteenth-century residential neighborhoods, these types of restrictions were common in land sales and defined the initial character of development on many streets on the Upper West Side and in Harlem. Why would landowners have restricted the use of property that they were hoping to sell to the highest bidder? In a new neighborhood that was untested in the real estate market, speculative investors demanded some guarantee regarding the future marketability of the property if they were going to pay high prices for plots. For example, an investor interested in erecting private houses might hesitate to buy property if the neighboring plot were soon to host a commercial livery stable with all of its attendant noise and objectionable smells. Thus, in the years before zoning was instituted in 1916, restrictive covenants made purchasing property more attractive and helped assure future profits from increased land values by requiring all buyers to adhere to the same land-use rules.[3] One developer concerned about the future of Morningside Heights wrote to Columbia's clerk John B. Pine in 1896 that "The restriction of a neighborhood to improvements of a high class, adds at once from 15 to 25 per cent to the value of the lots in the territory restricted. This has been invariably so."[4] Since Morningside Heights was seen as a natural extension of the Upper West Side, where similar restrictions were in force on certain blocks, it was assumed that Upper West Side developers, or others like them, would be the bidders for the properties put up for auction by the hospital. In addition, since the governors hoped to maximize their profit when the remainder of their property on Morningside Heights was finally offered for sale, it was important that construction on the auctioned lots be limited to quality buildings. Restricted sales would assure that such development would occur.

The auction took place at noon on April 4, 1889. A brochure printed prior to the event included the terms of sale, a map of the lots, and a note that the "property lies near the proposed New Cathedral, and is only a short distance from Morningside and Riverside Parks" (figure 8.2)[5] The auction was a success, with all lots selling at prices "considered satisfactory." [6] New York Hospital received a total of $500,400, with midblock lots averaging about $4,500, avenue lots selling for about $6,500, and corner sites ranging from $8,600 to $9,600. A few buyers bought a single lot, but most purchased two or three adjacent lots, while several assembled larger holdings of up to eleven lots each. Since these buyers purchased properties as investments rather than for immediate improvement, no development occurred immediately after the auction even though developers knew that both the Bloomingdale Asylum and the Leake and Watts Orphan Asylum were committed to leaving Morningside Heights. Some buyers quickly resold their purchases at a profit, while others held onto their lots, awaiting the day when they could either develop the sites themselves or sell at a higher price to those wishing to build.[7]

The first rowhouses on the heights, a lone pair at 633 and 635 West 115th Street near Riverside Drive, were built in 1891. These houses are unusual on Morningside Heights as they were not built on speculation, but were constructed for their own use by Columbia law professors Francis M. Burdick and Munroe Smith, who moved into No. 633 and No. 635 respectively as soon as the houses were completed. Since Burdick and Smith were not building houses on speculation, they did not commission a design from an architect who specialized in speculative rowhouse design. Rather, the pair of houses is a stylish Colonial Revival work designed by Henry Otis Chapman, a well-trained architect who, on his own and in partnership with John Stewart Barney, would receive

FIGURE 8.2

Announcement of the auction of a portion of New York Hospital's property on Morningside Heights, 1889.

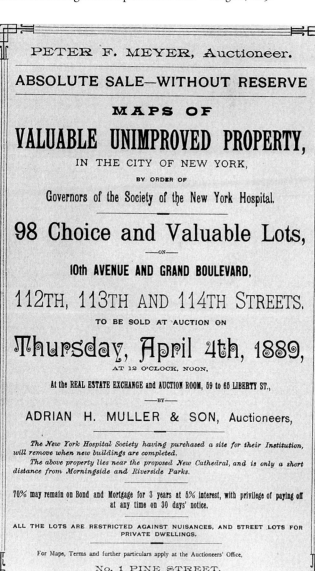

PETER F. MEYER, Auctioneer.

ABSOLUTE SALE—WITHOUT RESERVE

MAPS OF

VALUABLE UNIMPROVED PROPERTY,

IN THE CITY OF NEW YORK,

BY ORDER OF

Governors of the Society of the New York Hospital.

98 Choice and Valuable Lots,

—ON—

10th AVENUE AND GRAND BOULEVARD,

112TH, 113TH AND 114TH STREETS,

TO BE SOLD AT AUCTION ON

Thursday, April 4th, 1889,

AT 12 O'CLOCK, NOON,

At the REAL ESTATE EXCHANGE and AUCTION ROOM, 59 to 65 LIBERTY ST.,

—BY—

ADRIAN H. MULLER & SON, Auctioneers,

The New York Hospital Society having purchased a site for their Institution, will remove when new buildings are completed.
The above property lies near the proposed New Cathedral, and is only a short distance from Morningside and Riverside Parks.

70% may remain on Bond and Mortgage for 3 years at 5% interest, with privilege of paying off at any time on 30 days' notice.

ALL THE LOTS ARE RESTRICTED AGAINST NUISANCES, AND STREET LOTS FOR PRIVATE DWELLINGS.

For Maps, Terms and further particulars apply at the Auctioneers' Office,

No. 1 PINE STREET.

M. B. Brown, Printer and Stationer, 49 & 51 Park Place, N. Y.

many prestigious commissions for churches, banks, and homes. When Chapman received this commission, he had just begun his career and the Morningside Heights houses are among his earliest works.[8] The focal point on the facade of each of these simple beige brick dwellings is a magnificent entrance, an adaptation of the Federal style doorways found on New York's finest rowhouses of the 1820s. The door of each house, with its idiosyncratic panel capped by a swan's-neck pediment, is flanked by the attenuated colonettes typically found on early-nineteenth-century New York homes, and is crowned by an elegant, somewhat overscaled fanlight.[9]

It was generally believed that speculative development on Morningside Heights would have to await the construction of the subway. Indeed, in 1892, even after the Cathedral of St. John the Divine, St. Luke's Hospital, Columbia College, and Teachers College had all planned major construction projects on Morningside Heights, the *Real Estate Record and Builders Guide* predicted that "The advent of the speculative builder need not be feared until after the completion of the new West Side rapid transit line is assured; and that event, to put it mildly, is not dangerously imminent."[10] In 1892, discussions regarding a subway line that would traverse Morningside Heights were only in the earliest stages and this mass transit line would not finally open until 1904. Despite the lack of adequate transit facilities, and notwithstanding the *Real Estate Record's* assurances, a few speculators began building rowhouses in the area in 1894. Over the next five years, twelve speculative rowhouse projects, comprising 65 houses, were erected by seven different developers.

The pioneering speculative construction on Morningside Heights was undertaken by David T. and Carrie S. Kennedy, who were to be the most active rowhouse developers in the neighborhood, ultimately erecting thirty single-family homes. The Kennedys were experienced rowhouse builders, having already completed several rows on the Upper West Side. Their initial project was not built on land auctioned by New York Hospital, but on property on the north side of West 117th Street between Morningside Drive and Amsterdam Avenue.[11] This site was purchased in 1894 and 1895 from Dwight Olmstead, the realtor who had led the fight to force the relocation of the Bloomingdale Asylum (see chapter 1). With New York Hospital's pledge to transfer the asylum to White Plains within a few years, Olmstead was able to sell, at a profit, land he had purchased in 1868.

The Kennedys bought this property with the intention of erecting rowhouses. The land was sold to them without restrictions as to the type of development, but Olmstead undoubtedly relied on the fact that he was selling to developers active in the rowhouse market who would erect dwellings that would enhance the value of his and other landowners' holdings on Morningside Heights. Only a short time after completing their initial purchase, the Kennedys subdivided the property into lots of about eighteen feet in width, a lot size frequently used for rowhouses erected for middle-class households. The six initial houses (figure 8.3), begun in 1894, ten additional dwellings constructed the following year, and a single multiple dwelling on the Amsterdam Avenue corner were all designed by Neville & Bagge. The firm of Neville & Bagge was established in 1892 with offices on West 125th Street in Harlem, a site convenient to the uptown neighborhoods where construction was booming. Although Neville & Bagge was one of the most prolific firms active in New York at the turn of the century, almost nothing is known about either Thomas P. Neville or his partner George A. Bagge.[12] This lack of biographical information also holds true for most of the architects who designed speculative rowhouses. In general, these men had little formal training, were not associated with elite professional organizations, and received few prestigious commissions. Critics writing for professional architectural magazines, such as the *Architectural Record*'s Montgomery Schuyler, denigrated their work, dubbing architects such as Neville & Bagge "the speculative builder's draughtsmen."[13] These architects were, however, proficient in producing well-planned and well-appointed dwellings at the reasonable costs expected by developers.

Neville & Bagge's houses typify rowhouse design of the 1890s. The five-story Kennedy dwellings were designed in the Neo-Renaissance style, a loose amalgam of Italian Renaissance forms adapted to the urban rowhouse facade, then at the pinnacle of fashion for residential construction in New York. Each rowhouse had a rusticated limestone base, low stoop, and projecting limestone portico supported by Ionic columns. The upper stories were faced with buff-colored brick and trimmed with terra cotta; a galvanized-iron cornice and balustrade crowned the row. Although the Kennedy houses have been demolished, an extensive description, no doubt published as part of a sales campaign in 1895, provides detailed evidence of the architectural elements, design amenities, and

FIGURE 8.3
Neville & Bagge's design for rowhouses at 425–435 West 117th Street and a small apartment house at 437 West 117th Street (later Teachers College Hall), 1895.

decorative finishes expected by potential middle-class buyers.[14] Upon entering, one passed through a small vestibule with tile floor, oak trim, and leaded glass "in beautiful and appropriate tints," entering a reception room with an ornate stair leading to the main rooms on the second story. Middle-class households expected fine details and up-to-date conveniences. Thus, rooms were finished in oak, maple, birch, and olive, and main rooms had parquetry floors and marble fireplaces with wooden mantels; gas was provided for lighting and for gas logs in the fireplaces. There were two bathrooms with modern silver-plated plumbing. Closets, cupboards, wardrobes, mirrors, and modern kitchen appliances were all installed in the houses before they were sold.

What would have prompted the Kennedys to build on Morningside Heights in 1894–95 and why did they choose a site that in retrospect seems so inconvenient? Since a great deal of residential development, including the construction of a significant number of rowhouses, had occurred in the first half of the 1890s in the neighborhoods adjoining Morningside Heights, the Kennedys must have hoped for the possibility of a substantial return on an investment in middle-class rowhouses on Morningside Heights. Even the *Real Estate Record,* which only three years earlier had emphasized the area's lack of convenient mass transit, noted that the "location is superb" since there were several parks in the vicinity for recreation and fine views. The view to the south was uninterrupted as yet by intervening buildings, thus from these new houses one could see built-up parts of the city and even as far, according to the *Real Estate Record,* as the hills of Staten Island.[15] The siting, coupled with the impending opening of Columbia and the area's other new institutions, and the fact that the elevated station was close by, albeit difficult to reach, must have convinced the Kennedys that the time was ripe for investment in the area. Today, when most people entering Morningside Heights alight on Broadway from the subway or bus, West 117th Street between Morningside Drive and Amsterdam Avenue seems an odd place for a pioneering builder. In the 1890s, however, Broadway was not the area's main street, but merely a rough, unpaved boulevard. The neighborhood looked to the east, toward the streetcar line on Amsterdam Avenue and the elevated in Harlem which was accessible via a steep stairway at 116th Street. Thus, the choice of a building site at the far eastern end of the area was logical from the perspective of a developer attempting to sell middle-class housing in the mid-1890s.

Although a few speculative rowhouse developers rented out their newly constructed houses, this approach was exceptional and was generally adopted only by large landowners with long-term property interests.[16] Most developers, the Kennedys included, hoped to maximize their profits by selling their houses as quickly as possible at a price considerably higher than the initial investment in land, financing, and construction. The Kennedys' 117th Street dwellings were placed on the market in 1895 at a time when a financial panic had depressed the real estate market. As a result, sales were slow despite an article in the *New York Times* entitled "Reasons for Living on the Heights," which advised its readers of the many amenities Morningside Heights offered: "The city has extended the sewer and water systems throughout the whole territory, and all the main streets have been graded and paved with granite. Many of the side streets have been paved with asphalt. The gas and electric light companies have arranged for the supply of light, and the territory is as well policed and protected from fire as any part of town."[17] Nevertheless, between 1895 and 1897 only six of the Kennedys' houses were sold to people who would use these dwellings as their primary place of residence.[18] In addition, Columbia President Seth Low purchased no. 425 in 1896, possibly as a convenient place to sleep when attending construction meetings relating to the new campus being erected nearby, since his official residence continued to be on East 64th Street.[19] For unknown reasons, the ownership of three of the Kennedys' houses reverted to Dwight Olmstead. These were later converted to fraternities or boarding houses for students and university employees.[20] The remaining houses were not sold until the early years of the twentieth century, when they were purchased primarily as investments by absentee landlords. Several of these structures were also later converted into fraternities or boarding houses.[21]

Although the mixed success that David and Carrie Kennedy had selling their rowhouses failed to demonstrate that there was an overwhelming demand for single-family dwellings on the Morningside Plateau in the 1890s, they were successful enough to encourage investment in additional rowhouse construction between 1895 and 1899. Rowhouse developers were apparently responding to the increasing presence of people affiliated with the institutions who, they hoped, would wish to live in the area. They also sought to attract other New Yorkers who would want to purchase new homes near the prestigious cathedral, hospital, and colleges. The rows erected in the late 1890s ranged from the exceptionally narrow (fourteen and fifteen feet wide) and particularly banal group at 604–616 West 114th Street (E. R. & C. J. Lawson, 1896), to the more typical eighteen- to twenty-foot wide houses designed by architects such as Neville & Bagge, George F. Pelham, and George A. Schellenger, all of whom specialized in speculative rowhouses work (see appendix), to the larger and more expensive dwellings constructed at 414 and 415 Riverside Drive (George Pelham, 1897).[22] Much of this new construction took place on the West 113th and 114th street lots auctioned by New York Hospital in 1889 and still subject to the restrictions imposed by that sale. These houses were generally well-detailed Neo-Renaissance style brick dwellings with limestone bases, terra-cotta trim, and metal cornices (figures 1.12 and 5.35).[23]

The most interesting row architecturally is the one at 619–627 West 113th Street designed by C. P. H. Gilbert (figure 8.4). Unlike most of the architects who designed speculative housing, Charles Pierrepont Henry Gilbert had an extensive architectural education, having studied at Columbia College and the prestigious Ecole des Beaux-Arts in Paris. In the late 1880s he began designing speculative rowhouses, first in Brooklyn and later in Manhattan. The Morningside Heights row, dating from 1897–98, is among Gilbert's last middle-class residential designs, undertaken just before he began receiving commissions for mansions from the city's wealthiest families. Gilbert's success can be attributed to his ability to design proficiently in almost any style; for this Morningside Heights row, he chose Colonial-inspired motifs borrowed from eighteenth-century residential design on Beacon Hill in Boston. With their rounded bays and oriels, rectangular and segmental-arch entryways, leaded-glass transoms and fanlights, and paneled and splayed lintels, these houses are the most sophisticated rowhouses on Morningside Heights.[24]

The rowhouses on Morningside Heights were erected during a period when the traditional plan and exterior design of the rowhouse was undergoing a marked change. Since the early nineteenth century, when rowhouse construction began extending north up Manhattan Island, the most distinctive feature of the city's house fronts had been the high stoop. The stoop, developed in the early nineteenth century as a means of increasing usable space on New York's narrow and expensive lots, not only elevated the main parlor floor, lending a sense of grandeur to the rowhouse front, but also allowed for a raised basement that was more usable by the family in residence than a dark sunken one. The basement floor was set only a few feet below street level, with large windows permitting light and fresh air to enter the front room. This room was generally used as the dining room in most early-nineteenth-century rowhouses.[25] By the 1890s, when the Morningside Heights rowhouses were being erected, the stoop began to be viewed by some as an unfashionable protrusion, although many builders still chose to construct conservative high-stooped homes, perhaps because, as one real estate analyst reported, "The stoop has come to be looked upon, by some people, as the outward expression of respectability."[26] This continuing use of the high stoop is evident on 113th Street, where two rows erected in 1896 and 1897 are entered via stoops ranging from five to ten steps high.

As the popularity of the stoop began to decline, however, many new houses were erected with entrances

FIGURE 8.4

619–627 West 113th Street (C. P. H. Gilbert, 1897), 1937.

near street level. In some of these the basement was sunk below the level of the sidewalk and was reached by a steep stairway. Such dark subterranean basements were used entirely for service facilities such as the kitchen. This plan, popular on English rowhouses, never became very common in Manhattan. However, many of the Morningside Heights rowhouses, including the group designed by C. P. H. Gilbert, employ this English basement plan. A variant on this is the American basement plan, the most important rowhouse design to develop in New York in the late nineteenth century.[27] American basement houses were entered at or near street level and generally contained a small vestibule and entrance hall from which stairs rose to the main level one flight up. The kitchen and other service facilities were located at the rear of the ground floor, with the underground cellar used only for mechanical equipment and storage. American basement houses, such as the Kennedys' row on 117th Street (figure 8.3), were generally provided with a narrow service entrance set to one side of the main facade which permitted servants and tradespeople to enter and exit without coming into contact with the residents and their guests.

The rowhouses erected on Morningside Heights in the late 1890s were not universally successful. A few were sold shortly after their completion to Columbia professors or to middle-class families whose heads of household commuted to a job in Lower Manhattan. Other houses were initially leased and were not sold until the early twentieth century. Many of the houses remained vacant for years. Indeed, most of the rowhouses built on 112th to 114th streets do not appear in the 1900 census, indicating that they were unoccupied. The five houses designed by C. P. H. Gilbert are typical of the slow pace of residential sales on Morningside Heights. Although construction was completed late in 1898, only one house was occupied as of 1900 and it was not until 1906 that the last house was sold.[28] Most of the households in these Morningside Heights rowhouses consisted of four to six family members and one or two servants, almost always young women who were recent immigrants from Ireland or other countries in Europe.

Because of the slowness of sales to families, a number of the rowhouses were converted into fraternity houses or student boarding houses, rather than being sold as private homes as planned. Unlike in private homes, where servants were generally European immigrant women, the fraternities and rooming houses were almost always staffed by African-American men and women, most having moved north from Virginia. When, for example, the New York State census enumerator recorded a fraternity at 608 West 113th Street in 1905, the house was occupied by four students and two black servants—a male butler and a female cook.[29] Among the few jobs open to African Americans in the segregated job market of northern cities were menial positions in public facilities—restaurant waiters, cooks, railroad porters, elevator operators, etc. Relatively few were employed as live-in servants in New York City. Apparently, employment in fraternities and rooming houses was considered to be more akin to service work in a public facility than to domestic service in a private house.

As a result of slow sales, several of the builders of Morningside Heights row-houses lost their investment when their properties were foreclosed. In 1899 Marie Cook erected five houses at 523–531 West 113th Street and David Kennedy erected a row of nine around the block at 538–554 West 114th Street. Both owners lost their property in foreclosure actions—Cook in 1901 and Kennedy in 1902—without having sold a single dwelling. Such foreclosures made it clear that Morningside Heights was not to be fertile ground for rowhouse development. Even when Columbia College, Teachers College, and St. Luke's Hospital had finally relocated to Morningside Heights, few people wished to live in the area. Morningside Heights houses simply could not compete with the new row-houses for sale on the Upper West Side and in Harlem. Those houses were in more convenient neighborhoods, well-served by mass transit and by the shops, schools, churches, and social centers that defined desirable residential communities and that were still totally lacking on Morningside Heights. In addition, by 1900 apartment houses were beginning to become more attractive to middle-class New Yorkers than single-family rowhouses.

FIGURE 8.5

Proposed elevator in Morningside Park, 1900.

Thus, by 1900 residential development on Morningside Heights remained slow and erratic. The *New York Tribune* reported in 1900 that "The development of this beautiful hilltop has been retarded by its somewhat inconvenient accessibility."[30] The major access problem was the "series of long and circuitous flights of steps" leading to and from the 116th Street station of the elevated on Eighth Avenue. In order to alleviate this problem, several large property owners in the area commissioned designs for an elevator that would transport people up and down the cliff of Morningside Park (figure 8.5). As designed by civil engineers Percival Robert Moses and Samuel Osgood Miller, the elevator was to be a steel structure with two electric-powered cars. A walkway would extend out from Morningside Drive to the elevators and a cupola was to cap the open steel shaft. Although this was apparently a serious proposal, nothing came of it, perhaps because the Parks Department could not support a project in a public park that would primarily benefit private landowners unless there was extensive public backing.[31]

Although New York Hospital's 1889 deed restrictions controlled development on several blocks of Morningside Heights, most land on the Morningside Plateau remained vacant and without any restrictions as to the types of buildings that could be erected. Efforts had been made as early as the late 1880s to regulate property development in the area. In 1887, owners along Riverside Drive between 116th and 120th streets had sought to limit construction along that boulevard to three houses per block, thus assuring that only large homes for wealthy individuals would rise opposite Riverside Park and the Hudson River.[32] However, this proposal gained little support since interest in building in the neighborhood at that time was minimal. Morningside Heights' institutional owners, who were expending large sums to erect new buildings, were also deeply concerned about the nature and quality of future development on the plateau. Most of these institutions had purchased property on Morningside Heights after being forced from their previous homes as downtown areas became densely built up and increasingly noisy and commercialized. In order to ensure that their investments in land and buildings would not be wasted and that they would not be forced to vacate Morningside Heights for the same reasons, the institutions sought to prevent major commercial development and the construction of tenements or other types of housing that might diminish the prestige of the neighborhood. To that end, in 1896 the institutions organized the Morningside Protective Association with the objective of ensuring "the social and material improvement of that portion or district of the City of New York lying between Morningside Drive and 122d street on the east and north, and Cathedral Parkway and Riverside Drive on the south and west; and the bringing together of the residents of the district for their better acquaintance and mutual benefit."[33] The idea for a protective association apparently originated with the Board of Trustees of Teachers College, possibly because of concern that their location at the northern end of the area, close to the rundown houses of Manhattanville, would be surrounded by tenements. Indeed, by 1896, tenements were edging close to Teachers College's property. A group of six, for example, was erected that year at 520–530 West 123rd Street between Amsterdam Avenue and Broadway.

Initially, the Board of Directors of the Morningside Protective Association represented only the area's new institutional owners, but the directors realized that restrictions could not be promulgated and new construction controlled without also including local real estate owners on the board of directors. Thus, in 1897 landowners Charles T. Barney, John D. Crimmins, James J. Goodwin, Dwight Olmstead, and D. Willis James were invited to become members of the board, as were H. H. Cammann and Merritt Trimble, representatives of New York Hospital which still owned extensive property in the area.[34] The Morningside Protective Association opposed a number of projects judged undesirable for the plateau. They fought, for example, a proposal to erect an elevated railroad on Amsterdam Avenue since the noisy and dirty el would have been a blight on the property immediately adjacent. However, the major thrust of the Protective Association was to seek restrictions on all of the land between 110th Street and 122nd Street, limiting owners to the construction of single-family homes on the side streets and apartment buildings on the avenues.[35]

The Association's efforts were ultimately fruitless. By the time the group was organized and promulgated its proposed restrictions, Morningside Heights was already divided among many landowners. Much of the land was owned by individuals or corporations that had invested in long-term ownership, with a primary goal of profiting as development expanded in the vicinity. Even though some of these owners might have agreed to restrict some future development, it would have been impossible to acquire unanimous consent and it would have been prohibitively expensive for the institutions to purchase the land of recalcitrant owners. After the proposal to restrict the plateau failed, optimists continued to hope that the "sentiment of the principal owners" would assure quality development even without restrictions.[36] This assumption was based on the fact that much of the property was held by respected real estate interests, such as the Astor and Goelet families, and that other lots were in the hands of such long-term owners as the Society of the New York Hospital and the De Peyster family. This may have been nothing more than a rationalization on the part of the Morningside Protective Association's institutional members, who were unwilling or unable to spend the money necessary to assure the kind and quality of development that they desired. In any event, the area did develop in a "high class" manner, although not in the way that the founders of the Morningside Heights Association had hoped.

The Second Wave of Speculative Development: The Creation of a Middle-Class Apartment House Neighborhood

The transformation of noninstitutional property on Morningside Heights into a residential community occurred during a period of significant change in living patterns in New York City. While New York is generally perceived to be a city of apartment dwellers, it was not until the first years of the twentieth century that this mode of living became the common residence type for most prosperous middle-class Manhattanites. It is generally accepted that the first apartment building in New York City planned specifically to attract middle-class tenants was the Stuyvesant, commissioned by Rutherford Stuyvesant and erected in 1869–70 to a design by Richard Morris Hunt.[37] The Stuyvesant, located on East

18th Street between Irving Place and Third Avenue, was five stories tall, with four apartments on each of the lower four floors and artists' studios in the fifth-story attic. Although there were no elevators and the apartment plans were somewhat awkward, the Stuyvesant was built with amenities responsive to middle-class desires—two entrances and stairways minimized the number of people using public areas; sizable courts guaranteed light and air in every room; eight rooms per apartment provided space, privacy, and a degree of separation between private and public functions; a kitchen and a bathroom were equipped with up-to-date fixtures; a servant's bedroom allowed each household to have a single live-in servant; a service stair separated residents and their guests from servants and deliveries; and a concierge assured residents that no unwelcome visitors would be permitted to enter the building.

A few other middle-class apartment houses were erected in the years immediately following the completion of the Stuyvesant, but the financial crisis caused by the Panic of 1873 slowed construction of new buildings. By late in the decade, as the real estate market recovered from the panic, many new multiple dwellings were constructed. However, it was only in the 1880s that large, well-appointed apartment buildings were erected to attract the wealthy tenants or cooperative buyers who could also afford to live in single-family rowhouses. Among these buildings, which offered elevators, large units, and impressive amenities, were some of the city's most famous early apartment houses—the Dakota (1880–84), the Central Park Apartments (1882–85; demolished), the Gramercy (1883–85), the Osborne (1883–85), and the Chelsea (1883–85; now the Chelsea Hotel).

By the 1890s, the apartment house was becoming an acceptable choice of living accommodation for the middle class. Although no longer a novelty, apartments were not yet the most prevalent form of housing in Manhattan and they were not the only choice for affluent people. Even during the 1880s and 1890s, when many fine apartment houses were erected, most lots in the new middle-class neighborhoods continued to be developed with single-family rowhouses. The Upper West Side, Harlem, and Carnegie Hill in the East 90s experienced major rowhouse development during these decades. In each of these neighborhoods, a few apartment houses were built, but they were not the dominant residential type. On the Upper West Side, for example, although the Dakota established the acceptability of apartment living at the inception of residential development in the area, it was not until the first years of the twentieth century that other apartment houses were erected that rivaled it in grandeur and appointments. Thus, at the end of the nineteenth century, prosperous middle-class households in Manhattan could choose to live in an apartment house if they wished, but most such families chose the more traditional rowhouse.

By the early twentieth century, housing conditions were changing dramatically and single-family home construction virtually ceased. The *American Ar-*

chitect and Building News documented the construction of just over 100 single-family dwellings in Manhattan in 1901, in comparison to the 835 that had been built in 1890.[38] In fact, most of the new single-family homes were not speculative rowhouses, but individual townhouses commissioned by the very wealthy for plots on and adjacent to Fifth Avenue on the Upper East Side. The population of Manhattan Island grew significantly in the late nineteenth century and first decade of the twentieth century, rising above a million people by 1890. While many of the city's residents were poor immigrants who moved into overcrowded tenement districts such as the Lower East Side and Hell's Kitchen, the middle class was also growing as business and industry, and the city's intellectual, professional, and entertainment communities expanded. This increasingly large affluent population could not be accommodated in the city's limited supply of rowhouses. In addition, the displacement of large numbers of people from Midtown as commercial construction pushed north up the island increased pressure on the housing market, resulting in the construction of large numbers of multiple dwellings in uptown neighborhoods.

It was the subway that was to have the most profound influence on the patterns of residential construction in New York.[39] The subway's development had a twofold effect. First, it transformed undeveloped sections of the city into prime residential areas by making them accessible and thus convenient to those who worked downtown. Second, it raised land values in the developed areas through which it ran to such an extent that new single-family home construction became prohibitively expensive for developers and homes already built on some thoroughfares, such as West End Avenue, became so valuable that owners sold them to developers who planned to replace the rowhouses with apartment buildings.

Underground mass transit for New York City had been proposed as early as the 1860s, but weak political leadership, unable to fight the powerful streetcar and elevated railroad interests, delayed serious consideration of a subway until the 1890s. In 1895, a commission established by the New York State Legislature finally chose a route for a subway that would extend from City Hall north on Elm Street (now Lafayette Street) and Fourth Avenue (now Park Avenue South and Park Avenue) to Grand Central Terminal, then west to Times Square, and north up Broadway to 96th Street, where the line would split with one branch continuing north on Broadway (through Morningside Heights) and the other turning east to Lenox Avenue in Harlem, both continuing into the Bronx. In 1900, a franchise for construction of the city's first subway line was given to the Interborough Rapid Transit Company (IRT). This subway route traversed a widely varied series of neighborhoods—densely built up commercial sections north of City Hall, areas that had recently experienced residential construction such as the Upper West Side, and virtually undeveloped areas including Morningside Heights (figure 8.6). Service on the first IRT trains was inaugurated on

October 27, 1904. On that day, Morningside Heights was transformed into a conveniently located area, less than a thirty-minute commute to City Hall and even closer to downtown retail and industrial centers and to the burgeoning entertainment district around Times Square.[40]

The opening of the subway thus led directly to major investment in speculative apartment house construction on Morningside Heights and the area was rapidly transformed into a middle-class apartment house neighborhood. Although residential development in other areas of the city was also affected by the inception of subway service, especially in Hamilton Heights and Washington Heights to the north, in no other area was the overall residential character changed so rapidly and so completely. Because Morningside Heights was the Manhattan neighborhood still with extensive vacant property located closest to previously built up neighborhoods, developers immediately sensed the possibility of profitable residential development. In addition, the area boasted such attractive amenities for potential residents as Riverside Park and Drive, Morningside Park, close proximity to the northern sections of Central Park, a high elevation cooled by river breezes, and the presence of prestigious educational, charitable, and religious institutions. These factors were all conducive to the creation of a middle-class neighborhood, one that would be filled with what the real-estate industry referred to as "high-class" buildings. In order to meet the anticipated demand, virtually all of the new construction on Morningside Heights took the form of apartment houses.

As noted above, a few multiple dwellings had been erected on Morningside Heights before 1900 when most residential construction on Morningside Heights was rowhouses. The developers who erected these first few apartment buildings in the 1890s must have hoped that the faculty and staff at Columbia and Teachers College or the doctors and staff members at St. Luke's Hospital would welcome the convenience of living only a few minutes walk from their offices and classrooms. In addition, since the academic institutions had not yet committed themselves to the construction of dormitories, students who could not live at home would be seeking rooms or small apartments and might be accommodated in these new buildings. The earliest of these multiple dwellings were the anomalous pair of modest four-story tenements at 2848 and 2850 Broadway

FIGURE 8.6

Subway construction on Broadway looking northwest from 110th Street, May 22, 1901; saloons occupy the small wooden buildings and "for sale" signs advertise the availability of vacant land.

erected in 1886, long before other substantial buildings were built on the Morningside Plateau. The next multiple dwelling to appear on Morningside Heights was erected by the Kennedys in 1894 on the northeast corner of Amsterdam Avenue and West 117th Street as part of their larger rowhouse project. This five-story building was planned as a rooming house, arranged with small suites and single rooms without kitchens or individual baths. Shortly after its completion, the building was rented by Teachers College for its women students (see chapter 6). Known as Teachers College Hall, this experiment with off-campus housing was not a success and the building soon became a typical rental property with a diverse tenancy. It was demolished in 1926 for the construction of Casa Italiana. Other multiple dwellings erected prior to 1900, including several five-story walkup tenements and a few larger elevator buildings, did attract staff and students. The most popular buildings were the pair of apartment houses known as University Court at 417 and 419 West 118th Street. Erected early in 1899 with eighteen apartments in each building, the pair was ready for occupancy by the fall semester of 1899 and immediately attracted tenants affiliated with Columbia, Barnard, and Teachers.[41] As with the Kennedys' earlier rowhouses, University Court was sited on the east side of the neighborhood close to the Amsterdam Avenue streetcar line and the elevated station.

In anticipation of the opening of the subway on Broadway, widespread apartment-house construction on Morningside Heights began in the early years of the twentieth century while the subway was under construction; eight apartment buildings were begun in 1900, four in 1901, and four in 1902. By 1902 an observer of real estate conditions in the city correctly predicted the future of Morningside Heights as "a section of the city that will be immediately and profoundly affected by the subway. Within a couple of years its small area will be practically covered with apartment houses."[42] In 1903 apartment-house developers finally began large-scale investment in Morningside Heights, gambling that the subway would begin service as the buildings were completed and would ensure rapid rental of the new apartments and a profitable return on investment. That year permits were issued for ten apartment houses on streets close to the stations under construction at West 110th and West 116th streets. Five of these buildings, the Blennerhasset, Bertha, Kendal Court (figure 8.7), De Peyster, and Mumford were located on the north side of West 111th Street (nos. 507–535; figure 1.14) between Amsterdam Avenue and Broadway. These modest

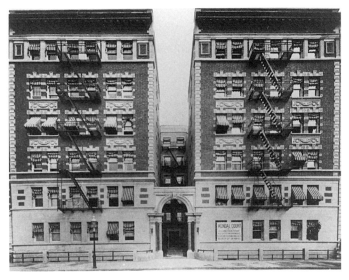

FIGURE 8.7

Kendal Court (Schwartz & Gross, 1903), 521 West 111th Street, c. 1904. The sign advertises "all latest improvements," including elevator, telephone, and a mail chute.

six-story structures with their ornate brick facades were described as "typical of what is to be expected soon in many other streets on the Heights."[43] In 1904, permits were issued for fifteen additional apartment houses located on blocks throughout the Morningside Heights neighborhood.

Once the subway opened in late 1904, apartment house construction accelerated. In 1905 alone thirty-seven new buildings were begun, with permits issued for an additional thirty-three the following year. Among the residential buildings begun in 1905 was one of the most unusual structures erected in the neighborhood, the Renaissance-inspired, nine-story Sesrun Club at 420 West 116th Street designed by Neville & Bagge as a residence for nurses ("Sesrun" is "nurses" spelled backwards).[44] This use for nurses' housing proved to be unsuccessful and the building was converted into a residential and transient hotel called the King's Crown. By 1906, construction of apartment houses on Morningside Heights was so rapid and of such a high quality that the *Real Estate Record* boasted that the area was already "probably the most distinctive high-class apartment house quarter in the city. Almost all the buildings are of that type; the few private residences are survivals for the most part, and it would seem some law has been passed against any other kind of a house than a great multi-family palace."[45] After a brief slowdown during an economic depression in 1907 (only eight new apartment houses were begun that year), speculative investment rebounded in 1908 and construction began on twenty-four buildings. This resurgence coincided with the impending expiration of the twenty-year restrictive covenants imposed by New York Hospital that limited construction on several side streets between Amsterdam Avenue and Broadway to single-family homes. After it became clear that Morningside Heights would not become a rowhouse neighborhood, owners of restricted lots held their property for later development. In 1906, the *Evening Post* speculated that "as soon as the private-house restriction shall be terminated . . . the vacant land there will be speedily given over to a high class of apartment house."[46] This is indeed what happened. In 1908 construction on eight apartment houses was begun on the restricted property on West 114th and 115th streets. This building actually occurred a year before the expiration of the covenants, but no one seems to have protested since it was clear that apartment buildings would soon rise on every available lot.

Building on Morningside Heights continued to boom in 1909, when an additional thirty-five buildings were erected, including six on property that had been restricted, followed by seventeen additional apartment houses in 1910, and twelve in 1911. This last burst of construction, from 1909 through 1911, included many of the neighborhood's grandest and most impressive residential structures. By 1911, most property had been developed. Over the next twenty years, the few remaining vacant sites—including four large plots on Riverside Drive, three on Cathedral Parkway, and one on Broadway—were gradually developed. Finally, in 1930 the last apartment building erected on a vacant site was begun

at 512 West 112th Street. Afterward, all new construction would entail the demolition of existing buildings, as when St. James House (figure 8.8), the area's final
pre-World War II apartment building, was erected in 1931 on the northwest corner of Amsterdam Avenue and West 113th Street, replacing a modest tenement
dating from 1897.[47]

Apartment House Builders and Their Architects

As with most of the earlier rowhouses on Morningside Heights, all of the apartment house construction in the area was undertaken by speculative developers
hoping to profit from their initiatives. They invested as little of their own
money in a project as possible, often borrowing half to two-thirds of the cost at
as low a rate of interest as could be obtained.[48] Once the building was completed, these developers were, in most cases, uninterested in actually managing
the property. Just as the builders of speculative rowhouses in the nineteenth
century generally sold these structures as rapidly as possible, apartment house
builders almost always sold their properties upon completion to people referred to in the real estate community as "investors."[49] This practice prevailed
on Morningside Heights, where almost every building was sold shortly after its
completion.[50] Management of apartment buildings fell to the investors who
sought profits over the long term by renting apartments at the highest rates the market would bear.

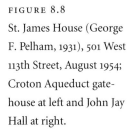

FIGURE 8.8
St. James House (George
F. Pelham, 1931), 501 West
113th Street, August 1954;
Croton Aqueduct gate-
house at left and John Jay
Hall at right.

The builders responsible for the development of most early-twentieth-century apartment houses in New York City and almost all of the apartment buildings on Morningside Heights reflect the major changes that were occurring in the city's ethnic composition during this period, espe-cially the immigration of hundreds of thousands of Italians and Eastern Eu-ropean Jews. The entry of immigrant Italians and Jews and the children of these immigrants into the worlds of real estate, building, and investment coincided with the advent of the apartment building as the most popu-lar form of middle-class residence in Manhattan. Speculative residential development had long been a field open to immigrants since the con-struction, sale, and leasing of such

buildings was not tied to social connections, as was the construction of private homes for the wealthy. In the nineteenth century, a substantial proportion of the city's speculative rowhouses had been erected by Irish builders, while German immigrants had erected many of the tenements on the Lower East Side. All one needed to become involved in speculative development was sufficient capital for the initial investment in land and construction, and the ability to get a loan. Many immigrants speculated in a small way, often risking money on only one or two projects. Others became professional builders, investing in the construction of many buildings.

The most active builders on Morningside Heights were members of the Paterno family, which had emigrated from Castelemezzano near Naples. Stories differ as to how the four Paterno brothers—Joseph, Charles, Michael, and Anthony—became involved in apartment house construction. The most romantic tale, as told in Joseph Paterno's *New York Times* obituary, has the young immigrant newsboy shivering at his post on Park Row, watching a tall office building rise. "'Papa,' he asked, 'why do they make the business buildings so high?' 'Because it pays,' his father replied.... [T]his is the American way.' The bright-eyed newsboy wrinkled his brow and frowned, while making change for a customer. 'But, papa, if this is so why don't they make the houses and tenements high, too, as they will bring more rent?' The father smiled and patted his son's curly head. 'You have an eye for business, my son. Perhaps some day you may build some high houses.'" From that day on, the story continues, "it became Joseph's ambition to build skyscraper apartment houses."[51] This story notwithstanding, it is far more likely that Joseph and his brothers became involved in construction because their father, John Paterno, had been a builder in Italy and eventually became a partner in the New York building firm of McIntosh & Paterno.

In 1898, John Paterno began construction on two of the earliest apartment houses on Morningside Heights, a pair of modest structures at 505 and 507 West 112th Street (demolished). At John's death in 1899, Joseph and his brother Charles were brought in to complete the unfinished buildings. From this beginning, the Paterno brothers went on to contribute significantly to the construction of apartment houses in New York City, undertaking their "most extensive construction in the Columbia University neighborhood."[52] In 1907, Charles Paterno established his own business, the Paterno Construction Company, with his brother-in-law Anthony Campagna. Working independently and in joint ventures, the members of the Paterno family built thirty-seven apartment buildings on Morningside Heights, ranging from modest six-story structures to the impressive Luxor, Regnor, and Rexor (figure 8.9) on Broadway at 115th and 116th Streets and the Colosseum (figure 8.14) and Paterno (figure 8.20) on Riverside Drive and 116th Street. The Paternos were active on Morningside Heights during the entire span of apartment house development in the area, beginning with John Paterno's modest apartment buildings on 112th Street in 1898 and ending with Joseph Paterno's enormous 1924 building at 425 Riverside Drive.[53] The Paternos were so proud of their buildings that the facades of some

of their grandest works are emblazoned with initials referring to the family—
"P" for Paterno, "JP" for Joseph Paterno, or "PB" for Paterno Brothers.[54] These
initials often baffle modern viewers, but were probably recognized by many
people at the time the buildings were erected, perhaps assuring potential renters
that these were quality apartment houses.

The vast majority of other builders active in the Morningside Heights neighborhood were Jewish. Many were small-scale builders involved with only a few
buildings, but others established major careers as apartment-house developers.
Some built under their own names or as corporations that bore their names,
but the most active Jewish builders incorporated as real estate firms with
names stripped of Jewish ethnic identity. For example, Edgar A. Levy, Jacob
Stein, and Leo S. Bing were partners in the Carlyle Realty Company, Jacob Axelrod was president of the West Side Construction Company, and Charles Newmark headed the Carnegie Construction Company.[55] Like the builders, many,
but by no means all of the architects commissioned by the speculative developers to design apartment buildings were also from Italian and Jewish backgrounds, including Gaetan Ajello, Simon Schwartz, Arthur Gross, George and
Edward Blum, and William Rouse.[56] However, the builders did not necessarily hire architects of their own ethnic background. While Paterno Brothers
commissioned three buildings from Italian architect Gaetan Ajello, the firm
was most loyal to the Jewish ar-
chitects Schwartz & Gross. The Jewish building company, B. Crystal &
Son (incorporated by Bernard and
Hyman Crystal), hired the Jewish
architectural firm of George & Edward Blum for two buildings, but
used Ajello for four additional structures, while the Jewish building firm
West Side Construction almost always hired the non-Jewish architect
George Pelham.

The architects who specialized
in apartment-house design rarely
trained at the leading architectural
schools or apprenticed in prestigious
offices. Rather, most were practition-
ers who, if they had any formal architectural training at all, had been
educated in less prestigious offices or
in technical schools.[57] Since these architects were not welcome in the
higher echelons of the architectural
profession because of their ethnic

FIGURE 8.9
Rexor (Gaetan Ajello,
1911), 600 West 116th
Street, 1912.

background and "inferior" training, they entered the field at the least presti-gious end, designing speculative apartment houses.[58] In fact, in the first decades of the twentieth century, few apartment house architects were members of the American Institute of Architects or the Architectural League of New York, bas-tions of the professional elite.

As a neighborhood that was part of the first wave of middle-class apartment-house construction in New York City, Morningside Heights contains an early concentration of speculative apartment buildings designed by these architects. Three firms, George Pelham, Neville & Bagge, and Schwartz & Gross, were re-sponsible for more than half of the apartment houses on Morningside Heights and, indeed, for thousands of other apartment buildings located throughout Manhattan. Thus, they were among the most prolific designers ever to work in New York City.[59] Although generally unheralded, it was Schwartz & Gross, George Pelham, Neville & Bagge, and other speculator architects who, by the sheer volume of their work, created the architectural character and texture of many of New York's neighborhoods, while more prestigious architects like McKim, Mead & White, Carrère & Hastings, and Delano & Aldrich designed only a small number of great monuments that are set amidst the city's more typical speculative buildings.

The Design of Apartment Buildings

The architects of speculative apartment buildings did not generally provide the builders who commissioned these designs with architectural masterpieces. Rather, they designed commercially viable buildings in popular stylistic idioms, using Italian Renaissance, French Renaissance, French Beaux-Arts, Gothic, and American Colonial forms, often in an unsophisticated manner. Facades were almost always of brick, the least costly material available, with one- or two-story limestone bases and terra-cotta ornamental trim on the upper stories. A pro-jecting pressed-metal cornice generally capped the street frontage. A typical ex-ample is George Pelham's Blennerhasset at 507 West 111th Street (figure 8.10), with its two-story rusticated limestone base, entry portico, red brick upper fa-cade highlighted with French-inspired Beaux-Arts white terra-cotta decorative features, and a metal cornice supported by brackets. A significant number of Morningside Heights buildings combined the ornamentation of Beaux-Arts de-sign with American Colonial brickwork. On these buildings, dark red brick was laid in Flemish bond with burned headers. Overscaled terra-cotta trim was em-ployed on some of these structures, such as on Schwartz & Gross's Revere Hall and Hudson Hall on West 114th Street. However, on the better examples of this type, such as George Pelham's Malvern and Barieford on Claremont Avenue (figure 8.11), and Lawlor & Haase's Brookfield on Riverside Drive (figure 8.27), the trim is used in a more understated manner. The prevalence of this type of composite design on Morningside Heights may reflect the influence of the Renaissance/Colonial design of Columbia's classroom buildings.

FIGURE 8.10
Blennerhasset (George F.
Pelham, 1903), 507 West
111th Street, c. 1904.

FIGURE 8.11
Malvern and Barieford
(George F. Pelham, 1906),
47 and 49 Claremont
Avenue, c. 1908.

Critics of the period abhorred the general quality of the speculative apartment buildings. In his 1910 critique for the prestigious *Architectural Record,* H. W. Frohne complained that builders spent their money "for sham and display," erecting apartment houses of "much superficial pretense, little substantial fulfillment."[60] Frohne explained that facades were designed "for the maximum of visual display" because the builders saw "The power of advertising" in applying a substantial amount of fashionable decorative trim to make a building readily visible and thus attract the attention of prospective tenants.[61] Whether creative or pedestrian, facade design was of paramount importance in the owner's campaign to rent apartments. In 1909, a critic of apartment house design commented:

> The vanity in human nature is a primal factor to be reckoned with. Most every man desires that the house in which he lives should be indicative of his prosperity and importance. A little skimping in the servants' bedroom will be condoned if the exterior appearance is thereby enhanced. Consequently the facade, entrance and hallway should be as elegant as possible in proportion to the total cost of the building.[62]

In advertisements, builders often included a photograph of the facade rather than a floor plan and particularly referred to architectural style, although the terms used to describe many buildings had little to do with the actual facade designs. The Castle Court, a building with only the vaguest eighteenth-century detail, was referred to as "Colonial"; Reed House, a Beaux-Arts work heavily laden with decorative cartouches (there are 63 on the two street elevations!) was referred to as "French Renaissance," as was the Brookfield (figure 8.27), a building with Colonial and Beaux-Arts features; the Fiora-Ville and Porter Arms, also with Colonial and Beaux-Arts detail, were marketed as "Parisian."[63] The exceptionally ornate white terra-cotta facades of Gaetan Ajello's Eton Hall and Rugby Hall (figure 8.20) on Claremont Avenue were described as following "the early period of the Italian Renaissance," although Brunelleschi and Alberti would have had trouble recognizing, let alone making sense of the decorative detail.[64] Ajello's even more flamboyantly vulgar white terra-cotta Mira Mar (figure 8.12) at 452 Riverside Drive was classified as being "in the early period of the Italian Renaissance, about the beginning of the fifteenth century, when there was still some prevailing sentiment for the Gothic as seen in some of the old palaces of Florence and Venice"![65] Although this latter description might have had little to do with the reality of the design precedents, it provided the ostentatious building with a respectable pedigree.

A few speculative apartment buildings did rise above the general level of design, but these were, as Frohne noted, "so much in the nature of the special case . . . that their effect on the rule is almost negligible."[66] Some of these "special case" apartment houses, designed with traditional stylistic features, have well-massed, finely proportioned, or handsomely detailed facades. Examples include the Hendrick Hudson (figure 8.13) on Riverside Drive between Cathedral

Parkway and West 111th Street, where architect William Rouse, exploiting a dramatic elevated site, created a large apartment house that resembles an Italian villa, complete with Spanish-tiled towers and an open loggia (all sadly removed); Schwartz & Gross's Colosseum (figure 8.14) and Paterno (figure 8.20), both with stone bases, well-placed Renaissance-inspired ornament, finely detailed cornices, and curved facades, frame the West 116th Street approach to the Columbia University campus from Riverside Drive (their curved facades follow the undulating route of the old Bloomingdale Road); and Neville & Bagge's pic-

FIGURE 8.14
Colosseum (Schwartz & Gross, 1910), 435 Riverside Drive, c. 1911.

turesquely gabled Riverside Mansions (figure 8.15) on Riverside Drive and 113th Street, with its massive base punctuated by a recessed driveway.[67]

The most unusual of the traditional buildings on Morningside Heights is the Britannia (figure 8.16) at 527 Cathedral Parkway, designed in 1909 by Waid & Willauer.[68] The building, referred to as "A shining exception to the generality of apartment houses," resembles an English Elizabethan or Jacobean manor house expanded vertically from three stories to nine.[69] It is faced in rough tapestry brick "of beautiful gradations, and of golden brown color," with buff limestone on the lower stories and tan terra-cotta trim.[70] The facade is enlivened by a series of projecting bays (not unlike those at Hatfield, Blickling, Burghley, and other well-known late-sixteenth- and early-seventeenth-century English country houses), tall gables, whimsical grotesque figures (figure 8.1), and spectacular multipaned windows (including 24-over-24 double hung sash). Architect Arthur Willauer hoped that developers would "see the profitable advantage in erecting buildings [such as the Britannia] which are homelike and domestic in appearance."[71] By "homelike and domestic," Willauer was clearly referring to the Anglo-Saxon precedents that elite architects and critics nostalgically advocated as models for American domesticity during a period of increasing non-Anglo-Saxon immigration.[72]

FIGURE 8.15

Riverside Mansions
(Neville & Bagge, 1909),
410 Riverside Drive, 1946.

FIGURE 8.15
Riverside Mansions
(Neville & Bagge, 1909),
410 Riverside Drive, 1946.

The most innovative speculative apartment house facade on Morningside Heights is that of the 1909 Phaeton (figure 8.17) at 539 West 112th Street. This six-story building, with its facade of brick laid in a diaper pattern, glass mosaic trim highlights, fire escapes treated like balconies and ornamented with fleur-de-lis, and elegant rooftop loggias (destroyed), was influenced by the design of contemporary progressive French housing. Not surprisingly, its architects, George and Edward Blum, were far better trained than most of their colleagues, having studied at the Ecole des Beaux-Arts in Paris. The brothers were of Alsatian-Jewish ancestry and had spent much of their youth living both in New York and France. Thus, they had a greater familiarity with contemporary French apartment house design than any of their peers. At the

FIGURE 8.16
Britannia (Waid &
Willauer, 1908), 527 West
110th Street, 1909.

FIGURE 8.17
George & Edward Blum's
design for the Phaeton,
539 West 112th Street,
1909.

Phaeton, their first building, they created a strikingly original design. Even Frohne, who was critical of most speculative apartment buildings, noted that "The use of color in the brickwork and the treatment of the fire escapes are worthy of notice."[73] The *Real Estate Record* described the building as "more artistic than what is usually met with in apartment houses."[74] In their marketing campaign, the owners of the Phaeton particularly touted the singularity of the facade (not surprisingly, since the apartment layouts are quite commonplace), proclaiming that the Phaeton "is beyond doubt one of the prettiest apartment houses in the city. Its general style of architecture is unique and radically different from other apartments."[75] George & Edward Blum also designed other exceptional buildings in the city, including five additional buildings on Morningside Heights, notably the Oxford Hall and Cambridge Hall at 454 and 456 Riverside Drive, ornamented with their trademark intertwining organic detail.[76]

Planning the Apartment Building

The construction of an apartment building was an extremely complex enterprise, governed by historic, legal, economic, and social variables. As one architectural writer noted in 1910, "Apartment houses, perhaps, require greater diversity in planning than any other type of structure. Not only have the elements of cost and the character of the prospective tenantry to be considered, but the question of light and air and the shape and size of the plot are very important factors."[77] The most basic constraint placed on construction in most parts of Manhattan was the regularized grid of blocks established by the Commissioners Plan of 1811.[78] In this plan, each east-west block was to be about 800 feet long and 200 feet deep. Lots were generally 25 feet wide, but could easily be split or merged to create narrower or wider building plots. While it was easy to create wider buildings by combining lots along a street, it was far more difficult to increase a building's depth since almost every New York lot is about 100 feet deep (actually 100'11" on Morningside Heights), one half the depth of the block. This extremely limited depth was a crucial factor in determining the form of apartment houses.

Besides the constraints of size and dimension that the grid plan placed on all construction, specific legal requirements also had a major impact on apartment building design. The most significant legal requirements governing construction of all apartment buildings on Morningside Heights, with the exception of a few extremely early structures, were the rules promulgated in the New York State Legislature's Tenement House Act of 1901, generally referred to as the "new law."[79] This law not only regulated living conditions in tenements erected for the poor, but also governed the size and arrangement of apartment houses planned for more affluent households. A major goal of the Tenement House Act was to ensure adequate light and air in every room of every apartment. In

limited depth [handwritten marginal note]

order to accomplish this goal, light courts were required. Unlike the tiny air shafts required in multiple dwellings erected prior to 1901, the new law mandated larger light shafts or courts and open rear yards for new buildings. In addition, every room had to have a window and every window had to open onto the street, the rear yard, or a light court. Although builders and their architects could manipulate the shape of the building and the arrangement of the open space, the law further required that buildings cover no more than 70 percent of their lot area (75 percent for corner buildings).

These design requirements resulted in several popular "footprints" for middle- and upper-middle-class buildings on midblock sites (figure 8.18). Relatively small lots, including the 50-foot-wide plots created by combining two traditional 25-foot-wide lots, often contained inverted T-shaped buildings with very narrow light slots running along the edges of the lot at the rear two-thirds of a building.[80] This plan was used on Morningside Heights both in relatively modest buildings such as 508 and 509 West 112th Street and at grander and more prestigious buildings, including six 12-story buildings on Riverside Drive between 116th and 119th streets. Cheaper buildings using a T-shaped footprint often have bedrooms arranged along the slots, but in the apartments erected for the well-to-do, only subsidiary rooms, such as kitchens, baths, and servant's bedrooms generally looked onto the light slots. Although this plan was legal and quite popular with builders, it was not especially effective in providing light

FIGURE 8.18
Building footprints
on West 111th and West
112th streets between
Amsterdam Avenue
(right) and Broadway
(left).

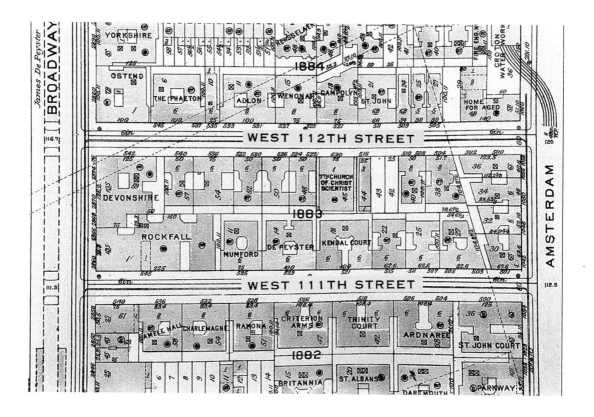

and air to rooms with windows on the narrow slots, and thus to a certain extent may have hindered rentals in a competitive market where other builders were offering apartments with better light.

More common than the T-plan for 50- to 75-foot-wide plots on Morningside Heights were buildings with an I-shaped footprint.[81] The light courts on either side of these buildings were shorter than the slits in the T-shaped structures, but they were wider, permitting more light and air to reach apartment windows. This plan also permitted unbroken front and rear facades. Side courts were especially effective for buildings with I-shaped footprints that were erected in groups, since the open spaces were combined and thus created even larger courts. This combination of light courts is evident, for example, in the 1905 construction of a pair of six-story buildings at 526 and 530 West 112th Street. A year later, three adjoining I-shaped apartment houses were erected, each drawing additional light and air from its neighbor's light courts. Paterno Brothers built a somewhat more impressive grouping using this form in 1908 at their Tennessee, Arizona, and San Maria apartments at 508, 514, and 520 West 114th Street.

The footprint of buildings on larger sites, generally 75 to 100 feet wide, often took the form of a modified O or a U. These buildings employ the light slots used on the T-shaped buildings, but also incorporate central courts to meet the requirements for light on a wider lot. The central courtyards of O-plan buildings are usually inaccessible to residents. Buildings with O-shaped footprints are scattered throughout Morningside Heights, ranging from early six-story structures, such as the De Peyster and Mumford of 1903 at 529 and 535 West 111th Street, to later structures, including the 1910 eight-story trio of the Ramona, Charlemagne, and Amele Hall at 528, 532, and 536 West 111th Street. The courts at U-shaped buildings generally open onto the street, with the building's entrance placed at the rear of the court. This plan was especially popular on midblocks, but such recessed courtyards had the potential disadvantage of becoming a "loafing place of tramps or other undesirables."[82] However, the front court could create a distinguishing entrance, as at the Kendal Court at 521 West 111th Street with its arched screen (figure 8.7). The largest buildings on Morningside Heights, located on lots with a width of 125 feet or more, often doubled the O or U plans incorporating two interior courts, as at the St. Valier at 90 Morningside Drive and the Paterno at 440 Riverside Drive, or adding a second open court to create an E-shaped plan as at the Iradell and the Laureate Hall, both on West 119th Street between Morningside Drive and Amsterdam Avenue. The footprints of corner buildings, with direct light guaranteed on two street elevations, vary depending upon the size of the lot and the number of apartments planned for each floor.

The predetermined depth of New York City lots and the various possible footprints for light courts required by law provided the base upon which builders and their architects chose the other elements of their speculative ven-

tures. The economics of construction and the expectations of the prospective
tenant class would then determine such features as the height of a building,
number of apartments, plan of each unit, size and number of rooms, design and
location of lobbies and vestibules, number and placement of elevators, facade
details, and interior amenities. Location within a neighborhood was also a key
factor in determining the quality of a building. Wealthy tenants, who could afford to pay substantial rents, demanded large apartments conveniently located
close to a subway station. Such tenants also preferred buildings on wide, light-
filled streets, especially those with scenic views. Land for such buildings was
more costly than property on less desirable plots, entailing a greater investment
on the part of the builder who would have to recoup these additional expenses
by charging higher rents from contented affluent tenants. In contrast, middle-
class households paid less rent for less spacious units with less light and fewer
amenities on narrower and less prestigious streets. While the individual apartment rents in such buildings were less than those in grander structures, the
costs of land and construction were also lower. The amalgam of lower rents
from a larger number of apartments would produce a sufficient profit if other
market conditions cooperated.

Given these competing factors, it is clear why there is a distinct hierarchy
among the residential streets of Morningside Heights.[83] At the top of the Morningside Heights hierarchy are Riverside Drive and Broadway. Land values were
extremely high on Riverside Drive, with its park frontage and panoramic views
of the Hudson River and New Jersey Palisades. This cost precluded modest development, fostering the construction of tall buildings with large apartments,
as is most evident on the long Riverside Drive frontage between 116th and 119th
streets with its impressive row of nine- to fourteen-story apartment buildings,
all erected in 1906–1911. The value of land on Broadway was even higher than
that on Riverside Drive. Although the noise and dirt from stores and from
streetcars and other traffic made this thoroughfare a somewhat less desirable
residential address than Riverside Drive, developers could expect even greater
profits by offering spacious apartments that commanded high rents in large
twelve-story corner buildings and also receiving a substantial additional income
from commercial tenants in ground-floor stores. Thus, the finest buildings
on Broadway—the Hendrick Hudson Annex, Rockfall, Devonshire, Allerton,
Forest Chambers (figure 8.19), Luxor, Regnor, and Rexor (figure 8.9)—offered
affluent families large, well-planned suites.[84] Although not so prestigious as
Riverside Drive and lacking the amenities of the finest Broadway buildings,
Cathedral Parkway between Amsterdam Avenue and Riverside Drive, West
116th Street between Broadway and Riverside Drive, and Claremont Avenue
from 116th Street to 119th Street (figure 8.20) also offered upper-middle-class
families large and well-designed apartments. The apartments lining the west
side of the long block of Claremont Avenue between 116th and 119th streets

are especially impressive, with their ornate facades, most clad in white brick with stone and terra-cotta trim.

For the less affluent middle-class renter seeking an apartment on Morningside Heights, Morningside Drive offered the best address. With its location along the edge of Morningside Park and its magnificent vistas to the east, it might have been expected that Morningside Drive would have offered the apartment-seeker a choice of tall apartment buildings of the highest class. Instead, most of the buildings facing Morningside Drive are only six-story structures (figure 8.21). Here, location was the determinant, for "the fact that it

is more remote from the subway has tended to lessen the land values."[85] The vast majority of middle-class buildings lined the narrower, less prestigious side streets. The mid-blocks with the highest land values were those between 111th and 116th streets west of Amsterdam Avenue because these sites were convenient to the subway. In contrast, land values in the northern part of the neighborhood above about 119th Street suffered because of their extreme distance from the subway stations located on Broadway at 110th, 116th, and 125th streets.[86]

Such depressed values were especially marked in the northeast corner of Morningside Heights along Morningside Drive and on adjacent

streets between 119th and 122nd streets. This problem was so serious that landowners in this area joined Teachers College, Union Theological Seminary, and Corpus Christi R.C. Church in lobbying for a subway station at or near 122nd Street. An initial effort to have a new subway station built was undertaken in about 1906, but the Rapid Transit Commission did not feel that there were enough residents in the area to warrant one. Within a few years both the resident population and number of commuting students had increased and "An Association for Obtaining a Subway Station at or Near 122nd Street and Broadway" was formed.[87] Realtor Albert E. Gibbs was confident that a new subway station "is an assured fact," but Union Theological Seminary's lawyer, Edmund Coffin, was "very much in doubt as to the success of such an application."[88] Coffin, as it turned out, was correct, for the Transit Commission made no effort to add an expensive new station that was only a few blocks from those already opened.

Development of an Apartment House Neighborhood

Early apartment house speculation followed the same pattern as speculative rowhouse development. Pioneering builders who invested in the construction of apartment buildings in an untested market, such as Morningside Heights, generally built on a modest scale, speculating that their capital and that of their

FIGURE 8.19
George & Edward Blum's design for the Forest Chambers, 601 West 113th Street, 1909.

FIGURE 8.20
Claremont Avenue north of West 116th Street, 1911; from left, Paterno (Schwartz & Gross, 1909), 440 Riverside Drive; Barnard Court (Schwartz & Gross, 1909), 15 Claremont Avenue; Sophomore (Schwartz & Gross, 1909), No. 21; Peter Minuit (Gaetan Ajello, 1909), No. 25; Eton Hall and Rugby Hall (Gaetan Ajello, 1910), Nos. 29 and 35; and Campus (Schwartz & Gross, 1910), No. 39.

FIGURE 8.21
Mont Cenis (Schwartz & Gross, 1905), 54 Morningside Drive, c. 1907; at right, La Valenciennes (Schwartz & Gross, 1905), 404 West 116th Street, and Sesrun Club (Neville & Bagge, 1906), 420 West 116th Street.

financial backers would yield profits. Few developers were willing to invest large sums constructing expensive apartment buildings before an area's residential character and attractiveness were confirmed. Only after more modest buildings proved to be marketable and profitable would grander buildings be erected. Development on Morningside Heights followed this typical pattern, even though overall development occurred over a period of only a few years.

In the late 1890s, a few five-story apartment houses without elevators were erected on Morningside Heights, but such buildings were not economically viable in an area with high land values. It was the six-story elevator building, first introduced in Morningside Heights in 1898, that became the most common apartment building type in the neighborhood, dominating construction during the first years of major development.[89] "The fact that builders have selected the 6-sty elevator house in preference to any other for present work," reported the *Real Estate Record* in 1906, "is clear proof that they pay better, and the inside fact is that they produce a very much larger net income than the non-elevator houses. . . . [T]hey rent for twice as much per room, but they do not cost twice as much per cubic foot."[90] These six-story buildings were relatively inexpensive to build since building laws permitted semi-fireproof construction in apartments up to this height as long as the structure had a street frontage of at least 40 feet.[91] Although concrete, brick, and terra cotta were the primary structural materials employed in the construction of these buildings, wood was used for studs and other interior features. The use of wood required fire escapes on the exterior elevations. On most apartment houses, the fire escapes were simply appended to the facades (figures 8.7 and 8.10), detracting from the visual appearance. On a few buildings, such as the Phaeton, the fire escapes are ornamented with decorative detail creating the illusion of elegant metal balconies (figure 8.17). A number of Morningside Heights buildings, notably a group designed by Schwartz & Gross for Paterno Brothers on or just off of Morningside Drive, are "not disfigured by projecting fire escapes," but instead have fire escapes that are recessed within the facade and detailed to resemble Parisian balconies (in fact an advertisement referred to the architecture as "Parisian"; figure 8.21).[92] After becoming the prevailing residential type for middle-class apartment buildings on Morningside Heights, the six-story, semi-fireproof elevator building also became the dominant form for middle-class apartment houses in other neighborhoods throughout New York City, with thousands erected in northern Manhattan, the Bronx, Brooklyn, and Queens.

Once Morningside Heights demonstrated that it was a viable market for the construction of respectable middle-class apartment buildings, builders began to invest in the construction of more expensive buildings on prime sites. By 1909, extensive construction was underway on impressive apartment houses on Riverside Drive, Broadway, Claremont Avenue, and Cathedral Parkway, leading the *Real Estate Record* to comment that Morningside Heights "has affirmed the doctrine that the best improvements come last."[93] The first of the grand apartment houses on Morningside Heights appeared in 1906. In that year, George F. Johnson and Aleck Kahn, developers who had already had great success with the construction of the luxurious Chatsworth Apartments on West 72nd Street and Riverside Drive, erected the eight-story Hendrick Hudson (figure 8.13) on the entire Riverside Drive frontage between 110th and 111th streets, only a short walk from the 110th Street subway station. This building is more notable for its impressive exterior design—a towered Tuscan palazzo (now sadly altered) of brick, limestone, and terra cotta set 105 feet above the Hudson, with a Mannerist entrance guarded by over-scaled figures—than for its awkward apartment layouts. Its success, however, provided the stimulus needed to attract other builders to line the neighborhood's best thoroughfares with impressive apartment houses of up to twelve stories. In August 1910, the *New York Times* proclaimed that "On Morningside Heights, surrounding the Columbia University buildings, some of the most imposing apartments in the city have recently been completed."[94] A month later, the *Times* indicated that the area had "some of the most palatial apartments on Manhattan," including "one of the finest rows of expensive structures in the City" on Claremont Avenue and "two of the stateliest apartment houses in the city," the Paterno (figure 8.20) and Colosseum (figure 8.14) on Riverside Drive and 116th Street.[95]

The Layout of Apartments

In addition to decisions regarding massing, scale, and exterior design, builders needed to pay particular attention to apartment layout, since room sizes and arrangements had to meet not only the requirements of the 1901 tenement law, but also the needs of discriminating renters of varying economic status and the desire of builders for maximum profits. Thus, the builders, working with their architects, manipulated the public spaces and apartment sizes and layouts to make the most effective use of a limited amount of rental space, while at the same time meeting the expectations of the particular class of tenants in a highly competitive market. Apartments planned for upper-middle-class households often contained spacious layouts and sizable rooms, while those designed for middle-class tenants contained fewer and smaller rooms, often awkwardly arranged.

To the prospective tenant, the ideal urban apartment would provide all of the amenities of a private home with the additional benefit of a well-integrated plan laid out on one floor (a simplex) or on two floors (a duplex). The well-integrated plan of this ideal apartment would contain three spatial divisions or zones, each clearly separated from the others—public rooms, private bedrooms, and service spaces.[96] The public rooms, such as the living room or parlor, dining room, and library, where the family gathered and where guests were received and entertained, were the largest. These spaces would be arranged conveniently near to the apartment's entrance and would flow into one another so that they could be combined for "gracious" entertaining. They would also be placed in the best location, with windows looking onto the street. At a discrete remove from these public rooms would be the family's private bedrooms (almost always referred to as "chambers" on floor plans) and bathrooms. The service spaces—kitchen, pantry, and servant's rooms—were separated from both the public and private spaces, although the kitchen had to be located adjacent to the dining room so that food could be efficiently served.

On Morningside Heights, this ideal division of spaces is realized in some of the more expensive buildings, such as the Paterno Brothers' Colosseum. This building was planned with only sixteen apartments, including twelve-room and eight-room simplex units and ten-room duplexes. Separate service and passenger elevators led to separate small public halls, from which employees and delivery personnel entered the service wing set in the rear of the building and tenants and their guests entered a foyer. In the largest apartments (figure 8.22), the foyer flowed directly into a sizable dining room, library, and parlor, which were laid out *en suite* overlooking Riverside Park and the Hudson River. A door from the foyer led into the service wing and another door led to a private hall along which were aligned five bedrooms (four of which had views toward the Hudson River), three baths, and a dressing room. Although slightly less ideal in arrangement, the smaller simplex units were arranged in a similar manner. In the duplexes, the zones were clearly differentiated by placing the bedrooms on a separate level from the public and service spaces. The Colosseum's duplex apartments are unusual on Morningside Heights where simplex units were far more prevalent. Architect Gaetan Ajello designed some of the best planned simplex apartments on Morningside Heights. For example, the four apartments on each floor of the Luxor (figure 8.23) at 600 West 115th Street, on the southwest corner of Broadway, may not be as expansive as those at the Colosseum, but they are well laid out, with clearly separated zones and well-lit and well-appointed rooms.

The ideal plan was rarely realized in New York apartment houses erected for the middle class since such an arrangement of rooms required more space than was generally provided in such buildings with their large numbers of rental units. While builders attempted to provide

FIGURE 8.22
Plan of the Colosseum
(Schwartz & Gross, 1910),
435 Riverside Drive.

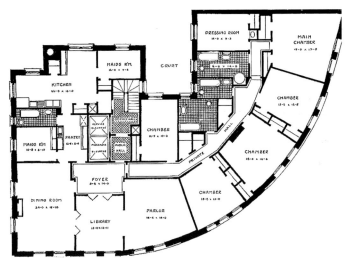

their prospective middle-class tenants with some of the attributes of the ideal plan, all requirements could not be accommodated. Middle-class apartment buildings are composed of smaller rooms, often awkwardly arranged, with public rooms frequently far apart and separated by bedrooms, kitchens awkwardly placed, and rooms generally arrayed along narrow dark halls. As the *Evening Post* noted, "in the cheaper houses the rooms are not so large as in the more expensive [apartment buildings], nor is as much care shown in separating the living and sleeping apartments."[97] This stark variance from the layout of the ideal apartment resulted from two factors—the location of the elevator and builders' attempts to place public rooms in the front of an apartment overlooking the street. The elevator was a crucial aspect of any middle-class apartment building since well-to-do people would not, in general, climb more than a few flights to reach an apartment. However, the builder needed to place this utilitarian ma-

FIGURE 8.23
Plan of the Luxor
(Gaetan Ajello, 1910),
600 West 115th Street.

West 115th Street

chine in a location where it would not take up valuable rental space. Since no builder wished to lose rentable space along the street front, the elevator was set toward the rear and was reached through a public vestibule and lobby. Usually only one elevator was provided, although in some buildings there are two, one for passengers and the other for service. On each apartment floor, a public hall or vestibule led to apartment doors. The resulting placement of the elevator and apartment entry doors toward the rear of a building caused a serious problem in apartment layout, since the public rooms were located in the front of the apartment, overlooking the street. As a result, as one critic bemoaned, entry into the apartment was through the "back door." [98] To provide a passage from this "back door" to the public rooms in front, architects employed an awkward narrow hall stretching from the entrance to the parlor. Such an arrangement is found in thousands of typical middle-class New York City apartments. While walking along this long hall, the tenants and guests were required to pass by bedrooms and service areas stretched laterally through the apartment. Thus, this arrangement significantly compromised the ideal of separating private from public spaces.

FIGURE 8.24
Plan of the Blennerhasset (George F. Pelham, 1903), 507 West 111th Street.

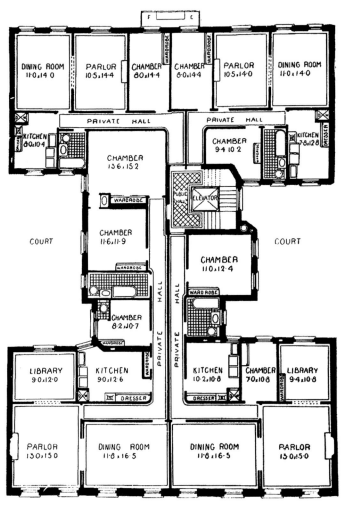

An examination of several Morningside Heights apartment plans demonstrates how this less than ideal type of room arrangement worked in typical New York City middle-class apartment buildings. I-shaped buildings almost always had four apartments per floor, as at the Blennerhasset (figure 8.24) on West 111th Street. There, the single elevator is placed about two-thirds of the way into the building. On each floor, the elevator opens onto a small public hall from which doors lead into the two front apartments and two smaller rear apartments. Since the building is 62.5 feet wide and about 85.5 feet deep, the four- to seven-room apartments are cramped, with rooms of only modest scale. In the front apartments, long narrow L-shaped halls pass chambers and a bathroom leading to the dining room and parlor overlooking the street. The rear apartments have shorter halls that also pass by bedrooms on their way to the public rooms.

Architect Neville & Bagge's Reed House (figure 8.25) at the corner of West 121st Street and Broadway has a plan that was called "typical" of this class of middle-class apartment house. "The arrangements of apartments in the Reed House meets the requirements of the most fastidious, in fact it would be difficult to improve on the layout of the rooms," boasted Albert E. Gibbs, Reed House's rental agent.[99] The plan of this building was typical of the O-shaped buildings on Morningside Heights, but it is far less ideal than Gibbs's self-interested puffery would suggest. The single elevator opens onto a long narrow public hall on each floor from which one has access to six apartments. The public rooms of the four front apartments overlook Broadway and are reached via exceptionally long narrow halls, some over 35 feet in length and others bending in an awkward L. These halls pass private bedrooms and, in the two largest apartments, the maid's room and kitchen as well. While the public rooms are well integrated, the spaces are small. Although the halls are shorter in the small rear apartments, their rooms are also smaller and a tiny chamber is tucked between the parlor and dining room.

Builders were certainly aware that these long narrow halls were not popular.

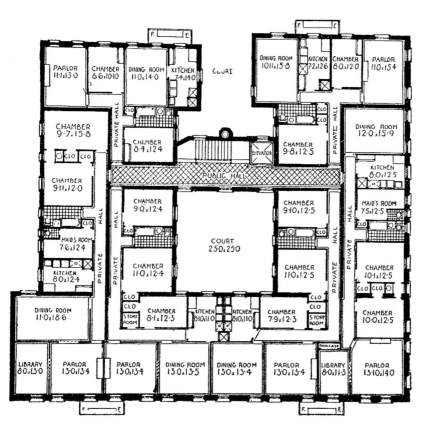

FIGURE 8.25

Plan of Reed House
(Neville & Bagge, 1905),
537 West 121st Street.

The Britannia's developers advertised that in their building "none of the apartments contains the long dark narrow hallway so objectionable to dwellers in apartments," while an advertisement for the Campolyn and Wenonah, a pair of well-planned I-shaped buildings on West 112th Street, boasted that the buildings were "unique, particularly in the elimination of the LONG HALLWAYS COMMON IN MANY HIGHER PRICED APARTMENT HOUSES [sic]."[100] Some builders and architects experimented with novel plans in order to separate functions and avoid the long dark hall. For example, B. Crystal & Son and their architect Gaetan Ajello attempted to create separate public and private zones in the two apartments on each floor of the U-shaped Mira Mar (figure 8.26) on Riverside Drive. The dining room, kitchen, and maid's room are placed in the rear of each unit, while the parlor and library are in the front, overlooking Riverside Park. A reception room oddly sited well within the apartment, adjacent to the parlor, and a long hall awkwardly connect the parlor and dining room. However, in this arrangement, the hallway does not pass by the four bedrooms, three of which are segregated in their own wing overlooking the court, with the fourth strangely set adjacent to the entrance foyer.[101]

FIGURE 8.26
Plan of the Mira Mar
(Gaetan Ajello, 1909),
452 Riverside Drive.

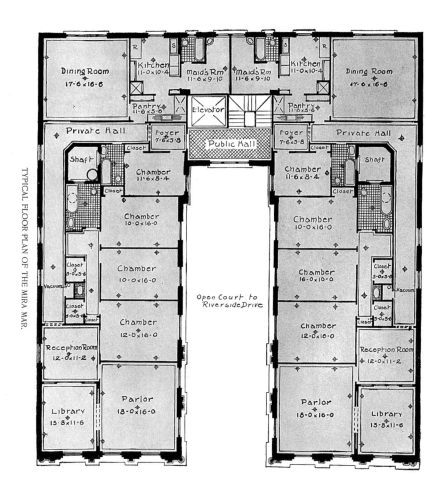

Apartment Amenities

Middle-class households also demanded technological and decorative amenities in their apartment buildings. Thus, builders were compelled to provided
those amenities to attract the economic and social class of tenant needed for the
financial success of each project. "The interior, the place where he [the tenant]
is going to live, and which his friends are going to criticise [sic] is vital. It was,
therefore, no surprise . . . to find that [in some buildings] the architects had
put more adornment inside than outside," noted one critic of a Morningside
Heights apartment building in 1909.[102] William L. Rouse, an architect who specialized in apartment house design, also noted that the cost of building an apartment house had increased by the early twentieth century because there was a
"higher standard of public requirements." The result of this "improvement in
the standard of public taste" was that "tenants and investors demand finer buildings than formerly . . . [resulting in the fact that] materials, workmanship and
equipment must be correspondingly
better."[103] Indeed, builders and their
rental agents gave prominence in
their advertisements, not only to the
design of the building's facade, but
also to its amenities, hoping to attract potential renters to visit the
building and lease an apartment.
Among these technological features
were electric lighting, steam heat,
modern kitchen appliances, nickel-
plated bathroom fixtures, garbage-
disposal and vacuum-cleaning systems, mail chutes, and local and long-
distance telephone service. Builders
also often advertised the presence
of service staff, such as switchboard
operators, superintendents, and uniformed doormen and elevator operators. The Tennessee and Arizona on
West 114th Street offered "trained
hall attendants, in neat fitting livery,
[who] are always at hand ready to
serve the tenant and answer to the
slightest beck and call."[104] The owner
of the Brookfield (figure 8.27) on
Riverside Drive, presuming the prejudices of potential upper-middle-

FIGURE 8.27

Lawlor & Haase's design
for the Brookfield, 450
Riverside Drive, 1908.

class tenants, went so far as to advertise "uniformed hall attendants (white boys) both day and night." [105]

Vestibule and lobby design were especially important since these spaces provided potential renters and residents' guests with their first impression of a building's quality and, by extension, that of its residents. William G. August, manager of the Strathmore on Riverside Drive and West 113th Street, described the importance of the lobby: "That part of the building which is most apt to create a favorable or unfavorable impression is obviously the entrance. While it is self-evident that all sections of the building should contribute toward the making of desirable impressions, yet the primary consideration must concern itself with the possible influence of that particular part of the building which first attracts attention, or the entire effect is lost." [106] Lobbies were decorated with floors of marble or, more commonly, with small round tiles, sometimes laid in complex patterns, walls of marble or plaster and marble, and ornate plaster ceilings. Much of the detail was inspired by fashionable Classical, Renaissance, or Gothic design. Lobby spaces were frequently furnished with chairs, tables, sofas, stained-glass windows and skylights, fireplaces, and rugs to create the aura of a fashionable private entry hall in this public space. For example, the vestibules and reception rooms of the Tennessee and Arizona on 114th Street were decorated with marble and tile and, noted an advertisement, "grouped artistically about the hall, furniture of special design, blending harmoniously in color with the hall itself, mak[ing] this a true poetical chamber of antique association." [107] Lobbies in some of the more expensive structures were quite expansive and magnificently appointed. Liveried attendants stood ready to assist residents in the lavish lobby of the Hendrick Hudson (figure 8.28) on Cathedral Parkway with its coffered ceiling, crystal chandelier, marble floor, area rug, table, benches, and potted plants; while at the Regnor (figure 8.29) on Broadway and 115th Street, marble floors were covered with Persian rugs, heavy portieres framed an archway, potted palms flanked elegant piers, and "antique" chairs, tables, and lamps created a "homelike" appearance.

In addition to the decorative and service amenities provided in public areas, builders also offered amenities in the individual apartments, including wood paneling, parquet floors, wooden shelves in dining rooms, fireplaces, and wall safes (figure 8.30). At the Mira Mar on Riverside Drive, standard features included "[Cuban] mahogany and quartered oak [trim], oak parquet floors, white porcelain pedestal bath fixtures, . . . a special grade of hardware, steam heat, electric lights, dumb-waiters, marble, tile, and mosaic, and a vacuum cleaning system"; while the Brookfield advertised separate passenger and service elevators, porcelain lined refrigerators, medicine cabinets, hardwood floors, tiled bathrooms with ceramic floors, linen closets, gas and electric light, steam heat, open fireplaces, basement storage rooms, and local and long distance telephone service. [108] The marketers of the Paterno, also on Riverside Drive, perhaps somewhat hyperbolically boasted that it was "designed to appeal

FIGURE 8.28
Lobby of the Hendrick
Hudson (Rouse & Sloan,
1906), 611 West 110th
Street, c. 1908.

FIGURE 8.29
Lobby of the Regnor
(Gaetan Ajello, 1911), 601
West 115th Street, 1912.

FIGURE 8.30
Dining room in an
apartment at the
Hendrick Hudson,
c. 1908.

to those who desire to enjoy the convenience of an apartment without giving up the spaciousness and privacy of a separate home" and that it left "nothing to be desired." In fact its "spacious drive" did lead into an exceptionally handsome lobby with uniformed attendants and its residents were provided with a barber shop, ladies' hairdresser, tailor shop, and "three noiseless elevators."[109] Of course, such luxurious features were not provided in every building. As would be expected, buildings with higher rents tended to have finer and more costly decoration and more amenities than those planned for less affluent tenants. However, even the more modest amenities provided in middle-class buildings were important factors in their success in the extremely competitive rental market.

Technological improvements and decorative amenities were not the only means used by owners to promote their buildings. The naming of apartment houses was exploited by builders to establish a unique and attractive identity for each building. Some names conjured up images of European elegance or grandeur (Devonshire, Clarendon, Yorkshire, St. Valier, La Touraine, Mont Ceris, and Fiora-Ville), others referred to the elevation and location of Morningside Heights (Cliff Haven, Monte Vista, Aqua Vista, and Broadview), or to its educational and charitable institutions (Sophomore, Campus, Barnard Court, University Court, Laureate Hall, Cathedral Court, and St. John Court), but most names were simply chosen as a means of lending a separate identity and, in many cases, a special cachet, to a building that was competing for tenants against many neighboring apartment houses. Names were frequently employed in the initial advertising, but, unless carved into the street elevation, their use generally faded after the initial rental campaign ended. Names already noted above—Mira Mar, Phaeton, Brookfield, Reed Court, Regnor, Iradell, etc.—are rarely if ever used today, but these and almost every other apartment building erected on Morningside Heights before World War I originally had a name (see appendix).

While the naming of an apartment building was usually a simple matter, builders could become embroiled in controversy if the wrong name was chosen. In 1910 construction began on 509 West 121st Street (figure 8.31) immediately across the street from Teachers College, one of several early works by Emery Roth that demonstrate his interest in the progressive architecture of the Vienna Secession. The building was planned with 108 small apartments

FIGURE 8.31
Emery Roth's design for the Bancroft (originally the Sethlow), 509 West 121st Street, 1910.

for "the professors and wealthier students" of the nearby universities.[110] The building was to be named the "Sethlow." Upon its completion, the building was advertised as the "Sethlow Kitchenette Apartments" and as the "Sethlow Bachelor Apartments."[111] However, Columbia's former president Seth Low was not consulted about having a speculative apartment house named after himself, only finding out about this dubious honor when he saw an advertisement in a newspaper. The *New York Times* reported that "Seth Low doesn't mind lending his name to cities, colleges, and charities when they think it may help them along, but when it comes to apartment houses—especially apartment houses which look right over Mr. Low's beloved Columbia University campus and which shock the finer sense of the young ladies who are studying art in Teachers College by alleged architectural incongruities—ex-Mayor Low firmly draws the line."[112] Low instructed his lawyers to seek an injunction to keep the owner from using his name. Not wishing to become involved in protracted litigation, the owners changed the name to the Bancroft.[113]

By 1912, most lots on Morningside Heights had been developed and the residential character of the neighborhood well established. Few poor or working-class people inhabited the area's apartments. Instead, the students at Columbia, Barnard, Teachers College, and other Morningside Heights institutions mingled with middle- and upper middle-class people, most native born.[114] The only poor people likely to be encountered on a walk through the neighborhood were the servants employed by the more affluent households. The economic and ethnic makeup of households living in two of Morningside Heights' apartment buildings in the early twentieth century demonstrate the character of local residents. The Blennerhasset on 111th Street was designed in 1903 with twenty-five modestly-scaled middle-class apartments. The enumerator for the 1905 New York State census recorded fifteen households in residence, totaling forty-four people. Only two households were headed by immigrants (from Germany and Austria). Occupations listed for employed male heads of household were glove importer, school supplies salesman, clerk, lawyer, physician, clothing manufacturer, cloak manufacturer, and photographer. Two households were headed by women, but none of the women who lived in the building worked outside of the home. In five apartments, young women in their twenties worked as live-in servants—two were American born, one Irish, one Finnish, and one Bohemian.[115]

At the far grander Colosseum on Riverside Drive and 116th Street, designed in 1910 with sixteen apartments, twelve households responded to the queries of the 1915 New York State census enumerator. Fifty people lived in the building, including several large families. There was only one woman listed as head of household. The men were employed in higher paying jobs than those at the Blennerhasset, but at both buildings people in business and the professions predominated. Residents at the Colosseum included a man in the Victrola business, a liquor merchant, a picture manufacturer, two Columbia professors, a mining engineer, president of a lithographic business, a railroad vice president, a coffee merchant, and real estate developer Joseph Paterno. Only Paterno and a German professor were of foreign birth. Eight servants lived in apartments, including two male butlers (one from Japan), and women servants from England, Switzerland, Finland, and Germany.[116]

Later Residential Development

After World War I, most of the few remaining vacant lots were sold and developed. Between 1921 and 1931, eleven additional apartment buildings were erected, mostly on vacant property, but in a few cases, they replaced earlier structures. Most of these new buildings were large apartment houses on prominent streets. The building at 535 Cathedral Parkway is typical (figure 8.32). Although the building is fifteen stories, it is no taller than its earlier twelve-story neighbors because apartments in buildings erected during the 1920s tended to have lower ceilings, thus permitting more floors in a building that still came within the height limitations of the building code. The apartments were also considerably smaller than in earlier buildings. There are ten units on each floor, most with smaller rooms and fewer amenities than in the grandest pre-World War I buildings. There are no maid's rooms in the individual apartments, reflecting a rapid decline in the number of live-in servants in middle- and upper-middle-class households after the war. A small number of servant's rooms were provided on the roof level, but not enough for all tenants. In most apartments there are no separate dining rooms and a few apartments have only kitchenettes. Of course, some amenities aimed at attracting tenants were still provided. Residents of the Cathedral Parkway Apartments entered through a sizable lobby with a coffered ceiling and stylish furnishings, two passenger and two service elevators were provided, and apartment details included paneled walls, parquet floors, electric plugs with twin outlets, built-in showers and tubs, steel medicine cabinets, mail chutes, and modern laundry facilities.[117]

The most unusual residential buildings of this period are Butler Hall on Morningside Drive and West 119th Street, and the former Explorers Club at 544 Cathedral Parkway. Butler Hall contained 316 one-, two-, and three-room suites on fifteen floors and was erected to meet what was seen as an "an urgent demand for modern housekeeping

FIGURE 8.32
Cathedral Parkway Apartments (Robert T. Lyons, 1922), 535 West 110th Street, 1953.

suites in small units near the university."[118] It was built of red brick in a style that harmonizes with Columbia's classroom structures. This design choice was especially appropriate for a structure named for Columbia's president (unlike Low, Butler did not threaten to sue to have the name changed). The Explorers Club on Cathedral Parkway looks like a typical apartment building, but it was erected in 1928–29 as the club's headquarters with meeting rooms, library, museum, and lecture hall, as well as floors of apartment suites that could be rented by members when they were not off on expeditions.[119]

Related Development on Morningside Heights

As Morningside Heights was being transformed into a neighborhood of apartment houses, few other types of buildings were erected on its residential streets. Only a small number of commercial buildings appeared since the apartment buildings along Broadway all incorporated street-level shops. The only exceptions are several "taxpayers" on Broadway, one- or two-story buildings erected to generate enough income to permit the owner to pay taxes and other expenses while awaiting a more favorable climate for full-scale development. The only architecturally notable extant commercial structure on Morningside Heights is 2832 Broadway on the northeast corner of Cathedral Parkway, an exceptionally handsome example of a taxpayer, designed by Townsend, Steinle & Haskell in 1911. The Renaissance-inspired design includes an ornate entrance leading to the second-story office space, fine polychromatic terra-cotta detail, and metal brackets supporting a Spanish-tiled roof. Two commercial garages were built in 1909–10, indicating that a considerable number of original Morningside Heights residents already owned their own automobiles.[120]

Since Morningside Heights' residential fabric developed so rapidly, there was too little time for public agencies or established religious and social organizations to anticipate the changing character of the area and to purchase land before land prices became prohibitively high or other interests had acquired the best sites. Thus, Morningside Heights has no public schools or other civic structures (with the exception of an early firehouse; see chapter 1), no social clubs, and very few churches. Only the Roman Catholics and Presbyterians erected church buildings during the period of major neighborhood development before World War I. The first of two Catholic churches was Corpus Christi on West 121st Street, which erected the chapel in 1906, replaced by the present Colonial Revival church and school building designed by Wilfred Edwards Anthony in 1935.[121] More prominently located is the Eglise de Notre Dame on Morningside Drive and West 114th Street. This church is an austere French Neo-Classical structure modeled by Cross & Cross after the Invalides in Paris. The interior of this grotto church has domes, vaults, and other features constructed of exposed Guastavino tiles.[122] On the exterior, the church was to be crowned by a tall dome and was to have a sculpted pediment, but these were never completed.[123] The only Protestant church erected on Morningside Heights before World War I was Broadway Presbyterian (figure 8.33), located on a prominent corner site purchased in 1910 on Broadway and West 114th Street. In 1911, Louis Jallade designed an unexceptional English Gothic structure faced with local Manhattan schist for this congregation, which moved to Morningside Heights from Park Avenue South and East 22nd Street. The design is closely modeled on the Brown Memorial Tower of Union Theological Seminary where Jallade was associate architect.[124] Episcopalians did not build any parish churches since they were well served on Morningside Heights by their cathedral, the chapel in St. Luke's Hospital, and St. Paul's Chapel at Columbia. However, members of other religious denominations were forced to travel outside of the area to attend services.[125]

In 1913, the *Evening Post* summed up the extraordinary development that had taken place on Morningside Heights in only a few years:

FIGURE 8.33
Broadway Presbyterian
Church (Louis E. Jallade,
1911), northwest corner
Broadway and West 114th
Street, 1913.

Less than twenty years ago Columbia University bought its first land on . . . Morningside Heights . . . and subsequently increased its possession, until to-day it controls a valuable tract of land made so because of the handsome educational buildings the College erected, but more so, because of the city of elegant apartment houses that honeycomb the whole of this

area, from the bluff [on Morningside Drive] over to the Hudson River, not occupied by the College.[126]

The commercial and social success of Morningside Heights as an early apartment-house neighborhood was replicated by similar development and redevelopment in other sections of Manhattan as the apartment house became the building type that defines New York City's twentieth-century residential neighborhoods.

Inside the illustration:

SHREVE LAMB & HARMON ASSOCIATES
ARCHITECTS
NEW YORK, N. Y.

A

COLUMBIA ··· FERRIS BOOTH HALL & 114ᵀᴴ STREET DORMITORY ··· NEW YORK

FIGURE AFTERWORD.1
Shreve, Lamb &
Harmon's design for
Ferris Booth Hall and
Carman Hall, c. 1957.

Morningside Heights in the Second Half of the Twentieth Century

BY THE 1930S, WHEN THE GREAT DEPRESSION VIRTUALLY HALTED building in New York City, the Morningside Plateau had been almost fully developed and the area had taken on the character that sets it apart from other areas of New York City — prestigious urban institutional complexes of great architectural distinction located within a neighborhood of middle-class apartment buildings. Virtually every lot in the neighborhood had been built upon or was part of an institutional campus where land was being held for future expansion. Except for a small number of apartment buildings that had been purchased by Columbia University and by Teachers College beginning in 1919 to house their students, faculty, and staff, and a number of rowhouses that had been purchased by Columbia or had been leased to or purchased by fraternities, the institutions and the residential community still operated in relatively separate spheres.[1] While some of the apartment-house residents were affiliated with the institutions, most apartments were still inhabited by middle-class households with no institutional affiliation.

This dual character of Morningside Heights began to change during the Depression and World War II, setting the stage for the conflicts that would divide the neighborhood during the following decades. The story of Morningside Heights in the second half of the twentieth century could easily take an entire separate study and will not be discussed in great detail here, but it is important to note briefly several trends that relate to issues of architectural and neighborhood development. Events on Morningside Heights in the decades after World War II reflected many of the major social and architectural forces and trends that shaped urban communities and urban institutions throughout America during that period. Morningside Heights was profoundly affected by the changing nature of higher education that resulted in efforts by Columbia and the other academic institutions to expand and modernize their facilities in order to meet the demands for specialized research and rapidly growing graduate and professional programs. Similarly, St. Luke's Hospital struggled to modernize its antiquated buildings and expand its facilities as the requirements of hospital care and new medical and technological advances demanded new facilities. As a result of these pressures, not only were new buildings erected on vacant land within the institutional complexes, but also a few older buildings within the complexes were demolished and replaced by new structures (notably at St. Luke's Hospital, where two of Ernest Flagg's original hospital pavilions were replaced with particularly banal buildings). In addition, a number of institutions expanded into the surrounding residential community, leading to conflicts with that community.

Tensions between the expanding institutions and their surrounding communities had also occurred elsewhere—for example in neighborhoods adjoining urban institutions in Chicago, Philadelphia, New Haven, and Boston. However, on Morningside Heights the problems were exacerbated not only by the institutions' aggressiveness, but also by the mediocrity of the new institutional buildings both on campus and off-campus. At a time when Harvard was commissioning major buildings from international leaders in Modern design, such as Le Corbusier, Alvar Aalto, and Jose Luis Sert, and Yale was working with such notable American architects as Eero Saarinen, Philip Johnson, Gordon Bunshaft, and Paul Rudolph, Columbia, Barnard, St. Luke's, and neighboring institutions were generally commissioning buildings from mediocre architectural firms and were building some of the most pedestrian institutional structures of the period (figure afterward.1), a development that is discussed in detail by Robert A.M. Stern and his coauthors in *New York 1960: Architecture and Urbanism Between the Second World War and Bicentennial.*[2]

In addition to the expansion of facilities by established Morningside Heights institutions in the post-World War II period, three new institutions also arrived in the neighborhood. In 1954, John D. Rockefeller, Jr., began planning for the construction of the Interchurch Center on the undeveloped block immediately south of Riverside Church. This building was to be a center for ecumenical Christianity, housing the offices of a variety of Christian denominations and organizations. Rockefeller purchased the property from Barnard College and commissioned a design from Voorhees, Walker, Smith & Smith and Collens, Willis & Beckonert (figure afterward.2). The result is an undistinguished, bulky limestone building (colloquially referred to in the neighborhood as the "God Box"), which opened in 1958.[3] Both of the other new institutions were private schools that erected large new buildings on Morningside Heights with the support of Columbia. The Bank Street College of Education, founded in 1916, and its progressive Laboratory School moved from Bank Street in Greenwich Village into a hulking building on West 112th Street between Broadway and Riverside Drive designed by Harry Weese & Associates of Chicago. The school, which replaced two apartment houses, was persuaded to relocate onto Morningside Heights by Columbia, which gave Bank Street substantial financial assistance.

The planned move was announced in 1963, but it was not until 1971 that the 112th Street building was completed.[4]

St. Hilda's and St. Hugh's, a coeducational Episcopal-affiliated ecumenical school founded in 1950, occupied four buildings in the Morningside Heights area, three rowhouses at 619–623 West 113th Street and the Schinasi Mansion on the northeast corner of Riverside Drive and 107th Street. Columbia sold the school two adjoining apartment houses on 114th and 115th streets between Broadway and Riverside Drive for the token sum of $1.00 and then Columbia and Remedco, a real estate investment company owned by nine of the institutions on Morningside Heights, lent money for the construction of a fortress-like new school building designed by Moore & Hutchins.[5] In contrast to the progressive Bank Street School, St. Hilda's and St. Hugh's, which moved into its new home in 1967, favored a more traditional educational philosophy, evidenced by Headmistress Rev. Mother Ruth's comment to a *New York Times* reporter "that no long-haired boys were welcome there."[6]

Columbia assisted both the progressive Bank Street College and the traditional St. Hilda's and St. Hugh's because it was anxious to improve primary education on Morningside Heights as part of its effort to make Morningside Heights a more attractive neighborhood for its faculty. Columbia hoped that the presence of these schools, with their modern facilities and contrasting educational philosophies, would induce both liberal and conservative faculty members to live on Morningside Heights rather than move to the suburbs. To community residents who opposed Columbia's actions in the neighborhood, the construction of these private schools was merely a means by which the Columbia community could abandon the neighborhood's integrated public schools.[7]

Even more significant for the changing character of Morningside Heights than the quality (or lack of quality) of most new institutional construction were the changes that occurred in the residential community and the response of the institutions to actual and perceived deterioration in the surrounding area. As we have seen, the residential fabric of Morningside Heights was almost entirely middle- and upper-middle-

FIGURE AFTERWORD.2
Voorhees, Walker, Smith & Smith and Collins, Willis & Beckonert's design for the Interchurch Center, 1955.

class apartment buildings (see chapter 8). During the Depression, the character of many of these buildings had begun to change as financial problems hit both owners and tenants. Tenants, for example, began taking in boarders as a means of helping to pay their monthly rent. Some buildings, especially those with large apartments, also began to experience financial problems as it became increasingly difficult to find tenants who could pay the rent that was necessary for profitability and upkeep. In order to maintain fully occupied buildings and maximize income, some owners subdivided the apartments. For example, at the Dartmouth at 509 Cathedral Parkway, built in 1908 with four apartments of from seven to nine rooms on each floor, the suites were reconfigured in 1934 into three- and four-room apartments and the rent roll rose from $33,000 to $70,000 per year.[8]

Other owners converted their buildings into single room occupancy hotels (SROs) by subdividing apartments into small, single-room units with shared bathrooms and kitchens. This type of transformation became popular during World War II, when thousands of single men and women moved to New York City for war-related jobs, while wartime federal rent regulations, which prevented owners from substantially raising rents in apartment buildings, spurred conversions to more profitable commercial hotels, which were not covered under these regulations. Conversions were often done in the cheapest way possible and many landlords were unconcerned about who moved into their buildings so long as rents were paid. The increase in what many referred to as "undesirable" residents became such a problem on Morningside Heights that the *New York Times* noted that the blocks between West 110th and 113th streets from Amsterdam Avenue to Broadway were placed off limits to Navy midshipmen training at Columbia because of the large numbers of prostitutes allegedly housed in SROs on those blocks.[9]

After World War II, many middle-class whites abandoned Morningside Heights for rapidly growing suburban communities. In many cases they were replaced by the poor black and Puerto Rican families who where moving to New York City in increasing numbers. This racial and ethnic shift is evident in population statistics for that period. In 1930 there had been approximately 70,000 people on Morningside Heights, almost all of whom were white. By 1950, the total population had remained the same, but there were now 6,671 African-Americans and 6,552 residents from Puerto Rico.[10] Many of these new residents could afford accommodations only in the deteriorating SROs, which also housed prostitutes, drug addicts, and other criminals. In the 1950s additional apartment buildings were converted into hotels as a way of avoiding the city's postwar rent-control regulations, which, like the wartime regulations they replaced, did not apply to leases in commercial hotels. Having been converted into hotels, grand apartment buildings, such as the Hendrick Hudson, Hendrick Hudson Annex, and Devonshire, rapidly deteriorated. In fact, in 1960 the *New York Times* referred to the once-elegant Hendrick Hudson, with its

1,500 tenants and hundreds of building, health, and sanitary code violations, as "one of the city's worst slum buildings."[11] As crime increased on Morningside Heights, tensions among the various communities and between the poor residents and the institutions intensified.

The changing character of the Morningside Heights neighborhood was of great concern to the area's institutions, which had enormous investments in property and infrastructure, and legitimately feared that they would have difficulty attracting students, faculty, and staff if the surrounding neighborhood were perceived as dangerous and deteriorating. The issues that faced Columbia and the other institutions on Morningside Heights as the urban population changed were not unique; New York University, the University of Chicago, the University of Pennsylvania, and other urban universities confronted similar problems. Whereas New York University entirely abandoned its Bronx campus designed by Stanford White, other institutions, such as Columbia, chose to remain in their historic locations, investing in what they believed was the stabilization and renewal of their immediate neighborhoods.

All of the institutions on Morningside Heights were concerned about conditions in the surrounding residential community, but those at the northern end of the neighborhood were especially uneasy, since their buildings abutted the poor residential community of Manhattanville north of 122nd Street and east of Broadway, where the plateau begins its steep descent at the historic northern boundary of Morningside Heights. This area, bordering on Harlem, was home to the area's largest concentration of African-American residents. As early as 1946, International House, the northernmost institution on the Morningside Plateau, commissioned a survey that suggested that the Morningside Heights institutions band together and undertake a long-range redevelopment project that would entail the demolition of much of the Morningside Heights residential community.[12] The Morningside Heights institutions had never before joined together on a major joint venture, but through the initiative of David Rockefeller (John D. Rockefeller, Jr.'s son), fourteen of the institutions organized Morningside Heights, Inc. in 1947.[13] The institutions hoped that by working together they could construct new housing, improve educational and recreational opportunities for neighborhood residents, increase public safety, and, most importantly, by improving housing conditions throughout the area, safeguard their interests.

The greatest fear of the institutions was what was euphemistically referred to as the "encroachment of Harlem," which symbolized to them the spread of slum conditions from the blighted blocks of Harlem and Manhattanville.[14] The term also unquestionably had a racial overtone since, by the 1950s, Harlem was almost entirely an African-American neighborhood. The institutions on Morningside Heights were afraid that their neighborhood might become entirely inhabited by black and Puerto Rican households and that this development might scare away their generally white and middle-class constituency. These were, however, also generally progressive institutions that supported civil rights and integration, at least on a limited scale. Thus, they hoped to stabilize Morningside Heights and stop middle-class white flight, while at the same time welcoming a small number of blacks and Puerto Ricans, generally to the fringes of the area.

The first major project undertaken by Morningside Heights, Inc., was the replacement of the apartment houses and tenements north of 122nd Street, largely populated by black households. Although contemporary reports referred to the area as a "slum" with "overcrowded and deteriorating tenements," there was actually a wide mix of residential buildings in the proposed renewal area.[15] There were many deteriorated and overcrowded late-nineteenth-century walkup tenements with cramped and poorly ventilated apartments, but the area also contained a significant number of six-story elevator buildings from the early twentieth century that were not unlike the middle-class apartment houses that line the streets between Amsterdam Avenue and Broadway from 111th to 114th streets. The area north of 122nd Street had not traditionally been considered a part of the Morningside Heights neighborhood (see Introduction), but as the area deteriorated and its population changed from largely Irish to heavily African-American, the neighborhood's northern boundary was now deemed by the institutions to extend to West 125th Street. This expansion permitted the institutions to claim a neighborhood interest in these blocks and lobby for their demolition and replacement with new housing projects (the neighborhood's southern boundary was also extended, often as far as 106th Street).

On October 1, 1951, the nine northernmost institutions on Morningside Heights (Barnard College, Columbia University, Corpus Christi R.C. Church, International House, Jewish Theological Seminary, The Juilliard School of Music, Riverside Church, Teachers College, and Union Theological Seminary) announced their sponsorship of Morningside Gardens, a slum clearance project that would replace the buildings on the two blocks north of 123rd Street between Amsterdam Avenue and Broadway with 984 middle-income cooperative apartments in six twenty-story buildings designed by the Rockefellers' favorite architectural firm, Harrison & Abramovitz (figure afterward.3).[16] At the public hearing before the New York City Planning Commission held late in 1952, Harry Emerson Fosdick, retired minister of Riverside Church, testified in favor of the project. He summed up the view of the institutions' leaders when he exclaimed "that what you are considering today is not just the fate of one housing project, but the possible future of one of the city's most important neighborhoods. It is a pioneer neighborhood where the American city confronts some of its most characteristic problems and where, if we solve them at all well, the whole world will know it."[17] In conjunction with the government-funded but privately sponsored Morningside Gardens cooperative project, the New York City Housing Authority planned General Grant Houses, a low-income housing project located to the north and east of Morningside Gardens, with 1,950 apartments in ten high-rise slabs designed by Eggers & Higgins (figure afterword.3).[18]

Demolition for the two housing projects entailed the relocation of 1,626 families. The Morningside Heights Housing Corporation, the official sponsor of Morningside Gardens, diligently assisted residents with their relocation, offering to locate reasonably priced apartments and pay moving costs. Not surprisingly, however, there was opposition from some of the residents who were to be displaced. They formed an organization called "Save Our Homes," which demonstrated at City Hall and charged that the renewal project was planned as a way to remove black and Puerto Rican households from the neighborhood.[19] The residents' group was unable to stop the projects and by 1957 both complexes were ready for occupancy. The institutions that sponsored Morningside Gardens hoped that both this middle-income cooperative and the low-income Grant Houses would be integrated. Original stockholders of Morningside Gardens were approximately 75 percent white, 20 percent black, 4 percent Asian, and 1 percent Puerto Rican, with nearly one-third of the residents drawn from the staffs of the sponsoring organizations. This racial and ethnic mix was con-

sidered a good balance at the time, since, as the *New York Times* noted, "Housing and integration experts believe that the chances of successful integration are best when Negroes and Puerto Ricans together make up no more than 25 percent of the tenants."[20] Grant Houses was less successful to these advocates of limited integration, since its population was 51 percent black, 38 percent Puerto Rican, and only 11 percent non-Puerto Rican white.

Morningside Gardens and Grant Houses thus created the northern barrier separating Morningside Heights from Harlem sought by the institutions. In fact, the alignment of the giant slabs of Grant Houses creates a virtual wall along the northern and northeastern corners of the neighborhood. This did not, however, solve the problem of deteriorating housing and white flight within the older residential community of Morningside Heights. This problem was of particular concern to the academic institutions, which were seeing many of their own faculty members leaving Morningside Heights for homes in the suburbs, thus undermining the sense of university life that had been a major concern since Columbia and the other academic institutions had first arrived on Morningside Heights. In order to control more directly conditions on the streets around their campuses, the institutions began buying property.[21]

Columbia had long been interested in buying land surrounding the original campus. As we have seen, South Field was acquired by Columbia in 1903, and in 1910–14 President Butler arranged for the university to purchase the block between West 116th and 117th streets to the east of the main campus (see chapter 5). Butler was interested in acquiring other property as well, suggesting to the trustees in 1925 "the need of taking early steps to protect the University site and to make possible its future development and expansion as conditions might from time to time make desirable or necessary."[22] In fact, when John D. Rockefeller, Jr., purchased the Morningside Drive blockfront between 117th and 118th streets several months earlier as a possible site for his ecumenical church, Butler criticized this purchase on the grounds that this was property that Columbia hoped to acquire (see chapter 2).[23] In January 1946, only a few months after his retirement as president of Columbia, Butler wrote a "confidential memorandum" to the trustees detailing his ideas for the future course of the university. One of his key points was "The great importance of the completion of the purchase of Morningside. . . . This would mean the purchase of all property lying between Amsterdam Avenue and Morningside Drive, from 114th Street to 122nd Street." This purchase would not only permit the eventual expansion of the university, but would also protect the neighborhood from what the bigoted Butler described as the "greatly feared invasion from Harlem which has been threatened more than once."[24]

Columbia had purchased its first apartment houses in 1919 (see chapter 5), but did not begin buying large numbers of residential buildings until the late 1950s. However, it was in the 1960s that the university acquired most of its holdings, purchasing more than one hundred buildings in that decade and transforming the character of real estate ownership in the community. In fact, Columbia became one of the largest landlords in New York City. Although Columbia purchased the largest number of buildings over the widest geographic area (from Cathedral Parkway between Amsterdam Avenue and Broadway to Claremont Avenue and Tiemann Place), it was not the only institution to buy apartment buildings in the post war years. Barnard College, Union Theological Seminary, Jewish Theological Seminary, and St. Luke's Hospital made similar, if less extensive, purchases.

The acquisition of apartment buildings by the institutions created tensions with the residential community, especially in buildings where the institutions attempted to gain possession of as many of the apartments as possible. Since SRO tenants were generally not covered by rent regulations, it was easy for the institutions to clear these buildings and either demolish them, restore them to apartment use, or convert them for other institutional needs.[25] At least nine SROs were torn down in the 1960s and, of the thirty-three SROs in existence in 1961, only two were still in use in 1997.[26] The institutions viewed the SROs as a blight, filled with alcoholics, drug addicts, and prostitutes, and felt that by demolishing or rehabilitating these buildings they were removing slum conditions from Morningside Heights.[27] Undoubtedly undesirable tenants were a segment of the SRO population, but the hotels also housed many law-abiding poor people who were often victimized by these other tenants and by owners who failed to adequately maintain these properties or screen prospective tenants.

Most of the residents of the SROs were poor blacks and Puerto Ricans, and their eviction heightened racial tensions in the area. In 1961, charges that Columbia was attempting "to drive Negroes and Puerto Ricans from the Morningside Heights area" were filed with the New York State Commission Against Discrimination.[28] This complaint grew out of attempts to remove tenants from the Devonshire at 542 West 112th Street on the southeast corner of Broadway, a once-elegant apartment house that had been converted into a hotel in 1952. Columbia, in coordination with several other Morningside Heights institutions, had agreed to invest $1.5 million to assist the owner of the Devonshire in upgrading the facilties so that units could be rented to institutional affiliates.[29] Columbia strongly protested the accusation of discrimination, stating that the university was interested in assisting the landlord in the creation of decent housing and also noting that none of the educational institutions on Morningside Heights discriminated in the acceptance of students. The State Commission reported early in 1962 that, while the institutional affiliates entitled to preferences in renting apartments in the Devonshire were "predominantly white," non-white students, teachers, and staff members were equally entitled to housing, thus, the commissioners found, there was no discrimination on the part of the university.[30] However, the Congress of Racial Equality (CORE) condemned Columbia and vowed to protest what it saw as Columbia's segregated housing policies; in 1964, the city's Commission on Human Rights announced an inquiry into a complaint "that the university was singling out Negroes and Puerto Ricans for eviction." [31]

In contrast to the SROs, the apartment houses fell under New York City's strict rent regulations, which did not permit the institutions to evict those with legitimate leases. However, as apartments were vacated, they could be rented to institutional affiliates. Beginning in 1962, all new tenants were required to sign an affiliation clause that permitted the university to terminate their tenancy when they left Columbia. Although Columbia saw this affiliation agreement as a way of assuring the availability of much-needed apartments for its faculty, students, and staff, some neighborhood residents and some of those forced to leave apartments when their Columbia affiliation ended disagreed. Tenant and community groups fought this rule, taking Columbia to court, but the state courts ruled in the university's favor and the affiliation clause has remained a controversial aspect of Columbia's tenancy policy. Other institutions on Morningside Heights were involved in similar disputes with tenant and neighborhood groups as they too increased the size of their real estate portfolios. Ownership of residential properties by Columbia and the other institutions became so widespread that some residents complained that they were living in a "company town." [32]

Besides using buildings to house their affiliates, some of the apartment buildings purchased by Columbia were converted for nonresidential academic uses. For example, the Ostend Apartments on the northeast corner of Broadway and West 112th Street, which had become the Oxford Residence Hotel before its acquisition by Columbia in 1965, was converted into the Goddard Institute of Space Studies and renamed Armstrong Hall, while Victor Hall (later known as the Princeton) at 622 West 113th Street, purchased by Columbia in 1965, was renamed McVickar Hall and converted into classrooms first for the School of International Affairs and then for the School of Social Work. [33]

While some residential buildings were converted to nonresidential use, others were demolished for institutional expansion. Columbia tore down sixteen rowhouses and five apartment buildings for the construction of East Campus, including the law school, School of International Affairs, a residence hall, and a raised platform and bridge over Amsterdam Avenue; Barnard demolished the six-story Bryn Mawr, an apartment building on the corner of Amsterdam Avenue and West 121st Street, which had become a hotel "notorious as a center of narcotics addiction, prostitution and other crime," and replaced it with Plimpton Hall, a sixteen-story dormitory; St. Luke's Hospital removed eight buildings on Amsterdam Avenue for its expansion; Union Theological Seminary demolished two apartment buildings on Riverside Drive, north of 122nd Street, for Van Dusen Hall (now International House North); and Jewish Theological Seminary demolished two apartment buildings for its library addition. [34]

Several plans for the improvement of the neighborhood would have entailed wholesale demolition of entire residential blocks. For example, in 1966 Columbia announced a proposal that included not only demolition of the East Campus block between 117th and 118th streets, but also the entire block of 115th and 116th streets between Morningside Drive and Amsterdam Avenue, except for the Morningside Drive frontage which the university did not own, and its replacement with an arts center. The plan also envisioned a gymnasium in Morningside Park and a proposal that architecture critic Ada Louise Huxtable believed was "even more explosive," the creation of a "south campus" by demolishing all of the midblock buildings between 111th and 114th streets and replacing them with a library extension and new dormitories and apartment houses.[35] A year later, Morningside Heights, Inc., the organization established by the neighborhood's institutions in 1947, promulgated the astounding suggestion that Columbia's south campus proposal be expanded to include the replacement of all of the residential buildings on the midblocks between 111th and 116th streets from Broadway to Riverside Drive with institutional buildings and new housing, that substantial new construction also be undertaken in the northern part of the neighborhood, and that most of the east-west streets through the neighborhood be closed to traffic.[36]

Since Columbia University ultimately did not pursue the "south campus" plan, it would be the university's efforts to build a gymnasium in Morningside Park that sparked the community explosion Huxtable predicted. Indeed, the gymnasium controversy was the most inflammatory event in the postwar history of Morningside Heights. Columbia proposed to build yet another mediocre building for an off-campus site in the middle of a public park, with only limited access for the residents of Morningside Heights and Harlem who shared its use. New York City's Board of Estimate reluctantly voted for Columbia's proposal, but increasing tensions on campus between students and the administration, exacerbated by this issue, led to demonstrations that closed down the university in the spring of 1968, forcing Columbia to abandon the gymnasium proposal.[37]

This was not, however, the only battle being fought against new development in the neighborhood. "While the battle of Morningside Heights has been raging on the Columbia University campus," wrote a *New York Times* reporter in May 1968, "two quieter fights are being waged against other institutions in the area."[38] One of these was a Rockefeller-funded proposal for the extension of the Interchurch Center, which would have entailed closing 119th Street between Claremont Avenue and Riverside Drive and demolishing two apartment buildings on Claremont Avenue and one on Riverside Drive. Opposition from tenants in the Concord Hall on the corner of Riverside Drive and 119th Street, aided by the Claremont-Riverside Residents' Association, forced the Rockefellers (who were averse to the type of bad publicity this proposal generated) to abandon the project.[39] The other project defeated by community opposition was a plan to replace eight buildings on Amsterdam Avenue between 111th and 112th streets with Morningside House, a nursing home designed by Phillip

Johnson.[40] In addition, community residents and students continued to condemn Columbia's policies toward tenants in institutionally-owned residential buildings, even briefly occupying 618 West 114th Street in May 1968, which Columbia planned to demolish for the expansion of the School of Social Work.[41]

The tensions between the institutions and the surrounding community that had peaked with the gymnasium crisis led Columbia to look inward for new development sites. Late in 1968, following the gymnasium defeat and criticism of the East Campus expansion, Columbia commissioned a new master plan from architect I.M. Pei, who, in 1970, recommended two enormous towers on South Field at approximately the location of McKim, Mead & White's proposed inner rank of dormitories. These buildings would house classrooms and faculty offices. In addition, a new science building was to be erected on the Green, behind Uris Hall. The most innovative aspect of Pei's proposal was the idea of building underground. A huge new gymnasium and student center would be built beneath South Field, and, in the only part of the Pei plan ever realized, an extension was to be erected for the architecture school beneath the courtyard shared by Avery, Fayerweather, Schermerhorn, and St. Paul's Chapel.[42]

The growth in institutional ownership of Morningside Heights residential properties in the late 1950s and 1960s continued into the final decades of the twentieth century, so that by the last years of the century, the institutions owned all but about fifty of the apartment buildings between 110th and 122nd streets.[43] In the southern portion of the neighborhood, on 110th and 111th streets between Amsterdam Avenue and Riverside Drive and on 112th Street between Broadway and Riverside Drive, the majority of the buildings remained in private hands, but almost all of the buildings farther north were owned by Columbia or one of the other local institutions. Even north of 122nd Street, on Claremont Avenue and Riverside Drive, a significant number of apartment buildings were held by Columbia. The institutions purchased buildings where, in many cases, maintenance had been neglected for many years. In general, however, the new institutional owners undertook few major restoration projects.

In 1979, a piece of masonry fell from the Regnor at 601 West 115th Street at the northwest corner of Broadway, a building Columbia had purchased in 1967, killing a Barnard student.[44] This tragedy prompted New York City to pass Local Law 10, which mandated an inspection every four years of the facade of every residential building over six stories. Unfortunately, this law did not result in the restoration of apartment facades on Morningside Heights. Rather, the financially strapped institutions often simply opted for the less expensive alternatives of removing cornices and, in the case of the Regnor, George & Edward Blum's Forest Chambers (figure 8.19) at 601 West 113th Street, and a few other Columbia-owned buildings, stripping virtually every bit of ornamental detail from the facades and crudely patching the street elevations, creating some of the worst eyesores in the community.[45]

In the final years of the twentieth century, relations between the residential community and the institutions, particularly Columbia, remained tense, as new construction projects were once again planned for residential blocks within the neighborhood. In 1986–87, Columbia erected a seventeen-story dormitory, Morris Schapiro Hall (Gruzen Sampton Steinglass, architect), on West 115th Street between Broadway and Riverside Drive that, in spite of efforts on the part of the architect to design a building compatible with neighboring apartment houses, was criticized for its height, partial setback from the street wall, and institutional use.

In the mid-1990s, Columbia began work on several projects that were also poorly received by the local community and by preservation groups around New York City. Renovations were undertaken on several of the historic McKim, Mead & White buildings, including a major redesign of the attic level of Journalism Hall by Pasanella + Klein Stolzman + Berg that included the addition of over-scaled dormers and a tall elevator bulkhead. Even more controversial was Bernard Tschumi's Alfred Lerner Hall (designed in association with Gruzen Sampton Associated Architects; figure afterword.4), a student center replacing the banal Ferris Booth Hall at the southwest corner of the campus (figure afterword.1), which had been completed in 1959. Lerner Hall, focusing on an expansive glass wall and ramp system facing north toward the main campus, has been judged by some as a dynamic modern counterpoint to McKim, Mead & White's buildings and by others as a desecration of the historic campus.[46] The Journalism and Lerner projects in turn generated a movement to have the en-

FIGURE AFTERWORD.4 Bernard Tschumi's design for Alfred Lerner Hall, 1996.

tire historic Columbia campus designated as a landmark by the New York City Landmarks Preservation Commission.[47]

Columbia also undertook widely criticized projects off campus during the 1990s. William C. Warren Hall, a sliver tower designed by Polshek and Partners for the *Columbia Law Review* and the law school's clinical programs, on the south side of 116th Street just west of Morningside Drive, has been criticized for its height, design, and materials. A business school and law school building designed by the Hillier Group for a site on Amsterdam Avenue and 115th Street has created controversy since it fails to include stores on what has traditionally been a commercial strip.[48] Although a number of the institutional building projects both on and off campus were criticized, others have been lauded, notably Barnard College's Iphigene Ochs Sulzberger Hall designed by James Stewart Polshek and Partners and the award-winning restoration of the exterior and auditorium of Casa Italiana and the creation of dynamic modern classroom and office interiors by Buttrick, White & Burtis in association with Italian architect Italo Rota.[49]

Columbia was not the only institution embroiled in battles with neighborhood residents in the last years of the century. In 1996 the Morningside Heights Residents Association lost a protracted legal battle to stop the Amsterdam House nursing home from constructing a major addition to its facility on Amsterdam Avenue and West 113th Street. The building, designed by the Geddis Partnership of Stamford, Connecticut, incorporates the Croton Aqueduct Gatehouse at 114th Street into the complex. It is an overscaled Postmodern work that reads almost as a parody of the neighborhood's historic buildings.[50] As this book was going to press, Jewish Theological Seminary was involved in an all-too-familiar battle with residents of two apartment houses on West 122nd Street, where residents want to save their homes and the seminary wishes to evict those residents who moved in after July 1, 1978, and are thus not protected by noneviction laws, in order to create much-needed student housing.[51] Frustrated with institutional management of the neighborhood's residential buildings and fearing that the area's institutions would continue to demolish residential buildings for new institutional construction, widespread community support developed in 1997 for the efforts of a local community group, the Morningside Heights Historic District Committee, to have the New York City Landmarks Preservation Commission designate a Morningside Heights Historic District that, the group hopes, will eventually include the entire neighborhood.

At the century's end, however, there were also some positive signs that even with their legitimate, but differing interests and needs, the institutions and the residential community can work together. When Teachers College began removing the unusual original copper cornice from Seth Low Hall (106 Morningside Drive) in the spring of 1996, an outcry from the community, from citywide preservation groups, and, refreshingly, from Columbia University's administration, led the college to halt this destructive act. After hiring the architectural firm of Beyer Blinder Belle to study the issue, the college agreed to restore the remaining portion of the cornice and reconstruct the section that had been removed. Even more promising was the planning study undertaken by Columbia University in 1996 at the behest of executive vice president Emily Lloyd. This study examined the original campus plan, individual campus buildings, university-owned buildings in the residential portion of Morningside Heights, and potential sites for new buildings, as part of an effort to treat the university's and community's physical fabric with greater sensitivity. The university hired an architect, landscape architect, garden designer, preservationists, and historian to study and analyze the campus and the neighborhood and make recommendations for the future.[52] The most promising part of this project was the formation of a working group, consisting of community activists, Columbia faculty, and representatives of preservation organizations, to participate in the project and critique its work. This working group, the university hopes, will be a model for future dialogue, so that even when the institutional and residential communities disagree, at least all opinions will be aired.

The results of this dialogue were evident in 1997 when architect Robert A.M. Stern presented preliminary designs for a proposed new dormitory on the northeast corner of Broadway and West 113th Street (incorporating the facade of the Colonial Revival style residence at 565 West 113th Street) to the community so that the final proposal could be developed in response to community concerns. In addition, Columbia has committed itself to improved stewardship of its residential buildings, promising, when possible, to restore rather than remove historic features and to undertake new work in a manner more sensitive to the historic character of the architecture.

In spite of their sometimes conflicting interests, by the late 1990s, the efforts of neighborhood residents and the area's institutions, had turned Morningside Heights into one of the New York City's more desirable neighborhoods. Columbia and the other institutions in the area had succeeded in creating a safe community where people want to live, although the manner in which this was accomplished was often controversial. The relatively safe streets, the urban environment, and the presence of prestigious institutions are attracting record numbers of applicants to Columbia and other institutions. Many faculty members are now anxious to live in the neighborhood and apartments in the private cooperative buildings are selling for record prices.[53] Despite the changes that occurred on Morningside Heights in the last half of the twentieth century, including the demolition of a small, but significant number of residential buildings, the construction of undistinguished new buildings, and inappropriate alterations to a few of the older buildings, the neighborhood retains most of its historic fabric.

The institutions that are the defining element of Morningside Heights have grown over the past one hundred years from modest organizations into universities, colleges, seminaries, hospitals, and churches of world renown. Many of the buildings erected by these institutions in order to establish their presence in the city are among the most beautiful and most significant institutional structures in America. In addition, the residential community of Morningside Heights, developed in a distinctive and rapid manner in response to the opening of the subway in 1904, remains one of the city's most notable apartment house districts. Morningside Heights developed in a manner that sets it apart from other New York neighborhoods and it remains a unique institutional and residential enclave in the great metropolis of New York.

Building List

This building list includes all extant buildings located between the south side of West 110th Street (Cathedral Parkway) and the north side of West 122nd Street; between Broadway and Riverside Drive, the list extends north as far as Tiemann Place. Important demolished buildings (excluding rural buildings erected in the 18th and early 19th centuries) are also listed. The neighborhoods institutional complexes are listed separately.

Buildings are arranged by street, odd number addresses followed by even number addresses. All buildings are apartment houses unless noted otherwise. Listings include address, original name (where applicable), name of original owner/builder, architect, and date building permit was issued.

Key

c:	commercial building
f:	fraternity house
i:	institutional building
p:	public building
s:	single-family house
d:	demolished building
des:	designed
cons:	constructed

Addr./Name		Original Owner/Builder	Architect	Date
AMSTERDAM AVENUE				
1101ᵈ	Parthenon	Polstein Realty & Construction Co.	George F. Pelham	1906
1105ᵈ	—	Polstein Realty & Construction Co.	George F. Pelham	1906
1109ᵈ	Mathilda	Polstein Realty & Construction Co.	George F. Pelham	1906
1113ᵈ	—	Polstein Realty & Construction Co.	George F. Pelham	1906
1117ᵈ	Pantheon	Polstein Realty & Construction Co.	George F. Pelham	1906
1121ᶜ,ᵈ	—	John Johnson	John Johnson	1909
1121ⁱ	—	Columbia University	Hillier Group	1997
1175ᵖ	Croton Aqueduct Gatehouse	New York City	unknown	c. 1880s

Addr./Name	Original Owner/Builder	Architect	Date
1241 —	C.M. Silverman & Son	Neville & Bagge	1905
1245 —	C.M. Silverman & Son	Neville & Bagge	1905
1249 —	C.M. Silverman & Son	Neville & Bagge	1905
1253 —	C.M. Silverman & Son	Neville & Bagge	1905
1255 —	C.M. Silverman & Son	Neville & Bagge	1905
1040[d] Fantana	Jaffer & Wittner	Moore & Landsiedel	1906
1046 Huldana	Jaffer & Wittner	Moore & Landsiedel	1906
1052[d] Helena	Jaffer & Wittner	Moore & Landsiedel	1906
1058[d] Sigfried	Jaffer & Wittner	Moore & Landsiedel	1906
1058 Echo Apartments	Ecumenical Community Housing Corp.	Harry Simmons	1990
1060[i,d] Home for Old Men & Aged Couples	Home for Old Men & Aged Couples	Cady, Berg & See	1897
1060[i] Amsterdam House	Amsterdam Nursing Home Corp.	Kennerly, Slomanson & Smith	1973
1064[i] Amsterdam House	Amsterdam Nursing Home Corp.	Geddes Partnership	1996
1068[p] Croton Aqueduct Gatehouse	New York City	unknown	1870
1086[d] Cathedral View	Jacob Weinstein	Stern & Morris	1906
1090[d] —	Jacob Weinstein	Stern & Morris	1906
1094[d] —	Jacob Weinstein	Stern & Morris	1906
1086[i] Medical Arts Pavilion	St. Luke's Hospital	Harry Prince	1968
1260 —	Lefkowitz & Horwitz	George F. Pelham	1905
1264 —	Lefkowitz & Horwitz	George F. Pelham	1905
1268 —	Louis & John Brandt	John Brandt	1898
1270 —	Louis & John Brandt	John Brandt	1898
1272 —	Louis & John Brandt	John Brandt	1898
1274 —	Louis & John Brandt	John Brandt	1898

BROADWAY

Addr./Name	Original Owner/Builder	Architect	Date
2851[c,d] —	Moses Sahlein	Arnold W. Brunner	1907
2861[c] —	Larimer Cushman	Frank Rooke	1908
2867[c] —	Thomas Graham	William C. Lester	1908
2869[c] —	unknown		
2875[c,l] —	Slawson & Hobbs	Lafayette A. Goldstone	1904
2915 —	William Drought	Neville & Bagge	1897
2925[i] Broadway Presbyterian Church	Fourth Avenue Presbyterian Church	Louis E. Jallade	1911
2929[c] —	Fourth Avenue Presbyterian Church	Louis E. Jallade	1911
3089[d] Buckingham	Times Realty Co.	Neville & Bagge	1907
3099[d] Hazelton Court	A.C.& A.M. Hall Realty Co.	Neville & Bagge	1907
3111 —	3111 Broadway Realty Co.	H.I. Feldman	1941
3115 —	Friedman Construction Co.	Harold L. Young	1911
3117 Fairview Court	Surety Construction Co.	George F. Pelham	1909
3133 —	George G. Jackson	Neville & Bagge	1898

Addr./Name	Original Owner/Builder	Architect	Date
3135 —	George G. Jackson	Neville & Bagge	1898
3137 —	George G. Jackson	Neville & Bagge	1898
3139 —	Emanuel Doctor	John Hauser	1906
3143 —	Emanuel Doctor	John Hauser	1906
3147 —	Emanuel Doctor	John Hauser	1905
3149 —	Emanuel Doctor	John Hauser	1905
3151 —	Emanuel Doctor	John Hauser	1905
3153 —	Emanuel Doctor	John Hauser	1905
3155 —	Emanuel Doctor	John Hauser	1905
3157 —	Emanuel Doctor	John Hauser	1905
3161 —	Arthur Silverman	George F. Pelham	1905
3163 —	Arthur Silverman	George F. Pelham	1905
3165 —	Arthur Silverman	George F. Pelham	1905
2828[c] —	Peter C. Eckhardt	James E. Cole	1898
2832[c] —	Robert E. Westcott Estate	Townsend, Steinle & Haskell	1911
2848 —	Ruth Stevenson	Cleverdon & Putzel	1886
2850 —	Ruth Stevenson	Cleverdon & Putzel	1886
2856[c,2] —	Joseph Kennelly	J. Harry O'Brien	1910
2900[d] —	Gunn & Grant	Henry Andersen	1899
2900[c] Chemical Corn Exchange Bank	Chemical Corn Exchange Bank	Alfred Easton Poor	1958
2906[c] —	Carvel & Murray	Thomas W. Lamb	1909
2910[i] St. Luke's Home for Indigent Christian Females	St. Luke's Home	Trowbridge & Livingston	1898

CLAREMONT AVENUE

15 Barnard Court	M.E. Paterno Realty Co.	Schwartz & Gross	1909
21 Sophomore	Paterno Bros. Inc.	Schwartz & Gross	1909
25 Peter Minuit	B. Crystal & Son	Gaetan Ajello	1909
29 Eton Hall	B. Crystal & Son	Gaetan Ajello	1910
35 Rugby Hall	B. Crystal & Son	Gaetan Ajello	1910
39 Campus	V. Cerabone Construction Co.	Schwartz & Gross	1910
47 Malvern	Robert Ferguson	George F. Pelham	1906
49 Barieford	Robert Ferguson	George F. Pelham	1906
89[i] Union Theological Seminary Gym	W.W. Carman	Louis E. Jallade	1912
99[d] Alderson	Clinton W. Kinsella	Neville & Bagge	1909
111[d] Dacona Hall	Dacorn Realty Co.	Moore & Landsiedel	1908
175 Fairview Court	Charles Hensle	Glasser & Ebert	1906
181 —	Charles Hensle	Glasser & Ebert	1905
183 —	River Clare Realty Co.	H.I. Feldman	1940
189 —	James O'Brien	Denby & Nute	1905
191 —	James O'Brien	Denby & Nute	1905

Addr./Name		Original Owner/Builder	Architect	Date
195	Crescent Court	Charles Hensle	Neville & Bagge	1905
122[d]	Hudson Grant View	Joel Marks	John C. Watson	1908
130[d]	Lincoln	William Walker	John Hauser	1908
140	Claremont Club Hotel	Tuscan Construction Co.	Neville & Bagge	1910
150	Brighton Court	Occidental Holding Corp.	Samuel Katz & Louis Allen Abramson	1921
160	—	Clementine Realty Co.	Maximillian Zipkes	1911
170	—	Occidental Holding Corp.	Samuel Katz & Louis Allen Abramson	1921
180	Springfield	John V. Signell Co.	Neville & Bagge	1905
182	Roselle	Jumel Realty Co.	Neville & Bagge	1905
184	—	Jumel Realty Co.	Neville & Bagge	1905
186	—	Jumel Realty Co.	Neville & Bagge	1905
188	—	Jumel Realty Co.	Neville & Bagge	1905
190	—	Jumel Realty Co.	Neville & Bagge	1905
192	—	Jumel Realty Co.	Neville & Bagge	1905
200	—	John V. Signell Co.	Neville & Bagge	1905

LASALLE PLACE

| 124 | — | George Jackson | Neville & Bagge | 1898 |
| 126 | — | Kantor & Sussman | Lorenz Weiher | 1906 |

MORNINGSIDE DRIVE

40[i]	Eglise de Notre Dame	Novitiate of the Fathers of Mercy	Daus & Otto	1909
40[i]	Eglise de Notre Dame[3]	Novitiate of the Fathers of Mercy	Cross & Cross	1914
40[i]	Eglise de Notre Dame[4]	Novitiate of the Fathers of Mercy	Cross & Cross	1913
44	Cathedral Court	Paterno Bros. Inc.	Schwartz & Gross	1904
53	La Touraine	Paterno Bros. Inc.	Schwartz & Gross	1905
54	Mont Cenis	Paterno Bros. Inc.	Schwartz & Gross	1905
70[d]	University Court	R.M. Silverman Realty & Construction Co.	George F. Pelham	1905
74[d]	Hague Court	West Side Construction Co.	George F. Pelham	1907
90	St. Valier	West Side Construction Co.	George F. Pelham	1911
100	Palmetto	Joseph H. Davis Building Co.	George F. Pelham	1909
106	Janus Court	Stevenson Construction Co.	John M. Baker	1910
110	Shelburne Hall	West Side Construction Co.	George F. Pelham	1909
114	Circle	W. Axelrod Realty Co.	George F. Pelham	1908
130	Rebelle Court	Krulewitch Realty Co.	Neville & Bagge	1908

RIVERSIDE DRIVE

| 375 | — | 375 Riverside Drive Corp. (Michael Paterno) | Gaetan Ajello | 1921 |
| 390 | — | Alart Building Corp. | Gaetan Ajello | 1924 |

Addr./Name		Original Owner/Builder	Architect	Date
395	—	Alart Building Corp.	Gaetan Ajello	1924
400	Fowler Court	Cummings Construction Co.	George F. Pelham	1908
404	Strathmore	Akron Building Co.	Schwartz & Gross	1908
410	Riverside Mansions	Emsworth Construction Co.	Neville & Bagge	1909
411 [s,d]	George Noakes House	George Noakes	Arthur Bates Jennings	1884
414 [s]	—	Alexander Walker	George F. Pelham	1897
415 [s]	—	Alexander Walker	George F. Pelham	1897
417	Cliff Haven	John J. Hearn Construction Co.	Denby & Nute	1909
420	Hamilton	Riverside Drive Realty Co.	Gaetan Ajello	1911
425	—	Joseph Paterno	Rosario Candela	1924
431	Columbia Court	William Rankin & Edgar Pruden	George Keister	1900
434 [f]	Alpha Club	Alpha Club	Wood, Palmer & Hornbostel	1898
435	Colosseum	Paterno Bros. Inc.	Schwartz & Gross	1910
440	Paterno	Paterno Bros. Inc.	Schwartz & Gross	1909
445	Stadium View	Paterno Bros. Inc.	Schwartz & Gross	1909
448	Shore View	Paterno Bros. Inc.	Schwartz & Gross	1909
450	Brookfield	Porterfield Construction Co.	Lawlor & Haase	1908
452	Miramar	B. Crystal & Son	Gaetan Ajello	1909
454	Oxford Hall	B. Crystal & Son	George & Edward Blum	1911
456	Cambridge Hall	B. Crystal & Son	George & Edward Blum	1911
460	Aqua Vista	M. E. Paterno Realty Co.	Schwartz & Gross	1909
464	Monte Vista	M. E. Paterno Realty Co.	Schwartz & Gross	1909
468	Concord Hall	Nathan Loewy Realty & Construction Co.	George F. Pelham	1906
470 [i]	Interchurch Center	Seatlantic Fund	Voorhees, Walker, Smith & Smith and Collens, Willis & Beckonert	1956
490 [d]	—	Clinton W. Kinsella	Neville & Bagge	1909
494 [s,d]	John J. Gibbons House	John J. Gibbons	Arthur Bates Jennings	1887
494 [d]	John J. Gibbons Stable [5]	John J. Gibbons	Charles S. Mott	1889
495 [s,d]	Joseph J. Kittel House	Joseph J. Kittel	Arthur Bates Jennings	1885
498 [d]	—	Clinton W. Kinsella	Neville & Bagge	1909
520 [i]	International House	Intercollegiate Cosmopolitan Club	Jallade, Lindsay & Warren	1922
524 [d]	Ardelle	Ardelle Realty Co.	Radcliffe & Kelley	1908
524 [i]	Van Dusen Hall	Union Theological Seminary	Rogers & Butler	1958
527 [d]	Veronique	Rutland Realty Co.	Lafayette A. Goldstone	1906
528	Ulysses	St. Paul Construction Co.	Lafayette A. Goldstone	1908
530	Claremont Court	Bergen Realty Co.	George Keister	1907
547	Hague Dwelling	Bergen Realty Co.	George Keister	1906
548	Montebello	Lispenard Realty Co.	George Keister	1906
549	Bordeaux	Calvert Construction Co.	Lafayette A. Goldstone	1905
550	Alabama	Riverside Viaduct Realty Co.	George F. Pelham	1908
552	Madrid	Silverson & London Construction Co.	George F. Pelham	1908
564	—	London Construction Co.	Gronenberg & Leuchtag	1911

Addr./Name		Original Owner/Builder	Architect	Date
TIEMANN PLACE				
31	Edgewood	Charter Construction Co.	Schwartz & Gross	1907
45	Whitestone	Charter Construction Co.	Emery Roth	1909
55	Claremont View	Israel Lippmann	Charles B. Meyers	1909
69	Tiemann Hall	Faultless Construction Co.	Charles B. Meyers	1911
WEST 110TH STREET (CATHEDRAL PARKWAY)				
501	Morris Hall[6]	Yorktown Realty Co.	Neville & Bagge	1908
509	Dartmouth	Carlyle Realty Co.	Schwartz & Gross	1908
515	St. Albans	Carlyle Realty Co.	Schwartz & Gross	1908
527	Britannia	Gracehull Realty Co.	Waid & Willauer	1909
535	Cathedral Parkway	Samuel Roseff	Robert T. Lyons	1922
543[c]	—	George Ehret	S. Edson Gage	1921
601	Hendrick Hudson Annex	Broadway & Cathedral Parkway Co.	Rouse & Sloan	1907
611	Hendrick Hudson	Hendrick Hudson Co.	Rouse & Sloan	1906
410	Cathedral Court	Cathedral Realty Co.	Sommerfield & Steckler	1909
412	—	Old Lyceum Building Co.	Walter Haefeli	1911
446	Cathedral Parkway Houses	Morningside Renewal Council and Harlem Urban Development Corporartion	Davis Brody & Associates and Roger Glasgow	1973
500	Irving Court	Irving Judis Building & Construction Co.	Bernstein & Bernstein	1908
504	Amherst	Carlyle Realty Co.	Schwartz & Gross	1909
510	Cortlandt	Carlyle Realty Co.	Schwartz & Gross	1909
514	Mark Anthony	Paterno Construction Co.	Schwartz & Gross	1911
520	Prince Humbert	Paterno Construction Co.	Schwartz & Gross	1911
542[s]	—	Smith & Thompson	Smith & Thompson	1985[7]
544[i]	Explorers Club	Explorers Holding Corp.	Charles E. Birge	1928
550[i]	Unity Congregational Church	Unity Congregational Society of New York	Hoppin & Koen	1921
610	—	610 West 110th Street Corp.	Schwartz & Gross	1921
WEST 111TH STREET				
503	Clara Court	Emanuel Doctor	John Hauser	1904
507	Blennerhasset	Max Liebeskind	George F. Pelham	1903
515	Bertha	Emanuel Doctor	John Hauser	1903
521	Kendal Court	Gunn & Grant	Schwartz & Gross	1903
529	DePeyster	Lorenz Weiher	Moore & Landsiedel	1903
535	Mumford	Lorenz Weiher	Moore & Landsiedel	1903
545	Rockfall	Rockfall Realty Co.	George & Edward Blum	1909
603	Antlers	Harvard Realty Construction Co.	William L. Rouse	1908

Addr./Name		Original Owner/Builder	Architect	Date
605	Markenfield	Markenfield Construction Co.	Lawlor & Haase	1905
611	Markenfield	Markenfield Construction Co.	Lawlor & Haase	1905
500	St. John Court	Gross & Herbener	Neville & Bagge	1908
504	Ardnaree	Roffler Construction Co.	Neville & Bagge	1909
518	Trinity Court	Samuel D. Davis	Bernstein & Bernstein	1909
526	Criterion Arms	Highwood Realty & Construction Co.	Lafayette A. Goldstone	1909
528	Ramona	Carnegie Construction Co.	Mulliken & Moeller	1910
532	Charlemagne	Carnegie Construction Co.	Mulliken & Moeller	1909
536	Amele Hall	Riverside Drive Viaduct Realty Co.	Mulliken & Moeller	1910
600	—	Alart Building Corp.	Jacob M. Felson	1925
610	Savoy	Harry Schiff	Neville & Bagge	1906

WEST 112TH STREET

505[d]	—	John Paterno	M.V.B. Ferdon	1898
507[d]	—	John Paterno	M.V.B. Ferdon	1898
509	St. Marino	John Paterno's Sons	M.V.B. Ferdon	1900
511	St. John	Michael Tully	S.B. Ogden & Co.	1902
521	Campolyn	Kaw Realty Co.	Lawlor & Haase	1910
523	Wenonah	Kaw Realty Co.	Lawlor & Haase	1910
533	Adlon	Hennessy Realty Co.	Schwartz & Gross	1909
535	Hotel Colonial[8]	University Construction Co.	Charles Steinmetz	1906
539	Phaeton	Advance Building Co.	George & Edward Blum	1909
545	Ostend	George E. Wilson	Neville & Bagge	1900
601	Claremont Hall	Max Vogel	Neville & Bagge[9]	1901
605	Clarendon	Trood Realty Co.	Thain & Thain	1904
611	Maranamay	Michael Tully	Israels & Harder	1903
504[d]	—	John Reilly	Frank H. Quimby	1902
508	Ordell	Frank Woytisek	Neville & Bagge	1903
512	—	E.S. Brandt Building Co.	George Miller	1930
516[i,d]	—	7th Church of Christ Scientist	Griffen & Wynkoop	1918
520[i]	—	7th Church of Christ Scientist	William Fryer	1987
520	Lionsgate	Morningside Development Association	William Fryer	1987
522	—	Seplow & Son	George F. Pelham	1906
526	De Boulogne	Kleinfeld & Englesberg	Stern & Morris	1905
530	Huguenot	Kleinfeld & Englesberg	Stern & Morris	1905
534[d]	Belvedere Court	Kleinfeld & Englesberg	Stern & Morris	1906
534[c,p]	Columbia Station Post Office	Columbia University	Kaeyer, Garment & Davidson	1996
540	Kiltonga	Brogan Construction Co.	Neville & Bagge	1903
542	Devonshire[10]	A.C. & H.M. Hall	Neville & Bagge	1907
604[i]	Bank Street College	Bank Street College	Harry Weese	1966

Addr./Name		Original Owner/Builder	Architect	Date
604[d]	Wenoit	Trood Realty Co.	Lawlor & Haase	1904
610[d]	Porterfield	Porterfield Construction Co.	Joseph M. Lawlor	1904

WEST 113TH STREET

Addr./Name		Original Owner/Builder	Architect	Date
501[d]	St. James	G. L. Lawrence	Neville & Bagge	1897
501	St. James House	St. James House Inc.	George F. Pelham	1931
507	Louisiana	Paterno Bros. Inc.	Schwartz & Gross	1908
511	Illinois	Paterno Bros. Inc.	Schwartz & Gross	1908
517	Michigan	Paterno Bros. Inc.	Schwartz & Gross	1908
523[s]	—	Marie Cook	Henry F. Cook	1899
525[s]	—	Marie Cook	Henry F. Cook	1899
527[s]	—	Marie Cook	Henry F. Cook	1899
529[s]	—	Marie Cook	Henry F. Cook	1899
531[s]	—	Marie Cook	Henry F. Cook	1899
535	Senior Arms	Paterno & Sons Contruction Co.	George & Edward Blum	1909
541	Cathedral Court	Sun Construction Co.	Benjamin W. Levitan	1908
549	Clearmont Court	Sun Construction Co.	Benjamin W. Levitan	1908
565[s]	—	Martha Dederer	George Keister	1903
601	Forest Chambers	George F. Johnson, Jr.	George & Edward Blum	1909
603	Versailles Palace	Scheer-Ginsberg Construction Co.	George F. Pelham	1910
611[d]	Sunnycrest	V. Cerabone Construction Co.	Schwartz & Gross	1907
617	Hunting Field	Huntingfield Construction Co.	Lawlor & Haase	1906
619[s]	—	D.R. Kendall	C.P.H. Gilbert	1897
621[s]	—	D.R. Kendall	C.P.H. Gilbert	1897
623[s]	—	D.R. Kendall	C.P.H. Gilbert	1897
625[s]	—	D.R. Kendall	C.P.H. Gilbert	1897
627[s]	—	D.R. Kendall	C.P.H. Gilbert	1897
500[p]	Engine Co. 47	New York City Fire Department	Napoleon Le Brun & Sons	1889
502	Stamford	Ferguson-Miller Realty Co.	George F. Pelham	1905
506	Arlington	Ferguson-Miller Realty Co.	George F. Pelham	1905
510[d]	Galanthea	Michael Paterno & Son	Schwartz & Gross	1909
514[c]	—	C.J. Zimmerman	Louis A. Sheinart	1910
526	Quidnet[11]	Champlin Realty Co.	Mulliken & Moeller	1909
530	—	530 W 113th Street Co.	Mulliken & Moeller	1910
536	Rensselaer	Keystone Investing Co.	Neville & Bagge	1909
540[s]	—	Frederick Wachsmuth	Charles Steinmetz	1897
542[s]	—	Frederick Wachsmuth	Charles Steinmetz	1897
544[s]	—	Frederick Wachsmuth	Charles Steinmetz	1897
546[s]	—	Frederick Wachsmuth	Charles Steinmetz	1897
548[s]	—	Frank E. Wise	Gilbert A. Schellenger	1896
550[s]	—	Frank E. Wise	Gilbert A. Schellenger	1896
552[s]	—	Frank E. Wise	Gilbert A. Schellenger	1896
554[s]	—	Frank E. Wise	Gilbert A. Schellenger	1896
556[s]	—	Frank E. Wise	Gilbert A. Schellenger	1896

Addr./Name	Original Owner/Builder	Architect	Date
558[s] —	Frank E. Wise	Gilbert A. Schellenger	1896
560[s] —	Frank E. Wise	Gilbert A. Schellenger	1896
562 Yorkshire	Isaac Mayer & Son	Neville & Bagge	1908
600 Allerton	Yorkshire Realty & Construction Co.	Neville & Bagge	1910
606 Altamonte	Louis & John Brandt	Louis & John Brandt	1898
508[s] —	Martha Dederer	George F. Pelham	1897
610 Grant Court	Nathan Loewy	George F. Pelham	1904
514[s] —	Ernest R. & Clarence J. Lawson	George F. Pelham	1897
516[s] —	Ernest R. & Clarence J. Lawson	George F. Pelham	1897
518[s] —	Ernest R. & Clarence J. Lawson	George F. Pelham	1897
622 Victor Hall	V. Cerabone Construction Co.	Schwartz & Gross	1908

WEST 114TH STREET

Addr./Name	Original Owner/Builder	Architect	Date
411 —	Phillips-Jullien Realty Co.	George A. Dessez	1909
417[d] St. Orimand	Joseph Spota	Neville & Bagge	1898
419[d] Aldean	Hennessy Realty Co.	Schwartz & Gross	1909
417 see St. Luke's Hospital			
605 Heathcote	Carnegie Construction Co.	Schwartz & Gross	1910
619[d] Evelyn Court	Central Building Improvement and Investment Co.	Henri Fouchaux	1904
619[i] St. Hilda's and St. Hugh's School	St. Hilda's and St. Hugh's School	Moore & Hutchins	1964
508 Tennessee	Paterno Bros. Inc.	Schwartz & Gross	1908
514 Arizona	Paterno Bros. Inc.	Schwartz & Gross	1908
520 San Maria	Paterno Bros. Inc.	Schwartz & Gross	1908
524[s] —	Ernest R. & Clarence J. Lawson	George F. Pelham	1897
526[s] —	Ernest R. & Clarence J. Lawson	George F. Pelham	1897
528[s] —	Carrie S. Kennedy	Neville & Bagge	1898
530[s] —	Carrie S. Kennedy	Neville & Bagge	1898
532[s] —	Carrie S. Kennedy	Neville & Bagge	1898
534[s] —	Carrie S. Kennedy	Neville & Bagge	1898
536[s] —	Carrie S. Kennedy	Neville & Bagge	1898
538[s] —	David T. Kennedy	Neville & Bagge	1899
540[s] —	David T. Kennedy	Neville & Bagge	1899
542[s] —	David T. Kennedy	Neville & Bagge	1899
544[s] —	David T. Kennedy	Neville & Bagge	1899
546[s] —	David T. Kennedy	Neville & Bagge	1899
548[s] —	David T. Kennedy	Neville & Bagge	1899
550[s] —	David T. Kennedy	Neville & Bagge	1899
552[s] —	David T. Kennedy	Neville & Bagge	1899
554[s] —	David T. Kennedy	Neville & Bagge	1899
604[s] —	Ernest R. & Clarence J. Lawson	Frank A. Lang	1896
606[s] —	Ernest R. & Clarence J. Lawson	Frank A. Lang	1896
608[s] —	Ernest R. & Clarence J. Lawson	Frank A. Lang	1896

Addr./Name		Original Owner/Builder	Architect	Date
610[s]	—	Ernest R. & Clarence J. Lawson	Frank A. Lang	1896
612[s]	—	Ernest R. & Clarence J. Lawson	Frank A. Lang	1896
614[s]	—	Ernest R. & Clarence J. Lawson	Frank A. Lang	1896
616[s]	—	Ernest R. & Clarence J. Lawson	Frank A. Lang	1896
618[d]	Rockland Hall	John J. Falahee	Moore & Landsiedel	1907
622	Revere Hall	Paterno Bros. Inc.	Schwartz & Gross	1905
628	Hudson Hall	Paterno Bros. Inc.	Schwartz & Gross	1905

WEST 115TH STREET

403	Park Court	Paterno Bros. Inc.	Schwartz & Gross	1905
411	Colonial	West Side Construction Co.	George F. Pelham	1904
415	Munroe	West Side Construction Co.	George F. Pelham	1904
419	Cragsmoor	West Side Construction Co.	George F. Pelham	1904
601	Regnor	Paterno Bros. Inc.	Gaetan Ajello	1911
605[d]	Bellemore	Moses Crystal	Neville & Bagge	1903
609[d]	Annamere Court	Herman Oppenheim	Neville & Bagge	1906
615[i]	Schapiro Hall	Columbia University	Gruzen Sampton Steinglass	1987
617	—	Wilmot Building Co.	Moore & Landsiedel	1909
627[f]	Lambda Association	Lambda Association	Little & O'Connor	1900
629	Overton Hall	Alcazar Realty Co.	William L. Rouse	1909
633[s]	—	Francis M. Burdick	Henry Otis Chapman	1891
635[s]	—	Francis M. Burdick	Henry Otis Chapman	1891
404[d]	Warren Hall	Paterno Bros. Inc.	Schwartz & Gross	1904
408	—	John Yule	John Brandt[12]	1898
410	—	John Yule	John Brandt	1898
412	—	John Yule	John Brandt	1898
600	Luxor	Paterno Bros. Inc.	Gaetan Ajello	1910
604	Wharfedale	Geraldine Broadbelt	Henry Anderson	1900
606[d]	Wharfedale	Geraldine Broadbelt	Henry Anderson	1900
610	Amesbury Hall[13]	Carnegie Construction Co.	Schwartz & Gross	1910
612	Duncan Hall	Frank Woytisek	Neville & Bagge	1905
616[d]	Arleigh	Philip Merowitz	Neville & Bagge	1903

WEST 116TH STREET

404	La Valenciennes	Paterno Bros. Inc.	Schwartz & Gross	1905
416[i]	William C. Warren Hall	Columbia University Law School	James Stewart Polshek & Partners	1995
420	Sesrun Hall[14]	Clinton W. Kinsella	Neville & Bagge	1906
424	—	Manhattan Heights Improvement Co.	George & Edward Blum	1920
430	Hillcrest	A.S. Luria	Neville & Bagge	1900
438	Fairmont	Morgenthau & Ehrich	Neville & Bagge	1901
600	Rexor	Paterno Bros. Inc.	Gaetan Ajello	1911
606	Broadview	Paterno Bros. Inc.	Schwartz & Gross	1907
610	Westerfield	Paterno Bros. Inc.	Schwartz & Gross	1908

Addr./Name		Original Owner/Builder	Architect	Date
612 [f]	Delta Phi	Delta Phi Fraternity	Thomas Nash	1906
616	Fiora-Ville	Paterno Bros. Inc.	Schwartz & Gross	1906
620	Porter Arms	Paterno Bros. Inc.	Schwartz & Gross	1906

WEST 117TH STREET

405 [s,d]	—	Carrie S. Kennedy	Neville & Bagge	1895
407 [s,d]	—	Carrie S. Kennedy	Neville & Bagge	1895
409 [s,d]	—	Carrie S. Kennedy	Neville & Bagge	1895
411 [s,d]	—	Carrie S. Kennedy	Neville & Bagge	1895
413 [s,d]	—	Carrie S. Kennedy	Neville & Bagge	1895
415 [s,d]	—	Carrie S. Kennedy	Neville & Bagge	1895
417 [s,d]	—	Carrie S. Kennedy	Neville & Bagge	1895
419 [s,d]	—	Carrie S. Kennedy	Neville & Bagge	1895
421 [s,d]	—	Carrie S. Kennedy	Neville & Bagge	1895
423 [s,d]	—	Carrie S. Kennedy	Neville & Bagge	1895
425 [s,d]	—	Carrie S. Kennedy	Neville & Bagge	1894
427 [s,d]	—	Carrie S. Kennedy	Neville & Bagge	1894
429 [s,d]	—	Carrie S. Kennedy	Neville & Bagge	1894
431 [s,d]	—	Carrie S. Kennedy	Neville & Bagge	1894
433 [s,d]	—	Carrie S. Kennedy	Neville & Bagge	1894
435 [s,d]	—	Carrie S. Kennedy	Neville & Bagge	1894
437 [d]	—	Carrie S. Kennedy	Neville & Bagge	1894

WEST 118TH STREET

401	East View	West Side Construction Co.	Neville & Bagge	1907
405	The Terrace	West Side Construction Co.	Neville & Bagge	1907
415	Invermere	John Robertson & William Gammie	Henry Anderson	1901
417	University Court	John Robertson & William Gammie	Henry Anderson	1899
419	University Court	John Robertson & William Gammie	Henry Anderson	1899
421	Elizabeth Court	Felt & Malakoff	George F. Pelham	1906
423	Winthrop	Felt & Malakoff	George F. Pelham	1906
414 [d]	Summit	James Brown	Henry Anderson	1900
416 [d]	Julian	James Brown	Henry Anderson	1900
418 [d]	St. Gothard	John Acker	Harde & Short	1902
420 [d]	Saville	John Acker	Harde & Short	1902
430 [d]	Melville	Hugo F. Hoeffler	Neville & Bagge	1900

WEST 119TH STREET

419	Kingscote	Jacobs Construction Co.	Schwartz & Gross	1911
435	Laureate Hall	Carnegie Construction Co.	Schwartz & Gross	1911
400	Butler Hall [15]	City Construction Co.	George F. Pelham	1924
420	Iradell	Ira Realty Co.	Sommerfeld & Steckler	1909
424	Rosmond Court	Jumel Realty & Construction Co.	Sommerfeld & Steckler	1908

Addr./Name		Original Owner/Builder	Architect	Date
WEST 120TH STREET				
411	Devinclaire Residence[16]	Mrs. Susan Devin	Lawlor & Haase	1913
417	Marquette	Patrick McMorrow	Neville & Bagge	1904
423	Edmund Francis	Edmund Francis Realty Co.	George F. Pelham	1912
414	Herodian Court	Joseph H. Davis Building Co.	George F. Pelham	1911
434	Poinciana	Carnegie Construction	Schwartz & Gross	1912
WEST 121ST STREET				
417[d]	Louise	Samuel Potick & Sidney Stern	John Hauser	1905
419[d]	Emma	Samuel Potick & Sidney Stern	John Hauser	1905
421[d]	Powers Court	Powers Court Realty	Moore & Landsiedel	1906
501	Kings College	Fichter & Simon	Neville & Bagge	1905
503	Fairholm	Joseph H. Davis	George F. Pelham	1905
509	Bancroft	Sethlow Realty Co.	Emery Roth	1910
519	Miami	West Side Construction Co.	George F. Pelham	1905
523	Spencer	West Side Construction Co.	George F. Pelham	1905
527	Gerard	West Side Construction Co.	George F. Pelham	1905
529[i]	Corpus Christi R.C. Church Rectory	Corpus Christi R.C. Church	Thomas Dunn & Frederick E. Gilson	1930
533[i,d]	Corpus Christi R.C. Church	Corpus Christi R.C. Church	F.A. de Meuron	1906
533[i]	Corpus Christi R.C. Church	Corpus Christi R.C. Church	Wilfred E. Anthony	1935
537	Reed House	A.C. & H.M. Hall Realty Co.	Neville & Bagge	1905
414	Carolyn Court	Robert Wallace, Jr.	George F. Pelham	1912
420[d]	Bryn Mawr	Israel Ruth	John Hauser	1905
420[i]	Plimpton Hall	Barnard College	Slingerland & Booss	1967
WEST 122ND STREET				
503	—	Lefkowitz & Horwitz	George F. Pelham	1905
505	—	Lefkowitz & Horwitz	George F. Pelham	1905
509	Ogontz	Mulligan & Tierney	Jacob H. Amster	1904
515	Simna Court	Krulewitch Realty Co.	Bernstein & Bernstein	1905
521	Marimpol Court	Krulewitch Realty Co.	Bernstein & Bernstein	1905
531[d]	Cathedral Ayrcourt Apartments	Cathedral Ayrcourt, Inc.	Henry Atterbury Smith & William P. Miller	1922
500	Reldnas Hall	Julius S. Sandler	John Hauser	1904
502	Alvernie	Huppert & Bernstein	Bernstein & Bernstein	1906
506	Wisteria	Huppert & Bernstein	Bernstein & Bernstein	1906
512	Sarasota	West Side Construction Co.	George F. Pelham	1905
514	Grant	West Side Construction Co.	George F. Pelham	1904
520	Delaware	West Side Construction Co.	George F. Pelham	1905

Addr./Name		Original Owner/Builder	Architect	Date
524	Riverview	Charles Shapiro	Bernstein & Bernstein	1906
526	Summit	Charles Shapiro	Bernstein & Bernstein	1906
530	Columbia	Charles Shapiro	Bernstein & Bernstein	1906
532ᶜ	University Garage	Corpus Christi R.C. Church	Lewis P. Fluhrer	1910
540	Castle Court	A.C.& H.M. Hall Realty Co.	Neville & Bagge	1905

Institutional Complexes

Name	Architect	Dates
BARNARD COLLEGE		
Milbank Hall	Lamb & Rich	1896–97
Brinckerhoff Hall	Lamb & Rich	1896–97
Fiske Hall	Lamb & Rich	1897–98
Brooks Hall	Charles Rich	1906–07
Students' Hall (now Barnard Hall)	Arnold Brunner	1916–17
Hewitt Hall	McKim, Mead & White	1924–25
Adele Lehman Hall	O'Connor & Kilham	1957–59
Helen Reid Hall	O'Connor & Kilham	1957–59
Millicent McIntosh Hall	Vincent Kling	1966–69
Helen Goodhart Altschul Hall	Vincent Kling	1966–69
Iphigene Ochs Sulzberger Hall	James Stewart Polshek & Partners	1986–89
Plimpton Hall, see 420 West 121st Street		

COLUMBIA UNIVERSITY		
Macy Villa (now Buell Center and Maison Française)	Ralph Townsend	1885
Low Memorial Library	McKim, Mead & White	1895–97
Schermerhorn Hall	McKim, Mead & White	1896–97
Fayerweather Hall	McKim, Mead & White	1896–97
Engineering Hall (now Mathematics Hall)	McKim, Mead & White	1896–97
Havemeyer Hall	McKim, Mead & White	1896–97
Gymnasium and Power Plant (base of University Hall)	McKim, Mead & White	1896–97
University Hallᵈ	McKim, Mead & White	1896; (des.) 1899–1900 (partial cons.) 1899–1900
Earl Hall	McKim, Mead & White	1900–1902
St. Paul's Chapel	Howells & Stokes	1903–7
School of Mines (now Lewisohn Hall)	Arnold Brunner	1904–5
Livingston Hall (now Wallach Hall)	McKim, Mead & White	1904–5
Hartley Hall	McKim, Mead & White	1904–5
Hamilton Hall	McKim, Mead & White	1905–7

Name	Architect	Dates
Kent Hall	McKim, Mead & White	1909–11
Philosophy Hall	McKim, Mead & White	1910–11
Avery Hall	McKim, Mead & White	1911–12
President's House	McKim, Mead & White	1911–12
Journalism Hall	McKim, Mead & White	1912–13
Furnald Hall	McKim, Mead & White	1912–13
Faculty Club	McKim, Mead & White	1922–23
Business School (now Dodge Hall)	McKim, Mead & White	1923–24
Johnson Hall (now Wien Hall)	McKim, Mead & White	1924–25
John Jay Hall	McKim, Mead & White	1925–27
Pupin Hall	McKim, Mead & White	1925–27
Chandler Hall	McKim, Mead & White	1925–28
Casa Italiana	McKim, Mead & White	1926–27
Schermerhorn Hall Extension	McKim, Mead & White	1928–29
South Hall (now Butler Library)	James Gambrel Rogers	1931–34
Brander Matthews Academic Theatre[d]	Eggers & Higgins	1940
Ferris Booth Hall[d]	Shreve, Lamb & Harmon (Harvey Clarkson, project architect)	1956–59
Carman Hall	Shreve, Lamb & Harmon (Harvey Clarkson, project architect)	1956–59
Law School (now Jerome Greene Hall)	Harrison & Abramovitz	1958–61
Seeley Wintersmith Mudd Hall	Voorhees, Walker, Smith, & Smith	1958–61
Uris Hall	Moore & Hutchins	1959–64
Seeley Wintersmith Mudd Hall Extension	Voorhees, Walker, Smith, Smith & Haines	1964–66
School of International Affairs	Harrison & Abramovitz	1966–70
Marcellus Hartley Dodge Physical Fitness Center	The Eggers Partnership	1971–74
Sherman Fairchild Center for the Life Sciences	Mitchell/Giurgola Associates	1974–77
Avery Hall Extension	Alexander Kouzmanoff & Associates	1977
Uris Hall Extension	Peter L. Gluck & Partners	1983–84
East Campus Housing	Gwathmey Siegel & Associates,	1977–81[17]
Computer Science Building	R.M. Kliment & Francis Halsband	1981–83
Havemeyer Hall Extension	Davis Brody & Associates	1984–88
Schapiro Center for Engineering and Physical Science Research	Helmuth, Obata & Kassebaum	1989–92
Jerome Greene Hall (Law School) Extension	Polshek & Partners	1995–96
Alfred Lerner Hall	Bernard Tschumi	1996–
Schapiro Hall, see 615 West 115th Street		
William C. Warren Hall, see 416 West 116th Street		

JEWISH THEOLOGICAL SEMINARY

Jacob H. Schiff Memorial Library	Gehron, Ross & Alley; David Levy, associate	1928–30
Teachers Institute	Gehron, Ross & Alley; David Levy, associate	1928–30
Louis S. Brush Memorial Dormitory	Gehron, Ross & Alley; David Levy, associate	1928–30
Seminary Extension and Library	Gruzen Partnership	1980–83

Name	Architect	Dates

Name	Architect	Dates
Institute of Musical Art	Donn Barber	1909–10
Institute of Musical Art extension[d]	Donn Barber	1924
Juilliard School of Music Addition	Shreve, Lamb & Harmon	1930–31
Mitzi Newhouse Pavilion	MacFadyen & Knowles	1969–70

RIVERSIDE CHURCH

Name	Architect	Dates
Riverside Church	Allen & Collens and Henry C. Pelton	1926–30
Parish House	Collens, Willis & Beckonert	1955–59

CATHEDRAL OF ST. JOHN THE DIVINE (chapel dates are date of completion)

Name	Architect	Dates
Cathedral of St. John the Divine (first building campaign)	Heins & La Farge	1893–1911
St. Saviour Chapel	Heins & La Farge	1911
St. Columba Chapel	Heins & La Farge	1911
St. Ambrose Chapel	Carrère & Hastings	1914
St. Boniface Chapel	Henry Vaughan	1916
St. James Chapel	Henry Vaughan	1916
St. Martin of Tours Chapel	Cram & Ferguson	1918
St. Ansgarius Chapel	Henry Vaughan	1918
St. Faith's House, Training School and Home for Deaconesses	Heins & La Farge	1909–10
Synod Hall	Cram, Goodhue & Ferguson	1911–13
Choir School	Cook & Welch	1912–13
Episcopal Residence (Bishop's House and Deanery)	Cram, Goodhue & Ferguson	1912–14
Cathedral of St. John the Divine (second building campaign)	Cram, Goodhue & Ferguson (later Cram & Ferguson)	1911 (des.) 1925–41 (cons.)

ST. LUKE'S HOSPITAL

Name	Architect	Dates
Adminstration Building (Muhlenburg Pavilion) and Chapel	Ernest Flagg	1892–96
Minturn Pavilion	Ernest Flagg	1892–96
Norrie Pavilion[d]	Ernest Flagg	1892–96
Vanderbilt Pavilion[d]	Ernest Flagg	1892–96
Ambulence Stable	Ernest Flagg	1892–96
Pathology Building[d]	Ernest Flagg	1892–96
Margaret J. Plant Pavilion	Ernest Flagg	1903–6
Travers Pavilion	Ernest Flagg	1908–16
Scrymser Pavilion	Ernest Flagg	1925–28
Florence Stokes Clark Building	York & Sawyer	1952–54
Stuyvesant Building	York & Sawyer	1955–1956
114th Street research pavilion	Harry M. Prince	1966–68

Name	Architect	Dates
Woman's Hospital Annex	York & Sawyer	1964–65
St. Luke's Hospital Nurse's Residence[d]	York & Sawyer	1936
Dorothy Doubleday Babcock Building	Skidmore, Owings & Merrill	1990–91
Medical Arts Pavilion, see 1086 Amsterdam Avenue		

TEACHERS COLLEGE

Main Hall	William Potter	1892–94
Macy Hall	William Potter	1892 (des.)
		1893–99 (cons.)
Milbank Memorial Hall	William Potter	1892 (des.)
		1896–97 (cons.)
Horace Mann School	Howells & Stokes and Edgar A. Josselyn	1899–1901
Whittier Hall (including Lowell, Longfellow, Whittier, and Emerson halls)	Bruce Price and J. M. A. Darragh	1900–19
Frederick Ferris Thompson Memorial Hall	Parish & Schroeder	1902–4
Household Arts Building (now Grace Dodge Hall)	Parish & Schroeder	1907–9
Russell Hall	Allen & Collens	1919 (des.)
		1922–24 (cons.)
Grace Dodge Hall Extension	Allen & Collens	1922–24
Thorndike Hall	Hugh Stubbins	1969–73

UNION THEOLOGICAL SEMINARY

Union Theological Seminary (Administration Building, Library, President's House, dormitory wing, faculty housing, and base of Brown Memorial Tower)	Allen & Collens	1906–10
James Memorial Chapel	Allen & Collens	1906–10
Charles Cuthbert Hall		
Refectory, Francis Brown Social Hall, and Brown Memorial Tower	Allen & Collens	1906–7 (des.)
		1925–28 (re-des./cons.)
McGiffert Hall	Allen & Collens	1931–32
Auburn Hall	Collens, Willis & Beckonert	1949–51
Dickinson Hall	attributed to Collens, Willis & Beckonert	1957–59
Van Dusen Hall, see 524 Riverside Drive		

WOMAN'S HOSPITAL

Hospital[d]	Allen & Collens	1902–6
Nurse's Residence[d]	Allen & Collens	1913–14
Thompson Pathological Building[d]	Allen & Collens	1913–15

RIVERSIDE PARK

Grant's Tomb	John Duncan	1890–97
122nd Street Viewing Pavilion	Theodore Videto	1909–10

Abbreviations

AA, *American Architect*
AABN, *American Architecture and Building News*
A&B, *Architecture and Building*
AR, *Architectural Record*
As&Bs, *Architects' and Builders' Magazine*
CUQ, *Columbia University Quarterly*
DAB, *Dictionary of American Biography*
EP, *New York Evening Post*
Herald, *New York Herald*
HT, *New York Herald Tribune*
HW, *Harper's Weekly*
JSAH, *Journal of the Society of Architectural Historians*
NCAB, *National Cyclopaedia of American Biography*
NYT, *New York Times*
RRBG, *Real Estate Record and Builders Guide*
SA, *Scientific American*
Spectator, *Columbia Daily Spectator*
Sun, *New York Sun*
Tribune, *New York Tribune*
World, *New York World*

BCA, Barnard College Archive
Columbiana, Columbiana Collection, Columbia University
CF, Central Files
CU, Columbia University
CUA, Columbia University Archives
CUL, Columbia University Library, Rare Book and Manuscript Library
JSMA, Juilliard School of Music Archive
JTS, Jewish Theological Seminary
LC, Library of Congress

LC-ROA, Library of Congress, Records of the Olmsted Associates

L&W, New-York Historical Society, Leake and Watts Orphan Asylum Papers

MMW, McKim, Mead & White Collection

NYHA, New York Hospital Archives

NYHS, New-York Historical Society,

RAC, Rockefeller Archives Center; RFA, Rockefeller Family Archives; OMR, Office of the Messrs Rockefeller

RSCA, Riverside Church Archive

StJA, Cathedral of St. John the Divine, Archive of the Episcopal Diocese of New York

StLA, St. Luke's Hospital Archive

TCA, Teachers College Archive

UTSA, Union Theological Seminary Archive

Notes

INTRODUCTION

1. "A Modern Acropolis," *Dayton Press,* January 21, 1896 (TCA, Newspaper Clippings).

2. For "New York's Acropolis," see "Old Columbia's Proudest Day," *Herald,* May 3, 1896, p. 5, and "A Great Public Benefaction," *Sun,* May 8, 1895, p. 6. For "America's Acropolis," see "At Morningside Heights," *NYT,* December 20, 1896, p. 23. The *New York Mail and Express* claimed that it had "christened" the area "the Acropolis of the New World"; see "Columbia's Dormitory," *Mail and Express,* November 28, 1896, p. 1.

3. *Uptown Visitor,* October 15, 1887, quoted in Morningside Park Association, *Description of the Region Between Morningside and Riverside Parks in the City of New York, Including Morningside Heights* (1891; in BCA, Box C, File C17).

4. Robin Francis Rhodes, author of *Architecture and Meaning on the Athenian Acropolis* (New York: Cambridge University Press, 1995) provided the author with information about the meaning of the Acropolis in Periclean Athens.

5. Christopher J. Schuberth, *The Geology of New York City and Environs* (Garden City: Natural History Press, 1968), pp. 65–80, and Edward Hagaman Hall, "A Brief History of Morningside Park and Vicinity," *Twenty-First Annual Report of the American Scenic and Historic Preservation Society, 1916* (Albany: J.B. Lyon Co., 1916), pp. 541–44.

6. "Morningside Plateau," *EP,* March 14, 1896, p. 21.

7. These streets had been officially closed by acts of the New York State Legislature in 1838 and 1884.

8. "Teachers' College Open," *NYT,* November 16, 1894, p. 8.

9. According to Elliot Willensky and Norval White in the *AIA Guide to New York City* 3rd ed. (San Diego: Harcourt Brace Jovanovich, 1988), p. 418, "from Cathedral Parkway north to West 125th Street, the western hilly side of Manhattan Island is Morningside Heights."

10. See, for example, "Morningside Heights," *RRBG* 63 (March 25, 1889), 520; "Morningside Plateau," *EP,* March 14, 1896, p. 21; and "Morningside Plateau," *RRBG,* 60

(October 16, 1897), 542. For later discussions that set the northern boundry at 122nd Street, see "Spires of Morningside," *NYT,* February 13, 1926, p. 12, and Abraham Steers (of Slawson & Hobbs, real estate brokers), "Transformation West of Park Now in Progress," *HT,* January 27, 1929, sec. 5, p. 13. When the Morningside Protective Association identified all of the landowners on Morningside Heights in c.1895, it listed only properties between 110th and 122nd streets; see "Alphabetical and Descriptive List of the Names of all the Owners of the Property on Morningside Heights between Morningside Avenue and Riverside Drive and between Cathedral Parkway & 122nd Street" (c.1895; Columbiana, Morningside Protective Association Box).

11. Hall, "A Brief History," pp. 540, 547.

12. For the use of "at Bloomingdale," see, for example, "A Good Step Forward," *New York Record,* December 26, 1891, p. 6. This terminology was in use as early as 1811, when the Society of the New York Hospital announced that it had purchased property "at Bloomingdale"; Society of the New York Hospital, *Minutes of the Board of Governors,* August 1, 1815. Bloomingdale was an anglicization of "Bloemendaal," the name that the Dutch gave to a small settlement and rural district that included much of today's Upper West Side. See, Peter Salwen, *Upper West Side Story: A History and Guide* (New York: Abbeville, 1981), pp. 13–21.

13. For Bloomingdale Heights, see, for example, "The World's Fair of 1892," *SA* 62 (January 4, 1890), 2, and Walter L. Hervey, "New York College for the Training of Teachers," *Review of Reviews* 5 (May 1892), 424. For Riverside Heights, see "Plans for the New Columbia," *NYT,* December 5, 1893, p. 1, and "Columbia's New Building," *EP,* October 30, 1894, p. 7. For Columbia Heights, see "Columbia's Dedication," *The Critic* 28 (May 9, 1896), 328; for University Heights, see "Dormitories at Columbia," *Tribune,* November 23, 1896, p. 6. Bloomingdale Heights and Riverside Heights are names that also appear to have been in use prior to the 1880s.

14. Quoted in Hall, "A Brief History," p. 562.

15. For the use of Morningside Plateau, see, for example, "Morningside Plateau," *EP,* November 12, 1892, p. 1, and "Columbia's Site is Safe," *World,* March 18, 1892, p. 10. For Morningside Hill, see, [editorial], *RRBG* 49 (January 23, 1892), p. 108, and [editorial], *RRBG,* 49 (May 14, 1892), 763.

16. Morningside Park Association, *Description of the Region,* p. 3 refers to "Morningside Hill (or Heights)." Newspapers began to use the name "Morningside Heights" in 1894; see "Columbia's New Location," *NYT,* September 26, 1894, p. 7.

17. Low to John B. Pine, February 19, 1895 (CUA, CF, Pine File).

18. Columbia University, *Minutes of the Board of Directors,* March 4, 1895 (CUA); Low to Potter, June 2, 1896 (CUA, CF, Potter File).

19. Columbia University, *Minutes,* June 1, 1896.

20. Low to Potter, June 2, 1896.

21. Low to Potter, June 2, 1896.

22. Columbia University, *Minutes,* March 1, 1897.

23. Resolution of the Common Council, April 13, 1897 (StJA).

24. "As To Names," [editorial] *Tribune,* October 5, 1898, p. 6.

25. Edward Hagaman Hall, *A Guide to the Cathedral Church of Saint John the Divine in the City of New York* (New York: Laymen's Club of the Cathedral, 1920), p. 9.

26. The *New York Mail and Express* campaigned for the establishment of the Public Library on Morningside Heights; see especially, "For the New Acropolis," *Mail and Express,* April 2, 1895, p. 10, and Phyllis Dain, *The New York Public Library: A History of Its Founding and Early Years* (New York: New York Public Library, 1972), pp. 73, 142, 152. George Macculloch Miller, who was instrumental in bringing both the Cathedral and St. Luke's Hospital to Morningside Heights, supported this plan; see "For the Acropolis," [letter to the editor], *Mail and Express,* April 5, 1895, p. 5. Miller also notes that the Historical Society "would be a fitting addition to the grounds [of Columbia]."

27. The National Academy of Design, one of New York City's oldest arts organizations, was established in 1826 as an art school and exhibition center. In 1897, after a proposed union with Columbia University fell through, it purchased a large site on Cathedral Parkway, Amsterdam Avenue, and 109th Street. Funds could not be raised to erect Carrère & Hastings' design. Instead, a temporary school was built on 109th Street and the rest of the property remained vacant and was sold to Woman's Hospital in 1948. The major published source for the history of the National Academy of Design is Eliot Clark, *History of the National Academy of Design, 1825–1953* (New York: Columbia University Press, 1954). The National Academy of Design's archive contains minute books, letters, and other material relating to the proposed move to Morningside Heights and the design competition.

28. "A Great Opportunity," *Christian Union,* January 30, 1892, p. 194.

29. "Removing Columbia College," [editorial] *NYT,* November 13, 1892, p. 4.

30. McKim, Mead & White to Low, April 10, 1893; letter printed in "Correspondence, Etc. Relating to Buildings Upon the New Site," in *Minutes of the Committee on Buildings and Grounds* (CUA).

31. Royal Cortissoz, "Landmarks of Manhattan," *Scribner's Magazine* 18 (November 1895), 541.

32. "Morningside," *Harper's Weekly* 41 (February 13, 1897), 162.

33. Montgomery Schuyler, "Architecture of American Colleges IV. New York City Colleges," *AR* 27 (June 1910), 447, 456.

34. St. Luke's Hospital rejected designs that were more sympathetic to the design of the Cathedral of St. John the Divine, notably those of James Brown Lord and of the cathedral's architect Heins & La Farge (see chapter 3).

35. Columbia specifically rejected the suggestion of architect Charles Haight to erect a Collegiate Gothic campus (see chapter 4).

36. The Union Theological Seminary competition requirements are in "The Program of a Competition for the Selection of an Architect and the Procuring of a General Plan for the Union Theological Seminary in the City of New York" (1906), p. 9 (UTSA, Box 2.3D).

1. AT BLOOMINGDALE: THE PREHISTORY OF
   MORNINGSIDE HEIGHTS

1. In the seventeenth century, all of the land on what would become known as Morningside Heights, with the exception of a small plot at the northeast corner of the area which was within the boundaries of the town of Harlem, was owned by New York City. This concentration of ownership resulted from a 1686 grant or "patent" issued by British-Colonial Governor Thomas Dongan that conferred title to all lands that had not yet been claimed by private individuals to the city government. In 1688, New York City erected a new city hall and ferry house, but did not have money to pay for these projects. Land had to be sold to raise capital. As a result, in 1701 all of the city's property on Morningside Heights was sold to Jacob De Key. The De Key family held the property until 1735, selling it in two sections to Adrian Hogeland (also spelled Hoogland and Hoglandt) and Harmon Vandewater. In 1784, Nicholas De Peyster purchased the Hogeland Farm and the following year his brother James took title to the Vandewater property. It was not until the nineteenth century that members of the De Peyster family sold any of their Morningside Heights land. See I. N. Phelps Stokes, *The Iconography of Manhattan 1498–1909,* vol. 6 (New York: Robert H. Dodd, 1928), pp. 96–98 and Edward Hagaman Hall, "A Brief History of Morningside Park and Vicinity," *Twenty-First Annual Report of the American Scenic and Historic Preservation Society, 1916* (Albany: J. B. Lyon Co., 1916), pp. 546–47.

2. The battle of Harlem Heights was a relatively minor skirmish with patriotic forces successfully holding back the British advance up Manhattan Island, thus permitting the escape of George Washington and his troops. The main action took place in a buckwheat field located at approximately 119th and 120th streets between Broadway and Riverside Drive; the battle ended just south of an orchard at approximately 112th Street and Broadway. The battle is commemorated on a bronze plaque affixed to the Broadway facade of Columbia University's Mathematics Hall by the Sons of the American Revolution in the State of New York on October 16, 1897. See New York Historical Society, *Commemoration of the Battle of Harlem Heights on its One Hundredth Anniversary* (New York: New-York Historical Society, 1876); Henry P. Johnston, *The Battle of Harlem Heights* (New York: Macmillan, 1897); and William R. Shepherd, "The Battle of Harlem Heights," *Half Moon Series,* vol. 2 (New York: Putnam, October 1898).

3. Stokes, *Iconography of Manhattan,* vol. 3 (1918), p. 977. "Claremont" became the property of New York City in 1873 and was leased as an inn that became a popular destination for pleasure drives and promenades. The house burned in 1953. Andrew Carrigan was a grocer and also president of the Emigrant Savings Bank. The Carrigan mansion was sold in 1874 to Janet Rudd and came to be known as the "Rudd" or "Carrington Rudd" house. See Stokes, *Iconography of Manhattan,* vol. 3, p. 977; "Big Investment Property in Demand," *Tribune,* January 8, 1911, p. 11; Henry Collins Brown, ed., *Valentine's Manual of Old New-York,* vol. 3 (New York: Valentine's Manual, Inc., 1919), p. 259; and Andrew Alpern, *Luxury Apartment Houses of Manhattan: An Illustrated History* (New York: Dover, 1992), p. 85.

4. Additional small plots were acquired between 1833 and 1846 to even out the boundaries of the site; a tiny parcel on West 120th Street just west of Amsterdam Avenue was purchased in 1853.

5. The most detailed history of New York Hospital's facilities for treating the insane and of the hospital's Bloomingdale Asylum is William Logie Russell, *The New York Hospital: A History of the Psychiatric Service 1771–1936* (New York: Columbia University Press, 1945).

6. *Medical Repository* 5 (1898); quoted in Russell, *The New York Hospital,* p. 70.

7. Russell, *The New York Hospital,* p. 49.

8. Russell, *The New York Hospital,* pp. 116–22.

9. Thomas Eddy, *Hints for Introducing an Improved Mode of Treating the Insane in the Asylum* (New York, 1815), pp. 15–17; quoted in Russell, *The New York Hospital,* p. 122.

10. Society of the New York Hospital, *Minutes of the Board of Governors,* August 1, 1815 (NYHA).

11. *Minutes of the Board of Governors,* August 1, 1815.

12. *Minutes of the Board of Governors,* June 1, 1816.

13. *Minutes of the Board of Governors,* January 9, 1817, February 4, 1817, and January 20, 1818.

14. In the *Minutes of the Board of Governors,* March 21, 1818, a resolution was passed to buy property from several different owners.

15. *Minutes of the Board of Governors,* January 1, 1821; Russell, *The New York Hospital,* p. 128; Franklin Toker, "James O'Donnell: An Irish Georgian in America," *JSAH* 29 (May 1970), 135. It is not known if the claim was paid because O'Donnell had actually designed the building or because the governors did not feel it was worth contesting the claim in court.

16. *Minutes of the Board of Governors,* May 5, 1818.

17. *Minutes of the Board of Governors,* May 5, 1818.

18. *Minutes of the Board of Governors,* May 6, 1826, November 13, 1827, May 5, 1827.

19. *Minutes of the Board of Governors,* January 9, 1829, January 16, 1829. For McComb, see Agnes Addison Gilchrist, "John McComb, Sr. and Jr., in New York, 1784–1799," *JSAH* 31 (March 1972), 10–21, and Damie Stillman, "John McComb, Jr.," in Adolf Placzek, ed., *Macmillan Encyclopedia of Architects,* vol. 3 (New York: The Free Press, 1982), p. 134. Although drawings for hospital structures by McComb survive at the New-York Historical Society, none of these can definitely be associated with proposals for the Bloomingdale Asylum.

20. For Dakin, see Arthur Scully, Jr., *James Dakin, Architect: His Career in New York and the South* (Baton Rouge: Louisiana State University Press, 1973), and Scully, "James Dakin," in Placzek, *Macmillan Encyclopedia,* vol. 1, pp. 489–91.

21. For the Green Building, see "A New Wing of the Bloomingdale Asylum," *Frank Leslie's Illustrated Newspaper,* April 3, 1880, pp. 75–76. At the time of his death, John C. Green was the president of the Board of Governors of New York Hospital.

22. The Bloomingdale Road north of 23rd Street had not been a part of the 1811 plan for New York City's streets, but various acts of the New York State Legislature between 1838 and 1865 had officially extended it as far as 106th Street. In 1868 its route north

of 106th Street was abandoned and what became known as the Boulevard (now Broadway) was extended north along the route of Eleventh Avenue; see Andrew H. Green, "Report Accompanying the Plan Adopted for the West Side of the City From 55th Street to 155th Street," in *Eleventh Annual Report of the Board of Commissioners of the Central Park For the Year Ending December 31, 1867* (1868), p. 161.

23. Macy Villa was shorn of its porches and moved by Columbia University to a site just south of St. Paul's Chapel. It is now shared by the Buell Center for the Study of Architecture and the *Maison Française*.

24. Edward Ruggles, *A Picture of New-York in 1846* (New York: C. S. Francis & Co., 1846), p. 43.

25. David J. Rothman, *The Discovery of the Asylum: Social Order and Disorder in the New Republic* (Boston: Little, Brown & Co., 1971), pp. 278–79.

26. Russell, *The New York Hospital,* p. 199.

27. *Minutes of the Board of Governors,* November 6, 1821.

28. Will of John G. Leake, June 2, 1827.

29. "New York City," *Churchman* 66 (August 6, 1892), 161.

30. Leake and Watts Orphan Asylum, *Minutes of the Board of Directors,* November 18, 1834 (NYHS, Leake and Watts Collection). The remainder of New York Hospital's property, located between 107th and 109th streets, was sold in 1835; see Russell, *The New York Hospital,* p. 136.

31. *Minutes of the Board of Directors,* December 31, 1834.

32. *Minutes of the Board of Directors,* June 15, 1835. For Town, see Jane B. Davies, "Ithiel Town," in Placzek, *Macmillan Encyclopedia,* vol. 4, pp. 220–23.

33. *Minutes of the Board of Directors,* July 13, 1837. Trench is an obscure figure best known as architect of the original A. T. Stewart Store on Broadway and Reade Street; see New York City Landmarks Preservation Commission, *Sun Building Designation Report,* report prepared by James Dillon (1986), p. 3.

34. Aspects of the design and construction are discussed in *Minutes of the Board of Directors,* May 18, 1835; June 15, 1835; September 14, 1835; October 29, 1835; December 28, 1835; June 17, 1835; August 22, 1836; July 13, 1837; and October 24, 1837.

35. For Samuel Thomson, see Geoffrey Carter, "Samuel Thomson: Prolific New York Builder," *Preservation League of New York State Newsletter* (Fall 1991), 4–5.

36. For a discussion of the building and its design, see Christopher Gray, "A Castoff in the Path of a Growing, Great Cathedral," *NYT* June 24, 1990, sec. 10, p. 6.

37. For the Croton Aqueduct, see John B. Jervis, *Description of the Croton Aqueduct* (New York: Slamm and Guion, 1842); F. B. Tower, *Illustrations of the Croton Aqueduct* (New York: Wiley and Putnam, 1843); Edward Wegmann, *The Water-Supply of the City of New York 1658–1895* (New York: John Wiley, 1896); and Charles H. Weidner, *Water For a City: A History of New York City's Problem from the Beginning to the Delaware River System* (New Brunswick: Rutgers University Press, 1973).

38. The 113th Street gatehouse is discussed in Christopher Gray, "Worthy Interests Clash on 113th St.," *NYT,* November 25, 1990, sec. 10, p. 7.

39. New York City acquired the land for this gatehouse in 1877.

40. In 1997 a high-rise nursing home structure was erected that abuts the 113th Street gatehouse. The gatehouse was converted for use by nursing home residents.

41. Andrew S. Green, "Communication from the Comptroller of the Park to the Commissioners of the Central Park relative to the District Between Fifty-Fifth Street and One Hundred and Fifty-Fifth Street, West of the Eighth Avenue and Around Central Park," in *Eleventh Annual Report of the Board of Commissioners of Central Park,* p. 148. The New York State Legislature had given the Central Park Commissioners jurisdiction over alterations to the street grid and the laying out of parks in northern Manhattan. The Commission was also responsible for the addition of Claremont Avenue to the street grid of Morningside Heights.

42. For Morningside Park, see Edward Hagaman Hall, "A Brief History of Morningside Park and Vicinity," *Twenty-First Annual Report of the American Scenic and Historic Preservation Society, 1916* (Albany: J. B. Lyon Co., 1916); Elizabeth Barlow and William Alex, *Frederick Law Olmsted's New York* (New York: Praeger, 1972), pp. 47–48, 114–15; and Jeffrey Simpson, *Art of the Olmsted Landscape: His Works in New York City* (New York: New York City Landmarks Preservation Commission, 1981), pp. 19–20. An excellent brief history of the planning of Morningside Park is supplied in David Schuyler and Jane Turner Censer, eds., *The Papers of Frederick Law Olmsted: The Years of Olmsted, Vaux & Company,* vol. 6 (Baltimore: Johns Hopkins Press, 1992), pp. 658–59.

43. Frederick Law Olmsted and Calvert Vaux, *A Preliminary Study by the Landscape Architect of a Design for the Laying Out of Morningside Park,* Board of the Department of Parks, Document No. 50 (1873), reprinted in Schuyler and Censer, *The Papers of Frederick Law Olmsted,* pp. 651–60; Hall, "A Brief History," pp. 565–71; and Albert Fein, ed., *Landscape Into Cityscape: Frederick Law Olmsted's Plans for a Greater New York City* (New York: Van Nostrand Reinhold, 1967), pp. 333–41.

44. Frederick Law Olmsted and Calvert Vaux, *General Plan for the Improvement of Morningside Park* (1887), reprinted in Fein, *Landscape Into Cityscape,* pp. 441–57.

45. "A Preliminary Study," in Fein, *Landscape Into Cityscape,* p. 335.

46. "General Plan," in Fein, *Landscape Into Cityscape,* p. 452.

47. For Riverside Park, see Barlow and Alex, *Frederick Law Olmsted's New York,* p. 48, 116–21; Simpson, *Art of the Olmsted Landscape,* pp. 17–19; New York City Landmarks Preservation Commission, *Riverside Park and Riverside Drive Designation Report,* report prepared by Elizabeth Cromley and Gail T. Guillet (1980).

48. Laws of the State of New York, Chapter 697 (1867).

49. Frederick Law Olmsted, *Report of the Landscape Architect upon the Construction of Riverside Park and Avenue,* Board of the Department of Public Parks, Document No. 60 (1875); reprinted in Fein, *Landscape Into Cityscape,* pp. 343–48.

50. Olmsted to Park Commissioner John Crimmins, in "General Grant's Monument: An Architect on its Position and Surroundings," *NYT,* August 8, 1885, p. 8. Also see, Barlow and Alex, *Frederick Law Olmsted's New York,* p. 120, and Laura Wood Roper, *FLO: A Biography of Frederick Law Olmsted* (Baltimore: Johns Hopkins University Press, 1973), pp. 398–99.

51. For the competitions and design, see David M. Kahn, "The Grant Monument," *JSAH* 41 (October 1982), 212–31, and Eric A. Reinert, *Grant's Tomb*, (Eastern National, 1997).

52. The land for the firehouse was acquired by New York City from the Leake and Watts Orphan Asylum.

53. In order to save money, the Fire Department often employed the LeBrun's designs more than once. Thus, a virtually identical firehouse to the one on 113th Street was erected on West 10th Street in Greenwich Village in 1891. Charles Savage, who is completing a dissertation on the LeBruns at Columbia University, supplied information on the architectural firm and its firehouses. For the firehouse, see New York City Landmarks Preservation Commission, *Fire Engine Company No. 47 Designation Report*, report prepared by Laura Hansen (1997).

54. Eva Elise vom Baur, "Dwelling In High Places," *EP Magazine*, May 17, 1913, p. 13. Conveyance records for property along 110th Street confirm ownership by William Dixon or members of his family. Property was purchased by members of the Dixon family beginning in 1857 on the blocks between Amsterdam Avenue and Broadway and between Broadway and Riverside Drive. The 1880 U.S. Census shows that most of the houses were occupied by families headed by laborers and other working-class individuals, many of whom were immigrants from Ireland or Germany.

55. "A Typical Apartment House District," *RRBG* 88 (September 16, 1911), 378; also see, "Building on Cathedral Heights," *RRBG* 84 (October 23, 1909), 721–22, and "A Unique Contrast on Cathedral Parkway," *RRBG* 86 (March 11, 1911), 437.

56. "The Riverside Drive," *RRBG* 61 (March 12, 1898), 453; also see "Riverside Drive," *RRBG* 70 (October 11, 1902), 518–19.

57. *New York City Directories*, 1880–1890. For Noakes, see "George Noakes, [obituary], *NYT*, April 9, 1941, p. 24; for Kittel, see "Wins Race With Death," [obituary] *NYT*, March 17, 1904, p. 1; for Gibbons, see Moses King, *King's Handbook of New York* (Boston: Moses King, 1893), p. 850, and Moses King, *King's Notable New Yorkers* (Boston: Moses King, 1899), p. 529. In 1889, John Gibbons erected a stable, designed by Charles S. Mott, at the rear of his property, facing onto Claremont Avenue.

58. Many of Jennings's buildings are illustrated in photographs in the A. B. Jennings Collection (NYHS, Architecture Collection). Among Jennings's few extant buildings in New York City are the row at 718–730 St. Nicholas Avenue (1889–90). Jennings later specialized in churches designed in a rather personal adaptation of the Romanesque Revival style. Two of his churches are extant in Brooklyn—the Bay Ridge Reformed Church (1896–97) on Ridge Boulevard and 80th Street, and the Bedford Presbyterian Church (1897) on Bedford Avenue and Dean Street.

59. The Noakes House is discussed and illustrated in "A Residence in Riverside Park, New York City," *SA Architects and Builders Edition* 11 (March 1891), 38 and supplement, and 11 (April 1891), 53 and 62; also see Andrew Alpern, *Luxury Apartment Houses of Manhattan: An Illustrated History* (New York: Dover, 1992), p. 85.

60. New York Hospital, *Annual Report* (1865), p. 37.

61. Amsterdam Avenue had been opened in 1855 and West 113th Street was opened in 1869.

62. *Minutes of the Board of Governors,* December 4, 1866.

63. *Minutes of the Board of Governors,* April 21, 1871, June 13, 1871. In 1871, the hospital had discussed designs for a new asylum with architects James Renwick, Jr., Edward D. Lindsey, and Vaux, Withers & Co., as well as with Hunt.

64. Joseph Cunningham and Leonard O. Dehart, *A History of the New York City Subway System Part 1: The Manhattan Els and the I.R.T.* (privately printed, 1976), p. 9.

65. For the Upper West Side, see Sarah Bradford Landau, "The Row Houses of New York's West Side," *JSAH* 34 (March 1975), 19–36, and New York City Landmarks Preservation Commission, *Upper West Side/Central Park West Historic District Designation Report* (New York: Landmarks Preservation Commission, 1990), pp. 9–20. For Harlem, see Andrew S. Dolkart, "The Architecture and Development of Harlem," in Andrew S. Dolkart and Gretchen S. Sorin, *Touring Harlem: Four Walks in Northern Manhattan* (New York: New York Landmarks Conservancy, 1997), pp. 9–16, and Gilbert Osofsky, *Harlem: The Making of a Ghetto . . . Negro New York, 1890–1930* (New York: Harper & Row, 1966), pp. 71–80. For Hamilton Heights, see Dolkart and Sorin, *Touring Harlem,* pp. 88–91, and New York City Landmarks Preservation Commission *Hamilton Heights Historic District Designation Report* (New York: Landmarks Preservation Commission, 1974).

66. The fight to remove the Bloomingdale Asylum from the city was first discussed in Russell, *The New York Hospital,* pp. 311–18, and is analyzed in greater detail in David Rosner, *A Once Charitable Enterprise, Hospitals and Health Care in Brooklyn and New York, 1885–1915* (New York: Cambridge University Press, 1982), pp. 164–86. A large collection of newspaper clippings relating to this topic is preserved at the New York Hospital Archive.

67. In Laws of New York State, Chapter 257 (1822), all of the property of New York Hospital was exempted from taxes. This exemption was attached to an act incorporating the Bank of Newburgh and may have been an attempt to sneak the provision passed unsuspecting legislators. In 1869 (Chapter 875), the act was amended to exempt only property used for hospital purposes. A further amendment in 1875 (Chapter 467) permitted the exemption of property from which no income was derived as long as it was used for purposes for which the society was chartered. This law permitted the continued exemption of the grounds of the Bloomingdale Asylum. Chapter 140 of the Laws of the State of New York (1838) prohibited the opening of streets between 114th and 120th streets. In 1882, the New York State Legislature passed the Consolidation Act (Chapter 410), a bill mandating that the city's Department of Street Openings cut through all of the unopened streets between 59th Street and 155th Street; there were no exemptions in this law. The Governors of the Society of the New York Hospital petitioned the legislature to amend it, and, in 1884 (Chapter 17), they were successful in reestablishing the right to keep the streets between 114th and 120th closed. This amendment was fought by real estate interests intent on developing the asylum property and land nearby.

68. "A Good Bill" and "A Bad Bill" (NYHA, Gerry Papers, Box 15/11).

69. "The Bloomingdale Insane Asylum," *RRBG* 37 (March 6, 1886), 284; see also "Must Bloomingdale Go?," *Herald* March 10, 1886, p. 8.

70. "A Bad Bill."

71. The questions asked in the memorial were published in "Now for Bloomingdale," *World*, March 11, 1888, p. 7.

72. These hearings, which occurred on March 10, 1888, March 17, 1888 (postponed from March 12, 1888 when "the 'blizzard' appeared—but not the committee," referring to the great blizzard of 1888), March 24, 1888, March 31, 1888, and April 7, 1888, are recorded in *Testimony Taken Before the Senate Committee on Taxation and Retrenchment*, New York Senate Document, 111th Session (1888).

73. Testimony of Leopold Friedman, in *Testimony Taken*, pp. 11–13.

74. "Bloomingdale An Incubus: A Blight on the West Side," *Herald*, March 18, 1888, p. 17; "Hot Shot For Bloomingdale: The Hollow Pretensions of a So-Called Charitable Asylum Scathingly Arraigned," *Herald*, February 10, 1888, p. 4.

75. *Testimony Taken*, p. 206.

76. "The Bloomingdale Asylum's Removal," *RRBG* 41 (May 26, 1888), 670.

77. Rosner, *A Once Charitable Enterprise*, p. 177.

78. The *Real Estate Record and Builders Guide* had reported in February that the asylum would move, but the official announcement was not made until May. See "The Bloomingdale Asylum to Move," *RRBG* 41 (February 18, 1888), 206; [editorial], *RRBG* 41 (May 26, 1888), 666; and "The Bloomingdale Asylum's Removal." As Rosner notes, there was opposition in the legislature to extending the tax exemption to the White Plains property, but a bill to this effect was finally passed; Rosner, *A Once Charitable Enterprise*, pp. 178–79.

79. Laws of the State of New York, Chapter 450 (1889); Rosner, *A Once Charitable Enterprise*, p. 179.

80. Leake and Watts Orphan Asylum, *Minutes of the Board of Directors*, May 17, 1887.

81. *Minutes of the Board of Directors*, October 25, 1887, November 2, 1887.

2. BUILDING FOR THE SPIRIT: THE CATHEDRAL OF ST. JOHN THE DIVINE AND RIVERSIDE CHURCH

1. The most thorough discussion of the Cathedral of St. John the Divine, focusing primarily on the design competition, is Janet Adams Strong, "The Cathedral of St. John the Divine in New York: Design Competitions in the Shadow of H. H. Richardson 1889–1891," unpublished Ph.D. dissertation, Brown University (1990). Also, see Robert A. M. Stern, Gregory Gilmartin, and John Montague Massengale, *New York 1900: Metropolitan Architecture and Urbanism 1890–1915* (New York: Rizzoli, 1983), pp. 396–402. Cathedral guidebooks are useful sources of information on the building's history and design; see Cathedral League, *Cathedral Church of Saint John the Divine* (New York: St. Bartholomew's Press, 1916); Edward Hagaman Hall, *A Guide to the Cathedral Church of Saint John the Divine in the City of New York* (New York: Laymen's Club, 1920 and later editions, New York: Dean and Chapter of the Cathedral Church); *The Cathedral of St. John the Divine: Its Progress Pictured* (1928); *A Pictorial Pilgrimage To the Cathedral of St. John the Divine in the City of New York* (New York: Laymen's Club of the Cathedral of St. John the Divine, 1930 and later editions);

Rt. Rev. William Thomas Manning, *The Progress of the Cathedral of St. John the Divine 1934* (1934); George W. Wickersham II, *The Cathedral Church of St. John the Divine: "A House of Prayer for All Nations,"* (197–); and Howard E. Quirk, *The Living Cathedral St. John the Divine: A History and Guide* (New York: Crossroad, 1993).

2. In 1890 New York County had 80 Episcopal church organizations with 37,597 congregants, out of a total population of 1,515,301. Although relatively small in number, Episcopalians were the largest single Protestant group. There were, in comparison, 16,447 Presbyterians, 14,998 Methodists, 14,207 Baptists, 386,200 Roman Catholics, and 35,085 Jews. See Henry K. Carroll, *Report on Statistics of Churches in the United States at the Eleventh Census: 1890* (Washington: Government Printing Office, 1894).

3. The early history of the cathedral project is discussed in George W. Wickersham II, *Crossroads: The Cathedral of St. John the Divine, New York* (n.d.), and is recounted in several contemporary newspaper articles, including "New Cathedral Planned," *NYT,* June 2, 1887, p. 5, and "The Cathedral," *EP,* December 27, 1892, p. 12. On November 17, 1828, Philip Hone recorded in his diary that the bishop "proposed in confidence the plan of a cathedral to be erected on Washington Square"; see Philip Hone, *The Diary of Philip Hone,* edited by Allan Nevins (New York: Dodd, Mead & Co., 1927), p. 7.

4. At Potter's death, his friends raised money to erect the City and Suburban Homes Company's Bishop Potter Memorial, a pair of model tenements on East 79th Street. Unfortunately, there has been no modern critical biography of this important figure in New York's history. For Potter, see George Hodges, *Henry Codman Potter Seventh Bishop of New York* (New York: Macmillan, 1915); James Sheerin, *Henry Codman Potter An American Metropolitan* (New York: Fleming H. Revell, 1933); "Bishop Potter Dies After Long Illness," *NYT,* July 22, 1908, p. 1; "Henry Codman Potter, *NCAB,* vol. 14 (New York: James T. White, 1910), pp. 35–36; and Joseph Cullen Ayer, "Henry Codman Potter," *DAB,* vol. 8 (New York: Scribner's, 1935), pp. 127–29.

5. New York was not unique in emulating European architecture. Urban elites across America sought to re-create European-inspired institutions and European architectural forms. This movement culminated in the "white city" erected at Chicago's World's Columbian Exposition of 1893, with its monumental Classical- and Renaissance-inspired pavilions, many designed by New York architects. The earliest examples of buildings in New York designed to emulate the great historic works of European culture include Richard Morris Hunt's William K. Vanderbilt House (1878–82; demolished), an adaptation of an early French Renaissance chateau, and McKim, Mead & White's Villard Houses (1882–85), modeled on the early Renaissance Cancellaria in Rome. For this period in American architecture, see Richard Guy Wilson, "The Great Civilization" and "Architecture, Landscape, and City Planning," in *The American Renaissance 1876–1917* (Brooklyn: The Brooklyn Museum, 1979), pp. 11–109. For the World's Columbian Exposition, see Stanley Appelbaum, *The Chicago World's Fair of 1893* (New York: Dover, 1980), and R. Reid Badger, *The Great American Fair: The World's Columbian Exposition and American Culture* (Chicago: Nelson-Hall, 1979).

6. The text of Bishop Potter's letter "To the Citizens of New York" was first published

in "A Great Cathedral," *New York Commercial Advertiser,* June 1, 1887, p. 1, and appeared in many other local and national newspapers on the following day; see, for example, "New Cathedral Planned," *NYT,* June 2, 1887, p. 5; "A Great Cathedral Plan," *Tribune,* June 2, 1887, p. 1; and "An Episcopal Cathedral," *World,* June 2, 1887, p. 2.

7. The King James version of the New Testament, Acts 21:39 reads, "But Paul said, I am a Jew, of Tarsus in Cilicia, a citizen of no mean city."

8. James to Potter, May 24, 1887 (StJA, Choir Chapels—General File). James donated $50,000 in December 1887 and another $50,000 in November 1888. James later donated funds for the purchase of Columbia University's property (see chapter 4) and was the major donor to Union Theological Seminary (see chapter 7).

9. This misperception on the part of many was noted in "Not to be Non-Sectarian," *New York Star,* May 23, 1889, p. 6, and in an editorial in *AABN* 32 (May 9, 1891), p. 7.

10. [Editorial] *Catholic News,* June 22, 1887, p. 4.

11. [Editorial] *Catholic American and Semi-Weekly Catholic Review,* October 15, 1887, p. 4. Several years later, the paper derisively proclaimed that St. John the Divine "will be cold and lifeless like the Protestantism it typifies," February 4, 1893, p. 4.

12. "The New Cathedral Site," *RRBG* 40 (October 15, 1887), 1286.

13. Rev. R.J. Nevin to George Macculloch Miller, May 25, 1887; Olmstead defended his actions in letters to Nevin, May 31, 1887, and June 8, 1887 (StJA, Cathedral Site—Selection File). Also see "For the Cathedral," *NYT,* June 10, 1887, p. 8; "The New Cathedral Site," *NYT,* June 11, 1887, p. 8; and "To Rival Old World Piles," *NYT,* November 6, 1887, p. 9.

14. George Macculloch Miller (1832–1917) was a wealthy lawyer and the president or a director of several companies involved with railroads and shipping. He was an original board member, appointed when the cathedral was incorporated in 1873, and was also president of the Board of Trustees of St. Luke's Hospital. See "George M. Miller Dead at 85 Years," *NYT,* November 15, 1917, p. 13; *NCAB,* vol. 28 (New York: James T. White & Co., 1940), p. 200; Lyman Horace Weeks, ed., *Prominent Families of New York,* vol. 2 (New York: The Historical Company, 1897), pp. 402–3; and Strong, pp. 455–56. It is Miller-family tradition that George Macculloch made a down payment of $500,000 on the site, but there is no evidence confirming this.

15. "Morningside Plateau," *RRBG* 60 (October 16, 1897), 542.

16. "Two Ways of Going to Work," *NYT* [editorial], November 27, 1887, p. 4; *Uptown Visitor,* October 15, 1887, quoted in Morningside Park Association, "Description of the Region Between Morningside and Riverside Parks in the City of New York, Including Morningside Heights" (BCA, Box C, File C17).

17. "The Purchase of the Cathedral Site," *RRBG* 40 (November 12, 1887), 1413.

18. All aspects of the competition are discussed in great detail in Strong, *The Cathedral of St. John the Divine in New York;* also see Stern, *New York 1900,* pp. 396–400, and Sarah Bradford Landau, *Edward T. and William A. Potter: American Victorian Architects* (New York: Garland Publishing, 1979), pp. 210–19.

19. According to Strong, *The Cathedral of St. John the Divine in New York,* p. 10, the fourteen invited architects were J. C. Cady, Carrère & Hastings, Henry Congdon, Frank

Furness, Robert Gibson, Charles Haight, Richard Morris Hunt, McKim, Mead & White, Renwick, Aspinwall & Russell, R. H. Robertson, Van Brunt & Howe, Henry Vaughan (who withdrew), Frederick Clarke Withers, and William Halsey Wood. All were leading New York City architects, with the exception of Furness (Philadelphia), Van Brunt & Howe (Kansas City), Vaughan (Boston), and Wood (Newark). Not all were Episcopalians; Cady, for example, was Presbyterian and Furness, Unitarian.

20. Since no list of entrants was maintained by the trustees, the exact number of entries is not verifiable, but sixty-eight is the number accepted by Strong, *The Cathedral of St. John the Divine in New York,* p. 12, and Landau, *Edward T. and William A. Potter,* p. 211. Twenty-one of the designs are illustrated in *Competitive Designs for the Cathedral of St. John the Divine in New York City* (Boston: Heliotype Printing Co., 189–; reprinted, New York: Da Capo Press, 1982). Eighteen designs, including some not illustrated in the above, appeared in *AABN* in 1889–90; see 26 (October 5, 19; November 2, 23; December 14, 21, 1889) and 27 (January 4, 1890).

21. "Art," *Churchman* 59 (May 4, 1889), 558.

22. See, for example, "New Cathedral Plans," *NYT,* May 17, 1889, p. 8; "For the New Cathedral," [discussion of Potter & Robertson and William Halsey Wood's designs] *EP,* May 15, 1889, p. 5, and "For the New Cathedral," [discussion of Huss & Buck's design] *EP,* May 17, 1889, p. 5.

23. "For the New Cathedral," *EP,* May 16, 1889, p. 5. Officially the design was that of Heins & La Farge and W. W. Kent. Kent claimed credit for the design in a letter to the Rev. Dr. Morgan Dix, April 2, 1891 (StJA, Architectural Competition, Principal Documents 1890–91 File) and unsuccessfully sued when Heins & La Farge refused to acknowledge his contribution; see Strong, *The Cathedral of St. John the Divine in New York,* pp. 29, 383. Kent's only involvement with the Heins & La Farge design was this early stage of the competition. The four finalists' designs were printed in *AABN* 32 (May 9, 1891). Each design was also illustrated and discussed in the *Churchman:* William Halsey Wood, 63 (April 4, 1891), 537–45; Huss & Buck, 63 (April 18, 1891), 623–27; Potter & Robertson, 63 (May 2, 1891), 711–17; Heins & La Farge 63 (May 30, 1891), 871–76. William Halsey Wood published his designs with commentary in William Halsey Wood, *A Description of the Design Presented in the First Competition for the Cathedral of St. John the Divine, New York, Accompanying the Plans Under the Signature of "Jerusalem the Golden"* [c.1890]. The interior of Potter & Robertson's design was published in *AR* 1 (January-March 1892), 260.

24. "The Cathedral Design," *NYT,* May 18, 1889, p. 8.

25. "The Cathedral Competition," *NYT,* May 26, 1889, p. 4. Newspaper articles from all over the country, commenting on dissatisfaction with the results of the competition, are collected in "Scrapbook" (StJA, Box 51).

26. Satterlee to Board of Trustees, February 20, 1891 (StJA, Architectural Competition— Principal Documents 1890–92 File). The text of this letter was published in many newspapers, including "To the Cathedral Trustees," *EP,* February 21, 1891, p. 5, and "Dr. Satterlee Speaks Out," *NYT,* February 22, 1891, p. 3; see Strong, *The Cathedral of St. John the Divine in New York,* pp. 28–29.

27. [Editorial], *AABN* 32 (May 9, 1891), 77; "Bishop Potter No Nepotist," *NYT,* June 24,

1889, p. 1; "They May Compete," *New York Press,* March 19, 1891, p. 6; "Potter & Robertson May Compete," *Sun,* March 19, 1891, p. 5. The bishop had recently been accused of nepotism when William Potter had won the competition for St. Agnes Chapel on West 93rd Street. The most detailed discussion of William Potter and his career is Landau, *Edward T. and William A. Potter;* the St. Agnes and Cathedral competitions are discussed on pp. 204–19.

28. "More Time Allowed," *NYT,* January 23, 1890, p. 9, and Strong, *The Cathedral of St. John the Divine in New York,* pp. 26–27.

29. "The World's Fair of 1892," *SA* 62 (January 4, 1890), 2; "The New York Exhibition of 1892," *SA* 62 (January 4, 1890), 1, 8; "New York as a Site for the World's Fair," *SA* 62 (January 18, 1890), 34; "The Great World's Fair—Addresses Before the Senate Committee," *SA* 62 (January 18, 1890), 33, 39.

30. Heins & La Farge, Huss & Buck, and William Halsey Wood submitted their designs by the deadline of March 2, 1891, but Potter & Robertson requested and was granted an extension. All of the designs went on exhibition at the National Academy of Design on April 6, 1891; Strong, *The Cathedral of St. John the Divine in New York,* pp. 28–30.

31. Editorial, *AABN* 32 (May 9, 1891), 77.

32. "Shall the Cathedral be Romanesque?," *NYT,* April 26, 1891, p. 4.

33. "The Architects Chosen," *NYT,* July 26, 1891, p. 9.

34. William Partridge, "Competition for Cathedral of St. John the Divine," manuscript (CU, Avery Library, William Ware Collection—Partridge, Cathedral of St. John the Divine File).

35. Ropes to Heins, September 7, 1892, and September 12, 1892 (CU, Avery Library, Heins & La Farge Collection); also noted in Strong, *The Cathedral of St. John the Divine in New York,* p. 41.

36. Strong, *The Cathedral of St. John the Divine in New York,* p. 145.

37. "The Cathedral Plans," *Tribune,* May 20, 1889, p. 7.

38. Francis W. Kervick, *Architects in America of Catholic Tradition* (Rutland, Vermont: Charles E. Tuttle, 1962), pp. 62, 78. Strong, *The Cathedral of St. John the Divine in New York,* p. 385, questions Heins's religious background, but notes an even greater irony in that the Episcopal cathedral was probably designed by two Roman Catholics and the Roman Catholic Cathedral by an Episcopalian (James Renwick, Jr.).

39. For biographical information on Heins and La Farge, see "Messrs. Heins & La Farge, The Architects of the Cathedral of St. John the Divine," *Churchman* 64 (September 26, 1891), 392; "George Lewis Heins Dead," *NYT,* September 27, 1907, p. 9; "C. G. La Farge, 76, Architect, Is Dead," *NYT,* October 27, 1938, p. 27; and Strong, *The Cathedral of St. John the Divine in New York,* pp. 381–89. The earliest buildings by Heins & La Farge in New York City (and possibly the firm's first commission) appear to be the rowhouses at 123–129 West 122nd Street from 1886–87. Significant later buildings in New York City include the original structures of the New York Zoological Park (the Bronx Zoo; 1896–1914) and the stations and other architectural features of the original IRT subway line (1904–5).

40. Heins & La Farge, *Description of the Design for the Cathedral of Saint John the Divine* (privately printed, 1891), p. 7, and C. Grant La Farge, "The Cathedral of St. John the Divine (New York)," *Scribner's* 41 (April 1907), 385.

41. *Description of the Design*, p. 18.

42. "To Revise Cathedral Plans," *NYT*, October 21, 1891, p. 2.

43. "A Compromise Cathedral," *NYT*, May 15, 1892, p. 4. The alterations are described in "The Episcopal Cathedral," *NYT*, December 19, 1891, p. 9, and "The New Cathedral in New York," *Churchman* 64 (December 26, 1891), 842–43, and are discussed in Strong, *The Cathedral of St. John the Divine in New York*, pp. 134–39. The revised design was illustrated in "The Proposed Cathedral of St. John the Divine, New York," *Churchman* 65 (February 13, 1892), 201.

44. "St. John's Cathedral," *NYT*, December 4, 1892, p. 15.

45. Heins & La Farge's position is detailed in a letter to Rev. E. A. Hoffman, February 27, 1893; also see Heins & La Farge to Trustees, March 22, 1892, and September 27, 1892 (StJA, Cathedral Site—Location on Site File).

46. *Report of the Committee of the Trustees of the Cathedral of St. John the Divine Appointed to Devise a Plan for the Naming of the Chapels to be Grouped about the Apse* (1902), n.p.

47. "The Progress of New York's Great Cathedral," *NYT*, October 18, 1908, sec. 5, p. 9.

48. The chapels, from south to north, are (dates given are those of dedication): St. James, the Spanish (Mozarabic Rite) chapel (Henry Vaughan, 1916), gift of Elizabeth Scrivan Potter (wife of Bishop Henry Codman Potter); St. Ambrose, the Italian Rite chapel (Carrère & Hastings, 1914), gift of Sara Whiting Rives; St. Martin of Tours, the Huguenot (Gallician) Rite chapel (Cram & Ferguson, 1918), gift of Clementina Furniss; St. Saviour, the Oriental Rite chapel (Heins & La Farge, 1911), gift of August Belmont; St. Columba, the Scots (British) Rite chapel (Heins & La Farge, 1911), gift of Mary Augusta King; St. Boniface, the Holland (German) Rite chapel (Henry Vaughan, 1916), gift of George and Julia Bowdoin and their children; and St. Ansgarius, the Swedes (Scandinavian) Rite chapel (Henry Vaughan, 1918), built in memory of William Reed Huntington, a cathedral trustee and rector of Grace Church. The first subscription for a chapel came in 1900 when August Belmont donated between $150,000 and $200,000 for the construction of the Chapel of St. Saviour as a memorial to his wife; see "To Build Cathedral Chapel," *NYT*, May 26, 1900, p. 1. The chapels are discussed in Edward Hagaman Hall, *A Guide to the Cathedral Church of St. John the Divine in the City of New York* (New York: Laymen's Club of the Cathedral, 1921), pp. 51–75. For Vaughan's St. James, St. Ansgarius, and St. Boniface chapels, see William Morgan, *The Almighty Wall: The Architecture of Henry Vaughan* (New York: The Architectural History Foundation, 1983), pp. 86–88. Also see "St. Ambrose Chapel Cathedral of St. John the Divine, New York City," *AR* 54 (September 1923), 233–37; "St. Ambrose Chapel Whiting Memorial in the Cathedral of St. John the Divine, New York," *AR* 36 (August 1914), 129–35; "St. Ansgarius Chapel Cathedral of St. John the Divine, New York City," *AR* 54 (August 1923), 157–67; "St. Ansgarius (Huntington Chapel), 14th Century English Gothic," *AR* 51 (March 1925),

plate 38; "St. James' Chapel, Cathedral of St. John the Divine," *Architectural Forum* 33 (October 1920), 121–22; and "St. James Chapel, 14th Century English Gothic," *AR* 51 (March 1925), plate 38.

49. "The Cathedral Corner-stone," *EP*, December 10, 1892, p. 1. The cornerstone ceremony was described in a number of newspaper articles, such as "The Cathedral," *EP*, December 27, 1892, p. 12; "A Church for the People," *NYT*, December 27, 1892, p. 1; and "Great Work Will Begin," *NYT*, December 28, 1892, p. 1.

50. "Cathedral Builders Puzzled," *NYT*, September 10, 1893, p. 8; "Cathedral Foundations," *EP*, October 31, 1893, p. 7; and "Religious News and Views," *NYT*, July 23, 1898, p. 5.

51. Sooy Smith to Building Committee, January 13, 1893 (StJA, Choir to 1895 File); also see [editorial], *NYT*, February 24, 1894, p. 4. William Sooy Smith was a prominent civil engineer who worked extensively on bridges and building foundations, especially pneumatic foundations. Smith was responsible for the foundations of many of the important Chicago skyscrapers erected between 1890 and 1910; see John I. Parcel, "William Sooy Smith," *DAB* vol. 9 (NY: Charles Scribner's, 1935), pp. 367–68.

52. "Its Foundation Rising," *NYT*, August 13, 1895, p. 9.

53. "Construction of the Foundations of The Cathedral of St. John the Divine," *Engineering Record* 32 (August 10, 1895), 189–90.

54. "The Cathedral Church of St. John the Divine," *AA* 99 (April 19, 1911), 147.

55. Miller records that Morgan said this to Potter; see Miller's draft of a cathedral history, pp. 3–4 (StJA, Box 48).

56. For the crypt, see Charles De Kay, "The Chapel in the Crypt," *New York Times Illustrated Magazine*, June 18, 1899, p. 10; W. H. Thomas, "Glass-Mosaic—An Old Art With a New Distinction," *International Studio* 28 (May 1906), lxxiii-lxxviii; *The Art of Louis C. Tiffany* (1914; reprint Poughkeepsie: Apollo Books, 1987), pp. 47, 49; Robert Koch, *Louis C. Tiffany Rebel in Glass* (New York: Crown, 1964), p. 77; and Hugh F. McKean, *The "Lost" Treasures of Louis Comfort Tiffany* (Garden City: Doubleday, 1980), pp. 37–45. Strong, *The Cathedral of St. John the Divine in New York*, p. 142, notes that the trustees initially rejected this gift from Celia Whipple Wallace of Chicago and only accepted it in 1898 as an expedient way of completing the crypt chapel. The chapel was closed in 1911. It was repossessed by Tiffany in 1916 and installed at his Long Island estate. The estate burned and the chapel was left derelict. The remnants are in the collection of the Morse Gallery of Art in Winter Park, Florida.

57. Donations for the columns are listed in Cathedral League, *Cathedral Church of Saint John the Divine* (New York: St. Bartholomew's Press, 1916), p. 79. The donors were Bishop Henry Potter in memory of his father Bishop Alonzo Potter of Pennsylvania, Ellen S. Auchmuty in memory of Colonel Richard Tylden Auchmuty, Georgia E. Morris in memory of Harry Manigault Morris, various donors in memory of Eugene Augustus Hoffman, Colonel John Jacob Astor in memory of John Jacob Astor, Mrs. John Divine Jones in memory of her husband, Mrs. George W. Collard in memory of Josiah Mason Fiske, and Sebastian D. Lawrence in memory of Joseph Lawrence and family (a donation of only $16,000).

58. A contract between John Peirce and the Cathedral was signed on March 11, 1899, for columns to cost $14,375 each (StJA, Choir—Column File).

59. The lathe and the method of turning the columns is described in detail in "The Production and Transportation of the Granite Columns for St. John's Cathedral, New York City," *Engineering News* 50 (December 3, 1903), 491.

60. Peirce to Heins & La Farge, March 25, 1902 (StJA, Choir—Column File).

61. An amended contract between Peirce and the Cathedral was signed on December 1, 1902, for two-part columns to cost $17,135 each, including cutting, delivery, and construction (StJA, Choir—Column File).

62. "The Production and Transportation of the Granite Columns"; "Moving and Erecting Large Granite Columns," *Engineering Record* 50 (November 19, 1904), 611–12; and "Moving the Columns of St. John the Divine," *SA* 89 (October 3, 1903), 240.

63. "Raising 90-Ton Columns at the Cathedral of St. John the Divine, New York City," *Engineering News* 52 (September 1, 1904), 183, notes that the wood for the derricks was fir from Washington that was shipped overland from Seattle. "Moving and Erecting Large Granite Columns," p. 612, states that the wood was pine from Oregon. "New York's Greatest Cathedral," *Munsey's* 31 (September 1904), 77, reports that the wood for the derricks was pine from Oregon and that it was shipped around Cape Horn. Possibly basing its information on the *Munsey's* article, the same information is provided in H. M. Riseley, "America's Greatest Monument to Christianity," *Overland Monthly* 45 (May 1905), 412.

64. The $25,000 figure is quoted in "Moving the Columns of St. John the Divine."

65. "Moving the Columns of St. John the Divine."

66. *Cathedral Church of Saint John the Divine*, p. 81, records that Morton actually contributed $575,000.06 between 1906 and 1911.

67. All contributions to the cathedral fund, ranging from $1.00 to hundreds of thousands of dollars, are listed in *Cathedral Church of Saint John the Divine*, pp. 66–83. Between 1887 and 1893, the cathedral received several donations of $100,000 or more, including $100,000 each from John Jacob Astor, William Astor, and Cornelius Vanderbilt, and $500,000 from J. P. Morgan paid in five annual installments. The level of donations rapidly declined in the late 1890s; in 1901 general donations totalled only $2061.36!

68. "The New Cathedral," [letter from D to Editor], *RRBG*, 40 (November 12 1887), 1412, and "A Compromise Cathedral," *NYT*, May 15, 1892, p. 4.

69. Henry C. Potter, "The Significance of the American Cathedral," *Forum* 13 (May 1892), 351–59; "An American Cathedral," *Munsey's* 19 (May 1898), 242–49; and "The Uses of a Cathedral," *Century Magazine* 63 (February 1902), 565–71.

70. Late-nineteenth-century Episcopal churches on the Upper West Side include St. Michael's (Robert Gibson, 1890–91), St. Agnes Chapel (William Potter, 1888–92; demolished), All Angels (John B. Snook & Sons, 1888–90; enlarged William Halsey Wood, 1896; demolished), and Christ Church (Charles Haight, 1888–89; enlarged, Renwick, Aspinwall & Renwick, 1892; demolished); churches in Harlem and adjoining neighborhoods of northern Manhattan include Holy Trinity (William Potter, 1887–89; now St. Martin's), St. Andrew's (relocation and major enlargement of ear-

lier building, Henry Congdon, 1889–90), and St. Luke's (R. H. Robertson, 1891–92).

71. "The Significance of the Cathedral," *RRBG* 50 (July 23, 1892), 49.

72. "Three More Arches to Follow the Eight Great Pillars," *NYT*, March 30, 1903, p. 9.

73. Trustee William H. Burr, an engineer, spearheaded the attack on the alleged instability of the arches and piers, particularly noting concerns about the south pier; Burr to Rev. William R. Huntington, May 22, 1906 (StJA, Stability of Great Arch File). Also see Strong, pp. 151–52, and "Warns Cathedral Trustees to Halt," *NYT*, June 24, 1911, p. 1. In that article, La Farge's partner Benjamin Wistar Morris related the history, as told to him by La Farge, of problems between La Farge and the cathedral trustees.

74. Peters to Huntington, July 11, 1905 (StJA, Rev. John P. Peters File).

75. Peters to Huntington, January 18, 1907 (StJA, Architects-Heins & La Farge 1907 File) notes that "there appears to be no question but that the architects have for a long period neglected their duty toward the Cathedral. . . . [I]f this were . . . private work we would discharge the architects tomorrow for failure to fulfill their regular contract obligations." In Peters to Huntington, June 1, 1907 (StJA, Rev. John P. Peters File), Peters comments that the cathedral had "lost an admirable opportunity either to secure efficient service or to rid itself of the present architects." Peters resigned from the building committee in 1908; see Peters to Huntington, March 27, 1908 (StJA, Rev. John P. Peters File).

76. "The Progress of New York's Great Cathedral," *NYT*, October 18, 1908, sec. 5, p. 9.

77. The anti-La Farge group was led by Canon Robert Ellis Jones and included two board members, engineer William H. Burr and the Rev. John P. Peters of St. Michael's Church. Ellis prepared a detailed report on the problems with Heins & La Farge and its design (StJA, bound report). Both Burr and Peters tried to resign from the Board when La Farge was retained. Strong, p. 155, notes that the trustees voted to retain the architect because they did not wish to impede progress and possibly endanger Levi P. Morton's promised $600,000 donation for the completion of the east end of the cathedral.

78. For the crossing dome, see "Disaster Defied on the Cathedral Dome," *Herald,* September 19, 1909, magazine section, p. 11; "Erecting a Large Dome Without Falsework," *Engineering Record* 60 (November 6, 1909), 508–10; "America's Largest Dome. Erected Without Scaffolding or Falsework Support, Two Hundred Feet Above the Ground," *Architecture* 21 (January 15, 1910), 12–13; "The Dome of the Cathedral of St. John the Divine," *International Studio* 40 (March 1910), xiv–xv; George Perrine, "The Construction of the Temporary Dome Over the Crossing of the Cathedral of St. John the Divine," *New York Architect* 5 (April 1911), 56–61; and H. B., "A Large Dome Built Without Centering," *Architectural Association Journal* 43 (October 1927), 131–35.

79. For Guastavino, see George Collins, "The Transfer of Thin Masonry Vaulting from Spain to America," *JSAH* 27 (October 1968), 176–201; Theodore H. M. Prudon, "Guastavino Tile Construction," *Progressive Architecture* (September 1989), 137–38; Janet Parks and Alan G. Neumann, *The Old World Builds the New: The Guastavino Company and the Technology of the Catalan Vault, 1885–1962* (New York: Avery Ar-

chitectural and Fine Arts Library, 1996); and Peter Salwen, "Visible City," *Metropolis* 3 (November 1983), 24–27. The Guastavino Company's records, preserved at Avery Library, Columbia University, contain material on the dome and other projects at the Cathedral.

80. Perrine, "The Construction of the Temporary Dome," p. 58; "The Dome of the Cathedral of St. John the Divine," p. xiv; and "Cathedral of St. John the Divine," *Saturday Evening Mail,* October 9, 1909, p. 14.

81. Quirk, *The Living Cathedral,* p. 127. The choir stalls were carved by the John Barber Company of Philadelphia.

82. A contract for these tiles was signed in March 1909 and specifications prepared in April (StJA, Choir File). Grueby tiles are also employed as highlights in the ambulatory. For Grueby, see Susan J. Montgomery, *The Ceramics of William H. Grueby: The Spirit of the New Idea in Artistic Handicraft* (Lambertville, N.J.: Arts & Crafts Quarterly Press, 1993). Heins & La Farge also used Grueby tiles on the frieze of the Lion House at the Bronx Zoo and on many of their subway stations.

83. "New Cathedral Dedicated with Majestic Rites," *Herald,* April 20, 1911, p. 1; "Rites at New Cathedral," *EP,* April 19, 1911, p. 1; "Dix at Consecration Services in Cathedral," *Tribune,* April 20, 1911, p. 5; "Eminent Men to See Chapels Consecrated," *World,* April 19, 1911, p. 7; "Great Cathedral is Consecrated," *NYT,* April 20, 1911, p. 5; and "Part of Cathedral is Consecrated," *Sun,* April 20, 191, p. 5.

84. "American Cathedrals," *Tribune,* April 20, 191, p. 6; "The Great Cathedral," *NYT,* April 20, 1911, p. 10; "The New Cathedral," *World,* April 19, 1911, p. 8; and *EP,* April 19, 1911, p. 8.

85. "The Cathedral Church of St. John the Divine," *AA,* 99 (April 19, 1911), 152.

86. For Cram, see Robert Muccigrosso, *American Gothic: The Mind and Art of Ralph Adams Cram* (Washington: University Press of America, 1980); Douglas Shand-Tucci, *Church Building in Boston 1720–1970 With an Introduction to the Work of Ralph Adams Cram and the Boston Gothicists* (Boston: Dorchester Savings Bank, 1974); Tucci, *Ralph Adams Cram, American Medievalist* (Boston: Boston Public Library, 1975); Tucci, "Ralph Adams Cram," in Adolf K. Placzek, ed. *Macmillan Dictionary of Architects,* vol. 1 (New York: Free Press, 1982); and Tucci, *Ralph Adams Cram: Life and Architecture, Volume I: Boston Bohemia 1881–1900* (Amherst: University of Massachusetts Press, 1995).

87. *Competitive Designs for the Cathedral of St. John the Divine.*

88. Ralph Adams Cram, "A Note on Church Architecture," *Churchman* 65 (March 26, 1892), 389, and Strong, *The Cathedral of St. John the Divine in New York,* pp. 153–54, 160–61.

89. GHB [sic] to La Farge, November 5, 1907 (CU, Avery Library, Heins & La Farge Collection). Strong, *The Cathedral of St. John the Divine in New York,* p. 154 notes that the condemnation of the cathedral design in "The Cathedral of St. John the Divine: A Criticism," *AA* 91 (May 18, 1907), 203–4, signed by the pseudonymous "Candidus," is often attributed to Cram, but there is no evidence to support this contention.

90. Cram to Miller, June 16, 1911 (StJA, Cram 1911 File).

91. "Oust Architect Who Designed the Cathedral" refers to this letter, but mistakenly dates it May 6; the probable date is May 16.

92. "Cram Will Build Gothic Cathedral," *NYT,* June 22, 1911, pp. 1–2.

93. Cram to Rev. William M. Grossman, Dean of the Cathedral, May 25, 1911 (StJA Cram 1911 File).

94. Henry Lewis Morris to Miller, October 20, 1911 (StJA, Cram 1911 File).

95. For the AIA see Cram to Rev. W. H. Grosvenor, June 26, 1911 (StJA, Cram 1911 File).

96. "Warns Cathedral Trustees to Halt," *NYT,* June 24, 1911, pp. 1–2. Cram's lack of response to Morris's comments was noted in "Cram Won't Answer Morris," *NYT,* June 25, 1911, p. 2.

97. "Architect of the Cathedral," *NYT,* June 25, 1911, p. 10. Two years later, when the *Times* published Cram's preliminary design, the short commentary recapitulated the story of La Farge's removal rather than analyzing the design, "First Pictures of Complete Designs For the Great Cathedral of St. John the Divine," *NYT,* November 16, 1913, sec. 8, p. 1.

98. "The Cathedral of Saint John the Divine New York City," *AR* 30 (August 1911), 185.

99. "Ousted Architect of Cathedral Back," *NYT,* June 28, 1911, p. 11.

100. Cram to La Farge, March 26, 1921, and La Farge to Cram, March 30, 1921 (CU, Avery Library, Heins & La Farge Collection). These letters refer to, Ralph Adams Cram, "The Cathedral of St. John the Divine," *Churchman* 123 (March 26, 1921), 18–24. In his letter, Cram claimed that only half of this article was his, the remainder "inserted by one of the Cathedral's officials without my knowledge or consent." In a letter to the editor, cathedral Canon Robert Ellis Jones notes that the latter half of the article was not written by Cram and apologizes to Cram "for causing him to appear to disregard the rules of professional etiquette"; "An Explanation," *Churchman* 123 (April 16, 1921), 24. Drafts of the article in the collection of the Cathedral of St. John the Divine's Archive show that Jones was in fact the author of the additions, although he does not admit this in his letter to the *Churchman.* Jones had long campaigned against Heins & La Farge's work.

101. This issue was explored by Ann S. Fowler in "Architects and Gentlemen: La Farge, Cram, and The Cathedral of St. John the Divine Commission," paper presented at Society of Architectural Historians Conference (1992).

102. Strong, *The Cathedral of St. John the Divine in New York,* p. 153.

103. "Cram Will Build Gothic Cathedral," *NYT,* June 22, 1911, p. 1.

104. Ralph Adams Cram, *My Life in Architecture* (Boston: Little, Brown & Co., 1936), p. 172.

105. Quoted in Alfred D. F. Hamlin, *A Study of the Design for The Cathedral of St. John the Divine* (1924), p. 17. Hamlin's work is the best analysis of Cram's design. Hamlin was a professor of architecture at Columbia University and an adviser to the cathedral's trustees. Cram described the design and the history of his association with the cathedral in *My Life in Architecture,* pp. 167–84.

106. Cram discusses these aspects of his design in *My Life in Architecture,* p. 173.

107. For the twin-spired proposal, see, for example, "Design Proposed for the Comple-

tion of the Cathedral of St. John the Divine, New York," *AA* 104 (December 17, 1913), plates, and George Martin Huss, "Should St. John the Divine Have One or Two Spires," *Art World* 3 (October 1917), 20–27. For the octagonal crossing tower, see, for example, Hamlin, *A Study of the Designs,* pp. 20–21, and "Contract Let for Nave of Cathedral of St. John the Divine," *RRBG* 115 (January 31, 1925), 7. For the square tower, see, for example, "Final and Accepted Design, Central Tower of the Cathedral of St. John the Divine, New York," *AA* 131 (February 20, 1927), 209–12, and Wilfred E. Anthony, "The New Crossing at Saint John the Divine," *Architecture* 55 (March 1927), 143–46. The design of the tower is discussed in Strong, *The Cathedral of St. John the Divine in New York,* pp. 166–70.

108. The pulpit was a gift of Olivia Egleston Phelps Stokes in memory of her sister Caroline Phelps Stokes. The two sisters had previously donated St. Paul's Chapel to Columbia University, also designed by Howells & Stokes (see chapter 5). The pulpit is illustrated in "Out of Doors Pulpit Cathedral of St. John the Divine Morningside Heights New York," *AA* 108 (September 8, 1915).

109. "Educational Building on Cathedral Grounds," *RRBG* 84 (August 21, 1909), 345; "Church Training School," *NYT,* May 1, 1910, p. 3; and "Training School Cornerstone Laid," *NYT,* May 8, 1910, p. 12. St. Faith's House was erected with funds provided in a bequest from Rev. Charles Comfort Tiffany in memory of his wife Julia Wheeler Tiffany. The building now houses the cathedral archives and library, offices, and residences for staff.

110. Cram to E. R. L. Gould, June 18, 1913 (StJA, Synod House File). Also see "Plan a Convention Hall," *NYT,* December 3, 1910, p. 5; "To Build New Synod Hall," *NYT,* November 29, 1911, p. 6; "Plan for New Synod Hall on Cathedral Heights," *NYT,* March 1, 1912, p. 6; "New Buildings on Cathedral Grounds," December 21, 1912; "New Buildings on Cathedral Grounds," October 11, 1913; Cathedral League, pp. 43–45; and "Synod House, Cathedral of St. John the Divine, New York," *AA* 104 (December 17, 1913), plates.

111. Cram to Dean Grosvenor, December 1, 1911 (StJA, Synod House File).

112. The full iconography is described in Hall, *A Guide to the Cathedral,* pp. 82–86. The subjects were chosen on the recommendation of Mrs. Bayard Cutting. The sculptor who created the often witty figures was John Evans & Co. of Boston. See, Cram to R. Fulton Cutting, March 4, 1913; Cram to Cutting, March 7, 1913; Cram to Dean Grosvenor, April 1, 1913; Cram to Cutting, March 8, 1913; and Cram to Grosvenor, February 4, 1914 (StJA, Synod House File).

113. The woodwork is by William F. Ross & Co. of Cambridge and the glass by Charles J. Connick of Boston.

114. "For a Cathedral Choir," *NYT,* April 1, 1906, sec. 4, p. 4, presents a picturesque preliminary design by Babb, Cook & Willard and Winthrop Welch, Associated; by the time the building was erected, only Cook and Welch were involved; "New Buildings on Cathedral Grounds, *RRBG* 90 (December 21, 1912), 1165; "New Buildings on Cathedral Grounds," *RRBG* 92 (October 11, 1913), 659–60; "Choir School at the Cathedral of St. John the Divine," *AR* 36 (August 1914), 142; and Cathedral League,

Cathedral Church of Saint John the Divine (New York: St. Bartholomew's Press, 1916), pp. 38–40. The Choir School was a gift of Mrs. J. Jarrett Blodgett in memory of her father John Hinman Sherwood.

115. Cram to Dean Grosvenor, September 16, 1912 (StJA, Cathedral House to 1912 File). The Bishop's House and Deanery were donated by Helen Slade Ogilvie as a memorial to her husband Clinton Ogilvie. The main floors of the Bishop's House are now offices for the cathedral, including the office of the dean. The bishop lives on the upper two floors. The Deanery retains its original use. "Start Bishop Greer's Home," *NYT,* November 9, 1913, p. 10; "The Bishop's House and Deanery at the Cathedral of St. John the Divine New York," *AR* 36 (August 1914), 136–41; "New Buildings on Cathedral Grounds" (October 11, 1913); and Cathedral League, *Cathedral Church of St. John the Divine,* p. 45.

116. Miller to Greer, April 26, 1912, and Greer to Miller, May 2, 1912 (in StJA, Cathedral House to 1912 File).

117. Cram to Dean William M. Grosvenor, September 16, 1912 (StJA, Cathedral House to 1912 File). This letter quotes an earlier letter from Grosvenor to Cram.

118. Cram to Grosvenor, September 16, 1912.

119. "Halt Work at Cathedral," *NYT,* November 19, 1916, p. 8.

120. Work on the baptistry began on May 29, 1924 and it was consecrated on April 15, 1928. The Stuyvesants donated a total of $305,861.13 for the baptistry and an additional $24,000, between 1929 and 1940, for adjoining passageways; see "Contributions made by the Stuyvesants" (StJA, Choir Baptistry 1927—File).

121. The full iconography is detailed in "A Description of the Baptistry in the Cathedral of St. John the Divine New York City," prepared by Cram & Ferguson and accompanied by a letter from Frank E. Cleveland (architect in the Cram & Ferguson Office) to Manning, March 13, 1928 (StJA, Choir Baptistry 1927- File).

122. "15,000 Pack Madison Square Garden in $15,000,000 Cathedral Fund Drive; Bishop Announces $4,100,000 Pledges," *NYT,* January 19, 1925, pp. 1–2; "Cathedral Likened to Shrines of Old," *NYT,* January 19, 1925, p. 3; "Crush at Garden; 5,000 Turned Away," *NYT,* January 19, 1925, p. 3; and "The Cathedral Appeal," [editorial] *NYT,* January 20, 1925, p. 20.

123. "Contract Let for Nave of Cathedral of St. John the Divine," *RRBG* 115 (January 31, 1925), 7, 10.

124. "Start Tomorrow on St. John Front," *NYT,* January 6, 1925, p. 1, and "Active Work Begun on Cathedral Front," *NYT,* May 7, 1925, p. 21.

125. "Cathedral of St. John the Divine, New York City," *Architecture* 53 (June 1926), 163. The north transept (still unfinished) was to be dedicated to the Blessed Mother.

126. "15,000 Pack Madison Square Garden," p. 2.

127. "Rockefeller Seeks Union in Cathedral," *NYT,* February 7, 1925, p. 1; also see "J. D. Rockefeller Jr. Subscribes $500,000 To Cathedral Fund," *NYT,* February 6, 1925, p. 1.

128. Manning to Rockefeller, February 5, 1925 (RAC, RFA, Religious Interests, Record Group 2, OMR, Box 18, File 117).

129. William T. Manning, "To the Builders of the Cathedral of St. John the Divine," introduction to *The Cathedral of St. John the Divine: Its Progress Pictured* (1928).

130. Rt. Rev. William T. Manning, D.D., "The Progress of the Cathedral of Saint John the Divine," *Living Church* 90 (May 26, 1934), pp. 945–48; reprinted as pamphlet (1934).

131. "10,000 in St. John's See Great Vista to Altar Opened," *NYT,* December 1, 1941, p. 1; "12,000 At Rites Opening Length of Cathedral," *Sun,* December 1, 1941, p. 3; and "15,000 at St. John's Cathedral See Entire Interior Opened," *HT,* December 1, 1941, p. 1.

132. Philip N. Youtz, "American Architecture Emerges from the Stone Age," *Creative Art* 10 (January 1932), 17–18.

133. "St. John's Halts Construction Until After War," *HT* January 6, 1943, p. 15.

134. "$10,000,000 Sought To Aid Cathedral," *NYT,* June 4, 1945, p. 1; "Manning Delays Cathedral Drive," *NYT,* October 15, 1945, p. 12; and "St. John's Fund Drive Halted by Bishop Manning," *HT* October 15, 1945, p.24.

135. Paul Goldberger, "St. John Cathedral: The Slow Finishing Touch," *NYT,* September 30, 1982, p. B17.

136. For Cathedral Stoneworks, see Stanley Abercrombie, "Stepping Stones," *Historic Preservation* 44 (September/October 1992), 28–37, 88,

137. William Bryant Logan, "The Gothic Cathedral According to Calatrava: Completion of the New York Cathedral," *Lotus International* 72 (1992), 64–69; Jayne Merkel, "A Nature Sanctuary: St. John Biosphere Competition," *Competition* 2 (Winter 1992), 15–21; Karen Salomon, "Ecological Sanctuary," *Architecture* 80 (September 1991), 35; and "Tree of Life," *Architectural Review* 190 (April 1992), 34–37.

138. "To Build Again," fundraising brochure (c. 1984) (CU, Avery Library, Guastavino Collection, St. John the Divine, File 1).

139. "Southern Rector Chosen to Lead St. John the Divine," *NYT,* September 28, 1996, p. 25.

140. Interview with vice president for planning and special projects Stephen Facey, February 18, 1997; also see "Chip, Chip, Chip . . . ," *NYT,* March 9, 1997, sec. 13, p. 2, and Nina Rappaport, "Resurrecting Religious Buildings," *Oculus* 59 (April 1997), 5.

141. For the development of Rockefeller's religious beliefs and their relationship to his philanthropic ventures, see Albert F. Schenkel, *The Rich Man and the Kingdom: John D. Rockefeller, Jr., and the Protestant Establishment* (Minneapolis: Fortress Press, 1995).

142. Rockefeller to Greer, January 24, 1917 (RAC, RFA, Religious Interests, Record Group 2, OMR, Box 17, Folder 116).

143. Manning to Rockefeller, June 11, 1924; an almost identical statement was made in a letter of October 17, 1924 (RAC, RFA, Religious Interests, Record Group 2, OMR, Box 17, Folder 116).

144. Rockefeller to Manning, February 4, 1925 (RAC, RFA, Religious Interests, Record Group 2, OMR, Box 18, Folder 117).

145. Wise to Rockefeller, February 9, 1925 (RAC, RFA, Religious Interests, Record Group 2, OMR, Box 17, Folder 116).

146. Manning to Rockefeller, February 5, 1925 (RAC, RFA, Religious Interests, Record Group 2, OMR, Box 18, Folder 117). For Manning, see E. R. Hardy, "William Thomas Manning," *DAB*, vol. 4 (New York: Scribner's, 1974), pp. 546–48.

147. "J. D. Rockefeller Jr. Subscribes $500,000 To Cathedral Fund."

148. Rockefeller to Manning, February 20, 1925 (RAC, RFA, Religious Interests, Record Group 2, OMR, Box 18, Folder 117). Almost a decade later, Andrew Landale Drummond commented on Manning's lack of interest in ecumenicism, noting that "this cathedral, built by the subscriptions of men of all creeds, is the metropolitan seat of an ecclesiastic like Bishop Manning, a High Churchman of limited outlook who makes every effort to restrain liberal Episcopalians from fraternizing with other denominations." Andrew Landale Drummond, *The Church Architecture of Protestantism: An Historical and Constructive Study* (Edinburgh: T.& T. Clark, 1934), p. 116; also quoted, in part, in Stern, *New York 1930*, pp. 155–56.

149. "Rockefeller Seeks Union in Cathedral," *NYT*, February 7, 1925, p. 4, and "Church Unity Is Rockefeller Jr. Cathedral Plea," *Tribune*, February 27, 1925, p. 4.

150. The most complete source on Fosdick is Robert Moats Miller, *Harry Emerson Fosdick: Preacher, Pastor, Prophet* (New York: Oxford University Press, 1985).

151. International House was organized in 1910 as the Intercollegiate Cosmopolitan Club to bring together foreign and American students as a means of fostering international brotherhood. This project appealed to Rockefeller since he was a strong supporter of the idea that peace would come only through international understanding. Accordingly, he had been a supporter of the League of Nations and would provide the land upon which the United Nations was erected. Rockefeller promised $1.8 million for the construction of International House, but eventually donated considerably more. "List of the Donations Made by Rockefeller," *HT*, May 12, 1960, p. 20 indicates that Rockefeller gave $6,663,000 to International House. The large, but simple building (Rockefeller insisted on a simple facade) had 525 small bedrooms and large public rooms. There is considerable material on International House at RAC, RFA, Educational Interests Series, 2, OMR, Boxes 10–11.

152. Edmonds to Rockefeller, January 20, 1925. (RAC, RFA, Religious Interests, Record Group 2, OMR, Box 72, Folder 559).

153. For the Park Avenue Baptist Church, see "The Park Avenue Baptist Church," *Architecture* 45 (June 1922), 175–80, plates 81–86; "Park Avenue Baptist Church, New York," *A&B* 54 (June 1922), 59–60 and plates; and Stern, *New York 1930*, p. 149.

154. James B. Colgate (board member of Park Avenue Baptist Church) to Rockefeller, January 12, 1925 (RAC, RFA, Religious Interests, Record Group 2, OMR, Box 72, Folder 559), and Schenkel, *The Rich Man and the Kingdom*, p. 175.

155. "Harry Emerson Fosdick Dies; Liberal Led Riverside Church," *NYT*, October 6, 1969, p. 47; also quoted in Miller, *Harry Emerson Fosdick*, p. 162, and Schenkel, *The Rich Man and the Kingdom*, p. 176.

156. Fosdick to Edward L. Ballard (board member of the Park Avenue Baptist Church),

April 17, 1925 (RAC, RFA, Religious Interests, Record Group 2, OMR, Box 72, Folder 558); Dr. Fosdick Called By Park Av. Baptists Insists on Changes," *NYT,* May 16, 1925, p. 1; "Park Avenue Baptists Call Dr. Fosdick," *HT,* May 16, 1925, p. 1; and Dr. Fosdick Accepts Call; Will Create a Liberal Church," *NYT,* May 29, 1925, p. 1.

157. "The Purpose of the Church," in *The Riverside Church in the City of New York: A Handbook of the Institution and its Building* (New York: The Riverside Church, 1931), p. 9. Since the Park Avenue Baptist Church had been completed only recently, there was some concern that members of the congregation would not support leaving the new building. The church board, which supported the move, promised that none of the cost of construction on the new church would be borne by members of the congregation; see memo, May 1925 (RAC, RFA, Religious Interests, Record Group 2, OMR, Box 72, Folder 558). There was dissension from about 15 percent of the congregation, both because of the abandonment of the Park Avenue site and because of Fosdick's liberal teachings, especially his request that the name of the new church exclude a denominational title. This issue is discussed in Miller, *Harry Emerson Fosdick,* p. 163–64.

158. Rockefeller to Collens, December 13, 1926 (RAC, RFA, Religious Interests, Record Group 2, OMR, Box 77, Folder 602).

159. T-Square, "The Sky Line," *New Yorker* 6 (November 29, 1930), 82.

160. Rockefeller actually purchased the Morningside Drive blockfront between West 117th and 118th streets (part of the site initially sought by the cathedral's trustees) which contained two apartment houses; see "Rockefeller Jr. Buys Plot Uptown," *NYT,* May 26, 1925, p. 8. This purchase irked Columbia's president Nicholas Murray Butler, who had hoped to purchase much of the land east of the university's campus. Rockefeller responded that Butler could not count on securing property at some later date; see Butler to Rockefeller, May 29, 1925, and Rockefeller to Butler, June 6, 1925 (RAC, RFA, Religious Interests, Record Group 2, OMR, Box 64 Folder 496). Rockefeller was most interested in a blockfront closer to the cathedral, between 115th and 116th streets. However, this location contained cooperative apartment houses and he was unable to complete negotiations with a few of the stockholders; Rockefeller to Fosdick, June 18 and July 6, 1925 (RAC, RFA, Religious Interests, Record Group 2, OMR, Box 72, Folder 558).

161. "Dr. Fosdick and the Church Tomorrow," *Churchman* 131 (May 23, 1925), 8.

162. The apartment houses were 498 Riverside Drive and the Alderson at 99 Claremont Avenue, both designed by Neville & Bagge in 1909, and the Dacona Hall at 111 Claremont Avenue designed by Moore & Landsiedel in 1908.

163. Harry Edmonds favored a Colonial-inspired design; see Edmonds to Rockefeller, January 20, 1925, and Rockefeller to Edmonds (RAC, RFA, Religious Interests, Record Group 2, OMR, Box 64, Folder 497). Architect Charles Collens suggested English Gothic; see Collens to Rockefeller, September 11, 1925 (RAC, RFA, Religious Interests, Record Group 2, OMR, Box 77, Folder 603).

164. Fosdick to Rockefeller, October 16, 1925 (RAC, RFA, Religious Interests, Record Group 2, OMR, Box 72, Folder 559).

165. Rockefeller to Fosdick, June 18, 1925 (RAC, RFA, Religious Interests, Record Group 2, OMR, Box 72, Folder 558).

166. Rockefeller to Fosdick, June 18, 1925 (RAC, RFA, Religious Interests, Record Group 2, OMR, Box 72, Folder 558).

167. Rockefeller to Fosdick, July 6, 1925 (RAC, RFA, Religious Interests, Record Group 2, OMR, Box 72, Folder 558). Presentation drawings for two schemes are in the collection of Columbia University's Avery Library.

168. Collens and Pelton to Rockefeller, October ? [sic], 1925 (RAC, RFA, Religious Interests, Record Group 2, OMR, Box 77, Folder 603).

169. Rockefeller to Fosdick, October 30, 1925 (RAC, RFA, Religious Interests, Record Group 2, OMR, Box 72, Folder 558).

170. See, for example, "$5,000,000 Church Edifice Planned for Riverside Drive and 122nd Street," *RRBG* 117 (February 20, 1926), 9. Pelton, Collens, and builder Robert Eidlitz are commemorated in three statues set above the arched portal on the west wall of the church's cloister.

171. Rockefeller to Fosdick, February 23, 1926, and Fosdick to Rockefeller, March 20, 1926 (RAC, RFA, Religious Interests, Record Group 2, OMR, Box 72 Folder, 559).

172. "Rockefeller Gets New Church Plot," *NYT,* May 2, 1926, p. 24.

173. "Plans Approved For $4,000,000 Fosdick Church," *Tribune,* December 27, 1926, p. 1; "Rockefeller's New Giant Church to Rise in 1928," *New York American,* December 27, 1926, p. 13; and "Church On Drive To Be The Largest," *World,* December 28, 1926, p. 13

174. Eugene C. Carder, *The Riverside Church As I have Known It* (RSCA, unpublished manuscript, c. 1955).

175. The design and its sources were initially discussed in an article by Charles Collens in the congregation's *Church Monthly* (December 1925). His comments were reprinted in "Plans Are Approved for $4,000,000 Riverside Church," *RRBG* 119 (January 1, 1927), 7–8, and in "The Building," *Church Monthly* (December 1930), 5–9; also see "Chartres Cathedral Model for New Riverside Church," *Telegram,* December 27, 1926, p. 2.

176. All of these design sources were noted by Collens in his 1925 article in *Church Monthly.*

177. This idea of employing design features from two styles, one earlier and one later, to give the appearance of age is found on other late-nineteenth- and early-twentieth-century churches. An excellent example of this is McKim, Mead & White's St. Paul's Episcopal Church, Stockbridge, Massachusetts (1883–85), a Romanesque Church with a west window that appears to have been altered, in a later century, into a Gothic design.

178. The structure is discussed in Emil Praeger, "Structural Features of Some Modern American Churches," *Architectural Forum* 49 (November 1928), 737–38.

179. Walter A. Taylor, "A Criticism of the Riverside Church, New York," *AA* 139 (June 1931), 32–33, 68, 70, 72.

180. Taylor, "A Criticism of the Riverside Church," 70, 32.

181. Taylor, "A Criticism of the Riverside Church," 72.

182. Charles Crane, "Why We Made It Gothic," *AA* 140 (July 1931), 26.

183. Youtz, "American Architecture Emerges from the Stone Age," 17. The critical reaction to the building is discussed in Stern, *New York 1930,* pp. 154–55. Other critics were also troubled by the design of Riverside Church. T-Square referred to the design as "Scrambled Gothic"; T-Square, "The Sky Line," *New Yorker* 6 (November 29, 1930), 82.

184. See, for example, "Einstein Among Angels on Church Arch," *World,* October 4, 1930, p. 4, and "Riverside Church Opens Doors Today," *NYT,* October 5, 1930, sec. 2, p. 5.

185. The Park Avenue Baptist Church building was sold to the Central Presbyterian Church which took possession of the property in October 1929 before construction on Riverside Church was completed. The Park Avenue congregation then temporarily worshipped at Temple Beth-El on Fifth Avenue, loaned, free of charge, by Temple Emanu-El (the two synagogues had recently merged), until Riverside Church was completed; see Miller, *Harry Emerson Fosdick,* p. 205.

186. "New Riverside Church Opening," *Sun,* October 4, 1930, p. 6; "Riverside Church Open," *EP,* October 4, 1930, p. 11; "Riverside Church Opens Tomorrow," *World,* October 4, 1930, p. 4; "New Riverside Church's First Services Today," *HT,* October 5, 1930, p. 4; "Riverside Church Opens Doors Today," *NYT,* October 5, 1930, sec. 2, p. 5; "Riverside Church Will Open Today," *World,* October 5, 1930, p. 6; "Crowds Turned Away at Riverside Church," *NYT,* October 6, 1930, p. 11; "Overflow Throng Is Turned Away As New Rockefeller Church Opens," *World,* October 6, 1930, p. 1; and "Visiting Throng Sees Riverside Church Opened," *HT,* October 6, 1930, p. 12.

187. "Bishop Manning Asks 10 Million For Cathedral," *HT,* October 6, 1930, p. 12; "Cathedral Needs $10,000,000 More," *EP,* October 6, 1930, p. 5; and "St. John's Asks For $10,000,000," *Sun,* October 6, 1930, p. 15.

188. Olmsted to Raymond Fosdick [Rockefeller's lawyer], May 18, 1927 (LC-ROA, Job 527). The Records of the Olmsted Associates contain extensive correspondence on this project.

189. The design is discussed in Leon Henry Zach [a designer on the staff of Olmsted Brothers], "Landscape Beauty and Use: Some Examples From Claremont Park," *Landscape Architecture* 26 (January 1936), 56–67; original manuscript in LC-ROA, Job 527.

190. Zach, "Landscape Beauty and Use," 57; "New Claremont Park Will Be Ready May 1," *NYT,* April 12, 1934, p. 23. In 1935, the park was renamed Sakura Park in recognition of a gift of 1,000 cherry trees from the Japanese government. "Sakura" is Japanese for cherry. The wall and path system planned by Olmsted Brothers are largely extant, as are most of the original linden trees.

191. "Statement," May 23, 1934 (LC-ROA, Job 527).

192. Rockefeller to Henry S. Coffin (president of Union Theological Seminary), May 23, 1930 (RAC, RFA, Religious Interests, Record Group 2, OMR, Box 82, Folder 648).

193. "St. Luke's Sues to Sell Land Gift: $1,000,000 Tract Is Too Far Away," *NYT,* October 22, 1933, sec. 2, p. 1, and "Rockefeller Gets Plot," *NYT,* March 29, 1935, p. 42.

194. Press release, April 24, 1955 (RSCA, South Wing Box, Minutes, Correspondence File).

195. "Fact Sheet on the New South Wing of the Riverside Church" (RSCA, South Wing Box, Minutes, Correspondence File).

196. "Riverside Votes for Parish House," *NYT,* May 6, 1955, p. 14; "Church Cars Put in Basement 'Lot,'" *NYT,* October 22, 1954, p. 31; "Morningside Building Boom Brightens the Area," *NYT,* March 8, 1959, sec. 8, p. 1; and "Riverside Church to Dedicate Wing," *NYT,* November 23, 1959, p. 36.

3 . BUILDING FOR THE BODY: ST. LUKE'S HOSPITAL AND OTHER HEALTH FACILITIES ON MORNINGSIDE HEIGHTS

1. For the early history of St. Luke's, see *History of St. Luke's Hospital with a Description of the New Buildings* (New York: Wynkoop & Hallenbeck, 1893). The Church of the Holy Communion still stands; in the late 1970s it was converted into a dance club known as the Limelight.

2. The acquisition of the Fifth Avenue and 54th street site was somewhat convoluted. The Free Anglo-American Church of St. George the Martyr had sought to establish a hospital for British immigrants. They had raised a small amount of money and had gained the support of Trinity Church. Since Trinity had a claim against the city for the Fifth Avenue property, the city agreed to release the property to St. George's as long as a hospital was erected within a specific number of years. St. George's effort to build a hospital was merged with the new St. Luke's enterprise and the property transferred to St. Luke's. See *History of St. Luke's Hospital,* p. 11, and Rev. J. F. Richmond, *New York and Its Institutions 1609–1871* (New York: E. B. Treat, 1871), pp. 367–68.

3. Richmond, *New York and its Institutions,* p. 368. Unlike other hospitals with a religious affiliation, the superintendent of St. Luke's had to be an Episcopal clergyman.

4. For the development of Fifth Avenue in Midtown, see M. Christine Boyer, *Manhattan Manners: Architecture and Style 1850–1900* (New York: Rizzoli, 1985), pp. 130–51, and Mosette Broderick, "Fifth Avenue New York, New York," in Jan Cigliano and Sarah Bradford Landau, eds., *The Grand Avenue 1850–1920* (San Francisco: Pomegranate Art Books, 1994), pp. 3–33. Development of this wealthy residential neighborhood culminated in the 1880s with the construction of several mansions by members of the Vanderbilt family. These included the twin residences erected by William H. Vanderbilt (John B. Snook, 1880–84) on Fifth Avenue between 51st and 52nd streets, and the William K. Vanderbilt House (Richard Morris Hunt, 1878–82) on 52nd Street. The area's most significant new churches were St. Thomas Episcopal (Richard Upjohn, 1868–70, burned in 1905 and replaced in 1911–13 by a structure designed by Cram, Goodhue & Ferguson) on Fifth Avenue and 53rd Street, and Fifth Avenue Presbyterian (Carl Pfeiffer, 1873–75) on the corner of 55th Street.

5. St. Luke's Hospital Board of Managers, *Minutes,* April 27, 1885, and October 26, 1885 (StLA). Although the minutes do not mention why a decision was made not to

move, on February 22, 1886, it became clear that this idea had been shelved when the managers considered building a residence for the superintendent adjacent to the hospital building.

6. "A Beneficent Union," *Tribune,* February 24, 1891, p. 6.

7. Miller to Rev. Charles F. Hoffman, October 13, 1886, and Miller to Potter, April 9, 1891 (StLA, Letterbook, 1886–1896).

8. Board of Managers, *Minutes,* February 19, 1892.

9. Board of Managers, *Minutes,* February 19, 1892.

10. On January 30, 1893, the Board of Managers voted to sell the Fifth Avenue hospital property for a minimum of $2.5 million. They soon rejected an offer for $2.25 million. Most of the property was sold in small parcels in 1895 and 1896. The last lot, at the northwest corner of Fifth Avenue and West 55th Street, was sold in 1901; see "The St. Luke's Hospital Site," *RRBG* 67 (February 9, 1901), 226. Revenues from the sale of all of the lots totaled $2,427,650.

11. "St. Luke's New Hospital," *NYT,* April 27, 1892, p. 9, and "St. Luke's Hospital Competition," *A&B* 16 (April 30, 1892), 222.

12. Board of Managers, *Minutes,* March 28, 1892, and St. Luke's Hospital Competition."

13. Besides Heins & La Farge, Lord, and Harney, the seven other competitors were Ernest Flagg; Charles Alling Gifford; George Keller; Henry Rutgers Marshall; Sinclair, Doan & Horsfall; Thom, Wilson & Schaarschmidt; and William Halsey Wood.

14. "St. Luke's Competition," *RRBG* 50 (August 18, 1892), 208. A letter to the editor, "Is It Favoritism?," *NYT,* August 29, 1892, p. 3, also commented on the mistake of permitting signed submissions.

15. The designs are described in "St. Luke's New Hospital," *NYT,* August 17, 1892, p. 9, and Walter B. Chambers, "Architects' Plans for New St. Luke's," *New York Mail and Express,* September 7, 1892, p. 7. Lord's proposal was published in *AABN* 41 (August 26, 1893).

16. "St. Luke's New Hospital."

17. Board of Managers, *Minutes,* September 26, 1892.

18. Board of Managers, *Minutes,* November 28, 1892. The most complete work on Flagg is Marges Bacon, *Ernest Flagg: Beaux-Arts Architect and Urban Reformer* (New York: Architectural History Foundation, 1986). Also see H. W. Desmond, "The Works of Ernest Flagg," *AR* 11 (April 1902), 1–104.

19. Bacon, *Ernest Flagg,* p. 63.

20. Flagg to Miller, November 22, 1892 (StLA). In a letter of November 24th, Flagg offered to pay Clinton's fee.

21. The garden facade of the Luxembourg Palace was redesigned in a Renaissance style by Alphonse de Gisors in 1836–41 based on the original conception for the facade by Renaissance architect Salomon de Brosse; see Bacon, *Ernest Flagg,* p. 93.

22. "St. Luke's New Hospital," *HW* 37 (January 7, 1893), 20.

23. New Columbia," *RRBG* 52 (December 16, 1893), 757.

24. Chambers, "Architects' Plans for New St. Luke's"; quoted in Bacon, *Ernest Flagg,* p. 91.

25. A beautifully rendered perspective drawing, a first-floor plan, and a brief commentary were published in *A&B* 17 (December 24, 1892), 311 and plates; the rendering was also published in "St. Luke's New Hospital," p. 17.

26. The development of the pavilion plan is discussed in detail in John D. Thompson and Grace Goldin, *The Hospital: A Social and Architectural History* (New Haven: Yale University Press, 1975), pp. 118–69.

27. Thompson and Goldin, *The Hospital*, pp. 175–87, and John Shaw Billings, *Description of the Johns Hopkins Hospital* (Baltimore: Johns Hopkins Hospital, 1890). Members of the St. Luke's Building Committee visited Johns Hopkins Hospital in December 1892; see "St. Luke's Hospital Affairs," *NYT*, December 24, 1892, p. 2.

28. "St. Luke's New Hospital," p. 20.

29. Benoni Lockwood [Secretary of the Board of Managers] to Aaron Ogden [Secretary of the Building Committee], December 3, 1892 (StLA, Letterbook 1).

30. The revised elevations and plans were published in *Brickbuilder* 5 (February 1896), plates 7–12.

31. For a history of surgery, see Charles Singer and E. Ashworth Underwood, *A Short History of Medicine*, 2nd ed. (New York: Oxford University Press, 1962), pp. 357–70.

32. Clinton to Samuel D. Babcock [chairman of the Building Committee], February 15, 1893; also Clinton to Babcock, April 5, 1893 (StLA, Letterbook 1).

33. The balcony of the chapel was enlarged in 1959 to accommodate 75 patients, including those in wheelchairs and on stretchers; see "Balcony is Dedicated," *NYT*, October 20, 1959, p. 42. The chapel was damaged in a 1959 fire and was restored and rededicated in 1961; "Hospital Chapel is Now Restored," *NYT*, May 6, 1961, p. 28.

34. The hospital initially planned to erect the administration building and the four pavilions to the east. It was apparently Flagg who proposed the construction of the central building and flanking pavilions, creating an impressive symmetrical design, rather than a lopsided and less impressive complex. The Clerk of the Works was Ralph Townsend, who had previously designed several of the buildings at the Bloomingdale Asylum, including the Macy Villa and Green Memorial Building; see Aaron Ogden to Miller, May 19, 1893 (StLA). The hospital and its new building are briefly discussed in Robert A. M. Stern, Gregory Gilmartin, and John Montague Massengale, *New York 1900: Metropolitan Architecture and Urbanism 1890–1915* (New York: Rizzoli, 1983), pp. 402–3.

35. Flagg had similar problems with other projects, notably the Corcoran Gallery and the United States Naval Academy; see Bacon, pp. 66–74.

36. Flagg to Building Committee, September 18, 1894 (StLA).

37. Robinson & Wallace to Building Committee, October 12, 1894 (StLA, Letterbook 2); this letter is a response to Flagg's letter to the Building Committee, October 3, 1894.

38. Flagg to Aaron Ogden [secretary of the Building Committee], April 4, 1895; Ogden to Cornell Iron Works, April 10, 1895; Miller to Ogden, April 11, 1895; Cornell Iron Works to Ogden, April 14, 1895; Flagg to Cornell Iron Works, April 29, 1895; J. B. & J. M. Cornell to Flagg, April 30, 1895; Flagg to J. B. & J. M. Cornell, May 1, 1895; J. B. & J. M. Cornell to Ogden, May 1, 1895; and J. B. & J. M. Cornell to Ogden, May 6,

1895 (StLA). For the J. B. & J. M. Cornell Ironworks, see Margot Gayle and Edmund V. Gillon, Jr., *Cast-Iron Architecture in New York: A Photographic Survey* (New York: Dover, 1974), pp. xiii–xiv, and David M. Breiner, "Architectural Development of the Tribeca East Historic District," in New York City Landmarks Preservation Commission, *Tribeca East Historic District Designation Report* (New York: Landmarks Preservation Commission, 1992), p. 25.

39. George Baker [Superintendent of the Hospital] to Building Committee, March 1, 1893 (StLA, Letterbook 1). Norrie had asked that his name not be mentioned and it does not appear in the *Minutes* until October 18, 1894.

40. A sketch of Holiday's original design is in Henry Holiday, *Stained Glass as Art* (London: Macmillan, 1896), figure 55b; the completed window is illustrated as figure 55 and the window is described on pp. 154–56. English stained-glass historian Dennis Hadley provided the author with information on Holiday's career and his work in America. Holiday visited the United States in 1890 and began obtaining many American commissions. In New York City, two other Holiday windows are extant at the Church of the Incarnation on Madison Avenue and East 35th Street.

41. Holiday to Baker, March 28, 1894 (StLA).

42. Holiday to Baker, April 20, 1894 (StLA).

43. Holiday to Baker, April 23, 1894 (StLA).

44. Annual Report of the Board of Managers of St. Luke's Hospital, New York (1894), p. 10.

45. "St. Luke's Partly Moved," *NYT,* January 25, 1896, p. 9.

46. Bacon, pp. 96–97, maintains that aside from the isolation of wards, the most progressive aspect of the design was the economical planning whereby identical services and facilities were stacked vertically.

47. "St. Luke's Hospital," *SA* 23 (January 1897), 16. Other reviews of the hospital include "The New Hospital of St. Luke's, Morningside Heights," *NYT-Supplement,* October 25, 1896, p. 9, and Katherine Hoffman, "A Model Hospital," *Munsey's* 22 (January 1900), 487–96.

48. Dr. Robert Abbe to Miller, May 22, 1902; reprinted in *Forty-Fourth Annual Report* (1902), p. 14.

49. *Fortieth Annual Report* (1898), p. 9.

50. Plant to Miller, October 19, 1903 (StLA).

51. *Forty-Sixth Annual Report* (1904), pp. 9–10; "The New Wing at St. Luke's Hospital," *NYT,* October 21, 1906, sec. 4, p. 4. The wing was donated by Margaret Graves (formerly Margaret Plant) from money inherited from her first husband Henry B. Plant.

52. "St. Luke's Hospital to be Enlarged," *RRBG,* 82 (December 5, 1908), 1070, and "New $200,000 Pavilion for St. Luke's," *NYT,* March 17, 1908, p. 8.

53. In 1952–54, St. Luke's filled the block purchased in 1892 with the construction of the ten-story Florence Stokes Clark Building on Amsterdam Avenue designed by York & Sawyer. This was followed in 1957 by construction of the Stuyvesant Building (also designed by York & Sawyer) on the site of Flagg's Norrie Pavilion. A third new structure, erected in 1966–68 on 114th Street (Harry M. Prince, architect), entailed the

demolition of the Vanderbilt Pavilion. The new buildings are briefly noted in Robert A. M. Stern, Thomas Mellins, and David Fishman, *New York 1960: Architecture and Urbanism Between the Second World War and the Bicentennial* (New York: Monacelli, 1995), p. 751; also see "Cornerstone Laid for New Hospital Unit Here," *NYT,* November 3, 1952, p. 29; "St. Luke's Hospital Relying on Faith for New Building," *NYT,* April 17, 1954, p. 26; and "St. Luke's Hospital Dedicates Addition," *NYT,* October 19, 1954, p. 29.

54. "St. Luke's Dome to Come Down," *NYT,* November 5, 1966, p. 23.

55. The first incursion onto surrounding blocks came in 1936 when a new nurses' residence was erected on the north side of 114th Street (York & Sawyer). Building continued on this block in 1966–68 when York & Sawyer designed an uninspired structure for the Amsterdam Avenue frontage that houses the Woman's Hospital Annex, erected as a result of the merger between St. Luke's and Woman's hospitals in 1952, and culminated in mid-1990s with Skidmore, Owings & Merrill's Dorothy Doubleday Babcock Building, which replaced the nurses' residence. A 17-story reinforced concrete staff building was erected on the southwest corner of Amsterdam Avenue and West 114th Street (Harry Prince, architect) in 1968.

56. Statement of Thomas P. Cummings, Chairman of the Committee on Admissions, *Sixth Annual Report of the Home for Old Men and Aged Couples* (1872), verso of front cover. The history of the Home for Old Men and Aged Couples is detailed in *Fiftieth Annual Report* (1923), pp. 5–6, and is briefly discussed in Stern, *New York 1900,* p. 403. For a history of St. Luke's Home, see Moses King, *King's Handbook of New York* (Boston: Moses King, 1893), pp. 442–43.

57. Cady, Berg & See was a curious choice since J. C. Cady was not an Episcopalian, but a devout Presbyterian. It was probably the firm's reputation for institutional design that prompted this commission. For Cady, see Kathleen Curran, *A Forgotten Architect of the Gilded Age: Josiah Cleveland Cady's Legacy* (Hartford: Trinity College, Watkinson Library, 1993); Andrew S. Dolkart, "J. C. Cady," in Adolf Placzek, ed., *Macmillan Dictionary of Architects,* vol. 1 (New York: Free Press, 1982), pp. 364–65 ; and Montgomery Schuyler, "The Works of Cady, Berg & See," *AR* 6 (April–June 1897), 517–56. The original home is illustrated in *A&B* 28 (February 19, 1898). Two apartment houses to the west were demolished for an expansion in the 1920s.

58. "Morningside," *HW,* 41 (February 13, 1897), 162. The only other buildings found to be "respectful" of the cathedral were those of Teachers College.

59. Amsterdam House was designed by Kennerley, Slomanson & Smith; see Stern, *New York 1960,* p. 752. In terms of organizational governance, Amsterdam House is the modern extension of the Home For Old Men and Aged Couples.

60. Suzanne Stephens, "Saving Traces: Hogan Hall, Columbia University, New York," *Progressive Architecture* 59 (March 1978), 62–63.

61. For the history of the Woman's Hospital, see James Pratt Marr, *Pioneer Surgeons of the Woman's Hospital* (Philadelphia: F. A. Davis, 1957), and Helen E. Hanson, "A Century of Service," *The Times: News of the Woman's Hospital* 7 (March 1955), 3–4; 7 (May 1955), 3–6; 7 (October 1955), 2–4, 8; 7 (December 1955), 3, 7–10.

62. The Central Park West site was sold for $345,000; Board of Governors, *Minutes,* November 14, 1898.

63. Designs were received from Augustus N. Allen; Allen & Vance; Cady, Berg & See; and James Brown Lord; Board of Governors, *Minutes,* March 3, 1899. Allen & Vance was selected on April 28, 1899. The design was published in "Architectural Additions to New York," *RRBG* 67 (June 2, 1900), 965.

64. The connection between the Thompsons and Frederick Allen was explained to the author by Thrya Waite, curator of Sonnenberg. Allen & Collens also designed the Canandaigua Post Office, a gift to the federal government from Mrs. Thompson.

65. Board of Governors, *Minutes,* January 13, 1902.

66. Board of Governors, *Minutes,* January 12, 1900; February 11, 1901; April 8, 1901; January 13, 1902; and February 10, 1902.

67. New York City Conveyance Records, Block 1864 (1902), and "Site for Woman's Hospital," *NYT,* February 11, 1902, p. 8.

68. Elevation, plans, and details were published in *AABN* 83 (February 20, 1904). The U-shaped design was somewhat controversial, with a minority of board members arguing that the design should have a straight elevation since the court would be dark in winter and poorly ventilated in the summer, and the east and west walls of the wings, where the largest wards were located, might be blocked by construction on adjoining lots not owned by the hospital; Board of Governors, *Minutes,* January 12, 1903.

69. The completed building is discussed in "New Woman's Hospital is Ready for Patients," *NYT,* December 6, 1906, p. 8, and "The New Woman's Hospital, New York," *AR* 21 (April 1907), 281–94.

4. BUILDING FOR THE MIND I: COLUMBIA UNIVERSITY AND THE TRANSFORMATION OF MORNINGSIDE HEIGHTS

1. The basic history of Columbia is *A History of Columbia University 1754–1904* (New York: Columbia University Press, 1904). Also see Brander Matthews, "Columbia," in *Four American Universities: Harvard, Yale, Princeton, Columbia* (New York: Harper & Brothers, 1895), pp. 157–202; John B. Pine, "King's College: Now Columbia University 1754–1897," in Maud Wilder Goodwin, Alice Carrington Royce, and Ruth Putnam, eds., *Historic New York: Being the First Series of the Half Moon Paper* (New York: Putnam, 1897), pp. 323–55; John William Robson, ed., *A Guide to Columbia University With Some Account of Its History and Traditions* (New York: Columbia University Press, 1937), pp. 3–16; Frederick Paul Keppel, *Columbia* (New York: Oxford University Press, 1914); Horace Coon, *Columbia: Colossus on the Hudson* (New York: Dutton, 1947); and Harold Wechsler, "Columbia University," in Kenneth T. Jackson, ed., *The Encyclopedia of New York City* (New Haven: Yale University Press, 1995), pp. 259–61. The early history of the college is also discussed in David C. Humphrey, *From King's College to Columbia* (New York: Columbia University Press, 1976).

2. The argument over the establishment of an Anglican versus a nondenominational school is discussed in Thomas Bender, *New York Intellect: A History of Intellectual Life in New York City, from 1750 to the Beginnings of Our Own Time* (New York: Knopf, 1987), pp. 18–25, and Humphrey, *From King's College,* pp. 18–54.

3. I am indebted to Professor Robert A. McCaughey of Barnard College for his insights on Columbia's irrelevancy to New York's professional and economic life in the nineteenth century and the process that transformed Columbia into a modern university, as presented in his lecture "From Barchester to Broadway: The Transfiguration of Columbia," Columbia University Seminar on the Morningside Heights Centennial, March 1996.

4. Adolf K. Placzek, "Design For Columbia College, 1813," *JSAH* 11 (May 1952), 22–23, and Paul Venable Turner, *Campus: An American Planning Tradition* (New York: The Architectural History Foundation, 1984), pp. 110–11.

5. The ideals that guided the founding of these institutions are discussed in Bender, *New York Intellect,* pp. 92–107. Columbia College's problems as an institution are summarized by Allan Nevins in his preface to George Templeton Strong, *The Diary of George Templeton Strong,* Allan Nevins and Milton Halsey Thomas, eds., vol. 1 (New York: Macmillan, 1952), p. xxx.

6. Resolution quoted in *A History of Columbia University,* p. 126.

7. *A History of Columbia University,* pp. 100–102.

8. Strong, *Diary,* vol. 2, p. 224.

9. Strong, *Diary,* vol. 2, p. 233; Everard M. Upjohn, *Richard Upjohn: Architect and Churchman* (New York: Columbia University Press, 1939), pp. 153, 223; and Montgomery Schuyler, "Architecture of American Colleges IV. New York City Colleges," *AR* 27 (June 1910), 446.

10. Strong, *Diary,* vol. 2, p. 225.

11. Strong, *Diary,* vol. 2, p. 264.

12. Strong, *Diary,* vol. 2, p. 283, and *History of Columbia University,* p. 129–130. Columbia purchased the asylum property in 1857, acquiring the block's Park Avenue frontage three years later.

13. In 1857, in order to fund the purchase of the Deaf and Dumb Asylum property, Columbia sold eighteen lots on and just off of Fifth Avenue between 48th and 49th streets to the Collegiate Church, which erected the Fifth Avenue Collegiate Church on a portion of the site. The remainder of the Upper Estate was leased for development. By the early twentieth century, several of the Fifth Avenue residences had been replaced by commercial buildings and most of the single-family rowhouses had become rooming houses or commercial establishments. Columbia sold the block between 47th and 48th streets in lots between 1904 and 1909 to pay for its development on Morningside Heights. All of the remaining buildings were demolished after Columbia leased the property between 48th and 51st streets to John D. Rockefeller, Jr., for the construction of Rockefeller Center. For a history of the Upper Estate, see Robson, *A Guide to Columbia,* pp. 12–13.

14. "City Intelligence: Columbia College," *EP,* May 9, 1857, p. 4.

15. "City Intelligence: Columbia College," *EP,* May 11, 1857, p. 2.

16. "City Intelligence: Columbia College" *EP,* May 11, 1857, p. 2; quoted (somewhat incorrectly) in *A History of Columbia University,* pp. 132–133.

17. For Barnard, see Marvin Lazerson, "F. A. P. Barnard and Columbia College: Prologue to a University," *History of Education Quarterly* 6 (Winter 1966), 49–64.

18. The architecture program was established in 1881 as part of the School of Mines; see Steven M. Bedford, "History I: The Founding of the School," in Richard Oliver, ed., *The Making of an Architect 1881–1981* (New York: Rizzoli, 1981), pp. 5–12.

19. As a result of these rejections Barnard College and Teachers College were established (see chapter 6).

20. *Tribune,* quoted in *Cap and Gown* 4 (January 1872), 83.

21. *A History of Columbia University,* pp. 160–61. The Washington Heights property was known as the Wheelock Estate.

22. These additions to Columbia's campus are discussed in "Columbia College," *Harper's New Monthly Magazine* 69 (November 1884), 824–26.

23. For Haight, see Montgomery Schuyler, "A Review of the Work of Chas. C. Haight," *AR,* Great American Architects Series 6 (July 1899), 1–102, and Caroline M. Mack, "Charles C. Haight," in Adolf Placzek, ed., *Macmillan Encyclopedia of Architects,* vol. 2 (New York: Free Press, 1982), pp. 296–97. Among Haight's Episcopal churches in New York City are Christ Church on West 71st Street (demolished), St. Ignatius Church on West End Avenue and West 87th Street, and the Chapel of St. Cornelius the Centurion on Governor's Island. For Trinity Church, Haight designed Trinity School on West 89th Street, the Trinity Offices (demolished) on the grounds of Trinity Church, and a number of warehouses on the extensive lower west side property owned by the church. The master plan for General Theological Seminary was prepared in 1883. Haight also designed more than a dozen buildings and gates for Yale University.

24. The only major published study on Low is Gerald Kurland, *Seth Low: The Reformer in an Urban and Industrial Age* (New York: Twayne Publishers, 1971). Much of what has been written about Low focuses on his political career; see, for example, Augustus Cerillo, Jr., "The Reform of Municipal Government in New York City From Seth Low to John Purroy Mitchell," *New-York Historical Society Quarterly* 57 (January 1973), pp. 51–71; Kenneth Finegold, *Experts and Politicians: Reform Challenges to Machine Politics in New York, Cleveland, and Chicago* (Princeton: Princeton University Press, 1995), pp. 35–44; Melvin G. Holli, *Reform in Detroit: Hazen S. Pingree and Urban Politics* (New York: Oxford University Press, 1969), pp. 165–167; and Steven C. Swett, "The Test of a Reformer: A Study of Seth Low, New York City Mayor, 1902–1903," *New-York Historical Society Quarterly* 44 (January 1960), 5–41. On Low and Columbia, see Bender, *New York Intellect,* pp. 279–84, and James Martin Keating, "Seth Low and the Development of Columbia University 1889–1901," unpublished Ph.D. dissertation, Teachers College (1973). Also see William Gilman Low, *Some Recollections for his Children and Grandchildren* (New York: Putnam, 1909); Benjamin Robbins Curtis Low, *Seth Low* (New York: Putnam, 1925); "Seth Low Dies at 66; In-

valid For Half Year," *Tribune,* September 18, 1916, p. 5; "Seth Low, Ex-Mayor of New York, Dies," *NYT,* September 18, 1916, p. 1; "Seth Low Dies at 66 After Long Illness," *Journal of Commerce,* September 18, 1916, p. 7; *NCAB,* vol. 6 (New York: James T. White, 1929), pp. 348–49; and Richard B. Morris, "Seth Low," *DAB,* vol. 6 (New York: Scribner's, 1933), pp. 449–50.

25. For Abiel Abbot Low and the China trade, see Robert Greenhalgh Albion, *The Rise of New York Port [1815–1860]* (New York: Scribner's, 1939), 201–203, 248; Richard C. McKay, *South Street: A Maritime History of New York* (Putnam, 1934), 323–27; Ellen Fletcher Rosebrock, "John Street's Abiel Abbot Low," *Seaport* 14 (Summer 1980), 15–17; and Conrad Edick Wright, "Merchants and Mandarins: New York and the Early China Trade," in David Sanctuary Howard, *New York and the China Trade* (New York: New-York Historical Society, 1984), pp. 40–50. Also see Richard B. Morris, "Abiel Abbot Low," *DAB,* vol. 6 (New York: Scribner's, 1933), pp. 444–45. In 1849, Abiel Abbot Low erected a stone warehouse at 167–71 John Street that is now owned by the South Street Seaport Museum.

26. The house was designed by German-emigré architect Frederick A. Peterson as part of a pair along with a house for another wealthy Unitarian, Alexander M. White; both houses were completed in 1857; see Elliot Willensky and Norval White, *AIA Guide to New York City* (San Diego: Harcourt Brace Jovanovich, 1988), p. 584. White's son, Alfred Tredway White, was an important social reformer, notable for his involvement in the construction of model tenements.

27. Keating, "Seth Low and the Development of Columbia," pp. 24–41, and Kurland, *Seth Low,* pp. 25–49.

28. The house was commissioned in 1882 from Parfitt Brothers, one of Brooklyn's pre-eminent late-nineteenth-century architectural firms. It has been demolished.

29. Keating, "Seth Low and the Development of Columbia," pp. 48–49.

30. Kurland, *Seth Low,* p. 43

31. Although Low's father and grandfather had been Unitarians, he was uncomfortable with Unitarian theology and, influenced by his Episcopalian stepmother, had joined the Episcopal church in 1872; see Kurland, *Seth Low,* pp. 20–21.

32. "The New President of Columbia College," *Century* 39 (February 1890), 635 (emphasis in original).

33. Low's initiatives are documented in John Burgess, "Reminiscences of Columbia College in the Last Quarter of the Last Century," *CUQ* 15 (September 1913), 328–31, and Kurland, *Seth Low,* pp. 55–60.

34. In 1896, the trustees officially changed the name of the school to Columbia University in the City of New York; see *A History of Columbia University,* p. 160. The official corporate name was not changed by the State Legislature until 1912.

35. Columbia College, *Minutes of the Board of Trustees,* May 4, 1891 (CUA). The appointment of this committee was reported in an editorial in *A&B* 15 (October 10, 1891), 170.

36. "Report of the Committee on Site," in *Minutes,* December 7, 1891, p. 2.

37. The committee did suggest that the Department of Architecture might not have to

move with the rest of the school, but could be relocated at the Metropolitan Museum of Art; "Report of the Committee on Site," p. 4.

38. The "clerk" was the secretary of the board; the title was later changed to "secretary."

39. Nicholas Murray Butler, "John B. Pine, '77, '779L, Lover of Columbia," *Columbia Alumni News* 14 (November 10, 1922), 77. Also see "J. B. Pine, Charity Head and Educator, Dies of Pneumonia," *Tribune,* October 29, 1922, p. 15, and "John B. Pine Dies of Pneumonia at 65," *NYT,* October 29, 1922, p. 30. Pine's contributions to Columbia are memorialized by the Pine Memorial Pylon at the south side of the 116th Street and Amsterdam Avenue entrance to the campus, which was dedicated in 1932, and by a tablet installed in the south transept of St. Paul's Chapel in 1924. He also served on the board of St. Luke's Hospital, was a trustee of Gramercy Park, led the campaign for the adoption of the city flag, and, in 1916, the year after the flag was officially adopted, wrote the lyrics to *The Orange, White & Blue,* a song, with music by Victor Herbert, that honored the new flag.

40. Low to Rives, October 22, 1891 (CUA, CF, Rives File).

41. John B. Pine, "Report of John B. Pine, Clerk to Special Committee on the Change of Site of the College," in "Report of the Committee on Site," *Minutes,* August 22, 1891, p. 11.

42. New York Hospital, Real Estate Committee, *Governors Minutes,* November 23, 1891 (NYHA).

43. David Rosner, *A Once Charitable Enterprise, Hospitals and Health Care in Brooklyn and New York, 1885–1915* (New York: Cambridge University Press, 1982), pp. 182–83.

44. An undated memo notes that the governors of New York Hospital refused to lower their price, but would agree to annual rather than semi-annual payments and to a ten year mortgage for $1,000,000 at 4 percent interest (Columbiana, Morningside Heights Box). This is also reported in "Report of the Committee on Site," p. 2.

45. "Report of the Committee on Site," printed report in *Minutes,* March 12, 1892, p. 3.

46. Burgess, "Reminiscences of Columbia College," p. 333. In a letter from Pine to Low, December 26, 1891 (Columbiana, Morningside Heights Box), Pine mentions "the complete failure of the appeal which was issued several years ago."

47. Pine to Low, November 27, 1891 (Columbiana, Morningside Heights Box).

48. Pine to Low, December 1, 1891 (CUA, CF, Pine File).

49. Pine to Low, December 26, 1891 (Columbiana, Morningside Heights Box).

50. The text of the speech was published in "Columbia's New Project," *NYT,* December 16, 1891, p. 5.

51. The trustees' statement was reprinted in "Columbia's Proposed Site," *EP,* January 20, 1892, p. 7. The alumni meeting and President Low's address at that gathering are reported in "Columbia's Future Home," *Tribune,* February 27, 1892, p. 1.

52. "A Good Step Forward," *New York Recorder,* December 26, 1891, p. 6. Other supportive editorials include "The Removal of Columbia," *World,* December 17, 1891, p. 4; "The Removal of Columbia College," *EP,* January 20, 1892, p. 6; and "Our Coming University," *World,* January 24, 1892, p. 4.

53. The urban site was questioned in "Columbia College," *NYT,* December 17, 1891, p. 4,

and "The Columbia College Option," *Tribune*, December 17, 1891. By February 1892, both papers were fully satisfied with Columbia's decision; see "A New Home for Columbia College," *Tribune*, February 27, 1892, p. 6, and "The Removal of Columbia," *NYT*, February 28, 1892, p. 4. The wisdom of moving out of the city was dismissed in "The New Site of Columbia College," *Sun*, February 29, 1892, p. 6.

54. [editorial], *New York Mercury*, December 27, 1891, clipping located in "Reports and Papers on the New Site of Columbia College," compiled by George L. Rives (Columbiana).

55. [editorial], *RRBG* 48 (December 19, 1891), 787.

56. "The Real-Estate Market," *EP*, December 19, 1891, p. 4.

57. New York University took an option on the estate of H. W. T. Mali in May 1891; see Theodore Francis Jones, ed., *New York University 1832–1932* (New York: New York University Press, 1933), pp. 149–50, 155–56.

58. Schiff apparently proposed the affiliation in a letter to Low written on December 22, 1891. Low responded the following day (CUA, CF, Schiff File). For Schiff and his philanthropy, see Cyrus Adler, *Jacob H. Schiff: His Life and Letters* (Garden City: Doubleday, Doran and Co., 1928).

59. In 1892, Schiff donated $5,000 to the fund for purchasing the Morningside Heights property; see John B. Pine, compiler, *Gifts and Endowments With the Names of Benefactors 1754–1904* (New York: Columbia University, 1904), p. 36. Schiff later gave additional gifts for scholarships and endowments, and was a generous donor to Barnard College; see Adler, *Jacob H. Schiff*, vol. 2, pp. 8–17.

60. Rives to Low, May 9, 1892 (CUA, CF, Rives File).

61. Pine to Low, December 29, 1891 (CUA, CF, Pine File); also see Jones, *New York University*, pp. 151–55.

62. The letters between Low and MacCracken are collected in "Correspondence Relating to a Union Between Columbia College and the University of the City of New York," printed report in *Minutes*, February 5, 1894.

63. Pine, *Gifts and Endowments*, p. 36.

64. Low to William Waldorf Astor [this letter is simply addressed to "Mr. Astor," but William Waldorf was the head of the family in the 1890s], January 20, 1892; Low to Andrew Carnegie, January 20, 1892; and Low to Theodore Havemeyer, February 4, 1892 (CUL, Seth Low Papers, Box 13). None of these men gave to the campaign.

65. [editorial], *EP*, March 3, 1892, p. 4.

66. "The Columbia Site" [editorial], *World*, March 13, 1892, p. 4.

67. Low to Plunkett, March 1, 1892 (Columbiana, Morningside Heights Box).

68. Many newspaper articles reported on the alumni petition, including many that listed the names of subscribers. See, for example, "Columbia and the Bloomingdale Site," *Tribune*, March 9, 1892, p. 6; "Streets Would Spoil It," *NYT*, March 9, 1892, p. 8; "Friendly to Columbia," *Tribune*, March 11, 1892, p. 4; "Added to the Protest," *NYT*, March 13, 1892, p. 8; "Adding to the List," *NYT*, March 16, 1892, p. 8; and "Many Sign the Protest," *NYT*, March 17, 1892, p. 6. Examples of supportive editorials include *EP*, March 3, 1892, p. 4; "Preserve Columbia's New Site," *Tribune*, March 4,

1892, p. 6; "The Conditions Changed," *Sun,* March 6, 1892, p. 6; and "The Columbia Site," *World,* March 13, 1892, p. 4.

69. *Minutes,* March 7, 1892.

70. "Friendly to Columbia," *Tribune,* March 11, 1892, p. 4.

71. "Columbia's Site is Safe," *World,* March 18, 1890, p. 10.

72. Laws of the State of New York, Chapter 230 (1892).

73. George William Curtis, "Editor's Easy Chair," *Harper's Magazine* 84 (March 1892),
67; "A Great Opportunity," *Christian Union,* January 30, 1892, p. 194; and [editorial],
RRBG 49 (May 14, 1892), 763.

74. Besides his work on behalf of Columbia, Rives served as Assistant Secretary of State
(1887–89); member of the New York City Rapid Transit Commission (1896–1902);
president of the commission to revise the charter of Greater New York (1900); corporation counsel of the city (1902–04) while Low was mayor of New York City;
trustee of the Astor Library (1883–88), the Lenox Library (1893–1895), and the New
York Public Library (1895–1914; president of the board, 1914–17); and governor of
New York Hospital (1904–17; president of the board, 1907–15). For Rives, see
"George L. Rives Dies at Newport," *World,* August 19, 1917, p. 7; "Geo. L. Rives Dies
in Newport Home," *Sun,* August 19, 1917, p. 7; "George L. Rives, Noted Lawyer,
Dies," *NYT,* August 19, 1917, p. 15; "George Lockhart Rives," *EP,* August 20, 1917, p. 4;
"George Lockhart Rives, '68, '73 Law," *Columbia Alumni News,* 9 (September 28,
1917), 18–19; *NCAB,* vol. 22 (New York: Janes T. White & Co., 1932), pp. 152–153; and
William R. Shepard, "George Lockhart Rives, *DAB,* vol. 8 (New York: Charles Scribner's Sons, 1935), pp. 634–635. Columbia honored Rives with a tablet installed on a
wall in the south transept of St. Paul's Chapel. Sara Whiting Rives donated the steps
leading from 116th Street to South Field and the Cathedral of St. John the Divine's
St. Ambrose Chapel as memorials to her husband.

75. Rives explained his ideas about planning a new campus in a lengthy handwritten letter to Low, April 8, 1892 (Columbiana, Morningside Heights Box).

76. "Report of the Faculty of Political Science to the Committee of the Trustees on
Buildings and Grounds," November 1, 1892; "University Faculty of Philosophy: Report of the Special Committee on Accommodation Needed at the New Site," November 4, 1892; "Report of the Faculty of Law to the Commission of the Trustees on
Buildings and Grounds," November 4, 1892; "Report of the Faculty of Mines to the
Committee of the Trustees on Buildings and Grounds," November 15, 1892; and "Report of the Librarian to the Committee of the Trustees on Buildings and Grounds,"
n.d.; all printed and bound in *Minutes of the Committee on Buildings and Grounds
1892–1895* (CUA).

77. Rives to Low, April 8, 1892.

78. "Columbia College Plans," *RRBG,* 49 (May 7, 1892), 720.

79. The architectural commission and other aspects of the design of Columbia are discussed in Francesco Passanti, "The Design of Columbia in the 1890s, McKim and
His Client," *JSAH* 36 (May 1977), 69–84, and are also discussed in Turner, *Campus,*
p. 177, and Robert A. M. Stern, Gregory Gilmartin, and John Montague Massengale,

New York 1900: Metropolitan Architecture and Urbanism 1890–1915 (New York: Rizzoli, 1983), pp. 404–10.

80. For Hunt, see Paul R. Baker, *Richard Morris Hunt* (Cambridge: MIT Press, 1980), and Susan R. Stein, ed., *The Architecture of Richard Morris Hunt* (Chicago: University of Chicago Press, 1986).

81. Bedford, "History I," pp. 8–9.

82. The most complete work on McKim, Mead & White is Leland Roth, *McKim, Mead & White, Architects* (New York: Harper & Row, 1983). Also see Albert Hoyt Granger, *Charles Follen McKim: A Study of His Life and Work* (Boston: Houghton Mifflin Co., 1913); Charles Moore, *The Life and Times of Charles Follen McKim* (Boston: Houghton Mifflin Co., 1929); Frederick P. Hill, *Charles F. McKim: The Man* (Francestown, N.H.: privately printed, 1950); and Richard Guy Wilson, *McKim, Mead & White Architects* (New York: Rizzoli, 1983).

83. Leland Roth, *The Architecture of McKim, Mead & White 1870–1920: A Building List* (New York: Garland Publishing Inc., 1978), p. 131.

84. Ware to Olmsted, April 15, 1893 (NYHS-MMW, CU, Box 224/226), and Olmsted, Olmsted & Eliot to Ware, April 17, 1893 (LC-ROA, Job File 242).

85. The withholding of information regarding the trustee's design preferences is documented in Pine to Low, December 22, 1892 (CUA, CF, Pine File); Low to Pine, January 12, 1893 (CUA, CF, Pine File); and Low to Schermerhorn, January 12, 1893 (CUA, CF, Schermerhorn File).

86. These specifications were provided to the architects in response to their questions; see "Report of the Committee on Buildings and Grounds in Relation to the Development of the New Site," (hereafter "Buildings and Grounds Report") printed report in *Minutes,* November 11, 1893, p. 2.

87. Haight, Hunt, and McKim to Low, April 7, 1893 (NYHS-MMW, CU Box 224/226).

88. These plans are discussed in Passanti, "The Design of Columbia," 71–73, and in Barry Bergdoll, "Laying the Cornerstone of the New Columbia University (Library) December 7, 1895," *Library Columns* 44 (Autumn, 1995), 14–15.

89. The three reports, "Report of Mr. Charles C. Haight," April 1893; "Report of Mr. R. M. Hunt," April 1893; and "Report of Messrs. McKim, Mead & White," April 10, 1893, are reprinted in "Correspondence, Etc. Relating To Buildings Upon the New Site May, 1892-April, 1893," pp. 10–19, in *Minutes of the Committee on Buildings and Grounds (1892–1895)* (CUA).

90. "Report of Mr. Charles Haight," p. 15.

91. Nikolaus Pevsner, *A History of Building Types* (Princeton: Princeton University Press, 1976), pp. 154–55. The influence of French hospital design is noted in Bergdoll, "Laying the Cornerstone," p. 14.

92. "Report of Mr. R.M. Hunt," p. 10.

93. "Report of Messrs. McKim, Mead & White," p. 17.

94. "Report of Messrs. McKim, Mead & White," p. 17. The Sorbonne was designed in the early 1880s by Henri-Paul Nénot.

95. "Report of Messrs. McKim, Mead & White,," pp. 17–18. Passanti, "The Design of

Columbia," p. 72, suggests that the approach from 116th Street with the main building on a podium may have been inspired by Olmsted's design for the approach to the U.S. Capitol. The similarity of approach is also commented on in "The Future Columbia," *Sun,* October 31, 1894, p. 7, and "New Columbia College Buildings," *Herald,* October 31, 1894, p. 9.

96. *Minutes,* June 5, 1893.

97. The trustees' endorsement of these elements is noted in "Report of Professor William R. Ware and Mr. Frederick Law Olmsted on the Occupation of the New Site," printed report in *Minutes,* May 26, 1893, p. 1.

98. Ware and Olmsted prepared seven alternatives; four are extant at Avery Library. Apparently only one was submitted for review to the trustees. That proposal is described in detail in "Report of Professor William R. Ware," pp. 2–11.

99. "Report of Professor William R. Ware," p. 3.

100. McKim to Haight, September 2, 1893; quoted in Moore, *The Life and Times of Charles Follen McKim,* p. 265.

101. Hunt, Haight, and McKim, Mead & White to Low, September 29, 1893 (NYHS-MMW, CU, Box 224/226). Perhaps out of respect, Olmsted's name was not mentioned in the condemnation of this design. Hunt and McKim had worked closely with Olmsted (notably at the World's Columbian Exposition) and may have been loathe to criticize a friend and close colleague. In addition, most of Ware and Olmsted's proposal dealt with architecture and not with landscaping, and had probably been written solely by Ware.

102. Hunt, Haight, and McKim, Mead & White to Low, October 9, 1893 (NYHS-MMW, CU, Box 224/226); reprinted in "Buildings and Grounds Report," printed report in *Minutes,* November 11, 1893, p. 5.

103. Hunt, Haight, and McKim, Mead & White to Low, October 9, 1893.

104. These conditions are detailed in "Buildings and Grounds Report," pp. 7–8.

105. Issues regarding the choice of an appropriate style are detailed in "Buildings and Grounds Report," pp. 9–12.

106. "Buildings and Grounds Report," p. 9.

107. The design of the University of Chicago is discussed in Charles E. Jenkins, "University of Chicago," *AR* 4 (October–December 1894), 229–46; Jean F. Block, *The Uses of Gothic: Planning and Building the Campus of the University of Chicago 1892-1932* (Chicago: University of Chicago Library, 1983); and Turner, *Campus,* pp. 175–77.

108. "Buildings and Grounds Report," pp. 10–11.

109. "Buildings and Grounds Report," p. 11.

110. "Buildings and Grounds Report," p. 11.

111. Seth Low, "The World's Columbian Exposition," *Columbia Literary Monthly* 2 (October 1893), 3.

112. "Buildings and Grounds Report," p. 11.

113. For White and the NYU design, see New York City Landmarks Preservation Commission, "Gould Memorial Library Interior Designation Report," report prepared

by Andrew S. Dolkart (New York: Landmarks Preservation Commission, 1981), and Leland Roth, *McKim, Mead & White*, pp. 185–90

114. On November 3, 1893, Low wrote to McKim, Mead & White announcing that the firm had been chosen as architect for Columbia; letter reprinted in "Buildings and Grounds Report," in *Minutes of the Committee on Buildings and Grounds, 1892–1895* (CUA). The firm of McKim, Mead & White and not McKim alone was hired by Columbia. Although McKim was the partner in charge of the project, and was largely responsible for the design, he wrote to Low on November 1, 1894: "though I have happened to be more directly connected with the work than my partners, no building is ever designed or goes out of this office that is not the result of our united effort" (CUA, CF, McKim, Mead & White File).

115. Low to Pine, February 26, 1894 (CUA, CF, Pine File). This is a response to a letter of February 25 (CUA, CF, Pine File) in which Pine informs Low of suggestions that he had given McKim for changing the layout of buildings. Similar conflicts are evident in Pine to Low, April 17, 1894; Low to Pine, April 18, 1894; Pine to Low, November 1, 1894; and Low to Pine November 2, 1894 (CUA, CF, Pine File). There appears to have been a strong animosity between McKim and Ware. McKim complained about Ware's comments on his plan in a letter to Frederick Law Olmsted, April 18, 1893 (LC-ROA, Job File 242). After it became clear in December 1893 that McKim would be chosen as architect, Ware apparently attempted to involve Charles Atwood of Chicago with the design project, an intrusion that McKim took personally; Ware to McKim, December 23, 1893 (NYHS-MMW, CU, Box 227). Ware also strongly criticized McKim's final design; Ware to Low, November 14, 1894 (NYHS-MMW, CU, Box 227).

116. The plan was printed in *Minutes*, May 7, 1894, in *Spectator* 34 (May 18, 1894), 61, and in "Columbia's Home on the Heights," *Herald*, May 20, 1894, sec. 5, p. 7.

117. Low to McKim, August 24, 1894 (NYHS-MMW, CU, Box 224/226).

118. McKim to Mead, July 6, 1894 (LC, McKim Papers); quoted in Moore, p. 192.

119. *Minutes*, October 1, 1894. This plan was published in "The New Columbia University," *HW* 38 (November 3, 1894), 1036; "The Proposed Building at Bloomingdale," *Spectator* 35 (November 9, 1894), 178; and Matthews, "Columbia," p. 192.

120. Memorandum, November 3, 1894 (NYHS-MMW, CU, Box 224/226).

121. Although McKim was familiar with this important building, there is scant evidence that it specifically inspired his Columbia library design. The only mention of the influence of the Rotunda identified in contemporaneous sources appears in "Columbia's Fine Library," *World*, October 31, 1894, p. 11, which simply asserts that the Rotunda was the model for Low Library. Jefferson's Rotunda was originally a two-story structure used as a library and administration building. McKim, Mead & White was commissioned to redesign the Rotunda after its interior was destroyed by fire, but this was not until the year after Columbia's design was unveiled; see Passanti, "The Design of Columbia," pp. 82–83; Roth, *McKim, Mead & White*, p. 195; Turner, *Campus*, p. 177; and George Humphrey Yetter, "Stanford White at the University of Virginia: Some New Light on an Old Question," *JSAH* 40 (De-

cember 1981), 324. The Pantheon and its significance are analyzed in William L. MacDonald, *The Pantheon: Design, Meaning, and Progeny* (Cambridge: Harvard University Press, 1976).

122. Memorandum, November 3, 1894.

123. Roth, *McKim, Mead & White*, p. 192.

124. The significance of the Library of Congress on McKim's library design is noted in Passanti, "The Design of Columbia," p. 79. For a discussion of the history of library design, see Pevsner, *A History of Building Types*, pp. 91–110.

125. Roth, *McKim, Mead & White*, p. 193, wonders "why it took McKim so long to achieve the final form of the Columbia Library, when White had already arrived at his centralized Gould Library for New York University."

126. The original form of the lecture hall at Havemeyer Hall is extant, but the hall at Schermerhorn Hall has been remodeled.

127. West 116th Street between Amsterdam Avenue and Broadway was closed to through traffic and presented to Columbia by the city in 1953 in honor of the school's 200th anniversary. Columbia purchased the property south of 116th Street in 1903 (see chapter 5).

128. The same effect could be experienced be entering the campus on Amsterdam Avenue and walking beside Kent Hall.

129. Herringbone-patterned brickwork can be found at the Forum in Rome and at other ancient Roman sites.

130. Low to McKim, Mead & White, December 5, 1894 (CUA, CF, McKim, Mead & White File).

131. "Statue At Columbia," *Tribune*, September 22, 1903, p. 7. In the summer of 1928, the statue was regilded; see *Minutes*, May 7, 1928 and October 1, 1928. In September 1962, the statue was sprayed with bronze paint to simulate the original gold leaf, but the reaction was so negative that the paint was immediately removed; see "Alma Mater, Formerly Green, Gleams With Bronze Brilliance," *Spectator*, September 27, 1962, p. 1; "Columbia Divided Over Redecorating Alma Mater Statue," *NYT*, September 27, 1962, p. 39; "The Ignoble Experiment," *Spectator*, October 2, 1962, p.2; "Kirk Doesn't Like Alma Mater Either," *Spectator*, October 15, 1962, p. 1; "Alma Mater's Color to Revert to Traditional Green Patina," *Spectator*, October 16, 1962, p. 1; "Columbia Alma Mater To Lose Coat of Gold," *NYT*, October 17, 1962, p. 28; and "Green Alma Mater Returns to Campus," *Spectator*, October 23, 1962, p. 1.

132. Robert Goelet, class of 1860, was a wealthy New York real estate owner, financier, and society leader; see "Death of Robert Goelet," *NYT*, April 28, 1899, p. 7, and *NCAB*, vol. 35 (New York: James T. White & Co., 1949), p. 417.

133. McKim to Harriette Gould, December 11, 1900 (CUA, CF, Alma Mater Statue File); quoted in Michael Richman, *Daniel Chester French: An American Sculptor* (New York: Metropolitan Museum of Art, 1976), p. 91.

134. McKim to Harriette Gould, December 11, 1900.

135. *Alma Mater* is discussed in "Statue At Columbia"; "Goelet Statue Unveiled," *EP*, September 23, 1903, p. 7; "Columbia Celebrates 150th Academic Year," *NYT*, Sep-

tember 24, 1903, p. 6; Richman, *Daniel Chester French,* pp. 90–96; Helen W. Henderson, *A Loiterer in New York* (New York: George H. Doran, 1917), p. 384; Margot Gayle and Michele Cohen, *Guide to Manhattan's Outdoor Sculpture* (New York: Prentice Hall, 1988), p. 296, and John Tauranac, *Elegant New York: The Builders and the Buildings 1885–1915* (New York: Abbeville Press, 1985), pp. 256–58.

136. Stern, *New York 1900,* p. 406.

137. Pine to Low, September 27, 1894 (CUA, CF, Pine File).

138. The plans were made public on October 30, 1894, and widely reported on in the press; see, for example, "Columbia's New Building," *EP,* October 30, 1894, p. 7; "Columbia's Fine Library," *World,* October 31, 1894, p. 11; "The Future Columbia," *Sun,* October 31, 1894, p. 7; "New Columbia College Buildings," *Herald,* October 31, 1894, p. 9; "Plans of the New Columbia," *NYT,* October 31, 1894, p. 9; "A Superb College Site," *Tribune,* October 31, 1894, p. 9; and "The New Columbia University," *HW* 38 (November 3, 1894), 1036 (this article includes a plan and, on the cover of the issue, a drawing of South Court, the facade of the library copied from the architect's model, and a view of the rear of the model of the library).

139. A.D.F. Hamlin, "The Modern Dome," *School of Mines Quarterly* 18 (November 1896), 118.

140. Memorandum, November 3, 1894.

141. McKim to Pine, November 30, 1894 (NYHS-MMW, Box 224/226). This letter was a reply to a now lost letter from Pine of November 27th criticizing the design of South Court; McKim quotes from Pine's letter in his reply.

142. McKim to Pine, November 30, 1894, and McKim, Mead & White to Low, December 7, 1894 (CUA, CF, McKim, Mead & White File).

143. McKim to Pine, November 30, 1894, and McKim, Mead & White to Low, December 7, 1894.

144. McKim to Pine, November 30, 1894.

145. Pine to Low, November 1, 1894 (CUA, CF, Pine File), and Low to Olmsted, Olmsted & Eliot, December 10, 1894 (LC-ROA, Job File 242).

146. Olmsted, Olmsted & Eliot to Low, January 1, 1895 (in CUA, *Minutes of the Committee on Buildings and Grounds*). In fact, there was some validity to Pine's criticism of the expansiveness of the paved court and, in 1906, Olmsted Brothers, with McKim's approval, removed some of the masonry and added the turf panels still extant at either side of the fountains (see chapter 5). Olmsted, Olmsted & Eliot was the successor firm to that of Frederick Law Olmsted, formed by Olmsted's nephew and stepson, John Charles Olmsted, son, Frederick Law Olmsted, Jr., and Charles Eliot.

147. Olmsted, Olmsted & Eliot to Low, January 1, 1895. The basins were erected as part of the initial construction of South Court, but the fountains were not installed until 1907; they were the gift of Marcellus Hartley Dodge (who also donated funds for Hartley Hall; see Chapter 5). The fountains no longer spurt water in the original forceful manner.

148. Low to Joseph W. Harper, May 21, 1894 (CUL, Seth Low Papers, Box 13).

149. Low to Harper, May 21, 1894.

150. "Another Call For Low," *Herald,* August 17, 1894, p. 5; "In Favor of Seth Low For Mayor," *NYT,* August 17, 1894, p. 12; and "They Want Seth Low For Mayor," *Tribune,* August 17, 1894, p. 3.

151. Low to Burgess, October 2, 1894 (CUL, Seth Low Papers, Box 13).

152. Nicholas Murray Butler, *Across the Busy Years: Recollections and Reflections,* vol. 1 (New York: Scribner's, 1939), p. 157.

153. Running on the Republican ticket, William L. Strong defeated Tammany Democrat Hugh Grant.

154. The four initial classroom structures were to house natural science and physics, chemistry, engineering and architecture, and the School of Arts; see "A Great City University," *Tribune,* May 7, 1895, p. 3. However, natural science and physics received separate buildings and a building for the School of Arts was not erected for many years.

155. *Minutes,* December 3, 1894.

156. Robson, *A Guide to Columbia,* pp. 60–61.

157. Pine to Low, September 27, 1894 (CUA, CF, Pine File).

158. "Plans of the New Columbia," *NYT,* October 31, 1894, p. 9.

159. Low to Trustees, in *Minutes,* November 5, 1894.

160. Schermerhorn to Low, April 20, 1895, copied into *Minutes,* May 6, 1895. William Colford Schermerhorn, class of 1840, was a lawyer and heir to one of New York's great commercial fortunes; see "W. C. Schermerhorn Dead," *NYT,* January 2, 1903, p. 1; "John B. Pine, "William Colford Schermerhorn, A.M.," *CUQ* 5 (March 1903), 188–91; and Robson, *A Guide to Columbia,* pp. 62–65.

161. Low to Trustees, May 6, 1895, in *Minutes,* May 6, 1895; also quoted in much of the newspaper coverage of the announcement; see "Generous Seth Low," *Herald,* May 7, 1895, p. 5; "Gifts to Columbia," *EP,* May 7, 1895, p. 8; "Lavish Gift to Columbia," *Tribune,* May 7, 1895, p. 1; "Low's Gift To Columbia," *Sun,* May 7, 1895, p. 1; "$1,300,000 To Columbia," *World,* May 7, 1895, p. 1; "Rich Gifts to Columbia," *NYT,* May 7, 1895, p. 1; and "Gifts to Columbia," *The Critic* 26 (May 11, 1895), 351. In exchange for providing funds for the library, Low required that the trustees agree to establish various scholarships and fellowships at Columbia College and Barnard College, many specifically for students from Brooklyn.

162. Passanti, "The Design of Columbia," 76–77.

163. "A Great Public Benefaction,"[editorial] *Sun,* May 8, 1895, p. 6, and "Columbia College Gifts," [editorial] *Commercial Advertiser,* May 7, 1895, p. 6. A significant number of newspaper clippings are preserved in CUL, Seth Low Papers, Letterbook C, Box 18.

164. Gilder to Low, May 8, 1895 (CUL, Seth Low Papers, Letterbook C, Box 18). Letterbook C contains many letters of appreciation sent to Low.

165. Low to McKim, May 10, 1895 (CUL, Seth Low Papers, Box 22).

166. "A Typical Act of a Typical American," *Congregationalist* (CUL, Seth Low Papers, Letterbook C, Box 18).

167. "The Gift of a Million," *Commercial Advertiser* (CUL, Seth Low Papers, Letterbook C, Box 18).

168. "The New Columbia," *Boston Evening Transcript*, May 8, 1895, p. 6 (CUL, Seth Low Papers, Letterbook C, Box 18). These voices of the merchant class overlooked, of course, the exploitation of seamen on ships and clerks in offices, and avoided comment on the fact that at least some of Abiel Low's fortune derived from the opium trade; Wright, *Merchants and Mandarins,* p. 48.

169. Quoted in many newspaper accounts, including "Rich Gifts to Columbia"; "Lavish Gifts to Columbia"; and "Gifts to Columbia."

170. Low to McKim, October 18, 1894 (NYHS-MMW, CU, Box 224/226).

171. Low to McKim, October 18, 1894.

172. McKim, Mead & White to Low, October 30, 1894 (NYHS-MMW, CU, Box 224/226).

173. McKim, Mead & White to Low, October 30, 1894.

174. *Minutes,* December 3, 1894.

175. Pine to Low, November 10, 1894, and Low to Pine, November 12, 1894 (CUA, CF, Pine File). The original section of the Harvard Club, at 27 West 44th Street, dates from 1893–94. The Edward J. Berwind House at 2 West 64th Street was designed by Nicholas Clark Mellon and erected in 1893–96. Both of these buildings are extant. Low again suggested the brick and black mortar on the Berwind House as a model in Low to McKim, Mead & White, October 22, 1895 (NYHS-MMW, CU, Box 224/226).

176. McKim, Mead & White to Low, January 14, 1896 (CUA, CF, McKim, Mead & White File) notes the firm's approval of Harvard brick, although the first choice was a grayish-yellow "Century" brick, probably a reference to the brick on McKim, Mead & White's Century Association Building on West 43rd Street. Low to McKim, Mead & White, January 17, 1896 (NYHS-MMW, CU, Box 224/226), informs the architect that the trustees had voted the previous day to use "Harvard brick."

177. See, for example, "Columbia's New Buildings," *HW* 40 (February 1, 1896), 116, and "Columbia's New Buildings," *EP,* November 19, 1895, p. 13.

178. Ware to Low, December 28, 1895 (NYHS-MMW, CU, Box 224/226).

179. The Harvard gates are discussed in Roth, *McKim, Mead & White,* pp. 147–48.

180. A.D.F. Hamlin, "Recent American College Architecture," *Outlook* 74 (August 1, 1903), 797.

181. Babb, Cook & Willard's Andrew Carnegie House is now the Cooper-Hewitt National Design Museum. Ernest Flagg's Clark House has been demolished.

182. *Minutes,* October 7, 1895.

183. Low to McKim, October 2, 1895 (NYHS-MMW, CU, Box 224/226).

184. "Columbia College's New Library," *NYT,* December 8, 1895, p. 2. The dedication of the site was widely discussed; see, for example, "Columbia's Dedication," *Harlem Local Reporter,* May 2, 1896, p. 1; "New Site of Columbia," *NYT,* May 3, 1896, p. 9; Old Columbia's Proudest Day," *Herald,* May 3, 1896, p. 5; "The Dedication of the New Site of Columbia University," *Science* 3 (May 8, 1896), 681–85; "Columbia's

Dedication," *The Critic* 28 (May 9, 1896), 328–29; "The New Columbia," *SA* 74 (May 16, 1896), 307; and Nicholas Murray Butler, "Columbia University and the City of New York," *HW* 40 (May 16, 1896), 485–86.

185. The gymnasium is discussed in "News of the Colleges: The University Hall at Columbia's New Site," *Mail and Express,* November 28, 1896, p. 7; "The New Gymnasium," *Spectator,* January 19, 1897, pp. 197–98; and "Columbia's New Gymnasium, *NYT Magazine,* November 6, 1898, p. 6.

186. For Engineering Hall, see Robson, *A Guide to Columbia,* pp. 77–78.

187. *Minutes,* April 6, 1896; "Columbia University," *EP,* April 7, 1896, p. 4; "Another Gift to Columbia," *EP,* April 8, 1896, p. 7; Columbia's New Halls, *Mail and Express,* April 8, 1896, p. 4; and "Gifts to Columbia," *Harlem Local Reporter,* April 12, 1896, p. 1. The Havemeyers' gift consisted of two plots of land worth an estimated $450,000: a site 100' x 125' at the southeast corner of Fifth Avenue and 82nd Street, and the blockfront on the east side of Park Avenue between 74th and 75th streets, stretching back 100 feet. Also see Robson, *A Guide to Columbia,* pp. 68–70.

188. Mead to Low, February 18, 1896 (CUA, CF, McKim, Mead & White File).

189. The lecture hall in Havemeyer is largely intact, while that at Schermerhorn has been altered.

190. Charles W. Stoughton, "Modern Brickwork–II," *International Studio* 38 (July 1909), xiv. The bricks were "laid on edge on a bed of cinders 12" thick and concrete 3" thick"; see Norcross Brothers to McKim, Mead & White (CUA, CF, Norcross File).

191. For the history of the brick and its early use, see Lorraine Schnabel, "The Brick Pavements of Columbia University New York, New York," unpublished report prepared for Columbia University Facilities Management (1994).

192. *Minutes,* January 4, 1897. McKim's design for South Court employs the ancient Greek feature of using a slight rise so that optically it will appear flat. William H. Goodyear notes that "McKim, Mead & White are probably the first among modern architects to make the experiment of using the Greek horizontal curves on an extended scale." See William H. Goodyear, "Horizontal Curves in Columbia University," *AR* 9 (January 1899), 82, and Hill, *Charles F. McKim,* p. 19.

193. Low to McKim, October 6, 1896 (CUA, CF, McKim, Mead & White File).

194. The Minerva is a copy of the Parthenon Minerva by Phidias and was executed in Athens by L. Droses for the Centennial Exposition in Philadelphia. It was donated by Dr. J. Ackerman Coles and Emilie S. Coles so that it would be on view on "the Acropolis of the Athens of the Western Hemisphere"; Coles to Low, December 15, 1896 (CUL, Seth Low Papers, Box 22). For the brass zodiac signs, see McKim to Low, September 4, 1896 (CUA, CF, McKim, Mead & White File), and *Minutes,* October 5, 1896.

195. The Trustees Room is illustrated in *AABN* 62 (October 29, 1898).

196. The four sculptures, representing Euripides (gift of Charles McKim), Demosthenes (W. Bayard Cutting), Sophocles (Dr. George G. Wheelock), and Augustus Caesar (Frederick A. Schermerhorn), were designed by Daniel Chester French and

carved by Piccirilli Brothers. They were installed in 1896; see *Minutes,* November 15, 1897.

197. Charles H. Caffin, "Architecture and Mural Painting," *HW* 41 (September 25, 1897), 955.

198. Ware to Low, March 6, 1896 (CUA, CF, Ware File). The dome is discussed in Edward R. Ford, *Details of Modern Architecture* (Cambridge: MIT Press, 1990), pp. 68–79.

199. For Norcross Brothers, see James F. O'Gorman, "O. W. Norcross, Richardson's 'Master Builder': A Preliminary Report," *JSAH* 32 (May 1973), 104–13, and Christopher Girr, "Mastery in Masonry: Norcross Brothers Contractors and Builders 1864–1924," unpublished M.S. dissertation, Columbia University School of Architecture, Planning and Preservation (1996).

200. Girr, "Mastery in Masonry," pp. 63–65; see also, O. W. Norcross to McKim, Mead & White, February 26, 1896; Ware to Mead, March 6, 1896; Ware to Low, March 6, 1896; O. W. Norcross to McKim, Mead & White, May 20, 1896; O. W. Norcross Brothers to Mead, May 25, 1896; amendment to building application, August 7, 1896; and Norcross Brothers to McKim, Mead & White, November 17, 1896; (NYHS-MMW, CU, Box 224/226); McKim to Low, July 15, 1896 (CU, Avery Library); Low to McKim, July 17, 1896 (CU, CF, McKim, Mead & White File); "Columbia University," *SA* 88 (March 26, 1898), 200–202; and Hamlin, "The Modern Dome," pp. 68–77.

201. Norcross Brothers to McKim, Mead & White, June 22, 1896 (NYHS-MMW, CU, Box 224/226).

202. White to MacCracken, September 11, 1896 (NYHS-MMW, NYU, Box M10/1968).

203. Caffin, "Architecture and Mural Painting," 955.

204. Low to McKim, September 18, 1896 (CUA, CF, McKim, Mead & White File).

205. Hill, *Charles F. McKim,* p. 21.

206. William Hallock, "Diffused Illumination," *Progressive Age* 16 (March 1, 1898), 107–109; "Columbia University," *SA,* p. 202; "Artificial Moonlight," *Baltimore American,* October 27, 1897 (article reprinted from the *World*) in "Scrapbook" (NYHS-MMW, CU). The "moon" was hung from the dome, but it is not known if the arc lights were ever placed in operation, or, if so, for how long they were in use. The "moon" is no longer extant.

207. Low to McKim, Mead & White, October 6, 1896 (CUA, CF, McKim, Mead & White File), and Pine to Low, March 25, 1896 (CUA, CF, Pine File). The controversy over inscriptions is noted in Bergdoll, "Laying the Cornerstone," p. 20.

208. Low to Pine, October 12, 1896 (CUA, CF, Pine File).

209. Low to McKim, October 6, 1896.

210. "University Notes: The Library," *CUQ* 18 (December 1897), 38, and Alexander Nelson, "The New Columbia," *The Library Journal* 22 (December 1897), 747. In comparison, the new University of Chicago did not yet have a library and books were scattered in various classrooms; Yale's library was divided between two buildings that could hold a total of 400,000 volumes; by 1899, Harvard's Gore library held

more than 365,000 books and an equal number of pamphlets, but was running out of storage space.

211. "University Notes: The Library," *CUQ*, 37–38, and "The New Columbia Rising," *Tribune*, April 19, 1896, sec. 3, p. 28.

212. J. M. Brydon and F. J. Burgoyne, "Public Libraries: I The Buildings," *Journal of the Royal Institute of British Architects* 6 (February 25, 1899), 222.

213. These statistics include only students at the Morningside campus, not students in the School of Medicine, College of Pharmacy, Barnard College, or Teachers College; see Pine to Committee on Finance, February 10, 1898, report printed as "Letter to the Committee on the Subject of Dormitories," and *Directory of Officers and Students 1915–1916*, pp. 95–96.

214. Butler to Pine, December 18, 1902 (CUA, CF, Pine File).

215. "Libraries of the United States—II," *AA* 77 (July 26, 1902), 28–29.

216. Montgomery Schuyler, "Architecture of American Colleges IV. New York City Colleges," *AR* 27 (June 1910), 447.

217. "The New Columbia," *HW* 40 (December 26, 1896), 1283.

218. The power plant is discussed in Edward Darling, "The Power Plant of a University," speech presented in May 1899 to the American Society of Mechanical Engineers and published in their *Transactions* 20 (1899), 1–58, and "Columbia University," *EP*, June 28, 1897, p. 4.

219. "University Hall," *CUQ* 2 (September 1900), 369–70.

220. "Fire Destroys University Hall; Pool and Power-House Saved," *Spectator*, October 10, 1914, p. 1.

221. "Columbia to Finish Unit Begun in 1896," *NYT*, February 11, 1941, p. 25. For Uris Hall, see Robert A.M. Stern, Thomas Mellins, and David Fishman, *New York 1960: Architecture and Urbanism, Between the Second World War and the Bicentennial* (New York: Monacelli Press, 1995), p. 739–40. The homely facade was partially covered in 1984–86 with an additional design by Gluck & Partners.

222. "The Removal of Columbia," [editorial], *NYT*, October 5, 1897, p. 6.

223. "The New Columbia," *The Library Journal* 22 (December 1897), 746.

224. The $6,879,011.90 included the purchase of a new site, preparation of the grounds, laying out of South Court, the construction of the library, four classroom buildings, and a gymnasium and powerhouse at the base of University Hall, and the removal of the university from 49th Street to 116th Street. More than half of this sum was paid with a loan at 4 percent interest; see *Annual Report of the President for the Academic Year Ending June 30, 1898* (1898), pp. 52–56.

225. For the 1897 election, see David C. Hammack, *Power and Society: Greater New York at the Turn of the Century* (New York: Russell Sage Foundation, 1982), pp. 115–17, 152–53.

226. "President Low to Stay," *NYT*, November 16, 1897, p. 1. Low served only one two-year term as mayor and his mayoralty has not generally been regarded as a great success; see Finegold, *Experts and Politicians*, pp. 40–44, and Holli, *Reform in Detroit*, pp. 166–167.

5. BUILDING FOR THE MIND II: THE GROWTH
AND EXPANSION OF COLUMBIA

1. For the 1901 election, see David C. Hammack, *Power and Society: Greater New York at the Turn of the Century* (New York: Russell Sage Foundation, 1982), pp. 154–56.

2. "William E. Dodge, Dead," *NYT*, August 10, 1903, p. 1, and *NCAB*, vol. 13 (New York: James T. White, 1906), p. 352.

3. Dodge expounded on these ideas in a letter to Low, May 16, 1900 (CUA, CF, William E. Dodge File). Dodge also asked Low to compose a formal letter in his name to the trustees explaining his ideas; Dodge to Trustees, May 23, 1900, in Columbia University, *Minutes of the Board of Trustees,* June 4, 1900 (CUA), and quoted in "Students Hall," [editorial] *CUQ* 2 (September 1900), 367, and expanded on in *CUQ* 3 (December 1900), 40.

4. *Minutes,* October 1, 1900.

5. The remainder of West Hall was demolished in 1913; see "West Hall is Gone," *Columbia Alumni News* 5 (October 10, 1913), 43–44.

6. The dome employs Guastavino tile arch construction, but unlike the use of these tiles at St. Paul's Chapel, the Cathedral of St. John the Divine, Union Theological Seminary, and other installations, the tiles are not visible. For the Guastavino installation, see William Dunn, "The Principles of Dome Construction.—II.," *Architectural Review* 23 (1908), 108, 110 and CU, Avery Library, Guastavino Collection, File 6.193.

7. Earl Hall is illustrated in *A Monograph of the Works of McKim, Mead & White* (1915; reprinted with an introduction by Leland Roth, New York: Benjamin Blom, 1973), plates 200, 202.

8. Pine to Butler, November 8, 1902 (CUA, CF, Pine File).

9. Thomas Bender, *New York Intellect: A History of Intellectual Life in New York City, from 1750 to the Beginnings of Our Own Time* (New York: Knopf, 1987), pp. 292–93, and Harold S. Wechsler, *The Qualified Student: A History of Selective College Admission in America* (New York: Wiley, 1977), pp. 140–41. In 1911, Low opposed Butler's insistence that Christian groups could freely use Columbia's facilities, but that Jewish groups could not. As a result, he withdrew from active participation on the board and resigned in 1914. The most detailed study of anti-Semitism at American universities, with a focus on Columbia, is Wechsler, *The Qualified Student,* especially pp. 131–85; also see Leonard Dinnerstein, *Antisemitism in America* (New York: Oxford University Press, 1994), pp. 84–87. Both Bender (pp. 287–88) and Wechsler (p. 134) note that Catholic immigrants would also have been unwelcome at Columbia, but since Catholics had established their own educational system, including Fordham University, founded in 1841, restrictive policies did not become as central an issue for them as it was for Jews.

10. Bender, *New York Intellect,* pp. 284–86.

11. "Columbia College Dormitories," *Harlem Local Reporter,* December 24, 1892, p. 1.

12. For a history of American university design, see Paul Venable Turner, *Campus: An American Planning Tradition* (New York: Architectural History Foundation, 1984).

13. "Columbia and Her New Student Life," *Herald,* November 28, 1897, sec. 5, p. 3.

14. Henry F. Osborne, "The Dormitory System for Columbia," *Spectator,* December 22, 1892, p. 92. At the time he wrote this article, Osborne was dean of the Faculty of Pure Science.

15. "Flats For College Men," *EP,* March 7, 1903, supplement, p. 3, is a humorous discussion of student apartment life. In 1898, only 37 Columbia students and 41 professors and staff members lived on Morningside Heights; *Directory of Officers and Students 1898–1899* (Columbia University, 1898).

16. Both George C. Palmer and Henry Hornbostel were graduates of Columbia; Palmer was a member of the Alpha Club. The design was published in "Alpha Club, Riverside Drive, New York," *Architecture* 8 (September 1903), plate lxviii; also see Robert A. M. Stern, Gregory Gilmartin, and John Massengale, *New York 1900: Metropolitan Architecture and Urbanism 1890–1915* (New York: Rizzoli, 1983), pp. 416–17.

17. "Delta-Phi Club-House," *AABN* 91 (April 20, 1907), plates. Delta Phi is now Columbia's Casa Hispanica.

18. "Dormitories For Columbia," *Tribune,* October 3, 1894, p. 4; see also "The Dormitory Question," *NYT,* March 31, 1895, p. 29.

19. *Minutes,* November 16, 1896; quoted in "Dormitories at Columbia," *EP,* November 21, 1896, p. 2.

20. "Columbia's Dormitory," *Mail and Express,* November 28, 1896, p. 1.

21. "News of the Colleges: Columbia University," *EP,* December 5, 1896, p. 20, and "Columbia's Dormitory."

22. Pine to Committee on Finance, printed as "Letter to the Committee on Finance on the Subject of Dormitories," February 10, 1898, p. 9. In 1899, a privately funded dormitory was proposed for Amsterdam Avenue and 113th Street; see "Dormitories for Columbia," *NYT,* May 6, 1899, p. 14. The following year a dormitory was announced for a site on the corner of Amsterdam Avenue and 116th Street: see "A Dormitory for Columbia," *NYT,* January 2, 1900, p. 7; "Proposed Dormitory," *Spectator* January 5, 1900, p. 1; and "Dormitories Again," *CUQ* 2 (June 1900), 267. In 1903, Knowlton Hall, a new apartment building at Broadway and 124th Street was adapted to dormitory purposes, but the project was a failure; see "Columbia Dormitory," *RRBG* 71 (June 6, 1903), 1121; "Students at Knowlton Hall," *Spectator,* January 11, 1904, p. 1; and "Knowlton Hall Closes," *Spectator,* February 24, 1904, p. 1.

23. Pine to Committee on Finance, pp. 17–18.

24. Pine to Low, December 8, 1898 (CUA, CF, Pine File).

25. *Minutes,* November 16, 1898; "Dormitories," *CUQ* 1 (December 1898), 60–63; Low to Pine, June 23, 1898 (CUA, CF, Pine File); Seth Low, *Annual Report of the President for the Academic Year Ending June 30, 1898* (1898), pp. 62–64.

26. "Columbia and Her New Student Life."

27. "Columbia's New College Spirit," *Sun,* February 15, 1903, sec. 2, p. 20.

28. Pine to Low, June 2, 1892 (CUA, CF, Pine File).

29. William R. Ware and Frederick Law Olmsted, "Report of Professor William R. Ware and Mr. Frederick Law Olmsted on the Occupation of the New Site," printed report in *Minutes,* May 26, 1893, p. 16; "The Morningside Acropolis," *CUQ* 2 (March 1900), 150.

30. Society of the New York Hospital, *Governors Minutes,* Real Estate Committee, March 30, 1899, and February 2, 1900 (NYHA).

31. Butler to J. Edward Simmons (and identical letter to Cornelius N. Bliss), May 2, 1902 (NYHA-Secretary-Treasurer Papers, Box 34/6), and Stillman, Speyer, and Fish to Trustees, June 23, 1902, in *Minutes,* October 6, 1902.

32. Bangs to Stillman, Speyer, and Fish, June 28, 1902 in *Minutes,* October 28, 1902.

33. *Minutes,* June 1, 1903, and "South Field Secured Dormitories Given," *Spectator,* June 10, 1903, p. 1.

34. "Purchase of South Field," *NYT,* October 2, 1903, p. 14.

35. "Report of the Special Committee on the Development of South Field and Proposed Resolutions to be Submitted to the Trustees at Their Meeting on November 2, 1903," printed report of the trustees, October 1903, pp 7–9 (CUA), and "Supplementary Report of the Special Committee on the Development of South Field and Proposed Resolutions to be Submitted to the Trustees at Their Meeting on December 7, 1903," printed report of the trustees, December 1903, pp. 4–5 (CUA).

36. McKim, Mead & White's proposal is detailed in "Report of the Special Committee on the Development of South Field." The plan of South Field is discussed in Leland M. Roth, *McKim, Mead & White, Architects* (New York: Harper & Row, 1983), pp. 280–81.

37. Both of these designs are preserved in watercolor drawings at Avery Library (CU, Avery Library, MMW, Drawings and Archives).

38. "Suggestion For the Development of South Field" (NYHS-MMW, Tube 276 annex/1950).

39. "Suggestions for the Development of the Buildings and Grounds of the University" (Columbia University, 1914).

40. "Layout of South Field," drawing on tracing paper, c. 1907 (NYHS-MMW, Tube 280 annex/1950). This plan is undated, but it includes grass panels on South Court which were not proposed by Olmsted Brothers until the fall of 1906.

41. The *Sun* reported that this was the proposed site for the president's house, although there is no evidence that this was a serious consideration; "Columbia's Newest Buildings: Plans for Making South Field One of the City's Show Places," *Sun,* November 20, 1904, p. 8.

42. "Birds Eye View of Columbia Grounds," NYHS-MMW, South Field Drawing. The best-known version of the South Field plan, published in 1915 in *A Monograph of the Works of McKim, Mead & White,* plate 47, shows a relatively shallow building on 114th Street (see figure 5.16).

43. "Layout of South Field."

44. Butler to Kennedy, December 22, 1904 (CUA, CF, Kennedy File). The gift was announced in *Minutes,* May 1, 1905, but Kennedy's name was not reported, even to most other trustees, until 1909. Kennedy was also a large donor to the American Museum of Natural History, the Metropolitan Museum, NYU, and the New York Public Library (a bust of Kennedy is set on the wall of the south stair at the library). He was especially interested in social work, providing the money for the construction of

the United Charities Building on Park Avenue South and East 22nd Street and the establishment of the School of Philanthropy. He gave generously to Presbyterian causes, including Presbyterian Hospital and the construction of the Presbyterian Building on Fifth Avenue and West 20th Street. For Kennedy, see "J. S. Kennedy Dead of Whooping Cough," *NYT,* November 1, 1909. p. 11, and W. B. Shaw, John Stewart Kennedy," *DAB,* vol. 5 (New York: Scribner's, 1932), pp. 334–35.

45. For the original design of College Hall, see John Pine, "College Hall," *CUQ* 3 (June 1901), 246–48, and "The New Columbia," *HW* 45 (June 15, 1901), pp. 605–607. Hamilton Hall, as built, is discussed in "Columbia's New Buildings," *EP,* September 22, 1906, p. 7; *CUQ,* Hamilton Hall Number 9 (March 1907); and Robson, pp. 92– 94. The building is illustrated in "Hamilton Hall, Columbia University," *Architecture* 15 (March 1907), plate 23, and *Monograph,* plate 313. The marble doorway surround and clock at the office of the Dean of Columbia College, set on axis with the main entrance to Hamilton Hall, was a 1908 gift of the class of 1884 (*Minutes,* January 4, 1909). The class of 1880 donated beautiful sliding iron grilles for the three front doors. These were designed by McKim, Mead & White and are extant, but are frozen in their pockets. Just outside of the building are the original gates to the Hamilton Hall that stood on the Midtown campus.

46. "Marcellus Hartley Dodge Dies; Ex-Remington Arms Chairman," *NYT,* December 26, 1963, p. 27. Also see "Sudden Death of Marcellus Hartley," *NYT,* November 9, 1902, p. 9, and "Mrs. G. W. Jenkins Dies at Age of 73," *NYT,* April 25, 1934, p. 22. In 1965, the former business school building was renamed Dodge Hall in honor of Marcellus Hartley Dodge. Dodge was the grandson of William Earl Dodge, Sr., and was, therefore, related to William Earl Dodge, Jr., who donated Earl Hall to Columbia and was a supporter of Union Theological Seminary, and to Grace Dodge, a founder and supporter of Teachers College.

47. Butler to Mrs. George W. Jenkins, March 13, 1902 (CUA, CF, Helen Hartley Jenkins File). The $300,000 initially pledged proved inadequate and an additional $50,000 was successfully solicited from the donors; see Butler to Marcellus Hartley Dodge, February 3, 1904, and Dodge to Butler, February 8, 1904 (CUA, CF, Marcellus Hartley Dodge File)

48. "South Field Secured Dormitories Given," p. 2.

49. Butler to Dodge, February 3, 1904. Livingston Hall was named in memory of Robert R. Livingston of the class of 1765.

50. The Hankey Memorial Window, a stained-glass window made by Mayer & Co. of Munich, representing Sophocles and Virgil, was transferred from the library of the old campus and installed in Hartley Hall; see Robson, p. 109. To the left of the fireplace in the Livingston Hall lounge was a memorial window donated in 1909 by members of the Livingston family as a memorial to Chancellor Livingston. It was designed by architect William Kendall and artist George W. Maynard; see "The Livingston Window, *CUQ* 12 (December 1909), p. 77, and Robson, *Guide to Columbia,* p. 110. To the right of the fireplace was a window by Heinigke & Bowen donated in 1916 as a memorial to Chief Justice John Jay; see *Minutes,* June 5, 1916, and Robson,

Guide to Columbia, p. 110. All of these windows have been removed and their whereabouts are not known.

51. Butler to Dodge, February 3, 1904.

52. Butler to Kennedy, December 22, 1904.

53. *Directory of Officers and Students 1915–1916* (New York: Columbia University, 1915).

54. Advertisement for Cathedral Plaza Apartments, 100 Cathedral Parkway, *Spectator,* October 10, 1914, p. 6.

55. Butler to Mrs. Francis P. Furnald, November 20, 1911 (CUA, CF, Furnald File).

56. For Furnald Hall, see Robson, *Guide to Columbia,* pp. 110–12, and *Monograph,* plate 201.

57. "Big Field on Hudson," *Tribune,* March 5, 1906, p. 1; "Columbia Plans $1,000,000 Stadium," *World,* March 5, 1906, p. 16; "Columbia's New Field," *EP,* March 5, 1906, p. 5; "New Field For Columbia," *Sun,* March 5, 1906, p. 3; "A $1,000,000 Stadium For Columbia Athletes," *NYT,* March 5, 1906, p. 1; "Will Rob Hudson For Big Stadium," *Herald,* March 5, 1906, p. 5. McKim, Mead & White's landscape plan for South Field may have been prepared as a result of this proposal.

58. "Columbia's Water-Front Stadium," [editorial] *World,* March 6, 1906, p. 6.

59. "Big Field On Hudson." The idea for the water gate was apparently that of Daniel LeRoy Dresser of the class of 1889. Palmer & Hornbostel's proposal is illustrated in *Architecture* 16 (August 15, 1907), 140–41.

60. "The City's Front Door," *Evening Mail,* March 6, 1906, p. 4.

61. "Agree on Plans for Big Riverside Stadium," *Sun,* December 13, 1912, p. 6; "Agree on $10,000,000 Riverside Pantheon," *NYT,* December 13, 1912, p. 12; "Columbia and Riverside Park," [editorial] *NYT,* April 24, 1912, p. 12; and "Agree on Plans For Big Riverside Stadium," *Sun,* December 13, 1912, p. 6. In 1910, a competition was held for a Robert Fulton Memorial, a water gate on the Hudson River at 116th Street, not including a Columbia stadium. The competition was won by H. Van Buren Magonigle; see "Accepted Design For a $2,500,000 Water Gate on the Hudson in Memory of Robert Fulton," *Tribune,* May 22, 1910, sec. 2, pp. 1, 8.

62. Among the more important gifts were the granite exedra opposite the entrance to St. Paul's Chapel (Edward Pierce Casey, 1911), given by the class of 1886; the bronze torchères that flank the entrance to the chapel (Arturo Bianchini of Florence, sculptor), given in 1908 by the class of 1883; the "Grecian" well head (actually from Venice), now in the Avery/Fayerweather courtyard, given by the class of 1887; a replica of sculptor Constantin Meunier's *Le Marteleur* (The Hammerman), given in 1914 by the class of 1889; *The Great God Pan* by George Grey Barnard, given in 1907 by Edward Sevrin Clark; the Class of 1885 Sundial (McKim, Mead & White with sculptor William Ordway Partridge, 1910–14); the Class of 1890 Pylon on the south side of the 116th Street and Broadway campus entrance (McKim, Mead & White, with sculptor Charles Keck, 1916); the Class of 1900 Pylon on the north side of the 116th Street and Broadway entrance (McKim, Mead & White, with sculptor Charles Keck, 1925); the Dwight Memorial Pylon and the Pine Memorial Pylon at the

116th Street and Amsterdam Avenue entrance (McKim, Mead & White, 1932); the Van Amringe Memorial in the Van Amringe Quadrangle (McKim, Mead & White, with sculptor William Ordway Partridge, 1918–22); the class of 1906 clock (1916) between Hartley and Livingston halls; a statue of Alexander Hamilton, set in front of Hamilton Hall (William Ordway Partridge, 1908), a gift of the Association of the Alumni; a statue of Thomas Jefferson, set in front of Journalism Hall (William Ordway Partridge, 1914), a gift, in part, of the estate of Joseph Pulitzer; the entrance gate and steps behind Earl Hall (1916) given by the class of 1891; and the Edward A. Darling Memorial Fountain (1903) in Low Library, given by Edith Pennington Darling in memory of her husband who was Superintendent of Buildings and Grounds.

63. In 1901 the Stokes sisters funded Woodbridge Hall at Yale with the same stipulation requiring that I. N. Phelps Stokes design the structure. Olivia Stokes also donated the open-air pulpit to the Cathedral of St. John the Divine (also designed by Howells & Stokes) in 1913 as a memorial to Caroline. For the Stokes sisters, see "Olivia Egleston Phelps Stokes and Caroline Phelps Stokes," *DAB*, vol. 9 (New York: Scribner's, 1935), p. 68.

64. Butler to McKim, September 17, 1903 (CUA, CF, McKim File).

65. Stokes was also a housing reformer, historian of New York City, print collector, and author of the extraordinary six volume *Iconography of Manhattan Island* (New York: Robert H. Dodd, 1915–28). For Stokes, see I. N. Phelps Stokes, *Random Recollections of a Happy Life* (privately printed, 1932; revised, 1941); "I. N. Phelps Stokes, Architect, 77, Dead," *NYT,* December 19, 1944, p. 21; "I. N. Phelps Stokes, Historian and Housing Expert, Dies at 77," *HT,* December 19, 1944, p. 16; and Marvin E. Gettleman, "Isaac Newton Phelps Stokes," *DAB,* sup. 3 (New York: Scribner's, 1973), pp. 743–44. Special thanks to Deborah Gardner for sharing her research material on St. Paul's Chapel, collected for a forthcoming biography of Stokes. The ashes of Stokes and his wife Edith Minturn are set into the south wall of the choir arch of St. Paul's Chapel. John Mead Howells, the son of novelist William Dean Howells, was related to McKim's partner William Rutherford Mead.

66. Howells & Stokes to Butler, October 7, 1903; also Howells & Stokes to McKim, October 5, 1903 (NYHS-MMW, CU, St. Paul's Chapel, Box 615, Folder 1).

67. Butler to Howells & Stokes, October 16, 1903 (NYHS, CU, St. Paul's Chapel, MMW/1950, Box 615, Folder 1). Stokes was the main architect for the project, with his partner having little involvement. On July 16, 1904, Stokes informed his aunts that Howells had not been involved with the design; Stokes to Olivia and Caroline Stokes, July 16, 1904 (NYHS-Stokes Papers, Letterbook 2).

68. Howells & Stokes to McKim, October 20, 1903 (NYHS-MMW/1950, CU, St. Paul's Chapel, Box 615, Folder 1).

69. Russell Sturgis, "St. Paul's Chapel," *AR* 30 (February 1907), 92. Many design sketches are in the collection of Avery Library; the proposals that include a campanile are in Stokes Collection, Folder 42b.

70. Stokes to Pine, June 10, 1904 (CUA, CF, Stokes File).

71. James Hall, *Illustrated Dictionary of Symbols in Eastern and Western Art* (London: John Murray, 1994), p. 42.

72. The cherubs in the column capitals and the grape vines of the central entrance, as well as other exterior details in limestone, were carved by Gutzum Borglum, the sculptor most famous for his work at Mt. Rushmore; see Borglum to Howells & Stokes, February 2, 1905 (CU, Avery Library, Stokes Papers, Box 2, File 33).

73. "Report of the Committee on Buildings and Grounds," in *Minutes,* October 7, 1912. The setting of the chapel includes the class of 1886 exedra, a semicircular stone bench designed by architect Edward Pierce Casey in 1911, and two wrought-iron gates dating from 1769 that originally stood in front of the North Dutch Church on Fulton and William streets; see "Old Iron Gates Given Columbia," *Sun,* August 6, 1938, p. 7.

74. Stokes to Olivia and Caroline Stokes, July 16, 1904.

75. Stokes to Pine, June 10, 1904.

76. Stokes to Olivia and Caroline Stokes, July 16, 1904.

77. Difficulties arose when Butler accepted a gift for the chancel windows without seeking Olivia and Caroline Stokes's permission. They insisted that they pay for these windows; see Stokes to Olivia and Caroline Stokes, May 26, 1905, and June 16, 1905 (NYHS-Stokes Papers, Letterbook 2), and Butler to Stokes, June 19, 1905 (CU, Avery Library, Stokes Papers, Box 2, File 9). In July 1905, Olivia and Caroline Stokes agreed to pay the additional cost of furnishing the chapel; *Minutes,* October 2, 1905.

78. The church was designed in 1891 by Henry Kilburn with a rectory of 1889 by Carrère & Hastings.

79. Howells & Stokes to John La Farge, November 2, 1904 (CU, Avery Library, Stokes Papers, Box 2, File 13).

80. William H. Goodyear, "The Columbia University Chapel," *Brickbuilder* 15 (December 1906), 266. This article also notes that the mortar chosen for the interior was "a deep purple color" (p. 265).

81. Howells & Stokes to Weinman, June 12, 1905 (CU, Avery Library, Stokes Papers, Box 4, File 59).

82. Janet Parks and Alan G. Neumann, *The Old World Builds the New: The Guastavino Company and the Technology of the Catalan Vault, 1885–1962* (New York: Avery Architectural and Fine Arts Library, 1996), pp. 26–27, and Dunn, "The Principles of Dome Construction," 111. Also see, CU, Avery Library, Guastavino Collection, Files 6.189–6.192.

83. "Brick Restored to its Sovereignty at Columbia — The Chapel of Saint Paul," *Craftsman Magazine* 11 (February 1907), p. 562.

84. Stokes to Olivia and Caroline Stokes, May 26, 1905 (NYHS-Stokes Papers, Letterbook 2).

85. Howells & Stokes to La Farge, October 6, 1904 (CU, Avery Library, Stokes Papers, Box 1, File 13). For La Farge's stained-glass work, see Henry A. La Farge, "Painting with Colored Light: The Stained Glass of John La Farge," in *John La Farge,* exhibi-

tion catalogue, Carnegie Museum of Art, Pittsburgh (New York: Abbeville Press, 1987), pp. 194–223.

86. Memorandum, Butler to Howells & Stokes, December 5, 1905 (CU, Avery Library, Stokes Papers, Box 2, File 9). Butler claimed that the choice of St. Paul preaching on Mars Hill was his idea.

87. These windows commemorate, beginning at the north, Ambrose C. and George L. Kingsland (class of 1856), Robert B. Minturn (1856), Mahlon Sands (1861) and Philip J. Sands (1863), Louis M. Cheesman (1878), Philip Van Cortlandt (1758), Anthony Lispenard (1761), Abraham de Peyster (1763) and Frederic de Peyster (1762), Egbert Benson (1765), Gerard Beekman (1766), Philip Pell (1770), Thomas Barclay (1772), DeWitt Clinton (1786), William C. Rhinelander (1808), Nathaniel G. Pendleton (1813), Nicholas Fish (1817), and Gouverneur M. Ogden (1833); see Maitland Armstrong & Co., "Proposed Scheme for Placing Memorials — St. Pauls [sic] Chapel Columbia University, N.Y.," January 17, 1906 (CU, Avery Library, Stokes Papers). The large transept windows by Henry Wyndyoung and J. Gordon Guthrie were not installed until the 1920s.

88. Stokes, *Random Recollections* (1932), p. 138; (1941), p. 131. In this autobiographic reminiscence, Stokes incorrectly notes that the Coppedé firm was from Genoa.

89. Stokes to Dr. William MacKenzie, May 1, 1905; Stokes to Mariano and Figli Coppedé, June 16, 1905; and Stokes to Pine, July 19, 1905 (NYHS-Stokes Papers, Letterbook 2); Mariano Coppedé to Stokes, July 20, 1905, and Stokes to Mariano and Figli Coppedé, May 2, 1906 (CU, Avery Library, Stokes Papers, Box 2, File 2).

90. A. D. F. Hamlin, "Saint Paul's Chapel, Columbia University: The Interior," *Inland Architect* 48 (December 1906), 51.

91. Sturgis, "St. Paul's Chapel," p. 90.

92. Montgomery Schuyler, "Architecture of American Colleges IV. New York City Schools," *AR* 27 (June 1910), 452. Also see, "St. Paul's Chapel: Columbia University, New York, N.Y.," *AABN* 87 (March 25, 1905), plates; "The New Buildings of Columbia University," *As&Bs*, 38 (February 1906), 194–198; "St. Paul's Chapel: Columbia University, New York, N.Y.," *AABN* 89 (June 30, 1906), plates; "Columbia's New Chapel," *RRBG* 78 (September 29, 1906), 522; "St. Paul's Chapel: Columbia University, New York, N.Y.," *AA* 91 (February 9, 1907), 72 and plates; "Columbia University Chapel," *Christian Art* 1 (April 1907), 16–18; Parker B. Fiske, "A Rational Standard of Quality in Face Brick," *RRBG* 83 (April 3, 1909), 632–33; Charles W. Stoughton, "Modern Brickwork–II," *International Studio* 38 (July 1909), xiv, xvii; and Robson, *Guide to Columbia*, pp. 51–58.

93. Memorandum, Butler to Howells & Stokes, December 5, 1905.

94. Nicholas Murray Butler, *Annual Report of the President* (1906), p. 2.

95. Butler to McKim, March 11, 1904 (CUA, CF, McKim, Mead & White File)

96. Butler to McKim, Mead & White, April 3, 1905 (NYHS-MMW/1950, Box 564, misc. folder, and CUA, CF, McKim, Mead & White File).

97. For Lewisohn, see "Adolph Lewisohn Dies At Age of 89," *NYT*, August 18. 1938, p. 1,

and Geoffrey T. Hellman, "Adolph Lewisohn," *DAB*, sup. 2 (New York: Scribner's, 1958), pp. 383–84.

98. It may seem incongruous that Lewisohn would donate a building to a school which engaged in restrictive anti-Jewish policies. However, when the School of Mines was donated to Columbia, Butler had been president for only two years and had yet to firmly establish restrictive admissions policies. Wechsler, *The Qualified Student* (p. 132), comments that at least until 1905 Columbia showed little concern for the ethnicity of its student body.

99. Arnold W. Brunner, Architect, Dies," *NYT*, February 15, 1925, p. 26.

100. The School of Mines Building is illustrated in *Architectural Review* 11 (December 1904), plates lxv–lxvi, and *Architecture* 12 (November 1905), plates xcviii–xcix.

101. Drawings for each of these buildings are in NYHS-MMW, Tube 276 annex. The drawings are referred to as "building east of Mining," "building east of Engineering," "building west of Physics," and "building west of Journalism" (Journalism was originally planned for the site later given to Philosophy).

102. Robson, *Guide to Columbia,* pp. 47–49.

103. At the east end of the library is the Wildey Memorial Window, a large and exceptionally fine stained-glass window by J. S. Lamb and Company donated in 1913 as a memorial to Pierre Washington Westcott Wildey, an 1860 graduate of Columbia College and 1863 graduate of the law school; see "Report of the Committee on Buildings and Grounds," *Minutes,* February 3, 1913, and Robson, *Guide to Columbia,* p. 48. Kent Hall and its library are illustrated in *Monograph,* plates 314–316, 319.

104. Jenkins to Butler, March 6, 1910 (CUA, CF, Jenkins File), and Robson, *Guide to Columbia,* pp. 49–51. Philosophy Hall is illustrated in *Monograph,* plates 317–318.

105. Butler to Avery, January 14, 1910 (CUA, CF, Avery File).

106. Avery to Butler, February 18, 1911, in *Minutes,* March 6, 1911. For Avery Hall, see C. Matlock Price, "The Design of the Avery Architectural Library," *AR* 33 (June 1913), 533–539; Edward R. Smith, "The Henry O. Avery Architectural Library of Columbia University, New York," *Royal Institute of British Architects Journal* 21 (June 13, 1914), 497–512; Robson, *Guide to Columbia,* pp. 58–60; and *Monograph,* plates 314, 315, 317.

107. Butler to Avery, May 13, 1910 (CUA, CF, Avery File).

108. The courtyard was redesigned by Alexander Kouzmanoff, and much of its geenery removed, as part of the construction of an underground extension to Avery Library in the late 1970s.

109. Quoted in Richard Terrill Baker, *A History of the Graduate School of Journalism Columbia University* (New York: Columbia University Press, 1954), p. 23; a draft memo, with Pulitzer's offer, was prepared in August 1902 and a letter sent to Butler on March 24, 1903; see Baker, pp. 26–27.

110. [editorial], *RRBG* 72 (August 22, 1903), 333.

111. "Report of the Committee on Buildings and Grounds in Relation to the School of Journalism," December 4, 1911 (CUA), and Robson, *Guide to Columbia,* pp. 96–101. Journalism Hall is illustrated in *Monograph,* plates 314, 316.

112. Roth, *McKim, Mead & White*, p. 334. McKim is commemorated by a large plaque placed near the center of South Court in front of *Alma Mater* in 1910.

113. Roth, *McKim, Mead & White*, p. 336; "William Mitchell Kendall," *NCAB*, current volume A (New York: James T. White, 1930), pp. 551–52; "William Kendall, Architect, 85, Dies," *NYT*, August 9, 1941, p. 15; "William M. Kendall," *Pencil Points* 22 (September 1941), 65.

114. The raised brickwork that appears on Earl Hall is evidence of the fact that Kendall was responsible for detailing this structure.

115. Nicholas Murray Butler, *Annual Report of the President* (1910), p. 6.

116. "Money Floods Heights," *Tribune*, February 6, 1910, sec. 2, p. 5.

117. "Report of the Committee on Buildings and Grounds," *Minutes*, December 5, 1910. Columbia purchased the northeast corner of Amsterdam Avenue and 116th Street at auction and the remainder of the north side of 116th Street in a private sale; see Robson, *Guide to Columbia*, p. 115.

118. *Minutes*, October 5, 1914, and "Columbia Acquires $500,000 More Land," *Sun*, October 28, 1914, p. 14.

119. *Minutes*, May 1, 1911.

120. Christopher Gray, "An Elegant 1912 Home With a Vacancy Sign Out," *NYT*, May 12, 1991, sec. 10, p. 6. The building is illustrated in *Architecture* 27 (February 1913), 24, and *Monograph*, plates 352–53.

121. Olmsted to McKim, May 27, 1904 (CUA, CF, Olmsted File).

122. McKim to Butler, May 31, 1904 (CUA, CF, McKim File).

123. Olmsted Brothers to Frederick A. Goetze [Superintendent of Buildings and Grounds], September 10, 1906 (LC-ROA, Job File 242); reprinted in a report to the trustees (1906).

124. Olmsted Brothers to Goetze, September 10, 1906.

125. Buildings and Grounds Committee, *Minutes*, May 6, 1907.

126. Memo, April 16, 1906 (LC-ROA, Job File 242); Olmsted Brothers to Goetze, April 24, 1906 (LC-ROA, Job File 242 and NYHS-MMW/1950, Box 616, Folder 1); Olmsted Brothers to McKim, April 26, 1906 (NYHS-MMW/1950, Box 616, Folder 1).

127. Butler to McMillin, October 18, 1916 (CUA, CF, McMillin File).

128. McMillin to Butler, November 13, 1916 (CUA, CF, McMillin File).

129. Butler to McMillin, January 9, 1919; McMillin to Butler, January 10, 1919; and Butler to McMillin, January 13, 1919 (CUA, CF, McMillin File).

130. Thurman W. Van Metre, *A History of the Graduate School of Business Columbia University* (New York: Columbia University Press, 1954) pp. 33–34. The trustees had earlier noted the importance of the Faculty Club as "an intellectual and social center"; *Minutes*, December 4, 1916.

131. "The Faculty Club, Columbia University, New York City," *A&B* 55 (August 1923), 83, plates 170, 171.

132. For the construction of the Business School, see James C. Egbert, "A Home for the School of Business," *Columbia Alumni News* 15 (December 14, 1923), 175–76. Also see "Building for School of Business, Columbia University, New York City," *A&B*

57 (January 1925), 2–3, plates 16–17. The building was renamed Dodge Hall in 1964 in honor of Marcellus Hartley Dodge.

133. This drawing is in the collection of the New-York Historical Society.

134. The theater was redesigned in the early 1990s and renamed Miller Theater.

135. Nicholas Murray Butler, *Annual Report of the President* (1919–1920), p. 32.

136. *Annual Report* (1919), p. 35.

137. Plans and elevations for Pierce Hall are in the Collection of Columbia University's Avery Library (MMW Collection, Group C). The design for Pierce is similar to the 1907 design for a building on that site.

138. "Nicholas Murray Butler," *DAB,* p. 136

139. Henry Lee Norris [Director of Works, Columbia University] to McKim, Mead & White, October 7, 1926 (NYHS-MMW, Tube 3B). This letter refers in detail to a lost letter from Butler, dated August 5, 1926.

140. "Columbia University Resumes Its Vast Building Program," *RRBG* 113 (May 24, 1924), 9; "Two Huge Buildings Costing $2,150,000 Begun at Columbia," *EP,* November 23, 1924, p. 5; "Columbia's New Laboratories," *Columbia Alumni News,* 18 (January 28, 1927), 312–13; "Chemistry Building, New York City," *A&B* 58 (October 1926), 118, plate 204; and Robson, *Guide to Columbia,* pp. 65–76.

141. For Pupin see "Two Huge Buildings Costing $2,150,000 Begun at Columbia"; "Physics Building, Columbia University, New York City," *A&B* 58 (December 1926), 130, 136, plate 246; Robson, *Guide to Columbia,* pp. 73–76; and "Columbia's New Laboratories," *Columbia Alumni News,* 18 (January 28, 1927), 312–13.

142. For delineator Fritz Steffens's proposal for the art building, see NYHS, Photograph File C-8L.

143. *Annual Report* (1919–20), p. 33.

144. *Annual Report* (1922), p. 7, 20. The old gymnasium was to be converted into an auditorium (*Minutes,* October 1, 1923).

145. *Annual Report* (1922), p. 7.

146. Many of the proposals for Students Hall are in NYHS-MMW, Tube 314.

147. *Minutes,* October 1, 1923.

148. "Casa Italiana, Columbia University New York City," *A&B* 59 (November 1927), 351–52, plates 219–22; and New York City Landmarks Preservation Commission, "Columbia University Casa Italiana Designation Report" (New York: Landmarks Preservation Commission, 1978).

149. The auditorium was beautifully restored in 1994–96 by the architectural firm Buttrick, White & Burtis, in association with Italian architect Italo Rota; see Stephen A. Kliment, "Rescue Transforms Columbia Landmark," *AR* 184 (July 1996), 80–83.

150. *Annual Report* (1919–1920), p. 32. Following World War I, New York City experienced a severe housing crisis as apartments filled and construction slowed because of the volatility in prices for materials and labor; see "Still a Shortage of Housing," *RRBG* 105 (January 10, 1920), 37.

151. Butler first advocated constructing a woman's dormitory in his *Annual Report* (1916–17), pp. 28–29.

152. *Minutes,* October 2, 1922. Johnson Hall was named for Samuel Johnson, first president of King's College, and his son William Samuel Johnson, first president of Columbia College.

153. *Minutes,* October 2, 1922; Robson, *Guide to Columbia,* p. 118. The Women's Faculty Club was later used by the School of Arts. In 1977, the space was redesigned by Robert A. M. Stern for use by the law school and was renamed Jerome L. Greene Hall (now Greene Annex); see Suzanne Stephens, "Making It Legal: Jerome L. Greene Hall, Columbia University, New York," *Progressive Architecture* 59 (March 1978), 64–65.

154. For Johnson, see "Johnson Hall, Columbia University, New York City," *A&B* 57 (April 1925), 35–35, plates 87–88.

155. The use of Colonial imagery is discussed in Karal Ann Marling, *George Washington Slept Here: Colonial Revivals and American Culture, 1876–1986* (Cambridge: Harvard University Press, 1988). A similar use of Colonial forms is apparent at Barnard College's dormitories (see chapter 6).

156. Sketches for McKim, Mead & White's proposals are in NYHS-MMW, Tube 311/1950 and at CU, Avery Library.

157. The name John Jay Hall was chosen by the Committee on Buildings and Grounds and reported to the trustees at their meeting of December 7, 1925 (see *Minutes*), because they felt that "The College Quadrangle would then be surrounded by buildings bearing the name of Hamilton, Livingston and Jay, three of the greatest names on Columbia's rolls and three of the most distinguished in the history of the United States. The Committee feel that association with these names would offer to generations of College students an inspiration and a stimulus that could not be had in any other way." For John Jay, see "John Jay Hall, Columbia University New York City," *A&B* 59 (April 1927), 141, plates 82–86.

158. The balcony in the entrance lobby has been blocked off, but its railing is extant. The grill room has been destroyed. The dining room is extant.

159. Bender, *New York Intellect,* pp. 289–90, and Wechsler, *The Qualified Student,* pp. 162–68.

160. "Report of the Committee on Finance," in *Minutes,* April 5, 1920.

161. Virginia Gildersleeve, *Dean's Annual Report* (Barnard College, 1919), p. 8.

162. Columbia purchased the Sophomore, Eton, Rugby, and Campus apartment buildings, renaming them Daniel D. Tompkins Hall, John Jay Hall (later renamed Charles King Hall), Gouverneur Morris Hall, and DeWitt Clinton Hall; see "Columbia Extends Housing Program," *NYT,* November 23, 1919, sec. 2, p. 1, "Columbia Confronted by Serious Housing Problem," *Tribune,* November 23, 1919, sec. 2, p. 8.

163. "Statement of the President," in *Minutes,* January 3, 1921.

164. Butler proposed this idea in his *Annual Report* (1921–22), p. 37, and also discussed the issue in *Annual Report* (1925), pp. 43–45.

165. The history of library expansion and the construction of Columbia's new library are detailed in Michael Stoller, "Columbia's Library For the Twentieth Century:

The Rise of South Hall," *Library Columns* 45 (Autumn 1996), pp. 4–17; Williamson's letter is discussed on p. 6.

166. *Minutes,* June 2, 1931.

167. For Harkness, see "Edward S. Harkness Dies at 66, Gave $100,000,000 to the Public," *NYT,* January 30, 1940, p. 1, and James W. Wooster, Jr., "Edward Stephen Harkness," *DAB,* sup. 2 (New York: Scribner's, 1958), pp. 283–85.

168. Rogers acknowledged that he was hired in order to increase the chances of funding the library project in a letter to William Kendall, February 13, 1931 (NYHS, CU, General File no. 70, 1950 Collection). Stoller, p. 10, notes that Williamson and Rogers were corresponding as early as the summer of 1928. Also see Butler to Rogers, June 26, 1930 (CUA, CF, Rogers File).

169. Rogers to Kendall, February 13, 1931.

170. Late in 1929, members of Columbia's Board of Trustees had apparently criticized the work of Kendall and other McKim, Mead & White architects who had worked on projects after McKim's death; see McKim, Mead & White to [trustee] Gano Dunn, December 26, 1929 (NYHS, MMW, Columbia General File No. 70). In its letter, McKim, Mead & White had to remind the Columbia board members of all of the buildings that the firm had completed for Columbia, providing a complete list of these projects.

171. Stoller, "Columbia's Library," pp. 7–11; the article includes illustrations of two proposed plans.

172. Butler to Rogers, June 26, 1930, and Rogers to Henry Lee Norrie [Columbia University Director of Works], October 1, 1930 (CUA, CF, Rogers File); and Butler to Malcolm P. Aldrich [assistant to Edward S. Harkness], December 9, 1930 (RAC, Commonwealth Fund Collection, Record Group Harkness Family Material, Box HR1, 1–22, A-H, Folder 11, and CUA, CF, Harkness File); also see Stoller, "Columbia's Library," p. 11. Had the gymnasium and power plant been rebuilt on another site, the cost of this already exorbitant proposal would have skyrocketed.

173. Butler to Aldrich December 9, 1930.

174. Bender, *New York Intellect,* p. 284.

175. Butler to Aldrich, February 21, 1931 (RAC, Commonwealth Fund Collection, Record Group Harkness Family Material, Box HR1, 1–22, A-H, Folder 11, and CUA, CF, Harkness File).

176. Butler to Aldrich, February 27, 1931 (RAC, Commonwealth Fund Collection, Record Group Harkness Family Material, Box HR1, 1–22, A-H, Folder 11, and CUA, CF, Harkness File). The design and redesign are discussed in Stoller, "Columbia's Library," pp. 11–13; the initial proposal is illustrated on p. 4.

177. The cost estimate was prepared on April 9, 1931 and sent by Butler to Aldrich on April 10, 1931 (RAC, Commonwealth Fund Collection, Record Group Harkness Family Material, Box HR1, 1–22, A-H, Folder 11, and CUA, CF, Harkness File). For the revised design, see Stoller, "Columbia's Library," pp. 11–13.

178. Butler to Aldrich, May 4, 1931 (RAC, Commonwealth Fund Collection, Record

Group Harkness Family Material, Box HR1, 1–22, A-H, Folder 11, and CUA, CF, Harkness File).

179. Harkness to Butler, May 8, 1931 (RAC, Commonwealth Fund Collection, Record Group Harkness Family Material, Box HR1, 1–22, A-H, Folder 11, and CUA, CF, Harkness File); also see "Harkness To Build Library at Columbia for 4,000,000 Books," *NYT,* May 18, 1931, p. 1, and "New Library Harkness Gift For Columbia, *HT,* May 18, 1931, p. 1.

180. "New Library Site Scored at Columbia," *NYT,* May 19, 1931, p. 29; "Columbia Protest on Library Grows," *NYT,* May 20, 1931, p. 45; and "Defends South Field for Columbia Library," *NYT,* May 22, 1931, p. 6. Although organized sports activity now took place on Baker Field, South Field was used for unofficial sports activities, as it still is today.

181. "Columbia to Build New Library on South Field," *Columbia Alumni News* 22 (May 22, 1931), 5; quoted in "Defends South Field for Columbia Library."

182. Rogers to Butler, February 13, 1931 (CUA, CF, Rogers File).

183. The design of the building is discussed in Aaron Betsky, *James Gamble Rogers and the Architecture of Pragmatism* (New York: Architectural History Foundation, 1994), pp. 202–206. Its features are described in a series of short essays in *South Hall Columbia University New York* (New York: Columbia University, 1935). For Rogers's extensive work at Yale, see Patricia D. Pierce, *Sparing No Detail: The Drawings of James Gamble Rogers for Yale University, 1913–1935* (New Haven: Yale University Art Gallery, 1982).

184. Butler to Rogers, May 10, 1932, May 13, 1932, August 25, 1933, and other letters (CUA, CF, Rogers File). Butler chose a conservative group of literary figures for the frieze: Homer, Herodotus, Sophocles, Plato, Aristotle, Demosthenes, Cicero, Virgil, Horace, Tacitus, St. Augustine, St. Thomas Aquinas, Dante, Cervantes, Shakespeare, Milton, Voltaire, and Goethe.

185. Betsky, *James Gamble Rogers,* p. 204.

186. Butler to Harkness, November 5, 1931 (RAC, Commonwealth Fund Collection, Record Group Harkness Family Material, Box HR1, 1–22, A-H, Folder 11).

187. William Barclay Parsons to Harkness, December 29, 1931 (RAC, Commonwealth Fund Collection, Record Group Harkness Family Material, Box HR1, 1–22, A-H, Folder 11). Also see "Honors For Dr. Butler Planned at Columbia, *NYT,* December 5, 1931, p. 19.

188. "Butler Unfolds Plan For Future Columbia," *Columbia Alumni News* 29 (March 18, 1938), 5; "Butler Outlines Columbia Need of $50,000,000," *HT,* March 28, 1938, p. 1; and "Columbia Program Seeks $50,000,000," *NYT,* March 28, 1938, p. 1.

189. These buildings and others erected by Columbia after World War II are discussed in Robert A. M. Stern, Thomas Mellins, and David Fishman, *New York 1960: Architecture and Urbanism Between the Second World War and the Bicentennial* (New York: Monacelli Press, 1995), pp. 735–51.

190. For James Stewart Polshek's plan, see *James Stewart Polshek Context and Respon-*

sibility: Buildings and Projects 1957–1987 (New York: Rizzoli, 1088), pp. 70–71. For Sherman Fairchild, see Ada Louise Huxtable, "A Stylish New Building At Columbia," *NYT,* December 11, 1977, sec. 2, pp. 35–36; Martin Filler, "Hail Columbia," *Progressive Architecture* 59 (March 1979), 54–59; and Stern, *New York 1960,* pp. 749–50. For the Computer Science Building, see Margaret Gaskie, "Classical Complexity," *AR* 172 (March 1984), 126–33, and "Computer Science Building, Columbia University," *Architecture and Urbanism* 168 (September 1984), 38–46.

191. The Sterling building is illustrated in *James Stewart Polshek Context and Responsibility,* p. 70.

192. "For Columbia, a New $68 Million Student Center," *NYT,* January 28, 1996, sec. 9, p. 1.

6. BUILDING FOR THE MIND III: BARNARD COLLEGE AND TEACHERS COLLEGE — WOMEN'S EDUCATION ON MORNINGSIDE HEIGHTS

1. The general histories of Barnard College are Alice Duer Miller and Susan Myers, *Barnard College: The First Fifty Years* (New York: Columbia University Press, 1939), and Marian Churchill White, *A History of Barnard College* (New York: Columbia University Press, 1954). Barnard's early history is also detailed in Emily James Putnam, "The Rise of Barnard College," *CUQ* 2 (June 1900), 209–17, and in William P. Trent, "Barnard College," in *A History of Columbia University 1754–1904* (New York: Columbia University Press, 1904), pp. 397–408. The school's history and its buildings are examined in Helen Lefkowitz Horowitz, *Alma Mater: Design and Experience in the Women's Colleges from Their Nineteenth-Century Beginnings to the 1930s* 2nd edition (Amherst: University of Massachusetts Press, 1993), pp. 134–42, 247–61.

2. For the history of women's higher education, see Barbara Miller Solomon, *In the Company of Educated Women: A History of Women and Higher Education in America* (New Haven: Yale University Press, 1985), and John Mack Faragher and Florence Howe, eds., *Women and Higher Education in American History: Essays From the Mount Holyoke College Sesquicentennial Symposia* (New York: Norton, 1988).

3. Solomon, *In the Company of Educated Women,* pp. 50–53. The earliest state universities admitting women were Iowa (1855), Wisconsin (1867), Kansas (1869), Indiana (1869), Minnesota (1869), Missouri (1870), Michigan (1870), and California (1870). Although women were admitted to religious and secular coeducational institutions, they were not always permitted to follow the same curriculum as men or attend classes with men.

4. Solomon, *In the Company of Educated Women,* p. 47.

5. "Barnard College," *HW* 34 (December 6, 1890), 954. The Society for the Collegiate Instruction of Women was officially incorporated in 1882; see Patricia M. King, "The Campaign for Higher Education for Women in Nineteenth-Century Boston," *Proceedings of the Massachusetts Historical Society* 93 (1982), 65–66.

6. For Radcliffe, see Hugh Hawkins, *Between Harvard and America: The Educational Leadership of Charles W. Eliot* (New York: Oxford University Press, 1972), pp. 193–97. The president of Harvard cosigned Radcliffe degrees.

7. Moses King, *King's Handbook of New York* (Boston: Moses King, 1893), p. 570.

8. Columbia University *Minutes of the Board of Trustees*, November 3, 1879 (CUA).

9. Frederick A. P. Barnard, *The Higher Education of Women: Passages Extracted From the Annual Reports of the President of Columbia College Presented to the Trustees in June, 1879, June, 1880, and June, 1881* (New York, 1882).

10. Quoted in Annie Nathan Meyer, *Barnard Beginnings* (Boston: Houghton Mifflin, 1935), p. 8.

11. "Barnard College."

12. "Barnard College."

13. "Barnard College." The Latin translates as "we have nothing to discuss with you."

14. Meyer, *Barnard Beginnings,* p. 18.

15. Meyer, *Barnard Beginnings.* Meyer's contribution to the establishment of Barnard College and the later ambivalence of the college toward that contribution are discussed in Lynn D. Gordon, "Annie Nathan Meyer and Barnard College: Mission and Identity in Women's Higher Education, 1889–1950," *History of Education Quarterly* 26 (Winter 1986), 503–22. Gordon argues that Meyer's contribution to the founding of Barnard was not adequately celebrated because she was Jewish.

16. Meyer, *Barnard Beginnings,* p. 30.

17. Annie Nathan Meyer, "The Higher Education For Women in New York," *Nation* 26 (January 21, 1888), 68–69; reprinted in Meyer, *Barnard Beginnings,* pp. 167–74. So important was this article in the history of the college that a copy was placed in the cornerstone of Milbank Hall, one of original buildings erected for Barnard on Morningside Heights.

18. Meyer, "The Higher Education For Women in New York," p. 68. Meyer notes her mathematical mistake in *Barnard Beginnings,* p. 167.

19. The full list of names appears in Meyer, *Barnard Beginnings,* p. 175. Also see, "Will The Columbia Trustees Yield," *Tribune,* March 4, 1888, p. 2, and "The Columbia Annex For Women," *Tribune,* March 5, 1888, p. 8.

20. Columbia University, *Minutes,* March 5, 1888, and *EP,* March 6, 1888, p. 7.

21. Columbia University, *Minutes,* May 7, 1888.

22. Meyer, *Barnard Beginnings,* p. 76; "Women At Columbia College," *EP,* November 17, 1888, p. 9; and "The Women Win At Last," *Tribune,* November 17, 1888, p. 7.

23. Columbia University, *Minutes,* May 7, 1888.

24. Meyer, *Barnard Beginnings,* p. 121.

25. In order to save money, the school rented the front room on the second story to the Women's University Club for two years and permitted the owner to use the top story; see Meyer, *Barnard Beginnings,* p. 150.

26. Meyer, *Barnard Beginnings,* p. 140; also see White, *A History of Barnard College,* p. 17.

27. White, *A History of Barnard College,* p. 19, and Trent, "Barnard College," p. 402;

Miller and Myers, *Barnard College,* p. 18, claims that there were only nine degree candidates.

28. Schiff to Meyer, March 18, 1892 (BCA, Meyer Papers, Box 3 File 2). Schiff resigned from the board in 1893.

29. "Agreement Regarding Gift—Mrs. Brinckerhoff," May 19, 1892 (BCA, File K2), and "A Gift To Barnard College," *EP,* May 28, 1892, p. 8.

30. Horowitz, *Alma Mater,* p. 138.

31. "Barnard College," [editorial] *EP,* May 28, 1892, p. 6.

32. Pine to Low, June 2, 1892 (CUA, CF, Pine File).

33. Olmstead to Silas Brownell [trustee], June 6, 1892 (BCA, Box C, File 19). Olmstead was interested in selling the north side of 117th Street between Morningside Drive and Amsterdam Avenue. This property would soon be sold to David and Carrie Kennedy, and was the location of the earliest speculative rowhouses on Morningside Heights (see chapter 8). Other real estate offers are in BCA, Box G and File K.

34. "Barnard Would Follow Columbia," *Tribune,* February 15, 1895, p. 12.

35. "Money For Barnard College," *EP,* February 19, 1895, p. 8; also see "Gifts to Barnard College," *NYT,* February 19, 1895, p 3.

36. See for example, "More Aid For Barnard College," *NYT,* February 27, 1895, p. 9; "Working For Barnard College," *NYT,* March 2, 1895, p. 8; "More Money For Barnard College," *NYT,* March 8, 1895, p. 16; and "For Barnard College's Land Fund," *NYT,* March 22, 1895, p. 4.

37. See, for example, "Barnard College," *EP,* March 2, 1895, p. 7, and "Barnard College," *A&B* 24 (April 25, 1896), 193−94.

38. "Barnard College," [editorial] *HW* 40 (May 23, 1896), 507.

39. For Anderson, see Lilian Brandt, "Elizabeth Milbank Anderson," *DAB,* vol. 1 (New York: Scribner's, 1927), pp. 263−64, and "Mrs. A. A. Anderson, Philanthropist, Dies," *NYT,* February 21, 1921, p. 13.

40. "She Gave Barnard Million," *Sun,* March 8, 1903, p. 1.

41. Horowitz, *Alma Mater,* p. 139, and Meyer, *Barnard Beginnings,* p. 59.

42. Rich had designed "Milbank," the Greenwich, Connecticut, estate built by Elizabeth's father in the early 1880s. Only the gates of this estate survive; see Junior League of Greenwich, *The Great Estates of Greenwich, Connecticut 1880−1930* (Canaan, New Hampshire: Phoenix Publishing, 1986), pp. 58−61. Just how the Milbank family and Rich became acquainted or whether they had a familial relationship is not known. In New York City, Anderson is known to have had Rich design a public bath for the New York Association for Improving the Condition of the Poor on East 38th Street (demolished) and the Bryant Park Studios at 80 West 40th Street.

43. Anderson to Smith, October 8, 1895 (BCA, Trustees Correspondence 1899−1904).

44. Officially the architect was the firm of Lamb & Rich, but Charles Rich was responsible for the design.

45. "Charles A. Rich, 88, Architect Is Dead," *NYT,* December 5, 1943, p. 66.

46. For the Dartmouth building, see Montgomery Schuyler, "Architecture of American Colleges VI: Darmouth, Williams and Amherst," *AR* 28 (December 1910), 425−34.

For Wesleyan, see Schuyler, "Architecture of American Colleges VII: Brown, Bowdoin, Trinity and Wesleyan," *AR* 29 (February 1911), 161–66.

47. Annie Nathan Meyer, "The New Home For Barnard College," *Harper's Bazaar* 29 (November 7, 1896), 938.

48. The terra cotta was manufactured by B. Kreischer's Sons of Kreischerville, Staten Island; see Heinrich Ries, "Clays of New York: Their Properties and Uses," *The University of the State of New York Bulletin of the New York State Museum* 7 (June 1900), 762.

49. *Barnard College New York City: Plans of the New Building on the Boulevard at One Hundred and Nineteenth Street* [c.1896], n.p. (pamphlet in BCA, File E); Meyer, "The New Home For Barnard College," 939; Herbert M. Richards, "The Curriculum and the Equipment of Barnard College," *CUQ* 12 (March 1910), 176; and Horowitz, *Alma Mater,* p. 141.

50. "On Barnard's New Site," *NYT*, July 4, 1896, p. 8, notes that "the style will be a combination of Italian and Colonial"; "Barnard College Buildings," *EP,* July 7, 1896, p. 9, claims that "the architectural style of the three buildings will be composite, of Italian Renaissance and Colonial."

51. Anderson to Dean Smith, c. May 28, 1897, and December 2, 1897 (BCA, Trustees Correspondence 1889–1904); agreement between Barnard College and Tiffany Glass and Decorating Company, July 7, 1897 (BCA, Box G); and "Barnard's New Building," *NYT,* October 3, 1897, p. 14. Only the mantel survives in the former library. Rich also designed a small theater in the southern section of Brinckerhoff; his design has been altered.

52. "Barnard College," *EP,* May 8, 1897, p. 16.

53. Fiske Hall was a dormitory from its opening in October 1898 until June 1902. It was then remodeled as science laboratories and lecture halls; see John William Robson, ed., *A Guide to Columbia University With Some Account of Its History and Traditions* (New York: Columbia University Press, 1937), p. 130

54. "Barnard College," *New York Times Illustrated Magazine,* October 9, 1898, p. 2; and List of Subscribers (1898; BCA, File F).

55. Not all graduate programs were open to women. It was not until 1917 that the medical school admitted women and 1927 when women finally were permitted to enroll at the law school.

56. "$400,000 For Barnard," *NYT,* April 1, 1902, p. 16.

57. Beginning in April 1902, many real estate companies wrote to New York Hospital expressing an interest in acquiring the property on Broadway between 116th and 119th streets (NYHA, Secretary-Treasurer Papers, Box 34, File 5).

58. Laura Drake Gill, *Dean's Annual Report* (1902), p. 186.

59. Plimpton to Cammann, February 23, 1903 (BCA, File L, Administration 1889–1904 Miscellaneous).

60. According to "She Gave Barnard Million," *Sun,* March 8, 1903, p. 1, which leaked the name of the donor, Anderson had offered to buy the property several weeks earlier. Anderson formally offered the land to Barnard in a letter to the trustees, April 17,

1903 (BCA, File L, A. A. Anderson File). Also see, "Mrs. Anderson and Her Million Dollar Gift," *Herald,* March 15, 1903, sec. 4, p. 4, and "Mrs. Anderson's Gift To Barnard College," *NYT,* April 19, 1903, p. 12.

61. Barnard College, *Minutes of the Board of Trustees,* April 17, 1903 (BCA).

62. West 119th Street between Broadway and Claremont Avenue was given to Barnard and closed to traffic in 1952.

63. Barnard College, *Minutes of the Buildings and Grounds Committee,* June 5, 1903, June 29, 1903 (BCA).

64. "Barnard College," *Architecture* 10 (November 1904), 173; this article also published Rich's design, pp. 174–75.

65. "Urge Big Park Purchase," *NYT,* January 24, 1906, p. 2.

66. [editorial], *Architecture* 13 (April 15, 1906), 50.

67. "The West Side Park," [editorial] *NYT,* January 25, 1906, p. 8. The *Tribune* was also critical; see "New Plans at Columbia," [editorial] *Tribune,* March 6, 1906, p. 6.

68. Elsie de Wolfe, "List of Decor in Brooks Hall," 1907 (BCA, Buildings and Grounds Committee File); also see "Dormitory for Barnard," *EP,* May 14, 1906, p. 3, and "New Barnard Dormitory," *EP,* September 7, 1907, p. 2. For de Wolfe, see Jane S. Smith, *Elsie de Wolfe: A Life in the High Style* (New York: Atheneum, 1982); the Barnard commission is mentioned on pp. 123 and 156.

69. "Barnard College is Crying Aloud For Funds," *NYT Magazine,* December 14, 1913, p. 10.

70. Barnard's new main entrance was embellished in 1921 by the Geer Memorial Gateway designed by Polhemus & Coffin. This gateway was donated by Helen Hartley Jenkins and Grace Hartley Jenkins as a memorial to Helen Hartley Jenkins Geer, class of 1915; see John William Robson, ed., *A Guide to Columbia University* (New York: Columbia University Press, 1937), p. 130. The gateway is illustrated in Architectural League of New York, *Yearbook* (1922), n.p.

71. Schiff to Plimpton, August 24, 1915 (CUA, CF, Schiff File).

72. Schiff to Low, October 8, 1915 (CUL, Seth Low Papers, Box 66).

73. Schiff to Plimpton, August 24, 1915. Rich would never again design for Barnard; with Anderson's death in 1921, the link between Rich and the college was broken.

74. The tablet reads "THIS BUILDING IS THE GIFT OF JACOB H. SCHIFF TO BARNARD COLLEGE TO PROMOTE THE WELFARE OF WOMEN STUDENTS OF COLUMBIA UNIVERSITY MCMXVII."

75. Robson, *A Guide to Columbia,* p. 132

76. Meyer to Plimpton, February 14, 1934 (BCA, Buildings and Grounds File 5, Folder 10).

77. Meyer to Plimpton, February 14, 1934; also noted in Gordon, "Annie Nathan Meyer," p. 518, and Horowitz, *Alma Mater,* p. 259.

78. For Dean Gildersleeve's views on Jewish students, see Gordon, "Annie Nathan Meyer," 515–21, and Horowitz, *Alma Mater,* pp. 258–59.

79. Gordon, "Annie Nathan Meyer," 516, and Horowitz, *Alma Mater,* p. 260.

80. "Hewitt Hall, Barnard College, New York City," *A&B* 58 (January 1926), p. 1, plates 1–3.

81. "Both Restraint and Beauty in the Designing of Hewitt Hall, the Residence for Women at Barnard College," unidentified newspaper article, c. 1925 (BCA, Buildings and Grounds File 5, Folder 16).

82. It is no coincidence that in 1926, only a year after Hewitt Hall was completed, Dean Gildersleeve established the Seven College Conference, an organization of elite eastern women's colleges (Barnard, Bryn Mawr, Mount Holyoke, Radcliffe, Smith, Vassar, and Wellesley) that became known as the "seven sisters"; see Horowitz, *Alma Mater*, p. 260.

83. "Barnard Planning To Build On Drive," *NYT*, December 6, 1935, p. 29.

84. The new buildings were Helen Reid Hall (O'Connor & Kilham, 1957–59), a dormitory that completed the east arm of the complex begun with Brooks and expanded with Hewitt; Adele Lehman Hall (O'Connor & Kilham, 1957–59), a concrete and terra-cotta library; a student center named Millicent McIntosh Hall (Vincent G. Kling, 1966–69); and the twelve-story Helen Goodhart Altschul Hall (Vincent G. Kling, 1966–69). Barnard also erected a dormitory called Plimpton Hall (Slingerland & Booss, 1966–69) on the southeast corner of Amsterdam Avenue and West 121st Street. All of these buildings are discussed in Robert A. M. Stern, Thomas Mellins, and David Fishman, *New York 1960: Architecture and Urbanism Between the Second World War and the Bicentennial* (New York: Monacelli Press, 1995), p. 740.

85. "Holding Court," *AR* 177 (October 1989), 112–15, and "Centennial Hall, Barnard College," *Architecture and Urbanism* 242 (September 1990), 88–95.

86. A major source for the early history of Teachers College and the intent of its founders, benefactors, and deans is Bette C. Weneck, "The 'Average Teacher' Need Not Apply: Women Educators at Teachers College, 1887–1927," unpublished Ph.D. dissertation, Columbia University (1996). Also see Lawrence A. Cremin, David A. Shannon, and Mary Evelyn Townsend, *A History of Teachers College, Columbia University* (New York: Columbia University Press, 1954), and Franklin T. Baker, "Teachers College," in *A History of Columbia University 1754–1904* (New York: Columbia University Press, 1904), pp. 409–41.

87. The development of Social Christianity is discussed in Mina Carson, *Settlement Folk: Social Thought and the American Settlement Movement 1885–1930* (Chicago: University of Chicago Press, 1990), pp. 10–19.

88. For Dodge, see James E. Russell, "Grace Hoadley Dodge: The Influence of Miss Dodge on Teachers College," Seth Low, "Grace H. Dodge and the Making of Teachers College," and Lucetta Daniell, "Impressions of Miss Dodge," addresses given at a service in memory of Dodge on January 4, 1915, printed in *Teachers College Record* 16 (March 1915), pp. 1–17, and reprinted in *Grace H. Dodge: Her Life and Work* (New York: Arno Press, 1974); "Grace Dodge Dead: Noted For Charities," *NYT*, December 28, 1914, p. 9; Sarah G. Bowerman, "Grace Hoadley Dodge," *DAB*, vol. 3 (New York: Scribner's, 1930), pp. 346–47; *NCAB*, vol. 18 (New York: James T. White & Co., 1922), p. 310; Abbie Graham, *Grace H. Dodge: Merchant of Dreams* (New York: The Woman's Press, 1926); and Ellen Condiffe Lagemann, *A Generation of Women: Education in the Lives of Progressive Reformers* (Cambridge: Harvard University Press, 1979), pp. 9–31.

89. This was true during the early years of Teachers College's development, but, as Lagemann, *A Generation of Women* (pp. 27–28) and Weneck, "Average Teacher" (p. 48) note, as the school became increasingly professionalized, Dodge's active role became more limited, although she remained a powerful force on the board of trustees.

90. Dodge also organized and supported the Travelers' Aid Society (which assisted women and girls traveling alone as they arrived at railroad stations and ship piers), the Working Girls' Association of Clubs, and the Girls' Public School Athletic League.

91. Quoted in Lagemann, *A Generation of Women*, p. 27.

92. Kitchen Garden Association, *First Annual Report* (1881), 17. The Kitchen Garden system was invented by Emily Huntington, who first experimented with the method of teaching in New York City in 1877. Her ideas were published in Emily Huntington, *The Kitchen Garden or Objective Lessons in Household Work* (New York, 1878). Also see Grace H. Dodge, *A Brief Sketch of the Early History of Teachers College* (New York: Maynard, Merrill & Co., 1899), p. 3, and Weneck, "Average Teacher," p. 42.

93. Kitchen Garden Association, *First Annual Report*, p. 9.

94. Kitchen Garden Association, *First Annual Report*, p. 9.

95. Dodge, *A Brief Sketch*, p. 16, and Weneck, "Average Teacher," pp. 43–47.

96. Lawrence A. Cremin, *The Transformation of the School: Progressivism in American Education, 1876–1957* (New York: Knopf, 1969), pp. 36–41 notes that by training workers outside of the established apprenticeship system, these schools also tended to bypass the unions.

97. For an overview of the manual training movement, see Cremin, *The Transformation of the School*, pp. 23–41, and Marvin Lazerson and W. Norton Grubb, *American Education and Vocationalism: A Documentary History 1870–1970* (New York: Teachers College Press, 1974), pp. 1–14.

98. Dodge, *A Brief Sketch*, p. 20.

99. *Classified and Descriptive Directory to the Charitable and Beneficent Societies and Institutions of the City of New York* (New York: Charity Organization Society, 1887), pp. 54–55, 125.

100. Union Theological Seminary moved in 1884 to a new complex designed by William Potter on Park Avenue between 69th and 70th streets (see chapter 7).

101. "College for the Training of Teachers," two page catalogue (TCA).

102. Weneck, "Average Teacher," p. 38.

103. Baker, *Teachers College*, p. 411.

104. Nicholas Murray Butler, "The Origins of Teachers College and the Horace Mann School," printed text of address at the 40th anniversary of the Horace Mann School delivered on January 22, 1927, pp. 5–6 (TCA).

105. Weneck, "Average Teacher," p. 62.

106. New York College for the Training of Teachers, *Minutes of the Board of Trustees,* December 8, 1892 (TCA).

107. "Summary," *Teachers College Bulletin* 1 (January 1894), p. 18 (emphasis in original).

108. Nicholas Murray Butler, "The Beginnings of Teachers College," *CUQ* 1 (September 1899), 345.

109. Weneck, "Average Teacher," p. 70, notes that in 1887, 16 of 18 matriculating students were women and 61 of 86 special students. In 1888, 49 of 50 matriculating students were female, as were 142 of 161 special students.

110. *Minutes,* October 30, 1890.

111. Letters written in November 1891 offered sites on West 14th Street, 79th Street and Columbus Avenue, and Central Park West between 66th and 67th streets (TCA, Walter L. Hervey Papers, Other Administrative Records).

112. Potter was elected chairman on November 24, 1891; *Minutes,* November 24, 1891.

113. *Minutes,* December 17, 1891, notes a resolution establishing a special committee to consult with President Low of Columbia.

114. Nicholas Murray Butler, *Across the Busy Years: Recollections and Reflections,* vol. 1 (New York: Scribner's, 1939), p. 168. Butler's recollections are not always truthful. It is clear, however, that the Teachers College trustees were aware of Columbia's negotiations with New York Hospital.

115. *Minutes,* February 18, 1892; "Another College To Be Near Columbia," *Tribune,* February 7, 1892, p. 2; and "College For Teachers," *NYT,* February 26, 1892, p. 8.

116. At the ceremony formally opening Teachers College's Morningside Heights building, held on November 15, 1894, Columbia's president Seth Low stated, "It is an interesting circumstance, naturally not known to many, that the Teachers' College had under consideration this present site before it was known that Columbia was likely to move here. . . . It is significant that two distinct bodies of people interested in education should have selected these Heights as the natural home in New York city for educational institutions seeking to find a permanent footing in the midst of the resistless growth of the metropolis." (Quoted in "The Teachers' College," *EP,* November 15, 1894, p. 5). Although it was true that Teachers College purchased its land before Columbia finalized its deal with New York Hospital, Low's statement was misleading. Perhaps Low was attempting to justify the wisdom of his decision to move Columbia to an urban site on Morningside Heights by accenting Teachers College's independent decision to buy property in the same area of the city. Curiously, Low's comments do not appear in the official transcript of his speech, see "Address of President Low," *Teachers College Bulletin* 5 (January 1895), 7–9.

117. *Minutes,* January 19, 1892, and Potter to Trustees of Columbia College, January 27, 1892 (TCA).

118. These issues are discussed in Weneck, "Average Teacher," p. 102.

119. Columbia College, "Report Submitted on Behalf of the University Council on the Proposed Consolidation of the College for the Training of Teachers With Columbia College," February 23, 1892 (TCA), and Columbia College, "Report of the Special Committee on the Proposed Alliance of the College for the Training of Teachers With Columbia College," May 2, 1892 (TCA).

120. *Minutes,* February 18, 1892.

121. No letter of resignation is recorded and there is no information about whether Potter undertook the design of the Teachers College buildings on a *pro bono* basis or charged his regular fee. The last board meeting that he attended was on February 18, 1892. The major source for Potter is Sarah Bradford Landau, *Edward T. and William A. Potter: American Victorian Architects* (New York: Garland Publishing, 1979); also see, Montgomery Schuyler, "The Work of William Appleton Potter," *AR* 26 (September 1909), 176–96.

122. Potter's finest extant church is the Church of the Holy Trinity (now St. Martin's Episcopal Church, 1887–89) on Lenox Avenue and West 122nd Street. Union Theological Seminary's complex on Park Avenue (demolished) was erected in 1881–84. Among Potter's work at Princeton are Chancellor Green Library (1871–73), John C. Green Science Building (1872–74), Witherspoon Hall (1875–77), and Alexander Hall (1891–94). At Union College, Potter designed Powers-Washburn Hall (1880–83). For a complete list of William Potter's buildings, see Landau, pp. 465–83.

123. "Plans of the New Teachers College"; "A New College Building," *EP,* January 20, 1894, p. 2; and "Teachers' College," *Harlem Local Reporter,* February 14, 1894, p. 1.

124. "Plans of the New Teachers' College," *RRBG,* 49 (April 16, 1892), 599; "Plans for the Teachers; College," *RRBG* 50 (August 27, 1892), 265. The designs were published in William A. Potter, *The New Buildings for the New York College for the Training of Teachers* (New York, c.1893); "New York College for the Training of Teachers, New York, N.Y.," *AABN* 36 (August 27, 1892), p. 136 and plates; "New Buildings for the Teachers' College, New York, N.Y.," *AABN* 40 (April 15, 1893), 46 and plate; and *A&B* 21 (October 13, 1894), plates.

125. The porch was demolished for the construction of Russell Hall in 1922.

126. The choice of architectural style for Teachers College is discussed in Landau, *Edward T. and William A. Potter,* pp. 342–44.

127. Teachers College slowly acquired most of the remainder of the block through purchases and gifts between 1892 and 1908; see New York City Deeds and Conveyances, block 1975. The east elevations of Main and Macy halls were eventually hidden by later construction. The west facade of Milbank Hall is still visible.

128. *Minutes,* February 16, 1893.

129. *Minutes,* February 16, 1893.

130. For V. Everit Macy, see *A Souvenir of New York Old and New* (New York: New York Commercial, c. 1917), p. 91; William Bristol Shaw, "Valentine Everit Macy," *DAB,* vol. 7 (New York: Scribner's, 1933), pp. 179–80; and "Everit Macy Dies in Arizona Hotel," *NYT,* March 22, 1930, p. 19.

131. "The New Teachers College," *Tribune,* September 22, 1894, p. 7.

132. *Minutes,* October 18, 1894, record the move into the new building, although the official dedication ceremony was not held until November 15, 1894; see "To Open the New Building," *Tribune,* November 11, 1894, sec. 2, p. 1; "The Teachers' College," *EP,* November 15, 1894, p. 5; and "Teachers' College Open," *NYT,* November 16, 1894, p. 8.

133. "How to Reach Teachers College," *Teachers College Bulletin* 4 (November 1894), back of front cover.

134. *Minutes,* November 22, 1894.

135. *Minutes,* March 26, 1896.

136. "Joseph Milbank's Gift," *Tribune,* May 26, 1897, p. 3. In 1897, Milbank became a Teachers College trustee.

137. "Gift to Teachers' College," *NYT,* March 19, 1893.

138. "Joseph Milbank's Gift."

139. Weneck, "Average Teacher," p. 131.

140. The interior is described in "Joseph Milbank Gift," and "Milbank Memorial," *Teachers College Bulletin* 9 (October 1897), 3–4. The original seating has been removed.

141. *Minutes,* January 19, 1899.

142. Among Teachers College's major donors were Grace Dodge (a Presbyterian), the Macy family (Quakers), Mary Thompson (a Congregationalist), and Josiah Milbank and John D. Rockefeller (both Baptists).

143. *Minutes,* January 16, 1899. The building cost approximately $550,000.

144. The below-market price paid by Teachers College resulted from the fact that the property was owned by James H. Jones, son-in-law of trustee A. Newbold Morris, who had "taken a lively interest in the growth of the Teachers College" and had held the land for several years waiting for the college to raise money for its acquisition; "Horace Mann School Land," *Tribune,* April 8, 1899, p. 1. According to this article, the site was actually worth $150,000. Teachers College paid $10,000 in cash and took out a note, at no interest, for the remaining $90,000, which was paid off in 1900 through gifts from Seth Low, Charles Harkness, and others. Also see "Teachers' College Buys Land," *NYT,* April 8, 1899, p. 9.

145. Comparing the facade of the completed Horace Mann School with other buildings designed by Howells & Stokes, it is probable that this firm designed the exterior. The patterned brickwork at Horace Mann resembles the exceptional use of brick at other Howells & Stokes buildings, notably the Royal Insurance Company buildings in New York and San Francisco. The firm's competition design for Union Theological Seminary (just across the street from Teachers College) uses a diaper pattern similar to that on Horace Mann.

146. *Minutes,* October 12, 1899.

147. See Macy to Russell, May 9, 1899 (TCA, Russell Papers, Series 3, Folder 124).

148. James Russell, *Teachers College Dean's Report* (1900, TCA), 28. For a history of the Horace Mann School, see Harold J. Bauld and Jerome B. Kisslinger, *Horace Mann-Barnard: The First Hundred Years* [1986].

149. Schiff to Russell, July 20, 1899 (TCA, Russell Papers, Series 6, Folder 599). This file contains many letters written by Schiff, Russell, Grace Dodge, and others between June and September 1899 relating to this issue.

150. Prettyman to Russell, August 14, 1899 (TCA, Russell Papers, Series 6, Folder 599).

151. James Russell, "Report of the Organization and Administration of the Proposed

Extension of the Experimental (Settlement) School," in *Minutes,* May 8, 1901.

152. Jesse D. Burks [acting principal], "History of the Speyer School," in "The Speyer School: Part I.—Its History and Purpose," *Teachers College Record* 3 (November 1902), 9–10.

153. For the Speyer School, see Burks, "The Speyer School," pp. 1–28, and Christopher Gray, "The Speyer School: 'Essentials of Wholesome Living' In a 'Settlement House' Setting," *NYT,* October 18, 1987, sec. 9, p. 14.

154. *Minutes,* November 11, 1901.

155. *Minutes,* March 6, 1902. For the Thompsons, see "Frederick F. Thompson Dead," *NYT,* April 11, 1899, p. 3, and "Mary C. Thompson Dead," *NYT,* July 29, 1923, p. 6.

156. *Minutes.* February 20, 1913.

157. The Dodges frequently employed Parish. In 1903, Ellingwood & Parish undertook alterations on Cleveland Dodge's Riverdale home and, in 1909–11, Parish & Schroeder did additional work on this home. Between 1900 and 1904, Parish & Schroeder designed alterations to William Earl Dodge's Riverdale house. The firm was also responsible for the Household Arts Building at Teachers College and an office building on Cliff Street (demolished) planned in 1908 for Cleveland Dodge. It was undoubtedly through Cleveland Dodge's influence as president of the YMCA that Parish & Schroeder received the commission for the West Side Branch on West 57th Street (demolished).

158. "Columbia's New $400,000 Gymnasium for Women," *Sun,* October 26, 1904, sec. 2, p. 3.

159. For Grueby tiles, see Susan J. Montgomery, *The Ceramics of William H. Grueby: The Spirit of the New Idea in Artistic Handicraft* (Lambertville, N.J.: Arts & Crafts Quarterly Press, 1993), p. 64; the leaf and berry border is illustrated in *Catalogue of the Grueby Faience Company* (c. 1900–1909; collection of the Andover Historical Society, Andover, Massachusetts). For the St. Gaudens sculpture, see "Physical Education Now Open to All at Columbia," *Herald,* November 17, 1907, magazine section, p. 5.

160. *Teachers College Hall 1899–1900* advertising brochure (1899), p. 7.

161. *Directory of Officers and Students 1899–1900* (New York: Columbia University, 1899).

162. *Minutes,* February 8, 1900.

163. *Minutes,* February 15, 1900.

164. "Certificate of Incorporation of the Morningside Realty Co." (TCA, Russell Papers, Series 15, Folder 862).

165. For Price, see Russell Sturgis, "The Works of Bruce Price," *AR,* Great Architects Series (1899), and Samuel Huiet Greybill, Jr., "Bruce Price, American Architect, 1845–1903," unpublished Ph.D. dissertation, Yale University (1957).

166. "New Model Apartment to Cost $1,000,000 Will Contain Cheap Rooms For 400 Teachers," *World,* August 26, 1900, p. E6.

167. "An Attractive Hotel For Single Women," *San Francisco Chronicle,* December 2, 1901 (in TCA, Newspaper Clippings).

168. James Russell, "Report to the Directors of the Morningside Realty Co., New York City," p. 1 (TCA, James Russell Papers, Series 15, Folder 862).

169. Russell, "Report to the Directors," p. 6.

170. James Russell, *Dean's Report* (1909), p, 10, and "New Year Gift to Columbia," *NYT,* January 1, 1909, p. 6.

171. Whittier and Longfellow are still dormitories for Teachers College students. Emerson and Lowell now house Teachers College faculty and staff.

172. Eva Elise vom Baur, "Dwellings In High Places," *EP Magazine,* May 17, 1913, p. 9.

173. Vom Baur, "Dwellings in High Places."

174. John D. Rockefeller, Jr. (writing on behalf of his father) to Russell, October 20, 1902, in *Minutes,* October 20, 1902.

175. Rockefeller's gift was widely reported in American newspapers. A large collection of these articles is preserved in TCA, "Newspaper Clippings."

176. Rockefeller was especially interested in women's education. He established the University of Chicago as a coeducational school. In 1902, besides his donation to Teachers College, he also gave $200,000 to Vassar College and $250,000 each to Barnard College and Bryn Mawr College; see "Notable Donations in 1902 to Science, Education and Charity," *Herald,* January 1, 1903, p. 5.

177. *Minutes,* February 16, 1905, lists donors who subscribed to pay off the debt. They included James Speyer ($50,000), William Dodge ($50,000), V. Everit Macy ($25,000), Grace Dodge ($5500), A. Newbold Morris ($5000), and Spencer Trask ($5000).

178. [editorial], *HW* 46 (November 8, 1902), 1639.

179. "The New Household Arts Building, Teachers College, Columbia University," *Teachers College Record* 10 (1909), p. 73. The resemblance to the Founder's Tower at Magdalen is minimal.

180. "The New Household Arts Building," p. 73.

181. Parish & Schroeder to John H. Ingram, January 6, 1909 (Mercer Archive, Doylestown, Pennsylvania); Ingram was an agent for the Moravian Tile Works, with an office in Philadelphia.

182. Cleota Reed, *Henry Chapman Mercer and the Moravian Pottery and Tile Works* (Philadelphia: University of Pennsylvania Press, 1987), p. 103.

183. Grueby tiles are also used in the halls of the Household Arts Building and in the halls of Parish & Schroeder Thompson Hall. Grueby also made the tiles for the floor of the choir and ambulatory of the Cathedral of St. John the Divine (see chapter 2).

184. *Minutes,* February 18, 1909.

185. "The New Household Arts Building," p. 72.

186. "The New Household Arts Building," pp. 72–73.

187. "Teaches Household Arts, Even Plumbing," *World,* November 7, 1909, sec. 2, p. 2.

188. "The New Household Arts Building," p. 77. "Housewifery" was a course that "treats of the kinds of service needed in various part of the household and the systematic planning of the daily routine." The course included classes in care of the

kitchen and other rooms, bed making, cleaning and ventilating the bathroom, and the use of "tools" such as brooms, brushes, and soap; *Teachers College Annual* (1909–1910), 138.

189. "The New Household Arts Building," p. 76.

190. The woodwork, wall lamps, and floor survive in what is now known as the Tudor Room.

191. For the Arts & Crafts movement, see, for example, Leslie Greene Bowman, *American Arts & Crafts: Virtue in Design* (Los Angeles: Los Angeles Museum of Art with the Bulfinch Press, 1990); Eileen Boris, *Art and Labor: Ruskin, Morris, and the Craftsman Ideal in America* (Philadelphia: Temple University Press, 1986); and Richard Guy Wilson, "Introduction," in *From Architecture to Object: Masterworks of the American Arts & Crafts Movement* (New York: Hirschl & Adler Galleries, 1989).

192. James Russell, *Dean's Report* (1911), p. 5. Russell reports that Teachers College had 1,571 matriculated students, 377 summer students, and 1,838 nonmatriculating students, plus 1,320 Horace Mann students, for a total of 5,106 (p. 5).

193. *Dean's Report* (1911), p. 21.

194. *Minutes,* November 16, 1916.

195. *Minutes,* April 19, 1917.

196. *Minutes,* January 19, 1919, and November 13, 1919.

197. Teachers College, *Treasurer's Report,* November 6, 1920, p. 1.

198. *Minutes,* April 30, 1919, and May 8, 1919.

199. Laws of New York State, Chapter 137 (1920).

200. Columbia had similar problems gaining the use of apartments in the four buildings that it purchased on Claremont Avenue at the same time that Teachers College was buying its first residential structures. "Report of the Committee on Finance," in Columbia University, *Minutes of the Board of Trustees,* December 5, 1921 (CUA).

201. Clark Williams (board treasurer) to Russell, in *Treasurer's Report,* March 20, 1922 (TCA).

202. *Minutes,* March 28, 1923.

203. Russell Hall is illustrated in "Library Building, Teachers College, Columbia University, New York," *AA* 126 (September 10, 1924), plates 84–88.

204. *Report of the Committee of Buildings and Grounds,* November 13, 1924 (TCA). This property contained a sawdust business and stable, deemed "an offense to the residents of Whittier Hall." The business predated Teachers College's purchase on the block. The college had been unable to acquire the property until 1924. The president's house, designed by J. Gordon Carr, was built of limestone with a granite base.

205. Stern, *New York 1960,* pp. 748–49.

206. "Education Schools: No.1 Teachers College, Columbia," in "Best Graduate Schools, *U.S. News & World Report* (1997), 46.

207. In 1906, Teachers College joined an unsuccessful campaign to persuade the Interborough Rapid Transit Company (IRT) to add a subway station at 122nd Street (see chapter 8).

208. As of 1997, the Teachers College buildings had not been designated as landmarks, a conspicuous oversight on the part of the New York City Landmarks Preservation Commission.

7. BUILDING FOR THE MIND AND SPIRIT: THEOLOGICAL SEMINARIES AND A MUSICAL INSTITUTE ON MORNINGSIDE HEIGHTS

1. The juncture of Manhattan Avenue and Broadway is just north of what was once 129th Street (now St. Clair Place). Manhattan Avenue has become a section of 125th Street.

2. The major study of Union Theological Seminary is Robert T. Handy, *A History of Union Theological Seminary in New York* (New York: Columbia University Press, 1987); also see Henry Sloane Coffin, *A Half Century of Union Theological Seminary 1896–1954* (New York: Scribner's, 1954).

3. Handy, *A History of Union Theological Seminary,* p. 18.

4. William Adams, *Theological Seminaries: A Discourse in the Madison Square Presbyterian Church* (New York: Trow & Smith, 1870), p. 36.

5. Handy, *A History of Union Theological Seminary,* p. 56.

6. The seminary initially purchased ten lots on Park Avenue at a cost of $275,000. In 1883 three additional lots were purchased and one more was added to the parcel in 1885. See "Introductory Note," in *Services in Adams Chapel at the Dedication of the New Buildings of the Union Theological Seminary* (New York: William C. Martin, 1885), p. 4.

7. The Park Avenue complex is discussed in Sarah Bradford Landau, *Edward T. and William A. Potter: American Victorian Architects* (New York: Garland Publishing, 1979), pp. 329–32. Potter and Lord were probably chosen as architects for this building because of their association with the Brown family (of the banking firm of Brown Brothers & Co.), who were important supporters of Union Theological Seminary. William Potter's half-brother, Howard Potter, was a partner in the Brown Brothers firm and James Brown Lord was related to the Browns. Since Potter was an Episcopalian, he might not have received this commission if it had not been for the Brown connection, especially since the seminary had previously commissioned J. C. Cady, a Presbyterian architect, to design a library addition for the University Place complex. In the 1880s, Cady was becoming increasingly well known for his -institutional work and he would have been a likely choice for the Presbyterian seminary.

8. William Adams Brown, *Statement of the Most Important Facts and Dates Connected with the History of the Union Theological Seminary from the Election of President Charles Cuthbert Hall, D.D., LL.D. to the Laying of the Corner Stone of the New Buildings on Morningside Heights* (New York: Irving Press, 1909), p. 9.

9. Brown, *Statement of the Most Important Facts,* p. 10. William Adams Brown was a professor at Union and the son of John Crosby Brown.

10. Brown, *Statement of the Most Important Facts,* p. 10; "Gift of $1,100,000 to Union Seminary," *NYT,* February 2, 1905, p. 1, and "$1,100,000 Has Been Given to Union Seminary," *World,* February 2, 1905, p. 1. Since James wished the gift to be anonymous, his name was not on the property deed. Title was held by Edmund Coffin (James's lawyer), who transferred ownership to the seminary (New York City Conveyance Records, Block 1992).

11. Brown, *Statement of the Most Important Facts,* p. 7. The issue was extensively covered by local newspapers, many placing Union's announcement on the front page; see, for example, "Union Seminary Drops Westminster Confession," *NYT,* November 27, 1904, p. 1, and "Union Drops the Confession," *Sun,* November 27, 1904, p. 1.

12. "Union Seminary Drops Westminster Confession."

13. Brown, *Statement of the Most Important Facts,* p. 9; also see Handy, *A History of Union Theological Seminary,* p. 117.

14. James donated $100,000 to the cathedral in 1887 and 1888; see James to Bishop Potter, May 24, 1887 (StJA, Choir Chapels—General File). James also donated $50,000 to Columbia's campaign to raise funds for the purchase of the Morningside Heights site. James's fortune, like that of William Earl Dodge who donated Earl Hall to Columbia (see chapter 5), came from the Phelps, Dodge & Co. mining business (James's mother was a Phelps). For James, see William Bristol Shaw, "Daniel Willis James," *DAB,* vol. 5 (New York: Scribner's, 1932), pp. 573–74; "D. Willis James Dies in New Hampshire," *NYT,* September 14, 1907, p. 9; "Death of D. Willis James," *EP,* September 13, 1907; and [editorial], *EP,* September 24, 1907, p. 6.

15. Union Theological Seminary, Building Committee, "Cash Statement as of October 6, 1911 (UTSA, Series 8, Box 2).

16. Union Theological Seminary, Committee on Site and Buildings, *Minutes,* January 9, 1906 and April 19, 1906 (UTSA, Series 8, Box 2).

17. "The Program of a Competition for the Selection of an Architect and the Procuring of a General Plan for the Union Theological Seminary in the City of New York" (UTSA, Box 2.3D).

18. "The Program of a Competition." Many of these requirements were established by the Committee on Site and Buildings; see *Minutes,* October 6, 1905.

19. "The Program of a Competition," p. 9.

20. "The Program of a Competition," p. 9.

21. Committee on Site and Buildings, *Minutes,* October 29, 1906.

22. *Minutes,* December 13, 1906. The competition entry of Allen & Collens and the three runners up, Howells & Stokes, Carpenter, Blair & Gould, and Pell & Corbett are illustrated in *Architecture* 15 (January 15, 1907), 2–8. These four designs as well as those of fifth place J. H. Freedlander and sixth place Cass Gilbert are in Adam Benedict Lacey, ed., *American Competitions* (New York: T-Square Club, 1907), pp. ix–xiv and plates (in UTSA, Series 2B, Models and Pamphlets, Box 1+); for Cass Gilbert's entry, also see "The Design of Mr. Cass Gilbert, Submitted in the Recent Competition for the Presbyterian Union Theological Seminary of New York," *Christian Art* 1 (Au-

gust 1907), 219–28. The jury awarded seventh place to Jackson & Brown with J. Henry Eames, associate, and eighth place to Lord & Hewlett (*Minutes,* December 13, 1906).

23. [editorial], *Architecture* 15 (January 15, 1907), 1.

24. In New York City, Allen & Collens also designed the Neo-Gothic Park Avenue Baptist Church on Park Avenue at East 64th Street (see chapter 2) and the French Romanesque-inspired Cloisters in Fort Tryon Park. The firm was also responsible for a number of Colonial Revival style churches, including the Flatbush Congregational Church (now the Flatbush-Tompkins Congregational Church) on Dorchester Road between East 18th and East 19th streets in Brooklyn. Allen & Collens was also the architect for Union benefactor Arthur Curtiss James's Elizabethan-inspired mansion on Park Avenue and 69th Street (1916; demolished). Notable Gothic-inspired academic buildings by Allen & Collens are Andover Theological Seminary, the Thompson Memorial Chapel at Williams College, and men's and women's dormitories at Hartford Theological Seminary.

25. Jallade would also be associated with Allen & Collens for the Flatbush Congregational Church project in 1910. Jallade was the architect of the Broadway Presbyterian Church on Broadway and West 115th Street, a rather uninspired essay in Neo-Gothic design clearly modeled on the design of Union (see chapter 8); he also designed International House (1921–25) located northwest of Union's complex (see chapter 2).

26. The revised final design is discussed in "The New Union Theological Seminary Buildings," *AA* 95 (January 20, 1909), 17–20 and plates, and "The New Union Theological Seminary Buildings, New York—Messrs. Allen & Collens, Architects—(Concluded)," *AA* 95 (January 27, 1909), 28–30 and plates.

27. The Committee on New Buildings suggested that the dormitory be extended along Broadway rather than splitting the quadrangle; *Minutes,* December 3, 1907.

28. Committee on Building, *Minutes,* November 9, 1908. The *Minutes* report that the Board of Directors had suggested this idea in a resolution of March 12, 1908.

29. "Sample Wall for the New Theological Seminary," *RRBG* 82 (July 25, 1908), 176.

30. "Manhattan Supplying Manhattan," *RRBG* 82 (October 10, 1908), 689.

31. "Noted Divines See New Site Dedicated," *NYT,* November 18, 1908, and "To Build a $250,000 Chapel," *NYT,* January 15, 1909, p. 5.

32. "Union Seminary's Dedication," *EP,* November 29, 1910, p. 14; "Church Unity Plea Opens New Seminary," *NYT,* November 30, 1910, p. 12; "New Seminary Dedicated," *Tribune,* November 30, 1910, p. 9; "Seminary's New Home Grows," *Sun,* November 30, 1910, p. 4; "The Union Theological Seminary," [editorial], *Sun,* November 30, 1910, p. 8; and *The Dedication of the New Buildings of the Union Theological Seminary in the City of New York* (1910; UTSA).

33. Architect Frederick R. Allen reported that the use of wooden wainscot beneath the windows was inspired by a similar design element at Kings College Chapel, Cambridge; Allen to Brown, August 1, 1908 (UTSA, "Scrapbook I, Series 8, Box 3).

34. "Union Seminary's Dedication." The chapel was altered in the late 1970s to create a

more flexible worship space. Architect Philip Ives removed the woodwork from the walls and replaced all of the original pews and chancel furnishings with chairs; see Handy, *A History of Union Theological Seminary,* pp. 331–32.

35. "Union Seminary's Quadrangle," *EP,* May 4, 1910, p. 9, and CU, Avery Library, Guastavino Collection, Files 6.203–6.205.

36. The dormitory and faculty housing are discussed in "Union Seminary's 'Quad,'" *EP,* May 4, 1910, p. 9.

37. "Dr. Charles C. Hall Dead," *NYT,* March 26, 1908, p. 7; "D. Willis James Dies in New Hampshire," *NYT,* September 14, 1907, p. 9; and "John Crosby Brown Dead," *NYT,* June 26, 1909, p. 7.

38. "Union Seminary's Dedication," *EP.*

39. "The New Home of the Union Theological Seminary," *Outlook* 96 (December 3, 1910), 803.

40. "English Scholastic Gothic," *RRBG* 85 (January 29, 1910), 216, and "New Buildings of Union Seminary," *RRBG* 85 (June 4, 1910), 1197.

41. "The Union Theological Seminary Group in New York as Executed," *AA* 98 (October 12, 1910), 128.

42. Montgomery Schuyler, "Architecture of American Colleges IV. New York City Colleges," *AR* 27 (June 1910), 457, 460.

43. Handy, *A History of Union Theological Seminary,* p. 133.

44. Robert Moats Miller, *Harry Emerson Fosdick: Preacher, Pastor, Prophet* (New York: Oxford University Press, 1985), p. 319.

45. Handy, *A History of Union Theological Seminary,* p. 157. Handy, pp. 97–98, notes that the first woman was admitted to Union classes in 1895. Although the number of full-time women students remained small in the early twentieth century, their admission at all was seen as a "a significant step" (p. 98). Union accepted its first black student in the late 1850s (Handy, p. 41), but it was not until the mid-1920s that more than an occasional African-American student was enrolled (Handy, p. 178).

46. "$50,000 Gift For Gymnasium," *NYT,* March 21, 1912, p. 10. Union used the gymnasium until the 1930s. The building then served as a housing shelter for homeless men during the Depression and was later occupied by the Uptown Branch of the YMCA. During World War II, Columbia University used the building for training midshipmen in the Naval ROTC program. In 1957, the building was purchased for Riverside Church by John D. Rockefeller, Jr., and renovated for use as a community gym and youth center (RSCA, Stone Gym Box).

47. "Union Theological Seminary: Plan For Expansion, April 1921" (UTSA, Series 17, Box 8, File 19.14). This was a confidential report sent only to members of the board of trustees.

48. Handy, *A History of Union Theological Seminary,* p. 154; Miller, *Harry Emerson Fosdick,* p. 320; and Albert F. Schenkel, *The Rich Man and the Kingdom: John D. Rockefeller, Jr., and the Protestant Establishment* (Minneapolis: Fortress Press, 1995), pp. 179–80. According to Miller, Rockefeller donated $1,083,333; Harkness, $1,250,000 (Harkness, like Rockefeller, was the son of a founder of the Standard Oil Company;

he also supported the construction of Russell Library at Teachers College and paid for Butler Library at Columbia University); and James, $365,000.

49. "Memorial Tower For Union Seminary," *NYT,* December 12, 1924, sec. 2, p. 1; "Union Seminary Plans Memorial to John Crosby Brown," *HT,* December 14, 1924, p. 15; "A Tower of Union," [editorial], *NYT,* December 15, 1924, p. 16; and Handy, *A History of Union Theological Seminary,* pp. 154–55. Cost constraints led Allen & Collens to reduce the planned height of the corner tower, creating a design that is in fact better proportioned to the remainder of the complex. The refectory was also lowered a story, leaving a scar on the north elevation of the chapel tower that provides evidence of the scale of the building originally proposed by Allen & Collens.

50. "Apartment House for Furloughed Missionaries" (pamphlet, UTSA, Series 17, Box 8, File 19.11).

51. "Missionary Residence Begun By Seminary," *NYT,* January 3, 1927, p. 8.

52. Besides Rockefeller, Harkness and James also contributed funds for the construction of McGiffert Hall; Handy, *A History of Union Theological Seminary,* p. 167; "Seminary To Erect $500,000 Building," *NYT,* February 24, 1931, p. 44; and "New Seminary Unit Begun," *NYT,* July 31, 1931, p. 12.

53. Handy, *A History of Union Theological Seminary,* pp. 198–99.

54. Union Theological Seminary, *Minutes of the Board of Directors,* May 17, 1949 (UTSA).

55. *Minutes,* January 8, 1957. In 1958–63, Union erected a rather pedestrian dormitory, Van Dusen Hall, designed by Rogers & Butler for sixty married students and twelve faculty members on a large Riverside Drive site, some distance from the Seminary complex, immediately north of International House; see "Union Seminary Plans Expansion," *NYT,* May 12, 1958; "Seminary Getting New Residence," *NYT,* January 30, 1961, p. 18; and Handy, *A History of Union Theological Seminary,* p. 226. The dormitory was sold to International House in 1989, as Union's enrollment decreased. The building is now known as International House North.

56. Susan Doubilet, "Let There Be Light," *Progressive Architecture* (June 1984), 84–87, and "The Burke Library Renovation," *Process: Architecture* 81 (March 1989), 68–73.

57. Holly Sraeel,"Hastings Hall Union Theological Seminary," *Buildings* 84 (June 1990), 86–89, and "Hastings Hall, Union Theological Seminary," *Architecture and Urbanism* 242 (September 1990), 100–103.

58. For Frank Damrosch, see George Martin, *The Damrosch Dynasty: America's First Family of Music* (Boston: Houghton Mifflin Co., 1983); Richard Frank Goldman, "Frank Heino Damrosch," *DAB,* supplement 2 (New York: Scribner's, 1958), pp. 140–41; and "Frank Damrosch, Musician, Is Dead," *NYT,* October 23, 1937, p. 17. Frank Damrosch was the brother of conductor Walter Damrosch, for whom Damrosch Park at Lincoln Center is named.

59. For Loeb, see Ashton Rollins Sanborn, "James Loeb," *DAB,* supplement 1 (New York: Scribner's, 1944), pp. 503–04; "James Loeb Dies On German Estate," *NYT,* May 29, 1933, p. 13; and Stephen Birmingham, *"Our Crowd": The Great Jewish Families of New York* (New York: Harper & Row, 1967), pp. 254–55. Loeb was a graduate

of Harvard and gave generously to his alma mater, including gifts supporting Harvard's music programs.

60. Moses King, ed., *King's Handbook of New York City* (Boston: Moses King, 1893; reprinted New York: Benjamin Blom, 1972), p. 289.

61. For a history of music in New York City, see James M. Keeler, Nancy Shear, Barbara L. Tischler, and Victor Fell Yellin, "Classical Music," in Kenneth T. Jackson, ed., *The Encyclopedia of New York City* (New Haven: Yale University Press, 1995), pp. 239–44.

62. Martin, *The Damrosch Dynasty*, p. 224, and Frank Damrosch, *Institute of Musical Art 1905–1926* (New York: Juilliard School of Music, 1936), p. 9.

63. Martin, *The Damrosch Dynasty*, p. 225.

64. Damrosch, *Institute of Musical Art*, p. 4, and Martin, *The Damrosch Dynasty*, pp. 226–27.

65. Damrosch, *Institute of Musical Art*, pp. 4, 15.

66. "Endowed Music School," *Tribune*, April 29, 1904, p. 1; also see, "For a Music Conservatory," *NYT*, April 30, 1904, p. 9.

67. For the roster of original board members see Damrosch, *Institute of Musical Art*, p. 13.

68. Loeb to Damrosch, April 29, 1904 (emphasis in the original) (JSMA, General Administrative Records, James Loeb 1904–1914 File).

69. "Endowed Music School."

70. Carnegie to Damrosch, February 9, 1905 (Library of Congress, Manuscript Division, Andrew Carnegie Papers, vol. 3). Also see Loeb to Damrosch, April 29, 1904; Paul Warburg to Loeb, January 3, 1905; and Loeb to Damrosch, January 6, 1905 and January 17, 1905 (JSMA, General Administrative Records, James Loeb 1904–1914 File).

71. Thomas Fortune Ryan lived across Fifth Avenue and had purchased the Lenox House to protect his property. The music school occupied the house rent free, but had to pay the taxes of about $6,000 per year. Ryan promised to give the school one year's notice when he wished to end the arrangement.

72. Institute of Musical Art, *Minutes of the Board of Trustees*, October 25, 1905 (JSMA).

73. "Bright Outlook for the New Institute of Musical Art," *NYT*, October 8, 1905, sec. 3, p. 3.

74. *Prospectus of The Institute of Musical Art of the City of New York* (1905).

75. Damrosch, *Institute of Musical Art*, p. 49.

76. Damrosch, *Institute of Musical Art*, p. 81.

77. Institute of Musical Art, *Minutes*, September 29, 1909.

78. Loeb to Damrosch, May 19, 1909 (JSMA, General Administrative Records, James Loeb 1904–1914 File). Loeb offered to buy the four adjoining lots for construction of a men's and a women's dormitory "as an investment of my own and thus to enable the students from distant parts to have the kind of life that makes the happiest memories in later years." This was never done.

79. The architects are mentioned in Loeb to Damrosch, June 8, 1909 (JSMA, General Administrative Records, James Loeb 1904–1914 File). The third architect may have

been John P. Leo, an architect primarily of residential buildings, with an office in Harlem, or Richard Leo, a partner in the firm of Janes & Leo, which designed such prominent apartment buildings as the Dorilton on Broadway and West 71st Street, and the Manhasset on Broadway between 108th and 109th streets.

80. Loeb to Damrosch, June 8, 1909.

81. For Barber, see *A Souvenir of New York City Old and New* (New York: New York Commercial, c. 1917), p. 166; Clarence Clark Zantzinger and Talbot Hamlin, "Donn Barber," *DAB,* vol. 1 (New York: Scribner's, 1927), pp. 587–88; and "Donn Barber Dies in His Sleep at 53," *NYT,* May 30, 1925, p. 9.

82. Barber referred to the style in a somewhat curious manner, describing it as "a free adaptation of the Adams architecture of Bath, England, treated in a French Renaissance manner"; *New York Architect* 4 (November 1910), 1 (no author's name is listed for this article, but since Barber was the editor of the magazine, it was undoubtedly written by him). Even odder was a description in the *Real Estate Record,* which referred to the building "as one of the finest examples of French Gothic style in New York"; "Institute of Musical Art Erecting Four-Story Extension," *RRBG* 114 (July 5, 1924), 10.

83. Frank Damrosch, speech at laying of the cornerstone, March 26, 1910; text printed in Damrosch, *Institute of Musical Art,* p. 99.

84. Damrosch, *Institute of Musical Art,* p. 99, and "The Institute of Musical Art, New York," *As&Bs* 43 (December 1910), 119.

85. Loeb to Damrosch, August 13, 1909 (JSMA, General Administrative Records, James Loeb 1904–1914 File).

86. Damrosch to Loeb, September 13, 1909 (JSMA, General Administrative Records, James Loeb 1904–1914 File).

87. *Minutes,* September 29, 1909. This loan was eventually forgiven; see Damrosch to Paul Cravath, January 11, 1926 (JSMA, Office of the President, General Administrative Records 1904–1938, Paul D. Cravath File). Lists of donors to the building effort are found in *Minutes,* November 9, 1909, and Damrosch, *Institute of Musical Art,* pp. 91–92.

88. "Dedicate Musical Institute," *NYT,* November 6, 1910. The building was widely published in the architectural press; see "The Institute of Musical Art, Donn Barber, Architect," *AA* 97 (May 25, 1910), 208 and plates; *New York Architect* 4 (November 1910), 155–58 and plates; "Institute of Musical Art, Claremont Avenue, New York," *AA* 98 (November 2, 1910), plate; "The Institute of Musical Art, New York," *As&Bs* 43 (December 1910), 119–22; "Institute of Musical Art," *Architectural League of New York Yearbook* 25 (1910); "The Institute of Musical Art of the City of New York, Claremont Avenue and 122nd Street, New York," *AR* 29 (April 1911), 338; and "The Institute of Musical Art of the City of New York, Claremont Avenue and 122nd Street, New York," *Architectural Year Book* (1912), 301–5.

89. Quoted in Damrosch, *Institute of Musical Art,* p. 132.

90. *Minutes,* December 9, 1919.

91. Damrosch, *Institute of Musical Art,* p. 193.

92. Barber's plans for the addition were approved by the board on February 27, 1924; *Minutes,* February 27, 1924.

93. Loeb to Damrosch, March 27, 1923 (JSMA, President's General Administrative Records, 1904–38, Box 1, File 6).

94. "Institute of Musical Art Erecting Four-Story Extension"; Damrosch, *Institute of Musical Art,* pp. 194, 201; "New Building For School," *NYT,* February 17, 1924, sec. 2, p. 5; and "Musical Art Annex," *NYT,* June 29, 1924, sec. 9, p. 1. Funds for construction were donated by James Loeb ($20,000), Eda Kuhn Loeb (wife of James's brother Morris; $15,000), Paul and Nina Loeb Warburg ($25,000), Felix Warburg ($25,000), Frieda Schiff Warburg (wife of Felix Warburg; $25,000), Guta Loeb Seligman ($10,000), and Therese Loeb Schiff (wife of Jacob Schiff; $10,000); see *Minutes,* May 27, 1924. The board decided to seek subscriptions from other trustees and supporters for the $30,000 needed to furnish the addition; $13,500 was raised (including an additional $1,500 from Felix M. Warburg); *Minutes,* May 27, 1924, and December 15, 1924.

95. W. B. Shaw, "Augustus D. Juilliard," *DAB,* vol. 5 (New York: Scribner's, 1932), p. 244, and "A. D. Juilliard Drygoods Man, Capitalist, Dies," *Tribune,* April 26, 1919, p. 14.

96. Initially the Juilliard bequest was estimated at about $5 million; see "Gives $5,000,000 To Advance Music," *NYT,* June 27, 1919, p. 1. When the money was transferred by the estate to the Juilliard Foundation, the bequest was estimated at $10 million; see "$10,000,000 To Go To American Music," *NYT,* February 23, 1923, p. 16. The sum of $13 million was later quoted in newspaper articles; see, for example, "Juilliard Trustees Plan Music Centre," *NYT,* January 25, 1926, p. 1.

97. "A Musical Foundation," *NYT,* January 26, 1926, p. 24.

98. John Erskine, *My Life in Music* (New York: William Morrow, 1950), pp. 52–53.

99. "Music Foundation Buys," *NYT,* February 2, 1924, p. 20. This building had been erected as the Vanderbilt family's guest house.

100. Damrosch, *Institute of Musical Art,* p. 199.

101. Damrosch to Loeb, June 6, 1924 (JSMA, President's General Administrative Records, 1904–38, Box 1, File 6).

102. "Juilliard Trustees Plan Music Centre"; "Juilliard Fund Merges Schools To Create Great Music Center," *HT,* January 25, 1926, p. 1; "Juilliard School Project Outlined," *World,* January 25, 1926, p. 3; and "Musical Art School and Juilliard Merge," *EP,* January 25, 1926, p. 5. Eugene Noble denied that there was any connection between the merger and the resignation of the advisory committee.

103. "New York's Music Center," *EP,* January 26, 1926, p. 8.

104. "Uniting Music Schools," *Sun,* January 26, 1926, p. 18, and "The Musical Foundation," *NYT,* January 26, 1926, p. 24.

105. Martin, *The Damrosch Dynasty,* p. 298.

106. Martin, *The Damrosch Dynasty,* p. 298.

107. In 1927, the Juilliard Foundation purchased the three-story residential structure on

the corner of Broadway and 122nd Street, and the Hudson-Grant View, a six-story apartment house at 122 Claremont Avenue (John C. Watson, 1908). In 1928, a small vacant lot on Broadway was purchased, as well as the Lincoln at 130 Claremont Avenue (John Hauser, 1908). In 1929, the foundation bought two additional six-story apartment buildings, the Buckingham and the Hazelton Court at 3089 and 3099 Broadway (both Neville & Bagge, 1907). The Institute of Musical Art already owned two small parcels on Broadway just north of 122nd Street. See, "Enlarges Holdings," *EP,* January 3, 1929, p. 19, and New York City Conveyance Records, Block 1993, Lots 1–11, 60–64.

108. Damrosch to Erskine, November 19, 1928 (JSMA, President's General Administrative Records, 1914–51, Box 2, Folder 9).

109. Erskine to Damrosch, August 9, 1929 (JSMA, President's General Administrative Records, 1914–51, Box 2, Folder 9). Harmon became a partner in the firm of Shreve & Lamb, forming Shreve, Lamb & Harmon in 1929 at the time when the Shreve & Lamb firm was involved with the design of the Empire State Building. For Harmon, see "Arthur Harmon, Architect, Dead," *NYT,* October 18, 1958, p. 21.

110. The addition is discussed in "For the Furtherance of Musical Art," *A&B* 63 (December 1931), 154–55.

111. Damrosch to Loeb, May 5, 1930 (JSMA, President's General Administrative Records, 1904–38, Box 1, Folder 6).

112. "The Juilliard School of Music," *AR* 71 (June 1932), 385.

113. "Cady, Lone Tenant, Plays in Luck; Gets $1,000 to Move for Wreckers," *World,* January 26, 1930 (JSMA, Juilliard Musical Foundation Scrapbook, vol. 1).

114. "Wreckers Are Defied by Book Shop Owner," *NYT,* June 22, 1930, p. 5; "Store is Flooded She Holds to Lease: Widow Refuses to Give up Book Store to Make Way for Building," *Pittsburgh Press,* June 26, 1930; "Sale of Bookshop Lease Opens Way for Music School," *Bronx Home News,* August 2, 1930; and "Battle of Books and Music Ends As Shop Makes Way for School," *New York Morning World,* August 3, 1930 (in JSMA, Juilliard Music Foundation Scrapbook, vol. 1).

115. "Juilliard School Dedicates Hall," *NYT,* November 8, 1931, p. D.

116. Albert Kirkpatrick, "A Tone Poem in Color," *Baton* 11 (November-December 1931), 15.

117. The interior is described in "The Juilliard School of Music," 385, and Kirkpatrick, "A Tone Poem in Color," 15.

118. Juilliard agreed to become a constituent part of Lincoln Center for the Performing Arts in 1957.

119. "Juilliard and Manhattan Open Their New Homes," *NYT,* October 3, 1969, p. 47.

120. For the history of the Jewish Theological Seminary, see Cyrus Adler, ed., *The Jewish Theological Seminary of America: Semi-Centennial Volume* (New York: The Jewish Theological Seminary, 1939), and "Historical Sketch," in Jewish Theological Seminary of America, "Dedication of New Buildings," program (October 19–26, 1930; JTS-Ratner Center). For the early history of the seminary, see Robert E. Fierstien, *A Different Spirit: The Jewish Theological Seminary of America, 1886–1902*

(New York: The Jewish Theological Seminary of America, 1990). The seminary's buildings are discussed in Jenna Weissman Joselit, "By Design: Building the Campus of the Jewish Theological Seminary of America," in Jack Wertheimer, ed., *Tradition Renewed: A History of Jewish Theological Seminary* (New York: The Jewish Theological Seminary, 1997), pp. 270–292. The author thanks Ms. Joselit for permitting him to read a prepublication copy of this essay. An excellent synopsis of the institution's building history is Cas Stachelberg, "The Jewish Theological Seminary of America: A History of the Institution and Its Architecture," unpublished paper (Columbia University School of Architecture, 1995; JTS-Ratner Center).

121. The ferment within the Jewish community in the final decades of the nineteenth century is discussed in Gerald Sorin, *A Time For Building: The Third Migration 1880–1920,* vol. 3 of *The Jewish People in America* (Baltimore: Johns Hopkins University Press, 1992), pp. 170–190.

122. Fierstien, *A Different Spirit,* pp. 115–18.

123. Fierstien, *A Different Spirit,* p. 127.

124. Cyrus Adler to Solomon Schechter, August 26, 1901, in Ira Robinson, ed., *Cyrus Adler: Selected Letters,* vol. 1 (Philadelphia: Jewish Publication Society of America, 1985), p. 90.

125. Adler to Schechter, August 26, 1901. For Adler, see Naomi W. Cohen, "Introduction," in Robinson, ed., *Cyrus Adler,* vol. 1, pp. xxv–xlii; Abraham A. Neuman, "Cyrus Adler," *DAB,* supplement 2 (New York: Scribner's, 1958), pp. 5–6; and "Dr. Cyrus Adler, 76, Educator, Is Dead," *NYT,* April 8, 1940, p. 1.

126. Adler to Schiff, November 11, 1919 in Robinson, ed., *Cyrus Adler,* vol. 1, p. 398.

127. Schechter arrived in New York in 1902; see "Jewish Theological Seminary Opening," *NYT,* November 21, 1902, p. 3.

128. Adler to Schechter, March 12, 1902, in Robinson, ed., *Cyrus Adler,* vol. 1, pp. 97–98. Details of the reorganization and merger are discussed in "Jewish Theological Seminary of America."

129. Adler to Schechter, August 26, 1901. Adler was especially disappointed with Lewisohn's gift of only $50,000. He wrote, "I had thought from the way Lewisohn talked and what I heard he said to you and others that almost any sum which was necessary might be expected from him." Schiff gave $100,000 and the Guggenheims $50,000; see Cyrus Adler, *Jacob H. Schiff: His Life and Letters,* vol. 2 (Garden City: Doubleday, Doran and Co., 1928), p. 53, and "Jewish Theological Seminary of America," *American Hebrew,* 70 (April 4, 1902), 598. Also see "Many Gifts For Education," *Tribune,* April 3, 1902, p. 1; "Historical Sketch," [p. 1]; and Joseph B. Abrahams, Oral History Tape No. 1 (1956), p. 3 (JTS-Ratner Center). Abrahams was on the administrative staff of Jewish Theological Seminary from 1901–1941; see "Joseph B. Abrahams, 84, Dead; Designer of Illuminated Citations," *NYT,* July 6, 1969, p. 43.

130. Sorin, *A Time For Building,* p. 185. This issue is also discussed in Fierstien, *A Different Spirit,* pp. 5–6.

131. "Jewish Theological Seminary of America," *American Hebrew,* p. 600.

132. Abrahams, Tape No. 1, p. 3.

133. "Jacob H. Schiff's Gift," *NYT*, January 9, 1902, p. 9, and "Land For Jewish Seminary," *Tribune*, January 9, 1902, p. 7.

134. Joseph B. Abrahams, "The Building of the Seminary," in Cyrus Adler, ed., *The Jewish Theological Seminary of America: Semi-Centennial Volume* (New York: The Jewish Theological Seminary, 1939), p. 66; "Historical Sketch, [p. 2]; Abrahams, Tape No. 1, p. 3 and Tape No. 3, p. 7. Schiff also established an endowment for the seminary and gave one half of the original $500,000 (Abrahams, Tape No. 1, p. 3).

135. "Jewish Theological Seminary Dedicated," *NYT*, April 27, 1903, p. 3; "Open Jewish Seminary," *Tribune*, April 27, 1903, p. 4; "Dedication of the Seminary Building," *American Hebrew* 72 (May 1, 1903), 792–94; and "Judaism's Home of Science," *Hebrew Standard* 44 (May 1, 1903), 1–2, 6.

136. The seminary did not officially use the term "Conservative" until 1940; see Sorin, *A Time For Building*, p. 187.

137. "Historical Sketch," [p. 3].

138. Cyrus Adler, *Report to the Board of Directors*, March 2, 1919, p. 10 (JTS Library).

139. The proposed library building is first discussed in a letter from Adler to Louis Marshall [a seminary trustee], July 4, 1923, in Robinson, ed., *Cyrus Adler*, vol. 2, p. 71.

140. Schechter's dormitory proposal is noted in Abrahams, Tape No. 3, p. 6.

141. Adler to Alexander Marx [seminary librarian], August 24, 1923, in Robinson, ed., *Cyrus Adler*, vol. 2, p. 75; also Adler to Mortimer Schiff in Robinson, ed., *Cyrus Adler*, vol. 2, p. 73.

142. The proposed Warburg gift is discussed in Adler to Marshall, November 16, 1927, in Robinson, ed., *Cyrus Adler*, vol. 2, p. 147.

143. Jewish Theological Seminary of America, *Register 1925–1926* (1925), pp. 30–31. Israel Unterberg was a shirt manufacturer; see "Israel Unterberg Dies at Age of 70," *NYT*, May 2, 1934, p. 21. Unterberg gave the gift in memory of his parents.

144. Abrahams, Tape No. 3, p. 8. The bequest was announced in March 1927; see "Brush's $1,000,000 to Seminary," *NYT*, March 3, 1927, p. 14, and "Jewish Seminary Gets $1,467,113 of Brush Estate," *NYT*, May 28, 1927, p. 21.

145. Jewish Theological Seminary, *Minutes of the Board of Directors*, February 22, 1927 (JTS Library); noted is Joselit, p. 15. The February board minutes and a letter of January 11, 1927, from board member Solomon M. Stroock to Adler (in *Minutes*, February 22, 1927), make it clear that Warburg had previously suggested this idea.

146. "65-Story Hotel Here To Be Part Church," *NYT*, September 1, 1925, p. 1, and "65-Story Hotel To Hold Church, Bank, Hospital," *HT*, September 1, 1925, p. 1; also see "$14,000,000 Building To Be Hotel-Church," *EP*, September 1, 1925, p. 8, and "Hotel to Be Tallest Building," *Sun*, September 1, 1925, p. 19.

147. "65-Story Hotel Here To Be Part Church," *NYT*, and Robert A. M. Stern, Gregory Gilmartin, and Thomas Mellins, *New York 1930: Architecture and Urbanism Between the Two World Wars* (New York: Rizzoli, 1987), p. 152. The proposal to erect the Christian Missionary Building was one of several unsuccessful projects to build the world's tallest skyscraper as a symbol of the prominence of religion in the life of

New York. Among the proposed skyscraper churches were Bertram Goodhue's design for the Convocation Tower on the site of Madison Square Garden, at Madison Avenue between East 26th and 27th Streets, and Broadway Temple, designed by Donn Barber (architect of the Institute of Musical Art) for a site on Broadway between 173rd and 174th streets; see Stern, *New York 1930,* pp. 147–52.

148. "Tallest Building In World Is Begun," *NYT,* January 19, 1926, p. 15; "World's Tallest Building for Missionary Work to Cost $14,000,000," *RRBG* 117 (January 30, 1926), 8; "Blast For Skyscraper," *NYT,* February 26, 1926, p. 23; "New York's Acropolis Grows in Glory," *NYT,* March 7, 1926, sec. 4, p. 5; and "Huge Rock Kills 5 In Pit On Broadway," *NYT,* March 31, 1926, p. 8. Curiously, no designs for this building appear to have been published and it is not known how far Konkle and Shreve & Lamb had proceeded with the actual design of the tower.

149. "Oscar E. Konkle, 89, A Realty Executive," *NYT,* November 25, 1954, p. 29.

150. "Jewish Seminary Buys Site," *NYT,* February 6, 1928, p. 23. On December 30, 1927, Oscar Konkle conveyed the property to Rose Freedman (an employee of seminary director Solomon Stroock), who transferred it, the next day, to the seminary; *Minutes,* February 1, 1928.

151. Adler to Felix Warburg, February 6, 1928, in Robinson, ed., *Cyrus Adler,* vol. 2, pp. 150–52.

152. Abrahams, Tape No. 3, p. 14. The fourth side of the seminary's quadrangle was not filled in until 1980–85 when Gruzen and Partners' sensitively designed addition was completed. This building, which includes a new library, auditorium, and classrooms was originally called the Ivan F. and Seema Boesky Family Library, but the name was removed when Boesky was convicted of embezzlement. For the library building, see "Urban Oasis," *AR* 174 (May 1986), 98–101.

153. Adler indicated discussing design ideas with Arnold W. Brunner Associates in 1928. Adler to Warburg, February 6, 1928, and *Minutes,* February 1, 1928. The name Gehron, Ross & Alley first appears in *Report of Dr. Cyrus Adler to the Board of Directors,* October 28, 1928 (bound in *Minutes*). According to architectural historian Joy Kestenbaum, who is completing a study of New York synagogue design, Gehron completed several of Brunner's projects after the latter's death. For Gehron, see "William Gehron Architect, 71, Dies," *NYT,* November 19, 1958, p. 37. Also see Abrahams, "The Buildings of the Seminary," p. 67, and William Gehron, "The New Great Buildings of the Seminary," *United Synagogue Recorder* 9 (April 1929), 2.

154. Louis S. Brush, Last Will and Testament, File 2747, Liber 1348, p. 34 (New York County Surrogate, 1926); reprinted in Board of Directors, *Extracts From the Minutes,* February 22, 1927 (JTS Library).

155. Abrahams, Tape 2, p. 6.

156. The William and Mary building that Abrahams and other seminary directors would have seen in 1928 was the 1867–69 reconstruction of the college designed by Alfred L. Rives, which included a tripartite arcaded loggia. Initial designs for a more faithful reconstruction of the original eighteenth-century building, with a five-part arcaded loggia, were not completed until 1929; see James D. Kornwolf, *"So*

Good a Design" The College of William and Mary: Its History, Background, and Legacy (Williamsburg: College of William and Mary, 1989), pp. 59–65.

157. Leonard Dinnerstein, *Antisemitism in America* (New York: Oxford University Press, 1994), pp. 58–69.

158. Dinnerstein, *Antisemitism in America,* pp. 81–83, and William B. Rhodes, "The Colonial Revival and the Americanization of Immigrants," in Alan Axelrod, ed., *The Colonial Revival in America* (New York: Norton, 1985), pp. 357–60.

159. Other Colonial Revival style buildings erected for Jewish individuals or organizations include Henry Street Settlement's Neighborhood Playhouse (1915), funded by members of the German-Jewish Lewisohn family; the Walter N. Rothschild House at 41 East 70th Street (1928–29); and synagogues such as Ansche Chesed in Harlem (1908), Temple Emanu-El in Brooklyn (1908), Sons of Israel in the Bronx (1911), and Derech Emunah (1904) and the Free Synagogue of Flushing (1926), both in Queens.

160. Lee Lawrie was responsible for a great deal of architectural sculpture, including work at Rockefeller Center, the Nebraska State Capitol, the Los Angeles Public Library, the Cathedral of St. John the Divine, and the Singing Tower at Lake Wales, Florida; see Hartley Burr Alexander, "The Sculpture of Lee Lawrie: An Appreciation of His Latter Work," *Architectural Forum* 54 (May 1931), 595–600 (the Jewish Theological Seminary panel is illustrated on p. 599). The burning bush was an ironic symbol for the entrance tower given that the interior would burn on April 18, 1966, destroying approximately 70,000 books. In 1996, Rabbi Myer Kripke and his wife Dorothy donated $7 million to repair the tower; see "Investment In the Divine," *NYT,* May 9, 1997, p. B1.

161. Myra Tolmach Davis, *Sketches in Iron: Samuel Yellin American Master of Wrought Iron 1885–1940* (Washington: George Washington University, 1971). The symbolism of the ornament on the gates is described in Abrahams, "The Buildings of the Seminary," p. 68 and in "Dedication of the Seminary Gates," (pamphlet JTS Library, Graphics Collection). The menorah is no longer extant.

162. The dormitory lounge, which may not actually have been constructed, is, in any event, no longer extant. The auditorium is intact, but is now a study hall. The manuscript room has been converted into administrative offices, but retains much of its detail and its two original chandeliers.

163. The stylized "semitic" decoration, drawing inspiration from Moorish and ancient Middle Eastern motifs, was first used by Walter S. Schneider and Henry B. Herts in their design of B'nai Jeshurun, a conservative synagogue on West 88th Street between Broadway and West End Avenue, erected in 1916–18; see "The Temple B'nai Jeshurun," *Architecture* 41 (January 1920), 18–19 and plates, and Israel Goldstein, *A Century of Judaism in New York: B'nai Jeshurun 1925–1925* (New York: B'nai Jeshurun, 1930), pp. 262–64. The beamed ceiling of the library reading room at Jewish Theological Seminary is actually concrete. The planned polychromatic detail was never executed. Instead, the beams were painted to resemble wood, lending an "ancient" aspect to the room. The library is now the seminary's synagogue. The ceil-

ing has been painted, but the original chandeliers and a double stair with its outer wall carved with book bindings are extant.

164. "Seminary Dedicates Two New Buildings," *NYT,* October 20, 1930, p. 3, and "Seminary Dedicates L. S. Brush Dormitory," *NYT,* October 27, 1930, p. 5.

165. The most serious alteration to the building was the removal of the multipaned windows from the Unterberg wing and their replacement with especially unpleasant tinted plate-glass windows with massive frames.

8. BUILDING FOR PROFIT: THE DEVELOPMENT OF A RESIDENTIAL COMMUNITY ON MORNINGSIDE HEIGHTS

1. New York Hospital, *Governors Minutes,* Real Estate Committee, March. 1, 1889 (NYHA). Ten lots facing onto 113th Street had rear lot lines on a diagonal due to the irregular shape of the Society's holdings. These lots ranged from approximately 45 feet deep to approximately 150 feet deep.

2. "Terms of Sale," in auction brochure, (NYHA, Governor's Papers, Secretary-Treasurer Records, Box 19, Folder 6).

3. In David Rosner, *A Once and Charitable Enterprise, Hospitals and Health Care in Brooklyn and New York, 1885–1915* (New York: Cambridge University Press, 1982), pp. 180–181, the author interprets these restrictions as a means by which the governors of New York Hospital sought to establish their social control on the development of the neighborhood at the expense of the city's poor and immigrant communities. This argument would be more convincing if the restrictions on property on Morningside Heights were different from those used on the Upper West Side and other neighborhoods that developed into middle-class areas in the late nineteenth century without any institutional involvement. Restrictive covenants determined the character of initial development on many streets on the Upper West Side. In fact, it was only upon the expiration of these covenants that many of the rowhouses on West End Avenue were demolished and replaced by apartment houses. New York Hospital appears to have been concerned primarily with maximizing the price of auctioned property, not with social control in the neighborhood. In addition, there were few poor immigrants in the areas surrounding Morningside Heights in the late nineteenth century and it was unlikely that immigrants would have moved to this isolated area, far from their jobs, or that the developers of tenements could have afforded land with the superb vistas and other amenities available on the Heights.

4. Letter of December 2, 1896 to Pine; author's name is illegible (NYHS-MMW, CU, Box 225).

5. Auction brochure.

6. *A History of Real Estate, Building and Architecture in New York City During the Last Quarter of a Century* (New York: The Real Estate Record Association, 1898), p. 107. The sale transactions are recorded in "Sales of the Week," *RRBG* 43 (April 6, 1889), 468, and in handwritten notations on a sales brochure in NYHA, Governor's Papers, Secretary-Treasurer Records, Box 19, Folder 6. The sale of eleven lots (ten on 113th

Street and one on 112th Street) had to be canceled because of title problems at the hospital's boundary where the lots abutted the old Asylum Lane.

7. *A History of Real Estate,* p. 107.

8. The initial owner of record for both houses was Francis Burdick. Chapman studied at Cornell where he may have met Burdick, who taught at Cornell before coming to Columbia. Among Chapman's finest works are Grace Chapel (now Immaculate Conception R.C. Church; Barney & Chapman, 1894–96) at 406–12 East 14th Street, the Church of the Holy Trinity (Episcopal) Complex (Barney & Chapman, 1897–99) at 316–332 East 88th Street, and the United States Mortgage and Trust Company (now Chemical Bank, 1921–22) at 940 Madison Avenue. Barney & Chapman's buildings are discussed in Montgomery Schuyler, "The Work of Barney & Chapman," *AR* 16 (September 1904), 204–96, and the firm's churches are discussed in Robert A. M. Stern, Gregory Gilmartin, and John Montague Massengale, *New York 1900: Metropolitan Architecture and Urbanism 1890–1915* (N.Y.: Rizzoli, 1983), pp. 113–16.

9. For Federal style rowhouses and their doorways, see Charles Lockwood, *Bricks and Brownstone: The New York Row House, 1783–1929. An Architectural & Social History* (New York: McGraw-Hill, 1972), pp. 1–53. Only two other private houses commissioned by someone who intended the house for personal use were erected on Morningside Heights, both built by hotelier Charles Dederer and his wife Martha, who first erected the yellow brick Colonial Revival building at 608 West 113th Street (George Pelham, architect) in 1897 and then moved from that house into the handsome red brick Colonial Revival townhouse at 565 West 113th Street commissioned in 1903 from architect George Keister.

10. "Morningside Heights," *RRBG* 49 (March 12, 1892), 393–94.

11. Conveyance records and building permits list Carrie Kennedy as the owner and builder of this row and several others in Manhattan, but she is not listed in city directories. Her husband, David T. Kennedy, is listed as a builder. Published articles attribute construction to David Kennedy; see "Morningside Heights," *RRBG* 60 (March 30, 1895), 502, and "Morningside Plateau," *EP* (undated article [c.1897] in Columbiana, Buildings and Grounds Box). Carrie Kennedy is listed as the builder of rows at 11–19 West 74th Street (1889), 6–14 West 71st Street (1891), and 150–160 West 77th Street (1891); see New York City Landmarks Preservation Commission, *Upper West Side/Central Park West Historic District Designation Report* (New York: Landmarks Preservation Commission, 1990), pp. 252, 338, 427. It was common practice in the nineteenth century for male property owners to list property in their wives' names.

12. *Upper West Side/Central Park West Historic District,* pp. A108–109, and Dennis Steadman Francis, *Architects in Practice in New York City 1840–1900* (New York: Committee for the Preservation of Architectural Records, 1980), pp. 13, 57. Neville & Bagge designed hundreds of rowhouses and apartment buildings between 1892 and the 1930s, and were especially active on Morningside Heights and in Harlem, Hamilton Heights, and Washington Heights.

13. Montgomery Schuyler, "The New New York House," *AR* 19 (February 1906), 84.

14. "Morningside Heights," March 30, 1895.

15. "Morningside Heights," March 30, 1895.

16. The major examples of rowhouses for rental were those developed by John Henderson on the East Side and the Clark family on the West Side. Henderson built 32 small rowhouses on Henderson Place, East End Avenue, East 86th Street, and East 87th Street in 1881, all of which were rented; see Andrew S. Dolkart, *Touring the Upper East Side: Walks in Five Historic Districts* (New York: New York Landmarks Conservancy, 1995), pp. 109–11. The Clarks, whose fortune came from the Singer Sewing Machine Company, were early builders on the Upper West Side. Edward S. Clark, president of the Singer Company, erected 28 rowhouses at 15–67 West 73rd Street (1882–85) near his Dakota Apartments and his grandson Frederick Ambrose Clark erected a row of 18 houses at 18–52 West 74th Street (1902–04). The Clark family rented all of the houses until the 1920s. See New York City Landmarks Preservation Commission, *Central Park West—West 73rd-74th Street Historic District Designation Report* (New York: Landmarks Preservation Commission, 1977).

17. "Reasons for Living on the Heights," *NYT,* April 7, 1895, p. 20.

18. No. 405 was sold in 1896 to Frederic A. Cauchois of F. A. Cauchois & Co., dealers in teas and liquors; No. 407 in 1896 to George R. Hill, manager of a company on Union Square East (Hill also purchased No. 435, apparently as an investment); No. 423 in 1897 to Jabez Burns of Jabez & Sons, dealers in machinery; No. 426 in 1895 to George Heeseman, whose occupation is not known (Heeseman lost the house in a foreclosure action in 1898); No. 431 in 1896 to lawyer William H. Reed; and No. 433 in 1896 to James R. Wheeler, a professor of Greek at Columbia.

19. By 1899, university secretary William H. H. Beebe was living in No. 424.

20. For example, in 1898, No. 417 West 117th Street housed eight students; *Directory of Offices and Students 1898–1899* (Columbia University, 1898).

21. Columbia University eventually acquired the entire block. Several of the houses became residences for deans and the entire row was known as "dean's row." The houses were demolished during the 1960s for construction of the School of International Affairs.

22. "New Riverside Drive Mansions," *RRBG* 62 (November 12, 1898), 701.

23. The row at 528–536 West 114th Street is briefly mentioned in "Trade Notes: New Dwellings on Cathedral Heights," *RRBG* 62 (November 12, 1898), 704, and is discussed in more detail in "Morningside Heights: Its Improvements, Beauties and Advantages for Residential Purposes," *RRBG* 63 (March 25, 1898), 520–21.

24. For Gilbert, see New York City Landmarks Preservation Commission, *Upper East Side Historic District Designation Report* (New York: Landmarks Preservation Commission, 1981), pp. 1243–45, and Dennis Steadman Francis and Mosette Glaser Broderick, "C. P. H. Gilbert," in Adolf Placzek, ed., *Macmillan Encyclopedia of Architects,* vol. 2 (New York: Free Press, 1982), p. 202.

25. Lockwood, *Bricks and Brownstone,* pp. 14, 70.

26. Cecil C. Evers, *The Commercial Problem in Buildings* (New York: Record and Guide Co., 1914), p. 120; also see Schuyler, "The New New York House," 84–85.

27. In Sarah Bradford Landau, "The Row Houses of New York's West Side," *JSAH* 34 (March 1975) 28, the author notes that the first American basement houses pre-date 1880.

28. United States Census, 1900; New York State Census, 1905; New York City Deed Conveyance records, block 1895, lots 43–46. No. 621 was the only house occupied in 1900. It was home to scientist George A. Black, his wife, a ward, and two Irish servants. Shortly after the census enumerator recorded this block in 1900, No. 627 was occupied by the household of iron and steel merchant G. B. Douglas. In 1905, G. B. Douglas's household consisted of Douglas, his wife, three daughters, and a Finnish servant. No. 625 was occupied by M. G. Dadirrian, a physician from Asia Minor, his wife Hosanna, two sons, five extended family members, and two servants—a cook and a butler—also from Asia Minor. Nos. 619 and 623 were still vacant in 1905.

29. New York State Census, 1905. The fraternity brothers at Alpha Delta Phi on 113th Street were served by a Japanese waiter, at a time when there were very few Asians in New York; thus, someone from Japan must have been seen by the fraternity brothers as an exotic "ornament" to fraternity life. For servants, see Faye E. Dudden, *Serving Women: Household Service in Nineteenth-Century America* (Middletown: Wesleyan University Press, 1983).

30. "Elevators for Heights," *Tribune,* October 7, 1900, sec. 2, p. 1.

31. "Elevators for Heights."

32. "A New Departure on the West Side," *RRBG* 39 (April 2, 1887), 434.

33. Morningside Protective Association, "Certificate of Incorporation Constitution and By-Laws" (1896).

34. "Minutes of the Morningside Protective Association," (Columbiana, Morningside Protective Association Box). According to the handwritten *Alphabetical & Descriptive List of the Names of all the Owners of the Property on Morningside Heights between Morningside Avenue, and Riverside Drive and between Cathedral Parkway & 122nd Street,* compiled by Robert T. Creamer for the Morningside Protective Association, probably in 1896, and a similar volume dated May 20, 1897, Barney owned 26 lots (in the name of John O. Baker), John D. Crimmins 12 lots, James J. Goodwin 11 lots, Dwight Olmstead 41 lots, and D. Willis James 18 lots.

35. The restrictions are discussed in "Charms of Morningside" and "Morningside Plateau," *RRBG* 60 (October 16, 1897), 542. The Association divided the Heights into six sections, three north of 116th Street and three to the south, with the east and west boundaries of each section marked by the major north-south avenues—Riverside Drive, Broadway, Amsterdam Avenue, and Morningside Avenue West (now Morningside Drive). These sections were carefully mapped and all owners listed. Restrictions were then drafted for each of the sections. The maps and the text of the restrictions for one section survive (Columbiana, Morningside Protective Association Box).

36. "Morningside Plateau," 542.

37. The early development of the apartment houses is discussed in detail in Elizabeth Collins Cromley, *Alone Together: A History of New York's Early Apartments* (Ithaca:

Cornell University Press, 1990); the Stuyvesant is discussed on pp. 62–103. An early synopsis of apartment house development is "New York Apartment Houses," *RRBG* 69 (April 5, 1902), supplement.

38. [editorial], *AABN* 75 (January 11, 1902), 9.

39. For the history of the subway, see Clifton Hood, *722 Miles: The Building of the Subways and How They Transformed New York* (New York: Simon & Schuster, 1993).

40. The subway that was constructed along Broadway is now part of the 1 and 9 lines.

41. Columbia University, *Directory of Officers and Students* (1899–1905). Besides the Kennedys' single building of 1894 and the two University Court buildings of 1899, two tenements were erected on Morningside Heights in 1897, and seven tenements and three apartment buildings in 1899.

42. "Morningside Heights," [editorial], *RRBG* 69 (June 14, 1902), 1092.

43. "Harlem Plains and Morningside Heights, *RRBG* 72 (October 31, 1903), 775.

44. The building was illustrated in *Architecture* 17 (April 1908), plate 37.

45. "Transformation of Morningside Heights," *RRBG* 78 (August 11, 1906), 255.

46. "Columbia University's Vicinity," *EP,* February 17, 1906, p. 6.

47. "20-Story Apartment Under Construction Morningside Heights," *Buildings and Building Management* 31 (July 13, 1931), 74.

48. "New Standards of Apartment Construction," *RRBG* 84 (September 4, 1909), 426, and George M. Hubbard, "Financing Apartment House Operations," *Building Management* 16 (March 1916), 46–47.

49. In H. W. Frohne, "Contemporary Apartment Building in New York City," *AR* 28 (July 1910), 66, the author notes that "the ability to dispose most rapidly of his crop is a measure of his [the builder's] ability to make money and continue to shape the future in a way entirely agreeable to his personal interests."

50. See for example, "Apartment Houses Sold on Morningside Heights," *NYT,* October 3, 1909, sec. 10, p. 1, which notes the sale of the three apartment buildings at 507, 511, and 517 West 113th Street that had been completed by Paterno Brothers several months earlier.

51. "Joseph Paterno Builder, 58, Dead," *NYT,* June 14, 1939, p. 23. A similar account is offered in "Joseph Paterno Dies: Builder, Skyline, Artist, *Tribune,* June 14, 1939, p. 20.

52. "Joseph Paterno Builder, 58, Dead."

53. On Morningside Heights, twenty-six apartment houses were erected by the firm of Paterno Brothers, Inc. Five were erected by Michael Paterno, three under the name M. E. Paterno Realty Co., and one each as Paterno and Son and 375 Riverside Drive Corporation) two by John Paterno, two by the Paterno Construction Company (Charles Paterno and his brother-in-law Anthony Campagna), and one each by Paterno & Sons, John Paterno's Sons, and Joseph Paterno. In addition, another Paterno brother-in-law, Victor Cerabone, also a builder, was responsible for three buildings. Besides Joseph Paterno's obituary, see "Paterno Bros., Inc.," *Apartment Houses of the Metropolis* (New York: G. C. Hesselgren Publishing Co., 1908), p. 61; "Joseph Paterno," *NCAB,* vol. 29 (New York: James T. White & Co., 1941), p. 247; "Dr. Paterno Dead, Realty Leader, 69," *NYT,* May 31, 1946, p. 23; "M. E. Paterno Dies, A Notable Builder," *NYT,* July 15, 1946, p. 25; "Anthony Paterno Dies," *NYT,*

December 21, 1959, p. 27; and "Victor Cerabone," [obituary], *NYT,* June 26, 1954, p. 13.

54. Examples on Morningside Heights are "PB" on the Luxor at 600 West 115th Street and "JP" on the Regnor at 601 West 115th Street, and on the Rexor at 600 West 116th Street. B. Crystal & Son is the only other builder on Morningside Heights to initial some of its buildings; the facades of the Peter Minuit, Eton Hall, and Rugby Hall (25, 29–31, and 35 Claremont Avenue) bear shields decorated with the letter "C."

55. Carlyle Realty erected four apartment buildings on Morningside Heights in 1908 and 1909; West Side Construction built twelve between 1904 and 1911; and Carnegie Construction was responsible for seven between 1910 and 1912. In 1924, Charles Newmark and his father Joseph Newmark, incorporated under the name City Construction Company, built Butler Hall at 400 West 119th Street. All of these firms were active in the construction of apartment houses in other neighborhoods as well. The religion of builders was verified in obituaries and death notices where possible.

56. In contrast with the apartment house architects, the architects of Morningside Heights' major institutions were among America's best trained and most prestigious designers. In addition, they were generally of northern European ancestry and most were Protestant, as were the leaders of the institutions for which they designed buildings.

57. Since biographical information on the architects who specialized in the construction of speculative apartment buildings is scarce, it is not always possible to pinpoint where they were trained. Simon Schwartz and Arthur Gross are both known to have trained at the Hebrew Technical Institute and William Rouse studied at the Stevens Institute of Technology in Hoboken, New Jersey.

58. It is notable that after 1910, when apartment houses began to be erected in large numbers on the Upper East Side for the city's wealthiest residents, builders commissioned designs not only from the speculator architects (mostly in the 1920s), but also from prominent architects not generally associated with apartment-house work, including McKim, Mead & White, Warren & Wetmore, Delano & Aldrich, C. P. H. Gilbert, Walter B. Chambers, York & Sawyer, Henry Otis Chapman, Walker & Gillette, and I. N. Phelps Stokes. The most popular designer of these luxury apartment houses was J. E. R. Carpenter, an MIT and Ecole des Beaux-Arts trained designer, who specialized in this type of work.

59. Of the 242 multiple dwellings on Morningside Heights, Neville & Bagge was responsible for the design of 38, George F. Pelham for 42, and Schwartz & Gross for 46. Pelham and Neville & Bagge had earlier designed some speculative rowhouses, including examples on Morningside Heights (see appendix). The work of Schwartz & Gross, including several buildings on Morningside Heights, is discussed in "Diversity of Planning in Apartment House Designs: Work of Schwartz & Gross, Architects," *As&Bs* 43 (December 1910), 95–112, and Dale H. Frens, *Schwartz & Gross: A New York Architectural Firm,* unpublished research paper (Columbia University, 1979). The firm Schwartz & Gross was established in 1903; Kendal Court at 521 West 111th Street is one of its earliest, if not its first, apartment buildings.

60. Frohne, "Contemporary Apartment Building," 62, 67.

61. Frohne, "Contemporary Apartment Building," 67.

62. H. J. Clemmons, "Planning Apartment Houses," *Building Management* 9 (September 1909), 45.

63. Numerous advertisements for Morningside Heights buildings are found in *Apartment Houses of the Metropolis* (New York: G. C. Hesselgren Publishing Co., 1908); *Apartment Houses of the Metropolis Supplement* (New York: G. C. Hesselgren Publishing Co., 1909); *New York American Annual Guide to High Class Apartments* (New York: New York American, 1910–1917); *The World's Loose Leaf Album of Apartment Houses* (New York: New York World, 1910); and *The New York Evening Post 1914 Apartment House Guide* (New York: New York Evening Post, 1914). For the Castle Court and Reed House, see *Apartment Houses of the Metropolis,* p. 118; for the Brookfield, see *World's Loose Leaf Album,* p. 54; for the Porter Arms and Fiora-Ville, see *Apartments of the Metropolis,* p. 60.

64. "New Apartments on Columbia Grounds," *RRBG* 85 (May 14, 1910), 1032.

65. "New Thoughts in Planning Apartments," *RRBG* 83 (June 26, 1909), 1299. Articles such as this appear to have been placed by the builders as part of the marketing of their buildings. The text in these articles is often identical to that in the builders' own advertisements.

66. Frohne, "Contemporary Apartment Building," 62, and "Contemporary Apartment Building," *RRBG* 85 (June 25, 1910), 1353. The latter is a discussion of Frohne's article.

67. For the Hendrick Hudson, see "To Be the Largest Apartment House in Manhattan," *RRBG* 78 (July 21, 1906), 111–12; "Luxury in the New Hendrick Hudson," *RRBG* 79 (January 26, 1907), 178–79; "Largest Apartment House of the Year," *RRBG* 81 (January 4, 1908), 36–37; "Apartment Houses," *As&Bs* 40 (February 1908), 199–200; "Big Apartment Project Now Nearing Completion," *NYT,* February 2, 1908, sec. 4, p. 5; William L. Rouse, "Architectural Criticism," *Architecture* 19 (March 15, 1909), 33; Albert E. Gibbs, "Opportunities Many on Morningside Heights," *RRBG* 82 (December 19, 1908), 1187–88; *World's Loose Leaf Album,* pp. 2–5; Andrew Alpern, *Apartments for the Affluent* (New York: McGraw-Hill, 1975), pp. 42–43; Andrew Alpern, *Luxury Apartment Houses of Manhattan* (New York: Dover, 1992), pp. 77–82; Stern, *New York 1900,* p. 418; and Christopher Gray, "A Decision to Save a Lump of Terra Cotta and Brick," *NYT,* December 29, 1996, sec. 9, p. 5. For the Colosseum, see "Diversity of Planning in Apartment House Designs, 102, 105–7; "Manhattan A City of Magnificent Apartments," *NYT,* September 8, 1910, sec. 7, p.1; *World's Loose Leaf Album,* pp. 16–16B; Alpern, *Apartments for the Affluent,* pp. 64–65; and Stern, *New York 1900,* pp. 302–4. For the Paterno, see "Diversity of Planning in Apartment House Design," pp. 102–4, 107; *New York American,* n.p.; and *World's Loose Leaf Album,* p. 18. The cornices of both the Colosseum and Paterno have been removed. The curving facades of the Colosseum and the Paterno reflect the original route of the Bloomingdale Road, which ran along the edges of these building's lots. For Riverside Mansions, see "Latest Apartments for Riverside Drive," *NYT,* January 23, 1910, p. 10; "The Hudson Mansions," *Tribune,* February 6, 1910, p. 12; and *World's Loose Leaf Album,* p. 14-LV.

68. For the Britannia, see "New Thoughts in Designing an Apartment House," *RRBG* 83 (January 30, 1909), 191; "Building on Cathedral Heights," *RRBG* 84 (October 23, 1909), 721–22 (this article incorrectly spells the building's name "Brittania"); *Architecture* 20 (December 1909), plate 110; Arthur E. Willauer, "The Modern Home in New York," *AA* 96 (December 22, 1909), 261–65; *Brickbuilder* 20 (February 1911), 43; "Typical Apartment House District," *RRBG* 88 (September 16, 1911), 378; "Homelike Apartments Desirable," *Building Management* 12 (February 1912), 59; *Apartment Houses of the Metropolis Supplement,* pp. 18–19; and Stern, *New York 1900,* p. 418. The building was also referred to as the Gracehull and the Tudor Gables.

69. "Homelike Apartments Desirable."

70. "Building on Cathedral Heights."

71. Willauer, "The Modern Home in New York," 263.

72. See, for example, Joy Wheeler Dow, "What House Architecture Should Be," *Arts and Decoration* 1 (January 1911), 114–15; C. Matlock Price, "English Derivations in American Architecture," *Arts and Decoration* 4 (November 1913), 9–12; and Julius Gregory, "On the Charm and Character of the English Cottage," *Forum* 44 (March 1926), 147–52, plates 33–40.

73. Frohne, "Contemporary Apartment Building," 66.

74. "Building on Cathedral Heights," 722.

75. *Apartment Houses of the Metropolis Supplement,* p. 74.

76. For the Blums and the Phaeton, see Andrew S. Dolkart and Susan Tunick, *George & Edward Blum: Design and Texture in New York Apartment House Architecture* (New York: Friends of Terra Cotta, 1993), pp. 1, 9–10. For the Oxford Hall and Cambridge Hall, see "A Riverside Drive Operation," *RRBG* 88 (September 2, 1911), 318, and Dolkart and Tunick, *George & Edward Blum,* pp. 13–15, 31–34.

77. "Diversity of Planning in Apartment House Design: Work of Schwartz & Gross, Architects," *As&Bs* 43 (December 1910), 95.

78. The most informative discussion of the grid plan is Edward K. Spann, "The Greatest Grid: the New York Plan of 1811," in Daniel Schaeffer, ed., *Two Centuries of American Planning* (Baltimore: Johns Hopkins University Press, 1988), pp. 11–39.

79. Laws of the State of New York, Chapter 334 (1901). Provisions of the law were amended several times between 1902 and 1908. For a discussion of the 1901 law and its impact, see Richard Plunz, *A History of Housing in New York City: Dwelling Type and Social Change in the American Metropolis* (New York: Columbia University Press, 1990), pp. 47–49.

80. Plunz, *A History of Housing,* pp. 47–49, 85–86.

81. The I-plan is discussed in E. S. Hanson, "Sitting in Judgment on Various Floor Plans That Bear Critical Analysis," *Building Management* 13 (November 1913), 28–29.

82. Hanson, "Sitting in Judgment," p. 38.

83. The issue of land values and rents on various streets is discussed in "A Typical Apartment House District," *RRBG* 88 (September 16, 1911), 377–78.

84. None of these buildings has a Broadway address—the Hendrick Hudson Annex is 611 Cathedral Parkway; the Rockfall, 545 West 111th Street; the Devonshire, 542 West 112th Street; the Allerton, 600 West 113th Street; the Forest Chambers, 601 West 113th

Street; the Luxor, 600 West 115th Street; the Regnor, 601 West 115th Street; and the Rexor, 600 West 116th Street. For the Hendrick Hudson Annex, see "Largest Apartment House of the Year," *RRBG* 81 (January 4, 1908), 36–37, and "Big Apartment Project Now Nearing Completion," *NYT,* February 2, 1908, sec. 4, p. 5. For the Rockfall and Forest Chambers, see "Building on Cathedral Heights," 722; Dolkart and Tunick, *George & Edward Blum,* pp. 2–3, 12; *World's Loose Leaf Album,* pp. 34B, 36C; and *New York American* (1911; Rockfall only), n.p. For the Forest Chambers only, see "George F. Johnson, Jr.'s Latest Operation,"*RRBG* 84 (November 20, 1909), 903. For the Devonshire, see *World's Loose Leaf Album,* p. 157, and *Apartment Houses of the Metropolis,* pp. 38–39, where the building is referred to as the Washington Irving. For the Allerton, see *New York American* (1911), n.p. For the Luxor, Regnor, and Rexor, see "Apartment Houses," *A&B* 44 (December 1912), 486, 489–90, and Christopher Gray, "On Broadway, the Odd Threesome," *NYT,* October 15, 1995, sec. 9, p. 7. For the Luxor, see "The Luxor," *Tribune,* August 20, 1911, sec. 4, p. 59, and *World's Loose Leaf Album,* p. 14-XLII. For the Rexor, see *New York American* (1916–17), n.p.. For the Rexor and Regnor, see "Block Front of Apartments Ready to Open on Broadway," *NYT,* June 23, 1912, sec. 8, p.1.

85. "A Typical Apartment House District," 377.

86. The subway station now known as 125th Street, on what was originally known as Manhattan Avenue, is at approximately 128th Street. Manhattan Avenue was renamed 125th Street in the early twentieth century.

87. "An Association for Obtaining a Subway Station at or Near 122nd Street and Broadway," c.1909 (circular in UTSA Correspondence Book II, Series 8, Box 5).

88. Albert E. Gibbs, "Opportunities Many on Morningside Heights," *RRBG* 82 (December 19, 1908), 1187, and Coffin to John Crosby Brown, January 25, 1909 (UTSA, Seminary Correspondence Book I, Series 8, Box 5). Also see "A Typical Apartment House District," 377, and "New Subway Station Needed," *Harlem Magazine* 2 (January 1914), 11–12.

89. The earliest six-story elevator apartment house was the St. Orimand at 417 West 114th Street (1898; demolished).

90. "New Standard of Apartment Construction," *RRBG* 84 (September 4, 1909), 426.

91. Laws of the State of New York, Chapter 334, Section 11 (1901).

92. *Apartment Houses of the Metropolis,* p. 150. Paterno and Schwartz & Gross employed this design at Cathedral Court (1904), 44 Morningside Drive ("Apartment Houses for Morningside Heights," *RRBG* 73 [February 27, 1904], 441); La Touraine (1905), 53 Morningside Drive (*Apartment Houses of the Metropolis,* p. 150); Mont Ceris (1905), 54 Morningside Drive (*Apartment Houses of the Metropolis,* p. 150, and *New York Evening Post,* n. p.); Revere Hall and Hudson Hall (1905), 622 and 628 West 114th Street between Broadway and Riverside Drive (*Apartment Houses of the Metropolis,* p. 178 [Hudson Hall only], and "More Riverside Drive Improvements," *RRBG* 74 [October 15, 1904], 788); Park Court (1905), 403 West 115th Street (*Apartment Houses of the Metropolis,* p. 216); Warren Hall (1904; demolished), 404 West 115th Street ("Apartment Houses for Morningside Heights," and *Apartment Houses of the Me-*

tropolis, p. 224); and La Valenciennes (1905), 404 West 116th Street (*Apartment Houses of the Metropolis,* p. 245). In a discussion of Revere Hall and Hudson Hall, the recessed fire escape design is described as "characteristic of the designs" of Schwartz & Gross ("More Riverside Drive Improvements"). George Pelham adopted this form at 522 West 112th Street (1906); the Stamford and Arlington (1905), 502 and 506 West 113th Street (*Apartment Houses of the Metropolis,* p. 256); and the Malvern and Barieford, 47 and 49 Claremont Avenue (1906; *Apartment Houses of the Metropolis,* p. 168).

93. "Building on Cathedral Parkway," *RRBG* 84 (October 23, 1909), 721.

94. "Riverside Drive a Great Parkway Lined with Palatial Apartments," *NYT,* August 21, 1910, sec. 6, p. 6.

95. "Manhattan a City of Magnificent Apartments," *NYT,* September 18, 1910, sec. 7, p. 1.

96. The ideal apartment house plan is discussed in Cromley, *Apartments for the Affluent,* pp. 173–85.

97. "Variety in Apartments," *EP,* September 21, 1903, p. 9.

98. Hanson, "Sitting in Judgment," p. 39.

99. "A Well Liked Floor Plan," *RRBG* 81 (March 28, 1908), 567.

100. For the Britannia advertisement, see "New Thoughts in Designing an Apartment House"; the same quote appears in another advertisement for the Britannia in *Apartment Houses of the Metropolis Supplement,* p. 18. For the Campolyn and Wenonah advertisement, see *Tribune,* January 29, 1911, sec. 4, p. 5; an advertisement in *Tribune,* October 16, 1910, p.5, notes "THERE ARE NO LONG HALLS IN THE APART-MENTS" [sic]. The Campolyn and Wenonah are illustrated in *Architecture* 23 (April 1911), p. 63 and plate 41.

101. The plan is published in "New Thoughts in Planning Apartments"; Frohne, "Contemporary Apartment Building," 62; and "The Apartment Houses of New York," *RRBG* 85 (March 26, 1910), 645.

102. Allen E. Beals, "New Ideas in Riverside Drive Apartment Houses," *RRBG* 84 (December 18, 1909), 1096. The building reviewed in detail in this article is the Dacona Hall at 111 Claremont Avenue on the southwest corner of West 122nd Street (demolished).

103. "New Standards of Apartment Construction," 425–26.

104. *Apartment Houses of the Metropolis Supplement,* p. 14.

105. *New York American,* n.p.

106. William G. August, "'First Impressions' Usually Governed by Appearance of Entrance Halls," *Building Management* 16 (August 1916), 28.

107. *Apartment Houses of the Metropolis Supplement,* p. 14.

108. For the Mira Mar, see "New Thoughts in Planning Apartments," *RRBG* 83 (June 26, 1909), 1299, and *World's Loose Leaf Album,* p 132. For the Brookfield, see *New York American,* n.p.

109. *New York American* (1911 and c.1913), n.p., and *Worlds Loose Leaf Album,* pp. 18–18B.

110. "A House for Columbia Professors and Students," *RRBG* 85 (June 18, 1910), 1300. Also see Steven Ruttenbaum, *Mansions in the Clouds: The Skyscraper Palazzi of Emery Roth* (New York: Balsam Press, 1986), pp. 56–57.

111. Advertisement, *NYT*, May 21, 1911, sec. 7, p. 7, and photo caption, *RRBG* 87 (May 27, 1911), 1006.

112. "'Sethlow' Building Can't Keep Its Name," *NYT*, July 4, 1911, p. 1.

113. The building is now owned by Teachers College. Ironically, when Teachers College purchased the Janus Court at 106 Morningside Drive in 1920, four years after Seth Low's death, it renamed that apartment building Seth Low Hall.

114. United States Census, 1900 and 1910; New York State Census, 1905 and 1915. The vast majority of families were headed by business and professional people, including many lawyers, doctors, manufacturers, merchants, engineers.

115. New York State Census, 1905.

116. New York State Census, 1915.

117. "The Cathedral Parkway Apartments," prospectus (New York City Department of Buildings File, block 1882 lot 8).

118. "$2,750,000 Operation for Columbia University Heights," *RRBG* (February 28, 1925), 9; also see prospectus (CU, Avery Library).

119. "Lay Cornerstone of Explorers' Club," *NYT*, June 17, 1928, sec. 2, p. 1; "A New Clubhouse For Explorers," *NYT*, June 24, 1928, sec. 9, p. 3; and "Explorers Club Has New Home," *NYT*, April 14, 1929, sec. 11, p. 12. The club lost the building during the Depression. It is now Harmony Hall, a Columbia University dormitory.

120. A garage at 2906 Broadway was erected in 1909 and University Garage at 532 West 122nd Street in 1910.

121. Under the pastorate of Father George Barry Ford, Corpus Christi became an important center for ecumenicism. Ford was friends with Harry Emerson Fosdick of Riverside Church. In his memoir, Father Ford recounts that "Later when the new building was erected for Corpus Christi, . . . and modelled . . . after early American church architecture, Dr. Fosdick said to me one day, 'It's odd that I have built a Roman Catholic structure and you are building a New England meeting house.' 'Well, Harry,' I answered, 'someone has to keep Protestantism alive on Morningside Heights.'"; George Barry Ford, *A Degree of Difference* (New York: Farrar, Straus & Giroux, 1969), p. 50.

122. Avery Library, Guastavino Collection, Folders 5.210–5.211.

123. The sanctuary of Eglise de Notre Dame was designed by Daus & Otto in 1909; the nave and facade by Cross & Cross date from 1914; see Dolkart, *Guide to New York City Landmarks*, p. 149, and *Church of Notre Dame: 75th Anniversary* (New York: Church of Notre Dame, 1985).

124. "New Fourth Ave. Presbyterian Edifice to Be Started," *RRBG* 86 (November 26, 1910), 884; "A Morningside Church," *RRBG* 88 (October 28, 1911), 628; "Church and Religious News Notes: Cornerstone of New Broadway Presbyterian Edifice To Be Laid This Afternoon," *Tribune*, March 16, 1912, p. 10; "Broadway Presbyterian Church," *Harlem Magazine* 2 (December 1913), 20, 26; "The Broadway Presbyterian Church at 114th Street, New York," *A&B* 46 (March 1914), 111.

125. Two additional churches were later erected: the Seventh Church of Christ, Scientist (Griffin & Wynkoop, 1918; demolished and replaced with a new church in 1987) on West 112th Street, and Unity Congregational Society (Hoppin & Koen, 1921; now Synagogue Ramath Orah) on Cathedral Parkway.

126. "The Week in Real Estate," *EP*, August 16, 1913, p. 14.

AFTERWORD: MORNINGSIDE HEIGHTS IN THE SECOND HALF OF THE TWENTIETH CENTURY

1. By 1930, Columbia owned eight apartment buildings and Teachers College, four.

2. Robert A.M. Stern, Thomas Mellins, and David Fishman, *New York 1960: Architecture and Urbanism Between the Second World War and the Bicentennial* (New York: Monacelli Press, 1995), pp. 734–56.

3. Extensive archival material on the Interchurch Center is at RCA, RFA, Religious Interests, Record Group 2, OMR, Boxes 62–63; also see "Morningside Building Boom Brightens the Area," *NYT*, March 8, 1959, p. 7; and Stern, *New York 1960*, p. 751. This block had been willed to St. Luke's Hospital by Mrs. Fitzgerald who had owned the property for many years. St. Luke's sold the block to Barnard College which intended to expand on the property. Rockefeller purchased the block from Barnard in 1954.

4. For Bank Street College, see "Bank St. College to Move Uptown," *NYT*, November 15, 1963, p. 23, and Stern, *New York 1960*, p. 752.

5. "Episcopal School Builds a Home In Morningside Heights Complex," *NYT*, August 28, 1966, sec. 8, p. 1. Remedco was established by Barnard College, Columbia University, Corpus Christi R.C. Church, International House, Jewish Theological Seminary, Riverside Church, St. Luke's Hospital, Teachers College, and Union Theological Seminary. The design of St. Hilda's and St. Hugh's brick and concrete building is out of place on residential 114th and 115th streets. Indeed, the building is almost as banal as Moore & Hutchins' design for Uris Hall, Columbia's Business School.

6. "Episcopal School Shows New Home," *NYT*, January 7, 1967, p. 19.

7. "Neighbors Assail Columbia Growth," *NYT*, January 18, 1964, p. 25.

8. Morgan Farrell, "Rebuilding New York's Apartments," *Architecture* 71 (March 1935), 124–26. The architect for the alteration was Voorhees, Gmelin & Walker.

9. "Slums Engulfing Columbia Section," *NYT*, June 9, 1958, p. 33.

10. "Slums Engulfing Columbia Section," p. 33.

11. "West Side Slum Regains Glitter," *NYT*, April 17, 1960, sec. 8, p. 1. The Hendrick Hudson became an SRO in the 1940s and was converted back into an apartment house in 1959–60.

12. This survey was undertaken by University of Chicago sociologist Wilbur G. Munnecke. See, Gertrude Samuels, "Rebirth of a Community," *NYT Magazine*, September 25, 1955, p. 26.

13. The fourteen charter members were Barnard College, the Cathedral of St. John the Divine, Columbia University, Corpus Christi R.C. Church, the Home For Old Men and Aged Couples, International House, Jewish Theological Seminary, The Juilliard

School of Music, Riverside Church, the St. Luke's Home, St. Luke's Hospital, Teachers College, Union Theological Seminary, and Woman's Hospital.

14. "Morningside Heights," Memorandum, February 25, 1954, discussing the early history of Morningside Heights, Inc. (RAC, RFA, Religious Interests, Record Group 2, OMR, Box 62, Folder 486).

15. See, for example, "Slum-Razing Housing Set For Uptown," *HT,* October 1, 1951, p. 1.

16. Morningside Gardens was the first housing project in New York City built under Title 1 of the National Housing Act. This act allowed cities to acquire designated slum properties and resell them at a low price to private developers, with the federal government paying two-thirds of the price and the city one-third. For Morningside Gardens, see "Slum-Razing Housing Set For Uptown"; Margaret Boulton Bartlett, "Morningside-Manhattanville," *American City* 68 (May 1953), 94–96; "City's 'Acropolis' Combating Slums," *NYT,* May 21, 1957, p. 37; Victoria Newhouse, *Wallace K. Harrison, Architect* (New York: Rizzoli, 1989), pp. 163–64; and Stern, *New York 1960,* pp. 734–35.

17. Quoted in Bartlett, "Morningside-Manhattanville," 94, and Stern, *New York 1960,* p. 734.

18. For Grant Houses, see City's 'Acropolis' Combating Slums, and Stern, *New York 1960,* pp. 734–35.

19. Samuels, "Rebirth of a Community," p. 37. This is a biased article that dismisses "Save Our Homes" as "an extreme left-wing group" whose "propaganda bitterly divided the community, many of whom could understand neither the language nor the issues."

20. "City's 'Acropolis' Combating Slums," 40.

21. Columbia briefly considered building faculty housing in the suburbs, but never actually pursued this idea; see "Columbia Weighs Suburb Housing," *NYT,* December 14, 1967, p. 55.

22. Columbia University, *Minutes of the Board of Trustees,* October 5, 1925 (CUA).

23. Butler to Rockefeller, May 29, 1925 (RAC, RFA, Religious Interests, Record Group 2, OMR, Box 64, Folder 496).

24. Nicholas Murray Butler, "Confidential Memorandum," January 7, 1946 (CUL, Butler Papers, Marcellus Hartley Dodge File).

25. Columbia has been accused of harassing the tenants of some SROs and apartment buildings, in order to force them to vacate more rapidly; see Roger Kahn, *The Battle for Morningside Heights: Why Students Rebel* (New York: William Morrow & Co., 1970), pp. 87–88.

26. The SROs are listed in Morningside Heights, Inc., *Morningside Heights Core Area Study* (c. 1967), appendix 12. The two surviving SROs are at 601 West 110th Street (Hendrick Hudson Annex) and 611 West 112th Street. Kahn, *The Battle For Morningside Heights,* states that during the 1960s, Columbia removed 6,800 SRO tenants from the neighborhood (p. 88).

27. "Neighbors Assail Columbia Growth."

28. "Tenants Accuse Columbia of Bias," *NYT.* October 4, 1961, p. 39.

29. "Tenants Accuse Columbia of Bias," and "Columbia Aiding Rundown Hotel," *NYT,* September 23, 1961, p. 21. Columbia sold shares of its mortgage to Remedco, the real estate investing company established by nine of the area's institutions. Columbia actually acquired ownership of this building in 1962.

30. "Housing Bias Case Won By Columbia," *NYT,* February 7, 1962, p. 40.

31. "Columbia, N.Y.U. Face Racial Fight," *NYT,* February 1, 1962, p. 17; "Housing Bias Case Won By Columbia"; "Columbia Named in Rights Inquiry," *NYT,* February 28, 1964, p. 15; and "City Slums vs. a University," *U.S. News and World Report* 56 (April 6, 1964), 76.

32. Controversies between the institutions and tenants and community groups are discussed in "Need For Housing Vexes Columbia," *NYT,* August 25, 1957, p. 70; "St. Luke's Hospital Seeks to Evict 44," *NYT,* March 6, 159, p. 27; "Hospital Assailed," *NYT,* March 7, 1959, p. 15; "Neighbors Assail Columbia Growth," *NYT,* January 18, 1964, p. 25; Ada Louise Huxtable, "600 Acres of Trouble," *NYT,* September 30, 1964, p. 34; "Columbia Jeered in Tenant March," *NYT,* September 22, 1968, p. 70; "Tenants Protest Eviction From Columbia's Housing," *NYT,* March 5, 1978, p. 30; "Tragedy Puts Columbia to New Test as Landlord," *NYT,* August 5, 1979, sec. 8, p. 4; "Columbia Picketed," *NYT,* January 15, 1980, p. B3; "Columbia: The Good Guy/Bad Guy Landlord," *NYT,* January 31, 1980, p. B1; Annette Fuentes, "Columbia Builds a Company Town," *City Limits* 11 (January 1986), 16–21; and "Troubled Tie: Neighborhood and Columbia," *NYT,* April 20, 1987, p. B1.

33. "Rename 6 Buildings to Honor CU Men," *Spectator,* March 3, 1966, p. 1.

34. Wallace K. Harrison's serious, if ultimately unsuccessful East Campus design entailed the construction of a raised platform and a bridge over Amsterdam Avenue. Three buildings were to be constructed on this platform — Harrison & Abramovitz's Law School, a faculty office building (later replaced by Harrison & Abramovitz's School of International Affairs Building), and a graduate dormitory (built as an undergraduate residence hall, designed by Gwathmey Siegel & Associates and reclad by Gruzen Sampton Steinglass after its original tile facade began to fall off). For the East Campus buildings, see "Columbia to Add to Campus and Build New Law School," *NYT,* March 28, 1956, p. 1; "Columbia's Fine Plans," [editorial] *NYT,* March 28, 1956, p. 30; "Columbia Project Criticized," letter to the editor from Nathan Glazer, *NYT,* April 9, 1956, p. 26; "Columbia Starts New Law Building," *NYT,* November 8, 1958, p. 23; "Columbia Plans Huge Expansion," *NYT,* April 19, 1961, p. 1; Allan Temko, "A Brilliant Plan Gone Awry?," *Columbia College Today* 10 (Fall 1962), 18–23; "Revson's Bridge Dedicated at Columbia," *HT,* November 24, 1965, p. 23; "Columbia to Erect Center for International Studies," *NYT,* February 24, 1966, p. 3; "Morningside Adds Buildings Other Than Gym," *NYT,* May 26, 1968, sec. 8, p. 1; "Columbia Plans a $20 Million Dorm Project," *NYT,* May 13, 1977, p. B2; "Columbia Dedicates New Suites and Town Houses for Students," *NYT,* June 4, 1981, p. B11; *Charles Gwathmey and Robert Siegel: Buildings and Projects 1964–1984* (New York: Harper & Row, 1984); Newhouse, *Wallace K. Harrison,* p. 322; and Stern, *New York*

1960, pp. 736–37. For the demolition and replacement of the Bryn Mawr, see "Barnard Acquires Bryn Mawr Hotel as Dormitory Site," *NYT,* February 19, 1966, p. 29; "Barnard to Build a New Dormitory," *NYT,* February 24, 1967, p. 21; "Morningside Adds Buildings Other Than 'Gym,'" *NYT,* May 26, 1968, sec. 9, p. 1; and "Plimpton Hall Dedicated," *NYT,* May 13, 1977, p. B2.

35. Ada Louise Huxtable, "Expansion at Columbia," *NYT,* November 5, 1966, p. 33. Columbia did not own all of the property on the proposed south campus.

36. *Morningside Core Area Study,* map 11.

37. For the Columbia Gym, see Eggers & Higgins, Sherwood Mills & Smith, "The New Columbia Gymnasium," (Columbiana). For the conflict, see Cox Commission, *Crisis at Columbia: Report of the Fact-Finding Commission Appointed to Investigate the Disturbances at Columbia University in April and May 1968* (New York: Random House, 1968); George Keller, "Six Weeks That Shook Columbia," *Columbia College Today* 15 (Spring 1968); "Columbia College Toady: 96 Pages That Distorted Six Weeks That Shook Morningside" (Columbiana); "Crisis at Columbia" An Inside Report on the Rebellion at Columbia from the Pages of the *Columbia Daily Spectator* (Columbiana); Kahn, *The Battle for Morningside Heights;* and Stern, *New York 1960,* pp. 743–46. The gym was approved by the Board of Estimate on October 25, 1967; see "Columbia Is Given Approval For Gym," *NYT,* October 26, 1967, p. 93. Columbia's was not the first proposal to build athletic facilities in Morningside Park. In 1909, the Parks Department had considered a proposal to erect a stadium adjacent to Morningside Avenue between West 118th and 120th streets. The proposal was vehemently opposed by nearby property owners. See "Athletic Field Project Hearing," *RRBG* 83 (March 20, 1909), 545.

38. "2 Buildings Are Fought In 'Heights,'" *NYT,* May 19, 1968, sec. 8, p. 1.

39. "Church Addition Is Halted Uptown," *NYT,* June 21, 1968, p. 82

40. "2 Buildings Are Fought In 'Heights,'" and Morningside Heights, Inc., *Morningside Heights Core Area Study,* n.p. The *Core Area Study* includes a sketch of Johnson's building. It appears that the building would have been of far higher quality than contemporary buildings on Morningside Heights and would have contributed to the character of the community far more than the banal Echo Apartments (Echo stands for Ecumenical Community Housing Organization), a senior citizen's housing project, that went up on a portion of this site in the late 1980s.

41. "Columbia Students Help Occupy Flats Run by University," *NYT,* May 18, 1968, p. 1. The protestors were evicted by the police; see "56 Columbia Rebels Seized Among 117 at Sit-In Here," *NYT,* May 19, 1968, p. 1. The apartment building was vacated and demolished; as of 1997, the site remained a vacant lot.

42. "Columbia Hires Pei to Project Its Growth for Decades Ahead," *NYT,* November 8, 1968, p. 1; I.M. Pei & Partners, *Planning For Columbia: An Interim Report* (1970); Ada Louise Huxtable, "Columbia Plan Includes Underground Expansion," *NYT,* February 18, 1970. p. 1; and Stern, *New York 1960,* p. 746. The architect for the Avery expansion was Alexander Kouzmanoff; see Suzanne Stephens, "Beneath the Hall of Ivy," *Progressive Architecture* 59 (March 1978), 60–61.

43. Most of the larger privately owned apartment buildings on Broadway, Riverside Drive, and 110th Street have been converted into cooperatives, as have a few of the smaller midblock buildings.

44. "Falling Masonry Fatally Injures Barnard Student," *NYT*, May 17, 1979, sec. 2, p. 3, and "Tragedy Puts Columbia to New Test as Landlord," *NYT*, August 5, 1979, sec. 8, p. 1.

45. Paul Goldberger, "What a Law Can Do to Architecture," *NYT*, January 18, 1983, p. C11.

46. "For Columbia, A New $68 Million Student Center," *NYT*, January 28, 1996, sec. 9, p. 1. For a particularly negative view of the project, see David Garrard Lowe, "Now They're Deconstructing the Columbia Campus," *City Journal* 7 (Autumn 1997), 84–97.

47. See, for example, Peg Breen [President of the New York Landmarks Conservancy] to Emily Lloyd [Executive Vice President for Administration], June 16, 1996 (New York Landmarks Conservancy Files).

48. For William C. Warren Hall, see "On a Narrow Lot, Legal Maneuvers," *NYT*, December 3, 1995, sec. 9, p. 1. Polshek and Partners also designed an addition to Jerome Greene Hall, the law school building, that was equally controversial. For the business and law building, see "A Building Reflecting Those on Main Campus," *NYT*, August 25, 1996, sec. 9, p. 1.

49. For Iphigene Ochs Sulzberger Hall, see "Nearing 100, Barnard Plans 18-Story Dormitory Tower," *NYT*, October 25, 1986, p. 29; "Holding Court," *AR* 177 (October 1989), 112–15; and "Centennial Hall, Barnard College," *Architecture and Urbanism* 242 (September 1990), 88–95. For Casa Italiana, see "In the Streetscape: The Casa and the Convent," *Oculus* 58 (April 1996), 6–7; Stephen A. Kliment, "Rescue Transforms Columbia Landmark," *AR* 184 (July 1996), 80–83; and "La Casa Italiana = The Italian House," *Ottagono* 31 (September-November 1996), 65–69. In 1997, the Casa Italiana project won a Lucy Moses Award from the New York Landmarks Conservancy in recognition of the quality of its restoration and adaptive reuse.

50. "Need for Nursing Home Beds vs. Effect on Cathedral of St. John the Divine," *NYT*, August 23, 1992, p. 23.

51. "Tenants Irked At Eviction By Seminary." *NYT*, December 15, 1996, sec. 13, p. 8. Material printed by the tenants group and the seminary are in the collection of Jewish Theological Seminary's Ratner Center.

52. The master plan team consisted of the architectural firm of Beyer Blinder Belle, landscape architect Thomas Balsley Associates, garden designer Lynden B. Miller, Higgins & Quasebarth, preservation consultants, and architectural historian Andrew S. Dolkart, the author of the present work.

53. In 1997 George Stephanopoulos, former adviser to President Bill Clinton, purchased a two-bedroom cooperative on Riverside Drive at 114th Street for what was then considered the extraordinarily high price of $550,000; see "The Pleasure of His Company; A Whirl Beyond the White House for Stephanopoulos," *NYT*, February 26, 1997, p. B1.

APPENDIX

1. The 1904 permit is for a one-story building. This was either demolished and later replaced by the present three-story building, or two stories were later added to this 1904 structure.

2. The facade of this building has been totally stripped and redesigned.

3. Completion of 1909 building.

4. Rectory located at 409 West 112th Street.

5. Stable was located at the rear of the lot, facing onto Claremont Avenue

6. This building was also referred to as Parkway Hall.

7. Two floors were built in 1985 and an additional two floors in 1987, creating three apartments and an office.

8. Erected as a "high class boarding house."

9. Original building permit for this building records owner Peter Wagner and architect George F. Pelham. Information on Vogel and Neville & Bagge pinned to original permit.

10. Called Washington Irving in *Apartment Houses of the Metropolis,* pp. 38–39.

11. Built as a student dormitory and apartment hotel.

12. Building permit notes that Brandt only prepared the plans for 408–412 West 115th Street.

13. Also known as Rena Hall.

14. Sesrun Hall was erected as nurses' housing. The idea failed and the building was converted into the King's Crown Hotel.

15. Butler Hall was built as a residential hotel.

16. Erected as a home for working girls.

17. Building reclad by Gruzen Sampton Steinglass in 1990–91.

Selected Bibliography

Alpern, Andrew. *Apartments for the Affluent: A Historical Survey of Buildings in New York.* New York: McGraw-Hill, 1975.

Alpern, Andrew. *Luxury Apartment Houses of Manhattan: An Illustrated History.* New York: Dover, 1992.

Apartment Houses of the Metropolis. New York: G. C. Hesselgren, 1908.

Apartment Houses of the Metropolis Supplement. New York: G. C. Hesselgren, 1909.

Bacon, Marges. *Ernest Flagg: Beaux Arts Architect and Urban Reformer.* New York: Architectural History Foundation, 1986.

History of St. Luke's Hospital with A Description of the New Buildings. New York: Wynkoop & Hallenbeck, 1893.

Bergdoll, Barry. "Laying the Cornerstone of the New Columbia University (Library) December 7, 1895." *Library Columns* 44 (Autumn 1995): 13–23.

Bergdoll, Barry, Janet Parks, and Hollee Haswell. *Mastering McKim's Plan: Columbia University's First Century on Morningside Heights.* New York: Miriam and Ira D. Wallach Art Gallery, 1997.

Brown, William Adams. *Statement of the Most Important Facts and Dates Connected With the History of the Union Theological Seminary.* New York: The Irving Press, 1909.

Butler, Nicholas Murray. *Across the Busy Years: Recollections and Reflections.* New York: Charles Scribner's Sons, 1939.

"Charms of Morningside." *New York Times,* August 2, 1896, p. 24.

Coon, Horace. *Columbia: Colossus on the Hudson.* New York: E. P. Dutton, 1947.

Cremin, Lawrence A., David A. Shannon, and Mary Evelyn Townsend. *A History of Teachers College Columbia University.* New York: Columbia University Press, 1954.

Cromley, Elizabeth Collins. *Alone Together: A History of New York's Early Apartments.* Ithaca: Cornell University Press, 1990.

Damrosch, Frank. *Institute of Musical Art 1905–1926.* New York: Juilliard School of Music, 1936.

Dodge, Grace H. *A Brief Sketch of the Early History of Teachers College.* New York: Maynard, Merrill & Co., 1899.

Dunlap, David W. *On Broadway: A Journey Uptown Over Time.* New York: Rizzoli, 1990.

Erskine, John. *My Life in Music.* New York: William Morrow & Co., 1950.

Frohne, H.W. "Contemporary Apartment Building in New York City." *Architectural Record* 28 (July 1910): 61–70.

Handy, Robert T. *A History of Union Theological Seminary in New York.* New York: Columbia University Press, 1987.

Haswell, Hollee. "Low Memorial Library: The Building of a Great University." *Library Columns* 44 (Autumn 1995): 25–31.

Hervey, Walter L. "New York College for the Training of Teachers." *Review of Reviews* 5 (May 1892): 424–28.

A History of Columbia University 1754–1904. New York: Columbia University Press, 1904.

History of Real Estate, Building and Architecture in New York City During the Last Quarter of a Century. New York: Record and Guide, 1896; reprinted, New York: Arno, 1967.

Horowitz, Helen Lefkowitz. *Alma Mater: Design and Experience in the Women's Colleges from Their Nineteenth-Century Beginnings to the 1930s,* 2nd edition. Amherst: University of Massachusetts Press, 1993.

Jackson, Kenneth T., ed. *The Encyclopedia of New York.* New Haven: Yale University Press, 1995.

Joselit, Jenna Weissman. "By Design: Building the Campus of the Jewish Theological Seminary of America." in Jack Wertheimer, ed., *Tradition Renewed: A History of Jewish Theological Seminary.* New York: The Jewish Theological Seminary, 1997.

Keating, James Martin. "Seth Low and the Development of Columbia University 1889–1901." unpublished Ph.D. Dissertation, Columbia University, 1973.

Landau, Sarah B. *Edward T. and William A. Potter: American High Victorian Architects 1855–1901.* New York: Garland, 1978.

Meyer, Annie Nathan, *Barnard Beginnings.* Boston: Houghton Mifflin Co., 1935.

Miller, Alice Duer and Susan Myers. *Barnard College: The First Fifty Years.* New York: Columbia University Press, 1939.

"Morningside." *Harper's Weekly* 41 (February 13, 1897): 162–63.

Morningside Heights, Inc. *Morningside Heights Core Area Study.* [c. 1967].

Nelson, Charles Alexander. *Columbiana: A Bibliography of Manuscripts, Pamphlets and Books Relating to the History of King's College, Columbia College, Columbia University.* New York: Columbia University, 1904.

New York American Annual Guide to High Class Apartments. New York: New York American, 1910–1917.

An Official Guide to Columbia University. New York: Columbia University Press, 1912.

Passanti, Francesco. "The Design of Columbia in the 1890s, McKim and His Client." *Journal of the Society of Architectural Historians* 36 (May 1977): 69–84.

Plunz, Richard. *A History of Housing in New York City.* New York: Columbia University Press, 1990.

Putnam, Emily James. "The Rise of Barnard College." *Columbia University Quarterly* 2 (June 1900): 209–17.

"Reasons for Living on the Heights." *New York Times,* April 7, 1895, p. 20.

Robson, John William, ed. *A Guide to Columbia College.* New York: Columbia University Press, 1937.

Roth, Leland. *McKim, Mead & White, Architects.* New York: Harper & Row, 1983.

Rothman, David J. *The Discovery of the Asylum: Social Order and Disorder in the New Republic.* Boston: Little, Brown & Co., 1971.

Russell, William Logie. *The New York Hospital: A History of the Psychiatric Service 1771–1936.* New York: Columbia University Press, 1945.

Schenkel, Albert F. *The Rich Man and the Kingdom: John D. Rockefeller, Jr., and the Protestant Establishment.* Minneapolis: Fortress Press, 1995.

Schuyler, Montgomery. "Architecture of American Colleges IV. New York City Colleges." *Architectural Record* 27 (June 1910): 443–69.

Solomon, Barbara Miller. *In the Company of Educated Women: A History of Women and Higher Education in America.* New Haven: Yale University Press, 1985.

Stern, Robert A. M., Gregory Gilmartin, and John Massengale. *New York 1900: Metropolitan Architecture and Urbanism 1890–1915.* New York: Rizzoli, 1983.

Stern, Robert A. M., Gregory Gilmartin, and Thomas Mellins. *New York 1930: Architecture and Urbanism Between the Two World Wars.* New York: Rizzoli, 1987.

Stern, Robert A. M., Thomas Mellins, and David Fishman. *New York 1960: Architecture and Urbanism Between the Second World War and the Bicentennial.* New York: Monacelli Press, 1995.

Stokes, I. N. Phelps. *The Iconography of Manhattan 1498–1909.* New York: Robert H. Dodd, 1918–1928.

Stoller, Michael. "Columbia's Library for the Twentieth Century: The Rise of South Hall." *Library Columns* 45 (Autumn 1996): 5–17.

Strong, Janet Adams. *The Cathedral of Saint John the Divine in New York: Design Competitions in the Shadow of H. H. Richardson 1889–1891.* Unpublished Ph.D. Dissertation, Brown University, 1990.

"Typical Apartment House District." *Real Estate Record and Builders Guide* 88 (September 16, 1911): 377–78.

Wenick, Bette C. *The 'Average Teacher' Need Not Apply: Women Educators at Teachers College, 1887–1927.* Unpublished Ph.D. Dissertation, Columbia University, 1996.

White, Marian Churchill. *A History of Barnard College.* New York: Columbia University Press, 1954.

The World's Loose Leaf Album of Apartment Houses. New York: New York World, 1910.

Index

Italic page references indicate illustrations. Named thoroughfares are entered under their names, e.g., Broadway; numbered avenues are entered under the spelled-out form of the numeral, e.g., Fifth Avenue; numbered cross streets are entered under "East" or "West" as appropriate, e.g., West 116th Street.

Photo Credits

FIGURE 5.15. *Christian Art* 1 (April 1907), 16

FIGURE 5.16. Columbia University, Columbiana Collection

FIGURE 5.17. Columbia University, Columbiana Collection

FIGURE 5.18. The Collection of The New-York Historical Society

FIGURE 5.19. The Collection of The New-York Historical Society

FIGURE 5.20. McKim, Mead & White Office Records, vol. 10, p.36; Avery Architectural and Fine Arts Library, Columbia University in the City of New York

FIGURE 5.21. The Collection of The New-York Historical Society

FIGURE 5.22. McKim, Mead & White Office Records, vol. 10, p. 40; Avery Architectural and Fine Arts Library, Columbia University in the City of New York

FIGURE 5.23. Columbia University, Columbiana Collection

FIGURE 5.24. Columbia University, Columbiana Collection

FIGURE 5.25. The Collection of The New-York Historical Society

FIGURE 5.26. Columbia University, Columbiana Collection

FIGURE 5.27. The Collection of The New-York Historical Society

FIGURE 5.28. The Collection of The New-York Historical Society

FIGURE 5.29. The Collection of The New-York Historical Society

FIGURE 5.30. Columbia University, Columbiana Collection

FIGURE 5.31. Columbia University, Columbiana Collection

FIGURE 5.32. Columbia University, Columbiana Collection

FIGURE 5.33. Columbia University, Columbiana Collection

FIGURE 5.34. *Architecture and Building* 59 (April 1927), 132

FIGURE 5.35. Columbia University, Columbiana Collection

FIGURE 5.36. Copyright Richard Wurts, from the collection of the National Building Museum.

FIGURE 5.37. Courtesy of Cervin Robinson, photograph by Cervin Robinson

FIGURE 6.1. Barnard College Archives

FIGURE 6.2. Barnard College Archives

FIGURE 6.3. Barnard College Archives

FIGURE 6.4. *Barnard College New York City: Plans of the New Building on the Boulevard at One-hundred-and-Nineteenth Street* (Barnard College Archives)

FIGURE 6.5. Barnard College Archives

FIGURE 6.6. Barnard College Archives

FIGURE 6.7. Barnard College Archives

FIGURE 6.8. Barnard College Archives

FIGURE 6.9. Columbia University, Columbiana Collection

FIGURE 6.10. Columbia University, Columbiana Collection

FIGURE 6.11. Barnard College Archives

FIGURE 6.12. Columbia University, Columbiana Collection

FIGURE 6.13. (c) Jeff Goldberg/Esto

FIGURE 6.14. Special Collections, Milbank Memorial Library, Teachers College, Columbia University

FIGURE 6.15. Special Collections, Milbank Memorial Library, Teachers College, Columbia University

FIGURE 6.16. The Collection of The New-York Historical Society

FIGURE 6.17. Special Collections, Milbank Memorial Library, Teachers College, Columbia University

FIGURE 6.18. Special Collections, Milbank Memorial Library, Teachers College, Columbia University

FIGURE 6.19. Special Collections, Milbank Memorial Library, Teachers College, Columbia University

FIGURE 6.20. Andover Historical Society

FIGURE 6.21. Special Collections, Milbank Memorial Library, Teachers College, Columbia University

FIGURE 6.22. Special Collections, Milbank Memorial Library, Teachers College, Columbia University

FIGURE 6.23. Special Collections, Milbank Memorial Library, Teachers College, Columbia University

FIGURE 6.24. Special Collections, Milbank Memorial Library, Teachers College, Columbia University

FIGURE 6.25. Special Collections, Milbank Memorial Library, Teachers College, Columbia University

FIGURE 7.1. Burke Library of the Union Theological Seminary in the City of New York

FIGURE 7.2. The Collection of The New-York Historical Society

FIGURE 7.3. Library of Congress

FIGURE 7.4. Burke Library of the Union Theological Seminary in the City of New York

FIGURE 7.5. *American Architect* 95 (January 20, 1909), 000

FIGURE 7.6. New York Public Library, Astor, Lenox and Tilden Foundations, United States History, Local History and Genealogy Division

FIGURE 7.7. Burke Library of the Union Theological Seminary in the City of New York

FIGURE 7.8. Library of Congress

FIGURE 7.9. The Juilliard School Archives, Samuel Gottscho, photographer

FIGURE 7.10. The Juilliard School Archives, Samuel Gottscho, photographer

FIGURE 7.11. The Juilliard School Archives, Samuel Gottscho, photographer

FIGURE 7.12. Courtesy of the Ratner Center for the Study of Conservative Judaism, Jewish Theological Seminary

FIGURE 7.13. Courtesy of the Ratner Center for the Study of Conservative Judaism, Jewish Theological Seminary

FIGURE 7.14. The Library of the Jewish Theological Seminary of America

FIGURE 7.15. Courtesy of the Ratner Center for the Study of Conservative Judaism, Jewish Theological Seminary

FIGURE 8.1. *American Architect* 96 (December 22, 1909), 262; courtesy Office for Metropolitan History

FIGURE 8.2. Courtesy of the Medical Archives, New York Hospital-Cornell Medical Center

FIGURE 8.3. *Real Estate Record and Builders Guide* 60 (March 30, 1895), 502

FIGURE 8.4. Office for Metropolitan History

FIGURE 8.5. *New York Tribune,* October 7, 1900, sec. 2, p. 1; Special Collections, Milbank Memorial Library, Teachers College, Columbia University

FIGURE 8.6. The Collection of The New-York Historical Society

FIGURE 8.7. Museum of the City of New York, Wurts Collection

FIGURE 8.8. Office for Metropolitan History

FIGURE 8.9. *Architecture and Building* 44 (December 1912), 489

FIGURE 8.10. Museum of the City of New York, Wurts Collection

FIGURE 8.11. *Apartment Houses of the Metropolis* (New York: G. C. Hesselgren, 1908), p. 168; Avery Architectural and Fine Arts Library, Columbia University in the City of New York

FIGURE 8.12. *Architecture and Building* 44 (December 1912), 491

FIGURE 8.13. *Apartment Houses of the Metropolis* (New York: G. C. Hesselgren, 1908), p. 11; Avery Architectural and Fine Arts Library, Columbia University in the City of New York

FIGURE 8.14. Copyright Richard Wurts, from the collection of the National Building Museum

FIGURE 8.15. Office for Metropolitan History

FIGURE 8.16. *Architecture* 20 (December 1909), plate 110

FIGURE 8.17. *Apartment Houses of the Metropolis Supplement* (New York: G. C. Hesselgren, 1909), p. 74; New York Public Library, Astor, Lenox and Tilden Foundations, United States History, Local History and Genealogy Division

FIGURE 8.18. *Atlas of the Borough of Manhattan* (Philadelphia: G. W. Bromley, 1921), plate 126

FIGURE 8.19. "George F. Johnson, Jr.'s Latest Operation," *Real Estate Record and Builders Guide* 84 (November 20, 1909), 903

FIGURE 8.20. Library of Congress

FIGURE 8.21. Museum of the City of New York, Wurts Collection

FIGURE 8.22. *The World's Loose Leaf Album of Apartment Houses* (1910), p. 16; New York Public Library, Astor, Lenox and Tilden Foundations, United States History, Local History and Genealogy Division

FIGURE 8.23. *The World's Loose Leaf Album of Apartment Houses* (1910), p. 14–xlii; New York Public Library, Astor, Lenox and Tilden Foundations, United States History, Local History and Genealogy Division

FIGURE 8.24. *Apartment Houses of the Metropolis* (New York: G. C. Hesselgren, 1908), p. 226; Avery Architectural and Fine Arts Library, Columbia University in the City of New York

FIGURE 8.25. *Real Estate Record and Builders Guide* 81 (March 28, 1909), 567

FIGURE 8.26. *The World's Loose Leaf Album of Apartment Houses* (1910), p. 132; New York Public Library, Astor, Lenox and Tilden Foundations, United States History, Local History and Genealogy Division

FIGURE 8.27. *The World's Loose Leaf Album of Apartment Houses* (1910), p. 54; New York Public Library, Astor, Lenox and Tilden Foundations, United States History, Local History and Genealogy Division

FIGURE 8.28. *Apartment Houses of the Metropolis* (New York: G. C. Hesselgren, 1908), p. 14; Avery Architectural and Fine Arts Library, Columbia University in the City of New York

FIGURE 8.29. *Architecture and Building* 44 (December 1912), 490

FIGURE 8.30. *Apartment Houses of the Metropolis* (New York: G. C. Hesselgren, 1908), p. 15; Avery Architectural and Fine Arts Library, Columbia University in the City of New York

FIGURE 8.31. *Real Estate Record and Builders Guide* 85 (June 18, 1910), 1300

FIGURE 8.32. Office for Metropolitan History

FIGURE 8.33. The Collection of The New-York Historical Society

FIGURE Afterword.1. Columbia University, Columbiana Collection.

FIGURE Afterword.2. Riverside Church Archives

FIGURE Afterword.3. Burke Library of the Union Theological Seminary in the City of New York.

FIGURE Afterword.4. Courtesy of Bernard Tschumi Architects.